Grand Rounds on Medical Malpractice

Francis X. Campion, MD

The Risk Management Foundation of the Harvard Medical Institutions Incorporated

American Medical Association

Printed in USA.

Additional copies may be purchased from:

Book and Pamphlet Fulfillment, OP630690
American Medical Association
P.O. Box 2964
Milwaukee, WI 53201-2964

ISBN: 0-89970-388-7
GF42:90-185:3.5M:12/90

This book is dedicated to my parents, Ann and Frank Campion, who by their example showed me the joy of caring for patients, and to my wife, Colleen, and son, Timothy, for their boundless inspiration and support.

"One of the essential qualities of the clinician is interest in humanity, for the secret in care of the patient is in caring for the patient."

Francis Weld Peabody, MD

Table of Contents

Acknowledgments xi
Publisher's Commentary xiii
Introduction 1
How to Use This Book 4

Chapter 1 The Physician-Patient Relationship

Case: Physician-Patient First Encounter 6
Overview
Establishing and Nurturing the Physician-Patient Relationship/ Record Keeping/ Confidentiality/ The Legal Contract 9
Tables
1.1 Recommendations for a Healthy Physician-Patient Relationship 17
1.2 Fundamental Elements of the Patient-Physician Relationship 19
Articles
1.1 Malpractice Risk and Patient Relations. Paul Sommers. *Journal of Family Practice*. March 1985 20
1.2 Good Medical Records Can Be Strongest Malpractice Defense. *Michigan Medicine*. January 1983 23
1.3 Clinical Confidentiality: Dilemmas and Guidelines. L.D. Hankoff, C. Nattland. *New Jersey Medicine*. October 1986 27
1.4 Patient Abandonment: From a Legal Perspective. Harold Hirsh. *Urban Health*. February 1985 34
Annotated Bibliography 42

Chapter 2 Negligence

Case: Failure to Diagnose 46
Overview
The Tort System/ Elements of Negligence/ Standards/ Expert Witnesses 48
Table
2.1 Most Common Allegations by Specialty 62
Articles
2.1 Medical Malpractice and the Tort System. Peter D. Jacobson. *Journal of the American Medical Association*. December 1989 63

2.2 Standards for Patient Monitoring During Anesthesia at Harvard Medical School. John H. Eichhorn, Jeffrey B. Cooper, David J. Cullen, Ward R. Maier, James H. Philip, Robert Seeman. *Journal of the American Medical Association.* August 1986 76
2.3 The Advent of Clinical Standards for Professional Liability. James F. Holzer. *Quality Review Bulletin.* February 1990 82
2.4 Practice Guidelines and Practicing Medicine: Are They Compatible? Robert H. Brook. *Journal of the American Medical Association.* December 1989 94
2.5 Statement on Qualifications and Guidelines for the Physician Expert Witness. Council of Medical Specialty Societies. March 1989 101
2.6 Diagnostic Issues Generate Most Expensive Claims. St. Paul Fire & Marine Insurance Co. *Physicians & Surgeons Update.* 1989. 102
Annotated Bibliography 105

Chapter 3 Informed Consent

Case: Surgical Consent 109
Overview
The Doctrine of Informed Consent/ Medical Uncertainty/ Special Circumstances When Consent Is Not Required/ Documenting 111
Tables
3.1 A Physician's List of "Do's and Don'ts" on Informed Consent 118
3.2 Sample Consent Form for Medical/Surgical Procedures 119
3.3 Sample Consent Form for Glaucoma Surgery 120
3.4 Authorization for Thoracentesis 121
3.5 Sample Procedure Consent Form 123
3.6 Sample Consent Form for Testing of Patient Blood for the Presence of HIV Antibody 124
3.7 Medical Interventions Requiring Written Informed Consent 125
Articles
3.1 Informed Consent: Are "Miracle, Mystery and Authority" Better Medicine? Jay Katz. *Connecticut Medicine.* July 1986 126
3.2 Malpractice Prevention Through the Sharing of Uncertainty Thomas Gutheil, Harold Burszatjn, Archie Brodsky. *The New England Journal of Medicine.* July 1984 131
3.3 Minors' Rights to Consent to Medical Care. Angela R. Holder. *Journal of the American Medical Association.* June 1987 134
3.4 Informed Consent and Incompetent Medical Patients. Mark R. Munetz, Charles W. Lidz, Alan Meisel. *The Journal of Family Practice.* March 1985 139
3.5 Two Models of Implementing Informed Consent. Charles W. Lidz, Paul A. Applebaum, Alan Meisel. *Archives of Internal Medicine.* June 1988 146

3.6 Informed Consent in Malpractice Cases: A Turn Toward Reality. William J. Curran. *The New England Journal of Medicine.* February 1986 ... 153
Annotated Bibliography ... 156

Chapter 4 Adverse Outcomes

Case: Peripartum Complications ... 159
Overview
Frequency of Adverse Events/ What to Do/ Talking With the Patient and Family/ Documentation/ Risk Management/ Peer Support ... 161
Table
4.1 Do's and Don'ts When Faced With A Malpractice Suit ... 170
Articles
4.1 Facing Our Mistakes. David Hilfiker. *The New England Journal of Medicine.* January 1984 ... 171
4.2 A Primer for Physicians. Douglas Danner. From *Medical Malpractice: A Primer for Physicians.* 1986 ... 176
4.3 Physician Management of Patients With Adverse Outcomes. William B. Applegate. *Archives of Internal Medicine.* November 1986 ... 186
4.4 Current Concepts in Risk Management. James F. Holzer. *International Anesthesiology Clinics.* 1984 ... 193
4.5 The Malpractice Stress Syndrome. Edward G. Reading. *Maryland Medical Journal.* March 1987 ... 207
Annotated Bibliography ... 210

Chapter 5 The Impaired Physician

Case: Operating Under the Influence ... 214
Overview
Residency Training/ Caring for the Impaired Physician ... 216
Tables
5.1 Warning Signs of Physician Impairment Due to Alcoholism or Drug Addiction ... 222
5.2 Suggestions for Coping With Stress ... 223
Articles
5.1 The Effects of Stress on Physicians and Their Medical Practice. Jack D. McCue. *The New England Journal of Medicine.* February 1982 ... 224
5.2 House Officer Responses to Impaired Physicians. David B. Reuben and Sarah Noble. *Journal of the American Medical Association.* February 1990 ... 231
5.3 Impaired Physicians: The Dilemma of Identification. G. Douglas Talbott, Earl B. Benson. *Post Graduate Medicine.* 1980 ... 237
5.4 Elements of the Impaired Physicians Program. G. Douglas Talbott. *Journal of the Medical Association of Georgia.* November 1984 ... 241
Annotated Bibliography ... 244

Chapter 6 Professional Liability Insurance

Case: Choosing the Right Coverage 249
Overview
Occurrence Policy/ Claims-made Policy/ Insurance Providers/ Making the Decision/ Malpractice Crisis and Reform/ Current Trends in Claims and Insurance 251
Table
6.1 Questions to Ask When Purchasing Professional Liability Insurance 261
Articles
6.1 Possible Claim? Role of Insurer and Legal Counsel. Donald P. Wilcox. *Texas Medicine.* July 1986 262
6.2 Malpractice Insurance—What Can Happen if You Don't Have It. William S. Hunt. *Hawaii Medical Journal.* June 1985 266
6.3 Medical Malpractice: "Crisis" and Reform. F.X. Campion. 1990 269
6.4 A Proposed Alternative to the Civil Justice System for Resolving Medical Liability Disputes: A Fault-Based, Administrative System. Executive Summary. *AMA/ Specialty Society Medical Liability Project.* January 1988 279
6.5 Liability Insurance Issues in Anesthesiology James F. Holzer. *International Anesthesia Clinics.* 1989 284
Annotated Bibliography 295

Chapter 7 Peer Review

Case: Surgical Complication 298
Overview
The Peer Review Process/ Hospital Liability/ Medical Staff Privileges/ Licensure and Discipline/ Antitrust Law/ Health Care Quality Improvement Act/ PROs 301
Table
7.1 Verification of Certain Credentials Can Be Obtained From the Following Sources 312
Articles
7.1 Practical Safeguards for Peer Reviewers. Marva West Tan. *Forum.* September-October 1987 313
7.2 Hospital Liability for Physician Negligence. William B. Smith. *Journal of the American Medical Association.* January 1984 316
7.3 Answers to Physicians Questions About Reporting Claims Experience. Peggy B. Martin, Marva West Tan, Sally T. Trombly. *Forum.* May-August 1988 319
7.4 An Overview of State Medical Discipline. Richard P. Kusserow, Elisabeth A. Handley, Mark Yessian. *Journal of the American Medical Association.* February 1987 322
7.5 Peer Review After *Patrick.* Jack Bierig. *Journal of Health and Hospital Law.* June 1988 330

7.6 Health Care Quality Improvement Act of 1986. AMA Office of General Counsel. *The Citation*. January 1987 336
Annotated Bibliography 339

Appendix
Physician-owned Insurance Companies 342
Medical Malpractice Joint Underwriting Associations 346
State Patient Compensation Funds 347
Ten Largest Commercial Medical Malpractice Insurance Carriers 348

Glossary
Glossary of Medical-Legal and Insurance Terms 349

Index
Index to text and reprinted articles 359

CME Test
Order CME Test Packet or additional copies of *Grand Rounds on Medical Malpractice* .... Inside Back Cover

Acknowledgments

This publication is the fruit of several years of cooperation between the Risk Management Foundation of the Harvard Medical Institutions Inc. and the American Medical Association Office of the General Counsel. At the Risk Management Foundation, Attorney James F. Holzer had the vision to recognize the need for high-quality instruction for physicians on the complex issues of medical malpractice. This is one example of his nationally recognized leadership in the field of health care risk management. Jim and his staff in the Department of Loss Prevention give depth and expertise in all related aspects of the field. Attorney Holzer has recently become the chief operating officer of the Ophthalmic Mutual Insurance Company in San Francisco. I would like to thank Jock Hoffman for his creative and meticulous work as managing editor. Ongoing editing contributions to the text were received from Marva West Tan, Peggy Berry Martin, Sally T. Trombly, Lynn A. Volk, and Meg O. Crossan. Tireless organization was maintained by Diane Falter Butera, Alison K. Anderson, and Lynnette Robinson. Former members of the Foundation, Russell Localio, Elizabeth Bowyer, Karin Byrne, and William J. McDonough, also gave expert advice.

I must thank the AMA Board of Trustees and the AMA House of Delegates who developed the objective of educating all physicians in the rudiments of professional liability and risk management. It is a massive undertaking led, in great part, by Dr. James S. Todd, AMA President. The multifaceted approach includes pursuing scholarly work through AMA journal publications, orchestrating the many voices of organized medicine through the AMA Task Force on Professional Liability and the AMA/Specialty Society Medical Liability Project, and developing sound educational materials for physicians. The Office of the General Counsel, directed by Attorney Kirk B. Johnson, has been the focal point of activities via its Department of Professional Liability and Insurance. Attorney Martin J. Hatlie, director of the department, has charted the course of this book through rigorous peer review and consensus building. His legal expertise and keen knowledge of the needs of practicing physicians have contributed greatly to the effectiveness of the book. Attorney Ilene D. Johnson contributed editorial review. Charlotte Miller, project manager, coordinated the input of many technical offices at the AMA headquarters in Chicago. Dr. Dennis K. Wentz, director of the Division of Continuing Medical Education, has planned all activities related to the offering of this text for Continuing Medical Education (CME) credits. Julie Breo, marketing manager, developed design, production, and promotion strategies for the book and will help guide its distribution. Design of this book was developed by Herb Hinkelman in Chicago, with contributions from Pam Pepper. Jim Hutchinson designed promotional materials and the CME Test Packet. Patricia A. Coleman did the copyediting and the index was constructed by Lisa Mirabile. Important support for the success of this book was made by Dr. Ronald Arky, Professor of Medicine, Harvard Medical School. Roger B. Dworkin, Professor of Law, Indiana University School of Law, gave helpful critique. James Lapinski of the National Practitioner Data Bank and Adam Wilczek of The Medical Inter-Insurance Exchange of New Jersey also made contributions to the text.

It is my earnest hope that your reading the product of our work will be as rewarding as my experience working with these many talented people.

F. X. Campion, MD

Publisher's Commentary

James S. Todd, MD
Executive Vice President
American Medical Association

The Malpractice Problem

For many years, this country has grappled with the growing inability of the tort system to resolve medical liability claims in a rational, timely, and cost-effective manner. The debate has intensified during the past two decades as medical liability crises have escalated and receded, and as society has borne the lingering effects of the crises.

It is imperative that health care professionals become familiar with the liability system and how they may be asked, or required, to interact with it. Medical liability is a fact of life for the medical profession. The average practicing physician has a 40 percent chance of being sued at least once in his or her career, and for some specialists the rates are much higher. In addition, many health care professionals will be asked to participate in litigation as expert consultants. Others may serve on medical boards of licensure, on institutional peer review or professional society membership committees or in numerous other capacities that are concerned with professional liability issues.

In seven chapters, *Grand Rounds on Medical Malpractice* presents the kind of basic orientation to the professional liability problem that I believe physicians need, but do not necessarily find in their formal medical training. In particular, the book's discussion of negligence in Chapter 2 will acquaint the reader with the fundamental concepts and terms of art used in the legal process. The discussion of the physician-patient relationship in Chapter 1 and the review of informed consent issues—a notoriously muddy part of the law—in Chapter 3 also should be mastered by every practicing physician.

Some Common Fallacies

In getting a grasp on what the medical liability problem is, it is helpful to dispel some common myths about what it is not. First, we must remember that the liability crisis is not confined to being a problem of bad medicine. I firmly believe that medical care today is safer than it has ever been. True, the administration of health care to persons who are not well will always carry inherent risks, but the fact remains that most health care providers are competently delivering quality health care to the vast majority of patients. A major study completed by the Harvard School of Public Health in 1990 showed that only 1 percent of patients hospitalized in New York State in 1984 were injured by negligent care of any kind, and three-quarters of these injuries were classified as minimal or moderate in degree. In other words, medical care is safe for 99 percent of all hospitalized patients and, for the most part, we the medical community are doing a very good job.

But as small as this injury rate statistic is, when extrapolated nationwide it means that thousands of patients are harmed by negligent medical care every day. And while we cannot hope to be perfect, physicians can continue to do better. The bottom line is that from our patients' point of view, no avoidable medical injury is ever acceptable. *Grand Rounds on Medical Malpractice* can serve as a valuable tool in this continuous self-improvement process. The book outlines many of the roles physicians can and need to play, from participating in risk management programs (Chapter 2), to engaging in peer review activity (Chapter 7), to being vigilant in identifying and helping rehabilitate physicians whose judgment may be impaired due to drug or alcohol use (Chapter 5).

A second fallacy is the frequently heard allegation that the medical liability problem is the fault of a few "bad" doctors. In fact, it is the risk associated with a particular medical condition or treatment, not the competency of the provider, that correlates most closely with the likelihood of being sued. Almost 90 percent of obstetricians will experience a liability claim at some time in their careers, making them the specialty at highest risk in most states. Are we to then conclude that there are more "bad" obstetricians than surgeons or pediatricians, who have less than a 60 percent or 10 percent chance, respectively, of being sued? Of course not. Such a conclusion would be completely unfounded.

Physicians are often sued not because they are negligent, but because they practice an imperfect science, one that is subject to myriad variables that can produce unpredictable and sometimes unfortunate results. President Bush acknowledged this fact in a recent speech at Johns Hopkins University, during which he called for restoring "common sense and fairness" to the current medical liability system. The President stated: "We've got to remember a simple truth: not every unfortunate medical outcome is the result of poor medicine, and you cannot make life risk-free." (*The New York Times*, February 23, 1990.)

But communicating the real risks of medical treatment in the informed consent process can be exceedingly difficult to accomplish. In some cases, the patient may not have the technical knowledge to thoroughly understand and weigh the available treatment options and all of their attendant risks. In others, it may be just too frightening to psychologically accept the information given. For the doctor, acknowledging that a course of treatment has not been successful, and effectively dealing with the disappointment or anger of a patient or family member, may be just as hard. Yet intervention following an adverse outcome with appropriate interpersonal care can be crucial in deflecting a medical liability claim. *Grand Rounds'* treatment of these issues in Chapter 4 is very well done.

It is by now well documented that all doctors, even the best doctors, can and do make mistakes. Indeed, in crafting an effective solution to the professional liability problem, it is the medical community's particular responsibility to do whatever it can to minimize harm to our patients. I am happy to say that health care providers—often working together with the liability insurance industry—are committed to a broad range of efforts to accomplish this goal.

Our Responsibility for Patient Safety

Providing medical care today involves complex systems of persons and equipment that rely on all components functioning properly to bring about the safe and effective delivery of care to the patient. While science and technology have greatly advanced the frontiers of medicine, providers must also contend with multiple systems problems inherent in today's medical care—training problems, communication problems, equipment problems, and documentation problems, just to name a few.

Over the past decade, the profession has vigorously addressed these systems issues under several different rubrics, including "patient safety," "loss prevention," "risk prevention," and "risk management." All aim at the common goal of preventing patient injury. All call upon us to examine what we do or fail to do, and how we do it. When problems are detected, solutions are developed and implemented. Some of these solutions are remarkably simple, little more than the systematic application of practical wisdom. Others are far more sophisticated, derived from complex sampling and statistical analysis techniques.

To take one example, in the early 1980s groups of anesthesiologists, concerned with the incidence of loss in their high-risk specialty, began to study the circumstances underlying alleged negligent anesthesiology events. The Harvard Risk Management Foundation's groundbreaking role in this effort is chronicled in Chapter 2.

Analyzing liability insurers' closed claim files, the studies done by the Harvard Risk Management Foundation and others determined that, for the most part, anesthesia losses could not be anticipated from the claims history of individual physicians. Rather, the incidents occurred almost randomly. The studies' results confirmed that liability was not simply the problem of a few bad apples in the profession. Certain scenarios were identified, however, during which an error was more likely to occur. With these findings, informational materials and guidelines were developed that enabled providers to identify high-risk situations and avoid injury. As a direct result of this effort, adverse events in the anesthesia field were dramatically reduced and the specialty's insurance classification and premiums dropped substantially.

The phenomenal success of this risk management approach led to the adoption of anesthesia protocols as a condition of insurance by virtually every liability insurer that covers the specialty, a very effective private regulatory mechanism. Just as important, it fueled the interest in all quarters of the medical community in developing what has now become a broad and prolific assortment of patient safety initiatives encompassing closed-claims studies, practice guidelines and policy statements, seminars, self-assessment surveys, and self-study programs, among many others.

These efforts have been furthered and often led by the physician-owned or institution-based "captive" insurance companies, which embraced early on the gospel of risk management and invested substantial resources in promoting it. Increasingly, insurance companies also play an active role in policing the profession through aggressive underwriting practices which deny coverage to physicians who fail to practice safely. Commercial insurers are also developing and implementing risk-management programs and are providing incentives for their insureds to avoid loss.

Organized medicine also is contributing to the patient safety movement. Certainly, the American Society of Anesthesiologists played a strong leadership role in promulgating practice standards and guidelines among its members, and encouraging ongoing research through its Anesthesia Patient Safety Foundation. In 1986, the AMA, together with more than 30 national medical specialty organizations, established the AMA/Specialty Society Medical Liability Project (AMA/SSMLP) to jointly address liability issues. Among its purposes, the AMA/SSMLP is dedicated to furthering innovation in the loss prevention field and has a standing Patient Safety/Risk Management Subcommittee. Through this subcommittee, the AMA/SSMLP monitors patient safety initiatives and disseminates information to hospitals, medical societies, insurers and others to promote the exchange of ideas and approaches.

The AMA/SSMLP also has undertaken the development of several practical risk management tools. In 1988, it published, together with the Physician Insurers Association of America, the *Compendium of Patient Safety and Medical Risk Management Programs*, a 175 page catalog of the risk management activities of state and national medical societies, insurers, and others, complete with subject matter index and the identities of key contact people to facilitate networking among professionals across the country.

The AMA/SSMLP followed this initial contribution with a May 1990 document entitled *Risk Management Principles & Commentaries for the Medical Office*. Developed in consultation with nationally known experts over a two year period, the publication sets forth in 12 chapters pragmatic risk management advice primarily for office-based practices. The chapters cover such topics as obtaining informed consent, establishing good communication with patients, developing workable follow-up systems for responding to patient telephone calls and missed appointments, instituting schedules for the maintenance and calibration of equipment, and evaluating the safety of office and parking area grounds, among others. As is true with all good risk management tools, the material collected in this work is data-based, drawn from the experience of insurers, defense lawyers and professional risk managers.

Also on the agenda of the AMA/SSMLP is finalizing an integrated risk management program now being pilot tested by the Oregon Medical Association. The program's two-fold purpose is to offer risk prevention advice and collect data to be used as a continuous feedback mechanism on the effectiveness of loss prevention efforts. The program consists of an office self-assessment survey, a self-study course, and an office site visit and assessment by a professional risk manager, which together constitute a single learning process that is adaptable to any specialty. The pilot phase is expected to be completed in late 1990, and the program is designed to be easily implemented by state, county and local specialty societies across the nation.

In addition to these profession-based actions, in 1987, the Joint Commission on Accreditation of Healthcare Organizations (JCAHO) began implementing a revolutionary quality improvement mandate in the nation's hospitals. Called the "Agenda for Change," its objectives are to create standards that provide a foundation for continual quality improvement activities within health care facilities, establish performance monitoring indicators, and improve assessment of facility compliance with JCAHO standards. The Agenda also calls for the development of "clinical indicators of quality" to enable better analysis of the quality of patient care. In addition, the Agenda encompasses an ongoing data collection and monitoring system to provide continuous feedback to institutions regarding the quality of care.

These efforts clearly represent a new era in the medical community's ability to respond aggressively to patient safety concerns. It should be noted that the frequency of medical liability claims filings appears to have stabilized and, in some states, even decreased since approximately 1986. While it is still too early to evaluate the meaning of this trend conclusively, the tremendous growth of patient safety activities in the 1980s may indeed be a contributing factor.

Forging A Real Solution

As we enter the 1990s, the debate on medical liability issues remains heated. However, a legacy of the 1980s is that much more data about where the problems really lie are now available. Numerous studies done in the latter half of the 1980s—by sources such as the United States Department of Justice, a Department of Health and Human Services Task Force, the General Accounting Office, the National Academy of Sciences, Institute of Medicine, and the Harvard School of Public Health—all confirm what physicians have been saying for

15 years: The legal system is broken and needs to be fixed. We strongly believe that the patient safety movement currently being implemented by the medical community is the optimal source of information for providers on injury prevention issues. Unfortunately, physicians themselves cannot solve the many legal inefficiencies that contribute to the medical liability crisis.

Most recently, this conclusion was reconfirmed by the Harvard study of medical liability in New York, which indicates that the current civil justice system simultaneously denies access to the majority of patients who may have been injured by negligent care, yet has no adequate mechanism to screen out non-meritorious claims that are clogging the wheels of justice. The end result is that the risk of being sued bears almost no relation to whether the physician or other health care provider practiced good medicine. In other words, the tort system does not deliver a focused deterrence of unsafe medical practices. Rather, it teaches every physician to regard every patient as a potential litigant, to practice defensively by ordering additional tests merely to document medical judgments that have already been made, and to avoid certain patients or treatment modes that are perceived to be too risky.

For those patients who do gain access to the civil justice system, the delay in resolving their claims is almost inexcusable—six to 10 years in most urban areas. Other data show that, even when patients receive compensation, they are not the primary beneficiaries of the system. Rather, attorneys' fees and expenses (both plaintiff and defendant) account for 38 percent of total monies spent on resolving medical liability claims. Although the purpose of the legal process is to compensate the injured, only 43 cents of every dollar spent in medical liability litigation reaches patients.

The tort system needs to be fixed to meet the needs of the real parties at interest, patients and health care providers. Patients injured by medical negligence are entitled to fair compensation and should be provided a reasonable opportunity to obtain it. Health care institutions, physicians, and other professionals should bear the responsibility for negligent mistakes when they occur and for preventing such mistakes to whatever extent possible. On the other hand, the unhappy truth must be acknowledged that physicians and other health care providers are mere mortals, and we do not have the power to guarantee an optimal treatment result in every instance. Society—the patient collective—must come to terms with the escalating cost of liability insurance, which tripled in the 1980s; the fact that the civil justice system is not fair or cost-effective in distributing these premium dollars to injured patients; and the impact that these liability costs have on the cost and availability of health care for everyone.

The AMA and state medical societies have worked to achieve litigation reform for over 15 years, typically in state legislative battles that were bitterly contested by the organized plaintiffs' bar. While a handful of states have achieved effective reform that has helped stabilize liability costs and expedited the resolution of claims, initiatives in most jurisdictions have been stalled or diluted. After 15 years of legislative battles, court challenges and exponential premium growth, in most places the tort system is as broken as ever.

It is not the goal of the authors of *Grand Rounds on Medical Malpractice* to convert its readers into ardent tort reformers. But the fact remains that when our patients are convinced that physicians care about their safety, and that reform proposals are fair, the possibility exists for more effective physician-patient alliances. Physicians must learn to advocate with sincerity our patients' concerns as well as our own if we expect public support for tort reform to be forthcoming. I hope *Grand Rounds* will prove to be a useful tool for the profession in emphasizing the importance of our patient safety responsibilities and in reinforcing the foundation of trust so essential to a successful physician/patient relationship.

Introduction

Professional liability is now a daily concern of all practicing physicians. Approximately 37 percent of all clinicians have been sued for malpractice at least once. Insurance industry figures show that the annual total expenses for medical malpractice losses escalated from $817 million in 1977 to $5.9 billion in 1986.

Malpractice insurance premiums rose dramatically during the 1980s, far in excess of the inflation rate. The average premium for a self-employed physician in 1987 was $15,000. The range, however, is vast. Some neurosurgeons and obstetricians in Florida and New York pay close to $200,000 per year for professional liability insurance. Statistics such as these command our attention and invite closer scrutiny.

More profound than the financial strain of malpractice insurance on physicians are the associated changes in the practice of medicine, medical education, and the entire health care system. Seventy percent of physicians surveyed by the American Medical Association (AMA) in 1984 said they engaged in "defensive medicine." The American College of Surgeons reported that 28 to 40 percent of surgeons have discontinued performance of certain procedures due to concern for potential liability. In many areas of the country, access to medical services has been limited due to such changes in practice. Physicians' and hospitals' escalating liability costs have become a primary component of the seemingly unchecked inflation of health care expenditures in the United States.

The very cornerstone of good medical care, the physician-patient relationship, is also showing signs of strain. As acknowledgment of the liability problem grows, so does the perception that each new patient is a potential legal adversary. Blossoming medical technology has, in many cases, intruded on the caring bonds between patients and physicians. Changes in our medical care delivery system have also interrupted established avenues of communication, as physicians and patients are increasingly brought together by prepaid insurance programs instead of traditional physician-physician referrals.

Systemic changes have greatly expanded the scrutiny of medical decisions beyond the physician community. The laws by which society conducts business and the insurance system we use to protect ourselves have undergone significant change in recent decades. The current system we use to compensate persons injured in the course of receiving medical care is based on establishing fault on the part of health care providers such as physicians or hospitals. It has been shown, convincingly, to be an extremely costly, slow, and inefficient system. Some experts suggest that it is time to reassess the merits of this system and implement a new one, which might serve to compensate the injured patient in a just and timely fashion and acknowledge the inevitability of adverse outcomes in medical care.

All too often, discussions of liability issues are marked by a lack of information and runaway emotions. Fortunately, reliable data are now being generated. A sample of 31,000 patient hospital discharges in New York state was analyzed in the Medical Practice Study directed by the Harvard School of Public Health. The study results, released in February 1990, revealed that 3.7 percent of hospitalized patients sustained an injury in the hospital that resulted in a measurable disability. Of those injuries, 28 percent were caused by the negligence of some provider. Such facts about professional liability are important to medical students and physicians as they work to develop effective patient-safety initiatives. Ongoing research concerning malpractice claims data and development of risk management education programs should be led by the physician community.

Every physician, including residents and medical students, should be aware of available loss prevention resources and play an active role in implementing effective risk management. This includes becoming involved in peer review, the establishment of medical care standards, the promotion of unbiased expert medical testimony, care for impaired physicians, and patient education toward realistic expectations of medical care.

It is the purpose of this resource book to increase physicians' understanding of liability and risk management issues and the opportunities to make positive changes benefiting both patients and physicians. This book examines the fundamentals of physician-patient communication; organizes the known facts of the insurance/liability cost crisis; and familiarizes medical students, physicians-in-training; and practicing physicians with important medicolegal and risk management issues. Seven general topics—The Physician-Patient Relationship, Negligence, Informed Consent, Adverse Outcomes, The Impaired Physician, Professional Liability Insurance, and Peer Review—are discussed and illustrated through specific clinical cases. Current articles reprinted from the medical literature describe the state-of-the-art knowledge of this young but rapidly expanding field. In the familiar style of hospital "grand rounds," particular subjects are presented by respected physicians and attorneys in authoritative medical and legal professional journals. A detailed, annotated list of references accompanies each chapter. Every attempt has been made to use articles and references from the medical literature that are comprehensible to the medical professional. The glossary of legal and insurance terms will be useful for the reader who studies these pages closely.

With the knowledge of our individual responsibilities as physicians as well as the roles of the institutions where we practice, we can confidently work for change and dispel the shadow of liability that currently casts itself over the day-to-day practice of medicine.

How to Use This Book

Medical students, house officers, and physicians at every stage of their career can benefit from instruction on how to improve communication with their patients and better understand the basics of professional liability. This book has been designed with flexibility in mind. It can be used as a primer and resource for a medical school or residency program course on professional liability issues in medicine. With the accompanying examinations, it can be used by practicing physicians or health care providers to obtain continuing medical education (CME) credits in risk management. The topical arrangement of this book makes it a useful teaching guide for a lecture or workshop series on professional liability. The extensive bibliographies and glossary will also make this book a ready reference for further inquiry into this evolving field.

The Physician-Patient Relationship, Negligence, Informed Consent, Adverse Outcomes, The Impaired Physician, Professional Liability Insurance, and Peer Review form the basis of the seven chapters of this book. A detailed medical case, portraying a realistic scenario, introduces each chapter. Discussion questions, which accompany each case, help readers explore their reactions to common as well as some unusual occurrences in daily practice. Each chapter contains a brief overview of the topic and key articles from the medical literature that represent timely information from respected authors. Annotated bibliographies, found at the end of each chapter, expand the scope of selected subtopics and are intended to provide an appreciation for previous work performed in the field and to guide future study.

Use as a Course Primer or Resource Book

Medical students, house officers, and physicians usually prefer "hands-on," case-oriented learning experiences to dry lectures (which tend only to be interrupted by dysfunctional slide projectors). The medical case introducing each chapter can, for example, be read aloud or acted out before a lecture hall or small group audience. While the cases do not include exact scripts, the description of characters and their situation sets the scene and allows individuals to act on their own best judgment. During the five to 10 minutes required to read or act out each scenario, the participants will be forced to make decisions and offer comments, just as they must do on hospital units or in private offices in daily practice. Discussion questions will assist the transition to a more formal lecture or can be the basis of an extended discussion of the cases themselves.

The arrangement of subtopics will assist in the planning of daily lectures and discussions. Participants should read all of the reprinted articles found in the book to gain a foundation of fundamental information. Additional reading assignments can be easily selected from the bibliographies at the end of each chapter. The glossary provides a useful guide to legal and insurance terminology.

Gaining CME Credits

Several states now require CME credits in professional liability and risk management. Some carriers of medical malpractice insurance offer discounts on premiums to those physicians proving competence in these areas. The topical arrangement of this book allows physicians to gain that knowledge in a manageable, organized fashion. The companion CME Test Packet for this book contains seven tests corresponding to the book's seven chapters. Each test is worth two Category I CME credits applicable toward the AMA's Physician Recognition Award.

Developing a Lecture Series

Presentations to practicing physicians in the field on the subject of professional liability during the past several years have often been hurriedly prepared in reaction to local fervor regarding a specific lawsuit, newly enacted legislation, or notification of rising insurance premiums. No easily accessible guide has been available to organize the confusing detail and information. A dearth of reliable statistics has also hampered coherent analysis and action. By focusing on related topics and gathering relevant data in the field, this book offers an overview of the range of issues encompassed within the area of medical professional liability.

The materials in this book can be used to structure informal lunchtime talks, more formal endeavors such as special evening presentations, or even lecture hall marathons. Active participation and a dynamic discussion leader are the keys to a successful program. Each of the seven chapter topics can serve as foundation for a single lecture. Subtopics may be mixed and matched to meet the desires of a particular audience. Specific issues, such as record keeping, professional peer review, and legislative reform, have been covered in selected chapters but are pertinent to virtually every discussion concerning medical liability.

Before each lecture or workshop, a reading assignment from the chapter may be valuable. As described above, role playing one of the medical cases will encourage audience participation. The overview section of each chapter provides a ready template for use by a knowledgeable person in the field who is chosen to give a lecture. Selected references may be distributed to workshop participants.

Your Critique

Only a limited handling of the wide variety of specific concerns related to medical professional liability could be accomplished in this first edition. We welcome your suggestions for additional articles, cases, issues, and questions that you believe will make this text more useful.

Chapter 1

The Physician-Patient Relationship

Case: Physician-Patient First Encounter

A "big-city" cardiologist cares for an elderly woman who requires replacement of her pacemaker. She was referred to him by a primary care physician in a "small community."

Mrs. Percy, who is from a small town in southern Maine, is referred to Dr. Randall at a large university hospital in Boston for replacement of her pacemaker. She is 75 years old and very active as the secretary of the local church meals programs.

Mrs. Percy had her pacemaker implanted five years ago in her community hospital, and it has generally functioned quite well. For the past 12 months, however, she has experienced fainting spells once every few weeks. Her family physician ascribed her symptoms to dehydration during the very hot summer weather when she first complained of syncope. He has changed her anti-hypertensive medications several times since then in an attempt to resolve this problem. Unfortunately, Mrs. Percy has continued to have fainting spells and is afraid that she may fall and break her hip.

Mrs. Percy recently spent six days in a local community hospital for workup of her syncope. She underwent numerous tests including electrocardiography, 24-hour Holter monitoring, echocardiography, carotid ultrasound examination, and electroencephalography. Mrs. Percy knows that the tests were performed to find out why she is fainting. She is fatigued by all of the testing and complains that she slept poorly during her hospitalization. She was quite upset when her family physician told her that her pacemaker will likely need replacement and that she would need to go to Boston for the procedure. While awaiting transfer to the Boston teaching hospital, Mrs. Percy drew up the following list of questions to ask Dr. Randall, whom she has never met:

- Why am I fainting?
- Do I have to have all those tests repeated?
- How long am I going to live?
- Do I have to have an operation? (She does not want "open heart surgery" because she had a friend who died during open heart surgery.)
- What if I still have fainting spells after the pacemaker is replaced?
- Will I save money if I continue to use the old battery in the new pacemaker?

- Will Medicare pay for a health aide to assist me in my daily chores after I leave the hospital?

Dr. Randall is highly regarded as a cardiac arrhythmia specialist. He is a busy physician with teaching duties and is involved in an ongoing research study of new cardiac medication. He has 10 patients in the hospital at this time.

Dr. Randall has heard Mrs. Percy's story over the telephone from her family physician. Dr. Randall requested only that her old electrocardiograms be sent with her. He plans to get his own baseline electrocardiogram, echocardiogram, and 24-hour Holter monitoring. He will not repeat the electroencephalogram or the carotid noninvasive studies. Dr. Randall concludes that Mrs. Percy's pacemaker is probably malfunctioning periodically, causing low cardiac output and resulting in syncope. He believes her pacemaker should have been replaced at least six months ago and is surprised it took her family physician 12 months from her first episode to refer the case. Dr. Randall has already scheduled operating room time for removal of the old pacemaker and implantation of a new one. One of the two cardiology fellows working under him will be in charge of Mrs. Percy's care.

Discussion Questions

1. What documentation should the referring family physician send to Dr. Randall?

2. Who should explain to Mrs. Percy the purposes and outcomes of certain tests?

3. Should Dr. Randall tell Mrs. Percy that her family physician erred by not having her pacemaker replaced six months earlier? What should he say to the referring family physician?

4. Who is ultimately responsible for her care: the cardiology fellow, the medical student on the case, the resident, or the attending physician?

5. What, if anything, should Dr. Randall explain about the cardiology fellow and his or her role in Mrs. Percy's treatment?

6. How should Dr. Randall handle the question, "How long am I going to live?"

7. How can Dr. Randall explain the causal relationship between a malfunctioning pacemaker and fainting spells? What analogies, aids, or devices might be helpful in explaining this complex topic?

8. How would you respond to Mrs. Percy's concerns regarding fainting spells of other etiology?

9. How would you explain the financing of her care when she asks if she can save money by using her existing pacemaker battery?

10. What are Dr. Randall's responsibilities regarding the preparation and payment mechanisms for his patient's home health care? Is it a physician's responsibility to remain informed about the economic and political climate in which our health care system is continually changing?

11. What, if anything, should Dr. Randall say if he knows that available home health care services will not meet all of Mrs. Percy's needs?

Overview

Technical skills and medical therapies are the acquired elements common to all physicians in the delivery of health care. Unique to each clinician, however, is the care and style with which medical histories are taken and physical examinations performed.

Physicians who carefully listen to their patients and comfortably share medical information with them have discovered the cornerstone of the art of medicine. A healthy physician-patient relationship can make a devastating diagnosis more bearable for a patient. It can help a resistant patient understand the need for medication and allow the physician to develop a realistic plan for continuing care. When a physician's relationship with a patient is marked by mutual trust and open communication, a giant step has been taken toward the assurance of patient satisfaction.

Evidence shows that a clear, two-way conversation is a key element in the prevention of malpractice claims. In fact, many episodes of patient dissatisfaction triggered by an iatrogenic injury or other "adverse outcomes" can be defused by a calming explanation from the physician who has previously established a good basis for communication. On the other hand, inadequate communication and misunderstanding are often the inciting agents that transform a poor medical outcome into a legal action against a physician even when quality care was delivered. Most studies show that a significant percentage of initiated legal actions against physicians are ultimately settled without any indemnity payment to the patient.[1,2] Many risk managers believe that a large number of these non-meritorious cases could be avoided if physicians talked more or listened more attentively to patients who experience less-than-optimal treatment outcomes. Techniques for increasing patient satisfaction through improved communication are now widely recommended for malpractice claims prevention.[3,4]

Because "poor communication" itself is not a legal cause of action, it is never listed as a primary legal allegation in a malpractice suit. Consequently, it is difficult to prove definitively the widely held opinion that poor communication leads to malpractice suits. Unfortunately, there is a common perception by both physicians and the public that the physician-patient relationship has weakened during the past 20 years.[5-7] Its disintegration is marked by a decline in physician credibility and patient trust. A recent survey of sued and non-sued physicians and suing patients attempted to describe the differing views of patients and physicians.[5] It found that sued physicians believed that their relationship with the patient, prior to the malpractice claim, was open (62 percent) and honest (78 percent). In contrast, only 38 percent of suing patients believed that their pre-claim relationship with their physician was open and only 44 percent described the relationship as honest. Two thirds of both groups agreed that better physician-patient communication was the most effective method for reducing malpractice litigation.

Establishing and Nurturing the Physician-Patient Relationship

Just as styles of practice are unique to individual physicians, so are the expectations of patients. Some patients desire an authoritative physician who relates to them only a minimal amount of information; others seek detailed facts concerning each medical decision. Most physicians encounter patients all along this spectrum. For this reason, clinicians must be sensitive, listen well, and be attentive to the individual needs of patients and flexible in their responses. Patients should be given the amount of medical data and opinion with which they feel comfortable and then be encouraged to assist in making decisions relevant to their care. A patient's ability to identify those physicians who are insensitive to his or her needs and interests should never be underestimated. With the selective use of educational materials and explanation, most patients can understand complex issues to the degree needed to participate in decisions regarding their care.

Fortunately, some interpersonal communication skills can be acquired and/or improved. Medical students are usually given some instruction in fostering physician-patient rapport during courses on the physical examination and introduction to clinical medicine. After the third year of medical school, however, there is too often too little time spent reinforcing these concepts. Students should be encouraged to accompany appropriate role models to patients' bedsides to learn the art of talking, touching, and listening to their patients. Recognition and avoidance of those verbal and nonverbal behaviors that detract from a constructive physician-patient relationship are equally important. These invaluable lessons, combined with the conscious practice of some common-sense guidelines, can make communication with patients a powerful tool (see Table 1.1).

It is a common perception that physicians are hurried individuals with crowded waiting rooms. Patients may assume that the physician's time is too valuable to be wasted on questions not directly related to their chief complaint. Unfortunately, these impressions are often reinforced when physicians do not take the steps needed to help the patient understand important information. As a result, patients may leave the physician's office confused about their health status and uncertain of the details of their therapy. Under such conditions, it is easy to understand why patients are sometimes reluctant to fill prescriptions or modify their life-styles as directed by the physician. Cultural and economic constraints may also render a medical plan impractical. Before blaming a patient for noncompliance with a medical regimen, it should be ensured that the plan is understood and accepted and that it is manageable for all parties involved.

Maintaining the Relationship

The clinical case that introduced this chapter illustrates other important stresses on the physician-patient relationship. Mrs. Percy has been referred for admission to a large teaching hospital under the care of a specialist whom she has never met. This practice is probably more common now than it was in the past. New health care delivery arrangements have been devised that sometimes restrict the patient's choice of medical specialist and hospital. A list of her rights as a patient, as recently adopted by the AMA, can be found in Table 1.2.

Because she is some distance from her home, Mrs. Percy may not have any family or friends visiting during her hospitalization. There will, however, be a wide range of nurses, physicians, students, and ancillary personnel seeing her during her stay. It is the responsibility of the attending physician, Dr. Randall, to sketch for her the overall plan for her care. He should relate to her his expectations for the scope of her treatment and the duration of her hospitalization and introduce the various personnel who will be involved in her care.

Mrs. Percy has definite concerns about the cost of her care. She may be worried that she will not have comprehensive third-party coverage or personal resources to pay her medical bills. It is important for both Mrs. Percy and her physician that she understand the extent of her insurance coverage. She has heard stories of patients being discharged early from the hospital and is concerned that she will require medical assistance at home after she leaves the hospital. Fiscal constraints within the health care environment have led to prospective payment systems and the institution of Diagnosis Related Groups (DRGs) for Medicare beneficiaries. Health care financing is undergoing dramatic changes that can affect the availability of services to patients. It is incumbent on the physician to be aware of the changes that pertain to his or her patients and to help them understand how these changes affect their medical care. The physician should also be able to provide the patient appropriate referral for further patient information regarding coverage and financing.

Although the importance of the physician-patient relationship has long been acknowledged, it is the most difficult aspect of medicine to quantify and test objectively. Descriptions of the physician-patient relationship range from the very paternalistic to recent writings on physician-patient accommodations and the concept of a "shared relationship." The annotated bibliography for this chapter includes a chronology of articles reflecting the maturation of the physician-patient relationship during the past several decades. Recent articles attempting to establish a link between patient satisfaction and medical outcomes are also included. In Article 1.1, "Malpractice Risk and Patient Relations," Paul Sommers stresses that even perceived negligence arising from an unhealthy physician-patient relationship can lead directly to a malpractice suit. He succinctly describes specific communication problems from the viewpoint of a non-physician and makes suggestions for their resolution.

Record Keeping

While quantifying the quality of the physician-patient relationship is difficult, a documentation of significant communication between those parties exists in the form of the patient's medical record. No longer simply a notebook of shorthand symbols for communication between physicians, today the medical record has become a reflection of the quality of the physician-patient relationship as well as an accounting of tasks completed. The medical record may still be the legal property of the individual physician or hospital, but now other parties often have guaranteed legal access to the information in that record. Patients, insurance reviewers, and legal advisors now scrutinize the written word of physicians. In a court of law, that which is not written down may be perceived as never having occurred.

The practicalities of record keeping are often taken for granted in medical education, yet cries over illegible, incomplete, or tardy patient records are heard daily in virtually every medical facility.

Standard formats for writing progress notes include S.O.A.P. (Subjective information, Objective data, Assessment, and Plan) notes, problem-oriented notes, or organ-system notes. The list of procedures requiring formal "procedure notes" and those requiring separate informed consent forms, with the signature of the patient and physician, varies among hospitals. Students beginning their clinical clerkships should be taught the standard formats for writing admitting orders, procedure notes, pre-operative and operative notes, labor and delivery reports, patient discharge instructions, discharge summaries, pharmacy prescriptions, and shorthand for reporting laboratory values. Allowing students to learn record keeping simply by mimicking their superiors can frequently perpetuate bad habits.

Documentation of important conversations, including significant telephone calls, with patients and their families may also be instrumental in explaining the course of medical decisions and ensuring proper follow-up. Clearly identifying the relationship between physical findings and subsequent therapy will allow reconstruction of the case at some future date when memories fail to recall the details. Physicians should describe the differential diagnoses considered and the potential therapies that may also be indicated. Specific documentation as to why a given course of action was taken, including critical decision points, should be included in the medical record.

Knowing what not to write in the medical record is just as important as knowing what to include. The patient record should not contain vague terms that invite varied interpretation. Consulting physicians should summarize medical facts and offer their recommendations for patient care. Open criticism of another physician's judgment should not be included in the medical record. Gratuitous remarks relative to a patient's personality or appearance are not useful. The standard procedure for documenting physician orders, informed consent, and the resuscitative status should be familiar to all personnel involved in direct patient care. (Documentation of informed consent raises specific issues that are addressed in Chapter 3.)

In the case presented in this chapter, Dr. Randall should write an admitting note as well as subsequent daily progress notes. The resident physician and cardiology fellow working under Dr. Randall will likely leave more detailed notes and also write the physician's orders. Dr. Randall ultimately will be responsible for the medical record, including the documentation of informed consent, procedure notes, and preparation of a timely discharge summary. He may co-sign information in the chart with which he agrees.

It is particularly important that any person making corrections in the record follow standard procedure. This entails drawing a single line through each unwanted word, writing the word "error" above the incorrect entry, writing in the corrections, and then initialing the change. Of course, corrections are to be made only by the original author of the incorrect entry. If the correction is made after the original text is completed, it should be labeled as such with the time and date, as should any addendum.

Record keeping in the private office and in the hospital requires special attention to ensure that tests and procedures done at other facilities are properly filed. The attending physician of record for the patient is responsible for acknowledging all abnormal laboratory and test results as well as responding to all consultation remarks found in the chart.

An area of growing concern is the use of computerized medical records. Some records employ a check-off list of pertinent positive facts to describe a given medical condition. It is equally important to document the pertinent negative facts, the physician's thought process, and the patient's emotional state to complete the medical record. The Michigan State Medical Society has published guidelines on record keeping that are reproduced in Article 1.2, "Good Medical Records Can Be Strongest Malpractice Defense."

From a legal perspective, medical records are considered the private property of the physician in the case of office records, and the hospital in the case of hospital records. It is appropriate, however, to provide copies of the record to a patient or his or her agent when properly requested. Some states specifically grant patients a right of access to their medical information and a copy of their records.[8] Even where no right of access exists by statute, some courts may routinely recognize such a privilege.[9] It is customary to supply copies of records within a reasonable period of time for a nominal copying charge. In no case is it appropriate to withhold the transfer of records due to an unpaid medical bill. The release or transfer of medical record information should always be authorized in writing by the patient. Laws also vary as to exactly what must be disclosed. Generally, all objective data, such as laboratory values and radiology reports, must be included. A summary of the physician's subjective opinion and diagnoses should accompany the report.

In many states, laws guarantee most patients the right to read their own medical record. Clinicians should ensure that such a reading is an informed one. A physician should be present to translate medical terms and to explain the record if a hospitalized patient reviews his or her own chart.

Confidentiality

Disclosure to a physician of personal habits, beliefs, and emotions is a very trying experience for many patients. It is generally understood that the physician will use the information to better understand and help the patient, all the while protecting the privacy of that know-ledge. Maintaining trust in the physician-patient relationship relies heavily on preserving confidentiality. The law usually protects confidentiality between physician and patient even in the delivery of medical care for minors. Physicians, however, must be prepared to address the concerns of parents in an understanding manner. The division of care among a team of consultants, residents, students, nurses, technicians, and administrators can easily compromise the privacy of information and lead to mistrust between patient and physician. The use of computerized data bases, care rendered at multiple institutions, and review of cases by third-party insurers further heighten the potential for breach of confidentiality. It is imperative that health care facilities make and enforce clear rules regarding personnel who have access to medical records. The discussion of patient information in public areas such as elevators and stairwells is, of course, not appropriate. Physicians and students need to be mindful of the many potential pitfalls regarding confidentiality and must be sensitive to this issue.

Legal precedent and state legislation form the laws governing "privileged communication" between physicians and patients. In Massachusetts, the 1985 case *Alberts v. Devine* illustrates this process. Psychiatrist Donald Devine was found liable for discussing the diagnosis of his client, William Alberts, with Alberts' clerical supervisor. Alberts alleged that he was not reappointed as a church minister because of a breach of confidentiality and sued for subsequent financial losses and mental anguish (*Alberts v. Devine, 395 Mass. 59 1985*). Massachusetts laws now protect the availability of hospital records (M.G.L. c.111, §70 and §70E). In the special instance of care delivered by a psychotherapist, medical records can sometimes be considered privileged communication and in many instances are not admissable in court (M.G.L.c.233, §20B).

There are instances, however, when the protection of the health and welfare of society, or specific individuals, necessitates the sharing of medical details without the consent of the patient. The California Supreme Court faced this issue in 1975 in the landmark case of *Tarasoff v. Catlin*. In that decision, the California court determined that a psychotherapist, who knew that his patient had intentions of committing a serious crime against another party, had a duty to prevent foreseeable potential harm his patient could have caused to third parties.[10]

In Article 1.3, "Clinical Confidentiality: Dilemmas and Guidelines," Hankoff and Nattland provide a discussion of the ethical and legal history of current laws regarding privileged communication between physicians and patients. They describe four examples of information, such as the suspicion of child abuse, that physicians are legally required to report to appropriate officials in the state of New Jersey (laws vary from state to state). These and other scenarios that may require a breach of confidentiality are the subject of three clinical cases discussed in the article.

The Legal Contract Between Physician and Patient

The legal and medical professions have long acknowledged the physician-patient relationship to be a special and privileged one. The decision to enter into a relationship is the prerogative of the physician once the patient has assented. Once initiated, however, the physician does not have exclusive power to terminate the relationship. The relationship can be legally concluded only if: (1) it is ended by the parties' mutual consent, (2) it is revoked by the patient, (3) the physician's services are no longer needed, or (4) the physician withdraws from the case after reasonable notice to the patient. Limitations can be put on the contract if they are stated at the outset.[11] During the term of the physician-patient contract, the physician must be fully informed of the patient's illness and treat the patient accordingly. When a patient decides to terminate the physician-patient relationship, complete documentation in the medical record is essential. The physician is encouraged to send a letter to the patient acknowledging the patient's decision to discontinue the relationship and summarizing the patient's current medical status and any requirements or recommendations for continued medical care. Arrangements for referral to another physician and orderly transfer of medical records should be included where appropriate. The physician may wish to request that the patient sign a copy of the letter to document further that the termination decision is mutually understood.

Abandonment is the unilateral severance of the relationship by the physician, without reasonable notice, at a time when there is still need for continuing medical attention. Harold Hirsh, MD, JD, differentiates "classical" and "constructive" abandonment in Article 1.4, "Patient Abandonment: From a Legal Perspective." He describes the legal responsibilities inherent in various physician-patient scenarios in this detailed article.

Although no legal obligation to treat exists, a physician may feel morally compelled to accept a patient when no other physician is available or in an emergency situation. Furthermore, the ethics manual of the American College of Physicians states, "The physician may be technically free to select his patients to the exclusion of those who cannot pay, but as a professional he has a moral obligation to contribute some of his services to the neglected and underprivileged and to give good medical care to all his patients irrespective of their ability to pay."[12] In this era of cost containment and expensive health insurance, some 30 to 40 million Americans who are without medical insurance rely heavily on an uncompensated care system.

Summary

The special bond between physician and patient is the most gratifying aspect of medicine for the majority of physicians. New diseases and therapies evolve over years, but the personalities presenting with medical complaints change each time the physician enters the examining room. It is vital for patients to understand the boundaries within which a physician will care for them. For example, the limited scope of care that a specialist offers may not be readily apparent or relevant to an individual who is unfamiliar with the idiosyncracies of our health care system. It is a responsibility of the physician to update and communicate this information to the patient.

It is a virtual certainty that the physician will encounter a tremendous variety of challenges and opportunities in the relationships he or she has with patients on a daily basis. The good that can come from a simple word of reassurance or a considerate touch can truly be a healing act. When proper attention is paid to this powerful therapeutic aid, the healthy physician-patient relationship has the potential to play a significant role in reducing the possibility of a malpractice claim.

References

1. Cheney FW, Posner K, Caplan RA, Ward RJ. Standards of care and anesthesia liability. *JAMA*. 1989; 261: 1599-1603.

2. *Medical Malpractice: Characteristics of Claims Closed in 1984*. Washington, DC: 1986; U.S. General Accounting Office document HRD-86-50.

3. Moser RH. Medical liability: no magic bullets for malpractice. *Quality Rev Bull*. 1986; 12: 118-120.

4. Mechanic D. Sounding board: public perception of medicine. *N Engl J Med*. 1985; 312: 181-183.

5. Shapiro RS, Simpson DE, Lawrence SL, Talsky AM, Sobsinski KA, Schiedermayer DL. A survey of sued and non-sued physicians and suing patients. *Arch Intern Med*. 1989; 149: 2190-2196.

6. Velente CM, Antlitz AM, Boyd MD, Troisi AJ. The importance of physician-patient communication in reducing medical liability. *Maryland Med J*. 1988; 37: 75-78.

7. Hirsch PJ, Hirsch SA, Reedman L, Weiss A. Twenty-five ways to avoid malpractice suits. *New Jersey Med*. 1987; 84: 101-103.

8. Kern SI. Maintenance and release of medical records. *New Jersey Med*. 1988; 83: 649-650.

9. Mitchell MW. Legally speaking: physician medical records—patient access. *J Arkansas Med Soc*. 1987; 84: 273-274.

10. Stone AH. The Tarasoff decision: suing psychotherapists to save society. *Harvard Law Review*. 1976;90:358-378.

11. Hirsh HL. Patient abandonment: from a legal perspective. *Urban Health*. February 1985: 34-37.

12. American College of Physicians ethics manual. *Ann Intern Med*. 1989; 111(3): 245-252 and (4): 327-335.

Table 1.1

Recommendations for a Healthy Physician-Patient Relationship

Risk management begins the moment you establish a professional relationship with a patient. Understanding, compliance, and satisfaction ultimately depend on oral and written communication. The following general points will be helpful as you build each physician-patient relationship. The result should be a mutually rewarding experience for both the physician and patient.

1. Introduce yourself to every new patient and describe your relationship with other health care providers, such as students, nurses, physician assistants, residents, fellows, consultants, and the relevant attending, referring, and primary care physicians.

2. Address your patients appropriately and modify your greeting as your relationship progresses. It is best to begin with formal titles, then, if both sides are comfortable with doing so, shift to something less formal. If possible, use a translator to help communicate with patients who speak a foreign language with which you are unfamiliar.

3. Sit down close to the bedside, if possible, and make frequent eye contact. Be attentive to the patient's non-verbal communication. Offer your own encouraging feedback through gestures and words.

4. Begin with open-ended questions to allow patients to talk of their symptoms, previous care, impressions of their prognosis, and the role of family members in decision making. Focus questioning to obtain specific information.

5. Ask for the patient's expectations of your care. Involve the patient and family directly in the care as much as possible.

6. Limit the use of medical jargon. Relate information at an appropriate level of understanding for the patient. Use pictures and models to help explain complicated concepts. Summarize and state your understanding of the patient's condition and, finally, the medical plan.

7. Provide emotional support to grieving, anxious, frightened, or depressed patients. Reassure your patients that you will be helping them throughout the course of their medical problems and will be available to answer questions as they arise.

8. Schedule a future meeting to discuss problems not related to the current medical concern if time does not permit discussion at the present visit. Be punctual for meetings with patients and families.

9. Avoid criticizing another physician's management of your patient with words or gestures. The other physician may have had different data and resources available at the time of initial decision making. Medical problems usually appear more clearly when viewed retrospectively.

10. Never guarantee the outcome of a treatment, orally or in writing. Prepare patients for pain, discomfort, and disability that they can reasonably expect from diagnostic and therapeutic interventions. Make clear the necessity and effectiveness of intervention if disability is the expected result.

11. If a complication or adverse outcome does occur, inform the patient of it promptly. Discuss the change in medical plan and role of referrals as the needs arise.

12. Send a written summary of your findings and the medical plan to your patient's primary physician following a hospital stay or major office visit. When multiple clinicians are involved, clearly delineate roles among the parties and convey this to the patient in a manner that will facilitate coordination of patient care.

Table 1.1 (continued)

13. Provide the patient with a similar written summary of care rendered appropriate to the individual's level of understanding and focusing on discharge instructions pertinent to the episode of care.

14. When it is necessary to discuss fees, be open and frank concerning the cost of care. Where appropriate, help educate patients concerning today's often confusing health care system. You might consider providing an estimate of the cost of an anticipated course of therapy or operation.

15. Be aware of the state and federal laws regarding health care for your patient population. Information on childhood vaccinations, prenatal nutrition programs, Medicare benefits, and other topics are vital for proper care of your patients.

16. An established, open relationship with the patient and family will facilitate future discussions of the termination of life support, organ donation, and the benefits of an autopsy.

Table 1.2

Fundamental Elements of the Patient-Physician Relationship

From ancient times, physicians have recognized that the health and well-being of patients depends on a collaborative effort between physician and patient. Patients share with physicians the responsibility for their own health care. The patient-physician relationship is of greatest benefit to patients when they bring medical problems to the attention of their physicians in a timely fashion, provide information about their medical condition to the best of their ability, and work with their physicians in a mutually respectful alliance. Physicians can best contribute to this alliance by serving as their patients' advocate and by fostering these rights:

1. The patient has the right to receive information from physicians and to discuss the benefits, risks, and costs of appropriate treatment alternatives. Patients should receive guidance from their physicians as to the optimal course of action. Patients are also entitled to obtain copies or summaries of their medical records, to have their questions answered, to be advised of potential conflicts of interest that their physicians might have, and to receive independent professional opinions.

2. The patient has the right to make decisions regarding the health care that is recommended by his or her physician. Accordingly, patients may accept or refuse any recommended medical treatment.

3. The patient has the right to courtesy, respect, dignity, responsiveness, and timely attention to his or her needs.

4. The patient has the right to confidentiality. The physician should not reveal confidential communications or information without the consent of the patient, unless provided for by law or by the need to protect the welfare of the individual or the public interest.

5. The patient has the right to continuity of health care. The physician has an obligation to cooperate in the coordination of medically indicated care with other health care providers treating the patient. The physician may not discontinue treatment of a patient as long as further treatment is medically indicated, without giving the patient sufficient opportunity to make alternative arrangements for care.

6. The patient has a basic right to have available adequate health care. Physicians, along with the rest of society, should continue to work toward this goal. Fulfillment of this right is dependent on society providing resources so that no patient is deprived of necessary care because of an inability to pay for the care. Physicians should continue their traditional assumption of a part of the responsibility for the medical care of those who cannot afford essential health care.

AMA Council on Ethical and Judicial Affairs.
Adopted by the American Medical Association June 26, 1990.

Article 1.1

Malpractice Risk and Patient Relations

Paul A. Sommers, PhD. The Journal of Family Practice, March 1985.

Malpractice claims result from both real and perceived negligence. Three areas account for claims: (1) standard of care within a specialty, (2) legal obligations, and (3) patient relationships. Information from the risk-management service division of St. Paul Fire and Marine Insurance Company shows that about 1 in 100 hospitalized patients could legally bring a negligence action against their medical-care provider for failing to act, or for acting improperly. Yet, less than 10 percent of them do. Why? Often the answer lies with the type of relationship the patient has with his health care provider. The more positive the relationship, the less the malpractice risk.

The development of good relationships with patients occurs, not by chance, but by prospective planning, systematic training, and ongoing evaluation. Furthermore, all staff functioning as part of the service delivery team must become patient oriented, not just the physician. Considerations for approaching the human aspect of patient care is the topic of this paper.

Patient Relationships

The patient-physician relationship is interpersonal by design and predicated upon trust. Without trust, patient compliance becomes suspicious and anticipated results can be tenuous. Liability, by definition, refers to something that works to one's disadvantage. The less trust a patient has in the physician, the more liability becomes a factor. Reduction of such liability can be easily facilitated by providing patient-oriented services.

By placing oneself in the patient's shoes, it is possible to better understand what expectations are being placed on the medical and paramedical staff. Too often patients are routinely expected to follow rigorous directions and procedures that may be common sense to the physician, but are fuzzy, at best, to the lay person.

The entire medical community can benefit from timely examination and reasonable modification to improve less-than-favorable service. A review of procedures conducted at nurses' stations, appointment desks, and examination rooms, as well as within the administrative section of any organization, is needed if patient satisfaction is to be attained.

Physicians might well ask each patient to write out the questions for which they are seeking answers. This exercise would allow for a review of problems in sufficient detail before examining the patient to make sure that all concerns are properly addressed.

Medical services are too often designed around the physician's schedule with patients filling available slots. This priority must change. Consideration for such important concerns to patients as vacation schedules, distance from their home to the clinic, school hours of their children, available transportation, preference for male or female physicians, lodging accommodations, and coordinating more than one appointment on the same day should be accorded high priority by physicians. A helpful rule of thumb is to treat the patient as you would like to be treated.

Problem Prevention

An appropriate communication pattern must be initially established with new patients by the office staff and physician. Dialogue must set in motion a clear, meaningful relationship between patient and physician. Briefly outlining what will be taking place during the appointment allows the patient to prepare for what is to come. Training oneself to actively listen, with all attention focused on the individual patient at hand, is an essential interpersonal skill. Physicians should be willing to openly discuss differences with patients, while respecting the patient's views.

Complaints are inevitable. Each problem or issue between two or more individuals should be viewed from each person's perspective. Most disagreements can be resolved if time is taken to clearly identify all related aspects of the case from each point of view; then the proper action is initiated without accusing or holding anyone to blame.

Many forms of consumer participation are possible. For example, including consumers on health-care advisory boards, committees, or task forces is a common practice. In this way, as policies and procedures relating to the delivery of health services are adopted by an organization, consumers are involved through committee work. However, what typically happens in this form of consumer participation is that friends of the organization are often appointed, elected, or otherwise recruited. Such a process defeats the purpose of seeking unbiased consumer input to help objectively determine satisfaction. Effective consumer-participation efforts must go beyond such token involvement. If a physician wants accurate information about patient-care services, he must consistently appraise patient perceptions. He must compare patient satisfaction with the care provided.

Patient participation can be of value on at least two levels: (1) by improving care for individual patients by solving problems as they are identified, and (2) by aggregating individual patient information into group data and monitoring the overall satisfaction level with the service system. Patients are appreciative of opportunities to ask questions of the physician, to comment on appointment scheduling, and to reflect on their progress following treatment.

Although many problems are resolved during the office visit, some cases necessitate additional arrangements. In these instances, follow-up contact with the patient after the visit is important. Although brief and typically inexpensive, this contact affords an opportunity to monitor results of medical intervention, promotes a continuing linkage between patient and physician, and facilitates examination of patient satisfaction.

The patient-physician difference of opinion concerning services received compared with what was expected can be called an index of satisfaction. To develop this index, it is necessary to continue thinking about services from the patient's point of view. What does the patient expect to hear when he calls or writes for an appointment? Is it possible to set up appointments that consider the patient's vacation schedule? Can the physician's hours be extended to accommodate patients who choose not to take off work? Can multiple department appointments be scheduled for different services on the same day?

Patient-Oriented Care and Follow-Up

Some standard services found in patient-oriented systems are availability and ease of securing appointments, personalized communications, effective evaluation and treatment planning, and individualized follow-up care. The referral system must encourage accessibility of appointments and be capable of handling each case, whether it be for a routine physical examination with one physician, or require multiple services and laboratory studies from four or five different specialists. For some patients, it may be advantageous to schedule all appointments on the same day with a staffing at the end to summarize the findings. Appointments should be available by telephone, letter, or in-person requests. Referrals should be encouraged from any source including patients themselves. It is helpful if prospective patients are provided informational literature describing a program or service. Such literature would let the patient know about available services and how to obtain them. This procedure can help to set the patient at ease about going to the physician, particularly one whom he has never met before.

Questions about fees, insurance, or related financial needs should be brought up as an appointment schedule is developed. Too often patients are given double talk by staff when the subject of cost is discussed, and many times patients are not aware of the financial impact until a bill is received. As patients are responsible for paying bills, they should know approximately how much the charges are going to be and how much their insurance will pay. If the patient has insurance, he or she may need guidance to help verify the extent of his coverage prior to clinic visits, as insurance policies vary.

Effective patient follow-up activity can take a variety of forms. The questions written out by the patient about problems to which he seeks answers from the physician should be answered at the end of the examination. Although this procedure is not a substitute for protocol information obtained during a comprehensive health examination, it provides insight into a patient's primary expectation of results. Additionally, the questions will serve as benchmarks for future care consideration, and can be used to reflect satisfaction with services by determining whether appropriate answers and results were obtained.

If a patient is seen by more than one staff member throughout his or her evaluation, it is recommended that the primary physician summarize the findings. Every visit should be followed up with a letter, telephone call, or report to the patient. Such follow-up has proven to positively influence patients' feelings about their health care.

Telephone follow-up has proven especially valuable in cases where medications are being used, a patient is recovering from surgery, or time is needed to determine appropriateness of the treatment. Follow-up contact re-establishes a personal link between physician and patient long after the office visit. If the treatment plan is not working, changes can be made during a telephone conversation, or a return appointment can be set up. An alternative is to have the patient call the physician at specified intervals, or as the need should arise. This option gives the patient confidence that help is only a telephone call away. Some organizations provide toll-free or collect numbers, thus promoting this convenience.

When patients believe their needs are being met, they will remain undaunted in their support and trust for the case. Although the follow-up procedures that have been described are little more than common courtesy, they have been proven to influence positive patient attitudes and minimize malpractice risk.

Sommers PA. Malpractice risk and patient relations. J Fam Pract. 1985; 20(3): 299-301.

Reprinted with permission from the author and Appleton & Lange, Inc.

Article 1.2

Good Medical Records Can Be Strongest Malpractice Defense

Michigan Medicine, January 1983.

Following is the outline of the pertinent, to the point course on good medical records keeping from the new MSMS risk management course for Michigan physicians.

Medical liability experts estimate that 35 to 40 percent of all medical malpractice suits are rendered indefensible by problems with the medical record. A bad result added to a bad record equals liability, regardless of the facts and regardless of the standard of care practiced.

The significance of medical records, both in the office and in the hospital, can be appreciated when one realizes that medical malpractice suits may come to trial anywhere from two to 10 years after the incident in question. At that point the physician will have little independent memory of contact with any single patient. The medical record therefore becomes invaluable to the defense because memory alone is worthless.

In addition, the medical record should reflect the complexity of a difficult clinical problem. If it does, it will demonstrate to a court that proper professional attention has been given to the medical problem. The law does not ask much more.

Mechanically, the record should be carefully prepared, complete, accurate, legible, germane, relevant, timely and generously informative.

Basic Principles

A. All entries should be neat, legible and in ink.
B. Never erase—draw a single line through the incorrect entry, write the word 'error' above. If the error is noted at a later time, make a marginal note as to the date and time of the correction.
C. Use only hospital approved abbreviations and symbols—do not use ditto marks or initials.
D. Do not skip lines or leave blank spaces. Do not squeeze in extra words on a line. Draw a line through the empty space at the end of an entry.
E. Sign each entry (first and last name, professional designation).
F. Date and time each entry.
G. Date each page.
H. Use a supplemental page if necessary to record missed notes and indicate as a late entry.
I. Patient's name should appear on every page.

Medical Records Should Include:

A. Names and signatures of nurses and physicians.

B. Notations of the patient's condition on admission and complete professional nursing assessment.
C. Progress notes on changes in conditions, both positive and negative.
D. Accounts of unusual incidents or injuries sustained while in the hospital.
E. Records of insertion and removal of drains and radium.
F. Patient's response to care and treatment, including refusal to cooperate or follow prescribed plan of care.
G. Patient's degree of mobility, appetite, orientation, mental attitude, and degree of independence.
H. Medications, treatments, vital signs, specimens obtained and where sent.
I. Visits of physicians, consultants and specialists, and contacts with, or attempts to contact, physician.
J. Informed consent for surgery and special procedures.
K. Deathbed statements of patient.
L. Accountability of patient's private property.
M. Teaching of patient or family, including instructions, medications and dietary rules.

Objective Versus Subjective

Use objective, rather than subjective, observations and language. Do not use the term "apparently," or "It appears that..." State facts, not conclusions.

State specifically what you:

1. **See**—bleeding; pallor; deformities; type of drainage; color of urine.
2. **Hear**—the patient's complaints; moaning; stertorous breathing.
3. **Smell**—alcohol on the patient's breath; malodorous drainage; fecal odor in vomitus; acetone breath.
4. **Feel**—motion at a fracture site; crepitus of subcutaneous emphysema; a firm, hot area of induration.
5. **Do** for the patient, and what the response to treatment is—whether cervical traction relieves the neck pain or makes it worse.
6. **Do** to protect the patient—put the side rails up and lock them in place; put soft restraints on; help to ambulate when the patient is unable to walk alone.

Problem Items

A. Use of vague phrases such as "better, fair, c/o pain."
B. Meaningless charting, such as "linen changed."
C. Failure to record observations and follow-through steps, when vital signs are abnormal.
D. Failure to record patient's tolerance, response and outcome to medications and treatment.
E. State facts, not conclusions. If a patient is found on the floor, document that fact. If a patient says, "I got up, lost my balance, and fell," document that quotation. Do not say, "Patient apparently fell."
F. Do not enter "an incident report has been filled out" in a patient's medical record. Only objective information on patient care should be included in the medical record. Incident reports are designed to alert hospital personnel to problem areas and potentially dangerous trends so that corrective action can be taken.
G. Do not joust in the medical record. Avoid a criticism, complaining or arguing with another professional or department.

Injections and IV's

A. Record time and site of intramuscular, subcutaneous, intradermal and intravenous injections.
B. Site of infusion and appearance.
C. Type and size of needle.
D. Type and amount of fluid; medications added; rate administered.
E. Note conditions of the site and number of drops per minute on each shift.

Medications

A. Note the type of medications given, and time and route by which medication is administered.
B. If medication requires taking vital signs, medications nurse should take signs and chart them personally.
C. If for pain, note the site of the pain, and its severity.
D. If relief from pain is obtained, state when.

Operating Room Records Should Include:

A. Patient identification, level of consciousness and understanding of anticipated procedure.
B. Verification of allergies, NPO status and physical limitations, if any.
C. Condition of skin and skin preparation.
D. Patient support mechanism and position.
E. Identification of prosthetic implants, medical devices, wound drains, catheters, packing, medical equipment and their location. Serial numbers and lot numbers should be included where applicable.
F. Sponge, needle and instrument count verification.
G. Output summary.
H. Specimen disposition.
I. Identification of type and location of patient monitoring device.
J. Location of electrosurgical grounding equipment.
K. Condition of patient upon transfer to post-receiving area and time.
L. Anesthesiologist's record.
M. Surgeon's operative note.
N. Pre-operative checklist.
O. Authorized observers in OR.
P. X-rays taken.
Q. Consent forms.
R. Post OP visit.
S. Consent should be signed and witnessed before preop. meds. given (date and time).

Discharge Instructions Should Include:

A. Diet, either by the dietician or with the nursing staff.
B. Activity, such as restrictions on activity, importance of rest periods, exercise programs. Restrictive lifting should be documented.
C. Medications, with the name of medication, reason for taking dosage and frequency and side effects.
D. Skin care and hygiene.
E. Specific treatments, such as colostomy care, Foley catheter care, dressing changes.
F. Follow-up appointments, such as clinic appointment with physician, appointment with physical or occupational therapist.

G. Appropriate agency referrals, such as social services.

H. Record and document:
   1. Patient and family's comprehension of instructions given.
   2. Patient's ability to give a return demonstration of a procedure taught.
   3. Booklets or written instruction sheets given to patient.
   4. Completed transfer forms, if patient is transferred to an extended care facility.
   5. Signed copies of instructions are helpful.

Documentation Guidelines

Michigan statute MCLA 600.-2146 states, "Any writing or record whether in the form of an entry in a book or otherwise, made as a memorandum of any act, transaction, occurrence or event shall be admissible in evidence in all trials, hearings and proceedings in any cause of suit in any court, or before any officer, arbitrators, or referees, in proof of said act, transaction, occurrence or event if it was made in the regular course of any business and it was the regular course of such business to make such memorandum or record at the time of such act, transaction, occurrence or event or within a reasonable time thereafter. All other knowledge by the entrant or maker, may be shown to affect its weight but not its admissibility. The term "business" shall include business, profession, occupation and calling of every kind. The lack of an entry regarding any act, transaction, occurrence or event in any writing or record so proved may be received as evidence that no such act, transaction, occurrence or event did, in fact, take place. Any photostatic or photographic reproduction of any such writing or record shall be admissible in evidence in any such trial, hearing or proceeding by order of the court, made within its discretion, upon motion with notice of not less than 4 days. All circumstances of the making of such photostatic or photographic reproduction may be shown upon such trial hearing or proceeding to affect the weight but not the admissibility of such evidence."

Record of Physicians: Availability of Information to Other Physicians

The interest of the patient is paramount in the practice of medicine, and everything that can reasonably and lawfully be done to serve that interest must be done by all physicians who have served or are serving the patient. When a colleague who is presently treating a patient requests records from another physician who has formerly treated the patient, that former physician should promptly make his records available to the attending physician.

No set rule can be laid down to cover the manner in which the records are to be transmitted to the attending physician. Under some conditions, a personal inspection of the records might suffice; under others, an oral report of what is contained in the records would be of help; or in other circumstances, a summary of the records might be made. In extreme cases, a physician might lend his complete record to the attending physician.

The manner of making the report—or the information contained therein—available to the succeeding physician is immaterial and will depend on the circumstances of each case. Certainly, however, the attending physician should not demand or expect more information from the former physician than is necessary to give the patient adequate care in the present illness.

It is assumed, of course, that proper authorization for the use of these records has been granted by the patient.

It is unethical for a physician who formerly treated a patient, to refuse for any reason to make his records of that patient promptly available on request to another physician presently treating the patient (from AMA Judicial Council Opinions and Reports—1977).

Sale or Purchase of Physician's Records

A physician retiring from practice may not ethically sell his patient's records to another physician. His records have been developed during the physician-patient relationship. To sell records would tend to make the patient subject to barter to the highest bidder. For the patient's benefit, however, but only with his consent, these records may be transferred to a physician of his choice. A reasonable charge for secretarial or duplicating service connected with such transfer is not improper.

Further according to Section 9 of the Principles of Medical Ethics, a physician may not reveal the confidences entrusted in him in the course of

AUTHORIZATION TO TRANSFER RECORDS

Date:___________

To:____________________, M.D.

I hereby authorize you to transfer or make available to ____________________, M.D., ____________________ all the records and reports relating to my case.

(address)

Signed____________________

American Medical Association, Office of the General Counsel,
Medicolegal Forms With Legal Analysis

medical attendance. The physician's records summarizing these confidences are cloaked with this same protection. To transfer a patient's records without his consent would violate this confidence.

A physician may not ethically purchase such records from a retiring physician or from the estate of a deceased physician. (From AMA Judicial Council Opinions and Reports—1977)

In Michigan, patients may review and obtain copies of hospital medical records. They may also request corrections or make addenda.

Miscellaneous Comments

Communication problems affect the physician-patient relationship. Illness is an emotionally charged experience for the patient. If a physician neglects needs of a patient, he may well feel very alienated by this lack of sensitivity. There are several categories of communication that can affect the physician-patient relationship.

1. Use of technical jargon—Many physicians will tend to use medical terms that are not easy for the patient to understand.

This may frustrate patients who never really understand their situation. In a case in which there is a bad result, the patient may feel that he was never informed or gave consent for the treatment or procedure.

Patients many times feel intimidated by the medical jargon that the physician provides. They may not feel comfortable in asking questions that could later become very important.

2. Colleague remarks—Remarks by physicians about treatments and procedures of other physicians can cause considerable communication, and ultimately legal, problems. Inappropriate colleague remarks—loose talk about colleagues—can lead to legal consequences.

Some physicians make inappropriate remarks as a means of bolstering their own ego and status with patients.

Inappropriate remarks can cause patients to believe that they were treated in a negligent or injurious manner and force a liability.

3. The telephone is an essential part of the physician's communication with the patient.

Good telephone communication between the physician or his employees and patient is absolutely essential. Many malpractice situations have developed or have been made worse by a communications breakdown that could have been avoided. Document phone calls in your medical record.

Calls that are emergencies or medical problems must receive priority for physician response.

Calls in which the patient threatens to sue should receive immediate priority since interventions at this point may stop a suit.

4. Communication of need of second opinion—Physician must be aware of the usefulness of second opinions and be willing to utilize them as a deterrent to liability.

Good medical records can be strongest malpractice defense. Mich Med. January 1983: 6-8.

Reprinted with permission from the Michigan State Medical Society.

Article 1.3

Clinical Confidentiality: Dilemmas and Guidelines

L.D. Hankoff, MD, and Candice Nattland, PsyD. New Jersey Medicine, October 1986.

The confidentiality of a patient's medical information is guarded by a fundamental medical ethic and reinforced by federal and state law. The privilege of medical information, however, is far from absolute and these same ethical and legal forces may require confidentiality to be breached.

The simple act of taking a medical history involves the physician into the most intimate recesses of the patient's life. This liberty is one of the powerful tools and facilitators of the treating relationship. The intimate disclosures of the patient, however, carry a grave ethical responsibility for the physician and, occasionally, seeds of deep conflict. This article is devoted to the understanding of the ethical and legal aspects of the confidentiality of information obtained in the clinical relationship of physician and patient. While the psychiatrist is most apt to be presented with information of a sensitive nature, any medical practitioner may encounter information which raises the question of confidentiality. Since the issue involves both general professional and legal aspects of significance, it is important that we consider the specific legal status of clinical confidentiality in New Jersey.

The issue of clinical confidentiality revolves around the definitional areas of a) the privacy of the communication; b) the confidentiality accorded the information; and c) the potential status of the communication as legally privileged.

Leon D. Hankoff, MD, is chairman of Elizabeth General Medical Psychiatric Center. Candice Nattland, PsyD, is a New Jersey Licensed Psychologist.

Privacy refers to the expected freedom from unauthorized intrusions into one's individual life in all of its aspects. Privacy is a possession of the individual and in the United States is rooted heavily in the Fourth Amendment which guarantees "against unreasonable searches and seizures." Once the information has been communicated to the physician, however, it no longer is private and the individual patient or client has lost possession of it. The protection of such information, now in the hands of the physician, depends on laws of confidentiality and privileged communication.

Confidentiality refers to the security surrounding personal information. It is a subset of the larger area of privacy (although the two terms often are misused interchangeably) and is an issue of information shared between the communicant and the recipient.

Privileged communication refers to the expectation by a communicator that the communication will be held confidential. This privilege may be derived from legal or ethical standards. Its strength lies in the value to society of protecting and fostering professional relationships of a confidential nature.

The existence of privileged communication is derived from the fact of testimonial compulsion, i.e., the demand by the legal system that an individual with pertinent information respond to the legal authority in providing that information. The development of privileged communication represented a hedging on the force of testimonial compulsion. It is the competition between the needs of the legal system and the value to society of the particular professional relationship which determines the changing limits of privileged communication.

The medical and other treating professions relate their principle of confidentiality back to a very ancient past. The Hippocratic oath states explicitly "that which ought not be spoken abroad" will not be revealed. This sense that the treater is privy to special information in a very special and treasured fashion runs through all of the treating professions and is reflected in many codes of professional conduct.

The 16th century is the time of the first recorded legal privilege for confidential information, granted to the relationship of attorney and client.[1] The first state to adopt a physician-patient privileged communication was New York in 1828.[1] In 1959, Georgia became the first state to adopt a law providing for psychiatrist-patient privilege. By 1962, 31 out of 50 states provided a law of privileged communication for clergy whereas 36 states provided such a privilege for physicians. The number of states providing privilege continues to increase: 38 states and the District of Columbia having physician-patient privilege statutes in 1984.[2,3] While privileged communication is an area of expanding concern and legal support, an accompanying trend has been toward restriction in the application of privilege. Thus, a wide range of specific limitations on privilege have evolved. In particular, there is a growing number of suspected abuses and crimes in which reporting is obligatory. All 50 states and the District of Columbia have enacted laws making it mandatory for the physician to report to the authorities information on child abuse.[2]

The Tarasoff decision has added a particular issue to the obligation to report.[4] In a crime committed in 1969 and decided in the California courts in 1975, it was adjudged that a psychotherapist with knowledge of an intended crime has an obligation to make a judgment as to the possibility of that crime and specifically to inform the intended victim. In the appeal decision which reaffirmed the original judgment, an additional stringency was added in that the police who had known of the intended crime were absolved for responsibility and the therapist left as the individual with the heaviest burden for initiating preventive acts against the patient.

While the Fourth Amendment is directed at privacy, there is no constitutional guarantee pertaining to the information which has been imparted to a physician by a patient. The legal rules pertaining to confidentiality are derived from case law, a welter of accumulated decisions which themselves can be in conflict. Case law has developed from debates regarding the disclosure of information and the appropriate stance of the physician as a source of evidence in such courts of law. Issues usually are resolved in terms of individual cases and the merits of disclosing information gained in the physician-patient relationship.

However, apart from individual case issues, the broader underlying philosophical question is that of the meaning to the profession of any change in the nature of its privileged communication status. In the debate over privileged communication and its value, the deciding factor in legal judgments often focuses on the balance between two sets of needs: 1) the physician-patient relationship that may be damaged if the information is subject to testimonial compulsion as against justice and 2) the needs of society that may be diminished if the relationship and if information remain privileged and immune to legal requirements.[1]

While the restrictions on privileged communication may come through case law and other statutes, there often is the important restriction on privilege posed by the patient. The patient may call on the physician or caregiver to provide information from the medical record to substantiate a point of view or advance a claim in a legal process.

Ethical and Legal Aspects of Confidentiality

The ethical code of physicians, as well as New Jersey law, provides for the confidential nature of the physician-patient relationship. The American Medical Association Code of Ethics, Section 9, states the relevant professional guidelines, "A physician may not reveal the confidences entrusted to him in the course of medical attendance or the deficiencies he may observe in the character of patients, unless he is required to do so by law or unless it becomes necessary in order to protect the welfare of the individual or of the community." New Jersey state law 2A:84A-22.2 provides physician-patient privilege exempting a physician from providing testimony and/or records regarding the patient. In fact, a physician may not disclose any information given to him by a patient within the context of the physician-patient relationship without risking civil liability charges.[5]

However, the physician often finds himself in conflict as medical information often is sought or demanded in the course of legal proceedings. Thus, the physician needs to know when it is permissible or even obligatory to violate confidentiality and when the privileged status of the physician-patient relationship is to be strenuously guarded.

New Jersey case law explicates specific situations in which confidentiality is waived so that other needs, which the courts have determined to be greater, can be met. The physician-patient privilege protecting the patient from having his physician testify in court or relinquishing treatment records is waived under two general types of circumstances: 1) when the patient poses a threat to himself or others, and 2) when the patient's behavior gives rise to an obstruction of justice.

There are four situations involving threat to self or others where confidentiality may be breached. 1) any case involving suspected or clear physical or sexual abuse of children (NJSA 9:6-8, 10; 9:6-8, 14); 2) any case in which the patient presents a "clear and imminent danger to self, another person, or to society"; 3) any case in which a patient must be involuntarily committed to a mental health facility (NJSA 2A:84A-22.3); and 4) any case in which certain health conditions exist including tuberculosis, venereal diseases (NJSA 26:4-15), gunshot wounds (NJSA 2C:58-8), and epilepsy (NJSA 39:3-10.4).

The duty to prevent harm to a third party has been considered in a New Jersey Superior Court which cited the Tarasoff decision. In this case, *McIntosh v Milano*, the court held that there is an affirmative duty by a psychiatrist or therapist "to take whatever steps are reasonably necessary to protect an intended or potential victim of his patient."[6]

Confidentiality also is to be waived in cases where to keep a patient's confidence might result in an obstruction of justice. These situations include: 1) evaluation for workman's compensation benefits; 2) a request for medical assistance to aid in the commission of a crime (NJSA 2A:84A-22.6); 3) the use of a patient's medical condition as an element of a claim or defense (NJSA 2A:84A-22.4); 4) the use of a patient's condition to contest the validity of a document such as a will (NJSA 2A:84A-22.3); 5) the use of a patient's condition in a legal dispute between individuals who are involved in a legally privileged relationship such as might occur in a malpractice claim (NJSA 2A:84A-22.7); and 6) if the court judges that nondisclosure is "contrary to public interest."

The Decision to Breach Confidentiality

Between the situations in which the physician is mandated to forego confidentiality, e.g., mandated reporting of child abuse, and those in which the patient freely and appropriately consents to release medical information are a range of possible situations in which questions regarding the breaking of confidentiality arise. The physician or other caregiver may be privy to information which may help to prevent a future crime or prevent a miscarriage of justice. When a physician, often a psychiatrist, is informed by a patient that a crime is being contemplated, the physician is confronted with the issue of violating patient confidentiality because of the obligation to society.

The uncommon situations in which the patient reveals self-incriminating information are apt to occur in the setting of psychiatric treatment or psychotherapy. The physician may need to anticipate such possibilities, to warn the patient that confidentiality is not absolute, and, on occasion, to obtain written informed consent regarding this understanding over confidentiality and privileged medical communication. The patient entering into psychotherapy may need to have an awareness of the fact that confidentiality has its limits. To the extent that a therapeutic contract is developed at the initiation of treatment, elements of informed consent may need to spell out this fact of the limit of confidentiality. For example, the client may need to know that if he reveals an ongoing situation in which he is injuring others, the psychotherapist may have an obligation to society or to the system of justice to forego confidentiality and inform authorities or possible targets of the patient's intentions.

If a physician determines that a case involves an issue which state law specifies must be reported, it is necessary to consider the manner in which confidentiality may be breached. Ideally, the process of reporting will result in a minimum of harm to the treatment relationship. In cases where the need to report is clear from the beginning, breaching confidentiality is relatively simple. A patient should be informed prior to treatment about his right to and the limits of confidentiality. Then, if information is to be reported, the physician should inform the patient he is doing so. For example, patients requesting evaluation for workman's compensation cases need to know that the doctor is obligated to report what he is told. Certain types of cases suggest the need for a thorough review of the limits of confidentiality. For example, physicians who work with potentially suicidal or homicidal patients often choose to explain at the beginning of treatment circumstances under which they will waive confidentiality.

The physician is faced with a more complex dilemma when, during the course of treatment and often because of the developing trust between doctor and patient, the patient reveals information which the physician is required to report. While this frequently is seen in the psychiatric practice, it also can occur in a general medical practice. For example, a man in treatment for venereal disease may reveal that he is involved in an incestuous relationship with his younger daughter. The physician might first encourage the patient to report himself to legal authorities. If the patient refuses, the physician, according to state law, must report this sexual abuse of a child. The physician first might ask the patient to provide written consent for him to report. If this strategy fails, the patient should be informed that confidentiality will be breached and told the exact information that will be reported.[7] The physician should be prepared to discuss the patient's reaction to his report in order to maintain the therapeutic relationship.

In the event that a patient waives his right to privilege, during court proceedings, a physician may receive a subpoena for information he obtained during the treatment of the patient. The physician should first consult an attorney to determine the nature of the subpoena and its legality. The privilege is that of the patient and must be asserted by the patient not the physician. If the physician is unable to avoid a court appearance, he should contact the patient and the patient's attorney to review the information which has been requested and demand written consent from the patient to release the information. The physician should indicate if the information may adversely affect the case. If the patient refuses to sign a written consent to release the information the physician may decide not to provide further information. At this point, he can request a private conference with the judge in an attempt to limit the information he must provide to the essentials of the case. Finally, the physician may appear in response to the subpoena and claim that the request for information is a violation of professional confidentiality and the patient's legal privilege.[7] A ruling then must be made by the court and then the physician will determine whether he/she must and can obey.

SPECIAL ISSUES IN MAINTAINING CONFIDENTIALITY

The private practitioner shares the issues and conflicts of confidentiality. The office practitioner also may have to deal with the specific challenges to confidentiality which accompany private practice and the office setting. Office assistants and professionals sharing in office practice are privy to the confidences of the patient which must be afforded the same consideration. The practitioner needs to consider the nature of communications and casual exchanges that may go along in relation to the office setting. For example, elevator conversations may reveal embarrassing details to other listeners. The office practitioner who utilizes a family member as a clerical or other form of assistant may engage in discussions with this fellow worker which represent violations of confidentiality. Furthermore, the exchanges of information by physicians in social situations also may represent violations of confidentiality which are carried out without due precaution because all of the participants in the conversation are professional colleagues.

The confidentiality of medical information imparted to the physician, nurse, or other caregiver working in a hospital or agency setting does not apply to other members of the treatment team. It is understood that such medical information will be shared in the course of coordinated care. This is a particular issue in a setting such as a community mental health center where interdisciplinary collaboration is basic to the treatment of most individual patients.[8] The patient may not always be aware of this coordination and mistakenly may regard this sharing as a breach of confidentiality. At times it may be necessary, in advance, to explain to the patient that information will be shared with other caregivers. This arises when the patient indicates a concern about the information or attempts to form a secrecy contract with the particular caregiver receiving information from the patient. The patient may be informed that, if he/she does not want information to be shared intramurally, it may be best for the patient not to disclose the specific item.

A similar issue arises when the patient agrees that information can be released from a past treating agency to a current treater. Consideration needs to be given to the amount and nature of information sent to the second agency in response to such pro forma requests. Although that patient has consented fully to such transmission of information, it is important to consider how the receiving agency will deal with the information. Is the information going to be utilized for treatment purposes? Will the information be exposed to an array of nonprofessional readers? If the information is going to be used solely for determining reimbursement, for example, it is ordinarily not necessary to disclose personal details or intimate aspects of the patient's life in order to satisfy the needs of the agency procedures.

When the patient is being prepared for discharge, various outside contacts may be necessary and information required in referral procedures. The content and form of the information released outside of the system should be looked at with discrimination. In making discharge plans and passing on discharge summaries, for example, the agency receiving the information should be considered in terms of its need for and use of the information and the nature of the staff who have access to such information. Information should be pointed to the specific need and unnecessary disclosure avoided.

Apart from the issues involved in transmitting medical information to other physicians or institutions, there exist concerns over access to information intramurally. The accessibility of medical records within an institution may allow the release of sensitive information to staff who may deliberately or unwittingly abuse this information. Such violations of confidentiality may come about as a result of outside technological forces. The enlarging use of computerized information banks makes accessibility to information by a wide variety of individuals possible. Thus, it is important that leaks in this system be attended to and that personnel relating to these sources of information be fully grounded in the dangers of information access. Hospitals in particular need to conduct regular training programs regarding confidentiality.

The computerized health record offers new problems in maintaining confidentiality.[9] In the large institutional setting where computer access is widely distributed for financial, administrative, audit, and educational use along with basic clinical record-keeping, the number and training of the staff involved spans the entire institution. As a consequence, there are many opportunities for casual violations of confidentiality. More seriously, however, is deliberate entry into the computerized medical record system by unauthorized individuals. Computer data banks have been penetrated for a variety of illicit purposes and various technological approaches are being developed to safeguard the stored data. In addition to technological safeguards, the staff having access to computerized medical records should be trained in the elements of confidentiality, both ethical and procedural. Without training, office and other personnel are not apt to appreciate fully the significance of guarding the confidentiality of the computerized medical record. Even the physician who has a general sense of confidentiality may not exercise the same sensitivity for the computerized records as he does for the verbalized information acquired in the course of routine medical history taking.

CASE EXAMPLES

Case 1. A couple learned that their five-year-old child is terminally ill. The pediatrician who diagnosed the child's illness becomes involved in helping the mother manage the care of the dying child. During this period the wife confides in the pediatrician that her husband frequently abuses her physically although he has never been abusive to the child. The pediatrician worries about what he should do about the wife's report of frequent physical abuse?

Comment. The pediatrician's role in this case is to help the couple manage the care of the terminally ill child. Unlike child abuse, the husband's physical abuse of the wife is not reportable. The pediatrician can offer support to the wife. In light of the complicated dynamics involved in physically abusive marriages, a referral to a competent mental health professional might provide the greatest likelihood for long-term resolution of the problem. Such a referral given to the couple would not involve a breach of confidentiality.

Case 2. Sally, a 30-year-old receptionist, diagnosed as a narcissistic personality disorder, was being treated in a psychiatric clinic in individual and group therapy and adjunctively with psychotropic medication. In the course of treatment, the patient took an overdose of her medication and was admitted to the hospital. She reported that a private physician was providing her with medication in large and inappropriate quantities. A month later, the patient's roommate attempted suicide. Sally, as a collateral source of information at the time in the emergency room, stated that she felt that her roommate had been stealing her medication and had used it in the suicide attempt. Her involvement with her roommate was a serious complicating factor in her already turbulent life. Sometime later in treatment, the patient announced that she was starting work as a counselor in a nearby child care agency.

Comment. The dilemma of confidentiality posed by the case involved the information provided by the patient which suggested that some form of intervention with a third party might serve to prevent further problems. The patient suggested that she was being given tranquilizer prescriptions by a private physician who, in effect, was abetting her abuse of drugs. She described her roommate as stealing her medication, both having used the medication in self injuries. Finally, we are confronted with the picture of this type of individual being in the role of caregiver to small children. In all of these situations there is insufficient cause for the therapist to violate confidentiality. The possible fact of past illegal acts does not in itself warrant a violation of confidentiality if there is no continuing danger or jeopardy to individuals. A past crime per se does not justify the violation of confidentiality. The possible danger to the children of the agency in which the patient plans to work also is insufficient basis for violating confidentiality. The dangers to others must be of a reasonably predictable nature to justify the involvement of third parties. Furthermore, the nature of the patient's personality points to a considerable degree of unreliability and dramatization in her expressed communication.

Case 3. Mrs. A., 29, married and the mother of two children, presented herself to the obstetrician-gynecologist who has been treating her intermittently for the past ten years. Her complaint was vaginal discharge with the question of venereal disease. The gynecologist did a routine Pap smear and culture which were reported by the laboratory as positive for venereal disease. Mrs. A. was asked to return to the office and a prescription was given. The gynecologist asked whether she would like a prescription for her husband and, if not, he requested that her husband be seen by his physician. Mrs. A. then tearfully said that she did not think she got the infection from her husband, as she had an incidental liaison with a friend who is a known philanderer. She thinks her husband may be fooling around too and believed she may have gotten the infection from him.

Comment. The dilemma begins with how to prevent the husband from becoming infected or, if he already is, how to treat him; how to treat the philanderer, if he should be treated at all; and how to prevent reinfection. In the case of a venereal disease, the physician has a specific duty under the law to warn a third party of possible exposure to infection. He also is required to report the wife's condition to the Department of Health which conducts communicable disease followup.

The dilemma of the gynecologist might be resolved without violating confidentiality. The information does not have to be transmitted to her husband against her wishes. It might be explained to the husband that her vaginal infection requires temporary abstinence from sexual activity and that treatment for him is a desirable adjunct. The issue of the venereal nature of the infection may not need to be introduced. This calls for a tactful explanation on the part of the gynecologist and a partial withholding of facts. It is this partial explanation that may provoke inquiries by the husband and place the gynecologist in a position of violating confidentiality. The possibility of damaging the marriage must be weighed and a careful discussion with the patient conducted beforehand regarding exactly how much information is to be imparted.

Conclusion

The burden of the physician and the health care system with regard to clinical confidentiality is a double one: on one hand, the confidentiality of medical information must be maintained scrupulously, the privacy of the patient must be protected by safeguards that keep pace with the advances in an age of information technology, and the ethical stance of the practitioner with regard to confidentiality must be continually refined and tested. On the other hand, ethical and legal directives must be followed which require that confidentiality be breached in specific instances. There are times when the welfare, even the life, of an outsider or society must be protected and the privacy of the medical patient compromised in order to achieve that protection. These are the rare times when our alliance with the patient must be put aside for the welfare of others.

References

1. Zenoff E: Confidential and privileged communications. JAMA 182 160-166, 1982.

2. DeKraii MB, Sales BD: Confidential communications of psychotherapists. Psychotherapy - Theory/Research/Practice/Training 21:3, 1984.

3. Medical Records, in Lasky PC: Hospital Law Manual, Vol. 1A. Aspen Systems Corporation, Health Law Center. 1981-84, pp.1-71.

4. Stone AA: The Tarasoff decisions: Suing psychotherapists to safeguard society. Harvard Law Review 90 358-378, 1976.

5. Robinson L, Popiel D: Patient's Rights: A Manual for New Jersey Community Mental Health Centers. Community Mental Health Law Project, 1981.

6. McIntosh v Milano. 168 Superior Court of New Jersey, Law Division, 1979, pp.466-496.

7. Schwitzgebel RL, Schwitzgebel RK: Confidential communications, in Schwitzgebel RL, Schwitzgebel RK (eds): Law and Psychological Practice. New York, NY. John Wiley & Sons, 1980. p.213.

8. Lewis M: Confidentiality in the community mental health center. Am J Orthopsychiat 37 946-955, 1967.

9. Opp M: The confidentiality dilemma. Modern Healthcare 49-54, 1975.

Hankoff LD. Clinical confidentiality: dilemmas and guidelines. New Jersey Med. 1986; 83(10): 655-659.

Reprinted with permission from the authors and New Jersey Medicine.

Article 1.4

Patient Abandonment: From a Legal Perspective

Harold Hirsh, MD, JD, FCLM. Urban Health, February 1985.

The Physician-Patient Relationship

The physician-patient relationship commences when the patient approaches the physician and the latter undertakes to render medical service. Ordinarily, this relationship endures as long as the occasion for care lasts.[1] This means, in the case of an illness, until the patient recovers or dies; in the case of a particular condition which requires a series of treatments in the physician's office, until the series is complete; and in the case in which the physician is called in consultation, when the consultation is completed.[2] The relationship starts and finishes in a situation in which a patient goes to the doctor's office for advice or examination and no reason for further service is discovered or mentioned.

The same would be true in the rare situation in which a doctor makes a "house call," and it is understood by both parties that the doctor will not return unless called again.The doctor-patient relationship begins and ends with this visit.[3] However, such cases must be distinguished from cases in which extended treatment or attention is needed. Also, it must be noted that the relationship may come to an end if the doctor becomes incapable of attending the patient, if, for example, the doctor becomes seriously ill, or insane, or dies.

During the life of the doctor-patient relationship, the physician is ordinarily obligated, in the absence of some countervailing agreement with his patient, to provide continued needed care. One who engages a physician to treat him impliedly engages his attendance throughout the illness or until his professional services have been dispensed with, that is to say, the doctor-patient relationship, once initiated, continues until:

1. it is ended by the parties' consent,
2. it is revoked by the patient,
3. the doctor's services are no longer needed,
4. or the physician withdraws from the case after reasonable notice to the patient.

It is usually held to be malpractice for a physician unilaterally to sever the doctor-patient relationship.

The relationship between a physician and his patient has been held by both the legal and the medical professions to be a special privileged relationship. Real and imaginary breakdowns in the relationship, however, have led to many malpractice actions against physicians. The entering into the physician-patient relationship is exclusively discretionary with the physician, but once the relationship is established its existence is not exclusively discretionary with the physician.[4] As a general rule, the length of the physician-patient relationship is proportionate to the need of the patient for the physician's care.

In entering into the physician-patient relationship, the physician is free to contractually specify a limitation on the time or nature of treatment; otherwise, the physician's continued attention to, and attendance upon his patient is obligatory. This obligation, which is absolute, includes keeping informed of the condition of the patient and progress of the patient's illness and continues during the patient's hospitalization.

The concept of abandonment is, by definition, in no way related to the physician's permissible refusal to enter into a doctor-patient relationship with a

Dr. Hirsch is Distinguished Visiting Professor, George Washington University; Past President, American College of Legal Medicine; Member, Board of Trustees, American Board of Legal Medicine; and Member, Board of Trustees, American College of Legal Medicine Journalism.

particular person. Thus, the refusal to respond to a call or render treatment to one not yet accepted as a patient is not within the abandonment concept. It follows that the doctor is not liable for abandonment if he does not choose to treat a case or, for that matter, if he does not choose to practice at all—even though he may be the only physician available. The act of regulating the practice of medicine is preventive; it is not a compulsory measure. In granting the license (permission) to practice, the State does not require, and the licensee does not engage that he will practice at all or on terms other than those he may choose to accept. [5]

It's Not All Over Until It's All Over

The patient may wish to terminate the relationship. He is, of course free to discharge the physician and end the contractual relationship at any time. The physician undoubtedly has a duty to warn him, in this situation, of the necessity for obtaining further medical care [and the] physician must also provide the successor physician with sufficient information to permit continuation of treatment without delay, but if these conditions are met, the original physician has no further obligation to the patient.

In such cases, written documentation of the patient's decision to terminate the relationship is highly advisable. The physician is best advised to write the patient a letter ("registered, return receipt requested") confirming that the patient has discharged him and reiterating the need for continuing treatment. If possible, the physician should obtain a signed statement of discharge from the patient, but a very disgruntled or rejected patient may refuse to comply with such a request. Written proof that the patient, not the physician, terminated the relationship is very important because these patients are the ones who, justifiably or not, are most likely to pursue legal action against the physician.[6]

Definition of Abandonment

Abandonment has been defined as the unilateral severance by the physician of the professional relationship between himself and the patient without reasonable notice, at a time when there is still the necessity of continuing medical attention.[7] Abandonment, of course, in its classical sense, involves an intent on the part of the physician to terminate improperly the contractual relationship. However, closely related to it is the situation in which there is no such intention by the physician, but he is so dilatory in his obligation that he does not see the patient as often as due care in treatment would demand, and the patient is thus denied the benefit of the physician-patient relationship. This would institute constructive abandonment. To further differentiate, classical abandonment gives rise not only to an action for negligence, but one for breach of contract.[8] Malpractice involving treatment which results either from failure to see the patient sufficiently often or from an incorrect conclusion that the patient's condition is such that no further treatment is necessary involves an action in negligence alone.[9]

The practical impact of the difference between the two is that in a case alleging negligent and inadequate treatment the patient must present expert medical testimony, as is true in all but a few types of medical malpractice suits. Juries are not, however, required to hear expert testimony for the plaintiff before declaring that the physician has abandoned his patient in an action for breach of contract.[9]

Abandonment of a patient can occur only where there is a bona fide physician-patient relationship. The North Carolina Supreme Court delineated the need for this relationship in *Easter v. Lexington Memorial Hospital, Inc.*[10]

In *Easter*, the defendant doctor was in charge of the emergency room. The doctor on duty—not the defendant—examined the patient and subsequently misdiagnosed his condition. The patient died shortly after being admitted. Even though the defendant doctor had never seen nor examined the decedent, the plaintiff sued him for abandonment. The court held that no action for malpractice could stand, for there was no relationship or even a brief encounter between the decedent and the physician. A physician-patient relationship must be established as a prerequisite for an actionable claim of abandonment.

The District Court in Kansas examined a factually more difficult case than in *Easter*. In *Doran v. Priddy*,[11] a physician was called upon to examine another doctor's patient who had been admitted to the hospital. The physician had some knowledge of the patient, but no knowledge of the treatment history nor of the arrangements that the patient's true doctor had made. The "counseling" doctor refused to treat the patient after the initial examination. The court held here that no abandonment occurred as no physician-patient relationship existed. Therefore, the "consulting" physician was under no duty to act toward the patient. In light of decisions in other cases, this physician was fortunate in not being held liable since he had become involved in the care and management of the patient under a legal theory designated as "holding self out." Usually, a little involvement means complete responsibility and liability.

The general principles concerning abandonment are jurisdictionally uniform. Basically, when a physician establishes a physician-patient relationship by agreeing to treat a patient, a duty of the physician is created. This entails the devotion of his best efforts to the treatment of the patient as long as needed, unless he is dismissed by the patient or he has given the patient sufficient proper notice of his withdrawal to allow the patient to find a competent medical substitute.

Physicians' Duties and Prerogatives

The duty of the physician not to abandon his patient includes the duty of the physician to continue treatment of the patient as long as is necessary. This duty encompasses not only the initial treatment but also any follow-up which may be warranted.

Vann v. Harden[13] started off appropriately. The defendant doctor had properly set and placed a cast on a fracture of the plaintiff's lower leg. However, on two subsequent calls, even though the patient complained of extreme pain, the doctor did nothing. He then left town, despite the fact that his patient's chart showed fluctuating fever and low blood count. When the patient's parents were unable to reach the defendant, they called another doctor who bivalved the cast and found evidence of acute infection.

When the defendant returned he refused to examine the patient's leg and instead discharged him from the hospital, although his temperature had continued to rise and he was still complaining of excruciating pain. Another physician was called. He removed the plaintiff's cast and observed necrotic spots. Eventually, it became necessary to amputate the plaintiff's leg. Upholding a verdict against the defendant, the Supreme Court of Virginia held that the jury could properly have found that his refusal to attend and treat the plaintiff was the cause of the ultimate injury, stating:

> After a physician has accepted employment in a case, it is his duty to continue his services as long as they are necessary. He cannot voluntarily abandon his patient. Even if personal attention is no longer necessary in the treatment of an injured limb, the physician, if the case calls for it, must furnish the patient with instructions as to care, and his failure to do so might become actionable negligence.

The physician may not withdraw in a peremptory manner from the treatment relationship or leave the patient stranded without medical attention.[14] He must give the patient reasonable notice, which, again for the physician's own protection, should be in writing and preferably sent "return receipt requested."[15] He must give the patient sufficient time to locate another physician who is willing to accept the case. The period of notice will obviously vary with the situation. However, as a rule of thumb, a period of at least a week from the date of mailing such a notice should be allowed before the first physician actually ceases to see the patient. Even if the physician is the party who withdraws from the relationship, he is obligated to provide sufficiently adequate records and information to his successor to insure proper continuing care. This, of course, assumes that there is a successor physician available. If a physician is, as is true in many communities of this country, the only one in town, it would appear that regardless of provocation he must continue to see the patient until some resolution of the problem is achieved for a reasonable time.

Duty Is Absolute

In an early case[16] decided by the Supreme Court of West Virginia, the physician was engaged to attend the patient during pregnancy and home delivery. Because of seemingly undue delay in the commencement of labor, he gave her medicine at 8:00 p.m. to induce labor. He stated it would probably be midnight before he would be needed, so he was going to his office. He further stated that he would return in two hours, but, if needed before that time, he was to be called at his office. By 11:00 p.m. the patient's pains had become very intense. A call for the physician at his office met with no response. A search for him at his home and in the neighborhood proved in vain. Shortly after 1:00 a.m. another physician was obtained, who promptly delivered her child. It was born at 3:00 a.m. and lived only an hour-and-a-half.

In the meantime, the first physician had attended another patient, also in childbirth, and did not return to the home of the patient until approximately 3:00 a.m. Finding another physician there, he did not enter. The patient described her condition from 11:00 p.m. to 1:00 a.m. as "agony," the progress of the fetus not being normal. She was substantiated by her husband and a neighbor woman.

The plaintiff claimed damages for the loss of the child and for impairment of her health and her extreme suffering prior to the delivery. The court held that the charge that the loss of the child was due to the defendant's absence was not proven. However, the defendant having given medicine to accelerate labor, it was his absolute duty to remain where he could be reached, or to provide a competent substitute. His leaving the plaintiff at a critical stage was a "culpable dereliction of duty," he was liable for the suffering caused, and the fact that he was attending another patient did not excuse him.

Limited and Special Practice

Although the physician's duty on one hand is absolute, on the other hand it is not always absolute. Depending upon contractual agreements, either express or implied, a physician may be able to limit his obligation based on what he is asked and agreed to do. If the physician-patient relationship is general in nature, then the physician has a duty to continue treatment and attention as long as it is necessary. The physician is under no obligation, however, to enter into such a general contract for treatment. He may limit his duty through a more specialized agreement. That is, a physician may be asked to treat only a particular illness or only for a strictly limited time or place. If such is the case, his duty is terminated upon completion of the specialized agreement.[17] It is important that the patient be in full approval of the limited relationship.

Because the relationship of doctor and patient is a consensual one, a physician is free to limit the scope of the relationship into which he is willing to enter.[18] He can restrict his practice to his office, and his refusal to make a house call will not constitute abandonment of the patient.[19]

The same principle applies to the physician who is brought into a case for consultation only or to conduct a specified series of tests. The doctor-patient relationship terminates when the consultation or testing is completed, and a refusal to provide additional professional services to the patient cannot be characterized as an abandonment of him.[20] By the same token, physicians, whether specialists or general practitioners, can limit their practice to certain ailments or injuries.

A physician has the professional and legal right to limit his practice both as to geographical area and as to subject matter. He is under no legal obligation whatever to treat patients who wish him to exceed those limitations, in the normal course of events.

An internist is not considered to have abandoned his patient when he realizes that a surgical problem is involved and insists that the patient consult a surgeon.[21] In one case, the defendant, an internist, thought that the patient had bacterial colitis and treated him for that complaint. When the patient's condition did not improve, the physician sent him to a surgeon, who diagnosed appendicitis and operated. The patient sued the internist for abandonment.

The court held that the internist was not compelled to perform surgery when he had excluded it from the limits of his practice. The patient was not damaged by a delay in the diagnosis. The original diagnosis was reasonable and the patient called a surgeon as soon as the internist advised him to do so. No harm resulted.

Since the physician has the right to make reasonable limitations on his practice,[21] he is under no legal obligation whatever to treat any patient who wishes to exceed the stated limitations of that practice. Many physicians do not make house calls, and their practice is limited to the office. This is quite common in specialty practice.

In order to avoid difficulty, physicians should inform patients of the limitations of their practice. In the event the physician's services are needed at a time other than during office hours, the patient may be referred to a hospital emergency room. A physician whose policy is not to make house calls is not obligated to do so and is perfectly justified in telling the patient to come to the office or to see him at the hospital.

Except in emergencies, it is established that a physician does not have to make house calls involving his own patient. A case[18] in point involves the defendant obstetrician who had delivered the patient's baby. Several days following her return home from the hospital she called and indicated that she was having various problems and was in severe pain. The physician explained that he was alone in his office with numerous patients to see and that he could not come to see her at home. She went to another physician's office for treatment and then sued the obstetrician for abandonment. The court dismissed the action. The physician had the right to tell the patient that he would see her only at his office or at a hospital. Further, the court pointed out that since the woman was well enough to go to a second physician's office, she could just as easily have gone to the defendant's office, and therefore she, not he, terminated the relationship.

An example of this proposition is seen in a case[21] in which the patient had an operation which caused an abortion. When she was dismissed from the hospital, the surgeon had told her that "if things do not go right" she should come back to see him at his office for further treatment. Within the next two or three days she called him and he refused to visit her at her home, which was in another city. The court held that the failure of the surgeon to go to her residence did not constitute negligence because, by the terms of the contract, he did not undertake to treat her except to give service at his office. He was not, therefore, liable for abandoning her.

The Physician's Right to Limit the Contract—Limit Scope of Practice

The physician has the perfect right to make various types of reasonable limitations on his relationship with the patient. The most obvious example of this is the specialist who is treating a patient for an ailment within his field of specialization but refuses to prescribe for another ailment outside his area. For example, if a pregnant patient comes to an ophthalmologist for treatment of an eye infection and brings up a cardiological complaint while she is there, the ophthalmologist is not only legally justified in refusing to advise her, but he probably would be subject to severe criticism if he did, or liable for malpractice if he treated her negligently.

In another case[23] a woman injured in an automobile accident was seen by an orthopedic surgeon who set her fractured leg. After the procedure he told her not to bear any weight on the leg and gave her other quite proper instructions. While she was still in the hospital under his care she developed a traumatic psychosis and was referred to a mental hospital. All her records, orthopedic and medical, were sent with her. While in the mental hospital, she claimed that she was forced to walk on her injured leg, and she sued the orthopedist for abandonment. He had resumed care of the patient when she was released from the mental hospital and returned to the first hospital. The court held that the physician did not have an obligation to follow his patient to the mental hospital and, in fact, could not have done so since he was not a member of its staff. He had made all records and instructions available to the physicians at the mental hospital and was not liable for their failure to follow them.

A physician may limit his practice in other ways as well. He may refuse to treat a patient at home because of the danger involved. This is the basis of a case[24] in which the defendant was an obstetrician whose patient wanted to deliver her baby at home. The physician refused to deliver her except in the hospital, so she told him she would hire a midwife.

When labor ensued, the midwife realized that complications had set in, and the physician was called and asked to come to the house and deliver the child. He again refused and told the woman's husband to bring her to the hospital. The husband attempted to contact several other physicians, but none would agree to deliver the child at home. After approximately six hours of attempting to find a physician who would deliver the child, the husband brought the patient to the hospital for delivery. The child was born dead.

The original obstetrician was sued for abandoning the patient, but the court dismissed the case. The opinion pointed out that the dangers to mother and child in a home delivery were so obvious that a physician is entirely within his rights and justified in refusing to do it. No abandonment occurred, moreover, because the physician told the husband that he would see his wife as soon as he brought her to the hospital. The husband, not the obstetrician, was responsible for the delay in medical help. The opinion pointed out that the obstetrician repeatedly told the patient's husband that he would see her as soon as she arrived at the hospital.

Geographic Limitations

A physician may make reasonable geographic limitations on his practice. Failure to exceed those at the request of a patient is not in any way a breach of any legal duty or abandonment. This concept is apparent in a reported case.[17] In this instance the plaintiff cut her leg badly, and her husband brought her to the defendant's home in the middle of the night. The defendant called his associate, who was on call for the entire group of physicians that night, and told him to meet the patient and her husband at his office. The cut was sutured and the patient was carefully instructed to return two days later for further examination. She did not do so. She and her husband went on a vacation to another town about twenty miles away. While there, she began to have problems with her leg and called the defendant. He told her that he would not come to the neighboring town to see her but issued instructions and told her what local physician she could call. She sued for abandonment, and the court's decision was that a physician is entirely justified in limiting his practice to his own community.

As has been reported, physicians may quite properly refuse to see their patients outside the limitations of their own communities. The physician does not have to go to another community to treat a patient.

A physician entered into a contract with a woman whereby he agreed to treat an elderly woman "at any time or place during any spell of indisposition," for the remainder of her life, in return for a fixed compensation to be paid at the beginning of his service or by her executor after her death. This contract was held not to require the physician to accompany her to any place she might go, but only to bind him to treat her at her permanent abode. The court therefore held that the physician had not breached the contract when he refused to accompany the patient, who was a resident of Chicago, to California for a year.[25]

Other examples of this practice appear in the legal literature. A patient had a boil on his finger. He appeared at his physician's office on a Sunday morning and the physician refused to lance it except during regular office hours which he conducted at one hospital in the community. The patient wished to be seen either in the physician's office or a second hospital, both of which the physician refused to do. The patient went to another physician, and sued the first physician for abandonment. The court held that the patient had no right to insist upon being treated at a certain place.[26]

Agreement for Surgery Only

Unless there is an agreement to the contrary, a surgeon may limit his duty to the operation itself. The court in *Sheridan v. Quarrier*[27] agreed with this theory. In *Sheridan* a staff doctor participated in an amputation of a toe at the request of the chief of staff so that he could supervise the intern in charge of the operation. The surgeon did not see the patient after the operation. Holding that the surgeon was brought in solely for the operation, the court further held that the surgeon was not liable for any harm resulting from post-operative care.

Agreement for a Single Visit or Consultation Only

As with the agreement for surgery only, an agreement for one-call only, explicit or implicit, may limit the duty of the physician to that one call. This frequently occurs in vacation spots where injured tourists visit a local physician to correct an immediate problem. Unless otherwise agreed, that local physician is under no obligation to perform further treatment.[28]

An implicit or explicit agreement for consultation or assistance only may also operate as the above-mentioned agreements to limit the duty of the physician. An obvious example would be a physician called in a case to help diagnose a perplexing illness. It has been held that a true physician-patient relationship with the consultant is not formed in this case. Therefore, the consulting physician would not be considered to have abandoned the patient in the true sense of the word if he was not further involved.

This is the rationale that the Federal Fourth Circuit Court of Appeals used in *Murray v. United States.*[29] *Murray* concerned a disabled veteran who was taken to the nearest Veteran's Administration Hospital for treatment of an apparent mental disorder. The physician on duty diagnosed the disorder as an episode of acute chronic alcoholism. As regulations prohibited the admission of a person suffering from alcoholism, the physician sent the patient to a nearby hospital, accompanied by an attendant and a guard.

In examining the relationship in this case, the court concluded that there was no physician-patient relationship as the physician was merely "assisting" the patient to a hospital where he would be able to receive treatment for his condition. Furthermore, it was done in the proper manner. Therefore, no abandonment by the physician could exist.

When a physician is called in consultation with another physician, it should be determined among all (the physicians and the patient) whether the consultant is to continue or not. Misunderstanding in this regard may be the source of later difficulty.[30] If the consultant is expected to recommend treatment and does prescribe, should he not continue to see the patient and observe the results of therapy? Not necessarily, if that is the extent of his engagement. A consulting physician who examines a patient at the request of a primary physician but who does not intend to continue to treat the patient certainly is not legally obligated to do so. When his services are to be limited to the initial consultation, such remarks should be stated to the patient, to the attending physician, and written in the chart. A letter to the physician and to the patient summarizing the consultation should contain a statement of the consultant's interest in the patient and perhaps an offer to continue if and when requested.

If this is not done, it is possible that the consultant may later be sued for abandonment. A physician who refers a patient to a specialist for treatment generally is held to have relieved himself of any further responsibility to the patient in the absence of an understanding that he will be associated with the specialist in caring for the patient.[31] Again, however, this should be explained clearly to the patient and the specialist in order to avoid any possibility of misunderstanding.

In another case[3] in point, a consultant was called in to examine a patient's diseased arm, and he did so properly. None of the arrangements between the parties indicated that the specialist expected to be called again or that the patient was in any doubt that the primary physician was again assuming responsibility for the case. The consultant was not liable for his failure to come when the patient called him.

References

1. Lewis v. Johnson, 86 P.2d 99 (Cal. Sup. Ct. 1939); Hall v. Nagel, 39 N.E.2d 612 (Ohio Sup. Ct. 1942); Spendlove v. Georges, 295 P.2d 336 (Utah Sup. Ct.1956).

2. Buttersworth v. Swint, 186 S.E. 770 (Ga. App. Ct. 1936); Childers v. Frye, 158 S.E. 744 (N.C. Sup. Ct. 1931); Rice v. Rinaldo, 119 N.E.2d 657 (Ohio Sup. Ct. 1951).

3. Nelson v. Farrish, 143 Minn. 368, 173 N.W. 715 (1919).

4. Capps v. Volk, 369 P.2d 238 (Kan. Sup. Ct. 1962); McManus v. Donlin, 127 N.W.2d 22 (Wis. Sup. Ct. 1964).

5. Hurley v. Eddingfield, 59 N.E. 1058 (Ind. Sup. Ct. 190).

6. Pearson v. Norman, 106 P.2d 361 (Colo. 1940); Duke Sanitarium v. Hearn, 13 P.2d 183 (Okla, 1932).

7. Stohlman v. Davis, 220 N.W. 247 (Neb. 1928); Mucci v. Houghton, 57 N.W. 305 (Iowa, 1894); Grace v. Myers, 29 SE 2d 553 (N.C. 1944).

8. Chase v. Clinton County, 217 N.W. 565 (Mich. 1928); Alexandridis v. Jewett, 388 F. 2d 829 (C.A.1, 1968).

9. Thomas v. Corose, 288 A. 2d 379, (Md. 1972).

10. Easter v. Lexington Memorial Hospital, Inc., 278 S.E. 2d 253 (1981).

11. Doran v. Priddy, 534 F. Supp. 30. (D. Kansas 1981).

12. Gray v. Davidson, 15 Wash. 2d 257, 130 P.2d 341 (1942). See also: Lathrope v. Flood, 6 Cal. Unrep. 637, 63P.1007, rev'd other grounds, 135 Cal.Rep. 458, 67 P.683 (1901).

13. Vann v. Harden, 187 Va. 555, 47 S.E. 2d 314 (1948).

14. Grimsby v. Samson, 530 P .2d 291 (Wash. 1975); Capps v. Valk, P. 2d 238, Kans. 1962).

15. Lee v. Dewbre, 362 SW 2d 900 (Tex. 1962); Burnett v. Layman, 181 S.W. 157 (Tenn. 1915).

16. Young v. Jordan, 145 S.E. 41 (W. Va. 1928).

17. McNamara v. Emmons, 36 Cal. App. 2d 199,97 P.2d 503 (1939).

18. Young v. Crescente, 39 A. 2d 449 (N.J. Sup. Ct. 1944).

19. Nash v. Meyer, 31 P. 2d 273 (Idaho Sup. Ct. 1934); Urrutia v. Patino, 297 S.W. 512 (Tex. Civ. App. 1927).

20. Tomer v. Aiken, 101 N.W. 769 (Iowa Sup. Ct. 1919); Nelson v. Farrish, 173 N.W. 715 (Minn. Sup. Ct. 1919).

21. Skodje v. Hardy 288 P. 2d 771 (Wash. 1944).

22. Rogers v. Lawson, 170 F. 2d 157 (D.C. C.A. 1948).

23. Clark v. Wichman, 179 A. 2d 809. (La. 1962).

23. Clark v. Wichman, 179 A. 2d 809. (N.J. 1961).

24. Vidrine v. Mayers, 127 So. 2d 809, (La. 1961).

25. Zeigler v. Illinois Trust and Savings Bank, 91 N.E. 1041 (1910).

26. Dabney v. Briggs, 121 So. 394. (Ala. 1929).

27. Sheridan v. Quarrier, 127 Conn. 279, 16 A. 2d 479 (1940).

28. Miller v. Blackburn, 17o Ky. 263, 185 S.W. 864 (1916).

29. Murray v. United States, 329 F. 2d 270 (C.A. 5 1964).

30. Podvin v. Eickhorst, 128 N.W. 523 (Mich. 1964).

31. Engle v. Clarke, 346 S.W. 2d 13 (Ky. 1961).

Hirsch HL. Patient abandonment: from a legal perspective. Urban Health. February 1985.

Annotated Bibliography

Models of the Physician-Patient Relationship

Abram MD. *On the 'shared relationship.'* Am Med News. May 30, 1986: 4.
The author calls for a "new" kind of doctor-patient relationship in which information is fully shared and decisions are jointly reached. He predicts that a higher degree of patient satisfaction and fewer liability suits would result if such practice became widespread.

Childress JF, Siegler M. *Metaphors and models of doctor-patient relationships: their implications for autonomy.* Theor Med. 1984; 5: 17-30.
Five models of the physician-patient relationship are examined, including the physician as parent, partner, contractor, friend, and technician.

Henderson LJ. *Physician and patient as a social system.* N Engl J Med. 1935; 212: 819-823.
The first clear description of the physician-patient relationship. The description is paternalistic, but it examines the different values and needs of both patients and physicians and the central importance of language and communication. Truth-telling is used as an example of how proper communication can improve patient care.

Siegler M. *The physician-patient accommodation: a central event in clinical medicine.* Arch Intern Med. 1982; 142: 1899-1902.
The accommodation model is based on negotiation and considers the particularities of the physician, the patient, and the patient's illness. The model emphasizes mutuality, voluntary participation, and respect for persons.

Szasz TS, Hollender MH. *The basic models of the doctor-patient relationship.* Arch Intern Med. 1956; 97: 585-592.
The three basic models discussed are activity-passivity (care for a comatose patient); guidance-cooperation (an adult patient seeks help for an acute illness); and medical participation (an adult seeks help for a chronic disease). Each model implies different concepts of disease treatment.

Nurturing the Physician-Patient Relationship

Almy TP. *The healing bond.* Am J Gastroenterol. 1982; 73: 403.
The most productive physician-patient relationship is based on listening, explaining, and maintaining continuity and dependability of services. Trust and genuine communication can be integral elements of therapy.

American College of Physicians ethics manual. Ann Intern Med. 1989; 111 (3): 245-252 and (4): 327-335.
This manual offers direction for physicians considering a wide range of ethical issues, including the physician-patient relationship, financial arrangements, the medical record, impaired physicians, the relation of the physician to government, physician unions, care for the hopelessly ill patient, genetic counseling, and clinical investigation. A thorough collection of annotated references expands the value of this publication.

AMA/Specialty Society Medical Liability Project. *Risk Management Principles & Commentaries for the Medical Office*. Chicago, Ill: American Medical Association; 1990.
General recommendations are applicable to all medical and surgical office practices. Guidelines comment on physician-patient communication, record keeping, scheduling, billing, consent, consultations, office personnel, and other areas of daily practice, emphasizing throughout how appropriate office procedures and administrative systems help foster good patient relations.

Austin B. *Showing compassion to grieving parents*. Am Med News. October 10, 1986: 13-15
This article describes the work of The Compassionate Friends, a nationwide support group for bereaved parents. Interviews with a nurse and a physician who have lost their own children to disease gives insight to the tensions experienced by both parents and health care workers when children are dying.

Duffy DL, Hammerman D, Cohn MA. *Communication skills of house officers*. Ann Intern Med. 1980; 93: 354-357.
Ten central communication skills were studied in 20 house officers during clinic visits. Underdeveloped skills included obtaining a social history, assessing a patient's understanding of his illness, and explaining disease to patients. Constructive recommendations for house staff training are included.

Greenfield S, Kaplan S, Ware JE. *Expanding patient involvement in care*. Ann Intern Med. 1985; 102: 520-528.
In this randomized controlled trial, 45 patients with peptic ulcer disease received a 20-minute "coaching," including an explanation of ulcer disease treatment and medical inquiry, as well as a review of the patient chart. The study group showed greater interaction with their physician and better functional outcomes than did controls.

Groves JE. *Taking care of the hateful patient*. N Engl J Med. 1978; 298: 883-887.
A psychiatrist discusses the physician-patient relationship with four difficult patient types: dependent clingers, entitled demanders, manipulative help-rejecters, and self-destructive deniers.

Inglefinger FJ. *Arrogance*. N Engl J Med. 1980; 303: 1507-1511.
Necessary ingredients of good medical care are some measures of paternalism, authoritarianism, and domination; but arrogance, marked by vanity and a lack of empathy, can be a very destructive force.

Mechanic D. *Public perceptions of medicine*. N Engl J Med. 1985; 312: 181-183.
A non-physician describes the economic, technological, and manpower constraints that have the potential to shake the time-honored physician-patient relationship. Administrative innovation and a strong commitment to patient care will guarantee the survival of a revered profession.

Putnam SM, Stiles WB, Jacob MC, James SA. *Patient exposition and physician explanation in initial medical interviews and outcomes of clinic visits*. Med Care. 1985; 23: 74-83.
Physician-patient interactions and outcomes of care were analyzed in 102 clinic visits. Higher indexes of physician explanation and patient understanding were correlated with greater patient satisfaction but not with increased patient compliance.

Quill TE. *Recognizing and adjusting to barriers in doctor-patient communication.* Ann Intern Med. 1989; 111: 51-57.
Dr. Quill gives instruction on the recognition of physician-patient conflict and resolution through a process of acknowledgment, exploration, empathy, and legitimation.

Shapiro RS, Simpson DE, Lawrence SL, Talsky AM, Sobosinski KA, Schiedermayer DL. *A survey of sued and non-sued physicians and suing patients.* Arch Intern Med. 1989; 149: 2190-2196.
A survey of 642 physicians and patients compares each perception of the physician-patient relationship. They differed significantly on issues of trust and openness in the relationship. All parties agreed that improving physician-patient communication is the best method for reducing malpractice litigation.

Sommers PA. *Malpractice risk and patient relations.* J Fam Pract. 1985; 20: 299-301.
Article 1.1

Record Keeping

Battista ME. *Malpractice risks of documentation.* Physician's Management. February 1985: 232-258.
A physician-attorney reviews the contents of a medical record in a typical private practice. Thorough review of consultation reports, records of a previous physician, and emergency department reports is stressed. He describes seven specific areas of high legal risk.

Gomella LG, Braen GR, Olding MJ. *Chartwork.* In: Clinician's Pocket Reference. 4th ed. Norwalk, CT: Appleton & Lange; 1986: 20-27.
This guide gives the standard format for writing orders, notes, summaries, prescriptions, etc. It also includes a section on the history and physical examination and many of the skills every medical student needs to master.

Good medical records can be strongest malpractice defense. Michigan Med. January 1983: 6-8.
Article 1.2

Gutheil TG. *Paranoia and progress notes: a guide to forensically informed psychiatric record keeping.* Hosp Community Psychiatry. 1980; 31: 479-482.
Dr. Gutheil describes the special problems of record keeping and confidentiality in modern psychiatry. He suggests that psychiatrists use a set of records utilizing separate "progress" and "process" notes.

Kern SI. *Maintenance and release of medical records.* New Jersey Med. 1986; 83: 649-650.
A review of the laws governing medical records in the state of New Jersey.

McDonald CJ, Tierney WM. *Computer-stored medical records: their future role in medical practice.* JAMA. 1988; 259: 3433-3440.
The authors predict a large-scale conversion of both hospital and office medical records to computer-based systems in the near future. They show examples of computer display screens from five programs currently in use.

White MD. *The growing demand for physician office records.* Forum (bimonthly publication of the Risk Management Foundation of the Harvard Medical Institutions). 1986; 7(1): 8.
There is growing demand for courtroom scrutiny of private physician records. White reviews the regulations pertinent to physicians in Massachusetts. She describes the time period for which records are required and explains who has authority to release records.

Confidentiality

Grossman M. *Confidentiality in medical practice.* Annu Rev Med. 1977; 28: 43-55.
This excellent review includes a historical perspective of the traditions, laws, and legislation that define confidentiality today. It also includes discussion of medical records, the reporting of communicable diseases, children and minors, the use of medical computers, and medical research as they relate to confidentiality.

Hankoff LD, Nattland E. *Clinical confidentiality: dilemmas and guidelines.* New Jersey Med. 1986; 83: 655-659.
Article 1.3

Plaut EA. *A perspective on confidentiality.* Am J Psychiatry. 1974; 131: 1021-1024.
Psychiatric, psychotherapeutic, and psychoanalytic interactions between psychiatrist and patient are compared and contrasted. Legal ramifications and professional responsibilities concerning confidentiality are discussed.

Sherlock R. *Reasonable men and sick human beings.* Am J Med. 1986; 80: 2-4.
The author discusses the significance of trust in the clinical relationship, stating that essential to this process of patient entrustment is communication with the patient about his or her illness, therapy, and prognosis.

Siegler M. *Confidentiality in medicine: a decrepit concept.* N Engl J Med. 1982; 307: 1518-1521.
Dr. Siegler states that confidentiality, as traditionally understood by patients and physicians, no longer exists. He describes a typical case, in a teaching hospital, in which more than 75 people had access to a single patient's medical record. He makes some suggestions for improvement.

The Legal Contract Between Physician and Patient

Curran WJ. *Breaking of the physician-patient relationship: another legal hazard.* N Engl J Med. 1982; 307: 1058-1060.
A case description and legal review outline the proper methods of terminating a physician-patient relationship.

Hirsh HL. *Patient abandonment: from a legal perspective.* Urban Health. February 1985.
Article 1.4

Chapter 2

Negligence

Case:
Failure to Diagnose

A middle-aged woman, who had seen her physician four months previously with a complaint of lower back pain, now returns with obvious signs of metastatic cancer. The physician failed to perform an adequate physical examination when she first presented and did not review X-rays that showed evidence of cancer.

Dr. Fisher is regarded as the finest family physician in his small community. He is very busy, seeing 30 patients in his office daily, delivering babies, and making house calls. He often feels overworked and would like to spend more time with his own family. Today, one of the many patients in his office waiting room is 56-year-old Mrs. Rogers. The Rogers family has fondly called him their family physician for the past 25 years. He delivered and cared for both of the Rogers' children.

Mrs. Rogers saw Dr. Fisher four months ago with a complaint of lower back pain of one month's duration. He performed only a cursory examination of her lower back, which, at that time, led him to prescribe aspirin and a heating pad for presumed arthritis. He also ordered X-rays of her lumbo-sacral spine so that he would have an objective baseline by which to evaluate future progression of her condition. The X-ray report from the local radiologist arrived at Dr. Fisher's office three and one half months earlier, but was filed away without his seeing it. Mrs. Rogers was billed by the radiologist and Dr. Fisher but never received any information concerning the X-ray findings. She reasoned that no news was good news, but she has now returned because the pain has not subsided. In fact, she is beginning to feel a new pain in her ribs.

Dr. Fisher retrieves the radiology report from his file on the way into the examining room to see Mrs. Rogers. It reads, "compression fracture of T-10, without evidence of significant osteopenia or arthritic changes, likely etiologies include severe trauma or a neoplastic process."

He now questions her thoroughly about constitutional symptoms. She describes anorexia and a 15-pound weight loss since her last visit, as well as nighttime sweats and chills. On physical examination, Dr. Fisher finds a two-centimeter, firm breast mass, unlikely to be anything other than advanced breast cancer. Mrs. Rogers had noticed the lump just prior to her visit with Dr. Fisher four months ago, but did not mention it to him because her back pain was of more immediate concern and he appeared to her to be very busy. She reasoned that because it never caused her any pain, she could wait to report it.

Dr. Fisher must now inform Mrs. Rogers of his findings.

Discussion Questions

1. What acts or omissions in the above scenario might place Dr. Fisher in a difficult position to defend a malpractice action?

2. How much time should he have spent with Mrs. Rogers on the first visit? What points of her medical history should he have reviewed? What physical examination should he have performed? What advice should he have given her?

3. When should Dr. Fisher have examined the X-ray and radiology report? Should the radiologist have called Dr. Fisher with a verbal report of the findings? Does the radiologist's failure to do so constitute negligence?

4. What do you think of Dr. Fisher's record keeping system? What would you do differently?

5. Should four months have elapsed between Mrs. Rogers' scheduled visits? Did Dr. Fisher have a responsibility to contact her during this interval? Would some written communication accompanying the bill for medical services have been appropriate?

6. What should Dr. Fisher say now concerning the X-ray?

7. Is it common for patients to deny symptoms and signs of serious disease such as breast cancer? What implication does this have for medical practitioners?

8. Should Dr. Fisher ask Mrs. Rogers not to sue him? Should he discuss the case with other physicians? Should he notify his malpractice insurance company? Should he seek independent legal advice?

9. What should Dr. Fisher write in Mrs. Rogers' medical record today?

10. What recourse does Mrs. Rogers have to address any injustice that she may perceive?

Overview

"Tort," "negligence," "plaintiff," "statute of limitations," "standard of care," and "expert testimony" are just a few of the common terms and phrases employed in the discussion of medical malpractice in the American health care system. Familiarity with these terms and other basic concepts of the legal and insurance worlds is crucial for today's practicing physicians. An explanation of these basics is the goal of this chapter.

Although the uproar concerning malpractice insurance premiums and non-meritorious claims has been spearheaded by physicians in several specialties at high risk of litigation—particularly obstetrics, neurosurgery, orthopedic surgery, emergency medicine, and anesthesiology—every practicing physician has been affected. During the 1980s, the average physician's malpractice premium tripled. Although the problems of rising costs and numbers of claims will not be easily resolved in the coming years, there are steps that individual practitioners can take on a daily basis to improve patient care and reduce their risk of being sued. The suggestions outlined throughout this book are applicable to all physicians, regardless of their specialty.

There are natural hopes and expectations whenever a physician and patient meet in a medical care setting. Both parties hope the patient's questions will be answered and health problems cured. Unfortunately, physicians are not always able to fulfill these expectations. The presenting complaint may progress, without explanation, and in some patients incurable disease processes are diagnosed. Under optimal conditions, unanticipated outcomes may surprise even those with the most rational set of expectations. Although medical science is in constant flux, there are generally accepted approaches to the diagnosis and treatment of disease. *Malpractice may simply be defined as the unwarranted departure from generally accepted standards of medical practice resulting in injury to a patient.*[1]

The Tort System

The United States system for compensating persons injured in the course of medical treatment, with a few exceptions, is based on fault. To bring a claim for medical malpractice, an injured patient must state or "allege" that he or she suffered an injury due to the wrongful actions or failure to act by the treating physician. Of course, hospitals, nurses, and other hospital personnel are often implicated as well.

In a small but significant percentage of claims, manufacturers of medical equipment or pharmaceutical companies are also involved. The legal standards that apply to such "product liability" claims against manufacturers are quite different from the fault-based standards applied in medical malpractice claims against health care providers. Beginning in the 1960s, product manufacturers have been held by the courts to be "strictly liable" for injuries caused by their products, regardless of whether they had any reason to know the product might endanger the safety of its users. Strict liability was adopted by state legislatures and courts on the premise that manufacturers are better able to bear the financial risks of product-related injuries than are the product users.

An incident with the potential to lead to a medical malpractice claim may be instantly apparent to the clinician involved, or it may not surface until the physician receives a patient's irate telephone call or refusal to pay a bill. It is important, and in many situations required, that physicians report certain incidents or adverse outcomes that may eventually trigger formal liability action. Certainly, not all incidents become claims and not all medical malpractice claims become lawsuits. Definition of a formal claim varies within the medical, insurance, and legal fields. Physicians are advised to check with their affiliated institutions and professional liability insurance providers for the specific definition each uses to define a claim. The National Practitioner Data Bank (detailed in Chapter 7) defines a medical malpractice claim as "a written complaint or claim demanding payment based on a physician's, dentist's, or other health care practitioner's provision of or failure to provide health care services."

Many claims are settled by the insurers of the physician or hospital before they become malpractice lawsuits ("suits" or "actions"). Only when a claim or "complaint" is filed by or on behalf of a patient ("the plaintiff") with the court clerk's office does it become a medical malpractice suit.

The plaintiff has a limited time within which to file the complaint. This limit, prescribed by state law, is known as the "statute of limitations." Although these vary significantly from state to state, most statutes of limitation allow plaintiffs two to three years from the date of injury to file their suit, with longer times for minors, incompetent people, and patients who do not immediately discover their injury.

While the patient is the primary plaintiff, a spouse or other family members may join in the suit with a complaint for loss of companionship ("consortium") or, in cases where the patient has died, loss of financial support.

Lawyers representing the parties to a medical malpractice claim are compensated very differently, depending on which side they represent. Plaintiff lawyers usually work for a "contingency fee," which frequently pays them 30 to 50 percent of the ultimate payment if the plaintiff gets an award but nothing if the verdict is for the defendant. In contrast, defense attorneys work for an hourly fee, usually paid by the insurance company, whether the defendant wins or loses. Plaintiff attorneys' contingency fees have been a target of legislative reform efforts in several states. The United States is one of the few countries where the contingency fee is used.

Medical malpractice suits are judged in the legal system according to the body of law known as "tort" law. A tort is a civil wrong for which an action can be filed in court to recover damages for personal injury or property damage resulting from negligent acts or intentional misconduct. Tort law is one category of civil law, as distinct from criminal law. Hence, while punitive damage awards may be given in medical malpractice cases where the judge or jury determines that there has been egregious wrongdoing, these damages are not construed as criminal "fines" and do not generate a criminal record. The body of tort law not only includes laws and regulations promulgated by state legislatures and Congress but also relies heavily on previous judge and jury decisions known as "precedent" or "case law." Tort law is therefore continuously subject to change and interpretation in both the legislatures and the courts.

The body of law governing medical malpractice differs significantly from state to state. Malpractice suits are usually filed in state courts. However, under certain, limited circumstances when the patient and the physician reside in different states, the suit may be filed in federal court. The federal judge must then decide which state's laws should apply.

In Article 2.1, "Medical Malpractice and the Tort System," attorney Peter Jacobson discusses recent trends in professional liability. He describes the relentless rise in claim frequency and severity in the 1980s, which has declined perceptibly (and perhaps just temporarily) only in the last two years. Jacobson reports on changes in legal doctrine and procedure, and provides insight on jury behavior and the expanded use of expert witness testimony.

The actual processing of a malpractice claim is outlined by attorney Douglas Danner in Article 4.2 (Chapter 4). The effects of past attempts to reform the tort system and a number of proposals for replacing that system are discussed in Chapter 6.

The Elements of Negligence

The most common allegation brought against health care professionals in a medical malpractice suit is negligence in the rendering of medical services. The tort of negligence has four elements: (1) the establishment of a duty owed to the plaintiff, (2) breach of that duty, (3) causation, and (4) damage. The plaintiff has the burden of proving all four elements before the "defendant" physician (or other health care provider) incurs legal liability for a negligent act or failure to act.

Duty and the Standard of Care

The plaintiff in a malpractice suit must first prove that the physician owed a duty to the person harmed. Generally, this is proved by showing that there was an established physician-patient relationship. The scope of this duty is determined by the applicable standard of care, which is typically established by medical expert testimony and/or published medical literature that is admitted by the judge in the case as evidence. The judge follows a set of rules to determine whether evidence is sufficiently reliable to be admitted.

The standard of care requires that the physician possess and exercise the degree of skill and care ordinarily exercised by other health care professionals rendering the same type of medical care at issue in the case. On the premise that medical information is widely accessible and that training programs have a certain degree of standardization, the majority of states now recognize a standard of care based on the skill and knowledge of all physicians with similar training or expertise regardless of their practice location or environment. That is, a general pediatrician in a rural community hospital is held to the same standard as the general pediatrician in an urban university hospital. In a few locations, however, there does exist a more localized standard of care based on the care delivered by other physicians in that local area, or "similar community." It is important that physicians be aware of the prevailing standard used in the state in which they practice.

Breach

Breach of the duty owed to the patient is proved by showing that the physician's act or failure to act (omission) was a deviation from the standard of care. An error in judgment itself is not malpractice if the error was a reasonable one. However, the judgment or data base used to formulate a clinical decision may be challenged as unreasonable or below an acceptable standard of care. Such challenges are usually asserted by an expert witness called by the plaintiff. A defendant physician must then prove that a given medical decision was reasonable by providing evidence through countering expert testimony and appropriate documentation that diagnostic and treatment techniques and reasoning recognized as acceptable by his or her peers were employed.

Causation

Proof of causation is often the most difficult part of a medical malpractice case. The plaintiff must show that a direct causal link or "proximate cause" exists between the alleged breach and the damage suffered by the patient. If a reasonable connection cannot be proved, then there generally is no resulting liability. It is often most difficult for a plaintiff to prove that his or her condition would not have deteriorated if the physician had not acted negligently. Where the injury is the abrupt and unanticipated death of the patient, the causal link may be clear. However, in cases where a negligent act or omission resulted in some partial change in medical status or some percentage increase in suffering, proving proximate causation of specific damages is much more complex.

Damage

The plaintiff must prove actual loss or damage resulting from the physician's breach of the standard of care. Damages may be physical, financial, or emotional. Juries often differentiate between "economic" and "non-economic" damages. Economic damages are those expenses that can readily be assigned an objective economic value, such as lost wages, medical bills, or the installation of wheelchair ramps. By contrast, non-economic damages attributable to the patient's emotional distress or physical pain and suffering are largely subjective. Similarly, loss of consortium—the deprivation to the family of the companionship or affection caused by a person's injury—is another category of non-economic damages that is particularly elusive to quantification. There are no exact formulas to translate mental anguish and physical pain into dollars and cents. The proof of damages and their causal relationship to a breach of duty can depend heavily on the sympathy of a judge or jury. In recent years, awards for non-economic damages have grown significantly and their limitation has become a principal objective of medical liability reform efforts.

Standards, Guidelines, Principles, Parameters, Policies, or Protocols

In the past, the establishment of prospective written standards for medical practice was deemed impractical.[2] At present, however, it appears that published standards, guidelines, principles, parameters, policies, or protocols will become increasingly influential in defining accepted medical practice. Some commentators argue that using previously designed protocols will diminish the freedom of physicians to specifically tailor diagnostic workups and therapy for their patients in the "real world" of daily practice. In the extreme, some physicians contend that this would define the physician as a technician who practices "cookbook medicine." Carefully designed standards, however, can present a benchmark or outside boundary that does not preclude the exercise of sound individual judgment in utilizing the diversity of diagnostic and therapeutic interventions consistent with the complexity of the medical question at hand. In many circumstances, such guidelines may enable the competent physician to prove compliance with the legal standard of care applied by the courts and potentially support his or her case before a jury.

There are two broad categories of medical practice standards: (1) those focused on controlling liability exposure in the health care delivery process with the exclusive goals of minimizing injury to the patient and reducing liability risk for the health care team; and (2) clinical guidelines or parameters developed to help organize medical decision making by delineating indicated diagnostic procedures and criteria as well as therapeutic options. These two types of standards are not mutually exclusive and both serve the ultimate purpose of delivering the highest quality of care to the patient. For example, many liability control standards are used to organize the process in a practice setting to avoid instances of patient injury. The broader clinical standards, however, are oriented toward multiple goals, including curbing the perceived overutilization of medical treatment modes. In general, these broader standards are being developed in the effort to define the minimal criteria of medical care by which physicians might be reviewed by colleagues in a quality assurance setting or by third-party reimbursers. Many of these clinical standards are also potentially discoverable and/or admissible in a malpractice action.

Liability Control Standards

Some of the first widely recognized standards were those developed in 1985 by a committee of the anesthesiology chiefs of the hospitals affiliated with Harvard Medical School. The anesthesiology chiefs first met to analyze the medical malpractice experience of their departments. It was determined that a significant proportion of the claims arose from potentially preventable patient injuries. In response, the committee developed specific patient safety/risk management guidelines that became required practice in their nine hospitals. Article 2.2, "Standards for Patient Monitoring During Anesthesia at Harvard Medical School," describes the specific requirements and the committee process that generated them. The American Society of Anesthesiologists subsequently adopted similar standards.[3]

In the few years since the creation of the standards, Harvard anesthesiologists have experienced a significant decrease in monitoring-related malpractice claims and a reduction in malpractice insurance premiums. This is an example of how liability control standards can have a direct impact on patient care. Attorney James Holzer discusses the evolution of other liability control standards in Article 2.3, "The Advent of Clinical Standards for Professional Liability." He gives several examples of guidelines developed by physician-owned professional liability insurance carriers in response to their own claims experience in obstetrics, anesthesiology, and radiology.

In May 1990, the AMA/Specialty Society Medical Liability Project published its *Risk Management Principles & Commentaries for the Medical Office*.[4] Prepared by physicians in consultation with leading medical risk management experts, the principles and commentaries offer practical advice on avoiding liability claims arising from deficiencies in record keeping, physician-patient communication, and coordination of medical services between the primary treating physician and consultants. Recommendations regarding billing and collection, obtaining informed consent, maintaining office equipment, medication prescribing practices, and other topics also are included. They are offered as an educational tool and intended to be adopted and/or adapted to the individual practices of physicians for the improvement of patient care.

Clinical Practice Standards

A variety of forces are driving the development of clinical practice standards, guidelines, or—as they are increasingly known within organized medicine—practice parameters. Cost containment pressures from the federal government and other third-party payers, an explosion of new and often very expensive medical technologies, and data showing large variations in clinical practice are fueling the drive for national standards of medical care. The goal is to assist physicians in assessing patients and instituting therapies based on objective medical criteria in the hope that physicians will provide care more efficiently and safely while avoiding costly, unnecessary treatment. Dr. Robert Brook of the RAND Corporation discusses these competing interests in Article 2.4, "Practice Guidelines and Practicing Medicine: Are They Compatible?"

Even when physicians and payers can agree that standards or guidelines are needed, a major obstacle still impedes their development. In many areas of medicine there exists a glaring lack of objective outcome data by which to compare methods of diagnosis or therapy. Particularly in areas where technology develops rapidly, new techniques become commonplace before they are rigorously evaluated. In cardiology, for example, indications and utilization patterns of pacemaker implantation, angioplasty, and coronary artery bypass surgery vary tremendously. Fortunately, large-scale trials and data collection are now being pursued in many previously understudied areas.[5-7]

Despite some objection and considerable debate over what they should be called, organized medicine has been quick to take on the challenge of formulating what the AMA has termed "medical practice parameters."[8] There is great concern that if physicians do not take the lead, government or insurance companies will proceed with their own parameters that might be unacceptable to practicing clinicians and their patients. It should be noted that clinical standards are also potentially discoverable and/or admissible as evidence of the standard of care in malpractice suits.

The AMA has undertaken to analyze and monitor the legal implications of such guidelines for physicians, third-party payers that implement them, and organizations that develop and promulgate them.[9] The AMA has concluded that while parameters probably will become a source of evidence that is admissible in medical malpractice cases, it is unlikely that they will create new liability for physicians. The AMA predicts that practice parameters will serve as one piece of evidence to clinical appropriateness, together with treatises, articles, expert testimony, and other materials. Parameters are not likely to be treated by courts as inflexible requirements that must be adhered to in every circumstance, because the standard of care in medical malpractice suits is determined by the jury and judge on a case-by-case basis. Only in the limited situation when a parameter is explicitly promulgated as an absolute standard might the parameter itself constitute a *per se* definition of the standard of care, and then only if a court determines that the parameter sets forth the standard of care without room for modification in any situation.

A process of consensus building between experts and participating clinicians is essential for the effective acceptance and utilization of practice standards. Some general consensus has been reached regarding the nature of clinical practice standards: They should include the latest scientific knowledge and allow for revision on a regular basis and as new information becomes available. Economic factors included in standards should be clearly identified as such.

Physicians must be allowed flexibility to deviate from written criteria when medical judgment dictates a different course of action. Variation of practice based on availability of resources should be acknowledged.[10]

It is apparent that a consensus-building process will take time, depending to a large degree on the complexity of the specific treatment modes that are evaluated and the availability of outcome data. Some of the earliest written clinical standards were those developed for the vaccination of children in the 1950s. In 1984, a joint task force of the American College of Cardiology and the American Heart Association developed guidelines for the implantation of permanent cardiac pacemakers.[11] Adoption of the guidelines for reimbursement by Medicare provides effective enforcement of these clinical standards. The American Academy of Ophthalmology developed very specific guidelines for the treatment of open-angle glaucoma.[12] The American Diabetes Association recently published its standards for managing diabetes.[13] Blue Cross/Blue Shield has tested the application of clinical guidelines through the implementation of precertification requirements for cardiac catheterization, endoscopy, adenoidectomy, and other procedures.[14] Currently, the AMA, working together with the RAND Corporation and several academic medical centers, is developing criteria to guide the formulation of practice parameters and to ensure their appropriateness. It is hoped that these appropriateness criteria will be widely accepted by medical groups in developing, disseminating, and updating practice parameters.[15]

The scope of written standards varies considerably. Some are only a few pages long; others comprise several volumes. The Harvard Anesthesia Standards describe minimal criteria for patient care. The pacemaker guidelines list appropriate and inappropriate uses of this medical device. The ophthalmology and psychiatric standards mentioned provide great detail on diagnostic and treatment strategies. It is important to recognize the specific intended purpose of a given set of standards so they can be utilized appropriately for the improvement of patient care.

Reviewing the Facts of the Case

It is instructive at this point to analyze the case that introduced this chapter. Could a juror find Dr. Fisher's care for his patient, Mrs. Rogers, negligent? Does she have grounds to bring a malpractice suit against him? If so, would she prevail?

First, there can be no question that Dr. Fisher owed a duty of care to Mrs. Rogers. The physician-patient relationship giving rise to the duty is well established.

Did Dr. Fisher breach his duty by deviating from the standard of care? It appears that Dr. Fisher did not perform a thorough physical examination of his 56-year-old patient when she presented with a complaint of back pain. In addition, he failed to review the X-rays of her back in a timely fashion. These two points may well be considered a deviation from the customary standard of care for the evaluation of back pain in a middle-aged woman.

But was there proximate causation between Dr. Fisher's omission and Mrs. Rogers' injury and, if so, what is the extent of her damages? She does have breast cancer that most likely had metastasized to the bones in her vertebral column at the time of her initial presentation. She has obvious damage from the disease process for which Dr. Fisher is not responsible. However, she also has endured several months of poorly treated pain and untreated cancer. When she is ultimately given the diagnosis of breast cancer, she will be several months closer to her death. This may be construed as time lost for preparation for the dying process and for dealing with family matters. Would a more prompt diagnosis of cancer have prolonged her life? The true answer may never be conclusively established and would be a focus of debate between the medical expert witnesses if the case should go to trial. Indeed, many legal experts and some precedents in the case law hold that one who hastens an event (such as death) is considered to have caused it. If a lawsuit were to be filed, these precedents must be evaluated by Dr. Fisher's lawyer as one primary factor in determining whether the case should be settled prior to trial.

Mrs. Rogers possesses strong evidence to provide an allegation of "delay in diagnosis." In our current legal system, a final judgment of causation and damages can only be determined by a judge or jury. It is very possible that she will not pursue any malpractice action due to the long-held respect and confidence she has had in Dr. Fisher. However, this episode, which raises the question of substandard medical care and lack of communication, may lead to a justifiably irate patient and family. Legal action against Dr. Fisher may follow.

It should be noted that even if Mrs. Rogers decides not to sue Dr. Fisher, she may still bring a suit against the radiologist. Was this physician's failure to follow up with a telephone call a deviation from the standard of care? Under the legal doctrine known as "joint and several liability," every defendant physician can be held liable for the entire amount of a plaintiff's proved damages even if only a small percentage of the proved negligence is attributable to him or her. This doctrine poses particular risks where the plaintiff fails to sue one or more of the health care providers involved. However, if the radiologist were sued he or she would probably be able to add Dr. Fisher as a defendant. The doctrine of joint and several liability has been another target of physicians' tort reform efforts, and it has been modified in several states.

Expert Witness

If Mrs. Rogers does decide to sue Dr. Fisher for malpractice and the case progresses to a jury trial, then her attorney will need to call an expert witness. The expert witness will almost always be a physician who will explain to the jury what standard of care Dr. Fisher should have upheld. He or she will give an opinion as to whether Dr. Fisher performed an appropriate physical examination, asked the right questions, ordered the indicated tests, and interpreted their results accurately and in a timely manner.

In most states, this "expert" may have trained in any field of medicine and need not prove that he or she even practices clinical medicine. The expert can come from any one of the 50 states. Naturally, the plaintiff attorney will attempt to choose an expert who supports the claim of malpractice.

The process for qualifying testimony as evidence that can be admitted in most states leaves significant room for potential abuse. Historically, few physicians were willing to testify against their colleagues. Hence, rules were relaxed to allow almost any person holding a medical license, from any location, to qualify as an "expert" for purposes of the court. In recent years, attitudes have changed and many physicians make a practice of being available to both plaintiffs and defendants. For some, this has become a full-time job. Today, there are numerous accounts of "hired gun" physicians who practice little medicine but have their bags packed and are ready to go anywhere and provide a medical opinion for the right price.

Experts are now typically paid between $125 and $300 per hour to review medical records and prepare depositions and between $1,200 and $5,000 per day for courtroom appearances.[16] Because there are few accepted, written standards of medical practice and a plethora of opinions in the medical literature, it is possible for an "expert" to quote published data and interpret them as strictly or loosely as need be to support his or her opinion before a jury.

The excesses of the system have been known for some time. Only recently, however, has action been initiated by organized medicine and lawmakers to develop guidelines addressing expert testimony. In 1986, the American College of Obstetricians and Gynecologists (ACOG) surveyed the directors of obstetrics/gynecology departments in academic medical centers across the country.[17] Twenty-eight percent of full-time faculty and more than seven percent of part-time faculty had given prior testimony. Only 10 percent of the departments surveyed had any written policy regarding the participation of faculty as expert witnesses. In a formal statement on expert testimony, the ACOG Committee on Ethics developed six guidelines ACOG members should follow when performing the duties of an expert witness.[18]

The American Academy of Pediatrics, the American Academy of Orthopaedic Surgeons, and the American Association of Neurological

Surgeons have also released statements and guidelines on expert witness testimony.[19-21] In March 1989, the Council of Medical Specialty Societies released its recommended qualifications for physicians and guidelines for professional behavior regarding expert witness testimony. See Article 2.5, "Statement on Qualifications and Guidelines for the Physician Expert Witness."

All such guidelines acknowledge the professional duty to provide credible medical testimony in court for the protection of the legal rights of both patients and physicians. This obligation is expressed in Opinion 9.07 of the AMA Council on Ethical and Judicial Affairs[22]:

> As a citizen and as a professional with special training and experience, the physician has an ethical obligation to assist in the administration of justice. If a patient who has a legal claim requests his physician's assistance, the physician should furnish medical evidence, with the patient's consent, in order to secure the patient's legal rights. The medical witness must not become an advocate or a partisan in the legal proceeding. The medical witness should be adequately prepared and should testify honestly and truthfully. The attorney for the party who calls the physician as a witness should be informed of all favorable and unfavorable information developed by the physician's evaluation of the case. It is unethical for a physician to accept compensation that is contingent upon the outcome of litigation.

A few state legislatures have begun debate regarding the selection of expert witnesses. The AMA has also developed model legislation setting forth minimum criteria for courts to consider in qualifying medical experts.[23] Criteria may require a medical expert to prove competence in the particular area of medical practice about which he or she testifies in court. An expert may be required to practice clinical medicine for some minimum percentage of professional time or to limit legal consulting activities to a certain maximum of professional time. More far-reaching proposals may require judges, rather than the plaintiff's attorney, to select an appropriate expert. Further changes are predicted as specialty societies, the courts, and legislators address the issue of expert witness testimony. Practicing physicians who are experts in their fields should participate in the legal process and ensure that complex medical decisions are accurately represented in the courtroom.

Specialty-Specific Concerns

Malpractice insurance companies review their malpractice claims experience to assist in the rating of insurance premiums and to develop risk management programs. The St. Paul Fire and Marine Insurance Company, the nation's largest insurer of physicians, releases data on malpractice allegations in its yearly reports. An excerpt from St. Paul's 1989 Annual Report is reprinted as Article 2.6, "Diagnostic Issues Generate Most Expensive Claims." Data refer to the malpractice claims reported to the company in 1987 and 1988 in the 38 states where St. Paul, at that time, provided professional liability insurance to physicians. The top three categories of allegations included improper performance of surgery, failure to diagnose, and improper treatment. The breadth of allegations encompass all medical and surgical specialties. Post-operative complications, failure to diagnose cancer, and improper treatment of birth-related problems were the three most common specific allegations. Almost 70 percent of all allegations (and 80 percent of all malpractice lawsuits) arose from medical care delivered in the hospital setting.

The cost of professional liability insurance reflects the cost of defending and settling malpractice suits within a given medical specialty. Debate concerning malpractice reform frequently focuses on those medical and surgical specialties that incur the highest malpractice insurance premiums. For example, obstetricians, neurosurgeons, and emergency department physicians pay significantly higher insurance premiums than do other groups such as family practitioners and psychiatrists. Because the degree of potential liability exposure is proportional to the potential impact of clinical decisions and procedures on patients' treatment outcomes, those specialties that are oriented toward performing invasive medical procedures have higher risk. Certain aspects of medical care provided by those high-risk specialty groups are particularly emotional and even a minor complication can yield major disappointment for a patient. In such instances, patients may seek to assign fault to a physician as a mechanism for dealing with their own frustration and loss.

Obstetricians deal with the critical moments of parturition. Expectations for healthy babies are maintained by anxiously awaiting mothers and fathers. The birth of other than a perfect or healthy infant yields disappointment and the search for a cause. Other aspects of procreation and pregnancy, such as sterilization and prenatal care, are also emotional areas. Unanticipated and often unavoidable results commonly lead to legal action. A 1990 survey of ACOG's membership found that almost 80 percent have had at least one claim directed against them sometime in their careers.[24]

Neurosurgery is perhaps the quintessential high-risk specialty. Residual nerve damage is often difficult to predict and is frequently debilitating. The emergent nature of much of this type of surgery also leads to difficult operating conditions and a highly charged emotional atmosphere. In addition, the neurosurgeon is unlikely to have the long developed physician-patient relationship from which many other specialists may benefit.

Similarly, *emergency department physicians* may have only a single encounter with a patient. The patient is usually already in distress over newly experienced pain, injury, or other dysfunction. Optimal medical resources and ready access to radiologists and other medical consultants are sometimes lacking in the middle of the night when many of the most difficult emergency medical problems present. Follow-up care rarely involves the emergency department physician, who is therefore without the benefit of reassessing a diagnosis or therapy over time.

Summary

Every medical discipline carries its own degree of potential liability (see Table 2.1). Even the lower-risk specialties experienced rapidly escalating premiums during the decade of the 1980s. It is important for physicians to become aware of the risks they are likely to encounter. Particular attention must be paid to the documentation of significant diagnoses and decisions for intervention. Patient education, especially discharge or follow-up instructions, should always be communicated clearly. Some medical specialty organizations are addressing these issues and are developing information specific to their own areas of liability exposure. The annotated bibliography at the end of this chapter includes references that may help physicians to familiarize themselves with areas of concern within their own specialties.

References

1. Danner D. *Medical Malpractice: A Primer for Physicians*. Rochester, NY: The Lawyers Co-operative; 1986.

2. Estes EH Jr, Sullivan RJ. Standards for practice: effectiveness and acceptance. *Ann Intern Med*. 1978; 89: 826-828.

3. *Standards for Basic Intraoperative Monitoring*. American Society of Anesthesiology; October 21, 1986.

4. *Risk Management Principles & Commentaries for the Medical Office*. Chicago, IL: AMA/Specialty Society Medical Liability Project; 1990.

5. Winslow CM, Kosecoff JB, Chassin M, Karouse DE, Brook RH. The appropriateness of performing coronary bypass surgery. *JAMA*. 1988; 260: 505-509. (See also accompanying editorial, pp 540-541.)

6. Greenspan AM, Kay HR, Berger BC, et al. Incidence of unwarranted implantation of permanent cardiac pacemakers in a large medical population. *N Engl J Med*. 1988; 318: 158-163. (See also accompanying editorial, pp 182-183.)

7. Ellwood PM. Shattuck lecture: outcomes management, a technology of patient experience. *N Engl J Med*. 1988; 318: 1549-1556.

8. *Practice Parameters*. Chicago, IL: American Medical Association; December 1989. Report EE of the American Medical Association Board of Trustees.

9. Johnson KB, Hirshfeld EB, Ile ML, et al. *Legal Implications of Practice Parameters*. Chicago, IL: American Medical Association; 1990.

10. *Attributes to Guide the Development of Practice Parameters*. Chicago, IL: American Medical Association, Office of Quality Assurance; 1990.

11. *Guidelines for Permanent Cardiac Pacemaker Implantation*, May 1984. Report of the ACC/AHA Joint Task Force on Assessment of Cardiovascular Procedures. *JACC*. 1984; 4: 434-442.

12. *Preferred Practice Pattern for Primary Open-Angle Glaucoma*. San Francisco, CA: American Academy of Ophthalmology Quality of Care Committee; 1988.

13. ADA issues new standards for management of diabetes. *Intern Med News*. July 1-14, 1989: 1,24.

14. Weinstein M. Medicine, mathematics meet in initial outpatient utilization review programs. *ACP Observer*. February 2, 1990: 1,6,9.

15. *Practice Parameters*. Chicago, IL: American Medical Association; June 1990. Report GG of the American Medical Association Board of Trustees.

16. Holthans D. States judge expert witnesses before they testify. *Hospitals*. March 5, 1988: 60-61.

17. *The Expert Witness: An ACOG Survey*. Washington, DC: American College of Obstetricians and Gynecologists; 1986.

18. *Ethical Issues Related to Expert Testimony by Obstetricians and Gynecologists*. Washington, DC: American College of Obstetricians and Gynecologists, 1987.

19. American College of Pediatrics Committee on Medical Liability: guidelines for expert witness testimony. *Pediatrics*. 1989; 83: 312-313.

20. *Qualifications and Guidelines for the Orthopaedic Expert Witness* [position statement]. Park Ridge, IL: American Academy of Orthopaedic Surgeons; 1989.

21. *Testimony in Professional Liability Cases* [position statement]. Park Ridge, IL: Ethics and Human Values Committee, American Association of Neurological Surgeons; 1987.

22. *Current Opinions of the Council on Ethical and Judicial Affairs*. Chicago, IL: American Medical Association; 1989.

23. Model legislation to provide for the regulation of expert witnesses in medical malpractice injury actions. AMA Department of State Legislation (October 1989).

24. Professional liability and its effects: report of a 1990 survey of ACOG's membership. Washington, DC: American College of Obstetricians and Gynecologists; 1990.

Table 2.1

Most Common Allegations by Specialty

General Surgery
1. Negligent trauma management
2. Negligent treatment of fracture
3. Damaged structures during surgery
4. Failure to diagnose and/or treat appendicitis
5. Nerve damage during surgery
6. Post-operative wound infection

Orthopedic Surgery
1. Negligent treatment of fracture
2. Failure to diagnose fracture
3. Post-operative complications due to negligent surgery
4. Post-operative nerve damage
5. Negligent total hip replacement
6. Surgery, wrong side/limb
7. Post-operative wound infection

Obstetrics/Gynecology
1. Negligent performance of elective sterilization procedure
2. Complications during vaginal delivery (involving mother)
3. Injury to infant at birth
4. Retained sponge, surgical instrument, etc.
5. Complications after total abdominal hysterectomy
6. Negligent pre-natal care

General/Family Practice
1. Negligent drug therapy
2. Failure to diagnose carcinoma
3. Negligent treatment of cardiac condition
4. Failure to diagnose fracture
5. Negligent management of diabetes
6. Negligent obstetrical care

Internal Medicine
1. Negligent drug therapy
2. Damaged structure during treatment
3. Negligent management of cardiac condition
4. Negligent administration of chemotherapy

Neurosurgery
1. Negligent treatment of head trauma
2. Negligent management of disc problems
3. Negligent treatment of back pain/injury
4. Post-operative emboli
5. Bovie burns during surgery
6. Post-operative wound infection

Radiology
1. Failure to diagnose fracture
2. Negligent administration and management of contrast media
3. Failure to diagnose carcinoma
4. Perforation of bowel during barium enema

Emergency Medicine
1. Negligent treatment of laceration
2. Failure to diagnose fracture
3. Negligent treatment of trauma
4. Failure to remove foreign body

Anesthesiology
1. Tooth damage
2. Damaged structures due to negligent anesthesia management
3. Cardiac arrest during surgery
4. Post-operative brain damage
5. Esophageal intubation

Pennsylvania Medical Society Liability Insurance Company's Risk Management Documentation.

Article 2.1

Medical Malpractice and the Tort System

Peter D. Jacobson, JD, MPH. Journal of the American Medical Association, December 1989.

Few topics in health care policy generate more contentious commentary than medical malpractice. To some, the recent trend of increasing liability awards and malpractice insurance premiums is a major crisis that affects the organization and practice of medicine. To others, it is a sign that the medical profession has not yet developed adequate controls to sanction deviations from standard practice. In either case, the escalation in medical professional liability awards raises important public policy issues concerning the underlying reasons for the awards and the potential effects on medical practice and service delivery.

While the full dimension of the crisis is difficult to specify, rising malpractice insurance premiums and increased claim frequency and award severity have been, until recently, its primary manifestations. Various explanations for these trends have been proposed, with little agreement as to the nature or causes of the problem.[1-8]

Although lawyers, the legal system, the medical profession, and the insurance industry have all been "blamed" for the current medical professional liability situation, there is a growing perception that something is wrong with the manner in which the tort system assesses liability and awards compensation in medical malpractice cases. Many physicians contend that the entire claim-settlement process fails to distinguish between negligent and nonnegligent behavior in assessing liability[5,9,10] and thus exposes them to liability for adverse outcomes as well as for negligent medical practice. Large jury verdicts and relatively easy access to the court system contribute to these perceptions.

In response, much of the recent debate has focused on reforming the tort system as a solution to the recurring malpractice crisis.[11] It is more likely, however, that this crisis results from complex interactions between the medical, legal, and insurance industries and cannot be blamed on any one source. Rising health care costs, for instance, contribute to larger jury verdicts, which in turn contribute to increased medical malpractice insurance premiums. As such, medical malpractice is not one problem but a series of interrelated problems that involve the regulation and social control of medical practice, quality of care, insurance markets, and the consistent assessment of liability by the courts.

To provide a broader context for the malpractice debate, this article will evaluate changes in legal doctrine and practice over time. The tort system operates to provide compensation to an injured party, to provide incentives for reducing the risks and costs of injuries (that is, deterrence), and to provide accountability for injurious conduct. Although this system has been criticized as being an economically inefficient regulatory mechanism whose costs vastly exceed its benefits, this article is neither an analysis of the tort system's strengths and weaknesses in resolving medical malpractice disputes[12] nor a broad critique of tort law.

Instead, I will analyze how evolutionary changes in legal doctrine and practice have contributed to increased claim frequency and award severity. I conclude that these changes do not provide a full explanation for the continued rise in awards and that no single doctrinal change has led to recent

From the Behavioral Sciences Department, The RAND Corp, Santa Monica, Calif.
The conclusions expressed in this article are those of the author and do not necessarily reflect those of The RAND Corp.

malpractice liability problems. Thus, changes in legal doctrine alone are not likely to reverse current trends, although tort reforms will help to stabilize and moderate award severity. Effective medical professional peer review, risk management, and the continued development of standards to define appropriate medical intervention are needed to reduce the incidence of substandard medical care.

The first part of this article is a review of medical professional liability data trends during the past 20 years. In the next section, I discuss legal trends during this period, focusing on several hypotheses that might explain the data. Finally, I suggest several public policy measures that might be undertaken in response to these trends.

Medical Professional Liability Data Trends: General Trends

Assembling data to analyze empirically recent trends in medical malpractice cases can be difficult. For the most part, malpractice data are not systematically collected and analyzed, making it difficult to estimate the scope of the malpractice problem.[7] We know very little about the incidence of negligent iatrogenic injuries, the relationship between quality of care and tort awards, or why people seek recovery through the tort system. Other gaps in available information include the deterrent effects of malpractice liability on medical practice, the effects of malpractice insurance premium increases on the availability of services for high-risk patients, and the effects of risk-management or loss-prevention programs on claim frequency and award severity.

Regardless of these gaps, the trend in claim frequency and award severity is unmistakable. No one disputes that from the 1970s until the mid-1980s, medical malpractice award severity and claim frequency increased sharply and without interruption. Nor is there much dispute that, although there is considerable unexplained variation, awards are systematically related to injury severity, and for permanent injuries, to life expectancy.[1,8,13,14]

The available data suggest that malpractice liability is not randomly distributed in the physician population,[15] but varies according to specialty and practice

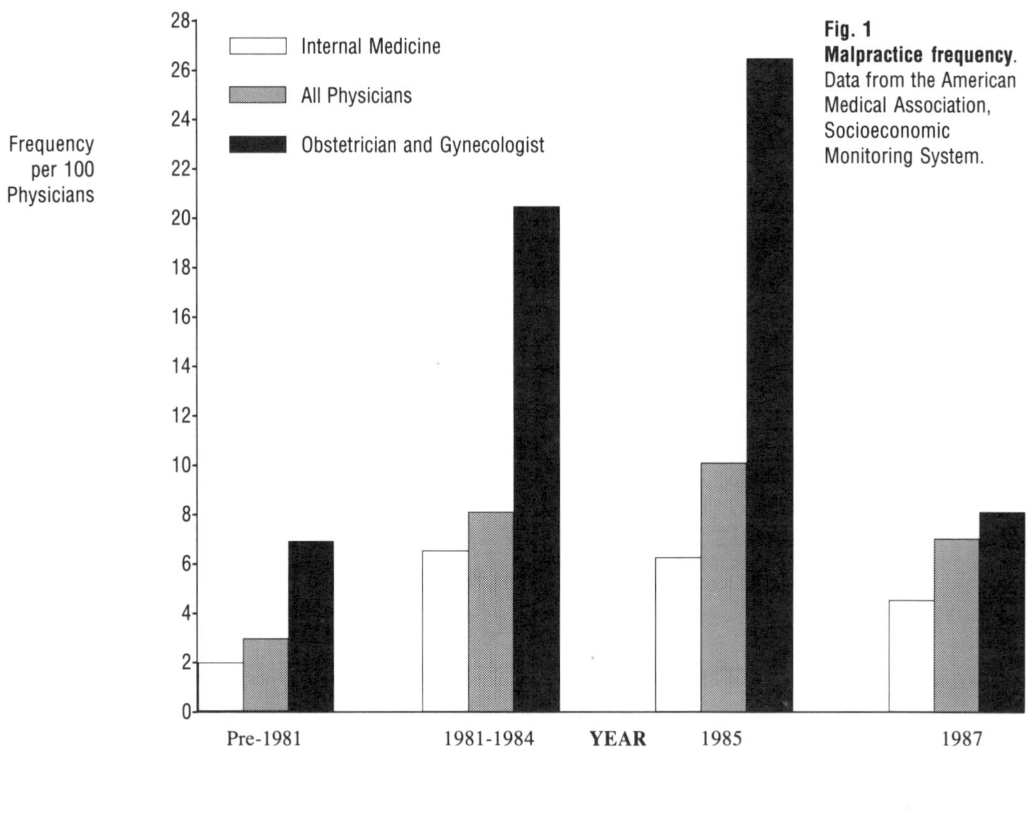

Fig. 1
Malpractice frequency. Data from the American Medical Association, Socioeconomic Monitoring System.

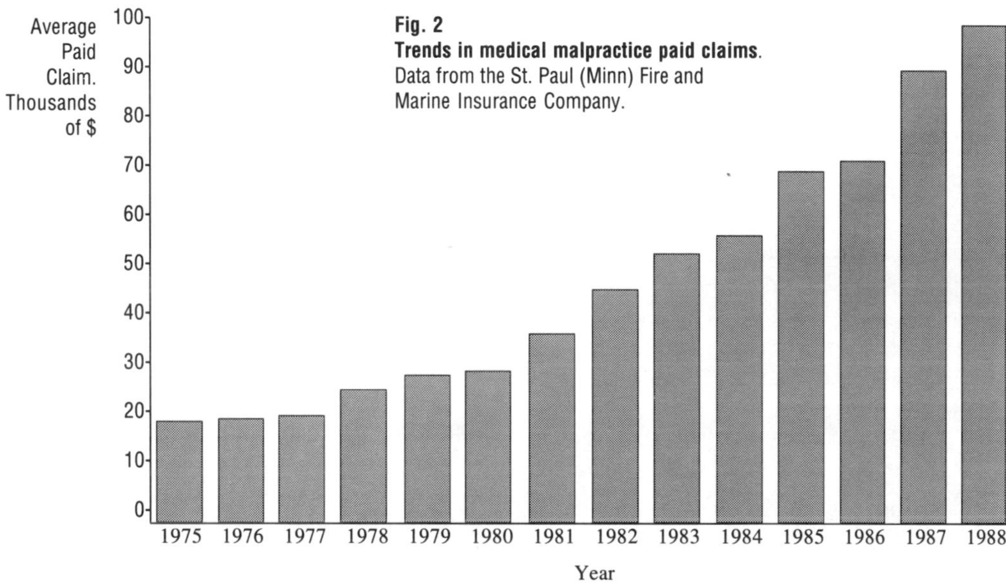

Fig. 2
Trends in medical malpractice paid claims.
Data from the St. Paul (Minn) Fire and Marine Insurance Company.

location. It does not appear, however, that only a "few" physicians are responsible for a disproportionate share of malpractice tort awards. Certain specialists (particularly surgeons and obstetricians and gynecologists) have a much higher risk of being sued and of being subjected to higher awards than other physicians,[1,6,16] although there is no reason to suspect that they are more negligent than other physicians. In all likelihood, this occurs because certain procedures have a higher probability of producing adverse outcomes in the absence of error. Also, errors in these specialties are more detectable and can result in more severely injured patients than in most other areas of medical practice.

It is also generally agreed that the proportion of potentially compensable malpractice incidents that reach the claim-settlement process or tort system is low.[8,17,18] According to the widely cited study by Mills,[17] only 1 in 10 legitimate malpractice incidents reaches the tort system. From this perspective, the problem is that too few, rather than too many, cases reach the tort system or claim-settlement process.[12,19] Of the cases in which a claim is filed, available data suggest that the tort system overcompensates those with modest losses while undercompensating those with very serious injuries and large losses.[1] In some cases, the tort system fails to compensate a negligently injured patient; in other cases, compensation may be awarded to someone who was not injured through substandard medical care.[10]

Claim Frequency and Award Severity

Looking first at the frequency of filed claims, Figure 1 shows sharp increases from the 1970s to the mid-1980s, with reductions occurring in the late 1980s. Between 1975 and 1985, claims per 100 physicians more than doubled,[20] while between 1976 and 1981, claims against obstetricians and gynecologists tripled. Because the proportion of incidents that results in claims is very low, claim filing could show major increases over time without suggesting any increase in substandard medical practice if the percentage of claims from legitimate malpractice incidents filed rises even slightly.

For the time being, the rise in claim frequency appears to have moderated, as some recent studies have indicated a drop or leveling in both claim and paid-claim frequency.[16,22-24] In Florida, for instance, Nye et al[6] suggest that claim filing peaked in 1984. Major medical malpractice insurers report similar trends beginning in 1986.[25] It is too soon to determine whether this is a statistical aberration, a leveling before new increases, the increased costs of litigating marginal claims, or the long-term effects of state tort reforms, hospital risk management efforts, and enhanced professional sanctions.

With regard to award severity (Figure 2), median awards have increased steadily over time in medical malpractice cases,[1,6,26,27] but the average verdict has soared.[6,8,28] Between 1975 and 1984, average medical malpractice verdicts increased at nearly twice the rate of the consumer price index.[8] In one study,[27] the average expected medical malpractice verdict in two jurisdictions was compared during two time periods, 1975 to 1979 and 1980 to 1984, showing a threefold rise in San Francisco, Calif, and a fivefold rise in Cook County, Illinois. Likewise, Nye et al[6] found that between 1975 and 1986 inflation-adjusted mean paid claims rose fivefold, while inflation-adjusted median paid claims rose nearly threefold. Average yearly increases reflect these trends.[28] In real terms, Nye et al[6] found that the average cost of a paid claim in Florida increased at a compound rate of 7.6% per year from 1975 to 1986.

Even with fewer claims, neither median nor average awards have yet declined, although the steep rise in average awards seems to have moderated. Thus, recent malpractice insurance premium reductions appear to result from declining total paid claim dollars rather than from declining median or average awards. Despite a reduced claim-filing rate, the average award paid by St Paul (Minn) Fire and Marine Insurance Company (a major underwriter of medical malpractice insurance) increased by 16% from 1986 to 1987 and by 6% from 1987 to 1988.[25] As with the decline in claim frequency, it is too soon to determine whether continuing tort reforms will ultimately result in reduced median and average awards, although local variations may result in greater reductions in certain areas.

The award severity data reflect a skewed distribution, attributable to an increase in large outlier awards. In the 1980s, million-dollar awards accounted for a disproportionate share of tort indemnity awards generally, and of medical malpractice awards in particular.[1,6,20,27] Recent data, however, suggest that the frequency of million-dollar awards has declined. If this trend continues, average award severity may also decline.

It seems likely that birth-injury cases have an inordinate effect on malpractice statistics. In 1984, according to the General Accounting Office,[1] obstetricians accounted for 10% of total claims, but 27% of total indemnity. The St Paul Fire and Marine Insurance Company[25] reports that birth-related injuries have replaced anesthesia-related injuries as the most costly claims. One study of California claims[29] found that by excluding birth-injury cases, average indemnity of reported large losses (verdicts and settlements of more than $50,000) would have declined by 28% from 1983 to 1986.

Finally, most claims are settled without any payment and defendants win most of the litigated cases.[24] A recent survey in three largely rural states reported that the defense prevailed in 81% of the litigated cases.[24] Data from the 1987 American College of Obstetricians and Gynecologists survey[23] indicate that defendants won 68% of all claims adjudicated by arbitration or jury verdict, although this was down from 81% reported in the 1985 American College of Obstetricians and Gynecologists survey.[30] At least in urban areas, however, plaintiffs may be winning a higher percentage of medical malpractice verdicts than 20 years ago. Peterson[27] reports that plaintiffs' victories in medical malpractice cases increased during a 20-year period from 27% to 53% in San Francisco, Calif, and from 25% to 49% in Cook County. This is consistent with other findings showing that urbanization is an important predictor of award severity.[8,31]

Data Constraints

In evaluating these data, some important limitations must be considered. Aside from major gaps in available data, the reported data cannot be compared easily. Each data-reporting system uses a different standard for defining the principal allegations of negligence, and each system uses different assumptions and numerical bases for data reporting. Some report data from all claims and expenses (ie, defense costs), including settlements and those in which no indemnity was paid. Others report averages only on a claims-paid basis or by looking at nonzero jury awards alone. Because many of the claims filed result in no indemnity payments, how those are incorporated into the figures makes a major difference in the apparent scope of the problem.

One result of these different approaches is that estimates of average verdicts vary widely (Figure 3), and statements about averages need to be scrutinized. As an example, Jury Verdict Research[32] reports that the annual average medical malpractice verdict rose from approximately $400,000 in 1980 to $1.4 million in 1986. Since this report only includes averages for initial jury verdicts (unadjusted for posttrial reductions), it provides a misleading picture in view of indications that large jury awards are often substantially reduced in posttrial proceedings. In medical malpractice cases, for instance, Shanley and Peterson[26] found an average posttrial reduction of 33%. They also found that reductions were disproportionate to large awards, with medical malpractice awards between $ 1 million and $ 10 million reduced by an average of 39%. Broder[14] found similar reductions. Thus, if the data regarding award severity disregard the effects of posttrial reductions, the averages misstate the dimension, although not the seriousness, of the medical malpractice problem.

Given the rise in health care costs over an equivalent period, it is not surprising that jury verdicts are higher. The soaring economic cost for treating permanent and total disabilities is no doubt a factor in many of these large verdicts. General rising salaries may also account for some portion of larger economic losses (*New York Times*. January 31, 1988;sect 3:2). This raises the question of what proportion of these large verdicts is for noneconomic damages. If most of a large verdict is for injury severity, as expressed through economic damages, and liability is accurately assessed over a range of cases, the rise in award severity may be a function of factors beyond control of the tort system. Unfortunately, the data are inconclusive on this issue, and further research is needed to isolate the effects of noneconomic damages on increased award severity relative to economic loss.[1,8]

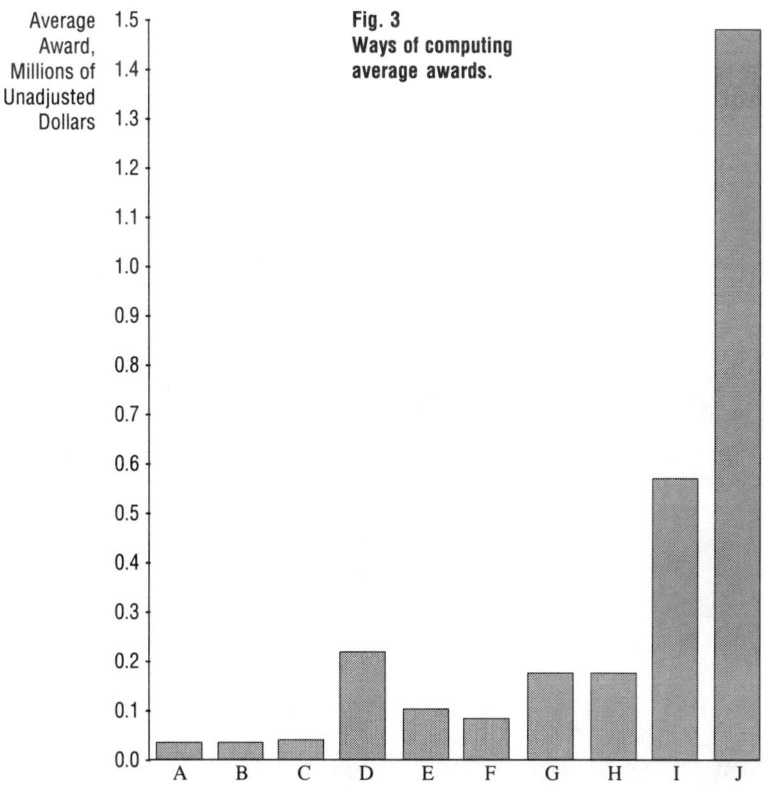

Fig. 3
Ways of computing average awards.

A. St. Paul, Minn, 1986, all claims

B. General Accounting Office (GAO) 1984, paid obstetrician and gynecologist

C. St. Paul 1981 to 1985, paid obstetrician and gynecologist

D. GAO 1984 paid obstetrician and gynecologist

E. St. Paul 1985, average paid losses

F. GAO 1984, paid claims

G. American College of Obstetricians and Gynecologists 1985, average claim

H. all California 1980 to 1984, expected award

I. San Francisco, Calif, and Chicago, Ill, 1980 to 1984, expected award

J. Jury Verdict Research 1986, verdict only

Legal Trends

The rise in claim frequency and award severity has occurred during a period of continued advances and improvements in medical care. It thus seems unlikely that a general deterioration in medical practice standards accounts for these trends. Nor is there any reason to believe that individual physicians are less skillful today than they were 20 years ago.[12,33]

What factors, then, account for the trends described previously? Whatever external factors may also be involved, such as increases in medical costs, it is appropriate to analyze changes in the tort system during the past two decades. Have standards for assessing liability changed so that physicians are now held to higher practice standards? Are courts and juries confusing adverse outcomes with physician error? If not, what other explanations might be explored? The following sections evaluate various hypotheses that link the rise in award severity to changes within the tort system.

Are Physicians Now Held to Higher Practice Standards?—One hypothesis often used to explain trends in medical malpractice liability is that courts and juries are holding physicians to higher liability standards, amounting to strict liability, instead of the traditional fault-based negligence standard of care. If this hypothesis were true, it could certainly explain much of the increase in claim frequency and award severity, as well as suggesting reasonable solutions.

In *strict liability*, a physician could be held liable for adverse outcomes regardless of fault. For a plaintiff to recover in *negligence*, he or she must show that the physician was at fault by failing to maintain the customary standard of care owed to the patient. *Customary care* is typically defined as the degree of care and skill ordinarily used under similar circumstances by members of the profession. In medical malpractice, the applicable standard of care is established by the medical profession itself through expert medical testimony.

Little evidence exists in the reported cases to confirm the strict liability hypothesis. In fact, a perusal of numerous medical malpractice cases decided within the past 20 years indicates considerable stability in the general common-law rules. The standard of liability remains what it has always been: a fault-based determination of whether the physician maintained the applicable standard of care.

Technological Change—A possible explanation for the perception of strict liability is that although the standard of care has not changed, how it operates in practice and what is necessary to meet the standard may have shifted over time. In large part, this change in how the standard operates is driven by advances in technology, improvements and changes in medical practice, and changes in legal organization and practice. As technology changes, medical standards change, and what constitutes a minimum standard of care also changes. Although difficult to quantify, it is likely that the introduction of new technology has raised what is considered to be customary care to much higher levels, giving the appearance of meeting a higher standard in court.

Along with opportunities for improved health care, technological advances create more opportunities for error, either in diagnosis or treatment, and those errors may result in more visible and more severe adverse outcomes. The availability of new technology is a particular problem for obstetric and gynecologic practice because much of it is controversial and may not add to improved health care,[35,36] while paradoxically contributing to a higher operating standard of care. Some technologies, such as genetic testing, electronic fetal monitors, and ultrasonography, carry the risk of increased liability either through failure to use in certain situations or for improperly interpreting the results.[36-38] Technological advances may have also helped to create an environment of perhaps unrealistic patient expectations that every neonate (or indeed any medical outcome) will be perfect. The ability to save a severely injured low-birth-weight infant, when that same infant would not have survived 20 years ago, carries with it the potential for litigation that blames the obstetrician for the injuries.

Expert Testimony—In addition, with the demise of the locality rule, which virtually limited testimony to the standard of care in the defendant's practice area, plaintiffs have access to a wider array of previously unavailable testimony from experts outside the local area. This moves the changing standard down to the practitioner much faster, particularly since out-of-state or academic experts may practice a different, that is, higher standard of care than practiced locally. However, this does not mean that a de facto strict liability standard has replaced the negligence standard. The question is how quickly these changes should be adopted by the average practitioner at a time when changes occur very rapidly.

Defensive Medicine—Another possible explanation for the perception of a higher standard of care is that the familiar problem of defensive medicine also operates to raise the standard of care. To the extent that physicians order additional tests as protection against subsequent liability, the added tests become part of the changing standard of care. This may, however, be as much a reaction to new practice standards as a cause of them. It is also difficult to distinguish defensive practices from those that are beneficial and would have occurred anyway,[9,39] and there appear to be no data that link them to increased claim frequency or award severity.

Jury Generosity—A second hypothesis is that "jury generosity" is a major reason for these trends. To be sure, it is possible that juries systematically confuse adverse outcomes with substandard care, disregard judicial instructions, and hold "deep pocket" defendants to a higher standard of care, or even confound the notion of liability with damages.[40] Individual juries may hold defendants in medical malpractice cases to a higher standard of conduct than would be applicable to an individual defendant. More broadly, critics of the tort liability system often allege that juries may view themselves as an instrumentality for redistributing wealth.

However, since there is very little systematic evidence regarding jury behavior, it is speculative to blame juries for not following the law when defendants win most of the litigated cases. Indeed, Danzon[8] concluded that available data refuted the assertion that juries disregard fault when assessing liability, and judges have the authority to overrule juries that clearly disregard either the evidence or the judge's instructions.[41] No doubt, some courts and juries assess liability incorrectly, but it has not been shown that courts or juries systematically assess liability improperly or impose an improper standard of care on physicians.

When evaluating jury behavior in medical malpractice cases, two interrelated issues should be considered. The absence of definitive research on appropriate outcomes from medical procedures (that is, the distribution of outcomes that can reasonably be expected from medical intervention) makes it difficult to establish whether the outcome in any given situation results from inappropriate care (negligence) or bad luck.[42] Confounding this problem is the equally difficult issue, particularly in birth-injury cases, of attributing an adverse outcome to a particular cause. Scientific notions of causation (established through probabilistic reasoning) are very different from the legal determination of proximate cause and can be difficult to reconcile in an individual case.

While a detailed discussion of the causation issue is beyond the scope of this article, one example might illustrate the problem. According to epidemiologic research, the incidence of newborns who have cerebral palsy has remained stable at anywhere from 1.3 to 2.7 per 1000 live births.[9] However, the etiologic factors that lead to cerebral palsy are not well understood and can rarely be predicted on the basis of perinatal events.[43,44] It is thus difficult to attribute an outcome of cerebral palsy to a preventable perinatal event or, in other words, to observed substandard medical care.[45,46] Nonetheless, a jury must decide what happened to an individual victim during the birthing process (based on the best available scientific evidence), hardly an easy task.

Juries may well be more sympathetic to a severely injured newborn in attributing causation to physician error,[35-37] but there is insufficient empirical or case support for that conclusion.[47] A review of reported obstetric and gynecologic cases is inconclusive on this point, and insurance company data are not available to confirm or refute this. Once again, the legal rule itself seems to be stable over time;[48-50] whether it operates differently in practice is harder to determine from the reported cases.

For example, it is possible that reduced standards of evidence make it easier for plaintiffs to show a causal connection, or that the availability of expert testimony allows "causation" cases to go forward. Perhaps a greater percentage of causation cases are now reaching the courts, resulting in larger verdicts.

A researchable hypothesis, for example, is that courts are seeing different types of cases, raising more difficult notions of causation, than those that were presented 20 years ago. If so, the trends described previously may be a function of judging a different class of issues rather than the unpredictability or randomness of jury verdicts.

Substantive Changes in the Law—Despite the previous discussion, the law has not remained static during the past 20 years; far from it. A third hypothesis is that there have been considerable proplaintiff substantive changes in the law that may affect claim frequency and award severity. Many changes have indeed been proplaintiff, such as the abolition of the locality rule, abolition of charitable immunity, expansion of informed consent, and expansion of *respondeat superior* (that is, employer liability for employee wrongdoing).

Proplaintiff Reforms—One of the unanswered empirical questions is the extent to which each change has contributed to changes in aggregate tort liability awards. Danzon[8] found statistically significant effects on claim frequency and award severity in jurisdictions that adopted the four proplaintiff doctrines listed previously, but the effects peaked in 1976 and then declined. In an analysis of data from the American Medical Association, Adams and Zuckerman[21] found that none of these doctrines had a statistically significant effect on claim frequency. Although the doctrine of informed consent in particular has generated considerable critical commentary and attention, it does not appear to have had a significant impact on award severity. The study by Adams and Zuckerman[21] indicates that informed consent had a statistically significant relationship to increased claim frequency between 1976 and 1981, but their study did not address award severity. Danzon,[51] however, found the effects of informed consent to be larger on claim frequency than on award severity. If so, this may add to the transaction costs of defending such cases (hence, increasing aggregate costs for insurers), but may not add that much to average award severity.

In view of these findings, it is unlikely that the proplaintiff changes are a major cause of the current malpractice crisis, although they may contribute to the rising percentage of plaintiffs' victories.[31] To be sure, these changes could also contribute to larger aggregate payouts if more claims are successful, even those of modest value.

Prodefendant Reforms—In reaction to the proplaintiff reforms, a "counterreformation" set in during the mid-1970s (and continued into the 1980s) as several prodefendant tort reforms were enacted. These included caps on noneconomic damages, mandatory collateral offset (that is, any award is net of other benefits), shorter statutes of limitation (the time period in which litigation must be initiated), and the use of arbitration panels. These reforms apparently have reduced award severity from levels they otherwise might have reached.[8,31] While the long-term effects of state tort reform efforts are still not fully known,[52] recent evidence suggests that the counterreformation is introducing greater stability and predictability on average. Over time, tort reforms are likely at least to limit the rate of increase in award severity and claim frequency. These reforms will perhaps reduce average or median awards, but will not reduce the underlying rate of medical malpractice incidents.

Liability Expansions—Finally, the types of cases in which liability might be determined have expanded during the past two decades. One example is the ability to recover emotional damages without showing a physical impact (although not adopted in all jurisdictions). Another example is recovery for loss of a chance of survival. Where the alleged medical malpractice reduces a chance of survival to an even lower probability, the injured victim may recover to the extent the malpractice reduced the chances of survival. For two reasons, however, this is unlikely to have a major effect on aggregate trends: first, the doctrine is not accepted in all jurisdictions; and second, awards are not likely to be large in any event because recovery is limited to damages that directly result from the premature death, such as lost earnings and additional medical expenses.[53,54]

An area of new liability that may be extremely troublesome to obstetricians and gynecologists is the tort of wrongful life or wrongful birth. Most jurisdictions deny liability for wrongful life (that is, a claim for damages brought by an impaired child's parents who allege that but for defendant's negligence the child never would have been born), but a growing number of jurisdictions allow recovery for wrongful birth (which is the parents' claim for damages that result from a prenatally detectable severe birth defect).[37,55] As discussed previously, the technological ability to save infants, albeit in imperfect condition, who would not have survived 20 years ago carries with it the potential for extensive liability awards. Genetic screening tests, although not now a liability problem, also have the potential for large indemnity awards if erroneous test results are imputed to physician error.

At the same time, there are indications that courts are beginning to restrain further expansions. Recent cases in New York have denied separate compensation for loss of enjoyment of life by an unconscious medical malpractice plaintiff. Such rulings may not reduce current award levels, but they may place upper bounds on aggregate award severity.

Changes in Procedural Rules—Beyond these changes in substantive law, there have been significant procedural changes (that is, the rules of evidence that govern how trials are conducted) that may also affect trial outcomes. Little is known empirically about the relationship between procedural changes and trial outcomes, but it is reasonable to expect that procedural changes can affect both claim frequency and award severity. By the mid-1970s, most state courts had adopted the more flexible federal rules of discovery and federal rules of evidence. These rules allow plaintiffs' lawyers greater opportunities for pretrial discovery and, hence, an expanded ability to discover and introduce into evidence factors that may either prove liability or increase a case's monetary value. In addition, courts have come to rely more heavily on expert witnesses, particularly economists, to estimate future health care costs. With access to a wider array of previously unavailable expert testimony, plaintiffs are able to present stronger cases and damage estimates to juries.[56] Such changes operate to facilitate the plaintiffs' burden of proof and allow any number of cases, which otherwise might not have gone very far, to achieve a positive settlement or to be decided by a jury.

The use and importance of expert witnesses is an aspect of medical malpractice litigation in need of further research. Like other procedural changes, the changing use and reliance on expert witnesses may be an important determinant of large awards, particularly in estimating future health care costs of neurologically impaired infants.

Changes in Legal Practice—An additional explanation for the data trends is that changes in the organization and practice of law may influence jury behavior[27] and certainly influence the types of cases brought to trial. Lawyers' courtroom presentations and tactics may be more sophisticated (shared information, better pretrial discovery, expert witnesses), so that their trial presentation is more convincing. For example, the use of videotapes and other litigation tools that show a day in the life of an injured patient enables a plaintiff's attorney to present a case more graphically to the jury than before. Juries may also be hearing stronger cases since lawyers may be more selective in cases taken to a jury.

This further suggests that there has been an important shift during the past 20 years in the balance between plaintiff and defense attorneys. Just as the practice of medicine has become increasingly specialized, so has the practice of law, mirroring trends throughout society (*New York Times*. September 9, 1988;sect A:19). In all probability, greater specialization permits larger capital investment in malpractice cases, sharing of knowledge and training with other specialists, and better preparation for litigation. Access to computer databases and institutional support mechanisms increases the likelihood of litigating the "right" cases for substantial awards. One consequence of this is to provide greater access to the tort system for injured patients (at least for those cases where the expected value exceeds the costs of litigation).

Ongoing changes in the organization and practice of law are not likely to affect outcomes to the same extent as changes in legal doctrine or procedure, but they can affect what types of cases reach a jury and how a jury might respond. More research is necessary to determine the extent to which these organizational and practice changes have affected trial outcomes.[52] When taken together, however, these changes provide a clearer picture of the legal system's role in explaining recent trends.

Public Policy Responses

If changes in the tort system over time are inadequate to explain fully the rise in claim frequency and award severity, then tort reform alone is unlikely to solve the malpractice problems faced by physicians. Indeed, focusing exclusively on tort reform is likely to obscure the inherent complexity underlying the malpractice conundrum and the need to develop broader approaches for ameliorating the problem.

At a time when demands for changing the tort system are increasingly articulated, the empirical basis for making sound policy decisions is inadequate. Nonetheless, it is quite possible, if not likely, that demands for change will not wait for the extensive research needs cited previously. Assuming that recent reductions in malpractice premiums provide a "window of opportunity" for further debate, several measures can be taken to better inform the policy process, regardless of what mechanism is used to resolve medical practice disputes.

First, and most important, the medical profession should expand work that has already begun to define what constitutes appropriate medical intervention and what the appropriate outcomes are from medical intervention.[42] Defining the range and probabilities of appropriate outcomes will provide a sounder basis for juries to differentiate between adverse outcomes from the natural course of disease and substandard medical care. In conjunction with appropriateness standards, the medical profession should also expand the use of medical practice protocols similar to the one developed for anesthesiology.[58]

Second, to the extent that the problem begins with substandard practice, the burden is on the medical profession to reduce the incidence of negligent iatrogenic injury.[59,60] The medical profession should continue to improve its sanctioning and risk-management and loss-prevention mechanisms. In the past, these have not been used effectively, and substandard medical practice has often not been punished.[61,62] As a result, the tort system has imposed certain social controls as a deterrent to substandard medical care. The burden should be shifted back to the medical profession to reduce injury costs through effective monitoring and sanctions. An important research question is the extent to which these self-policing mechanisms operate to reduce injury and litigation costs.

To assist the medical profession, states need to enact legislation that insulates peer review activity from liability except in cases that involve gross negligence or recklessness. In conjunction with the Health Care Quality Improvement Act of 1986, such legislation should provide sufficient protection to encourage active peer review.

Third, policymakers should consider whether cases that involve probabilistic causation, such as with neurologically impaired infants, should be removed from the tort system and resolved under a separate compensation mechanism similar to vaccine injuries. In cases where medical intervention is less likely to alter observed outcomes, such as cerebral palsy, it may be appropriate to spread the risk of birth injury through a separate compensation fund rather than trying to reconcile probabilistic and legal causation in an individual case. This would address a difficult problem facing physicians without undermining the tort system's general deterrence value. As the Virginia legislation dealing with neurologically impaired infants suggests, however, this is not an easy task.

Fourth, in conjunction with the previously mentioned measures, malpractice data need to be collected and arrayed in a more consistent and comprehensive manner to avoid comparability problems and to provide better information for injury prevention. In particular, insurance companies should take the lead in reporting disaggregated data by primary allegation (such as specific birth injury) and alleged treatment error (such as what caused a missed diagnosis). This would allow aggregate trends to be broken down into more discrete injury categories for closer evaluation. While initially more expensive, doing so should assist in reducing injury costs. Insurers should also report median awards and settlements (because they are more representative of the expected result than average awards),[63] and all claims (including claims with no payment and verdicts for the defense) as adjusted for posttrial reductions and increases in medical care costs.

Conclusion

As is so often the case when commenting on medical malpractice problems, more questions have been raised than answered. No single explanation of the medical professional liability crisis is likely to answer all questions. Changes in the tort system over time may help explain some of the reasons for increased claim frequency and award severity and may clarify the policy options for reforming the tort system. Tort reform by itself, however, is unlikely to be a panacea without an invigorated response from the medical profession. In the absence of effective sanctions from the medical profession, the tort system is likely to remain the dominant mechanism for monitoring injury prevention. At best, the tort system is an imperfect instrument for allocating risk and resolving medical practice disputes between physician and patient. No-fault and other alternative compensation systems are promising reforms, but whether they are superior alternatives to the tort system remains to be demonstrated.

Supplementary Information

Financial support was provided by The RAND Corporation and The Institute for Civil Justice of The RAND Corporation, Santa Monica, Calif, and G. D. Searle & Co, Chicago, Ill.

I would like to thank John Rolph, PhD, and Brian Mittman, PhD, for their insightful comments on an earlier draft of the manuscript. I am especially grateful to Debby Hensler, PhD, for thoughtful discussions about the legal system. Helpful comments at a 1987 Harvard University conference entitled "The Medical Malpractice Crisis in Obstetrics: The Economic, Medical and Health Policy Implications" were provided by Gary Schwartz, JD, Paul Weiler, JD, Harrison Pledger, JD, and J. Douglas Peters, JD. Three anonymous reviewers also provided thoughtful comments. The American College of Obstetricians and Gynecologists, Washington, DC, the St Paul (Minn) Fire and Marine Insurance Company, and the Physicians Insurers Association of America, Lawrenceville, NJ, provided valuable information.

References

1. Medical Malpractice: Characteristics of Claims Closed in 1984. Washington, DC: General Accounting Office; 1987. Publication GAO/HRD-87-55.

2. Report of the Task Force on Medical Liability and Malpractice. Washington, DC: Dept of Health and Human Services; 1987.

3. The Report of the Tort Policy Working Group on the Causes, Extent and Policy Implications of the Current Crisis in Insurance Availability and Affordability. Washington, DC: Dept of Justice; 1986.

4. Bovbjerg RR, Havighurst CC, eds. Medical malpractice: can the private sector find relief? Law Contemporary Problems. 1986;49:1-348.

5. American Medical Association and Specialty Society Medical Liability Project. A Proposed Alternative to the Civil Justice System for Resolving Medical Liability Disputes: A Fault-Based Administrative System. Chicago, Ill: American Medical Association; 1988.

6. Nye DJ, Gifford DG, Webb BL, Dewar MA. The causes of the medical malpractice crisis: an analysis of claims data and insurance company finances. Georgetown Law J. 1988;76:1495-1561.

7. Reynolds RA, Rizzo JA, Gonzales ML. The cost of medical professional liability. JAMA. 1987; 257:2776-2781.

8. Danzon PM. Medical Malpractice: Theory, Evidence and Public Policy. Cambridge, Mass: Harvard University Press; 1985.

9. The Medical Malpractice Crisis in Obstetrics: The Economic, Medical and Health Policy Implications. Cambridge, Mass: Harvard University; 1987.

10. Cheney FW, Posner K, Caplan RA, Ward RJ. Standard of care and anesthesia liability. JAMA. 1989;261:1599-1603.

11. Abraham KS. Medical liability reform: a conceptual framework. JAMA. 1988;260:68-72.

12. Bovbjerg RR. Medical malpractice on trial: quality of care is the important standard. Law Contemporary Problems. 1986;49:321-348.

13. Danzon PM. The Disposition of Medical Malpractice Claims. Santa Monica, Calif: The RAND Corp; 1980. Publication R-2622-HCFA.

14. Broder I. Analysis of Million Dollar Verdicts. Washington, DC: American Trial Lawyers Association; 1986.

15. Rolph JE. Some statistical evidence on merit rating in medical malpractice insurance. J Risk Insurance. 1981;48:247-260.

16. Physicians' & Surgeons' Update, 1988. St Paul, Minn: St Paul Fire & Marine Insurance Co; 1988.

17. Mills DH. Medical insurance feasibility study. West J Med. 1978;128:360-368.

18. Meyers AR. 'Lumping it': the hidden denominator of the medical malpractice crisis. Am J Public Health. 1987;77:1544-1548.

19. Abel RL. The crisis is injuries, not liability. In: Olson W, ed. New Directions in Liability Law. New York, NY: Academy of Political Science;1988:31-41.

20. Physicians' & Surgeons' Update, 1985. St Paul, Minn: St Paul Fire & Marine Insurance Co; 1985.

21. Adams EK, Zuckerman S. Variation in the growth and incidence of medical malpractice claims. J Health Polit Policy Law. 1984;9:475-488.

22. Neupauer R. 1987 California Large Loss Trend Study/ Malpractice. Oakland: Medical Underwriters of California; 1988.

23. Professional Liability Insurance and its Effects: Report of a 1987 Survey of ACOG's Membership. Washington, DC: Opinion Research Corp; 1988.

24. Hatch MA. Medical Malpractice Claim Study: 1982-1987. St Paul: Minnesota Dept of Commerce; 1989.

25. Physicians' & Surgeons' Update, 1989. St Paul, Minn: St Paul Fire & Marine Insurance Co; 1989.

26. Shanley MG, Peterson MA. Posttrial Adjustments to Jury Awards. Santa Monica, Calif: The RAND Corp; 1987. Publication R-3511-ICJ.

27. Peterson MA. Civil Juries in the 1980s: Trends in Jury Trials and Verdicts in California and Cook County, Illinois. Santa Monica, Calif: The RAND Corp; 1987. Publication R-3466-ICJ.

28. Kakalik JS, Pace NM. Costs and Compensation Paid in Tort Litigation. Santa Monica, Calif: The RAND Corp; 1986. Publication R-3391-ICJ.

29. Neupauer R. 1986 California Large Loss Trend Study/ Malpractice. Oakland: Medical Underwriters of California; 1987.

30. Needham, Porter, Novelli. Professional Liability Insurance and its Effect: Report of a Survey of ACOG's Membership. Washington, DC; 1985.

31. Danzon PM. New Evidence on the Frequency and Severity of Medical Malpractice Claims. Santa Monica, Calif: The RAND Corp; 1986. Publication R-3410-ICJ.

32. Current Award Trends, 1988 Edition. Solon, Ohio: Jury Verdict Research; 1988.

33. Brook RH, Brutoco RL, Williams KN. The relationship between medical malpractice and quality of care. Duke Law J. 1975:1179-1231.

34. Prosser WL. Handbook of the Law of Torts. 4th ed. St Paul, Minn: West Publishing Co; 1971.

35. Dobson T. Medical malpractice in the birthplace: resolving the physician-patient conflict through informed consent, standard of care, and assumption of risk. Nebraska Law Rev. 1986; 65:655-685.

36. Gilfix MG. Electronic fetal monitoring: physician liability and informed consent. Am J Law Med. 1984;10:31-90.

37. Heland KV. The professional liability crisis in obstetrics: can the causes suggest solutions? Quality Rev Bull. 1986 (special issue): 13-19.

38. Walker v United States, 600 F Supp 195 (D DC 1985).

39. Zuckerman S. Medical malpractice: claims, legal costs, and the practice of defensive medicine. Health Aff. 1984;3:128-133.

40. MacCoun RJ. Getting Inside the Black Box: Toward a Better Understanding of Civil Jury Behavior. Santa Monica, Calif: The RAND Corp; 1987. Publication N-2671-ICJ.

41. Rutherford v Zearfoss, 272 SE2d 225 (Va 1980).

42. Williams AP. Malpractice, Outcomes, and Appropriateness of Care. Santa Monica, Calif: The RAND Corp; 1988. Publication P-7445.

43. Sokol RJ. Perinatal risk and cerebral palsy. JAMA. 1984;251:1868-1869.

44. Nelson KB, Ellenbogen JH. Obstetric complications as risk factors for cerebral palsy or seizure disorders. JAMA. 1984;251:1843-1848.

45. Kitchen WH, Doyle LW, Ford GW, Rickards AL, Lissenden JV, Ryan MM. Cerebral palsy in very low birth weight infants surviving to 2 years with modern perinatal intensive care. Am J Perinatol. 1987;4: 29-35.

46. Niswander K, Elbourne D, Redman C, et al. Adverse outcome of pregnancy and the quality of obstetric care. Lancet. 1984;2:827-831.

47. Hippocrates Mertsaris v 73rd Corp, 470 NYS2d 792 (NY Ct App 1984).

48. Seattle First National Bank v Rankin, 367 P2d 835 (Wash 1962).

49. Long v Johnson, 381 NE2d 93 (Ind 1978).

50. Carter v Shirley, 488 NE2d 16 (Mass 1986).

51. Danzon PM. The Frequency and Severity of Medical Malpractice Claims. Santa Monica, Calif: The RAND Corp; 1982. Publication R-2870-ICJ/HCFA.

52. Carroll SJ. Assessing the Effects of Tort Reforms. Santa Monica, Calif: The RAND Corp; 1987. Publication R-3554-ICJ.

53. Herskovits v Group Health, 664 P2d 474 (Wash 1983).

54. King JH. Causation, valuation, and chance in personal injury torts involving preexisting conditions and future consequences. Yale Law J.1981;90: 1353-1397.

55. Louisell DW, Williams H. Medical Malpractice. New York, NY: Matthew Bender & Co Inc; 1988.

56. Trevino v United States, 804 F2d 1512 (9th Cir 1986).

57. Ensor v Wilson, 519 So2d 1244 (Ala 1987).

58. Eichhorn JH, Cooper JB, Cullen DJ, Maier WR, Phillip JH, Seeman RG. Standards for patient monitoring during anesthesia at Harvard Medical School. JAMA. 1986;256:1017-1020.

59. Julian TM, Brooker DC, Butler JE, et al. Investigation of obstetric malpractice closed claims: profile of event. Am J Perinatol. 1985;2:320-324.

60. Dubois RW, Brook RH. Preventable deaths: who, how often, and why? Ann Intern Med.1988;109: 582-589.

61. Kusserow RP, Handley EA, Yessian MR. An overview of state medical discipline. JAMA. 1987;257:820-824.

62. Medical Malpractice: A Framework for Action. Washington, DC: General Accounting Office; 1987. Publication GAO/HRD-87-73.

63. Localio AR. Variations on $962 258: the misuse of data on medical malpractice. Law Med Health Care. 1985;13:126-127.

Jacobson PD. Medical malpractice and the tort system. JAMA. 1989; 262(23): 3320-3327.

Reprinted with permission from the author and the American Medical Association.

Article 2.2

Standards for Patient Monitoring During Anesthesia at Harvard Medical School

John H. Eichhorn, MD, Jeffrey B. Cooper, PhD, David J. Cullen, MD, Ward R. Maier, MD, James H. Philip, MD, and Robert G. Seeman, MD. Journal of the American Medical Association, August 1986.

As part of a major patient safety/risk management effort, the Department of Anaesthesia of Harvard Medical School, Boston, has devised specific, detailed, mandatory standards for minimal patient monitoring during anesthesia at its nine component teaching hospitals. Such standards have not previously existed, and resistance to the concept was anticipated but not seen. The standards are technically achievable in all settings and affordable in terms of effort and cost. Early detection of untoward trends or events during anesthesia will result in prevention or mitigation of patient injury; this, in turn, may also help counter the explosive increases in anesthesia-related malpractice actions, settlements, judgments, and insurance premiums. The committee process used is applicable to the promulgation of standards of practice for all medical specialties and any organized group of medical practitioners.

Physicians traditionally have resisted standards of practice that prescribe specific details of their day-to-day conduct of medical care. In spite of this, as the first part of a risk management/quality assurance program, the Department of Anaesthesia of Harvard Medical School, Boston, has devised and implemented, at its nine component teaching-hospital departments, standards for minimal patient monitoring during anesthesia. Standards such as these have not previously existed at Harvard. Reported herein is the process used to balance physician autonomy in daily practice with the large general goal of improving patient care, which, in turn, should mitigate the malpractice crisis.

History

Adverse outcome from anesthesia has recently received increased attention.[1-3] Estimates of morbidity and mortality rates vary widely and are mostly extrapolated from comparatively small samples. Among the approximately 20 million patients anesthetized annually in the United States, 2000 or more may die of causes primarily attributable to anesthesia; the majority of these deaths are thought to be preventable.[1-3] The rate of preventable morbidity is even less easily estimated. Because major anesthetic accidents often lead to catastrophic results, consequent malpractice settlements and awards are frequently large (estimated to average over $100,000 and to range up to $41 million [United Press International, Sept 27, 1984]).

The nine teaching-hospital departments composing Harvard Medical School's Department of Anaesthesia include academic centers, specialty hospitals, and community-oriented hospitals. Together they administer approximately 100,000 anesthetics annually. All are insured under Harvard's own medical malpractice insurance company. The risk management arm of this insurance carrier expressed concern to the anesthesia department heads about the number of incidents and claims and the associated indemnity involving anesthesia care during the period 1976 through 1984. A risk management committee of six senior staff members was appointed to investigate the concerns and, if appropriate, suggest action.

The committee began by evaluating (without patient identification, to preserve confidentiality and prevent institutional bias) all the anesthesia-related claims and incidents on file with the insurance carrier. Of the cases involving major morbidity or death, most were believed to be preventable. Examining these cases, the committee concluded that more meticulous monitoring of the patients would help prevent such anesthesia accidents.

The committee reviewed practices of patient monitoring during anesthesia (then existing at Harvard, in the local community, and nationally). Controversy ensued about whether the committee should offer "suggestions," "guidelines," "recommendations," or actual "standards of practice." Basic monitoring practices were thought to be so important in accident prevention that they must be mandatory. Thus, "standards" was favored to ensure that each hospital department would *require* its members to institute a minimal level of monitoring for every patient anesthetized. The traditional resistance "on principle" to external imposition of methods of medical practice was anticipated. However, it was believed that this degree of emphasis was necessary to achieve the goal of anesthetic accident prevention. The anesthesia department heads unanimously joined the insurance carrier's enthusiastic support of this approach.

Only vague or general standards of practice exist in American medicine. Obstetrics/gynecology has organizational standards[4] detailing the makeup of a hospital service, privileges, record keeping, and stipulations, for example, that a history must be taken on a new patient. The American Academy of Pediatrics issues recommendations on vaccination protocols, breast-feeding, nutrition, and many other general topics. The Joint Commission on Accreditation of Hospitals has process-oriented standards that focus on organizational and physical structure, but relatively little on the details of actual daily medical practice. In anesthesia, there are voluntary product performance standards for many of the medical devices used, such as anesthesia machines, endotracheal tubes, and ventilators. These have been developed by committees comprising both manufacturers and anesthesia clinicians. The American Society of Anesthesiologists has general guidelines for practice, including, for example, that patients should be evaluated preoperatively. However, specific standards for the minute-to-minute conduct of anesthesia practice have never been promulgated.

Objectives of the Standards

The goals of the Harvard minimal monitoring standards are as follows:

1. To improve patient care, thereby reducing the number of adverse outcomes arising from anesthesia accidents. An additional secondary result should be a reduction in the number of malpractice claims, which will indicate improvement in care and also may slow the accelerating rise in insurance premiums or even lead to premium reduction for anesthesia practitioners.

2. To enhance detection of relatively low-frequency events, using principles derived from a large collective experience. An individual anesthetist's personal experience would suggest that preventable serious injuries or death occurs very rarely; therefore, it is unwarranted for individuals to develop standards of care based solely on their own adverse experiences.

3. To provide a means for objective evaluation. An individual practitioner, a supervisor, or a department head can observe (and quantify, if desired) whether actual patient monitoring practice measures up to clear criteria. This can help reinforce the subjective clinical impression that someone is a low-risk or, conversely, a high-risk anesthesiologist or anesthetist. Such observations are process audits, as distinct from outcome audits that evaluate the result of care, independent of how it was rendered. Studying relatively rare but serious adverse outcomes after they happen is valuable; focusing on the "process" or conduct of patient monitoring in anesthesia may *prevent* such an outcome.

4. To establish a precedent. The anesthesia risk management committee is in the process of developing additional standards of practice for other aspects of care for the Department of Anaesthesia at Harvard Medical School.

Criteria for the Standards

No experimental data exist from which a set of standards for minimal monitoring during anesthesia can be objectively derived. There is need for a balance between not enough and too much monitoring. It is assumed that the anesthetist will pay attention to the monitors and respond correctly to their output data. Among the factors weighed to optimize the set of measurements and alarms were availability; cost; simplicity of use; intraoperative distracting influence; the relative sensitivity, specificity, and predictability (freedom from breakdown or aberrant output) of each monitoring modality; and, finally, whether the standards represented "reasonable care"[5] consistent with applicable court decision precedents. Unable to use a classic scientific approach to analyze these factors, the committee adopted an intuitive approach requiring agreement to be forged from widely divergent opinions.

The actual daily practice in the anesthesia departments associated with Harvard Medical School was the starting point in evaluating what patient monitoring is desirable and then what should be mandatory. This was correlated with the insurance claim data. For example, one anesthesia death occurred when an old anesthesia machine without an oxygen monitor was used in an x-ray suite during a procedure. In the relative darkness, the wrong flowmeter knob was turned and the oxygen was shut off. This accident would have been prevented by a functioning oxygen monitor with a lower limit alarm. One of the standards mandates monitoring of breathing system oxygen during *all* general anesthetics.

The standards had to be realistic, technically achievable, and affordable in terms of both personnel and equipment utilization. It was recognized, however, that certain hospital departments would need to change some practices and add new equipment if the standards were fully implemented. The standards were written to make compliance easy and desirable for the individual practitioner.

During the development process (members' individual efforts plus about 20 hours of full committee meetings over eight months), committee members sought input from persons at all levels within their respective departments. Efforts were made to informally canvass senior members of all nine departments and others with known interest. One hospital department has a formal patient safety group that reviewed and accepted the proposed standards and also gave input to the committee. Suggestions were accepted or rejected by committee agreement.

The Standards

The standards for minimal monitoring during anesthesia are reproduced in the Table. The intent and reasoning for most of the specific items are self-explanatory. Their applicability was limited to situations under the control of the various departments of anesthesia (excluding, for example, nonanesthetists using heavy sedation in offices or clinics). While three of the standards apply to all regional anesthetics, epidural *analgesia* for labor or pain management was specifically excluded because the risk was judged to be extremely low (no related claims at Harvard from 1976 through 1985) and because the cost (requiring the physical presence of anesthesia personnel in each room throughout the entire duration of analgesic action) would be prohibitively high. The preface also reiterates that these standards describe *minimal* required monitoring, and that it is expected and appropriate that some or all of the requirements will be routinely exceeded.

The standard for continuous monitoring was the most difficult to formulate. It may appear too lenient. It was difficult to try to cover all situations without excessive detail or multiple exceptions. The standard is written to stress unequivocally that *intermittent* observations alone are insufficient. This is the only standard for which individual departments may change the criteria or add their own. Any such modification must be approved by the group of nine department heads to prevent any one department from circumventing the spirit of the standard by diluting it. Presently, seven of the nine hospitals have or are installing at least stand-alone end-tidal carbon dioxide monitoring, pulse oximetry (noninvasive arterial oxygen saturation monitoring), or mass spectrometry in every operating room. The committee expects that one or more of these monitoring modalities may be incorporated in future revisions of the Harvard standards.

Realities of practice were recognized. Most alarms for warning of breathing system disconnection during mechanical ventilation (one of the most frequent causes of major anesthesia accidents)[1-3] operate by sensing the absence of a cyclic pressure. While these alarms are valuable and important, there are several mechanisms for failing to detect a discontinuity in the breathing system (false-negative) with the potential for a serious accident, and this is noted in the standard.

The temperature monitoring standard includes a written rationale because of the intense debate within anesthesiology on the subject. Monitoring temperature is generally very useful. However, its utility as the primary diagnostic criterion for the very rare (but often catastrophic) syndrome of malignant hyperthermia is controversial. Also, the practicality of requiring temperature measurement during every single case, however brief, was weighed. If individual departments choose to mandate temperature measurement in all children or even in all patients, this is clearly their prerogative.

Table 1

Standards of Practice — I
Minimal Monitoring

Department of Anaesthesia
Harvard Medical School
Adopted March 25, 1985/Revised July 3, 1985

These standards apply for any administration of anesthesia involving department of anaesthesia personnel and are specifically referable to preplanned anesthetics administered in designated anesthetizing locations (specific exclusion: administration of epidural analgesia for labor or pain management). In emergency circumstances in any location, immediate life support measures of whatever appropriate nature come first with attention turning to the measures described in these standards as soon as possible and practical. These are minimal standards that may be exceeded at any time based on the judgment of the involved anesthesia personnel. These standards encourage high-quality patient care, but observing them cannot guarantee any specific patient outcome. These standards are subject to revision from time to time, as warranted by the evolution of technology and practice.

Anesthesiologist's or Nurse Anesthetist's Presence in Operating Room
For all anesthetics initiated by or involving a member of the department of anaesthesia, an attending or resident anesthesiologist or nurse anesthetist shall be present in the room throughout the conduct of all general anesthetics, regional anesthetics, and monitored intravenous anesthetics. An exception is made when there is a direct known hazard, eg, radiation, to the anesthesiologist or nurse anesthetist, in which case some provision for monitoring the patient must be made.

Blood Pressure and Heart Rate
Every patient receiving general anesthesia, regional anesthesia,or managed intravenous anesthesia shall have arterial blood pressure and heart rate measured at least every five minutes, where not clinically impractical.[1]

Electrocardiogram
Every patient shall have the electrocardiogram continuously displayed from the induction or institution of anesthesia until preparing to leave the anesthetizing location, where not clinically impractical.[1]

Continuous Monitoring
During every administration of general anesthesia, the anesthetist shall employ methods of continuously monitoring the patient's ventilation and circulation. The methods shall include, for ventilation and circulation each, at least one of the following or the equivalent.[2]

> **For Ventilation.** — Palpation or observation of the reservoir breathing bag, auscultation of breath sounds, monitoring of respiratory gases such as end-tidal carbon dioxide, or monitoring of expiratory gas flow. Monitoring end-tidal carbon dioxide is an emerging standard and is strongly preferred.
> **For Circulation.** — Palpation of a pulse, auscultation of heart sounds, monitoring of a tracing of intra-arterial pressure, pulse plethysmography/oximetry, or ultrasound peripheral pulse monitoring.

It is recognized that brief interruptions of the continuous monitoring may be unavoidable.

Breathing System Disconnection Monitoring
When ventilation is controlled by an automatic mechanical ventilator, there shall be in continuous use a device that is capable of detecting disconnection of any component of the breathing system. The device must given an audible signal when its alarm threshold is exceeded. (It is recognized that there are certain rare or unusual circumstances in which such a device may fail to detect a disconnection.)

Oxygen Analyzer
During every administration of general anesthesia using an anesthesia machine, the concentration of oxygen in the patient breathing system will be measured by a functioning oxygen analyzer with a low concentration limit alarm in use. This device must conform to the American National Standards Institute No. Z.79.10 standard.[1]

Ability to Measure Temperature
During every administration of general anesthesia, there shall be readily available a means to measure the patient's temperature. Rationale. — A means of temperature measurement must be available as a potential aid in the diagnosis and treatment of suspected or actual intraoperative hypothermia and malignant hyperthermia. The measurement/monitoring of temperature during every general anesthetic is not specifically mandated because of the potential risks of such monitoring and because of the likelihood of other physical signs giving earlier indication of the development of malignant hyperthermia.[1]

1 Under extenuating circumstances, the attending anesthesiologist may waive this requirement after so stating (including the reasons) in a note in the patient's chart.

2 Equivalence is to be defined by the chief of the individual hospital department after submission to and review by the department heads, Department of Anaesthesia, Harvard Medical School, Boston.

Implementation

After the committee achieved agreement, the standards were presented to the nine department heads who, after incorporating their few suggestions, voted unanimously to adopt them as official Harvard-wide policy. Each department head was then responsible for implementation within his department. The set of standards was presented to the members of the various departments as an accomplished fact, not open for further discussion of this edition. Some practitioners thought the standards too lenient, some too strict, and many predicted no impact on their practice because they already routinely met the standards.

Among the immediate tangible impacts were that one hospital purchased more oxygen monitors so that there would always be a replacement instrument available. Another hospital provided free earpiece stethoscopes to all staff, who previously had to purchase their own (few did). The purchase of pulse oximeters (including one for each operating room at three hospitals) at an average of about $5000 each was a capital expense encouraged, at least in part, by the standards process. Also, from their own clinical experience, committee members believe there was a heightening of awareness about anesthesia accidents and the use of patient monitoring to prevent them.

Audits (random visits to operating rooms during which an impartial observer completes a checklist of monitoring in use) of compliance with the standards have begun and are complete in two departments. In one, the continuous circulation monitoring standard was not met in half the observed cases. After discussion with the quality assurance committee of that department, remedial action to encourage adoption of new habits was instituted. In the other department, this circulation monitoring standard was not met in only 3% of cases, but the interruptions in continuous ventilation monitoring were more than "brief" in 25% of cases.

There is, as yet, no formal procedure for sanctioning noncompliance by either an individual or a department. The insurance carrier acknowledges that an accident occurring during known violation of the standards would be more difficult to defend in a malpractice action. However, legal counsel is of the opinion that documented compliance with the standards would be an aid to defense against a malpractice claim. Further, the committee believes that the positive effects of the standards outweigh any legal consideration. The insurance carrier is closely monitoring incidents and claims for a reduction in the number involving anesthesia care, but it is anticipated that it will take some time before sufficient data accumulate to make such an assessment.

Comment

Standards in medical care take many forms. They can be criteria for clinical teaching[6] or clinical skills.[7] A discussion of the outcome of care[8] raises the important question of whether standards in general should codify current practice and validate the existing, declare an ideal that may be impossibly high, or strike a balance in between. The latter is the course chosen by the Harvard Department of Anaesthesia risk management committee, which also agreed with the suggestion[9] that any standards, to be effective, must be limited and specific. Identifying a specific area (patient monitoring) related to a specific concern (adverse anesthesia outcomes) was the critical step that allowed formulation of a set of process standards that can be realistically expected to influence behavior in the target group of practitioners. Such definition would be a key element in efforts by other specialties to start writing detailed standards of practice, standards for either process or outcome of care.

Opinions and practices in medicine vary among institutions and regions. These standards illustrate that, with effort, agreement among several groups of practitioners with different approaches to the same type of activity can be achieved and a basic minimum standard developed. Such agreement could occur at the institutional, local, state, regional, or national level. The Harvard standards for minimal monitoring during anesthesia focus on behavior and habits rather than on expensive technology. They are fundamental minimal standards that would be achievable in the smallest rural community hospital. The average cost, per anesthetic administration, of providing for an electrocardioscope, oxygen monitor, and breathing system disconnection alarm is about $5,[1] much less than the present average per anesthetic cost of malpractice insurance (approximately $53 in 1985 at Harvard, ie, the total of anesthetist malpractice premiums divided by the number of cases). The expense for monitoring is minimal compared with the cost of *defending* even one minor malpractice claim (before including any possible settlement). It has been considered valid[10] for large academic medical centers to set standards that, over time, might be applied to smaller hospitals. While the committee is interested in seeing replication of this standard-setting process rather than the wide adoption of the Harvard standards, it was aware of this eventual possibility and deliberately avoided unrealistic requirements for extraordinarily costly and rapidly changing state-of-the-art high technology. Writers of standards (process or outcome) in other fields must continually be aware of these issues.

Virtually all US physicians are concerned over the very large increase in both the number of malpractice actions and the resulting monetary settlements and awards. The consequent astronomical increase in malpractice insurance premiums is causing modification or even closing of some physicians' practices.

Legislative relief or protection is being sought in many ways, with little sympathetic response from lawmakers.

Perhaps the best way to counter this seemingly out-of-control situation is to work even harder on patient safety and medical care quality assurance. Adherence to specific written standards of practice seems a logical component of these efforts. However, such standards have been avoided because of the traditional perception that physicians are automatically opposed to "big brotherism" imposition of authority. The Harvard Department of Anaesthesia experience demonstrates that this need not be the case. Referable to a laudable desire to improve care by reducing accidents and resultant injuries, realistic well-defined standards were created. They were accepted with minimal resistance for three reasons: (1) the desirable goal, (2) the lack of major or disruptive mandated changes in practice, and (3) the potential for reduction in malpractice claims and premiums.

These particular standards may not be applicable verbatim to all departments of anesthesia. What *is* applicable, however, is the process described above by which they were promulgated. While the strong commitment of chiefs of service to adopting and enforcing standards clearly helps the process, even in more loosely organized departments, groups, or specialties, with sufficient effort, this approach could be used. Insurance carriers may provide the impetus, but physician leadership is required. Even constituting a committee is a positive, consciousness-raising step. The Harvard anesthesia example is probably best applied to the other procedure-oriented specialties, but the model is valid for all of American medicine.

References

1. Pierce EC, Jr, Cooper JB (eds): Analysis of Anesthetic Mishaps. Boston, Little Brown & Co Inc, 1984, vol 22, No. 2.

2. Keenan RL, Boyan CP: Cardiac arrest due to anesthesia. JAMA 1985;253:2373-2377.

3. Emergency Care Research Institute: Death during general anesthesia. J Health Care Tech 1985;1:155-175.

4. Standards for Obstetric-Gynecology Services. Washington, DC, American College of Obstetricians and Gynecologists, 1985.

5. Philip JH, Raemer DB: Selecting the optimal anesthesia monitoring array. Med Instrum 1985;19:122-126.

6. Cormack JJC: Do standards improve patient care? Br J Med 1983;287:1683-1684.

7. American Board Internal Medicine: Clinical competence in internal medicine. Ann Intern Med 1979;90:402-411.

8. Palmer RH: The present range of provider performance in the United States, in Green R (ed): Assuring Quality in Medical Care. Cambridge, Mass, Ballinger Publishing Co, 1976, pp 113-136.

9. Estes EH, Sullivan RJ: Standards for practice: Effectiveness and acceptance. Ann Intern Med 1978;89:826-828.

10. Gravenstein JS, in Grundy BL, Gravenstein JS (eds): The Quality of Care in Anesthesia. Springfield, Ill, Charles C Thomas Publisher, 1982, p 57.

Eichorn JH, et al. Standards for patient monitoring during anesthesia at Harvard Medical School. JAMA. 1986; 256(8): 1017-1020.

Reprinted with permission from the authors and the American Medical Association.

Article 2.3

The Advent of Clinical Standards for Professional Liability

James F. Holzer, JD. Quality Review Bulletin, February 1990.

In 1983, hospitals and physicians paid more than $2.5 billion in malpractice insurance premiums.[1] That same year, a small group of anesthesiology chiefs from the Harvard University-affiliated hospitals risked the potential ire of their colleagues and began work on what would eventually be the first set of written patient-monitoring standards developed primarily to control professional liability claims.

With some notable exceptions, most clinicians within the Harvard system regarded the implemented standards as little more than codification of current practice. When the project was subsequently unveiled on the pages of the *Journal of the American Medical Assocation*[2] however, the standards were heralded by some physicians as a service to the legal profession and a disservice to practicing anesthesiologists.[3] Other parties, including consumer groups and the media, voiced support for the anesthesiologists' efforts.[4]

The skeptics notwithstanding, it appears that clinical standards are making significant inroads into risk management practices of the health care industry. More important, standards may even be doing what they were intended to do: reduce preventable morbidity, mortality, and malpractice costs.

Standards and the Law

Prior to the so-called medical malpractice crisis, the term "standard of care" no doubt was perceived by health care providers in a more favorable light than it is today. For decades, the term was associated more commonly with internally developed benchmarks of clinical performance and practice established by clinicians and monitored almost exclusively by providers. When, in the 1970s, it became more lucrative for lawyers to chase victims of iatrogenesis than those of motor vehicle accidents, organized medicine was suddenly exposed to an entirely new perspective on the use of clinical standards.

Most physicians have learned that an adverse clinical outcome is not, by itself, sufficient grounds for a malpractice action. In evaluating whether a clinical mishap constitutes potential negligence, risk managers and lawyers try to determine:

1. the *duty or standard of care* owed the patient by the practitioner or health care facility (the provider);
2. whether the provider's conduct *breached the required duty or standard* of care;
3. whether the conduct directly or *proximately caused harm* to the patient; and
4. whether the alleged harm constituted *legally compensable damages.*[5]

Although a plaintiff must affirmatively prove all four of these elements to win a negligence or malpractice lawsuit, the key element in most cases is convincing a jury that the required duty or standard has not been met.

When evidence in civil liability actions relates to the standards of professionals, such as doctors or architects, courts generally will not submit a case to a jury without some expert evidence relative to the defendant's conduct. As a general rule, this evidence depends primarily on the medical standards that physicians and health care institutions have established for themselves. This evidence is most commonly provided through the testimony of other

James F. Holzer, JD, is Vice President of Loss Prevention, Risk Management Foundation of the Harvard Medical Insititutions, Cambridge, Massachusetts, and a lecturer on the Faculty of Medicine at Harvard Medical School in Boston.

qualified clinicians. However, courts to a varying degree also rely on other sources of professional or customary standards, which can include

- a health care facility's own rules and policies;
- accrediting agencies' standards;
- statutes and official regulations;
- learned treatises, such as medical texts or articles; and
- policies and prescriptions from professional organizations and societies.[6]

Although such documents are not automatically admissible as evidence of customary or standard practice, they are of increasing probative value to juries because most courts tend to recognize national standards rather than the usual custom or practice of providers in a particular locality or community. This gradual erosion of the "locality rule" has been clearly articulated by many courts.[7]

As a general rule, then, the standard of care for doctors depends not on any community standard per se, but on whether the physician has exercised the degree of care and skill of an average qualified practitioner or specialist, taking into account the advances in the profession.[8] Similarly, the legal duty owed by health care facilities is moving toward a general national standard rather than a local one.[9,10]

Of course, the laws of negligence and rules of evidence are complex, confusing, and variable among states. The purpose of this article, therefore, is not to provide a comprehensive survey of the law but to demonstrate the growing reliance among risk managers, health care professionals, liability insurance companies, and the courts on the increasing use of standards to expedite the resolution of malpractice claims in a more uniform and equitable manner.

Standardmania

Separate from standards developed to control liability, there has been in recent years an explosion of proposed practice guidelines and specialty society standards. These guidelines, such as the parameters proposed by the American Medical Association, are focused broadly on *all* aspects of clinical practice and are concerned to some extent with cost containment. By contrast, standards developed for risk management purposes focus on clinical practices that give rise to malpractice claims.

This article discusses the latter type of standards and guidelines, those developed solely to reduce professional liability losses among health care providers, especially physicians. As such, these standards address an important component of the risk management process—"loss prevention"—by having physicians establish relevant benchmarks of clinical practice and conduct. Although intended to control liability, these standards can have the not insignificant effect of improving health care quality and controlling costs by reducing the incidence of unnecessary and inappropriate medical treatment.

Liability control standards also differ from standards that define how hospital risk management programs should work (e.g., the Joint Commission's new accreditation standards on risk management[11,12]), which relate more to administrative processes than clinical substance.

Incentive for Professional Liability Control Standards

In the early 1980s, malpractice insurance rates escalated sharply in response to dramatic increases in claims costs. Since then, physician insurance premiums nationally have continued to climb at an average annual rate of 19.5%.[13] Although the frequency and severity of claims have moderated, medical liability suits continue to be among the highest jury verdicts when compared with other types of personal liability actions.[14,15] In 1987, the average malpractice jury verdict against hospitals in the United States in all specialties was almost $925,000, only 3.5% lower than the average verdict five years earlier.[16]

Practitioners of high-risk specialties, such as obstetrics, continue to experience relatively large claims losses, disproportionate to their small number of claims and their representation in the medical profession.[1] An early study of malpractice claims, published in 1980, showed that a small number of anesthesia injuries also accounted for a disproportionately large percentage of dollars paid out.[17]

Spurred on by the risk management activities of newly formed doctor-owned and hospital-owned malpractice insurance companies, physicians in high-risk specialties started to take a closer look at their own claims activity. A few of the larger commercial underwriters, like the St. Paul Fire & Marine Insurance Company, also urged more interactive involvement among their physician insureds in analyzing high-risk claims loss. As the malpractice issue became more apparent to health care consumers, state legislatures began to look for ways to visibly respond to their political constituency.

A number of states mandated risk management regulations and enacted a flurry of tort reform provisions.[12] State and national specialty societies were asked (or directed) to work on ways to identify and eliminate the causes of malpractice.[10] Although the response among insurance companies, specialty groups, and states varied in scope and substance, there was considerable interest in the development of clinically oriented standards and guidelines based on major problems identified in claims analyses. Thus, the evolution of written standards tied primarily to the control of professional liability losses quickly became the cornerstone of many health care risk management initiatives. As will be discussed later in the article, the effort is not without its critics.

Clinically based standards developed primarily for risk management and liability control typically fall into three broad categories:

- Voluntary/physician-generated standards;
- Involuntary/underwriter-generated standards; or
- Statutorily imposed standards.

Voluntary/Physician-Generated Standards
Voluntary/physician-generated standards are voluntarily developed by physicians in specific specialties or practice settings. There generally are no insurance company sanctions or guaranteed financial benefits associated with such guidelines, although it is not unreasonable for providers and underwriters to mutually expect future premium decreases if the standards appear to be working.

The Harvard Experience. An example of physician-generated standards can be found in the experience of several clinical departments at Harvard University-affiliated medical institutions. The Risk Management Foundation of the Harvard Medical Institutions coordinates the professional liability insurance program for 15 Harvard-affiliated health care facilities and more than 5,000 physicians. The program began in 1976 with the formation of a provider-owned liability insurance company, which, among other things, closely monitored claims and loss-prevention trends through the auspices of the Foundation. It became clear in the program's first seven years that more extensive involvement among the Harvard clinical departments and insured physicians was needed to stem the rapid escalation in malpractice claims. Consequently, the Foundation and the insurance company adopted a multi-institutional effort based on the premise that teaching-hospital physicians practicing in high-risk specialties could be motivated to voluntarily develop and implement sound risk management/loss prevention strategies if permitted to review and analyze their group's own detailed malpractice claims data.

Harvard Anesthesia Standards. In 1983, the anesthesia chiefs from nine Harvard teaching hospitals became the first specialty group to collectively review their resolved and pending claims experience. The chiefs subsequently formed a risk management committee (RMC) of senior staff members from a cross section of Harvard anesthesia departments. The committee's charge was to investigate, discuss, and make recommendations on issues related to clinical practice of anesthesia at the Harvard medical institutions and, thus, to minimize related accidents, errors, and patient injuries associated with many of their prior malpractice claims.

The committee began by carefully reviewing anonymous case summaries of claims and incidents provided by the Foundation. As a result of this review in 1984, the committee believed that most of the cases involving major morbidity or death were preventable, and the members concluded that more meticulous monitoring of patients during anesthesia would help prevent such occurrences in the future.[2]

The RMC developed the following list of risk management problems and issues:

- Minimal monitoring during administration of an anesthetic and in the postanesthesia recovery period;
- Anesthetizing locations outside traditional operating rooms;
- Equipment standards, including preanesthetic equipment checkout;
- Equipment maintenance and servicing;
- Record keeping; and
- Preoperative and postoperative visits by anesthesia personnel.[18]

In spring 1985, the chiefs adopted the RMC's recommendations and implemented *Standards of Practice I: Minimal Monitoring*[19] within the Harvard system.

Prior to the adoption of those standards, Harvard's anesthesia malpractice losses had been approximately $5.5 million from April 1976 to April 1985. This amounted to a "loss per anesthetic" (LPA) for the nine-year period of $5.24. Following implementation of the standards, anesthesia losses for care rendered during 1986, 1987, and the first nine months of 1988 showed the significantly lower LPAs of $2.00, $1.84, and $.78, respectively. The average cost per claim also declined during the 12-year period.[15] It is possible, however, that these averages could change in future analyses because of increases in the amount allotted for open claims, subsequent payments on closed claims, and late reporting.

The reduction of anesthesia losses appears to coincide with adoption of the standards, although studies proving a direct statistical correlation are as yet unavailable. The improved loss experience has resulted in the 1989 malpractice premium for Harvard-insured anesthesiologists being reduced by almost one third over the 1988 rate. Effective April 1, 1989, anesthesiologists (premium class 3) paid an annual premium of $11,750, approximately one half of what they would have been assessed in their old 1985 rating group (premium class 5).

Since spring 1985, the RMC and the Harvard anesthesia chiefs have developed and implemented three additional sets of standards, as well as a protocol for handling anesthesia mishaps.[19] The standards apply to anesthetizing locations outside traditional operating rooms; equipment standards, including preanesthetic equipment checkout; and equipment maintenance and servicing.

What is perhaps most impressive about the effort is that the standards were not imposed by insurance company underwriters but were voluntarily developed and implemented by clinicians without assurance of future premium reductions. In short, the right steps were taken for the right reasons: a desire among clinicians for improved patient safety and a reduction of potentially compensable events.

Harvard Obstetrical Standards. The development of anesthesia standards also helped precipitate interest among other clinical departments. In October 1986, obstetrical department heads of three Harvard teaching hospitals convened to review the obstetrics-related malpractice claims managed by the Foundation over a 10-year period. After analyzing the blinded claims summaries, the chiefs decided to personally coordinate the development of a comprehensive set of 21 standards for Harvard-affiliated obstetrics services.[20] The topics addressed by the obstetrics standards are listed in Figure 1, below.

The objective of the standards was to influence physician behavior not only to improve outcomes but also to ensure that patient expectations are reasonable and informed. The document ultimately addressed such problems as recognition of fetal distress (see Figure 2), adequate record keeping, and informed consent. The standards also included a suggested list of outcome screens for use in departmental and institutional quality assurance programs to facilitate the early identification of adverse clinical events that could pose the threat of potential liability (see Figure 3).

It is still too soon to measure the impact of the standards because they were implemented only in January 1989. However, the department chiefs believe that physician compliance will ultimately reduce adverse events, large claims losses, and ultimately their liability insurance premiums, which are among the highest in the Harvard professional liability insurance program.

Harvard Radiology Standards. Although the dollar losses associated with radiology malpractice claims remain relatively low, the annual number of claims per 100 radiologists nationally remains somewhat higher than the rate for all physicians combined. The American Medical Association estimates that almost 41% of the nation's practicing radiologists have been sued at least once in their career since 1987.[13] The most significant malpractice claims losses in radiology appear to be associated with invasive diagnostic procedures, such as cardiac catheterization, computed tomography, and myelograms.[21] The introduction of low-osmolar contrast agents in radiology could also potentially increase the liability risk in the future.[22]

Topics Addressed by the Clinical Standards for the Obstetrical Services of the Harvard Medical Institutions

Medical Records and Documentation Standards
- Procedures for record keeping
- Preservation of fetal heart rate monitoring records

Informed Consent Standard
- Informed consent process and forms for labor and delivery-related consent

Professional Practice Standards
- Attendance of physician for patient in active labor
- Competency for interpreting electronic fetal heart monitoring tracings
- Obstetrician/patient case load in labor and delivery
- Physician coverage when away
- Professional nurse/patient staffing ratios in labor and delivery
- Requirements for consultations
- Resolution of clinical discord in labor and delivery

Patient Care Practice Standards
- Assessment of fetal maturity in normal gravidas prior to repeat cesarean delivery or elective induction of labor
- Protocol for vaginal cultures in premature rupture of membranes or premature labor
- Prolonged pregnancy
- Ordering of tocolytic (terbutaline) and uterotonic (oxytocin) drugs for the patient in labor
- Mandatory use of pumps for infusing oxytocin
- Assessment of fetal well-being in labor
- Blood pH sampling
- Use of vacuum extractor and forceps for midcavity application and midpelvic delivery
- Management of singleton breech presentation
- Prevention of retained sponges following vaginal delivery
- Screening for and reporting of adverse patient outcomes and untoward events

Figure 1. The chairpersons of the obstetrics and gynecology departments at hospitals affiliated with Harvard Medical School developed practice standards that focus on procedures and occurrences that have been the subject of most obstetric malpractice claims for a ten-year period.

Because of these factors, the Harvard radiology chiefs were asked to review their claims data and to consider voluntarily establishing related practice standards or guidelines. After considerable thought and occasionally heated discussions, the department heads formed an ad hoc risk management subcommittee, which subsequently proposed standards dealing with documentation, communication of radiologic information (see Figure 4) and safety measures during performance of examinations and procedures.

The draft standards were approved in concept by the chiefs in early 1989 and were similarly endorsed by the Foundation and Harvard's captive malpractice insurance carrier.[23] Implementation is pending. A newly constituted subcommittee of the Risk Management Foundation is currently working on the project's second phase, which will focus on more-detailed informed consent guidelines.

Ongoing Specialty Projects at Harvard. Under the auspices of the appropriate chiefs and clinical department heads, specialty-based claims review projects are currently under way in emergency medicine, general surgery, plastic surgery, otolaryngology, ophthalmology, and pathology. It is anticipated that orthopedics, neurosurgery, gynecology, and internal medicine will be encouraged to undertake similar efforts in the near future.

Physician-owned Insurance Programs. Other voluntary/physician-generated risk control standards have been created by a number of physician-sponsored insurance carriers. Without question, obstetrics has generated the greatest number of formal guidelines and recommendations.

One such effort was recently undertaken by The Doctors' Company, based in Santa Monica, California. The company established a special perinatal injury review panel, which examined the problem from 1982 through 1988, hoping to avoid such injuries in the future and make claims more defensible. The panel and company subsequently issued formal written recommendations to its insured physicians. The guidelines address such issues as response time and coverage, communications, delivery notes, standing orders, referral of problem cases, informed patient expectations, quality of hospital services, postdelivery-date pregnancies, perinatal evaluation, protocols for treating babies with depressed functioning, placental pathology, and electronic fetal monitoring. Although the guidelines are currently advisory in nature, the company states that is "holding in abeyance the implementation of stringent mandatory requirements as a condition of insurance."[24]

Other voluntary guidelines and recommendations are currently being advanced for obstetricians insured through other doctor-owned carriers. One such carrier is COPIC (a Colorado-based company), which offers a credit toward future premiums for voluntary compliance with its "participatory risk management system" in prenatal care. Other companies, such as the Washington State Physicians Insurance Exchange in Seattle, distribute comprehensive prenatal record forms to their insured providers to encourage standardized documentation practices. Commercial underwriters, like the St. Paul Fire & Marine Insurance Company, also issue a variety of written guidelines and recommendations to several thousand individual policyholders across the country.

Involuntary/Underwriter-Generated Standards
Involuntary/underwriter-generated standards are commonly developed by physician panels working on behalf of liability insurance companies. They are typically mandated as a condition of coverage or used to surcharge or cancel insured providers if a claim results from not following the guidelines. Many companies considering such programs are among the 41 doctor-owned insurance companies currently licensed in more than 32 states that provide professional liability insurance for more than one half of the nation's practicing physicians.[25]

Clinically based practice standards obviously take on less of an educational focus when stringently tied to underwriting policies or premium surcharges. Proponents of this system, however, argue its effectiveness in changing practice behavior more rapidly and uniformly, especially in high-risk specialty groups such as obstetrics and anesthesia.

The Maine Standards. One such effort was implemented recently by the Medical Mutual Insurance Company of Maine, a physician-owned-and-operated carrier in Portland. The company reports that physicians with expertise in obstetrics, anesthesia, and breast cancer diagnosis worked with hospital risk management representatives to develop what the carrier believes are "appropriate standards of care for Maine physicians based on current accepted national standards."[26] Underwriting guidelines reflecting the "participatory risk management criteria" were then developed and mandated as a condition of continuing insurance. New policy language states that "failure to practice in accordance with these guidelines may lead to nonrenewal of the physician's policy." The program also allows physicians to appropriately deviate from the guidelines with adequate justification that is well documented.

Utah Malpractice Insurance Requirements. In 1986 the Utah Medical Insurance Association in Salt Lake City established malpractice insurance requirements for those physicians requesting coverage for obstetrical care. The requirements, like all liability control standards, were not intended to define the minimum standard of care but rather to address the frequency and defensibility of claims in problem areas, including the following:

- Problems with regard to Cesarean sections (delay in performing or failure to perform; failure to interpret or use electronic fetal monitoring equipment properly);
- Misuse or mismonitoring of oxytocin administration;
- Mismanagement of hypertension in pregnancy;
- Mismanagement of patients' deliveries before or after their due dates; and
- Misuse of instrumentation, including forceps or vacuum extraction, during delivery.

Physicians applying for obstetrical coverage must agree in writing to comply with the requirements. Failure to comply could theoretically result in nonrenewal of the insurance policy or exclusion of coverage for obstetrics. Again, the carrier can grant exceptions.

Standard 16: Assessment of Fetal Well-Being in Labor

a. Prenatal patient education
During prenatal care every patient shall be informed about the various methods of assessment of fetal well-being during labor including electronic fetal heart monitoring.

b. Monitoring on admission to labor and delivery
Every patient admitted in labor with a live fetus of 24 weeks or more shall have an initial assessment of uterine contractility and fetal heart rate. An initial 20 minutes of continuous electronic fetal heart rate monitoring is recommended.

c. Monitoring during labor
If circumstances are entirely normal and none of the indications for continuous electronic monitoring apply (see below), then intermittent electronic monitoring, or monitoring with a hand-held Doppler instrument or acoustic obstetric stethoscope, may be substituted after the initial 20-minute observation. Such intermittent monitoring must be carried out and recorded at least every 15 minutes during the active phase of stage 1 labor and at least following every contraction in stage 2 labor. If any abnormality is detected, then continuous electronic monitoring is indicated thereafter until delivery.

d. Indications for continuous electronic fetal heart rate monitoring
Indications for continuous electronic fetal heart rate monitoring for live fetuses greater than 24 weeks of gestation throughout active labor include the following:

- Abnormal fetal heart rate pattern detected during initial twenty minutes of monitoring
- Gestational age less than 37 weeks or greater than 42 weeks
- History of abnormal antepartum fetal heart rate
- Breech presentation
- Multiple gestations
- Fetal growth retardation
- Serious maternal illness such as diabetes mellitus, hypertension, active asthma, where fetal perfusion could be compromised
- Labor induction or augmentation with oxytocin or prostaglandin
- Dysfunctional labor
- Prolonged labor (arrest of dilation, protraction disorders, arrest of descent, stage 2 longer than 2 hours)
- Passage of meconium
- Pregnancy-induced hypertension and toxemia
- Abnormal vaginal bleeding
- Placenta previa
- Placental abruption
- Abnormal fetal heart rate detected by intermittent monitoring during labor
- Epidural anesthesia

e. Monitoring in the delivery room
The standard for monitoring by auscultation shall be continued in the delivery room, that is at least following every contraction. If any abnormality is detected, the continuous electronic monitoring is indicated thereafter until delivery.

When continuous fetal heart monitoring has been used during labor, continuous electronic fetal heart monitoring shall be reestablished in the delivery room as soon possible after arrival in the delivery room.

"If internal monitoring is being used in patients who undergo cesarean delivery, the scalp electrode should be left attached to the fetus and the monitoring equipment until the abdominal preparation is complete. If external monitoring is used, it should be continued until the abdominal preparation is begun."*

If at any point during care, the physician believes that electronic fetal heart monitoring is clinically indicated and the patient refuses such monitoring, the refusal shall be documented in the medical record.

g. Institutional responsibility
The institution shall provide and maintain at least one electronic fetal monitoring apparatus for every labor bed.

*American College of Obstetricians and Gynecologists (ACOG): Standards for Ob-Gyn Services. 6th ed. Washington, DC: ACOG, 1985. p.36.

Figure 2. Assessment of fetal well-being is an issue frequently raised in quality assurance and risk management activities.

The Arizona Anesthesia Requirements. In March 1985, the Mutual Insurance Company of Arizona (MICA) implemented a similar program, requiring its insured anesthesiologists to sign a "preferred risk plan" and to agree to comply with MICA's new underwriting requirements on patient monitoring. Breach of any term in the agreement would theoretically result in a $25,000 surcharge on future annual premiums. The company also offers a 5% premium reduction for anesthesiologists submitting Advanced Cardiac Life Support (ACLS) certification.

Statutorily Imposed Standards

Another group of standards is mandated as part of a state or federal law or regulation to reduce the incidence of claims. As of January 1989, ten states had passed legislation or promulgated regulations requiring hospitals to implement risk management programs.[12] Some of these states, such as Massachusetts, incorporated the requirements as part of physician licensing regulations.[27]

The Massachusetts regulations, among other things, require anesthesiologists to comply with monitoring standards issued by the American Society of Anesthesiologists in 1986. The regulations further urge the state's specialty societies to develop their own clinical standards for liability control and suggest that the state's largest malpractice underwriter (the Medical Malpractice Joint Underwriting Association of Massachusetts [JUA], created by the legislature in 1975) provide financial incentives for physicians complying with these risk management guidelines. Consequently, JUA offered anesthesiologists premium discounts for agreeing to use such monitoring equipment as pulse oximeters and end-tidal carbon dioxide analyzers. Physicians would lose the discount if a claim resulted from their failure to use the monitoring devices.

Standards can be imposed by federal law as well. Statutes such as the Consolidated Omnibus Budget Reconciliation Act of 1986 contain specific clinical practice requirements in emergency medicine that, if violated, could give rise to malpractice action in federal court, as well as stiff fines and sanctions.[28]

Continuing Controversy

As discussed earlier, anything sporting the label "standard" understandably raises medical liability concern among providers and potential defendants. As evidenced by the negative response among some physicians to the publication of the Harvard anesthesia standards, there is continuing resistance to concise, written expressions of those things that traditionally have been confined to medical treatises or proffered by expert witnesses.

Arguments against the development and use of written clinical standards generally relate to one or more of the following positions:

1. Plaintiff lawyers will use the written standards to sue more physicians for malpractice;
2. Written standards are too inflexible and fail to address the unique clinical circumstances of each case (ie, "cookbook medicine");
3. Standards developed in one geographic region or clinical setting may be inappropriate for other settings (ie, urban/academic medicine versus rural/community-based medicine);
4. Medicine has done fine so far without formal written standards, guidelines, and protocols; or
5. There is no scientific evidence to prove that standards for liability control reduce the incidence and severity of malpractice claims or reduce patient morbidity and mortality.

Although these concerns are not wholly unreasonable in today's medicolegal climate, the following counterarguments can be offered in defense of professional liability control standards.

1. Courts generally will not routinely admit a written standard into evidence without a clear indication of its relevancy to the case.

As indicated earlier, the rules of evidence are complex and can vary among legal jurisdictions. A standard, like any piece of evidence, must clear a number of legal hurdles before it is permitted to be considered by a jury. For example, it is doubtful that a risk management standard dealing with the legibility of medical records would be admissable to prove a technical "breach of duty." However, it is likely that clinically based standards established to control professional liability will occasionally be allowed into evidence at the judge's discretion.

But if written standards are permitted to be used by plaintiffs to prove breach of duty, can they not also be used by the defense to show that the standard of

Standard 21: Screening for and Reporting of Adverse Patient Outcomes and Untoward Events

Routine screening of adverse patient outcomes or untoward events shall be conducted.
The following adverse patient outcomes or untoward events shall be reported to the designated hospital risk management or quality assurance representative as soon as observed or, when feasible, within 24 hours.

Birth Injury
1. Fractured clavicle
2. Brachial plexus palsy
3. Fractured skull
4. Fracture of any long bone
5. Tear of falx or subdural hematoma

Condition of Fetus at Birth
1. Seizures within first 24 hours
2. Apgar score of 4 or less at 5 minutes
3. Meconium aspiration
4. Iatrogenic respiratory distress syndrome (RDS) after elective induction or elective repeat cesarean section
5. Stillbirths and neonatal deaths in infants greater than 2500 grams unassociated with lethal congenital anomaly

Maternal Complications
1. Need for blood transfusion
2. Return to or need for delivery room or operating room postpartum excluding postpartum sterilization
3. Mother's transfer to intensive care unit
4. Length of stay greater than 5 days after vaginal delivery
5. Length of stay greater than 10 days after cesarean delivery

Figure 3. Screens, which were developed by physicians, include modifications to maternal and infant related occurrence screens developed by the Chicago Hospital Risk Pooling Program as published in the American Hospital's Medical Malpractice Task Force Report on Tort Reform and Compendium of Professional Liability Early Warning Systems for Health Care Providers (Chicago: American Hospital Association, May 1986), p.15.

care provided was appropriate? For the moment, however, it does not appear that there has been a major case in which a written standard exclusively developed for risk management purposes was used as pivotal evidence in a malpractice trial.

2. Standards that are carefully crafted to control liability will generally allow for appropriate deviations and exceptions.
It is well recognized that any clinically based standard, even those unrelated to risk management, must preserve the physician's right to tailor care in the best interests of his or her patient.[29] Almost all existing standards and guidelines encouraged or developed by liability insurance carriers expressly indicate that noncompliance may occasionally be warranted as long as the deviation is clinically appropriate and comprehensively documented. In emergency circumstances, for example, the Harvard anesthesia standards explicitly state that "immediate life support of whatever appropriate nature comes first with attention turning to...(the) standards as soon as possible and practical."[19]

3. Standards developed to control liability are generally intended to benefit a very specific class or pool of providers and not necessarily physicians in all national regions or practice settings.
With the exception of national specialty societies and large commercial liability insurance carriers, most clinical risk-control standards are intended to apply primarily to the setting in which they were created. For example, some providers complained that the Harvard anesthesia standards were forcing unnecessary changes in national practice, especially in regions of the country that could ill afford to spend money to acquire new technology or human resources. The Harvard Anesthesia Risk Management Committee responded by reminding providers that the standards were developed as part of a local risk initiative and applied only to Harvard-affiliated hospitals. The committee indicated that similar

standards developed by other groups could well vary by place and practice patterns.[3]

4. The careful development of consensus-based standards can benefit health care generally by reducing certain types of recurring preventable injuries and by eliminating the proliferation of so-called medical experts profiting from the malpractice litigation explosion.
The creation of most clinically based risk-control standards is essentially based on developing consensus among physicians to establish appropriate benchmarks of acceptable practice and outcome. This methodology is familiar to most scientists and clinicians and is perhaps more readily accepted when not linked to insurance and litigation. As McAfee suggested during a recent American College of Surgeons/American Cancer Society workshop on quality assurance, the process of developing consensus on appropriate forms of treatment begins by turning problem-oriented data over to physicians in a sanction-free environment.[30]

The codification of such consensus in written standards, particularly in those areas that recur frequently in malpractice litigation, may dampen the enthusiasm of so-called professional medical-legal experts allowed to testify on appropriate standards of care. The lack of formal specialty standards makes such "professional experts" a greater threat to those defendants who provide appropriate care but have little physical evidence to back up their defense.

5. Many physicians would prefer to put practical risk management guidelines to immediate use rather than wait for scientific validation studies or peer review.
Clinically based standards are occasionally attacked for lack of scientific evidence proving their effectiveness. Fortunately, many physicians prefer to use such guidelines immediately, particularly if the advice is intuitively reasonable and practical. For example, 60% of the physicians who received a controversial "Clinical Alert" issued by the National Cancer Institute in May 1988 supported the dissemination of the information before it was published in a refereed journal.[31] The alert was not meant to mandate care but to inform physicians of the important potential benefits of adjuvant therapy of node-negative breast cancer. It can be argued that standards developed to control risk offer essentially the same type of benefit.

Summary and Conclusion

The development of clinically based written standards to reduce the frequency and severity of medical malpractice loss appears to be gaining in popularity among provider specialty groups and professional liability underwriters. To date, such standards have addressed problems in specialties such as obstetrics and anesthesia where dollar losses associated with malpractice claims have been high. Guidelines can be developed and used by providers on a purely voluntary basis or

Selected Standards From Standards Group No. 7: Communication of Information

Objective: To transmit, in a timely fashion, radiologic information and reports to the individual responsible for patient care.

Standard 7.1: **Requests for Immediate Reports**
When the referring physician requests an immediate report, assuming that such requests are reasonable and medically justified, pertinent information shall be conveyed within **one hour** of the performance of the study **and sooner if medically indicated**, by face to face discussion, written note, telephone call, or electronic means. If the information is preliminary, it shall be so identified.

Standard 7.2: **Unexpected or Urgent Findings**
When a radiologic study reveals unexpected findings or findings of urgent clinical importance (i.e., a finding which will make an intervention necessary in the next 24 hours), information shall be conveyed within **one hour** and **sooner if medically indicated**. The communication of such information shall be documented with an entry in the patient's hospital record or with an entry in the final official or amended radiology report.

Figure 4. Communication of information is often critical to the prevention of adverse outcomes.

mandated on an involuntary basis by third parties such as malpractice insurance companies or legislators.

Because the advent of risk-control standards is a relatively new phenomenon, formal scientific studies on the long-term benefits of such guidelines have not yet been published. However, it appears that sharp reductions of malpractice losses in specialties such as anesthesia have coincided with the implementation of formal written standards specifically designed for liability control. This has led some liability insurance carriers to decrease premiums associated with specialists following such standards.

Many providers are understandably concerned about the potential use of written standards by plaintiff attorneys in medical malpractice suits. Although it is possible that such policies and guidelines could be admitted into evidence to show that a provider breached the legal duty or standard of care owed to a patient, it is uncertain whether these risk-control standards could ultimately pass the evidentiary rules of relevancy or materiality in a given lawsuit. It is clear, however, that the consensus-based process of creating clinical standards and guidelines specifically for controlling professional liability losses is itself a powerful and emerging standard for health care risk management programs.

References

1. U.S. General Accounting Office (GAO): Medical Malpractice: Characteristics of Claims Closed in 1984. Washington, D.C.: GAO, 1987.

2. Eichhorn JG, et al: Standards for patient monitoring during anesthesia at Harvard Medical School. JAMA 256:1017-1020, 1986.

3. Peterson AW: Standards for monitoring during anesthesia at Harvard (letter). JAMA 257:25, 1987.

4. Anesthesia safety saving lives: Report urges doctors to adopt anesthesia rules. Boston Globe, p.1, Aug. 22, 1986.

5. Prosser WL: Handbook of the law of torts, 4th ed. St. Paul, MN: West Publishing Co. 1971.

6. Macdonald MG. Meyer KC. Essig B: Health Care Law: A Practical Guide. NY: Matthew Bender, 1988.

7. Shilkret v. Annapolis Emergency Hospital, 276 Md. 187. 349 A.2d 245, 1975.

8. Brune v. Belinkoff, 354 Mass. 102, 235 N.E. 2d 793, 1968.

9. Darling v. Charleston Community Memorial Hospital, 33 Ill.2d 326, 211 N.E.2d 253, 1965.

10. Dickinson v. Mailliard, 175 N.W.2d 588 (Iowa), 1970.

11. Joint Commission on Accreditation of Healthcare Organizations: Accreditation Manual for Hospitals, 1989 ed. Chicago: Joint Commission, 1988.

12. U.S. General Accounting Office (GAO): Health Care: Initiatives in Hospital Risk Management, Washington, D.C.: GAO, 1989.

13. Slora EJ. Gonzales ML: Medical professional liability claims and premiums, 1985-1987. In Gonzalez ML, Emmons DW (eds): Socioeconomic Characteristics of Medical Practice, 1988. Chicago: American Medical Association, 1988.

14. Gastel RG: Medical malpractice. Data Base Reports pp 1-6, Dec 1989.

15. Holzer JF: Liability insurance issues in anesthesiology. Int Anesthesiol Clin 27:205-212, 1989.

16. Jury Verdict Research, Inc: Current Award Trends, 1989 ed. Solon, Ohio: Jury Verdict Research, Inc. 1989.

17. National Association of Insurance Commissioners (NAIC): Malpractice Closed Claims Study, 1975-1978, Milwaukee: NAIC, 1980.

18. Eichhorn JH. et al: Anaesthesia practice standards at Harvard: a review. J Clin Anesth 1:55-65, 1988.

19. Department of Anesthesia, Harvard Medical School: Standards for the Anesthesia Services for the Harvard Medical Institutions (internal document of the Harvard Medical Institutions). Department of Anaesthesia. Harvard Medical School, 1985.

20. Departments of Obstetrics and Gynecology; Harvard Medical Institutions: Clinical Standards for the Obstetrical Services of the Harvard Medical Institutions (internal document of the Harvard Medical Institutions). Department of Obstetrics and Gynecology. Harvard Medical School, 1988.

21. Bowyer EA: High radiology losses related to invasive procedures. Risk Management Foundation Forum 6:1-2,8. Jul/Aug 1985.

22. Jacobsen PD. Rosenquist CJ: The introduction of low-osmolar contrast agents in radiology: Medical, economic, legal, and public safety issues. JAMA 260:1586-1592, 1988.

23. Departments of Radiology, Harvard Medical Institutions: Clinical Standards for the Radiology Services of the Harvard Medical Institutions (internal document of the Harvard Medical Institutions). Department of Radiology, Harvard Medical School, 1989.

24. The Doctors' Company: Preventing Perinatal Injuries: An Update. Santa Monica, CA: The Doctors' Company, 1989.

25. Layton D (ed): Physician Insurers Association of America: 1989 Membership Directory. Wheaton, Ill: Layton Communications, Inc., 1989.

26. Medical Mutual Insurance Company of Maine (MMIC): Participatory Risk Management Program. Portland, ME: MMIC, 1988.

27. 243 CMR 3.10(4).

28. 42 USC sec 1395dd. 1986.

29. Page L: AMA, ASIM support practice guidelines as "ET" alternative. American Medical News 18:1 August 1989

30. McAfee RE: Medical staff enforcement: Dilemmas and decisions. Cancer 64:317-318, 1989.

31. Vanchieri C: Clinical alert stimulates changes in practice. Journal of the National Cancer Institute 80:1185-1187, 1988.

Holzer JF. The advent of clinical standards for professional liability. Quality Rev Bull. 1990.

Reprinted with permission from the author and Quality Review Bulletin.

Article 2.4

Practice Guidelines and Practicing Medicine: Are They Compatible?

Robert H. Brook, MD, ScD. Journal of the American Medical Association, December 1989.

Various factors, including increased financial pressures on the health system, the rapidity of the introduction of technology, and data showing high levels of inappropriate care, will coalesce into a movement that will yield practice guidelines. If the guidelines are developed with the aid of the best methods and if they are applied constructively, then the twin goals of increased health of the American public and physician satisfaction can be achieved.

A patient arrives at a physician's office. The patient may have an acute symptom and desire relief. The patient may be symptom free and represent the "worried well" in need of emotional support. The patient may be hanging on to life by a thread, and only a reflexive response by a well-trained medical team will prevent him or her from dying. The physician may know the patient. The physician may even have been trained in the specialty that is best able to treat the patient. Whatever the particular situation, the physician must act.

It is Monday morning in the boardroom of a large medical insurance company. The board is examining the bottom line for its fee-for-service business. The amount of red ink and losses is impressive. Will the board vote to give up its fee-for-service business?

It is Friday evening in the offices of a law firm that has been at work on a single case for 2 years. The verdict announcing its victory has just been handed down. The jury has concluded that some health maintenance organizations deliberately restrict access to care; all health maintenance organizations that use gatekeepers will suffer financial penalties.

It is budget time and a governmental decision needs to be made whether health insurance should be provided to everybody. Even though providing insurance is known to affect health positively,[1] the fear of increasing the rate of escalation in costs prevents any extension of coverage.

Finally, Mr. J. Q. Public gets some mild chest pain. Being a wise shopper, he goes to the library and checks out an out-of-date medical journal (the library also has cost problems). He discovers an ancient article, which was written in the 1980s,[2] that describes large variations in the use of medical care as a function of where one lives. He decides to experiment with his own health, and he visits several expert physicians across the country. He ascertains that there is confusion regarding the correct diagnostic path to follow. More importantly, he determines that each of the physicians believe firmly in their own recommendation. Therapeutic options are generally not presented, and if presented, the shortage of time makes it impossible for a detailed discussion to occur. The patient's own values regarding what components of his health he is interested in maximizing are not discussed. He leaves his last appointment confused. He makes the wrong decision, but lives anyway.

What do all of these vignettes have to do with practice guidelines? Physicians' need to act, the financial forces on the health system, and lack of even minimal health insurance for many have all increased pressure for physicians to define and justify what they are about. When these pressures are combined with changes in the technology of

Dr. Robert H. Brook is from the Departments of Medicine and Public Health, UCLA Center for the Health Sciences, Los Angeles, Calif; and The RAND Corp Health Sciences Program, Santa Monica, Calif.

medicine itself, then the development of practice guidelines appears even more urgent. It is to these changes that this article now turns.

Explosion of Technology

The technology explosion does not concern only the emergence of complex, expensive machines. Consider, for example, antihypertensive therapy. Additional drugs within a therapeutic class have become available. New classes of medications have been developed. The same medications are packaged differently, and the way the medicine is physically composed may affect how it is absorbed. Thus, the practicing physician is faced with many options. He or she does not have the time to read even the literature that summarizes the evidence that favors one drug regimen vs. another, let alone the original studies. If another physician refers a hypertensive patient to him or her, the physician may not be familiar with the antihypertensive drug that the patient is already taking. Finally, cost-benefit calculations of one therapy vs. another will almost certainly not be done by an individual practicing physician.

Consider a second example: the diagnostic evaluation of a patient who presents with mild chest pain. The physician could evaluate the digestive or cardiovascular system because abnormalities in either could produce chest pain. In addition, there are multiple tests that provide information about the same theoretical underlying cause of the chest pain. It is not surprising, then, that in the absence of practice guidelines, consultants, even if they are in the same subspecialty of medicine, will order different diagnostic tests on the same patient, which in turn will produce different outcomes and costs of care.

Emergence of Information Sciences and Decision Analysis

The choice of which test to order should at least partially be based both on information about how good (valid, reliable, and accurate) the test is in the setting in which the patient was treated and on an explicit estimate of the probability that the patient had the condition for which the test is useful. When choices were limited and benefits clearly exceeded risks, the ability to combine information from one test with that from another was not so critical. But today the situation is different. A test that produces an unexpected false negative may lead astray a physician who is not versed in information sciences, while a false-positive result may precipitate labeling a well person as sick.

For example, when evaluating patients with fatigue for potential problems such as hypothyroidism or anemia, carefully selecting the diagnostic tests to use and then using them in a specific order that is conditional on the results of previous tests will not only increase the probability that a correct diagnosis will be made, but also that it can be made in a cost-effective manner. Knowledge on how to combine information from multiple tests will not necessarily lead to fewer tests or reduced dependence on complex medical technology; rather, it will lead to better outcomes at the same expenditure level.

Although recent years have seen the emergence of journals devoted to decision analysis, their effect on practice has yet to be felt. The difficulty physicians face in obtaining clinical information when they need it may help explain the answers given by a nationally representative sample when asked how they would like to receive medical information. The majority of physicians wanted information presented in a concise format that told them what to do (i.e., practice guidelines).[3] As far as practicing physicians are concerned, lengthy textbooks of medicine that do not contain specific recommendations may not be as useful as authors of those textbooks would hope.

Increased Effect of Observer Variability

Even when medicine was simple (20 years ago), much was written about observer variability, and virtually every time this subject was examined startling results were obtained. Two cardiologists who listen to a patient's heart will often hear different murmurs. If a patient's blood is divided, placed into two test tubes, and sent to different laboratories, the resultant cholesterol measurements may differ widely. The decision to start a patient on a lifetime regimen of cholesterol-lowering therapy may be dependent on which laboratory received the blood sample. A roentgenographic study of the stomach is performed and the resulting films are read by two radiologists; one may conclude that an ulcer is present, the other that the results are normal.

Observer variability has always been present, but the explosion of technology has decreased our ability to cope with it. It is virtually impossible in the absence of guidelines to know how to account for variability when we make clinical decisions. Should a test be repeated if its results are not consistent with our diagnosis or if it was done by somebody else who we do not know we can trust?

Concern of Technology

In the recent past, almost all patients within a specified geographic area who had an unusual problem or disease (eg, Graves' disease) might have been seen by a few or even a single physician who then quickly became a clinical expert in that disease. In addition, a special test might have been performed in one laboratory and this laboratory was known to produce reliable results. However, for those Americans who currently receive care in the fee-for-service system, the world has dramatically changed. For example, the modal number of carotid endarterectomies performed by surgeons who do the procedure is one per year.[4]

Time, Appropriateness, and Guidelines

All of the aforementioned changes increase the pressure on physicians, especially in regard to allocation of time. Time to read the literature. Time to synthesize the literature. Time to interact with one's colleagues and try to reason together about how new technologies can be used. Time to do all this without much help, because it is difficult to get information in a user-friendly, timely manner. Physicians do not get paid for looking up or synthesizing information, and looking up information in the presence of a patient may actually tarnish the physician's image (this hypothesis needs to be formally tested). Unlike a lawyer, who employs a researcher to locate information, the physician is supposed to know the answer to a patient's question.

Appropriateness of Use

The literature on how to measure appropriateness (eg, does the health benefit of a procedure exceed its health risk by a sufficiently wide margin to make the procedure worth doing?) is sparse, and much remains to be done. Even when studies of the appropriateness of acute-care hospitalizations, procedures, drugs, and office visits are combined, there are less than 40 worthwhile studies.[5] Many of these use flawed methods or have a sampling frame that makes the results difficult to generalize. Nevertheless, a few conclusions can be made. First, methods for judging appropriateness have almost always been applied to people who received a procedure as opposed to people who have a complaint or a symptom. Thus, the literature can be used to say something about the potential overuse of services, but it does not contain information on detecting underuse. The reason for this bias in the literature is not an accident of fate. Just as quality-of-care assessment is concentrated in the hospital because it is easier to do there, appropriateness evaluation concentrates on measuring overuse because it is easier to assess. It is technically feasible to measure underuse, but doing so requires that agreement is first reached on the concept of an enrolled population and that the relevant population can be identified.
Second, because the scientific basis on which medical decisions are made will always be incomplete, we must determine how we can validly combine what is contained in the medical literature with expert judgment to arrive at a judgment of appropriateness.

Third, almost every study that has seriously looked for overuse has discovered it, and virtually every time at least double-digit overuse has been found. If one could extrapolate from the available literature, then perhaps one fourth of hospital days, one fourth of procedures, and two fifths of medications could be done without. Interpretation of the data, however, requires wisdom, is subject to debate, and will reflect the vantage point from which the data are examined. For example, at The RAND Corporation, we studied the appropriateness of use of three procedures in the Medicare population (nationally representative) in 1981.[6] The procedures were coronary angiography, upper gastrointestinal endoscopy, and carotid endarterectomy. For each procedure, we prepared a literature review, and then, based on the literature, developed a list of detailed clinical indications.

For each procedure, we then selected a nine-member multispecialty physician panel that was representative geographically and of the academic and private practicing communities. Using a modified Delphi procedure, we asked each physician, after reading the literature review, to rate the appropriateness of performing the procedure for each indication on a scale of 1 to 9. We then convened the physician

Perspectives on Appropriateness: Results From the RAND Health Services Utilization Study*

Procedure	Appropriate with Agreement, %	Appropriate, %	Equivocal, %	Inappropriate, %	Inappropriate with Agreement, %
Coronary angiography[a]	50	74	9	17	12
Carotid endarterectomy[b]	13	35	32	32	17
Upper gastrointestinal endocospy[c]	46	72	11	17	7
Overall	36	60	18	22	12

*The middle three colums add up to 100% (74+9+17=100; 72+11+17=100; and 60+18+22=100 [35+32=99 because of rounding]), and the column titled "Appropriate With Agreement" is a subset of the column titled "Appropriate"; the column titled "Inappropriate With Agreement" is a subset of the column titled "Inappropriate." See text for definitions of appropriateness, equivocal, inappropriateness, agreement, and disagreement.

a n=1677.
b n=1302.
c n=1585.

panel and discussed the indications and their rankings, and the panel rated them again.

We grouped indications into three categories: (1) appropriate — the panel's median rating was 7 to 9 and there was no disagreement; (2) inappropriate — the median rating was 1 to 3 and there was no disagreement; or (3) equivocal — the panel's median rating was 4 to 6 or there was disagreement. *Disagreement* was defined as three ratings of 1 to 3 and three of 7 to 9. *Agreement* was defined as having seven ratings fall within a three-point range, after discarding one extreme high and one extreme low rating. We then applied these ratings to 4564 elderly patients (about 1500 for each procedure). Patients were randomly sampled from five large geographic areas (average population of each area, 3 million).

What, then, did we find? The answer is dependent on how and from what perspective one views the data and what is one's view on how appropriateness guidelines should be used. A physician who believes in absolute clinical freedom might argue that only those procedures that the panel agreed were inappropriate should not be done (ie, "should not be done" could be translated as either not paid for from pretax or public dollars or it might mean not performed on the patient). In that case, 12% would be the number (Table). However, many physicians, even those believing in absolute clinical freedom and patient individuality, would probably consider a procedure inappropriate if there were not unusual clinical circumstances to justify its use and if a majority of physicians felt that way. In that case, the number would be 22%.

But now, let us consider the other side. A recession occurs, the deficit grows, and building a strong economy is vital to maintaining the health of the population, as well as an individual's health. A government official, especially one who is responsible for Medicare, might then ask what services must we provide. *Must* might be defined as those services that physicians agreed were appropriate. In that case, 36% of the services might be covered. (Note: procedures could be performed for other reasons, but expenses associated with them would not be reimbursed out of tax dollars.) A lot of medicine exists between these two extremes.

What does the patient want? The answer is not known. Patients, especially elderly patients, may be averse to risks, and they may agree with the government official and perhaps many physicians as well that they want only those procedures performed on them that the profession, as a whole, really believes in (36%). They may realize that all professionals believe in what they do and that belief often extends beyond what the scientific evidence can support.

On the other hand, some patients may want to believe totally in their physicians. This belief may even be essential to the modern healing process. Such patients may desire to have every possible test performed on them, as long as their physicians recommend it. Thus, they would believe in complete clinical freedom for physicians and want their physicians to provide them with everything in which they believe. Patients, of course, would want expenditures for such procedures completely covered by insurance.

The Future of Guidelines

Where, then, do we go from here? There are forces in place that cannot be stopped that will result in the production of timely information to physicians. This information will contain an element of the "should" or guidelines in it. Current medical textbooks do not fill this need; concise publications with explicit conclusions, such as the *Medical Letter*, might be better in this respect. New developments in computer technology and information sciences can make it easier to provide information to physicians in a user-friendly way at the time they need it. The physician of the future will most assuredly have on his or her desk a computer that will provide access to these guidelines with their explicit appropriateness ratings. These ratings could be shared with patients and thus transfer to them some of the responsibility of ensuring high quality of care.

On the other hand, people are worried that the production of practice guidelines may be accompanied by increased regulation or public release of sensitive information. Will more harm than good be done to patients? Will such a process destroy the ability of physicians to work together to improve constantly their own performance? Will the medical system be codified and will both experimentation and change be slowed? Will the interest in medicine as a career decline and, therefore, will the quality of the future practitioner be ever decreasing? Finally, will a regulatory system emerge that will actually cost more than it saves?

Even if all of these fears cannot be dispelled at this point in time, at least some part of the medical literature must become more specific and directive (ie, guidelines must be developed), and we can learn from past failures. Consider what happened during the Professional Standard Review Organization program. Perhaps more than 100,000 individual criteria sets were developed by hospitals to measure, for instance, the quality and appropriateness of hospital care for patients with heart attacks. Such criteria were developed by committees of physicians (3 to 7 per committee) who spent 1 to 2 hours in each of 2 to 3 meetings developing such criteria. Multiplying these numbers means that 2 million physician-hours (100,000 x 5 physicians x 2 hours x 2 meetings) were spent at $50/h, or $100 million, in developing practice guidelines, or appropriateness standards, for patients with heart attacks. However, even with this investment, there is no library from which a set of criteria for treating a patient with a heart attack can be checked out.

The reason for this sorry state of affairs is that an individual hospital or Professional Standard Review Organization committee did not have sufficient resources to do the criteria-setting process right. Doing it right might have cost $150,000 to $500,000 per condition and no single institution had that kind of money available. (Doing it right at least requires the following steps: performing an analytic literature review, developing supportable guidelines, testing their reliability and validity, bringing together research and clinical experts to evaluate the products, and developing a feasible system by which they can be used.)

Will we repeat the Professional Standard Review Organization process in the 1990s? It certainly seems that way, as everybody is still off doing their own thing. The bottom line is that such a process produces a low-quality product.

To avoid repeating our mistakes, we must create an institution that is capable of developing and maintaining practice guidelines for both common diagnoses and common procedures. Such an institution does not currently exist. The mission of the institution would not only be the development of such guidelines, but also testing them and reporting, on a periodic cycle, the results of their application. All guidelines would be outcome based and outcome justified. Before being used, guidelines must be either strongly considered by the profession or supported by the literature as resulting in better health, if adherence to them were the norm. In addition, the cost implications of adopting the guidelines would be considered. Adherence to some guidelines, even if that adherence improves outcome, may not be worth the cost, and this information will need to be produced along with the guidelines.

A report from such an institution might make the following points: On average, in the United States, 30% of coronary angiographies are inappropriate. In white women aged 65 through 75 years in the north central states the rate was 40%, but underuse was found among black men aged 45 to 65 years in the South, where 50% more procedures are required. A review of quality of care for patients with heart attacks indicates that about 15% of deaths from this condition were preventable, and most of the preventable deaths were due to failure to use clot-lysing agents in the first 2 hours of the hospitalization.

For such an institution to survive, it must not only report on appropriateness and quality, but it must also improve the methods to measure both of these attributes of medical care. This will require input from the spectrum of fields and disciplines associated with health services research: economics, sociology, psychology, clinical medicine, operations research, utility measurement, meta-analysis, decision analysis, and psychometrics. The institution must also be closely linked to developments in clinical science and technology assessment, so that the guidelines and standards can be kept current. The worst possible outcome of such an institution would be the adoption of methods and guidelines that lowered quality at great expense, and then codified the practice of medicine at that level.

What will happen if such information were made available on a routine basis? (1) Policy could be altered so that resources are better directed to need. This, of course, would require that guidelines be used to measure both underuse and overuse. For instance, expenditures on acute-care services might be lowered and those on long-term care increased. (2) The information, when displayed over time, might be used by local institutions, or groups of physicians, as a stimulus and means to self-improvement. (3) The information might be provided to the public on an institutional or provider basis, perhaps in the form of a consumer report. This might lead to "buy right" policies by businesses when they decide which health plans to offer employees, or by individuals when they decide which plan to join. (4) New textbooks of medicine organized around guidelines might be developed and the whole educational process could be altered, including a greatly expanded role for the information sciences in medical school. These changes could substantially increase the accuracy of a physician's clinical decision making. (5) Professional societies might develop performance-based review systems that would form the core of both their educational and recertification processes. To be a fellow in a college would require that appropriateness-of-care guidelines are met, as determined by a review of one's practice. Continuing medical education activities would be geared to improving practice behaviors. (6) Licensing bodies could base relicensing on compliance with guidelines and appropriateness standards. (7) Third-party payers could base their concept of a preferred provider and preferred organization on the above guidelines, and select only those providers that meet acceptable standards rather than those who simply offer an advantageous price schedule. (8) Third-party payers could use the information prospectively and deny or question reimbursement for care, after physician review and appeal, that does not fulfill the guidelines. (9) Patients and physicians could use the information cooperatively and could better share decision making, and patient utilities could be more correctly expressed in the final medical decision. (10) The legal system could base malpractice decisions on the guidelines, and by knowing what was expected, malpractice claims and rates could decline.

If any or all of the above come true, then medicine will have changed. Change is difficult and some of the above changes may not be desirable. Change is worth the agony if the public benefits both now and in the future, because the quality of care in America increases. If this is to occur, the satisfaction of American physicians with their work will also need to increase. There is reason to believe that both of these changes can occur. What changes are implemented and how successful they are will depend on who takes the leadership role in developing guidelines: the profession, business, the government, or insurance companies.

Supplementary Information
This work was supported by the John A. Hartford Foundation, New York, NY, and The RAND Corporation, Santa Monica, Calif.

I thank David Solomon, MD, and Jacqueline Kosecoff, PhD, for comments on earlier versions of the manuscript. I also thank Betsy Sullivan for her diligence in preparing and typing the manuscript.

References

1. Lurie N, Ward NB, Shapiro MF, Gallego C, Vaghaiwalla R, Brook RH. Termination of MediCal benefits: a follow-up study one year later. N Engl J Med. 1986; 314:1266-1268.

2. Chassin MR, Brook RH, Park RE, et al. Variations in the use of medical and surgical services by the Medicare population. N Engl J Med. 1986;314:285-290.

3. Kanouse DE, Winkler JD, Kosecoff J, et al. Changing Medical Practice Through Technology Assessment: An Evaluation of the NIA Consensus Development Program. Ann Arbor, Mich: Health Administration Press; 1989.

4. Leape L, Park RE, Solomon DH, Chassin MR, Kosecoff J, Brook RH. Relation between surgeons' practice volumes and geographic variation in the rate of carotid endarterectomy. N Engl J Med. 1989;321:653-657.

5. Brook RH, Kamberg CJ, Mayer-Oakes A. Appropriateness of Acute Medical Care for the Elderly. Santa Monica, Calif: The RAND Corp; 1989. Publication R-3717-AARP/HF/RWJ/RC.

6. Chassin MR, Kosecoff J, Park RE, et al. The Appropriateness of Use of Selected Medical and Surgical Procedures and Its Relationship to Geographic Variations in Their Use. Ann Arbor, Mich: Health Administration Press; 1989.

Brook RH. Practice guidelines and practicing medicine. JAMA. 1989; 262 (21): 3027-3030.

Reprinted with permission from the author and the American Medical Association.

Article 2.5

Council of Medical Specialty Societies Statement on Qualifications and Guidelines for the Physician Expert Witness

Approved by the Council of Medical Specialty Societies, March 20, 1989.

Preamble

Physicians are frequently called upon to serve as a medical expert witness in a variety of court proceedings. At the present time, in many courts, criteria or guidelines for expert witnesses are inadequate and, as a result, any physician can testify as an expert witness. It is in the public interest that medical expert testimony be readily available, objective, and unbiased. To limit uninformed and possibly misleading testimony, expert witnesses should be qualified for their role and should follow some clear and consistent set of ethical guidelines. Recommendations for each are set forth below. These recommendations are not meant to refer to the treating physician who is called upon to testify in that capacity.

I. Recommended Qualifications for the Physician Expert Witness

a. The physician expert witness must have a current, valid, and unrestricted license to practice medicine in the state in which he or she practices.

b. The physician expert witness should be fully trained in a specialty or a diplomate of a specialty board recognized by the American Board of Medical Specialties, and qualified by experience or demonstrated competence in the subject of the case. The specialty of that physician should be appropriate to the subject matter in the case.

c. The physician expert witness should be familiar with the clinical practice of the specialty or the subject matter of the case at the time of the occurrence, and should be actively involved in the clinical practice of the speciality or the subject matter of the case for three of the previous five years at the time of the testimony.

d. The physician expert witness should affirm that not more than twenty (20) percent of his/her professional activities involve serving as an expert witness.

II. Recommended Guidelines for Behavior of the Physician Expert Witness

Physicians have an obligation to testify in court as expert witnesses when appropriate. Physician expert witnesses are expected to be impartial and should not adopt a position as an advocate or partisan in the legal proceedings.

a. The physician expert witness should review the medical information in the case and testify to its content fairly and impartially.

b. The physician expert witness should review the standards of practice prevailing at the time of occurrence.

c. The physician expert witness should be prepared to state the basis of the testimony presented, and whether it is based on personal experience, specific clinical references or generally accepted opinion in the specialty field.

d. Compensation of the physician expert witness should be reasonable and commensurate with the time and effort given to preparing for deposition and court appearance. It is unethical for a physician expert witness to link compensation to the outcome of the case.

e. The physician expert witness should be aware that transcripts of depositions and courtroom testimony are public records, subject to independent peer review.

Qualifications and guidelines for the physician expert witness [position statement]. Chicago, IL: Council of Medical Specialty Societies; 1989.

Article 2.6

Diagnostic Issues Generate Most Expensive Claims

St. Paul Fire and Marine Insurance Company, Physicians' & Surgeons' Update, 1989.

Claims involving diagnostic issues continue to be the most expensive types of claims filed against physicians and surgeons insured by The St. Paul. These claims, with failure to diagnose cancer cited as the most frequent allegation, account for more than 34 percent of the total costs incurred for claims reported in 1987 and 1988.

Nearly 70 percent of the failure to diagnose cancer claims cite the physician's office or the clinic as the location for the allegation. These two areas are where the majority of the screening and diagnosing of the patients' symptoms occurs.

Surgical issues, dominated by the allegation of postoperative complications, continue to generate the highest number of claims. As would be expected, nearly all these claims occur in the hospital.

The birth-related allegation is the most frequent among the improper treatment issues. These types of claims continue to rank among the most costly.

A closer look at the claims alleging drug side effect revealed that eight drugs including DPT, prednisone, IVP dye, lidocaine, penicillin, indocin, anticoagulants and allergy injections, consistently were involved in these claims. The majority occur in the physician's office or clinic.

Just more than two-thirds of the claims continue to occur in the hospital setting and account for 70 percent of the total cost of all claims reported. The labor, delivery and nursery area of the hospital continue as the site of the most expensive claims and account for more than 21 percent of the total cost.

Claims data reflects all claims reported during 1987 and 1988, evaluated as of December 31, 1988. The total includes claims closed without payment.

Major Allegation Groups by Frequency

Group	Number	Percent of total Claims	Percent of total Incurred Cost
Surgery	2,867	28.8	25.8
Failure to Diagnose	2,771	27.8	34.4
Improper Treatment	2,672	26.9	29.7
Anesthesia	366	3.7	3.6
Other Issues	1,271	12.8	6.5
Total Claims	9,947	100.0	100.0

Surgery - Top Five Allegations

	Allegation	Claims
1	Postoperative Complications	1,474
2	Inadvertent Act	375
3	Postoperative Death	258
4	Inappropriate Procedure	233
5	Delay Complications	164
	Total Top Five	2,504

87.3% of Total Claims Alleging Surgical Issues

Failure to Diagnose - Top Five Allegations

	Allegation	Claims
1	Failure to Diagnose Cancer	607
2	Failure to Diagnose Fracture/Dislocation	304
3	Failure to Diagnose Infection	220
4	Failure to Diagnose Pregnancy Problems	217
5	Failure to Diagnose Abdominal Problem	190
	Total Top Five	1,538

55.5% of Total Claims Alleging Failure to Diagnose

Improper Treatment - Top Five Allegations

	Allegation	Claims
1	Improper Treatment/Birth Related	661
2	Improper Treatment/Drug Side Effect	288
3	Improper Treatment/Insufficient Therapy	277
4	Improper Treatment of Fracture/Dislocation	272
5	Improper Treatment/Infection	225
	Total Top Five	1,723

64.4% of Total Claims Alleging Improper Treatment

Top 10 Allegations by Frequency

	Allegation	Number of Claims	Average Cost*
1	Surgery/Postoperative Complications	1,474	$ 53,230
2	Improper Treatment/Birth Related	661	$ 129,123
3	Failure to Diagnose/Cancer	607	$ 96,462
4	Surgery/Inadvertent Act	375	$ 48,334
5	Failure to Diagnose/Fracture or Dislocation	304	$ 43,099
6	Improper Treatment/Drug Side Effect	288	$ 52,754
7	Improper Treatment/Insufficient Therapy	277	$ 59,411
8	Improper Treatment/Fracture or Dislocation	272	$ 45,806
9	Surgery/Postoperative Death	258	$ 97,609
10	Surgery/Inappropriate Procedure	233	$ 55,972

* The average cost includes the total value of the claim including legal and other expenses with no cap on individual claims.

Top 10 Allegations by Average Cost

(Based on the average cost of loss for allegations resulting in 24 claims or more)

	Allegation	Number of Claims	Average Cost*
1	Failure to Diagnose/Hemorrhage	73	$145,312
2	Failure to Diagnose/Bowel Lesion	24	$129,742
3	Improper Treatment/Birth Related	661	$129,123
4	Failure to Diagnose/Diabetes	28	$121,902
5	Failure to Diagnose/Myocardial Infarction	174	$106,961
6	Anesthesia/Cardiac Arrest	89	$101,370
7	Surgery/Postoperative Death	258	$ 97,609
8	Failure to Diagnose/Kidney Disorder	35	$ 96,977
9	Failure to Diagnose/Cancer	607	$ 96,462
10	Failure to Diagnose/Circulatory Problem/Thrombosis	196	$ 96,107

All Allegations by Location

Location & Allegation	Number of Claims	Percent of Total
Physician's Office/Clinic	2,855	28.7
Hospital by Location		
Surgery	3,076	30.9
Patient Care Area	1,255	12.6
Emergency Room	982	9.9
Labor/Delivery/Nursery	781	7.9
Outpatient Surgery	198	2.0
Other Hospital	469	4.7
Total Hospital	6,761	68.0
Other Non-Hospital	331	3.3
Total all Claims	9,947	100.0

*The average cost includes the total value of the claim including legal and other expenses with no cap on individual claims.

Annotated Bibliography

Standard of Care

American Board of Internal Medicine. *Clinical competence in internal medicine*. Ann Intern Med. 1979; 90: 401-411.
The American Board of Internal Medicine has detailed the abilities required for an individual to be clinically competent in the practice of internal medicine. The abilities are categorized into attitudes and habits, interpersonal skills, motor and technical skills, and intellectual abilities. This article does not cover patient care protocols for specific diagnoses.

Brook RH. *Practice guidelines and practicing medicine*. JAMA. 1989; 262(21): 3027-3030.
Article 2.4

Eichhorn JH, Cooper JB, Cullen DJ, Maier WR, Philip JH, Seeman RG. *Standards for patient monitoring during anesthesia at Harvard Medical School*. JAMA. 1986; 256: 1017-1020.
Article 2.2

Estes EH, Sullivan RJ. *Standards for practice: effectiveness and acceptance*. Ann Intern Med. 1978; 89: 826-828.
One highly specific treatment protocol, diagnosis and care for sore throat, has been shown to improve practice patterns in a group of physicians. However, improvement is dependent on constant feedback and a motivated physician group. The authors suggest that highly regimented standards are not practical but that more general standards may have some usefulness.

Frigoletto FD, Little GA, eds. *Guidelines for Prenatal Care*. 2nd ed. Elk Grove Village, IL: American Academy of Pediatrics/American College of Obstetricians and Gynecologists; 1989.
This volume offers a multi-disciplinary review of current scientific information, professional opinions, and clinical practices in prenatal care. Organization of prenatal services, as well as a wide range of clinical and social issues, are among the topics addressed.

Holzer JF. *The advent of clinical standards for professional liability* . Quality Review Bulletin. 1990; 16.
Article 2.3

McIlrath S. *Rules limit Medicare pay for heart transplantation*. Am Med News. April 17, 1987: 2,34.
The federal government has issued final regulations governing Medicare payments for heart transplantations. The rules define age and health requirements for patient selection and limit the number of facilities where the operation will be allowed. Spokesmen from the medical community raise concerns about the allocation of expensive medical technologies by third-party regulation.

Medicine by the book. Am Med News. January 6, 1989: 1.
This cover story article and seven related articles discuss the status of clinical practice standards or parameters from the view of clinicians, insurers, government officials, and malpractice risk managers.

Mulley AG. *What is inappropriate care?* JAMA. 1984; 260: 540-541.
Dr. Mulley describes the RAND-UCLA Health Services Utilization Study now in progress. An article entitled "The Appropriateness of Performing Coronary Artery Bypass Surgery" appears in the same issue.

Page L. *Blues crack down on test pay*. Am Med News. April 17, 1987: 9-10. Blue Cross and Blue Shield plans to deny reimbursements to some physicians by applying new guidelines prepared by the American College of Physicians. The guidelines describe the indications for chest X-rays, electrocardiograms, complete blood cell counts, and other diagnostic tests. The insurer hopes to save $6 million with the change. The College of American Pathologists opposes the new guidelines.

Schonfeld HK, Heston JF, Falk IS. *Standards for Good Medical Care.* Washington, DC: 1975. U.S. Dept. of Health, Education, and Welfare publication (SSA)75-11926.
This four-volume study describes standards of medical diagnosis and treatment for 242 diseases. It is written by professors of public health and is based on the opinions of clinicians associated with the Yale-New Haven Medical Center.

Standards for Obstetric-Gynecology Services. 7th ed. Washington, DC: American College of Obstetricians and Gynecologists; 1989.
This guidebook describes the facilities and organization needed to operate a sound obstetrics/gynecology practice. It includes maintenance of medical records, recommendations for obtaining informed consent, and general standards for medical care throughout pregnancy and for major categories of gynecologic disease.

Treatments of Psychiatric Disorders. Washington, DC: American Psychiatric Association; 1989.
This 3,000 page, four-volume set was drafted through a committee process and released for the first time in 1989. It defines clinical standards for diagnosis and treatment.

Expert Witness

Ethical Issues Related to Expert Testimony by Obstetricians and Gynecologists. Washington, DC: American College of Obstetricians and Gynecologists; 1987.
ACOG reports its guidelines for obstetricians/gynecologists acting as expert witnesses.

American Academy of Pediatrics. *Guidelines for expert witness testimony*. Pediatrics. 1989;83:312-313.
The Committee on Medical Liability reports its guidelines.

Statement on Qualifications and Guidelines for the Physician Expert Witness. Lake Forest, IL: Council of Medical Specialty Societies; 1989. Article 2.5

The Expert Witness: An ACOG Survey. Washington, DC: American College of Obstetricians and Gynecologists; 1987.
This survey of 112 academic Ob/Gyn departments reports the number of academic specialists serving as expert witnesses and a general lack of coordinated policies on the subject. The report was the impetus for the development of guidelines by ACOG and other specialty societies.

Specialty-Specific Experience

American College of Obstetricians and Gynecologists. *Professional Liability: A Resident's Survival Kit.*. Washington, DC; 1989.
ACOG easy-to-read booklet covers the basic elements of malpractice and liability for residents training in obstetrics and gynecology.

An Introduction to Medical Liability for Pediatricians. 3rd ed. Elk Grove Village, IL: American Academy of Pediatrics, Task Force on Medical Liability; 1986.
The American Academy of Pediatrics has published this 32-page report for its members. It includes chapters on "Malpractice and the Care of the Newborn," "Pediatrician and the Attorney," and "House Officers and Medical Liability."

Davis DA. *An analysis of anesthetic mishaps from medical liability claims.* Int Anesthesiol Clin. 1984; 22: 31-42.
Three senior anesthesiologists review 50 major medical malpractice claims related to anesthesia. They found that most errors were common ones usually emphasized in basic anesthesia training. Their analysis includes statistics concerning anesthesia mishaps nationwide and recommendations for claims prevention.

Epps CH. *Medical liability, 1986: problem, prescription, prognosis.* J Bone Joint Surg Am. 1986; 68: 1116-1124.
This annual presidential address delivered to the American Orthopaedic Association gives a brief history of the rising cost of malpractice insurance for orthopedists and compares the costs with those of other countries. Epps details recommendations for tort reform, record keeping, informed consent, the physician-patient relationship, and peer review in an overall approach to address the problem.

George JE. *Legal aspects of emergency care.* In: Mills J, Ho MT, Saunders CE, eds. Current Emergency Diagnosis and Treatment. Los Altos, CA: Lange Medical Publishers; 1985.
This chapter gives a useful summary of a diverse group of legal issues pertinent to the emergency department physician. Topics include good samaritan laws, reportable events and psychiatric emergencies.

Hamer MM, Morlock F, Foley HT, Ros PR. *Medical malpractice in diagnostic radiology: claims, compensation, and patient injury.* Radiology. 1987; 164: 263-266.
The authors studied malpractice claims brought against the United States government during a five-year period in Cook County, Illinois. Helpful charts include listings of types of claims/allegations and types of patient injuries/damages sustained.

Holzer JF. *Current concepts in risk management.* Int Anesthesiol Clin. 1984: 91-116.
Article 4.4

Holzer JF. *Loss prevention in the emergency room.* Forum (Bimonthly publication of the Risk Management Foundation of the Harvard Medical Institutions). 1988; 9(3).
This special edition of *Forum* includes a review of recent legislation, a closed claim abstract, and articles about specially designed risk identification screens to assist emergency room and ambulatory care physicians.

Milsten R, Turner M. *A review of urologic medical malpractice claims in New Jersey, 1977 to 1984.* New Jersey Med. 1987; 84: 35-37.
This detailed analysis of 104 cases closed without payment and 41 cases closed with payment includes a breakdown of costs and the reasons for claims. Three major categories of negligence were identified: problems with diagnosis, unnecessary surgery, and unintentional iatrogenic injury.

Pierce EC, Cooper JB, eds. *Analysis of anesthetic mishaps.* Int Anesthesiol Clin. 1984; 22.
This edition is devoted to medical malpractice as it pertains to anesthesiology.

Sager MS, Voeks S, Drinka P, Langer E, Grimstad P. *Do the elderly sue physicians?* Arch Intern Med. 1990; 150: 1091-1093.
Court records were reviewed from malpractice claims in the state of Wisconsin for 1983 and 1984. Only 10 percent of suits were initiated by elderly persons. A discussion of this relatively low rate is included.

Solazzi RW, Ward RJ. *The spectrum of medical liability cases.* Int Anesthesiol Clin. 1984; 22: 43-60.
The authors review 192 cases of anesthesia complications between 1971 and 1982 in the state of Washington. Fourteen specific types of complications are analyzed along with their medicolegal implications.

Towbin A. *Obstetric malpractice: the pathologist's view.* Am J Obstet Gynecol. 1986; 155: 927-935.
In this excellent article, a pathologist reviews the current literature concerning the pathogenesis of hypoxic brain damage and cerebral palsy. He contends that, at malpractice trials, the defense of obstetricians is often jeopardized by inadequate presentation of this information.

Edwards FJ. *Medical Malpractice: Solving the Cris*is. New York, NY: Henry Holt; 1989.
Dr. Edwards gives an illustration of the current tort system by detailing eight specific medical malpractice cases. Inequities and the high cost of the system lead the author to endorse an arbitration system as an alternative approach to resolving malpractice cases.

Malpractice Law

Holder AR. *Medical Malpractice Law.* 2nd ed. New York, NY: Wiley Medical Publications; 1978.
This detailed text, written by an attorney, is intended for both physicians and attorneys. Chapter topics include physician-patient relationship, specific categories of malpractice injury, and malpractice defense strategies.

Jacobson PD. *Medical malpractice and the tort system.* JAMA. 1989; 262(23): 3320-3327.
Article 2.1

Quimby CW Jr. *Law for the Medical Practitioner.* Washington, DC: AUPHA Press; 1979.
The author, a physician-attorney, discusses negligence, informed consent, contracts, medical records, and other topics with frequent reference to legal cases in this introductory text.

Chapter 3

Informed Consent

Case: Surgical Consent

A surgeon meets with parents whose son has a congenital heart defect, coarctation of the aorta, that causes high blood pressure and requires surgical repair.

Mr. and Mrs. Kravitz learned one week ago that their seven-year-old son, Timmy, has coarctation of the aorta, which is causing high blood pressure. They were told by their pediatrician that Timmy will need major surgery to correct this malformation and reduce his high blood pressure. He told them that Timmy should have surgery as soon as possible. The Kravitzes now meet with Dr. Vaughn, a pediatric cardiovascular surgeon. They have many questions concerning their son's condition. They wonder what harm is caused by high blood pressure and why it cannot be treated with medication in this case. They want to know why Timmy's high blood pressure was not detected earlier and whether their other children are at risk for the same disease. Neither parent has a medical background, but they do desire to know "all" the details of the proposed operation.

Dr. Vaughn is a highly talented surgeon and has a close professional relationship with Timmy's pediatrician. He has examined Timmy and reviewed his aortogram, which shows a significantly narrowed aorta. He now wishes to gain permission for Timmy's operation and is having some difficulty deciding how much information to give the Kravitz family.

Dr. Vaughn has prepared the following review of the medical literature: Coarctation is found in seven percent of patients with congenital heart disease. Commonly associated anomalies include bicuspid aortic valve, patent ductus arteriosus, and ventricular septal defect; it is twice as common in boys as it is in girls.

Usual clinical findings include midsystolic murmur, decreased lower-extremity pulses, and hypertension measured in the upper extremities with much lower, usually normal, blood pressures measured in the lower extremities. It is often detected in asymptomatic patients, such as Timmy, during a routine physical examination.

Surgical excision of the narrowed segment of aorta followed by end-to-end anastomosis is a common form of repair. Untreated coarctation may lead to complications of hypertension, including cerebral aneurysm and hemorrhage, rupture of the aorta, left ventricular failure, and kidney damage.

Surgical correction is best done between three and six years of age.

Inherent risks of thoracic surgery include hemorrhage, pneumothorax, and other complications. Chest tubes, surgical drains, antibiotics, and observation in an intensive care unit are commonly required during the post-operative period.

Special risks for coarctation repair include separation/dehiscence of the anastomosis leading to major bleeding, aortic dissection, and other complications. In the immediate post-operative period, paradoxic hypertension is often seen and generally lasts a day or two. Normal blood pressure usually follows shortly thereafter. Necrotizing panarteritis of small vessels of the gastrointestinal tract is a rare complication of this procedure.

Surgery fails to correct hypertension in a small percentage of patients and appears to be related to the duration of pre-operative hypertension. No sufficient alternate therapies are available.

Discussion Questions

1. What points should Dr. Vaughn disclose to the Kravitzes concerning Timmy's proposed operation?

2. What details concerning the need for the surgery, post-operative care, and potential complications should be discussed?

3. When should a signed form or other documentation indicating informed consent be obtained from the Kravitzes? Is it a legal requirement? Who should obtain it—Dr. Vaughn, his associate in group practice, or the resident on the case? Where should the informed consent document be kept?

4. What must be recorded? Who should sign the informed consent document? At what age will Timmy be allowed to sign for his own informed consent? Under what conditions would an individual's capacity to understand and give informed consent be called into question?

5. Should the Kravitz family obtain a second opinion? What factors determine the appropriateness or requirement of obtaining a second opinion?

6. Must Dr. Vaughn disclose that the resident, whom he is training, will be performing the bulk of the surgery under his guidance?

7. What procedures commonly performed in a private office or on a medical, surgical, or psychiatric ward require written informed consent? Who makes these decisions?

Overview

Informed consent is at the crossroads of medicine, law, and ethics. It represents one of the most important aspects of the physician-patient relationship. As medicine has become more complex, the number of physicians coming in contact with a single patient has grown and the number of therapeutic options available for the treatment of most illnesses has multiplied.

Diseases that were never before diagnosed are now recognized and treated. Likewise, the number of difficult therapeutic decisions to be made continues to rise exponentially. The public's interest in health care information and an ever-growing recognition by consumers of their rights have combined to create more medically sophisticated patients. New medical technologies, with their own inherent risks, have in many cases put greater distance between the clinician and his or her patient. As a result, patterns of communication between physician and patient continue to evolve in an era of the "shared relationship" within medical decision-making.[1-3]

The significance of appropriately documented informed consent to a judge and jury should not be underestimated. It tells them that the physician did explain the alternatives and risks of a given procedure or course of therapy. The care and completeness of the documentation also reflects the thoroughness of the physician's style of medical practice. Conversely, poor documentation of the consent process invites speculation about the credibility of the physician's oral testimony regarding the informed consent process and possibly even the care rendered. Absence of documentation of consent can be an important factor in a plaintiff attorney's decision to proceed with legal action on behalf of a disgruntled patient.

The case that introduces this chapter describes a fairly routine physician-patient encounter. It does not address an act of malpractice. In analyzing Dr. Vaughn's discussion regarding the young boy's need for major surgery, the scene takes on new meaning. In the eyes of the parents, their son is active and healthy, adding emphasis to their skepticism about the need for cardiothoracic surgery when they are told of its potential complications. How much detail should Dr. Vaughn supply to this couple? How much information concerning their son's disease and suggested therapy do they need to know to make the best decision on behalf of their son? How much information do they actually want to know?

The law's approach to the issues surrounding informed consent has always valued the preservation of individual decision-making on the part of the patient. This societal value is firmly established in case law and, in some states, by legislation.[4,5] However, uneasiness still exists in the actual delivery of information and the obtaining of consent. Malpractice suits citing insufficient or improper informed consent as an allegation are still common. Debate continues as to how much information should or must be told to the patient to ensure truly informed consent. In any situation, improved use of informed consent leading to better physician-patient communication and the sharing of medical uncertainty may prove to be the best form of malpractice prevention.

The Doctrine of Informed Consent

The key concept incorporated into the doctrine of informed consent is that a specific communication must transpire between physician and patient in arriving at important medical decisions. Captured in a standardized format, the process of informed consent is as follows[6]:

> A physician may not treat a patient until he or she has explained to the patient the risks and material facts concerning the treatment and its alternative, including nontreatment, and has secured thereafter the patient's competent, voluntary, and understanding consent to proceed.

Laws regarding informed consent vary significantly among states. Some states support a "patient-oriented" standard of disclosure. This standard judges the process from the patient's point of view and requires disclosure of information that a reasonable person should receive to make an informed decision about a given procedure. Although the patient-oriented standard is clearly the modern trend in the case law, many states still uphold a "physician-oriented" process, requiring disclosure commensurate with what an average physician deems reasonable in the particular circumstances of each case. Regardless of the standard used in a given state, the exchange of information should cover certain basics. Elements to be specifically discussed and documented in the medical record include[7]:

(1) the physician's diagnosis and prognosis;
(2) the suggested procedure, its purpose, and a brief description of what it involves;
(3) the chances of success or failure of the contemplated procedure;
(4) alternative methods of treatment—even if not preferable—or the possibility of nontreatment and the prognosis for such alternatives or nontreatment;
(5) an evaluation of the risks and benefits of alternatives to the contemplated procedure.

The institution of rules and standard procedures for obtaining informed consent is an example of a liability control standard meant to focus the physician and patient on this very important task. However, this ideal may not be fully reached in every case due to factors such as patient anxieties, physician attitudes, and the short time that physicians and patients have together or the reluctance of physicians to engage in these difficult and often emotional communications.

Without consent, physical contact between a physician and patient may constitute a battery.[8] Battery is an intentional tort, usually defined as an unpermitted touching. In actuality, a claim of battery is rarely invoked in medical malpractice cases today. Most malpractice suits that allege improper informed consent also allege negligent treatment on the part of the physician.

Medical Uncertainty and Informed Consent

Whether patients are able and willing to give informed consent is a key issue in this very subjective area of the law. Equally important is whether physicians are able and willing to make disclosures that allow patients to give meaningful consent. According to Dr. Jay Katz, author of Article 3.1, "Informed Consent: Are 'Miracle, Mystery and Authority' Better Medicine?" the data required to answer these questions have yet to be formulated. He describes the inherent uncertainties of modern medicine that continue to challenge both physicians and patients.

Transformation of those uncertainties into a therapeutic alliance requires empathy on the part of the physician, according to Thomas Gutheil, MD, et al, who, in Article 3.2, "Malpractice Prevention Through the Sharing of Uncertainty," describe the helplessness and anxiety patients experience during an illness. Physicians can also experience frustration and uncertainty during diagnosis and treatment. These stresses can potentially polarize the physician-patient relationship.

Through a process of mutual discovery, however, patients can come to understand the limitations of medical science and better judge their need for medical intervention. In this way, patients and physicians can together acknowledge the fact that medical science can be uncertain and proceed with a plan that realistically meets the patient's needs and desires.

Informed Consent in Particular Patient Settings

Several specific patient case settings pose unique considerations with regard to informed consent, including the many issues concerning the care of minors, human immunodeficiency virus (HIV) antibody testing, and mental incompetence. Particular details concerning consent for the care of prisoners, human experimentation, organ donation, do-not-resuscitate orders, and living wills, just to name a few, will be only briefly covered here. These issues are thoroughly dealt with in the book *Consent to Treatment: A Practical Guide* by Fay A. Rozovsky, JD, MPH. Articles concerning these topics and informed consent applicable to psychiatrists, radiologists, and plastic surgeons are included in the annotated bibliography at the end of this chapter.

Pediatricians and general practitioners are commonly confronted with consent issues in the case of legal minors and adolescents. During the past 20 years, courts have increasingly recognized the rights of adolescents to self-determination with respect to medical care. Confidential access to birth control, abortion services, treatment for venereal disease, and drug abuse counseling are guaranteed in many states.The historical development of these laws and definitions of "minor" and "mature minor" are discussed by attorney Angela Holder in Article 3.3, "Minors' Rights to Consent to Medical Care."

Testing for the presence of the antibody to HIV is posing new controversy in the arena of confidentiality and informed consent. State legislatures and individual health care facilities are now devising regulations regarding consent for testing and the protection of test results. A central issue in this deliberation is the fear that individuals may suffer from illegal discrimination in employment, housing, schooling, and other areas on the basis of HIV antibody status alone.[9] Debate concerning mandatory testing of prisoners, military personnel, marriage applicants, and other segments of the population is ongoing. Many testing centers now require an individual to sign a specific consent form before the HIV antibody test will be performed. In most cases, these forms include information concerning the existence of false-positive and false-negative test results and description of groups at high risk for HIV infection. One such form is reprinted later in this chapter as Table 3.6.

Special Circumstances: When Informed Consent Is Not Required

There are four situations in which the patient's informed consent is not required before a physician may proceed with the delivery of medical care: (1) emergencies, (2) cases involving therapeutic privilege, (3) instances where patients voluntarily and purposefully give up their rights to disclosure and autonomous decision-making, and (4) incompetency.

In an emergency, the patient may be unable to give consent or may incur greater harm if time is taken to explain medical interventions. The courts have recognized this fact and have waived the requirement of consent in medical emergencies.

Therapeutic privilege is the withholding of information by the physician based on his or her judgment that disclosure would be harmful to the patient. Recording and explaining this judgment in the medical record is essential, as the burden of justifying the use of therapeutic privilege falls on the physician.

When patients knowingly yield their right to informed consent, physicians should likewise document such and proceed in the best interest of their patient.

When used in the context of medical treatment decisions, "incompetency" is a legal term used to describe the situation where a person lacks the legal capacity to make certain decisions concerning his or her medical care. Legal incompetency must be determined by a court in a special proceeding. "Clinical incapacity," however, is a less technical term that can be applied to a determination made by a physician. Dr. Mark Munetz et al discuss the fine points of these legal doctrines in Article 3.4, "Informed Consent and Incompetent Medical Patients." It is common for patients on medical and surgical wards to experience temporary periods of time during which they are unable to reasonably register and process medical information from their caretakers. The effect of drugs, pain, isolation from familiar surroundings, language barriers, and disease processes can contribute to such lapses. It is important for physicians to recognize patients with a fluctuating mental status and those who are unable to form judgments due to chronic mental or physical handicaps. Under these circumstances, proper documentation and the timely involvement of family members in medical decisions are indicated. The physician should document the change in the patient's status, why it may have occurred, the steps being taken to ameliorate the condition, and the involvement of any new individuals (relatives or surrogates) in the consent process.

Obtaining Informed Consent

Proper documentation of informed consent for all major therapeutic and diagnostic procedures is a crucial risk management task. A timely and thorough entry in the patient's chart by the appropriate physician can become the single strongest piece of evidence in a malpractice trial. Unfortunately, some physicians erroneously believe that simply obtaining the patient's signature on the dotted line of a generic informed consent form provides them with complete legal protection.

Dr. Charles Lidz et al describe this mechanistic approach to informed consent as the "event model" in their Article 3.5, "Two Models of Implementing Informed Consent." They contrast this scenario with the preferred "process model," which seeks to "integrate informing the patient into the continuing dialogue between physician and patient that is a routine part of diagnosis and treatment."

A difficult challenge for the physician attempting to obtain informed consent lies in the determination of what information should be related to allow the patient to make a truly informed decision. The doctrine of informed consent sets broad goals concerning the review of treatment options and their inherent risks. As mentioned earlier, some states have chosen a standard based on what information the patient reasonably needs to know rather than what information the physician would customarily disclose. This patient-oriented standard requires the imparting of information measured by what a reasonable person in the patient's position would want to know when facing similar circumstances. The exact interpretation of the doctrine of informed consent does vary somewhat among states according to specific state laws and, more importantly, legal precedent. Attorney William J. Curran, a Harvard law professor and expert in legal medicine, reviews a case heard before the Massachusetts Supreme Judicial Court in Article 3.6, "Informed Consent in Malpractice Cases: A Turn Toward Reality." The case, *Precourt v. Frederick*, further defined the amount and quality of information a physician must disclose in Massachusetts in the informed consent process.

Attorney Douglas Danner provides an overview of helpful considerations in his list of "Do's and Don'ts" specific to the issue of informed consent (see Table 3.1). In particular, Danner recommends that physicians "disclose risks to a greater extent when the proposed treatment or procedure is experimental, new, novel, ultra-hazardous, capable of altering sexual capacity or fertility, or purely cosmetic in nature." He also recommends that physicians attempt to place themselves in the position of the patient by imagining how they might react were they or a member of their own family in the patient's position. Also, in Article 3.2, "Malpractice Prevention Through the Sharing of Uncertainty," Gutheil et al suggest specific styles of discussion that facilitate the informed consent process.

Documenting the Consent Process

Prepared consent forms may be an efficient way to record informed consent. These forms may be structured so that the physician can add information to the form to reflect special risks, benefits, and alternatives individual to a patient. Merely obtaining a signature on a consent form, however, does not ensure that proper communication actually transpired between physician and patient or that the patient fully understood what the physician said. A signed consent form can be challenged in court if there is evidence that the process of adequately informing the patient did not actually take place.

The format for consent forms varies. Examples are reprinted following this chapter as Tables 3.2 through 3.6. No one form is necessarily superior to another. The utility of each form depends on the physician who employs it. It should be emphasized that a carefully written note in the patient's chart, documenting the process of informed consent can be as effective as any standardized form. In addition to informed consent in the hospital, it is essential that documented consent be routine in settings outside the hospital where procedures are carried out and medications administered. As there is no uniform list of procedures that require informed consent, most hospitals or ambulatory clinics devise their own list based on the procedures performed within each institution. (See Table 3.7 for a listing of procedures that require written informed consent as outlined by the hospitals affiliated with Harvard Medical School.)

Summary

It is vital that medical students and physicians recognize the significance of informed consent in the daily care of patients. The legal definitions of informed consent, although not precise, do incorporate the discretion of physicians. The legal responsibilities attached to this discretion are relatively straightforward and should become routine within the practice of clinical medicine. Informed consent is more than another standardized form to be hurriedly checked off before an operation begins. It is a process of communication that becomes a useful aid when explaining to patients the uncertainties that exist in the delivery of medical care. Thorough informed consent encourages a relationship of collaboration between physician and patient and reinforces the understanding of a mutual responsibility for medical decision-making.

References

1. Abram MB. On the 'shared relationship.' *Am Med News*. May 30, 1986: 4.

2. Siegler M. The physician-patient accommodation: a central event in clinical medicine. *Arch Intern Med*. 1982; 142: 1899-1902.

3. Gutheil TG, Bursztajn H, Brodsky A. Malpractice prevention through the sharing of uncertainty. *N Engl J Med*. 1984; 311: 49-51.

4. *Stripek v. Bergamo*, 200 NJ Super 620, 491 A2d 1336, 1346 (1985).

5. *Logan v. Greenwich Hospital Association*, 191 Conn 282, 465 A2d 294.

6. Danner D. The informed consent doctrine: some practical guidelines. *Forum*. 1981; 1: 4.

7. Eisner JM, Tilson JQ, Agsten MA. A primer on informed consent for Connecticut physicians. *Conn Med*. 1986; 50: 391-398.

8. See, e.g., 56 A.L.R. 2d 695 (1957) and cases collected therein.

9. Sherer R. Physician use of the HIV antibody test: the need for consent, counseling, confidentiality, and caution. *JAMA*. 1988; 259: 264-265.

Table 3.1

A Physician's List of "Do's And Don'ts" on Informed Consent

1. Make sure the patient understands the nature of his or her medical condition.

2. Make sure the patient understands the nature of the proposed treatment or procedure.

3. Make sure the patient understands the possible alternative treatments or procedures.

4. Make sure the patient understands the medically significant risks of the proposed and alternative treatments or procedures.

5. Make sure the patient understands the chances of success or failure of the proposed and alternative treatments.

6. Disclose the identity of the chief surgeon when he or she is other than the attending physician.

7. Disclose any risk of death or serious harm.

8. Disclose the peculiar risks associated with a specific treatment or procedure.

9. Disclose risks to a greater extent when the proposed treatment or procedure is experimental, new, novel, ultra-hazardous, capable of altering sexual capacity or fertility, or purely cosmetic in nature.

10. Disclose the intent to perform procedures incidental to the principal procedure such as an appendectomy during a hysterectomy.

11. Make the disclosure yourself and do not ask or expect the nurses or paramedical personnel to do it for you.

12. Follow the rule "the greater the risk the less the chance of therapeutic benefit, the more you should explain to the patient to obtain his consent."

13. Act as if you or your family were on the receiving end of the treatment procedure.

14. Record your disclosures and the consent in a permanent way, either by a detailed writing in the medical or hospital records of what you disclosed, or by using an explanatory written consent form.

15. Make sure you fill in the blanks where the operative procedure or proposed treatment should be indicated.

16. Don't say you are going to do a routine operation as none is routine.

17. Don't inform the patient that the treatment or procedure is simple.

18. Don't tell the patient that no complications will occur because complications may occur.

19. Don't expect to obtain informed consent by merely answering the patient's questions because he or she won't ask you the right questions.

20. Don't expect a patient's signature on a consent form that was given to him or her just moments before the procedure.

Developed by Douglas Danner. Reprinted from Forum, Risk Management Foundation of the Harvard Medical Institutions, July-August 1981.

Table 3.2

Sample Consent Form for Medical and Surgical Procedures

You have been given information about your (the patient's) condition and the recommended surgical, medical or diagnostic procedure(s) to be used. This consent form is designed to provide a written confirmation of such discussions by recording some of the more significant medical information given to you. It is intended to make you better informed so that you may give or withhold your consent to the proposed procedure(s)

1. **CONDITION**: Dr.________________has explained to me that the following condition(s) exist in my (his/her) case: _______________________
____ Right☐ Left ☐

2. **PROPOSED PROCEDURE(S)**: I understand that the procedure(s) proposed for evaluating and treating my (his/her) condition is (are): _________
____

3. **RISKS/BENEFITS OF PROPOSED PROCEDURE(S)**:
   A. Just as there may be benefits to the procedure(s) proposed, I also understand that the medical and surgical procedures involve risks. These risks include allergic reactions, bleeding, blood clots, infections, adverse side effects of drugs, and even loss of bodily function or life, as well as risks of transfusion reactions and the transmission of infectious disease, including Hepatitis and Acquired Immune Deficiency Syndrome, from the administration of blood and/or blood components.
   B. I also realize that there are particular risks associated with the procedure(s) proposed for me (him/her) and that these risks include, but are not limited to, those enumerated in the attachment.

4. **COMPLICATIONS; UNFORESEEN CONDITIONS; RESULTS**:
I am aware that in the practice of medicine, other unexpected risks or complications not discussed may occur. I also understand that during the course of the proposed procedure(s) unforeseen conditions may be revealed requiring the performance of additional procedures, and I authorize such procedures to be performed. I further acknowledge that no guarantees or promises have been made to me concerning the results of any procedure or treatment.

5. **ACKNOWLEDGEMENTS**: The available alternatives, some of which include the potential benefits and risks of the proposed procedures(s), and the likely result without such treatment [_____________________________] have been explained to me. I understand what has been discussed with me as well as the contents of this consent form, and have been given the opportunity to ask questions and have received satisfactory answers. I also understand that the MEEI is a teaching and research hospital and that any tissue (including blood) that is recovered during surgery and not required for diagnosis may be used for research and/or teaching purposes.

6. **CONSENT TO PROCEDURE(S) AND TREATMENT**:
Having read this form and talked with the physicians, my signature below acknowledges that: I voluntarily give my authorization and consent to the performance of the procedure(s) described above (including the administration of blood and disposal of tissue) by my physician and/or his/her associates assisted by hospital personnel and other trained persons as well as the presence of observers.

X____________________	X _____	X_________________	X _____
Patient (or person authorized to sign for patient)	Date	Physician/Surgeon	Date

Table 3.3

Sample Consent Form for Glaucoma Surgery

Complications could occur days, weeks, months, or years later:

1. Loss of eye
2. As a result of the surgery, vision could be made worse or, rarely, totally lost
3. Abnormal collection of fluid in eye, necessitating a second operation
4. Bleeding in the eye
5. Chronic inflammation
6. Infection, early or much later
7. Early or late increase of pressure in eye (glaucoma)
8. Development or worsening of cataract
9. Irritation or discomfort in the eye that may persist
10. Failure to achieve intent of surgery, necessitating a reoperation
11. In spite of surgery, vision could become worse from continuing degenerative changes in the eye

Local complication of anesthesia injections around the eye:

1. Perforation of eye ball
2. Destruction of optic nerve
3. Interference with circulation of retina
4. Possible drooping of eyelid
5. Respiratory depression
6. Hypotension

Additional comments:

X ____

Patient (or person authorized to sign for patient)   Date

Table 3.4

Authorization for Thoracentesis

1. A thoracentesis has been recommended for me.
2. The nature and purpose of the procedure, its potential benefits and risks, the likely outcome without the procedure, and the available alternatives have been explained to me.
3. I understand that:

   a. A needle will be inserted between my ribs into the pleural space (between the lungs and rib cage), in order to remove accumulated fluid.

   b. This is done to determine the characteristics of the fluid for diagnostic purposes.

   c. Local anesthesia will be used to numb the skin.

   d. In spite of the anesthesia, I may experience a small amount of pain during the insertion of the needle (similar to that experienced when my blood is drawn).

   e. Possible risks include:

   - Allergic reaction to the anesthetic agent.
   - Rarely, the needle may puncture the lung causing a section of the lung to collapse. If a large section of the lung should collapse, a tube may have to be inserted between my ribs to bring about re-expansion of the lung.
   - Very rarely, the needle could cause bleeding into the pleural space. If the bleeding is severe, a tube might have to be inserted between my ribs to remove the blood. In rare cases, surgery may be required to stop the bleeding.

   f. Additional comments, if any:

4. I am aware that there may be other risks or complications not discussed that may occur. I also understand that during the course of the procedure, unforeseen conditions may be revealed requiring the performance of additional procedures. I authorize such procedures to be performed. I acknowledge that no guarantees or promises have been made to me concerning the results of the procedure or any treatment that may be required as a result of this procedure.
5. I understand what has been discussed with me as well as the contents of this form. I have been given the opportunity to ask questions and have received satisfactory answers.
6. I consent to the performance of the procedure described above by my clinician and/or my clinician's delegated associates.

Patient name (please print) ________________ HCHP No. _____

Patient signature* ________________________ Date _________

Clinician name/signature __________________ Date _________

*If patient is a minor or otherwise unable to sign, please complete back of form.

-Continued-

Table 3.4 (continued)

Please fill out information below if patient is a minor or otherwise unable to sign the consent form.

Printed name of patient ______________________ HCHP No. _____

Patient is a minor, __________________________ years of age.

Patient is unable to sign because ______________________________

I. WRITTEN CONSENT OF AUTHORIZED PERSON

I am the patient's ________________ (state relationship), and hereby consent to the procedure on his/her behalf.

Name of authorized person ___________ Signature ___________

Signature of clinician________________ Date ______________

II. TELEPHONE CONSENT OF AUTHORIZED PERSON

(to be signed by clinician)

Date ___________ Time _______(a.m./p.m.)

I have spoken by telephone with ____________________________ (state name of person you spoke with), the __________________ (state relationship) of the above-named patient. I have explained the necessity to perform the procedure described above. I have explained the potential benefits and risks, the likely result without treatment, the available alternatives, and the possibility of unexpected risk of complications. This person appeared to understand my explanation and gave me permission to do the procedure, with the anesthesia described (if applicable) and to treat any condition which arises during the course of the procedure.

______________________ ____________________________

Signature of clinician Signature of witness (monitoring conversation)

III. EMERGENCY PROCEDURE WITHOUT CONSENT

(to be signed by clinician)

Date_____________ Time _______(a.m./p.m.)

We have been unsuccessful in our attempts to contact______________ (name), the________________(relationship) of the above-named patient. I believe it is in the best interest of the patient to perform the procedure described above without further delay.

Signature of clinician______________________________________

Table 3.5

Sample Procedure Consent Form

DATE:

PATIENT:

UNIT NO:

PROCEDURE: Telescope Exam of the Lower Bowel (Colonoscopy) With Possible Biopsy or Polyp Removal

I have explained to the patient the nature of his/her condition, the nature of the procedure, and the benefits to be reasonably expected compared with alternative approaches.

I have discussed the likelihood of major risks or complications of this procedure including (if applicable) but not limited to loss of limb function, brain damage, paralysis, hemorrhage, infection, drug reactions, blood clots, and loss of life. I have also indicated that with any procedure there is always the possibility of an unexpected complication.

Additional comments (if any):

Colonoscopy is a valuable procedure for detailed examination of the large bowel (colon). If necessary, biopsies may be taken, and polyps removed. If polyps are present, it is important to remove them because as they grow larger, they can occasionally turn into cancer. Although colonoscopy is generally safe, some infrequent and possibly serious complications are inherent to the procedure. Drugs given during the colonoscopy may cause irritation of the vein, and occasionally patients are especially sensitive to their sedative action. More serious complications are bleeding and perforation (making a hole in the intestine), which may require hospitalization, blood transfusion, or surgery. These complications are slightly more frequent if polyp removal is carried out, but even so the serious problems occur in less than 1% of patients.

All questions were answered and the patient consents to the procedure.

________________________ M.D.

Dr.________________________
has explained the above to me and I consent to the procedure.

Signature __________________
If signature cannot be obtained, indicate reason in comments section above.

Reprinted with permission from Massachusetts General Hospital.

Table 3.6

Sample Consent for Testing of Patient Blood for the Presence of HIV Antibody

Your physician has requested that a test for HIV antibody be performed on a sample of your blood. The test is a voluntary one; you are not obligated to undergo the blood test. This test has been ordered because your physician feels it is necessary for the management of your care. HIV is an abbreviation of Human Immunodeficiency Virus, which is the cause of the Acquired Immunodeficiency Syndrome or AIDS. The HIV antibody test which will be performed is designed to detect the presence in the blood of the antibody formed by the body against the virus.

A positive test for HIV antibody indicates that the person has been exposed to HIV virus at some time in the past and has formed antibodies against the virus. Evidence indicated that many persons who have the antibody are able to transmit the virus to others by donating blood or by engaging in intimate sexual relations. The presence of the antibody to HIV does not necessarily mean that the person will get AIDS. At this time there are only limited estimates of the risk that AIDS will develop in a person who has been infected with the virus and has developed antibodies.

This test is not 100% accurate but is reliable in most cases. There are occasional false-positive test results. False-positive means that the tests are positive but they are positive for a reason other than the antibody to HIV. The following precautions will be taken to minimize the possibility of a false-positive test: Every blood specimen will be tested at least twice and blood specimens positive by one test method will be tested by a second method.

The test also has a small incidence of false-negative results, meaning that the test results are negative but the patient may nonetheless have been exposed to HIV virus in the past. Although the reported incidence of false-negative tests has been small, the existence of such results indicates that while the test is generally accurate, it is not perfect.

You should be aware there is concern that insurance companies may consider a person with a positive test to be a poor risk.

The results of the test will be conveyed to you by your physician who can provide additional information and counseling.

My signature confirms that I have read this consent form, have asked all of the questions I had about the reason for this testing and the nature of the test, and hereby agree to be tested for HIV antibody.

____________________ PLEASE PRINT NAME

____________________ DATE

____________________ L.C. NUMBER

____________________ SIGNATURE

____________________ WITNESS

Reprinted with permission from Lahey Clinic Medical Center.

Table 3.7

Medical Interventions Requiring Written Informed Consent*

Consent should be obtained for all major therapeutic and diagnostic procedures where disclosure of significant medical information, including major risks involved, would assist a patient in making an intelligent decision whether to undergo the proposed procedure. Such procedures include:

a. All surgical procedures performed under general/spinal anesthesia and selected procedures performed under local anesthesia;

b. Selected biopsies and excisions (including bone marrow);

c. Cardiac catheterizations and angiography;

d. All major endoscopies;

e. Bronchograms, lymphangiograms, myelograms, pneumoencephalograms, splenograms, ventriculogram, and radiation therapy;

f. Extracorporeal and peritoneal dialysis;

g. Cancer chemotherapy;

h. Electro-convulsive therapy;

i. Testing for human immunodeficiency virus (HIV);

j. Blood and blood product use (including blood donation and autologous and other blood transfusions);

k. Major radiologic and/or imaging procedures involving the use of contrast media;

l. Medications and/or other therapeutics with the potential for particularly severe side effects.

*This recommendation has been made by the Risk Management Foundation of the Harvard Medical Institutions for the benefit of its affiliates (March 1990).

Article 3.1

Informed Consent: Are "Miracle, Mystery and Authority" Better Medicine?

Jay Katz, MD. Connecticut Medicine, July 1986.

A fundamental tension inherent in the physician-patient relationship—the tension between patient choice and physician paternalism—was vividly portrayed by Dostoyevsky in the encounter between the Grand Inquisitor and his Prisoner, the son of God. Only the Grand Inquisitor spoke; his Prisoner remained silent throughout.

> Look what you have done...in the name of freedom! I tell you man has no more agonizing anxiety than to find someone to whom he can hand over with all speed the gift of freedom with which the unhappy creature is born. [For, it is] the nature of man [that he cannot] reject a miracle at the most fearful moments of life [and] stick to the free decision of the heart. [M]an is unable to carry on without a miracle, [and] he will create new miracles for himself; miracles of the witchdoctor and the sorcery of the wise woman....We have corrected your great work and based it on *miracle*, *mystery*, and *authority*. And men rejoiced that they were once more led like sheep and that the terrible gift [of freedom] which had brought them so much suffering had at last been lifted from their hearts....Tell me. Did we not love mankind when we admitted so humbly its impotence and lovingly lightened its burden....?[1]

Since the days of Hippocrates, many physicians have shared the Grand Inquisitor's view of the limitations of human nature. This view has shaped the conversation between doctors and patients in powerful and self-fulfilling ways.

Jay Katz, MD, is the John A. Garver Professor of Law and Psychoanalysis at Yale Law School and an Attending Psychiatrist at Yale-New Haven Hospital.

In theory, the legal doctrine of informed consent opposes this view, by asserting that "[e]very human being of adult years and sound mind has a right to determine what shall be done with his own body...."[2] Such a right, of course, makes sense only if it rests on the assumption that at least some human beings are not "sheep," are willing to accept "the terrible gift of freedom," and welcome making their own choices. But does this assumption hold true, for human beings in general, and more importantly for us, does the assumption hold true once human beings become patients? This question has provoked considerable controversy since the birth of the doctrine of informed consent. Opponents have insisted that patients have little capacity to make their own decisions and that asking them to do so is bad medicine.

I shall leave unexplored the question of whether patient self-determination or physician reliance on miracle, mystery, and authority are better medicine, even though I chose it as the title for my remarks. The choice was deliberate. I wanted to highlight that this question cannot be answered. All answers given so far are based on dubious data. The question will only be answered once medical scientists consider it worthy of scientific study. It is surprising and telling that such studies have not been undertaken, even though our ignorance of the answer to the question—what is the better medicine?—precludes a fuller understanding of the most significant concern in our professional work: the dynamics of cure.

I intend to demonstrate that we have to begin *de novo* and, therefore will discuss with you the ignorance, confusion, incoherence, and self-deception that underlie all the current talk about patient participation in decision making, now subsumed under the rubric of informed consent.

The confusion begins by not distinguishing between three fundamental aspects of informed consent: first, the idea of informed consent (based on the yet unproven belief that patients can play a greater role in medical decision making); second, the *legal doctrine* of informed consent (which endorses, although ambivalently, this belief); and third, *current practices* of obtaining informed consent, (still so thoroughly shaped by professional beliefs in the wisdom of delegating decision making to doctors). Physicians are instinctively aware of the confusion when they simultaneously express doubts about the idea of informed consent, complain of not knowing what to tell and what to withhold in order to comply with the legal doctrine, and profess compliance with both the idea and the legal mandate in their clinical practice.

What underlies the confusion, incoherence, and self-deception is that neither medicine nor law have taken the idea of informed consent seriously enough to answer the fundamental questions raised in the encounter between the Grand Inquisitor and his Prisoner: Are *patients* capable of giving, and willing to give, consent (the most frequently asked question); are *physicians* capable of making, and willing to make, disclosures that allow patients to give meaningful consent (a question infrequently asked); is the *science of medicine* sufficiently advanced to permit physicians to make adequate disclosures and, in turn, to obtain patient consent (a question virtually never asked).

I have been a student of informed consent for decades. One of the few *definitive* conclusions that I have come to is this: Neither its champions nor its critics sufficiently appreciate the complex nature of the problems that make informed consent so difficult to obtain. Let me mention in passing that critics of my work have overlooked that I have only championed *the idea* of informed consent, have written mainly about the obstacles that make the idea of informed consent so difficult to implement. I have not proposed an informed consent doctrine of my own. While, to the contrary, many doctors, lawyers, judges, and bio-ethicists have spoken about informed consent as if they knew what it meant either in law or in medicine, they have at best proposed *their* own doctrine. *The* doctrine cannot be discerned by looking to law or medicine.

You might be puzzled and ask: Is there not a legal doctrine of informed consent that can guide physicians' conduct? My answer is "no"; it cannot even guide judges' holdings. This is for two reasons:

First, the legal doctrine is, and always has been, in disarray. Consider its first formulation: "[I]n discussing the element of risk a certain amount of *discretion* must be employed consistent with the full *disclosure* of facts necessary to an informed consent."[3]
The disarray is, in part, a result of the existence of many legal doctrines, depending on the jurisdiction in which they were promulgated. Further, the legal doctrine attempts to reconcile conflicting interests and values in the law of torts: respect for patient self-determination and autonomy; protection of patients from "ill-considered, autonomous" decisions that "prudent" patients would not make; protection of patients from the harm of disclosure; elimination of the requirement of expert medical testimony out of fear over a "medical conspiracy" of silence; and/or the allocation of the economic cost of injurious consequences to the one most capable of bearing the cost, i.e. physicians and their insurance carriers.

Second, the legal doctrine provides little guidance to doctors as to their general lawful disclosure obligations. To be sure, law generally defines only unlawful conduct. But the legal silence on a general medical disclose standard presents a dilemma, since disclosure and consent are concepts alien to medicine, and were imposed by law on medicine. Thus, questions arise: What must physicians learn to disclose to remain true to their professional obligations and at the same time avoid legal liability? Were judges obliged to learn more about the difficulties inherent in the practice of medicine before imposing foreign concepts on a profession that has little experience with disclosure and consent? As I have said in my book *The Silent World of Doctor and Patient*

> Judicial pronouncements calling for the revelation of "any facts [necessary to] an intelligent consent" confronted courts with the staggering assignment of specifying what these facts were. They would have had to address complicated questions involving sophisticated inquiry: What are the risks and benefits of the proposed treatment

and of no treatment? Which ones did physicians have to be aware of? How much are they required to disclose? The courts were largely unwilling and unprepared to undertake this task. Instead, they retreated to the time-honored professional standard of care, which resurfaced in disguised form even in jurisdictions that had adopted the new legal rule of disclosure.[4]

The verdict is this: Courts did not delve into the complexities of medical practice to give physicians meaningful instructions about their disclosure obligations.

The incoherence created by side-stepping these questions is most clearly revealed in the division between courts which follow the *Natanson* line of reasoning, holding that "the duty of the physicians to disclose...is limited to those disclosures which a reasonable medical practitioner would make..."[5] and those which follow the *Canterbury* line of reasoning, holding that "[r]espect for the patient's right of self-determination on particular therapy demands a standard set by law for physicians..."[6] The *Natanson* court, to underscore what I have already argued, overlooked that "a reasonable physician" has significant professional and personal reservations about disclosing a great deal to patients and, more importantly, that if a professional standard for disclosure exists at all, it is one that eschews disclosure. The *Canterbury* court's opinion, calling for a legal, rather than a medical, standard for disclosure and consent, can be easily misinterpreted, unless one keeps in mind that the court only set the limits of legal liability for *non-disclosure*. The opinion provided little guidance as to the *disclosure* standards physicians must establish for themselves in order to comply with the new and alien legal mandate.

This brief assessment of the current legal status of informed consent should not diminish the symbolic significance of judges' call for patient self-determination. However much judges and physicians might continue to try to evade, side-step, and rationalize the complex questions posed by informed consent, the new doctrine prevents them from banishing certain fundamental questions completely from their consciousness: Do patients have a voice in decisions affecting their medical lives? If so, what must a physician communicate so that patients' voices will not remain hollow echoes of medical recommendations?

I now turn from law to our own practices. Before we can explore our own professional views on the nature and scope of patient participation in decision-making, we must appreciate that disclosure and consent except in the most rudimentary fashion are obligations alien to our thinking and practice. We have no experience with patient participation in decision making. We have no body of knowledge to fall back on. *De novo*, we have to begin the slow ascent from our feudal past which demanded that good patients follow doctors' orders without question.

The task that confronts us is to think deeply about the three major tensions that the implementation of the idea of sharing the burdens of decision with patients will create: The first tension is one of *authority*. Physicians throughout history have maintained that patients' needs are best served by following doctors' orders. Yet, the idea of informed consent demands joint decision-making between physician and patient, a sharing of authority. Thus the question must be posed: Should either physician, patient, or both decide?

The second tension is one of *autonomy*. Meaningful decision making implies that both parties have the capacity to make choices. This notion is contrary to ancient medical beliefs that patients, by virtue of being ill, are more like children than adults and that therefore their capacity for choice is fatally impaired. Thus the question must be posed: Can anyone but a physician decide?

The third tension is one of *uncertainty*. Meaningful decision making requires that both parties have sufficient knowledge that can be imparted and understood. Medicine's vast ignorance about the etiology and treatment of disease places difficult, and at times insurmountable, burdens on physicians: first, to sort out for themselves knowledge from ignorance and, second, to communicate in a comprehensible fashion their certainties and uncertainties to patients. Thus the question must be posed: How can anyone, either physician or patient, make an informed decision?

Time does not permit me to address the barriers to informed consent created by our traditional notions of physician authority and patient lack of autonomy. I shall limit myself, and all too briefly at that, to the problem of uncertainty. I consider uncertainty the most formidable obstacle. If we wish to make meaningful disclosures to patients and obtain their consent, we must first learn to manage uncertainty better than we have in the past. Before listing a few of the problems that uncertainty poses for physician-patient communication and decision-making, let me make one thing crystal clear: I do not want to suggest that all the issues I shall now raise deserve discussion with patients. I only want to suggest that we must clarify for ourselves *why*, in the face of uncertainty, we might wish to withhold certain information and *what* the implications of withholding information are for the informed consent process.

(1) Alvan Feinstein has noted that "at a time of potent drugs and formidable surgery, the exact effects of many therapeutic procedures are dubious and shrouded in dissension—often documented either by unquantified data of experience or by grandiose statistics whose mathematical formulations are so clinically naive that any significance is purely numerical rather than biologic."[8] Must we communicate to our patients Feinstein's doubts about therapeutic efficacy and, if so, how? If we do not, what is the meaning of informed consent?

(2) Lewis Thomas has called attention to how little we know and understand about nature, that "the only piece of scientific truth about which [we can feel] totally confident is that we are profoundly ignorant about nature."[8] At the same time, Thomas goes on to say, "we are at least facing up to [our ignorance]," and no longer need to make up "stories to fill the gap."[9] Since we are committed to the practice of scientific medicine, does this major achievement of medical science, i.e. the ability to distinguish better between medical knowledge and ignorance, oblige us to communicate both knowledge and ignorance to our patients? If we do not, what is the meaning of informed consent?

(3) We base so many of our interventions on "clinical judgment and experience," often in the absence of, or even in contradiction to, scientific proof. Must we communicate the experiential, scientifically unproven, assumptions that underlie our recommendations to our patients? If we do not, what is the meaning of informed consent?

(4) In the treatment of breast cancer, as in many other therapies, controversy exists about the relative merits of various surgical treatments, chemotherapy, radiation therapy, hormone therapy or immunotherapy, or all of these in various combinations and permutations. Must we discuss these controversies with our patients and, if so, to what extent? If we do not, what is the meaning of informed consent?

(5) Specialization affects the choice of treatment. Must specialists inform patients that other specialists may treat their diseases differently even though their preferred treatment comports with acceptable medical practice? If we do not, what is the meaning of informed consent?

(6) Personal determinants affect treatment recommendations. A dramatic example to illustrate this point emerged in the reminiscences of George Crile, Jr. He remarked how for many years he had performed only radical mastectomies, while his father had always opted for a less mutilating surgical procedure. Once Crile, Jr. appreciated the errors of his ways, he asked himself: Was the "discounting of his fathers ideas [a consequence of his] having been a rebellious child?"[10] Can we moderate these personal influences? Will "training for uncertainty" during medical school help? If we do not try to educate future physicians to manage uncertainty better, what is the future of informed consent?

(7) Physicians by-and-large prefer action to inaction, believing that errors of commission are less reprehensible than errors of omission. In the light of uncertainty about *vis medicatrix naturae*, the healing power of nature, vs. our interventions, particularly since the latter can expose patients to many iatrogenic complications, must we communicate the relative merits of interventions or delay to our patients? If we do not, what is the meaning of informed consent?

(8) Many of our interventions are elective and nonintervention is often an alternative. Must we more clearly distinguish between interventions that are elective and those that are mandatory, even when we believe that intervention is the better choice? If we do not, what is the meaning of informed consent?

(9) Time costs loom large in our reluctance to discuss uncertainty with patients. If we sacrifice information for the sake of time costs, whenever we believe that good medical care dictates taking the time, what is the meaning of informed consent?

I could go on, but I hope that I have said enough, to paraphrase Shakespeare, that there are more things in informed consent's heaven and earth than we have begun to contemplate. Hamlet, in gently chiding Horatio about his ignorance, ends by uttering the well-known words:

The time is out of joint:—O cursed spite,
That ever I was born to set it right!—
Nay, come, let's go together.[11]

Physicians generally believe that "the time is out of joint," and that informed consent is in part responsible for this state of affairs. I agree, but for a different reason. My reason is not that the world of medicine was a better one when doctors made decisions for patients. My reason is that our world is out of joint because we too are uneasy about our traditional non-disclosure practices, yet feel so at sea about how to change them, how to reconcile societal with our professional obligations. Thus, we find our current communications unsatisfactory and wanting. This makes us anxious and in turn, angry. It should. We have been asked to assume, and we have assumed, a task that we cannot as yet perform according to the high standards of caring for our patients to which we are otherwise committed.

It is our current ignorance and incapacity, but not our ultimate ignorance and incapacity that I wanted to bring to your attention. "Cursed spite" notwithstanding, perhaps our generation and the next generation of physicians were "born to set it right." "Come lets [do it] together," so that we can learn both to gain patients' trust and to trust them. Informed consent requires mutual trust. Without mutual trust it will remain a charade.

References

1. Dostoyevesky F: The Brothers Karamozov. trans. D. Magarshack, Baltimore. Penguin Books. 1958.

2. Schloendorff v New York Hospital. 211 NY 125. 1914.

3. Salgo v Leland Stanford Jr. University Board of Trustees 317 P.2d 170. 1957.

4. Katz J: The Silent World of Doctor and Patient. New York. The Free Press. 1985.

5. Natanson v Kline. 350 P.2d 1093. 1960.

6. Canterbury v Spence. 464 F.2D 772. 1972.

7. Feinstein A: Clinical Judgment. Baltimore. Williams & Wilkins Co. 1967.

8. Thomas L: The Medusa and the Snail: More Notes of a Biology Watcher. New York. Viking Press. 1979.

9. Ibid.

10. Crile G Jr: How Much Surgery for Breast Cancer? Modern Medicine. June 11 1983.

11. Shakespeare W: Hamlet. Act I, scene V.

Katz J. Informed Consent: are "miracle, mystery and authority" better medicine? Conn Med. 1986; 50(7): 457-460.

Reprinted with permission from the author and Connecticut Medicine.

Article 3.2

Malpractice Prevention Through the Sharing of Uncertainty

Thomas G. Gutheil, MD, Harold Burszatjn, MD, and Archie Brodsky, BA.
New England Journal of Medicine, July 1984.

Informed Consent and the Therapeutic Alliance

Uncertainty presents a commonly acknowledged threat to the doctor-patient alliance[1]; anxious patients seeking doctors also seek the reassurance of medical certainty. But anxiety about undiscovered causes and undetermined outcomes sets doctor and patient apart if both react defensively; even worse, anxiety over uncertainty may evoke feelings of helplessness, hopelessness, and worthlessness.

Increasingly, patients and families who experience tragic disappointments in their expectations of medicine attempt to assuage their grief, helplessness, and despair by suing—that is, blaming—the physician. In doing so, they often fail to discriminate among errors of negligence, other errors, natural variations, and acts of fate. Under the stress of life-and-death decision making, physicians also readily experience negative outcomes as blows to their sense of competence and professional pride. In the midst of such tragedy the physician is tempted to terminate the relationship, saying, "There is nothing more I can do." For the patient, then, a malpractice suit becomes the mechanism by which to force the "abandoning" physician to share both the responsibility for the outcome and—less obviously—the experience of distress and rage occasioned by suffering.[2]

Informed Consent: A Double-Edged Sword

At first sight, the informed-consent procedure seems to offer a way of ameliorating these strains. Nonetheless, physicians by and large have not welcomed informed consent. Besides viewing it as "red tape" and the imposition of a legal constraint on the exercise of professional judgment, physicians have expressed misgivings about the clinical ramifications of informed consent.[3,4]

In fact, the clinical impact of informed consent is double-edged.[5,6] Despite its positive effects of clarifying options and stimulating mutual understanding, the procedure is not without risk. It can bring to a crisis latent problems that the patient may have in accepting uncertainty--problems that can take two strikingly opposite forms.

At one extreme, calling attention to risks (especially in the chilling style of an informed-consent form) can touch off feelings of helplessness by crystallizing the patient's awareness that the situation really is uncertain. At the other extreme, the seemingly authoritative list of complications with their numerical probabilities, which lay persons have been found to desire,[7] can be used as a magical ritual to dispel the uncertainty.[8] Ironically, such an overly tidy disclosure can inflate the magical hope that "all bases have been covered," and disappointment may lead to malpractice suits. The twin dangers, then, lie in exaggerating how little or how much the physician knows.

Ideally, the clinical utility of informed consent lies in bridging the gap between either of the two fantasies—helpless ignorance or omnipotent certainty—and a more complicated reality. To achieve this goal, however, physicians must stop thinking of informed consent as a formality (the recital of options and signing of the form) and enter into it with their patients as a process of mutual discovery.[9] Informed consent as we envision it here is not an empty gesture toward liability reduction but an interaction between physician and patient, a dialogue intended not only to satisfy this legal requirement but to do more as well. The real clinical opportunity offered by informed consent is that of transforming uncertainty from a threat to the doctor-patient alliance into the very basis on which an alliance can be formed.[1] This is particularly important, since a sense of working together with the doctor may be one of the major elements in avoiding negative reactions to treatment.[10] An approach to this problem is outlined below.

PRACTICAL CONSIDERATIONS

Understand the Origins of the Patient's Fantasies of Certainty

Patients invoke wishful or magical thinking as a defense against feelings of helplessness. The fears, doubts, and actual disablement of illness reactivate memories of childhood helplessness, and, in turn, of the grandiose and magical thoughts that are virtually the child's only defense. When illness presents a threat to one's well-being—to one's very being, in fact—one attempts to resolve the discrepancy between the perception of powerlessness and the wish for omnipotence by transferring the latter to the physician. The patient says to the physician, in effect, "Okay, I am not perfect, but you will make me good as new. I cede to you the magical powers of my infantile self."[11] The patient thus forms with the physician what psychiatrists call an "irrational" or "narcissistic" alliance, in which the patient approaches the physician as child to parent rather than as adult to adult.[12] In this context the patient is simply not receptive to any disavowal of certainty on the physician's part, hearing it instead as an alienating rejection of the omnipotent, magical role scripted for the physician.

Magical notions of science play a key part in such fantasies of cure. The physician is a representative of science, which is conceived of (certainly in the unconscious but consciously in some cases) as a source of absolutely certain knowledge.[1] Unfortunately, the trust in scientific omnipotence may easily generate into paranoid distrust; the patient, already a helpless victim of illness, now feels like the helpless victim of an all-powerful science as well. If the patient is allowed to remain in this dependent state, subsequent outcomes of a disillusioning nature may lead to further regression and refusal to assume responsibility for self-monitoring and self-care or, regrettably, to litigation.

Empathize with the Patient's Unrealistic Wishes

The physician should resist what might seem the logical move of dismantling the unrealistic foundation of the narcissistic alliance by confronting it head-on; one cannot expect to take away the wishful thinking (and the resulting unhealthy attachment to the physician) without providing a different kind of comfort—and attempting a different kind of alliance—in its place.

Paradoxically, the best way to effect this substitution is to empathize with the patient's wish for certainty and with its specific manifestations as understandable human reactions to a difficult and painful situation. Explicit identification with the patient's fantasies is conveyed through such remarks as, "I wish I could give you a medication that was sure to have only positive effects" and "There is just no guarantee you'll live through this—I wish there were," which invite the patient to exchange idealization for identification. The patient can now approach the physician not as a childhood fantasy ideal but as another vulnerable human being facing—and hence, sharing—the same uncertainty. The physician is linked with the realistic, adult part of the patient in what is called a "rational" alliance, with two adults collaborating to reach a reasonable agreement based in reality. Instead of squaring off defensively against each other, doctor and patient are brought together by the shared acknowledgment of clinical uncertainty and of the fantasies to deny it.

Wean the Patient from the Fantasy of Certainty

Once the patient and physician are looking at the fantasy together, the physician can guide the patient on seeing it for what it is. Indeed, the very words used to establish the identification and alliance between patient and physician can begin the work of separating the patient from the fantasy. Expressions like "I wish it were possible...," even as they validate the wish as a wish, imply tactfully that it is contrary to fact. Clarifying statements (e.g., "Many people do believe that one can specify in advance every possible complication of an operation") offer the patient tactful support in taking a critical look at beliefs that he or she may share with "many people."[13]

Having provided this emotional and interpersonal grounding, the physician can proceed to the explicit disavowal of omnipotence and the substantive education of the patient about uncertainty. Both the implicit and explicit teaching separate the reality of human science from the fantasy of godlike science. Now the patient is a participant-observer rather than, say, simply the object of the physician's "experiment." It must be stressed, though, that this alliance and the awareness it generates rest on assurance of the physician's continuing availability to share the uncertainty—expressed, for example, in statements such as, "I'll be there for you every step of the way." Implicit in this statement is the promise of a continuing relationship, even if there is a tragic outcome. When this promise is fulfilled, the patient is less likely to feel a need to force the physician to share the experience of the misfortune by means of a malpractice suit.

Note that our approach stresses the selection of what to say to patients rather than such advice as taking more time with patients or telling them more. In practice, less time is taken and more is understood; sound efficiency of communication, not mere volume of words, is the desideratum.

Conclusion

Informed consent need not be a mere formality with a limited medicolegal function. Rather, it can be a focal point in establishing a therapeutic alliance. Seen as a dialogue in which both the cognitive and affective implications of uncertainty are acknowledged and shared, informed consent is a powerful clinical tool. Through its use, helplessness is replaced by a degree of control as the patient becomes a coexperimenter rather than a passive object of experimentation. Hopelessness is replaced by a degree of hope as the patient comes to see that uncertainty does not imply irrationality, defeat, or abandonment. Finally, the alliance between the patient and physician, instead of being undermined by the specious denial of uncertainty, is strengthened by the mutuality of its acceptance.

The legal benefits flow from the clinical ones. The usual perfunctory approach to informed consent can be characterized as a form of defensive medicine. Undertaken primarily to protect the physician from legal liability, it often fails to do even that. In contrast, the therapeutic use of informed consent to enlist the patient in an active alliance with the physician discourages overly simplistic blaming and reduces the alienation from the physician that leads the patient to seek legal remedies for dissatisfaction. This is true malpractice prevention, which offers the physician stronger legal protection by allowing both doctor and patient to deepen their understanding while building a supportive and trusting relationship—a relationship based not on unrealistic certainty but on honesty in facing the uncertainty inherent in clinical practice.

References

1. Bursztajn H, Feinbloom RI, Hamm RM, Brodsky A. Medical choices, medical chances, how patients, families, and physicians can cope with uncertainity. New York DeLacorte, 1981.

2. Day M, Semrad EV. Paranoia and paranoid states. In Nichols AM, Jr. ed. The Harvard guide to modern psychiatry. Cambridge. MA. Harvard University Press 1978:243-52.

3. Harnish v Children's Hospital Medical Center, 387 Mass. 152 (1982).

4. Ingelfinger FJ. Informed (but uneducated) consent. N Engl J Med 1972; 287:465-6.

5. Cassell EJ. Informed consent in the therapeutic relationship: clinical aspects. In Reich WT. ed Encylcopedia of bioethics, Vol. 2 New York Free Press, 1978:767-70.

6. Katz J. Informed consent in the therapeutic relationship; legal and ethical aspects. In Reich WT, ed. Enclyopedia of bioethics. Vol 2 New York Free Press, 1978:770-8.

7. Keowen C, Slovic P, Lichenstein S. Attitudes of physicians, pharmacists and laypersons toward seriousness and need for disclosure of prescription drug side effects. Eugene, Oreg., Decision Research, 1981 Report 81-6.

8. O'Keefe DL. Stolen lightning: the social theory of magic. New York Continuum, 1982:263-348.

9. Katz J. Informed consent—a fairy tale law vision. Univ of Pittsburgh Law Rev 1977; 39:137-74.

10. Egbert LD, Battit GE, Welch CE, Bartlett MK.

Reduction of postoperative pain by encouragement and instruction of patients. N Engl J Med 1964:270-825-7.

11. Freud S. On narcism, an introduction. In Riviere J. ed. Collected papers: general psychological theory. New York: Viking 1963:56-113.

12. Gutheil TG, Havens LL. The therapeutic alliance: comtemporary meanings and confusion. In: Rev Psychoanal 1979; 6:467-81.

13. Havens LL. Taking a history from the difficult patient. Lancet 1978; 1:138-40.

Gutheil et al. Malpractice prevention through the sharing of uncertainty. N Engl J Med. 1984; 311(1): 49-51.

Article 3.3

Minors' Rights to Consent to Medical Care

Angela R. Holder, LLM. Journal of the American Medical Association, June 26, 1987.

A continuing issue in the everyday practice of pediatrics is the boundary of the right of a specific child or adolescent to make decisions about his or her own health care.[1-5] Since at least the mid-seventh century in England, a minor, defined as anyone under 21 years of age, was a chattel of his or her father.[6] A father had the right to sue a physician who treated his son or daughter without his permission, even if the treatment had been perfectly appropriate, because such an intervention contravened the father's right to control the child.

The Preadolescent Child

That is still the rule with a young child in a nonacute situation. If a 3-year-old is visiting his grandmother, and she brings him to a plastic surgeon to remove a birthmark the parents had decided to leave alone, the plastic surgeon is at substantial risk of suit from the parents if he operates without parental knowledge.[7,8]

In an emergency, however, any child, no matter how young, may be treated without parental consent.[9,10] An "emergency" is defined as any condition that requires prompt treatment, and is not restricted to a condition that may cause death or disability. If a 4-year-old is brought to the emergency department by a 12-year-old baby-sitter because he has cut his foot, and immediate attempts to locate a parent are unavailing, it is perfectly legal to suture the wound. In fact, it probably would be considered negligent not to treat the child if he were left frightened and in pain in an emergency room for hours because the physicians were more concerned about their own risk of liability than the child's condition.

Angela R. Holder, LLM, is from the Office of Medicolegal Affairs and the Department of Pediatrics (Law), Yale University School of Medicine and Yale-New Haven Hospital, New Haven, Conn.

In this situation, of course, the child's medical record should include a note from the physician that details the attempts to reach a parent. If the treatment entails any consequential risk (ie, use of general anesthesia), it is also prudent to obtain a second medical opinion on the advisability of proceeding without delay, and to have that opinion noted in the chart.

Adolescents

In the more usual situation, courts in a great many contexts are permitting adolescents much more decision-making autonomy than they had historically.

Social customs have undergone significant change within the past 30 years, and teenagers are much more independent in all areas of their lives. Courts have not been unaware of this.

The Emancipated Minor

For at least the last 200 years, courts in the Anglo-American system have recognized the concept of an "emancipated minor." This means one who is living on his or her own, is self-supporting, and is not subject to parental control.

The old concepts of emancipation included minors in the military or married minors. The concept has evolved nowadays to include college students, even when parents are completely responsible for paying the bills, or unmarried minor mothers, including those who have surrendered their babies for adoption[11]—and in some states, a pregnant minor is considered completely emancipated. In all cases, an emancipated minor may be dealt with medically as an adult, and no parental permission is ever required for treatment.

Minor Treatment Statutes

Because physicians were concerned about the legality of treating teenagers, many states in the 1960s and 1970s enacted what are known as minor treatment statutes. (Readers are encouraged to consult their state or county medical society for specifics regarding the law where they practice.) These provide a specific age, usually 16 years, but maybe as young as 14 years, at which a minor, now anyone under 18 years old, may be considered completely independent for all health care purposes and treatment may be given as if he or she were an adult. Even those states that have not enacted a statute allowing a minor to consent to general medical treatment now all have statutes giving a physician the specific right to treat any minor for venereal disease without parental knowledge. Almost all states also have similar statutes permitting treatment of any minor for drug or alcohol problems without parental knowledge. Most of the venereal disease, drug, and alcohol statutes in fact forbid informing parents (presumably unless the minor consents or asks that the parent be informed). This means, of course, that the parents should not receive a bill for the child's care, since they would find out about the problem from the bill.

The Mature Minor

Even in the absence of statute, there have been no cases reported within the past 30 years in which a parent successfully sued a physician for nonnegligent care of an adolescent without the parent's knowledge.[12-14] Courts have in effect bowed to modern reality, and decisions apply what has come to be known as the "mature minor" rule. In effect, the legal principle now applied is that if a young person (aged 14 or 15 years or older) understands the nature of proposed treatment and its risks, if the physician believes that the patient can give the same degree of informed consent as an adult patient, and if the treatment does not involve very serious risks, the young person may validly consent to receiving it.[4,12-14] In determining whether allowing a particular minor to make a particular decision is reasonable, therefore, the age and maturity of the patient must be considered, and the nature of the illness and the risks of the therapy are also very relevant.[15-17] A particular 14-year-old might be perfectly capable of giving informed consent to treatment of acne; no oncologist would consider treating the same 14-year-old for leukemia without his family's knowledge. If nonemergency medical care is given without contacting parents and obtaining their consent, particularly if the procedure is completely elective, courts usually hold that the parent is not responsible for payment of the bill.[18-20] Minors themselves are, of course, liable for their own bills[21] in this circumstance, but because adolescents usually have little or no money, collection is likely to be a problem.

For economic reasons, therefore, the issue of adolescents' rights to consent on their own to medical care almost always involves questions arising in the context of outpatient care. Clinic or office visits, which usually do not involve treatment entailing major risks, may well be available to adolescents who can pay for it or for whom the physician is willing to provide free care. Admission to a hospital is, however, an entirely different situation. Whatever autonomy rights the adolescent may theoretically have, hospital admitting offices are more interested in who is going to pay the bill than in freedom to consent. Few unemancipated adolescents have hospital insurance of their own; they are insured, if at all, as dependents on their parents' policies. It is therefore most unlikely that a hospital would permit a nonemergency admission of a minor without obtaining insurance information from the policyholder-parent. Moreover, presumably, the first calls a parent would likely make when a teenager is inexplicably absent from home would be to the local hospitals. So the possibility of inpatient admission for nonemergency procedures of which the parent is unaware is quite remote, whatever theoretical right the minor might have to consent to those procedures.

Refusal of Treatment

Where there is capacity and a right to consent to treatment, one must presume that there is a corresponding capacity and right to refuse. Competent adults certainly have a universally recognized right to refuse treatment, even if it is lifesaving. While there are few, if any, cases on a minor's right to refuse treatment outside the context of abortions, it is likely that any court would rule that a minor has the right to refuse any treatment to which he has the right to consent. Thus, if a 15-year-old could present himself to an outpatient clinic and be treated for acne or a sore throat without parental permission, he could refuse to accept therapy for those same conditions if his mother brought him to the physician. In fact, the teenager's right to refuse completely elective treatment is probably greater than his or her right to consent. If, for example, a surgeon refuses to accept a teenager for plastic surgery without parental consent (which would undoubtedly be the case), even if the young person's mother brought him to the surgeon for purely cosmetic surgery, the adolescent would undoubtedly have the right to refuse if he did not wish to undergo the surgery.

On the other hand, where treatment is necessary, even if not lifesaving, there is serious doubt that a minor has the right to refuse it. If a teenager has appendicitis and his parent consents to the appendectomy, a court would not consider it battery to take the minor to the operating room against his will.

Although an adolescent and his or her family might certainly decide to stop treatment that is in effect just prolonging death and opt, as do adults, for "death with dignity," I doubt that any court would permit an adolescent to refuse treatment that is likely to be lifesaving. There are, however, no reported decisions on this point. Many 16-year-olds with bone cancer would probably think that they would rather be dead than lose a leg; assuming parental consent (or a court order if the parent backs up the patient) and an excellent prognosis for long-term remission and perhaps cure following the surgery, I doubt that any court would agree that the teenaged patient has the right to make a decision to die.

The two specific situations in which the issue of an adolescent's consent or refusal of treatment most often arises involve contraception and abortion.

The Minor and Contraception

In 1965, the US Supreme Court first struck down state statutes making the prescription or use of contraceptives a criminal offense.[22] In 1972, the court held that the constitutional right of privacy that precluded state intervention in this matter applied to unmarried adults as well as married ones.[23] In 1977, the Court considered a New York statute that made it a criminal offense to sell nonprescription contraceptives to minors and held that minors do have a right of privacy that extends to contraception.[24]

In that opinion, Mr. Justice Stevens wrote in his concurring opinion about the use of the legal system to enforce what someone thinks is "proper" conduct by young people:

> Although the state may properly perform a teaching function, it seems to me that an attempt to persuade by inflicting harm on the listener is an unacceptable means of conveying a message that is otherwise legitimate...
> It is as though a State decided to dramatize its disapproval of motorcycles by forbidding the use of safety helmets. One need not posit a constitutional right to ride a motorcycle to characterize such a restriction as irrational and perverse.[14]

Title X of the Public Health Service Act of 1970 has a provision stipulating that federally funded family planning agencies are required to provide services without regard to age or marital status.[25] On Jan 26, 1983, however, the US Department of Health and Human Services published regulations requiring federally funded family planning facilities to notify a minor's parents within ten days of her visit to the facility that she had been given contraceptives. This "squeal rule" had provoked more than 120,000 comments when published as proposals in 1982. The regulations were scheduled to take effect in February 1983, but in one suit filed by New York State and another filed by Planned Parenthood in the District of Columbia, both courts found the regulations unconstitutional.[26-29]

From these decisions, it is now clear that an adolescent who requests contraception has a constitutional right to have it if she is seeking it at a federally funded facility. A private physician has the right to refuse to provide it, but if the girl is a regular patient, he or she may have an obligation to refer her to Planned Parenthood or a public clinic.

The Minor and Abortion

The Supreme Court, of course, in 1973 struck down state laws making abortion a criminal offense.[30,31] The court held that statutory restrictions on first-trimester abortions were unconstitutional, except that, like any other surgical procedure, it was legitimate to require that they be performed by a licensed physician. As soon as those cases were decided, many states enacted statutes requiring parental consent before a minor could obtain an abortion. In a series of cases, the Supreme Court held that statutes that required parental consent without any alternative procedures to determine the girl's capacity to decide for herself—thus giving parents an absolute veto over this decision—was an unconstitutional violation of the girl's right of privacy.[32-38]

What the Supreme Court seems to have done is to hold that state statutes will be constitutionally acceptable if they provide that if a girl does not choose to involve her family in this decision, she must have access to a judge, whose role is limited to a determination that she is mature enough to make the decision about abortion for herself.

In states where there is no statute, adolescents may consent to abortion as they may do as "mature minors" to any other procedure.

Where there is doubt in the physician's mind about the young adolescent's capacity to understand and to give informed consent to an abortion, presumably there is no alternative to parental notification. However, many physicians and social workers have reported to me anecdotal evidence that leads them to believe that a great many (perhaps most) pregnant 12- and 13-year-olds (and perhaps 14-year-olds) are victims of incest and/or sexual abuse within the household or extended family; they are not participants in sexual relationships, however misguided, with age-appropriate boyfriends. Since reporting the pregnancy to the parent in this situation can put the girl at great risk of harm, anyone presented with such a situation should make very careful, nonthreatening inquiries into the circumstances. It may become evident that regardless of the issue of pregnancy or abortion, child abuse agencies may need to become involved on an emergency basis.

While many teenagers may respond to inquiries about parental discussion with the statement, "If my father finds out I'm pregnant, he'll kill me," and while such a statement is presumably almost always adolescent hyperbole, in some cases it may not be. Thus, in situations where the physician is confronted with a very young (chronologically or developmentally) girl who wants an abortion, even if the physician has some doubts about the girl's abilities to understand the situation, the choice may be between proceeding with the abortion or putting the patient at risk of brutality or being told to leave the home.

The converse situation is the one in which a mother brings her pregnant teenager to a gynecologist because she thinks the girl should have an abortion, but the girl wants to have and keep her baby. There are few decisions on this issue, because gynecologists usually will not consider (court order or not) performing an abortion on someone who does not want one. Thus, few parents have bothered to seek court orders in these cases, but all courts that have considered the matter have concluded that the same right to privacy that allows a woman to conclude that she wants an abortion will protect an adolescent's decision to give birth.[39,40]

Conclusion

Adolescents are, in all aspects of our society, allowed to have much more freedom than was the case when their parents were the same age. Colleges and even boarding schools no longer consider their role to be one of in loco parentis. Adolescents are invited to sign up for charge accounts or credit cards, sometimes without parental consent; teenagers are getting pregnant at the rate of more than 1 million a year in this country and 400,000 of those have abortions[41]; and in all aspects of their lives, adolescents are engaging in more "adult" behaviors than many of the health care professionals caring for them would have believed possible during their own adolescent years. The courts and legislatures of this country have not been unmindful of these societal changes, and there is a definite trend toward allowing adolescents more freedom to make decisions, and to exercise autonomy and self-determination in their relationships with health care providers and with others in the social system.

References

1. Holder AR: Legal Issues in Pediatrics and Adolescent Medicine, ed 2. New Haven, Conn, Yale University Press, 1985, chap 5.

2. Gaylin W, Macklin R (eds): Who Speaks for the Child? The Problem of Proxy Consent. New York, Plenum Publishing Corp, 1982.

3. Morrissey JM, Hofmann AD, Thrope JC: Consent and Confidentiality in the Health Care of Children and Adolescents: A Legal Guide. New York, Free Press, 1986.

4. Munson CF: Toward a standard of informed consent by the adolescent in medical treatment decisions, 8 Dickenson Law Rev 431, 1981.

5. Melton GB, Koocher GP, Saks MJ: Children's Competence to Consent. New York, Plenum Publishing Corp, 1983.

6. Pollock F, Maitland FW: The History of English Law, ed 2. Washington, DC, Lawyers' Literary Club, 1859, p 436.

7. Bonner v Moran, 126 F2d 121 (DC Cir 1941).

8. Zaman v Schultz, 19 PaD&C 309 (1933).

9. Luka v Lowrie, 136 NW 1106 (Mich 1912).

10. Sullivan v Montgomery, 279 NYS 575 (NY 1935).

11. Bach v Long Island Jewish Hospital, 267 NYS2d 289 (NY 1966).

12. Carter v Cangello, 164 Cal Rptr 361 (Cal 1980).

13. Younts v St Francis Hospital and School of Nursing, 469 P2d 330 (Kan 1970).

14. Lacey v Laird, 139 NE2d 25 (Ohio 1956).

15. Wadlington W: Minors and health care: The age of consent. 11 Osgood Hall Law J 115, 1978.

16. Hofmann AD, Pilpel HF: The legal rights of minors. Pediatr Clin North Am 1973;20:1001.

17. Rait GE Jr: The minor's right to consent to medical treatment. 48 So Cal Law Rev 1417, 1975.

18. Accent Service Company v Ebsen, 306 NW2d 575 (Neb 1981).

19. Poudre Valley Hospital District v Heckart, 491 P2d 984 (Colo 1971).

20. Ison v Florida Sanitarium and Benevolent Association, 302 So2d 200 (Fla 1974).

21. Cidis v White, 336 NYS2d 362 (NY 1972).

22. Griswold v Connecticut, 381 US 479 (1965).

23. Eisenstadt v Baird, 405 US 438 (1972).

24. Carey v Population Services International, 431 US 678 (1977).

25. Public Health Service Act, 42 USC §§ 300-300a(8) (1970).

26. Planned Parenthood of America v Schweiker, 559 FSupp 658 (DDC), aff'd, 712 F2d 650 (DC Cir 1983).

27. State of New York v Schweiker, 557 FSupp 354 (SD NY 1983).

28. Memphis Association for Planned Parenthood v Schweiker, DC Tenn Civil No. 83-2060, temporary injunction granted Feb 24, 1983.

29. Hosek N: Minors' rights of privacy: Access to contraceptives without parental notification. 7 J Juvenile Law 99, 1984.

30. Roe v Wade, 410 US 113 (1973).

31. Doe v Bolton, 410 US 179 (1973).

32. Bellotti v Baird, 424 US 952 (1976).

33. Bellotti v Baird II, 443 US (1979).

34. Planned Parenthood Association of Missouri v Danforth, 428 US 52 (1976).

35. H.L. v Matheson, 450 US 398 (1981).

36. City of Akron v Akron Center for Reproductive Health, 462 US 416 (1983).

37. Planned Parenthood of Kansas City, Missouri v Ashcroft, 462 US 476 (1983).

38. Buchanan E: The Constitution and the anomaly of the pregnant teenager. 24 Ariz Law Rev 553, 1982.

39. In re Smith, 295 A2d 238 (Md 1972).

40. In the Matter of Mary P., 444 NYS2d 545 (NY 1981).

41. Panel on Adolescent Pregnancy and Childbearing, National Research Council: Risking the Future: Adolescent Sexuality, Pregnancy and Childbearing. Washington, DC, National Academy Press, 1987, p 1.

Holder AR. Minors' rights to consent to medical care. JAMA. 1987; 257(24): 3402.

Reprinted with permission from the author and the American Medical Association.

Article 3.4

Informed Consent and Incompetent Medical Patients

Mark R. Munetz, MD, Charles W. Lidz, PhD, and Alan Meisel, JD.
The Journal of Family Practice, March 1985.

The mentally incapacitated patient is frequently encountered in the general medical hospital. Incapacity is the clinical state in which a patient is unable to participate in a meaningful way in medical decisions. Mentally incapacitated patients relinquish the authority, that is the competent patient's right, to choose among professionally acceptable alternative treatments. Such patients, therefore, require a surrogate decision-maker. There are certain clinical situations in which questions of incapacity are especially important to consider. In a study for the President's Commission for the Study of Ethical Problems in Medical Biomedical and Behavioral Research, the most common problem in recognizing incapacity was found with previously capable patients who became transiently incapacitated during the course of hospitalization. Questions of incapacity or the authority of surrogate decision-makers also arose with comatose, mentally retarded, mentally ill, and physically handicapped patients. While standards to determine capacity remain unclear, a practical approach is to demonstrate that a patient is able to describe the physician's view of the situation and to understand the physician's opinion as to the best intervention. When a patient is deemed to be incapacitated, the physician should turn to family members, whenever possible, to make decisions.

While much has been written about the problem of informed consent with psychiatric patients,[1,2,3] there is relatively little written about the mentally incapacitated patient in the general medical setting. Yet the mentally incapacitated patient is not a rarity in the general medical hospital. In a recent study for the President's Commission for the Study of Ethical Problems in Medical Biomedical and Behavioral Research (PCEMR),[4] the authors intensively observed the interaction between staff and patients on a general surgery and a cardiology service of a teaching hospital. Patients were also interviewed in depth about their understanding of their illness and treatment. It was found that questions about competency were or might have been raised in 13 of 101 cases. Despite this surprisingly large proportion of questionably competent patients, medical staff paid little attention to questions of incompetency and how it affected patients' participation in medical decision-making.

The concept of competency plays a central role in the legal and ethical doctrine of informed consent, the doctrine that allocates authority to make decisions about health care within the physician-patient relationship. Patients are presumed to be competent and thus to possess ultimate authority to choose among professionally acceptable alternative treatments or even to reject treatment altogether. However, patients who are legally incompetent because they are "mentally incapacitated" or, more properly, because they lack "decisional capacity" relinquish this authority over decision-making and require that another person (a surrogate) be appointed to make their health care decisions. Not only does the informed consent doctrine promote patient autonomy in decision-making, it also seeks to encourage that the decisions the patients do make are rational ones. If a patient's reasoning is seriously impaired, this goal of informed consent is undermined. For the physician who seeks to comply with legal and ethical mandates while still promoting a patient's best health interests, the incompetent patient can present a serious clinical problem.

This paper, based on data from the PCEMR study, describes common clinical situations involving patients with impaired decision-making capacity in the general medical hospital. Case vignettes from observations are also reviewed to highlight some of the more common problems and misconceptions in this area. Finally, some general guidelines on the assessment of incompetency and the management of decision-making with incompetent patients are suggested.

The Informed Consent Doctrine

The informed consent doctrine has evolved over the past three decades to promote society's interest in the dual values of individual autonomy and personal health. The doctrine encourages active patient participation in medical decision-making and holds physicians liable for patient injuries if they have failed to obtain valid informed consent for a diagnostic or therapeutic intervention.

The informed consent doctrine envisions that decisions about health care are to be made through the joint efforts of health care professionals and patients. Professionals contribute technical information about therapeutic possibilities—treatment options, the risks and benefits of those options, the nature and purpose of the procedures, and any other information that would be relevant to making a decision. Health care professionals also contribute professional judgment and serve as advisors to patients. Patients, however, are entitled to make the final decisions. To do this, they apply their own personal values, goals, and beliefs to the technical information and advice that they receive from health care professionals and other such information that they may already have acquired. Patients ask questions, seek advice from professionals (and possibly family and friends), and then decide, or possibly decide that someone else such as a physician or a spouse should make the decision.

There are four exceptions when disclosure of information or consent is not required: the emergency, the therapeutic privilege (whereby the physician withholds information based on his belief that disclosure would be harmful to the patient), the waiver (whereby the patient elects to forego disclosure or decision-making), and incompetency.[5] While the focus of this paper is on the incompetency exception, there frequently is overlap with the other three exceptions.

Distinguishing Legal Incompetency and Clinical Incapacity—Defining Terms

Discussion and understanding of the role that the concept of incompetency plays in health care decision-making are complicated by the vagueness of some of the terms used in the discussion and by the lack of agreement on the meaning of many of the terms.

At the outset, there is the meaning of the term *incompetency* itself. Technically, incompetency is a legal term referring to a determination by a court, that is, an adjudication that a person lacks the capacity to make a particular kind of decision. The consequence of an adjudication of incompetency is that the person adjudicated incompetent loses the legal authority to make decisions for himself. Adjudications of incompetency may be general or specific. In general incompetency the individual is globally incapacitated so that he or she is unable to make even basic decisions about everyday life. Inability to make medical decisions is only one aspect of the generally incompetent person's disability. Specific incompetency may occur, as the term suggests, regarding a specific medical decision in an individual otherwise competent to manage his or her affairs. Henceforth, the term *incompetency* will refer only to a legal state, and the terms *limited capacity* and *incapacity* will refer to the clinical state in which a patient is unable to participate in a meaningful way in medical decisions.

Whether a person is adjudicated generally or specifically incompetent, the basis for the determination is some sort of deficiency in the person's decision-making process. The source of the deficiency may be a physical handicap (such as deafness), an intellectual deficiency (mental retardation), a mental illness, substance abuse, or a medical illness (such as delirium). There is, however, no one-to-one correspondence between any of these kinds of impairments and legal incompetency. Rather, the determining factor is the extent to which the patient's impairment affects his ability to make decisions.

Finally, there is no agreed-upon set of criteria for ascertaining whether a person lacks decision-making capacity; nor are there any accepted tests that can be administered to a patient to determine capacity. Discussion of these matters so far has been largely confined to scholarly journals; neither courts nor legislatures nor other law-making bodies seem to be aware of these issues, or if they are, they prefer to disregard them.

These difficulties make the clinician's situation, when confronted with a possibly incompetent patient, even more difficult. Legally, all patients are presumed to be competent unless otherwise adjudicated. Judges, not physicians, have the legal duty to determine incompetency. While only a few patients in general medical settings are legally adjudicated incompetent, many are limited in their capacity to make medical decisions. It is the physician's duty to recognize incapacity prior to accepting a patient's consent to or refusal of treatment because the legal validity of a consent or refusal of an incapacitated patient is questionable.

Clinical Presentations of Possibly Incapacitated Patients

The following different types of presentations provide examples of typical ways in which incapacitated patients present themselves in a university-based teaching hospital. Case vignettes illustrate some typical problems and misconceptions that arise when dealing with patients of limited capacity.

Comatose Patients

A comatose patient is the clearest example of an individual who can be considered generally incapacitated. As with a severely retarded individual or a patient with profound organic brain syndrome, there is little doubt that a comatose patient is unable to make informed decisions. In these cases, a surrogate decision-maker must be obtained. The following case vignette illustrates the appropriate use of a surrogate decision-maker for a comatose patient but also points out the limitations on the authority of a surrogate to make decisions.

Case I: The Limits of Surrogate Consent

Mr. A. was an 89-year-old married man admitted to the hospital in a coma with a diagnosis of ischemic bowel disease. Immediate surgery was recommended, albeit hesitantly, because of his medical status. His wife was consulted, and she refused to grant permission for the surgery because she believed that her husband was terminally ill and she preferred that he die in peace. The surgeon honored her decision without argument. Unexpectedly Mr. A. improved with medical treatment alone and awoke from his coma long enough for some discussion with his wife. At that point Mrs. A. requested that the surgeon proceed with surgery. By then, however, the surgeon viewed surgery as too risky and agreed to operate only if certain specific complications arose in the future. Mrs. A. readily agreed to this plan. Mr. A. died a short time later.

There was no difficulty in this case in assessing incapacity. Nor was there difficulty in designating a surrogate decision-maker. The case highlights an important issue, however. Although a competent patient or an appropriate surrogate decision-maker is usually entitled to refuse an intervention, rarely can either insist that an active intervention be undertaken if it is one to which the physician is opposed.[5] In this case the surrogate went along with the physician's decision not to proceed with surgery, just as earlier the surgeon respected the surrogate's decision to refuse that intervention. If a conflict had arisen, the surrogate could have sought or been referred to another physician. Alternatively, review of the conflict before a hospital committee or a court might have been appropriate.[6]

Transient Incapacity

It is common for severely ill patients to lose full control over their mental functioning transiently. Medications that affect the central nervous system, such as narcotic analgesics, sedatives, or hypnotics, are commonly prescribed in hospitals and may cause transient incapacity. Patients may also suffer various insults to their central nervous system as part of the disease process itself. Thus, previously capable persons may be temporarily limited in their capacity to participate in decision-making during the course of treatment. If transient incapacity is not recognized, inappropriate decision-making can result. The following case illustrates how easy it is to miss transient incapacity.

Case 2: Transient Incapacity

Mr. B., a 66-year-old man, was treated in the coronary care unit (CCU) for a myocardial infarction. He was doing well and, in part because he pressed for it, was transferred out of the unit to a regular room. The next day he experienced severe chest pains and what turned out to be a second myocardial infarction. During the acute episode, Mr. B. was alert and helpful to the physicians in assessing his condition. Because he was in severe pain, he was given a considerable amount of morphine. Three days later, while he was recovering in the coronary care unit, it was discovered that he had no memory of the events prior to the second myocardial infarction. He even forgot being transferred from the CCU back to the floor and back again to the CCU. Yet, at no time was the clinical staff aware of any compromise in Mr. B.'s mental function.

Whether the memory loss resulted from the stress of a myocardial infarction or from heavy doses of morphine, it is likely that there was a period of time when Mr. B. would not have been a fully capable decision-maker. Indeed, his loss of memory was probably instrumental in his repeated requests to be allowed to go home prematurely. Yet, as is common with so many cases in the hospital, the alteration in Mr. B.'s mental capacity was not noticed, or at least not attended to, by the treating staff.

The Mentally Retarded

Mentally retarded patients require careful assessment to determine their capacity to participate in decision-making. Such an assessment, however, should not consist simply of evaluating the patient's intelligence quotient but should consider the complexity of the decision at hand with a careful assessment of the patient's sense of personal autonomy and experience making like decisions.[6]

Mrs. C. was a 54-year-old widow admitted to the hospital for a partial resection of the bowel. She had a previous diagnosis of mental retardation, but lived in the community with her daughter and son-in-law. Mrs. C.'s daughter functioned as a surrogate decision-maker in all matters. Indeed although Mrs. C. was perfectly willing to be interviewed for the purposes of the study, she insisted that the interviewer discuss the matter with her daughter. Her daughter also discussed all of Mrs. C.'s medical care with the surgeon and the house staff. Mrs. C. was told only what would happen next and asked to assent. Although this approach was consistent with the patient's ordinary procedure for decision-making, it did not solve all problems. For example, Mrs. C's medical condition caused her surgeon to consider the possibility of a temporary colostomy. She repeatedly stated that she did not want "the bag." The surgeon promised that he would do his best and was therefore pleased when a colostomy proved unnecessary. Nonetheless, Mrs. C. complained bitterly that she had to have "the bag" and was not very cooperative. Only several days later, during an interview with her, was it learned that she had not understood anything about the potential colostomy and had used "bag" to refer to the Foley catheter about which she was now upset.

The case points out that discussion of treatment with patients serves more than just legal and ethical functions. That Mrs. C. could not give informed consent did not mean that there was no need to explain, in very simple terms, the consequences of the operation. For the mentally retarded patient with a limited ability to make decisions and to understand medical problems, a good model might be that of recent regulation concerning children's participation in research.[7] In these cases, the surrogate decision-maker is the one to consent and the patient is only required to "assent," i.e., to agree to the procedure.

Mental Illness and Emotional Problems

Patients with psychiatric problems or diagnoses also need careful assessment of their decision-making ability, but like everyone else, should be assumed capable until proven otherwise. The mere fact of a history of a psychiatric disorder is not evidence that an individual is incompetent to decide about medical treatment or even psychiatric treatment.[8] Even active psychosis is not such evidence. As is always the case, the determinative issue is the patient's ability to make a specific decision, not the patient's mental health.[1]

Nonetheless, a high index of suspicion of incapacity should be maintained for patients with severe psychiatric symptoms. Two patients with long-standing significant psychiatric illness were observed during the course of the PCEMR study, one patient with chronic schizophrenia and the other with a bipolar affective disorder. Neither exhibited acute psychotic symptoms at the times that they were seen for their physical problems, and although neither patient seemed to understand particularly well the nature of the treatment they were receiving, there was no reason to believe that they lacked substantial capacity to understand.

A particularly thorny problem occurs when a patient's mental status interferes with his ability to make rational decisions despite maintaining full intellectual capacity. The following case illustrates this difficulty along with several other clinical problems.

Case 4: Irrational but Capable Refusal

Mr. D., a 61-year-old married man, was admitted to the coronary care unit following a cardiac arrest. During the first week in the hospital he was intermittently disoriented and agitated, presumably from anoxic brain injury, and had to be physically restrained. The basis for his confusion was explained to his wife, and her help in reorienting him was enlisted, but all treatment decisions were made by the medical team. Despite continued hypoxia secondary to aspiration pneumonia, Mr. D.'s delirium slowly resolved. However, he remained a difficult patient to manage as he repeatedly removed his oxygen mask and began requesting discharge.

Eleven days after admission, the medical staff began trying to explain his condition to him so that they could obtain permission to perform a cardiac catheterization. The patient stated that he understood the procedure but four days later vehemently refused the catheterization or to consider future surgery. Despite vigorous attempts by his physician and his wife to convince him of the seriousness of his condition and the need for the test, Mr. D. insisted on discharge. The patient was interviewed at the time of his discharge "against medical advice," and it was learned that his confusional syndrome had cleared and that he knew where he was and what he was doing. However, he did not demonstrate an understanding of the seriousness of his heart condition and seemed to be denying that he had had a myocardial infarction.

Although Mr. D.'s delirium had cleared at the time of discharge and there was no clear evidence of incapacity, still his demand to be discharged and his refusal of the catheterization was irrationally based on a denial of the seriousness of his illness. From the clinical point of view, such patients should be offered as much help as possible, including psychiatric consultation, to help them deal psychologically with their illness so that they are free to make rational decisions. Still it is important to note that Mr. D.'s physicians were correct in interpreting the informed consent doctrine. It is well accepted that bad judgment as such does not constitute incompetency. As frustrating as it may be to clinicians, all individuals are entitled to make bad judgments.[6]

The Physically Handicapped

Some physical difficulties may cause special problems for patients' participation in medical decision-making. For the physically handicapped, these problems may be more formal than substantive. For example, communications between physicians and deaf patients may be difficult, and blind patients are not able to read ordinary consent forms. There is an obvious need to alter the informed consent process for such patients. Blind patients must, of course, have someone read them the consent form if a consent form is used. Deaf patients may cause a more serious problem because of their difficulty in asking questions. A translator should be provided for speakers of American Sign Language or other means of establishing a dialogue should be developed. There is no reason, however, to remove the ultimate decision from the hands of the patient.

Assessing Capacity to Decide

It is probably easier to assess the capacity of individual patients to make decisions than it is to set standards for each assessment. The physician may well sympathize with former Supreme Court Justice Potter Stewart, who, wrestling with the problem of developing a standard for obscenity, opined that he could not develop a clear rule but "I know it when I see it."[9]

It is not the physician's role to assess legal incompetency. The physician is responsible, however, for assessing a patient's capacity to provide informed consent to or refusal of treatment. A variety of standards have been proposed to help the clinician assess incapacity. Unfortunately there is no authoritative law to guide in the selection of a test.

Appelbaum and Roth[10] have proposed four standards for judging capacity: (1) the ability to evidence a choice about treatment, (2) the capacity to have a factual understanding of the information that the average patient would consider material to making the health care decision in question, (3) the ability to rationally manipulate the information, and (4) the capacity to appreciate the nature of the specific situation.

While Appelbaum and Roth suggest that these standards can be arranged in a hierarchy, with the exception of "evidencing a choice," it is not clear that they can be easily ranked from less to more stringent. Rather than viewing each standard as a hierarchically arranged criterion for competency, it is probably better to view them as four components of competency. The ideally competent patient then would show ability in all of these areas; he would be able to evidence a choice, to understand factually the information disclosed to him, to manipulate the information rationally, and to apply it to his own situation.

Just how well a patient must do on each of these components is not established in law. Presumably, the nature of the clinical situation should determine how stringent the criteria for determining incapacity should be. The physician should increase the stringency of his criteria for determining decision-making capacity with the increasing riskiness or intrusiveness of the proposed intervention.[6] High-risk interventions demand clearly capable decision-makers.

While the search for a single, simple test of incapacity may be futile, certain practical suggestions may be made. For example, a patient may be viewed as capable of making decisions if he or she is able to describe, although not necessarily to accept the physician's view of the situation and understands the physicians's option as to the best intervention. For example, in Case 4, Mr. D. would not be considered incapacitated if he were able to say that his physician thought he had a heart problem requiring cardiac catheterization. That Mr. D. himself did not believe that he had a serious heart condition and would not consider the proposed procedure would not, in and of itself, constitute evidence of incapacity.

It cannot be too strongly emphasized that incapacity is a clinical state that should be assessed for each patient prior to his participation in medical decision-making. While it is tempting to consider incapacity only when patients refuse treatment or diagnostic intervention, it is equally important to consider whether a patient who consents to treatment has the capacity to do so. Such determinations can be easily made in most cases and do not impose an inordinate burden on the physician. The important issue is that clinicians consider the possibility of incapacity for each patient, not that they devote a great deal of time to its routine assessment.

As described above, patients with physical handicaps, intellectual deficits, or psychiatric illness should be assessed carefully for possible incapacity, even though they too must be presumed capable until proven otherwise. Patients with acute illnesses that can affect the central nervous system or who are medicated with central nervous system depressants should have their capacity assessed repeatedly over time. The most common error observed in the PCEMR study was a failure to consider that a previously fully capable patient might have become temporarily incapacitated as a result of either his treatment or his underlying illness. Finally, the possibility of incapacity should be especially carefully evaluated in patients for whom major intrusive or risky interventions are being proposed.[6] From a practical point of view, it is more important for incapacity to be recognized prior to consent for open heart surgery than for a routine chest roentgenogram.

Decision-Making for Patients Who Are Mentally Incapacitated

When a patient does not possess the capacity to make health care decisions for himself, someone else—a surrogate—must make the decisions on his behalf. Only in an emergency, when there is not time to consult with the surrogate without seriously endangering the patient's life or health, is this authority conferred upon the attending physicians. It has been customary in the medical profession to turn to close family members when patients lacked decisional capacity, although only occasionally have positive laws recognized familial authority to make health care decisions for other family members (with the exception of minor children). The express denial to family members of the authority to make such decisions is, however, quite rare. In general, therefore, physicians should turn to family members to make decisions for patients who lack decisional capacity or whose capacity is in doubt.

There are, however, situations in which the presumption that family members should decide can be overcome. If a surrogate makes a decision known to be contrary to a patient's wishes expressed while competent, the surrogate's authority should be called into question. Similarly, a decision clearly not in the best interests of the patient, but one that favors the selfish interests of the surrogate or some other party besides the patient should not be automatically honored. Finally, a surrogate who himself lacks capacity to make decisions should not be permitted to make binding health care decisions for a patient.[6] In cases in which the surrogate's authority is questionable, health care providers have a responsibility not merely to ignore the decision of the surrogate and substitute their own judgment, but to seek some sort of impartial review both of the surrogate's authority and of the decision. Unfortunately, in many jurisdictions the only available impartial review is the judicial system, which is often slow and expensive. Increasingly, though still almost imperceptibly, health care institutions have begun to create internal review committees to deal with such situations, a solution the PCEMR strongly endorsed.[6]

The absence of family members (or close friends) to act on behalf of incompetent patients also poses increasingly frequent and serious problems. In the absence of family, the medical custom is to administer routine medically indicated treatments and diagnostic procedures to patients who lack decisional capacity without seeking the judicial appointment of a surrogate. Where procedures involving substantial risk must be undertaken, however, a court-appointed surrogate should be sought and obtained. As a practical matter, this can be time consuming, expensive, and difficult—difficult because it is often impossible to find someone to act as the surrogate for the patient.

Conclusions

The patient of limited capacity is frequently encountered in the general medical hospital. Physicians, however, often are not aware of their patients' limitations as informed decision-makers and seem not to have a clear understanding of the informed consent doctrine and its exceptions.

This paper has tried to clarify how the informed consent doctrine is to be applied to patients with limited capacity. Its goal has not been to make physicians competent as lawyers but rather to help them better perform their clinical role. Toward this end some of the typical problems in both understanding and implementing the informed consent doctrine have been illustrated and some broad guidelines have been offered for managing decision-making with patients of limited capacity in the medical setting.

Acknowledgment

This work was supported in part by a grant from the President's Commission for the Study of Ethical Problems in Medical Biomedical and Behavioral Research, and by the National Institute of Mental Health.

References

1. Meisel A: Making mental health care decisions: informed consent and involuntary civil commitment. Behav Sci Law 1983; 1:73-88

2. Roth LH: Involuntary civil commitment: The right to treatment and the right to refuse treatment. Psychiatr Ann 1977; 7:245-257

3. Barnhart BA, Pinkerton JL Roth RT: Informed consent to organic behavior control. Santa Clara Lawyer 1977; 17:39-83

4. Lidz CW, Meisel A: Informed consent and the structure of medical care. In President's Commission for the Study of Ethical Problems in Medicine and Biomedical and Behavioral Research: Making Health Care Decisions: The Ethical and Legal Implications of Informed Consent in the Patient-Practitioner Relationship. Government Printing Office, 1982, vol 2, pp 317-410

5. Meisel A: The "exceptions" to informed consent: Striking a balance between competing values in medical decision-making. Wisconsin Law Rev 1979; 1979:413-488

6. President's Commission for the Study of Ethical Problems in Medicine and Biomedical and Behavioral Research: Making Health Care Decisions: The Ethical and Legal Implications of Informed Consent in the Patient-Practitioner Relationship. Washington, DC, Government Printing Office, 1982

7. Department of Health and Human Services: Additional protections for children involved as subjects in research. Federal Register 1983;48 (March 8):9814-9820

8. Rogers v Okin, 478 F Supp 1342, 1361 (D. Mass, 1979)

9. Jacobellis v Ohio, 378 US 184 (1964) Stewart J. concurring)

10. Appelbaum PS, Roth LH: Competency to consent to research: A psychiatric overview. Arch Gen Psychiatry 1982; 39:951-958

Munetz MR, et al. Informed consent and incompetent medical patients. J Fam Pract. 1985; 20(3): 273-279.

Reprinted with permission from the authors and The Journal of Family Practice.

Article 3.5

Two Models of Implementing Informed Consent

Charles W. Lidz, PhD, Paul A. Appelbaum, MD, and Alan Meisel, JD.
Archives of Internal Medicine, June 1988.

The doctrine of informed consent has been controversial since its inception. In spite of the professed ideal of improving physician-patient communication, many commentators have argued that it interferes with the relationship. However, the problem may not be the doctrine itself but rather the manner in which it is usually implemented. This article describes two different ways in which informed consent can be implemented. The event model treats informed consent as a procedure to be performed once in each treatment course, which must cover all legal elements at that time. The process model, in contrast, tries to integrate informing the patient into the continuing dialogue between physician and patient that is a routine part of diagnosis and treatment. We suggest that the process model has many benefits.

Since the concept of "informed consent" was first used in 1957,[1] it has become central to both legal and ethical regulation of American medicine, and much of the new subdiscipline of bioethics has been built around it.[2-5] The legal doctrine of informed consent specifies that physicians should disclose to patients all information "material" to making a decision whether to undergo or forgo a proposed treatment or diagnostic procedure. Thus, physicians must disclose the nature, purpose, risks, benefits, and alternatives of the proposed treatment. The patient is then allowed to consent to or refuse this recommendation.[6]

In contrast, the ethical "idea of informed consent," developed largely by theorists from underlying values and goals that informed consent is intended to promote, contemplates that patients should collaborate with physicians in developing and evaluating treatment options, with patients having a veto over any proposed treatment.[7,8] Both legal and ethical commentators have argued that informed consent will produce many benefits, ranging from a reduction in medical mistakes to greater compliance with treatment.[9-11]

In spite of its enthusiastic reception in bioethics and law, the doctrine's reception in medical circles has been mixed. Many have noted that the legal requirements have led to few positive changes in the physician-patient relationship.[12,13] Indeed, both empirical research and clinical observations indicated that informed consent often becomes an empty ritual in which patients are presented with complex information that they cannot understand and that has little impact on their decision making.[14,15] Many see informed consent as directly interfering with the care of patients by wasting valuable time and leading patients to reject medically desirable care.[16,17]

While some elements of this critique are legitimate, we suggest that the problem lies not so much in the idea of informed consent, or even in its legal requirements, as in its *implementation* in the clinical setting. This article contrasts two models of implementing informed consent. Although both of these models may satisfy the legal requirement and thereby provide some protection against suit, their effects on physician-patient relationships are quite different. Clinicians employing the first model approach the task of obtaining informed consent as an event that occurs at a single point in time. We refer to this as the *event model* of obtaining informed consent. The second model treats informed consent as an integral and continuous part of the relationship between patients and physicians embedded in the treatment process. For this reason, we call it the *process model.*

Consent as an Event

The event model of informed consent treats medical decision making as a discrete act that takes place in a circumscribed period of time, usually shortly before the administration of treatment, and emphasizes the provision of information to patients at that time. Physicians are expected to provide patients with material information about treatment and then allow patients to decide whether to accept their recommendations.

The event model emphasizes the importance of complete, accurate information and thus satisfies most legal requirements. The law of informed consent has also focused on the validity and comprehensiveness of the disclosure and has shied away from evaluating such considerations as whether patients actually understand the disclosure.[5,6] The consent form, with its detailed recital of risks and benefits, can be seen as the central symbol of the event model.

Implementation of the event model contains little process. Consent begins when the "time to get consent" arrives and the physician introduces the consent form and lists the risks of treatment. Anything said prior to this point is usually considered irrelevant to consent. Anything that is said after the form is signed is also irrelevant. In the event model, informed consent is not directly concerned with improving the quality of the decision-making process or the patient's comprehension of treatment; rather, the emphasis is on the physician's provision of the information that a hypothetically rational person would want.

The event model has several advantages. First, it provides both physicians and patients with a clear idea of their responsibilities and privileges. Moreover, except for the form signing, informed consent does not interfere with the ordinary relationship between physician and patient. Also, the consent form is a clear-cut document for the attorneys to use in the event of litigation; a well-crafted consent form may provide some protection for physicians against a lawsuit claiming that informed consent was not obtained.

Finally, the event model fits easily into the organization of hospital- and clinic-based medicine. Most modern health care organizations divide the care of patients into specialized tasks assigned to different care givers. House staff may be in charge of admission paperwork; attending physicians are responsible for overseeing patients' care; laboratory technicians perform the tests used in the diagnosis. Likewise, informed consent is usually assigned to one member of the health care team, often a house-staff physician or nurse.[14]

There are, however, problems with the event model. Since patients often fail to understand the information they receive, and sense that their participation in decision making is not really desired, the event model fails to implement fully the idea of informed consent, although it may meet the minimal legal requirement. Physicians, too, sense the futility of the event model, which reinforces their disdain for informed consent as a waste of time. Furthermore, the event model often seems to make the interaction between physicians and patients more bureaucratic and less humane. For physicians who are committed to improved care for patients, this model of informed consent often seems detrimental to patient care.

If we ignore the ideals of patient participation espoused in the idea of informed consent and are simply concerned about protection from legal liability, the event model may be acceptable. However, there is an alternative approach that satisfies both sets of desiderata.

Consent as a Process

The process model of informed consent is built on a vision of active patient participation in decision making. While the event model inserts an extra step—informed consent—into otherwise unchanged decision making, the process model, by contrast, integrates informed consent into the physician-patient relationship as a facet of all stages of medical decision making.

If patients are to participate in the decision-making process, we must recognize that medical decisions are rarely made at one point in time. Rather, decisions about care frequently begin with the suspicion that something is wrong and that medical treatment may be necessary, and end only when the patient leaves follow-up care. Although some points in treatment involve more active decision making than others, treatment decisions are being made continually, even if the decision is merely to continue to observe patient's progress.

Conditions of the Process Model

There are three conditions that must be met before a process model can be implemented. First, the role expectations of both patients and physicians need to be modified. The classic physician-patient relationship involves a diffuse acceptance of the physician's authority to direct treatment and the patient's obligation to cooperate, predicated on psychological regression by the patient and re-creation of many features of the parent-child relationship.[18] This relationship works for patients with acute illnesses, but continuous dependency can injure patients' sense of autonomy and lead to a type of behavior vis-a-vis physicians that shares many features of adolescent rebellion. Moreover, the role of passive patient interferes with the type of decision making envisioned by the idea of informed consent.[19]

The goal of patient participation in medical decision making is aided by role expectations that view patients as members of treatment teams with specific expertise. Levy and Howard[20] identified four types of patient expertise, including (1) knowledge of important historical and contextual facts unavailable to other treatment team members; (2) the ability to evaluate symptoms within complex contexts only patients understand (eg, differentiating heart-burn from angina pectoris depends, in part, on patients' assessments, such as whether their pain feels like heart-burn, on how anxiety-producing the day has been, and on a subjective sense of the quantity of pain involved); (3) the responsibility for initiating health care in most situations; and (4) the responsibility for implementing self-care and life-style changes critical to the success of long-term treatment.

A second condition for successful participation by patients in decision making is a matching of illness models between patients and physicians. Physicians and patients often have very different ideas about medical problems and their ramifications. For example, physicians' expectations about the course of juvenile-onset diabetes differ substantially from those of new diabetics, whose concerns are likely to focus on the discomforts of insulin injections.

Patients enter their doctors' offices with a great deal of "folk wisdom" about medical problems. Some sectors of our society hold theories of disease that emphasize causation through spirits, nutritional deficiencies, energy imbalances, and spinal blockages.[21] Even when pieces of patients' knowledge are correct, they are often combined in ways that are not. Unless physicians recognize that their models of illness may differ from their patients' and adjust their discussions accordingly, they will lack much of the basis for collaboration on the selection of treatment.

The final condition for an informed consent process is a clarification of the values and expectations of both participants. For example, in treating chronic pancreatitis, a disease that is often a result of alcohol abuse, the acute pain can sometimes be alleviated by removing all or part of the pancreas. However, such a decision often leads to considerable morbidity of its own. Moreover, the effectiveness of a partial pancreatectomy is highly dependent on patients refraining from further alcohol abuse. Only with some clarification of the relative values each participant places on life span, pain relief, and alcohol use, will doctor and patient be able to reach agreement on treatment. Often, patients will not be able to identify their values about issues they have not previously considered; they must be given time to reflect and discuss the issues with friends and relatives, as well as with their physicians.[22]

The Role of Mutual Monitoring

A successful collaborative decision-making process requires that role expectations be modified, that illness models be matched, and that the values of both parties be made explicit. This can be accomplished only if both parties engage in a continual dialogue that we call *mutual monitoring*.[5] This involves using the routine, ongoing discussions of patients' problems as an opportunity to discuss both sides' expectations; understandings of the illness, values, and expectations for the treatment; and, of course, their views of the advantages and disadvantages of the various treatment options.

Current practice often involves only limited mutual monitoring. Physicians begin by asking for descriptions of the problems (or their current status) that brought patients in. Patients respond with simple accounts of their symptoms. Physicians then ask a long series of "close-ended" questions about patients' current physical condition and their history. An examination usually follows. Finally, physicians either announce what the problems are and prescribe treatment or state that further workup will be necessary. Sometimes physicians will ask if patients have any questions, or patients may ask on their own initiative, but these are typically brief and focus on details of compliance rather than on the choice of treatment. Evidence that patients do not understand the problem or have unrealistic goals for treatment is often ignored.[23]

While these interactions involve tacit discussions of the goals of treatment, and an observant physician may be able to pick up some information about the illness model that the patient uses, there is little place in this type of interaction for either patients or physicians to explain in depth what they are thinking about.[24] Even when patients are given clear reliable information on a single occasion and are allowed to ask questions, it is no substitute for mutual monitoring over the course of treatment, because both patients' and physicians' understanding of the problems are constantly changing.

The continued changes in both patients' and physicians' perceptions of medical problems occur, in part, because the medical problems evolve and, in part, because patients and physicians, like everyone else, continue to ruminate on what they know. While continual reordering of knowledge facilitates human creativity, it also makes for a great deal of misunderstanding between physicians and patients. Each new event, each new comment from a colleague or a friend, may become the occasion to rethink and reconsider what each party already knows about the disorder and the treatment. Even in the absence of new stimuli, both parties reorganize and rethink their knowledge about the treatment so as to build a relatively simple cognitive field consistent with the decisions that have already been made.[25] Moreover, the course of the illness itself will change patients' perceptions of their problems. At the extreme, a patient facing death may find that what seemed important before is now trivial, and new issues and concerns arise. Thus a process model of informed consent requires continual dialogue between physicians and patients.

Informed Consent and the Phases of Patient Care— The process model can be clarified by describing its effect on the different phases of treatment. Treatment of individual patients follows unique patterns, making generalization difficult, but for our purposes we will refer to five phases in the treatment process: establishing responsibility, defining the problem, setting goals, selecting an appropriate treatment, and extended treatment and follow-up.

Establishing Responsibility.—An essential part of the beginning of any treatment relationship is the establishment of the physician's responsibilities for the patient's care. The extent of that process varies. When a profusely bleeding patient arrives in an emergency room, responsibility is usually established tacitly. More commonly, however, physicians will want to establish overtly three basic points: (1) the physician's role in treatment, (2) the substantive area of responsibility, and (3) the expected duration of the responsibility.

Sometimes these will be obvious. A patient who appears in an emergency room with a cut hand will probably assume that the physician who is providing care will focus on the cut and that the duration of the physician's responsibility will be short. Often, however, these issues will not be obvious. In all cases, patients need to know whether the particular physician will be in charge of care, will act as a consultant, or is only assisting others. Moreover, patients need to understand the areas of physicians' expertise and responsibility so that they can direct their questions appropriately. Finally, patients must know whether they will see a physician repeatedly or whether the present moment is the only chance to ask questions.

Defining the Problem.—Diagnosing patients' problems may seem a purely technical matter in which patients play no roles. In fact, however, most nonemergency treatment involves a complex negotiation between physicians and patients about the definition of patients' problems.[23,24] Physicians who ignore patients' definitions of their problems often find that patients are dissatisfied and resistant to medical recommendations. Conversely, when physicians and patients share a definition of the problem and thus an orientation to particular treatment approaches, patients are more likely to follow through with treatment.[26] Appropriate physician approaches to patients can facilitate an open negotiation about the problem to be treated. First, it is important for physicians to ask open-ended questions about the nature of a problem.[27]

Although it is often useful to review the functioning of all organ systems with patients, this should only be done following open-ended questions directed at eliciting patients' complaints. Equally important, physicians must listen to the responses and not simply view the interaction as an opportunity to correct errors in patients' thinking. Patients are often more concerned with an illness' interference in their daily lives than with underlying pathologic processes. Although the response to the problem cannot ignore the underlying pathology, treatment is much more likely to gain patients' acceptance if it addresses the problems that trouble the patient most.

Setting Goals for Treatment.—Even once physicians and patients agree about problems, there is often substantial misunderstanding between them about goals of treatment. Patients' expectations of treatment are often based on surgery or on the therapy of acute infectious diseases. They expect to be "cured" of their problems with little work on their part and often assume that treatment has failed if they are not.

Yet, assessing the risks and the benefits of particular treatments depends critically on what sort of goals can reasonably be expected. The potential benefits and risks of treatment are quite different if the patient has acute bronchitis and may have no lasting problems than if the problem is end-stage, metastatic cancer.

Selecting an Approach to Treatment.—Once the goals of treatment have been defined, patients and physicians must reach a decision on how to achieve them. This aspect of treatment decision making has attracted the most attention in informed consent law, and the legal requirements must play a part in determining physician behavior. Physicians must address the nature, purpose, risks, and benefits of the proposed treatment and any alternative treatments. Determining exactly which information to disclose is not a simple matter. The legal standards—information that a reasonable patient would find material to making a decision, or information that a reasonably prudent physician would disclose—are not particularly helpful in this regard.

Regardless of what standard applies, the emphasis should not be merely on the disclosure of "risks" but on a broader approach that describes both the advantages and disadvantages of treatment. Another critical part of choosing treatment is discussion of the therapeutic options. In most cases, treating physicians will have preferences for particular approaches to care. Indeed, in many cases there may be no medically acceptable alternatives. Provided physicians continue to understand that patients may see the matter differently, and that such views must be respected even if not agreed with, there is no reason why physicians should hesitate to state their point of view. One reason patients go to physicians is to gain access to their judgments about what should be done.

Extended Treatment and Follow-up.—The informed consent process during extended treatment and follow-up can be integrated into the ordinary process of monitoring patients' conditions. The standard question, "How is it going?" provides patients with an opportunity to express ideas about what continuing problems should be the focus of treatment. It needs to be remembered, however, that some patients hesitate to introduce their thoughts about treatment and that it is often necessary to ask repeatedly about patients' current views of their problems, goals, and preferred approaches. These may change for many reasons, including the effects of the disorder, pain and other side effects of treatment, and changes in patients' personal lives.

Patients' ruminations about the problem have the potential to provide insights that will help both patients and physicians better to understand the disorder, but initially they may leave patients confused about what is happening. A few strategic questions concerning what patients think about any new problem can help monitor patients' understanding of their disorders and treatment.

To maintain the informed consent process, a description of the next step in the treatment plan is essential. This may come to no more than explaining to a patient the need to stay in bed a few more days, or it may involve explaining what additional tests are needed and why. In either case, such an explanation provides an opportunity for patients to make sense of the seemingly chaotic series of procedures that they are expected to undergo.

Most interactions between physicians and patients should be terminated with a review of the overall treatment plan and how it contributes to the maintenance or improvement of patients' conditions. If physicians and patients meet frequently, it may become a test of a physician's ingenuity to keep the review from becoming monotonous. Nonetheless, such a review helps patients to keep a hopeful eye on the future and to justify the often painful present.

As episodes of treatment come to a close, the final task is to reestablish patients' responsibility for their own health care. Because illness, particularly illness that involves hospitalization, often induces profound emotional regression and dependence on the physician, follow-up care must concentrate on the reestablishment of patients' responsibility for themselves. This is the final phase of implementing an idea of the physician-patient relationship that seeks to maintain patients' sense of autonomy.

The reestablishment of personal autonomy is a normal part of the process of getting well again, and patients will generally undertake much of this emotional work on their own. Unfortunately, this is sometimes accomplished by projecting their anger at their dependence onto their physicians. The result is, occasionally, a lawsuit. Much more often it is an abiding sense of bitterness and selection of a new physician. It is important to understand that whether or not the anger is justified by the facts, its roots are often based in discomfort about the dependency that patients who are very ill typically feel.

The Limits of the Process Model

In spite of the ethical and clinical advantages of the process model, it is not universally applicable. Many physicians, eg, anesthesiologists or emergency care specialists, provide specialized services to their patients and have almost no relationship with their patients before or after the procedure is performed. In other cases, eg, house staff in an academic center, physicians may have quite brief relationships with their patients. In these instances, practices regarding disclosure and consent will, of necessity, closely approximate the event model. However, it is important that, even in these discussions, patients be fully informed of the physicians' thinking and that they be referred back to their attending physicians for further information. Especially when responsibility for care is diffused, the attending physician and the patient should be certain to review periodically the progress of treatment.

Another substantial limit on the process model concerns the economics of physicians' time. While there is reason to believe that such discussions are cost-effective, third-party payers have been reluctant to accept their importance. Although the process model need not consume great amounts of time, it is nonetheless important to begin modifying the reimbursement system to allow for such discussions. Current efforts to increase reimbursement from third-party payers for nonprocedural, "cognitive" services may be a step in the right direction.

Conclusions

Informed consent has been praised as "therapy" for the physician-patient relationship,[10] but it has also been criticized for not having any substantial positive effect on that relationship. The idea of informed consent emphasizes the need for patient participation in treatment decision making. There is ample reason to believe that such participation is not to be valued merely for its own sake, but that it contributes to therapeutic outcomes. However, the typical implementation of informed consent, bolstered by a narrow vision of the legal doctrine, focuses on the presentation of information at one time, on what we have called the "event model" of informed consent. This information presentation is often too complex for the patient to understand without reflection and dialogue, and frequently constitutes a formalistic effort to comply with the law, at the expense of real collaboration.

We have emphasized that more effective implementation of the doctrine of informed consent requires its integration into the decision-making process, which takes place over time. The resulting process is neither an arbitrary legal imposition on clinical care nor a ritual disclosure that the patient cannot understand.

We recognize that no physician perfectly implements the standards for interacting with patients that we have described here and that sometimes there are practical impediments to their implementation. Nonetheless, we hope that we have provided a direction in which to move.

References

1. Salgo v Leland Stanford Jr University Board of Trustees, 154 Cal App2d 560,317 P2d 170 (1957).

2. Engelhart HT: The Foundations of Bioethics. New York, Oxford University Press, 1980, pp 250-335.

3. Beauchamp TL, Childress JF: Principles of Biomedical Ethics. New York, Oxford University Press, 1979, pp 56-96.

4. Faden RF, Beauchamp TL: A History and Theory of Informed Consent. New York, Oxford University Press, 1986.

5. Appelbaum PS, Lidz CW, Meisel AM: Informed Consent: Legal Theory and Clinical Practice. New York, Oxford University Press, 1987.

6. US Department of Health and Human Services: Final regulations amending basic HHS policy for protecting human research subjects. Federal Register 1981;46(Jan 26):8366-8386.

7. Katz J: The Silent World of Doctor and Patient. New York, Free Press, 1984.

8. President's Commission for the Study of Ethical Problems in Medicine and Biomedical and Behavior Research: Making Health Care Decisions. Government Printing Office, 1982, vol I: Report.

9. Katz J: Informed consent: A fairy tale? Law's vision. Univ Pittsburgh Law Rev 1977;39:137-174.

10. Restructuring informed consent: Legal therapy for the doctor-patient relationship. Yale Law J 1970;79:1533-1576.

11. Stone GC: Patient compliance and the role of the expert, J Soc Iss 1979;35:34-59.

12. Ingelfinger FJ: Informed (but uneducated) consent. N Engl J Med 1972;287;465-466

13. Faden RR, Beauchamp TL: Decision making and informed consent: A study of the impact of disclosed information. Soc Indicators Res 1980;7:314-336.

14. Lidz CW, Meisel AM, Zerubavel E, et al: Informed Consent: A Study of Decision Making in Psychiatry, New York, Guilford Press, 1983.

15. Lidz CW, Meisel AM: Informed consent and the structure of medical care, in President's Commission for the Study of Ethical Problems in Medicine and Biomedical and Behavior Research Making Health Care Decisions. Government Printing Office, 1982, vol 2, pp 317-410.

16. Katz RL: Informed consent: Is it bad medicine? West J Med 1977;126:426-428.

17. Patten BM, Stump W: Death related to informed consent. Tex Med 1978;74:49-50.

18. Parson T: The Social System. Glencoe, Ill, Free Press, 1951, chap 10.

19. Lidz. CW, Meisel AM, Munetz M: Chronic disease and patient participation. Cult Med Psychiatry 1985;9:1-17.

20. Levy S, Howard J: Patient-centric technologies: A clinical-cultural perspective, in Milton T. Green C, Meather R (eds): Handbook of Clinical Health Psychology. New York, Plenum Publishing Corp, 1982, pp 221-156.

21. Gillick ME: Common sense models of health and disease. N Eng J Med 1985;313:700-703

22. Lidz CW: The weather report model of informed consent. Bull Am Acad Psychiatry Law 1980; 8:152-170.

23. Lazare A, Eisenthal S. Frank A, et al: Studies on a negotiated approach to patient hospitalization, in Gallagher EB (ed): The Doctor-Patient Relationship in the Changing Health Scene, US Dept. of Health, Education, and Welfare publication 28-183. Government Printing Office, 1978, pp 119-139.

24. Fisher S: Doctor talk/patient talk: How treatment decisions are negotiated in doctor-patient communication, in Fisher S, Todd AD (eds): The Social Organization of Doctor-Patient Communication. Washington, DC, Center for Applied Linguistics, 1983, pp 135-158.

25. Festinger L: A Theory of Cognitive Dissonance. Evanston, Ill, Row Peterson, 1957.

26. DiMatteo MR, DiNicola DD: Achieving Patient Compliance. Elmsford, NY, Pergamon Press Inc, 1982.

27. Mischler EG: Discourse of Medicine: Dialectics of Medical Interviews. Norwood, NJ, Ablex Publishing Corp, 1984.

Lidz CW, et al. Two models of implementing informed consent. Arch Intern Med. 1988; 148: 1385-1389.

Article 3.6

Informed Consent in Malpractice Cases: A Turn Toward Reality

William J. Curran, JD, S.M. Hyg. The New England Journal of Medicine, February 1986.

For at least two decades, American law in the malpractice field has often imposed unrealistic burdens on physicians in regard to informed consent.[1] The courts have, in my opinion, turned the proper ethical obligation of a physician into an expansive intellectual exercise that is of dubious benefit to sick and worried patients. In an angry essay some years ago, Franz Ingelfinger referred to the legal rules as creating informed, but uneducated, consent.[2]

Perhaps worse is the fact that the doctrine of informed consent in its most severe form—which requires a physician to inform the patient of all potential risks of a treatment or operation, no matter how remote—too often makes the physician a guarantor of good results when, unfortunately, events that are only remotely foreseeable do sometimes occur. Thus, when the courts, after the fact of severe injury and nondisclosure, impose the doctrine, they encourage application of the concept of strict liability of the physician, without proof of negligence, and require the payment of inflated tort-law damages, often in six- or seven-figure amounts. On the other hand, every proposal for the enactment of a no-fault system of medical liability at least replaces the tort-law rule with a much lower scale of recovery for actual damages suffered.[3]

Until the latest decision of the Massachusetts Supreme Judicial Court in *Precourt v. Frederick*,[4] the trend of unrealistic and oppressive damages decisions seemed unbroken across the country. In fact, it was not expected that the Massachusetts court would issue an important opinion in this direction, because it had only recently adopted the modern rules of informed consent, including what seemed to be highly detailed standards of full disclosure.[5]

In the trial of the Precourt case, the evidence indicated that the patient, a 33-year-old electrical construction worker, had been hit in the left eye at work. A piece of metal was removed from the eye at a local hospital, but a smaller piece remained deeply embedded. After removal of the larger piece, the patient was referred to the defendant, Dr. Frederick, at Massachusetts Eye and Ear Infirmary. The physician advised surgery for the removal of the smaller fragment and explained to the patient the risks and possible benefits of the procedure. The patient consented to the operation, which was successful in removing the metal. After the surgery, Dr. Frederick recommended a course of treatment with prednisone, a corticosteroid, to control inflammation. The patient took the prednisone for 90 days after the surgery. The court record and testimony did not indicate the dosage. The patient's vision improved at first, but later deteriorated until he was blind in the injured eye. Despite this, the patient returned to work.

Several months later, the defendant and plaintiff discussed an operation to remove scar tissue from the eye. Dr. Frederick indicated that this second procedure had only a 10 percent chance of restoring vision. Nevertheless, the patient elected to undergo the surgery. The procedure was performed and much of the scar tissue was removed, but sight was not restored. After the surgery, Dr. Frederick again prescribed corticosteroid treatment, and the patient took the drug for 55 days. Again, the record of the case and the court opinion did not indicate the dosage.

About three years later, the plaintiff was found to have aseptic necrosis in both hips. By the time of the trial, he had had bilateral hip-replacement operations.

It was agreed at the trial that the defendant had not told the plaintiff of a risk of aseptic necrosis associated with prednisone treatment. The doctor indicated that he considered it a very remote risk. Dr. Frederick testified that since 1963, he had treated 50 to 75 percent of the eye patients in his practice with corticosteroid after surgery and that aseptic necrosis had never developed as a result of administration of those drugs. He admitted, however, that aseptic necrosis was listed in the *Physician's Desk Reference* as 1 of the 41 potential complications known to be associated with use of the drug. An expert witness for the plaintiff testified that the "high dose" and "long course of treatment" had, in his opinion, caused the aseptic necrosis in the patient's hips. The witness also said that physicians should warn patients about the "possibilities" that such conditions may result from sustained corticosteroid use by persons who, like the patient in this case, have a history of alcohol use and slightly elevated blood pressure.

On the basis of this evidence, the trial court refused to direct a verdict favorable to the defendant and sent the case to a jury. The jury returned a verdict of $1 million against the defendant ($800,000 to the plaintiff for his injuries and $200,000 to his wife for loss of companionship and marital relations —a so-called loss of "consortium"). The judge denied a motion for a new trial, with the condition that the damages to the wife be reduced to $100,000—a sum that she accepted to avoid a new trial. Dr. Frederick appealed the decision to the Massachusetts Supreme Judicial Court.

The trial court's action shocked and distressed many physicians in Massachusetts. An amicus curiae brief was submitted to the high court by the Massachusetts Medical Society, the Massachusetts Society of Eye Physicians, and the Massachusetts Eye and Ear Infirmary. The brief took the position that the case was of great importance in establishing standards for disclosure of risks in the "ubiquitous area of prescribing drugs and medications" and that the effect of the trial court outcome, if not clarified, would be to make Massachusetts physicians

> virtual insurers of all risks of every drug they prescribe and every medical procedure they undertake, however infinitesimally remote, unless they explain every potential side effect of every drug and procedure to every patient, at a cost of time and resources that will be detrimental to good patient care and medical practice in Massachusetts.[6]

The brief cited the testimony of an expert for the defense in the trial, who testified that the risks of "most of the side effects" of prednisone, presumably including those that led to the patient's condition, were extremely remote—i.e., they occurred in only about one of tens of thousands of cases. This witness also indicated that he had conducted a computer search of 29,000 articles on the subject and had not found a single report of aseptic necrosis resulting from treatment with prednisone after eye surgery. Other ophthalmologists also testified that they were unaware of any reports of such side effects of the use of corticosteriods after eye surgery. It was also asserted that the plaintiff's expert witness had not contradicted this observation.

The Massachusetts high court, in an opinion written by Justice O'Connor, held that the verdict in the case should be reversed in favor of the defendant. All the justices agreed with this opinion, although Justice Liacos did write a separate concurring statement on the case. He did, however, agree with the results.

Justice O'Connor concluded, "In this case, there was no evidence [submitted by the plaintiff] that a person would develop aseptic necrosis after taking prednisone or that [Dr.] Frederick knew or should have known that the likelihood was other than negligible." The court found that the opinion of the plaintiff's expert witness, who said that the risk of this side effect was "high," did not constitute adequate evidence to support a verdict for the plaintiff. Justice O'Connor also observed that "high" was a relative term and could mean "one in ten, but it could just as well mean one in a million." Presumably, the court found the evidence too speculative in this case, in which the plaintiff had the burden of proof.

Most important, Justice O'Connor stressed that the earlier Harnish case had established the standard that there must be a balancing, an accommodation, among the patient's right to know, fairness to physicians, and society's interest that medicine be practiced "without unrealistic and unnecessary burdens on practitioners."

There seems little doubt that this decision will be helpful in moving American law away from serious collision with the realities of what physicians can and cannot do to inform their patients of the risks and benefits of proposed treatments.

I do not argue against reasonable disclosure of important risks of treatment, nor do I argue against the need to offer alternatives to patients when alternatives are available. Every physician has an ethical obligation to involve patients in decision making about their care.[7,8,9] However, prudent medical practice must incorporate limits to disclosure in regard to different types of procedures, as well as divergent emotional and intellectual assessments of a patient's capacity to deal with medical information at a particular time in an illness.

The Harnish case in Massachusetts, the forerunner to the present decision, involved elective surgery that was important primarily in relation to a young woman's physical appearance. Such a situation seems to call for full disclosure because the procedure is neither urgent nor highly effective in combating disease or disability. Under such circumstances, the patient should consider the remote but serious risks thoughtfully in deciding, for example, to undergo elective plastic surgery of the neck. In the Precourt case, on the other hand, the patient was seeking restoration of sight—a goal for which considerable risk might be justified and disclosure of negligible, remote risks might not be warranted in the view of either patient or physician.

I am, however, rather surprised at the brevity of the court's opinion in the Precourt case and at its failure to review the evidence in depth or to lay down a range of obligations for physicians in different types of clinical situations. My own suggestion in regard to the situational differences between the Harnish case and the Precourt case is not included in either opinion, nor are other examples given or evaluated. The decision of Justice O'Connor is more impressionistic than analytical. It clearly conveys the feeling that the justices thought that, in this case, the application of a full-disclosure standard would be unfair, and that the risk of necrotic hip disease was too remote to have required disclosure and culpability to the tune of nearly $1 million. Beyond this, however, the opinion offers little future guidance. We must await further decisions in the common law traditions of the courts to flesh out the details of the true meaning of this step in the right direction.

References

1. Rozovsky, FA. Consent to treatment: a practical guide. Boston: Little, Brown, 1984.

2. Ingelfinger FJ. Informed (but uneducated) consent. N Engl J Med 1972;287:465-6.

3. Curran WJ, Shapiro ED. Law, medicine, and forensic sciences. 3rd ed. Boston: Little, Brown, 1982:517-36.

4. Precourt vs. Frederick, 395 Mass. 689(1985).

5. Harnish vs. Children's Hospital Medical Center, 387 Mass. 152(1982).

6. Brief of Amicus Curiae, typescript copy to the court, October 23, 1985:3-4.

7. Rennie D. Informed consent by "well-nigh abject" adults. N Engl J Med 1980;302:917-8.

8. Chapman CB. Physicians, law, and ethics. New York: New York University Press, 1984.

9. Katz J. The silent world of doctor and patient. New York: Free Press, 1984.

Curran WJ. Informed consent in malpractice cases: a turn toward reality. N Engl J Med. 1986; 314(7): 429-431.

Annotated Bibliography

Informed Consent

Curran WJ. *Informed consent in malpractice cases.* N Engl J Med. 1986; 314: 429-431.
Article 3.6

Eisner JM, Tilson JQ, Agsten MA. *A primer on informed consent for Connecticut physicians.* Conn Med. 1986;50:391-398.
This is a thorough review of laws and cases on informed consent in Connecticut. It includes sections on consent forms, consent of minors, substituted consent, child abuse, non-therapeutic sterilization and living wills and discusses special consent situations.

Gutheil TG, Bursztajn H, Brodsky A. *Malpractice prevention through the sharing of uncertainty.* N Engl J Med. 1984; 311: 49-51.
Article 3.2

Hollander RD. *Changes in the concept of informed consent in medical encounters.* J Med Educ. 1984; 59: 783-788.
The author reviews recent changes in the conceptualization of informed consent in medical encounters to help provide a better understanding of the concept and of some difficulties that exist in philosophical justifications for the requirement of informed consent.

Katz J. *Informed consent: are 'miracles, mystery and authority' better medicine?* Conn Med. 1986;50:457-460.
Article 3.1

Napier JA. *Informed consent: an issue of substance.* Advisory (Quarterly Publication of the MMI Family of Companies). July 1986.
A risk manager provides a set of methods to help physicians meet the requirements of informing and obtaining patient consent.

Sherlock R. *Reasonable men and sick human beings.* Am J Med. 1986; 80:2-4.
The author discusses the significance of trust in the clinical relationship; essential to this process of patient entrustment is communication with the patient about his or her illness, therapy, and prognosis.

Special Issues in Informed Consent

President's Commission for the Study of Ethical Problems in Medicine and Biomedical and Behavioral Research. Compensating for Research Injuries: *A Report on the Ethical and Legal Implications.* Washington, DC: U. S. Government Printing Office; 1982.
This report analyzes the question, "Are subjects who deserve compensation for research injuries not receiving it?" It concludes that insufficient data exist and that a model compensation system tested.

President's Commission for the Study of Ethical Problems in Medicine and Biomedical and Behavioral Research. *Protecting Human Subjects.* Washington, DC: U.S. Government Printing Office; 1982.
This report reviews the adequacy of regulations in the federal departments of Health and Human Services, Housing and Urban Development, and Transportation regarding the protection of human research subjects. It identifies a few problem areas but concludes that the regulations are generally adequate.

The Doctrine of Informed Consent

Beck JC, Staffin RD. *Patients' competency to give informed consent to medication.* Hosp Community Psychiatry. 1986; 37: 400-402.
A psychiatrist and mental health worker collaborate on a study to determine whether uninformed state hospital patients can learn to make an informed decision about antipsychotic medication after being given an explanation of the risks and benefits of the medication.

Cassileth BR, Zupkis RV, Sutton-Smith K, March V. *Informed consent: why are its goals imperfectly realized?* N Engl J Med. 1980; 302: 896-900.
Two hundred cancer patients were quizzed on their recall of information from consent forms they had signed. Only 60 percent understood the purpose and nature of the procedure. Further analysis and recommendations are included. See also the accompanying editorial.

Danner D. *The informed consent doctrine: some practical guidelines.* Forum (bi-monthly publication of the Risk Management Foundation of the Harvard Medical Institutions.) 1981; 1(3): 4.
An attorney outlines the legal definition and elements of informed consent.

Grundner TM. *On the readability of surgical consent forms.* N Engl J Med. 1980; 302: 900-902.
A non-physician educator applies standardized readability formulas to five separate consent forms. All of the forms required a reading ability found in upper-division college students or greater. See also the accompanying editorial.

Holzer JF. *The process of informed consent.* Bull Am Coll Surgeons. 1989; 74 (9): 10-14
Attorney Holzer proposes that an improved sharing of information between patients and surgeons could yield more realistic expectations on the part of patients regarding the care they receive. This can help limit the number of nonmeritorious malpractice suits. Sharing of information from the time of the surgeon-patient first encounter through the time of post-operative recovery constitutes the "process of consent" to be differentiated from the simple signing of a consent form.

Lidz CW, Appelbaum PS, Meisel A. *Two models of implementing informed consent.* Arch Intern Med. 1988; 148: 1385-1389.
Article 3.5

Lo B, McLeod GA, Saika G. *Patient attitudes to discussing life-sustaining treatment.* Arch Intern Med. 1986; 146: 1613-1615.
A study focusing on patient characteristics and wishes about decision-making and care in a group of elderly patients without chronic illness.

Perry CB, Applegate WB. *Medical paternalism and patient self-determination.* J Am Geriatr Soc. 1985; 33: 353-359.
The authors contend that the complexity of the patient/physician relationship condones paternalism in various clinical settings, that some paternalistic acts may not violate the patient's rights of autonomy, that other such acts may be a function of respect for patient autonomy, and that other subgroups may only suspend or momentarily infringe on patient autonomy.

Redden E, Baker DC, Meisel A. *The patient, the plastic surgeon, and informed consent: new insights into old problems.* Plas Reconstr Surg. 1985; 75: 270-276.
An overview of informed consent focusing on the issue of the patient's understanding and recall of pre-operative information.

Reuter SR. *An overview of informed consent for radiologists.* Am J Radiol. 1987; 148: 219-227.
This article provides a thorough but concise discussion of the legal and ethical bases for informed consent. Specific issues, such as the injection of X-ray contrast agents and the variability of state laws, are highlighted.

Competency and Informed Consent

Drane JF. *Competency to give an informed consent.* JAMA. 1984; 252: 925-927.
A model with guidelines is provided to aid the physician who is called on to make a determination of competency.

Holder AR. Minors' rights to consent to medical care. JAMA. 1987; 257: 3400-3402.
Article 3.3

Munetz MR. *Informed consent and incompetent medical patients.* J Fam Pract. 1985; 20: 3273-279.
Article 3.4

Chapter 4

Adverse Outcomes

Case: Peripartum Complications

An obstetrician speaks with the parents of a newborn female infant who may have brain damage. This condition may have been due to insufficient oxygenation of the brain caused by compression of a twisted umbilical cord during birth.

Dr. Morton is a well-respected obstetrician-gynecologist who has delivered several hundred babies. The Roberts are young professionals in their mid-30s who feel fortunate to have had Dr. Morton deliver their two older children, a four-year-old daughter and a two-year-old son. Dr. Morton delivered the Roberts' second daughter just 30 minutes ago.

Mrs. Roberts had an uncomplicated, full-term pregnancy. However, her 11-hour labor culminated in a difficult and prolonged vaginal delivery. During labor, Dr. Morton had considered performing a cesarean section. She had not specifically recommended a cesarean section during labor but did recall from prenatal counseling that the Roberts were against the procedure unless absolutely necessary. During careful monitoring of labor there were no signs of fetal distress, and Dr. Morton opted to proceed with a vaginal delivery. The Roberts' daughter was born with a nuchal cord wrapped twice around her neck. Her Apgar scores were two and five. She was brought immediately to the neonatal intensive care unit by the pediatricians on duty.

Dr. Morton has just come from examining the infant; the child is less responsive than normal babies and she has diminished suck, grasp, and Moro reflexes, with labored respirations. She is receiving oxygen but is not on a respirator. She has no gross physical anomalies, seizures, or apparent cardiac defects. She weighs 6 1/2 pounds and is 20 inches long.

The Roberts were frightened by the speed with which their daughter was taken to the neonatal intensive care unit. They were confused by the terms used by the delivery room staff and detected the concern of the pediatrician who recited the infant's Apgar scores. Dr. Morton is aware of the neonate's serious condition. She knows the twisted umbilical cord may have diminished oxygen to the child's brain for the five to 10 minutes required to induce neurologic damage. It is too early to make a diagnosis of cerebral palsy, which is best determined after serial examinations during a period of months to years.

Dr. Morton has another expectant mother entering the delivery room within the next 10 minutes. She only has a brief moment to speak with the Roberts at this time.

Discussion Questions

1. Clearly, a poor or unfavorable medical outcome has occurred in this case, but has "malpractice" occurred? What is the difference?

2. What should Dr. Morton tell the Roberts in the 10 minutes she has before returning to the delivery room to deliver another baby?

3. Should she explain the role of the pediatrician who took the baby away, why the infant is being taken to the intensive care unit, what Apgar scores are, and what a twisted umbilical cord means? Should they be directed to speak with the pediatrician at this time?

4. Should Dr. Morton mention the possibility of cerebral palsy? What are the potential legal implications of using the term "cerebral palsy?"

5. Should she describe to the Roberts those features of their newborn daughter that appear normal? Should she tell them what appears abnormal? What level of concern should she raise with them in the immediate postpartum period? What should she say if asked by the Roberts if their baby is "normal?"

6. What should Dr. Morton record in the medical record at this time? Are there any terms or labels she should use cautiously?

7. What questions or behavior might the Roberts ask or display at this time? How should Dr. Morton respond?

8. What emotions might be evoked in Dr. Morton? How might this unfavorable outcome affect Dr. Morton's performance later the same evening or during the next year?

Overview

A sampling of adverse medical outcomes reveals how varied they are: a penicillin-induced drug rash, steroid-induced necrosis of the hip, post-surgical infections or wound complications, pregnancy following vasectomy or tubal ligation, a lacerated esophagus as a result of endoscopy, a fall and fracture of a rib in a radiology suite, a missed diagnosis of pancreatic cancer, anoxic brain damage in an infant, suicide in a depressed patient undergoing treatment, radiation-induced skin changes, and ventricular fibrillation experienced during a cardiac catheterization.

Because none of these is an expected or desired event, they can be considered adverse or poor outcomes associated with medical intervention. As our ability to diagnose and treat expands, so does the probability of iatrogenic injury or disease.[1-3] Some adverse outcomes may seem routine to the medical professional who observes them; others can be very disturbing. To the average patient and his or her family, however, all of these outcomes are worrisome and can be devastating.

How the patient and family perceive an adverse outcome may ultimately determine whether a malpractice claim is filed against the physician. It has been calculated that up to 63 percent of medical malpractice claims arise from minor and emotional injuries.[4] It is a common perception among health care risk managers that the majority of lawsuits could be prevented if opportunities for direct although often difficult physician-patient communication were optimized.[5] When an adverse outcome occurs, the lines separating negligence, equipment malfunction, and natural disease progression may be blurred, further complicating the patient's and family's perception of physician wrongdoing. The clinical case that introduces this chapter is a good example.

The Roberts are confused, scared, and concerned about their newborn daughter's condition. Dr. Morton has only an initial impression of the child's status. She may never know if different action on her part would have resulted in a healthier outcome for the infant. Perhaps she did act negligently; perhaps there was no way to avert the child's medical condition. Such emotional turmoil can consume the physician, the patient, and the patient's family. David Hilfiker, MD, describes the emotional turmoil he experienced when dealing with an adverse outcome in the treatment of a patient he had always enjoyed caring for. In Article 4.1, "Facing our Mistakes," he writes,

> . . . although I told them everything they wanted to know and described to them as completely as I could what had happened, I never shared with them the agony that I underwent trying to deal with the reality of the events.

As discussed in the previous chapters, good physician-patient communication, careful record keeping, and a thorough informed consent process are essential to protect against patient dissatisfaction. When an adverse outcome does occur, however, it is also essential to understand the physician's responsibilities following such an event. It is also valuable for physicians to understand their role in institutional risk management programs and the need for peer support among physicians given the growing acknowledgment of a "medical malpractice stress syndrome."

The Frequency of Adverse Events

How often do adverse events occur as a result of medical care? What is the frequency of negligent medical care? How debilitating to patients are adverse medical outcomes, and what percentage of them are the result of substandard medical practice? Answering these questions is vital to the effort to implement strategies for the reduction of patient injuries.

The prevalence of adverse events and negligent care in the outpatient setting has not yet been thoroughly studied. However, given that approximately 80 percent of malpractice suits arise from care delivered in the hospital setting, we are fortunate to have two large-scale studies on the incidence of adverse events in hospitalized patients. In the mid-1970s, the California Medical Association and the California Hospital Association sponsored the Medical Insurance Feasibility Study.[6] Investigators found that 4.6 percent of 20,000 hospital inpatient records studied showed evidence of significant patient disability during hospitalization. Seventeen percent of those injuries (representing 0.8 percent of all hospitalized patients) were believed to be caused by negligence.

In February 1990, the Medical Practice Study was released by the New York State Department of Health. This study was mandated by the New York state legislature and conducted by the Harvard School of Public Health.[7] Medical records from 30,195 hospitalizations during 1984 were analyzed. Among all patient charts reviewed, the study found that 3.7 percent of patients sustained injury during hospitalization that resulted in prolongation of hospital stay or measurable disability at the time of discharge. Twenty-eight percent of these injuries (representing 1.0 percent of all patients in the sample) were deemed to have been caused by negligence. The similarity in the findings of both the California and New York studies suggests that the 0.8 to 1.0 percent figure adequately represents the prevalence of negligent medical injuries in hospitalized patients.

Among all patient injuries reviewed in the New York study, most were minor, with 57 percent of patients recovering completely within one month and 70 percent recovering completely within six months. Surgical complications made up almost half of all injuries. Fourteen percent of injuries were fatal, with more than half of the fatal injuries the result of negligent medical care. The fact that one percent of all hospitalized patients sustain injury due to negligence is, on the one hand, a testament to the safety of medical care for the majority of patients. On the other hand, it certainly points to room for improvement in medical care provided by physicians.

Unlike the California survey, investigators in the New York study did have access to malpractice claims data for all the patient charts that were reviewed. The total number of malpractice claims was approximately 10 percent of the number of negligent injuries. Only two percent of patients who sustained injury due to negligence filed claims as of 1989 (within five years of the injury). Just as startling a finding is that up to 80 percent of cases where malpractice claims were initiated contained no evidence of negligent injury, according to the expert reviewers.[8] These data confirm what medical risk managers have long known: that the preponderance of malpractice suits is brought by patients who have not been the victims of negligent injury. These data also suggest that if physicians communicate the risk and occurrence of adverse events more satisfactorily to patients, many claims may be avoided.

What to Do After an Adverse Outcome

Prompt clinical response to an adverse outcome should begin with immediate requests for consultation, as needed. If equipment malfunction is suspected, the equipment should be promptly removed from service, tagged, and stored in a secure location until further evaluations can be made. Other pertinent physical evidence, such as catheters, medication ampules, and empty transfusion bags, should be preserved. The integrity and security of medical records, X-rays, and other documentation should be ensured. Staff should be reminded of patient confidentiality guidelines. The hospital risk manager should be notified immediately to assist staff, as necessary, in handling the events surrounding the adverse outcome. The risk manager may also be helpful in determining when and if a malpractice insurance carrier or legal counsel should be notified.

Attorney Douglas Danner summarizes advice for thinking and acting after a patient has begun legal proceedings against a clinician in the reprinted excerpt from his book *Medical Malpractice: A Primer for Physicians* (see Article 4.2). He gives an excellent description of the legal process, including information on completing depositions, the trial, the jury, appeals, and settlement. He discusses how the malpractice suit can affect a physician's medical practice and the role of legal representation. Suggestions regarding what actions the physician should take following notice of the suit are outlined in Table 4.1.

Talking With the Patient and Family

It is important that physicians do not isolate themselves from a patient or his or her family after an adverse outcome has occurred. Rapport between physician and patient may be a key factor in determining whether legal action will ever be considered by the patient. Given that the physician is the head of the health care team, talking only to nurses or other hospital personnel may not be satisfactory to the patient or the family. Prompt contact and factual discussion are essential and the hallmarks of a good physician-patient relationship, regardless of its duration or the presence of an adverse occurrence.

Careful consideration should be given prior to any admissions of guilt or failure, and the physician is strongly advised to consult with a hospital attorney, risk manager, or his or her personal attorney before taking this step. It is quite possible that the patient has not entertained the thought of failure or culpability on the part of the physician. Expressions of concern for a patient's pain or circumstance are encouraged and should not be construed as an admission of negligence. At least one state has a specific safeguard for physicians, ensuring that any statements, writings, or benevolent gestures relating to the suffering of the victim of an accident are inadmissible in court as evidence of liability.[9]

Sensitivity to the new emotional and financial burdens facing the patient will also engender a positive relationship. Thorough investigation of patient complaints and prompt planning for follow-up care may be appropriate responses to an adverse outcome. In some cases, it may be appropriate for the physician or the hospital to offer to provide subsequent treatments free of charge. This should only be done in consultation with the hospital or insurance company risk manager. When meeting with the patient and family, no attempt should be made to cover up the fact that an undesirable outcome has occurred. Communication of clinical data should be maintained, but remarks concerning liability insurance coverage or the fault of others, which are rarely constructive and can have significant adverse implications later, should be avoided. An ongoing review of the treatment should follow an adverse outcome. Dr. William Applegate analyzes the need for information and the emotional dynamics after an adverse event on the part of both the patient and physician. In his Article 4.3, "Physician Management of Patients With Adverse Outcomes," he, too, emphasizes the need for open communication.

Consider again the case of Dr. Morton, the Roberts, and their newborn child. Dr. Morton has only 10 minutes with the Roberts before she must deliver another child. She should sit down and reassure them that their daughter's heart is pumping fine and her eyes, ears, mouth, and limbs all appear to be normal. She should then discuss with the Roberts the following issues: (1) the normal and abnormal physical findings of their new daughter; (2) the child's abnormal breathing; (3) the degree of uncertainty as to the cause of their daughter's respiratory problem; (4) that she is being managed expertly; and (5) that they will be kept apprised of her condition.

Dr. Morton should briefly tell the Roberts the name of the pediatrician and his or her role in their daughter's care. The pediatrician will most likely determine when the parents can visit the newborn.

Dr. Morton should also comment on the health of Mrs. Roberts, as she is most definitely her patient. She should make them aware that she needs to care for another expectant mother and that she plans to meet with them later, at a specific place and time. An effective physician-patient relationship nurtured from the very first encounter will facilitate the resolution of problems as they arise throughout a course of care.

At their subsequent meeting, Dr. Morton should listen to the Roberts' questions, prompted perhaps by a few open-ended questions of her own, e.g., "Is there anything you'd like to ask me?" Listening can be as important as reporting information in this situation. Unanswered questions can harden into anger, thereby triggering a claim that could have been avoided. Conversely, honest answers and a caring demeanor can strengthen the physician-patient bond and discourage a lawsuit.

Documentation Considerations

The significance of complete medical records and proper informed consent becomes magnified when adverse outcomes occur. As discussed in Chapter 1, the medical record can be a physician's best malpractice defense. However, a poorly maintained medical record can suggest negligent practice, even where it technically does not exist.

Complete and accurate documentation of all the medical facts concerning a poor outcome should be maintained. A factual description of conversations between physician, patient, and family should be documented, as they may be important elements of medical decision-making. If augmentations to prior entries must be made, they should be clearly marked as such. Errors in current documentation should be corrected by a straight line drawn through the error, which is then dated and initialed; errors should not be obliterated completely. Likewise, personal or judgmental comments about the patient or another health care professional should not be made in the record, nor should documentation of notice to a risk manager, a malpractice insurer, or an attorney. Incident reports should be completed according to individual hospital policy and procedure; however, no mention of the completed incident report should be made in the patient's record. Terms that might inappropriately imply causation should not be used. For instance, the terms "birth asphyxia" and/or "perinatal asphyxia" should not be included in the medical record unless there is collaborative biochemical evidence to support their use.[10]

The safe preservation of all medical records and other pertinent documents is essential. Dr. Morton should ensure that the pertinent details of the labor and delivery are promptly recorded and all fetal monitoring tracings and nurses' notes are kept. Considering the nature of the child's condition, notes concerning the timing of labor and the details of anesthesia will be important elements in any future review of the case.

Risk Management

At the very least, a physician should properly document an adverse outcome, maintain communication with his or her patient, and form a medical plan for dealing with the complication. In addition, the physician may wish to review this information with professionals who are trained to deal with medical mishaps and their potential legal consequences. Many health care facilities, either voluntarily or through the mandate of an accrediting, insuring, or governmental agency, have developed the position of risk manager to assist physicians and coordinate these resources.

Hospital risk managers are skilled health professionals from a variety of backgrounds, including nursing, law, insurance, and business administration. Many have special training, education, and certification in hospital risk management. Occasionally, physicians and lawyers are employed specifically for their skills in risk management and loss control.

The risk manager is likely to be the person responsible for coordinating the identification of and response to various sources of potential liability for the hospital. Among other responsibilities, hospital risk managers may be involved in issues related to environmental safety, ancillary services, and insurance purchasing as well as the monitoring of nursing care and physician practice. Risk managers receive information through incident reports, chart reviews, occurrence screening, and direct communication with medical staff and non-medical employees (particularly patient representatives). Many health care institutions have developed departments of quality assurance, which assist in the monitoring of patient care, and utilization review functions, which assess the use of hospital resources and assist in resource planning. Much of the data they generate can be directly used by risk managers. Departments of quality assurance and risk management share the common goals of efficient and safe medical care delivery.

In January 1989, the Joint Commission on Accreditation of Healthcare Organizations (JCAHO) updated the formal risk management activities it requires for accreditation.[11] It now mandates broader participation by medical staff physicians in risk identification, analysis and risk reduction/loss prevention. While the JCAHO does not specify exact methods for data collection and analysis, it does require hospitals to have objective, ongoing review of clinical services and asks that they identify potential high-risk areas for patient injury.[12] Hospitals are required to demonstrate that staff physicians are actively involved with the development and assessment of corrective actions taken in response to problem identification.

Risk managers can assist physicians when specific cases of malpractice or adverse outcomes arise. It is of greater benefit, however, for risk managers to identify and coordinate correction of systemic problems within an entire hospital department or practice setting.

Attorney James Holzer gives a detailed example of risk management principles applied to a department of anesthesia in Article 4.4 "Current Concepts in Risk Management." Holzer emphasizes the need for commitment and participation of all physicians in the risk management process. When a problem area is identified or a specific case is reviewed, sensitive information is discussed with the physician. A patient's diagnosis and the physician's management of a particular case may be scrutinized. For the development of effective and acceptable review procedures, problem solving procedures, and methods of malpractice prevention, physician input is essential. Also included in Holzer's article is an historical account of the development and philosophy of risk management.

Risk management is more than just the careful practice of good medicine by physicians in a hospital. It is a method of liability prevention as well as a means of dealing with existing allegations of negligence. By its very nature it must be interdisciplinary, involving all persons who provide patient care and all who maintain health care facilities. Risk management practices are not limited to the hospital but should be extended to solo office practices, group practices, nursing home facilities, and health maintenance organizations (HMOs). Many professional risk management companies provide services to large and small health care organizations. Most liability insurance carriers offer loss prevention assistance in addition to settling claims.

Peer Support for Physicians

An adverse outcome or malpractice suit causes tremendous emotional stress for all involved. Often, it may take years to settle a claim or to try a lawsuit, and the proceedings may call into question a physician's competence or integrity. Even an unsubstantiated suit can mar a career of hard work and long-term service. Despite the fact that physicians in certain specialties have a high probability of being sued and the fact that malpractice suits have become more common, when an actual suit does arise, the physician is often unprepared and can be emotionally devastated by the experience.[13,14] Infrequently, a physician may also face substantial financial losses, depending on the status of his or her malpractice insurance and the nature of the settlement.

Understandable emotional reactions may lead the physician to publicly malign the patient and plaintiff's lawyer. Such behavior is discouraged and is not a constructive means for settling the dispute. Detailed discussion of the case with colleagues, although essential, should be limited to peer review settings where some legal protections are afforded. Some review of details may be required with nurses and other staff; however, these discussions should be limited to objective fact finding.

Peer support and understanding, however, are essential to avert a sense of abandonment. Support groups for physicians involved in malpractice litigation have been organized in several localities. Reverend Edward G. Reading, who has developed the concept of "malpractice stress syndrome," describes the work of the Litigation Stress Support Group in New Jersey in Article 4.5. This self-help group assists physicians and their families in dealing with the isolation and emotional distress associated with a malpractice suit.

The leaders of such support groups remind us that they are not a substitute for psychiatric counseling. Anxiety, depression, and suicidal ideation can become overwhelming. Physicians and their family members may require professional counseling or psychiatric care and should be referred for such assistance when indicated.

Summary

That adverse medical outcomes cannot always be avoided is a reality with which both the public and the health care community must come to terms. Out of necessity, many medical decisions are made with inadequate or unavailable data. Changing patient preferences, variations in patient compliance, or limited resources may all add to the uncertainty that physicians encounter. The nature of medical training and high expectations of medical science emphasize perfect results. Thus, disappointment and anger result when an adverse outcome occurs. Medical students and residents ultimately learn how to make decisions in the face of such uncertainty; however, better training on how to communicate this uncertainty to patients is needed.

In addition, improved public understanding of the limitations of medical care and scientific discoveries should be fostered in all available forums. Some information has already begun to emerge as a result of the consumer rights movement. Data concerning iatrogenic morbidity, such as hospital-acquired infection rates and surgical outcomes, have also appeared in the lay press. Knowledgeable discussion of these topics can help familiarize people with the potential hazards of sophisticated medical care. It is vital that unbiased physician input be included for the sake of both accurately informing patients and improving their care.

References

1. Steel K, Gertman PM, Crescinze C, et al. Iatrogenic illness on a general medical service at a university hospital. *N Engl J Med*. 1981; 304: 638-642.

2. Lambert EC. *Modern Medical Mistakes*. Bloomington, IN: Indiana University Press; 1978: 11-14

3. D'Arcy PF, Griffin JP. *Iatrogenic Disease*. 2nd ed. New York, NY: Oxford University Press Inc.; 1979: 19-44

4. *Medical Malpractice*. Washington, DC: Secretary's Commission on Medical Malpractice; 1973. U.S. Dept of Health, Education and Welfare publication (OS) 73-88.

5. Improving patient-staff relations key to loss reduction. *Hospital Risk Management*. 1975; 7: 3.

6. California Medical Association and California Hospital Association. In: Mills DH, ed. *Report on the Medical Insurance Feasibility Study.* San Francisco, CA: Sutter Publications; 1977.

7. *Medical Practice Study: Executive Summary.* New York, NY: New York State Health Department; 1990.

8. Hiatt HH, Barnes BA, Brennan TA, et al. A study of medical injury and medical malpractice: an overview. *N Engl J Med.* 1989; 321: 480-484. Special Report.

9. Mass.Gen.L.c.233, §23D (1986).

10. Ryan, EM. Causation issues in cerebral palsy. *Forum* (bi-monthly publication of the Risk Management Foundation of the Harvard Medical Institutions). 1990; 11(2): 9.

11. *1989 Accreditation Manual for Hospitals.* Chicago, IL: The Joint Commission on the Accreditation of Healthcare Organizations; 1988.

12. *Draft Scoring Guidelines for Hospital Risk Management Functions, 1989.* Chicago, IL: The Joint Commission on Accreditation of Healthcare Organizations; 1988.

13. Epps CH. Medical liability, 1986: problem, prescription, prognosis. *J Bone Joint Surg Am.* 1986; 68: 1116-1124.

14. General Accounting Office. *Medical Malpractice: Characteristics of Claims Closed in 1984.* Washington, DC: U.S. General Accounting Office; 1986. Document (GAO) HRD-86-50.

Table 4.1

Do's and Don'ts When Faced With A Malpractice Suit

DO	DON'T
1. Notify your insurer at once.	1. Do not change your records in any way.
2. Cooperate with your insurer.	2. Do not transfer your assets.
3. Gather all your records.	3. Do not discuss the case with anyone except your claim representative or your defense attorney.
4. Dictate or write down immediately all you know about the incidents and the parties involved.	4. Do not talk to the plaintiff, the plaintiff's friends or family, or the plaintiff's attorney.
5. Plan to teach your defense team all you can about the medical aspects of the case.	5. Do not talk to the media.
6. If suit has not yet been brought and the patient requests a meeting, consult with your claim representative.	6. Do not overreact to the summons.
7. If your patient's lawyer asks for your records, supply either a copy or an accurate written summary of your care and treatment of your patient that contains all the relevant data.	7. Do not be hostile to your insurance claim representative or your defense attorney.
8. Complete an "Initial Report Form" (*incident report*).	8. Do not expect that a counterclaim against the patient for malicious prosecution will be successful.

Excerpted from Douglas Danner's *Medical Malpractice: A Primer for Physicians*.

Article 4.1

Facing Our Mistakes

David Hilfiker, MD. The New England Journal of Medicine, January 1984.

Looking at the appointment book for July 12, 1978, I notice that Barb Daily will be in today for her first prenatal examination. "Wonderful," I think, remembering my joy as I helped her deliver her first child two years ago. Barb and her husband Russ are friends, and our relationship became much closer with the shared experience of that birth. With so much exposure to disease every day in my rural family practice, I look forward to today's appointment with Barb and to the continuing relationship over the next months.

Barb seems to be in good health with all the symptoms and signs of pregnancy, but her urine pregnancy test is negative. I reassure Barb and myself that she is fine and that the test hasn't turned positive yet. Rescheduling another test for the following week, I congratulate her on her condition and promise to get all her test results to her promptly.

But the next urine test is negative, too, which leaves me troubled. Isn't Barb pregnant? Had she had a missed abortion? I could make sure right now, of course, by ordering an ultrasound, but the new examination is available only in Duluth, 110 miles away from our northern Minnesota village, and it is expensive. I am aware of the Dailys' modest income. Besides, by waiting a few weeks, I'll find out for sure without the ultrasound. I call Barb on the phone and tell her about the negative test, about the possible abortion, and about the necessity of a repeat appointment in a few weeks if her next menstrual period does not occur on schedule.

It is, as usual, a hectic summer, and I almost forget about Barb's situation until a month later when she returns. Still no menstrual period, no abortion. She is confused and upset, since, she says, "I feel so pregnant." I am bothered, too, especially because her uterus continues to be enlarged. Her urine test remains definitely negative.

I break the bad news to her. "I think you have a missed abortion. You were probably pregnant, but the baby appears to have died some weeks ago, before your first examination. Unfortunately, you didn't have the miscarriage to get rid of the dead tissue from the baby and the placenta. If a miscarriage does not occur within a few weeks, I'd recommend a reexamination, another pregnancy test, and if nothing shows up, a dilation and curettage to clean out the uterus."

Barb is disappointed and saddened; there are tears. Both she and Russ have sufficient background in science to understand the technical aspects of the situation, but that doesn't alleviate the sorrow. We talk in the office at some length and make an appointment for two weeks later.

When Barb returns, Russ is with her. Still no menstrual period, no miscarriage, and a negative pregnancy test. It is difficult, but it also feels right to be able to share in friends' sadness. Thoroughly reviewing the situation with both of them, I schedule the D and C for later in the week.

Friday morning, when Barb is wheeled into the operating room, we chat before she is put to sleep. The surgical nurses in our small hospital are all friends, too, so the atmosphere is warm and relaxed. After induction of anesthesia, I examine Barb's pelvis. To my hands, the uterus now seems bigger than it had two days previously, but since all the pregnancy tests were negative, the uterus couldn't have grown. I continue the operation.

But this morning there is considerably more blood than usual, and it is only with great difficulty that I am able to extract any tissue. The body parts I remove are much larger than I had expected, considering when the fetus died, and they are not the decomposing tissue I'd anticipated. These are body parts that were recently alive! I suppress the rising panic in my body and try to complete the procedure.

I am unable to evacuate the uterus completely, however, and after much sweat and worry, I stop, hoping that the uterus will expel the rest within a few days.

Russ is waiting outside the operating room, so I sit with him for a few minutes, telling him that Barb is fine but that there were some problems with the procedure. Since I haven't completely thought through what has happened, I can't be very helpful in answering his questions. I leave hurriedly for the office, promising to return that afternoon to talk with them once Barb has recovered from the anesthesia.

In between seeing other patients in the office that morning, I make several rushed phone calls, trying to figure out what has happened. Despite reassurances from the pathologist that it is statistically "impossible" for four consecutive pregnancy tests to be negative during a viable pregnancy, the horrifying awareness is growing that I have probably aborted Barb's living child. I won't know for sure until several days later, when the pathology report is available. In a daze I walk over to the hospital and try to tell Russ and Barb as much as I know, without telling them all that I suspect. I tell them that there may be more tissue expelled and that I won't know for sure about the pregnancy until the next week.

I can't really face my own suspicions yet.

That weekend I receive a tearful call from Barb. She has just passed some recognizable body parts of the baby; what is she to do? The bleeding has stopped, and she feels physically well, so it is apparent that the abortion I began on Friday is now over. I schedule a time in midweek to meet with them and review the entire situation.

The pathology report confirms my worst fears: I have aborted a living fetus at about 13 weeks of age. No explanation can be found for the negative pregnancy tests. My consultation with Barb and Russ later in the week is one of the hardest things I have ever done. Fortunately, their scientific sophistication allows me to describe in some detail what I have done and what my rationale was. But nothing can obscure the hard reality: I have killed their baby.

Politely, almost meekly, Russ asked whether the ultrasound examination could not have helped us. It almost seems that he is trying to protect my feelings, trying to absolve me of some of the responsibility.

"Yes," I answer, "if I had ordered the ultrasound, we would have known that the baby was alive." I cannot explain to him why I didn't recommend it.

Over the next days and months, my guilt and anger grow. I discuss the events with my partners, with our pathologist, and with obstetric specialists. Some of my mistakes are obvious: I relied too heavily on one particular test; I was not skillful in determining the size of the uterus by pelvic examination; I should have ordered the ultrasound before proceeding with the D and C. Other mistakes become apparent as we review my handling of the case. There is simply no way I can justify what I have done. To make matters worse, complications after the D and C have caused much discomfort, worry, and expense. Barb is unable to become pregnant again for two years.

As physicians our automatic response to reading about such a tragedy is to try to discover what went wrong, to analyze why the mistakes occurred, and to institute corrective measures so that such things do not happen again. This response is important, indeed necessary, and I spent hours in such a review. But it is inadequate if it does not address our own emotional and spiritual experience of the events.

Although I was as honest with the Dailys as I could be in those next months, although I told them everything they wanted to know and described to them as completely as I could what had happened, I never shared with them the agony that I underwent trying to deal with the reality of the events. I never did ask for their forgiveness. I felt somehow that they had enough sorrow without having to bear my burden as well. Somehow, I felt, it was my responsibility to deal with my guilt alone.

Everyone, of course, makes mistakes, and no one enjoys the consequences. But the potential consequences of our medical mistakes are so overwhelming that it is almost impossible for practicing physicians to deal with their errors in a psychologically healthy fashion. Most people—doctors and patients alike—harbor deep within themselves the expectation that the physician will be perfect. No one seems prepared to accept the simple fact of life that physicians, like anyone else, will make mistakes.

By the very nature of our work, we physicians daily make decisions of extreme gravity. Our work in the intensive-care unit, in the emergency room, in the surgery suite, or in the delivery room offers us hundreds of opportunities daily to miscalculate, often with drastic consequences.

And it is not only in these settings but also in the humdrum of routine daily care that a physician can blunder into tragedy. One evening, for instance, a local boy was brought to the emergency room after an apparently minor automobile accident. One leg and foot were injured, but he was otherwise fine. After examining him, I consulted by telephone with an orthopedic surgeon in Duluth, and we decided that I would try to correct what appeared on the x-ray film to be a dislocated foot. As usual, I offered the patient and his mother (who happened to be a nurse with whom I worked regularly) a choice: I could reduce the dislocation in our small hospital or they could travel to Duluth to see the specialist. I was somewhat offended when they decided they would go to Duluth. My feelings changed considerably when the surgeon called me the next morning to thank me for the referral. He reported that the patient had not had a dislocation at all but a severe posterior compartment syndrome, which had hyperflexed the foot, causing it to appear dislocated. The posterior compartment had required immediate surgery the previous night in order to save the muscles of the lower leg. I felt physically weak as I realized that this young man would have been permanently injured had his mother not decided on her own to take him to Duluth.

Although much less drastic than the threat of death or severe disability, perhaps the most frequent result of physician misjudgment is the wasting of money, often in large amounts. Every practicing physician spends thousands of dollars of patients' money every day in the costs for visits, laboratory examinations, medications, and hospitalizations. An unneeded examination, the needless admission of a patient to the hospital, even the unnecessary advice to stay home from work can waste large amounts of money—frequently, the money of people who have little to spare. One comes to feel that any decision may have important consequences.

The cumulative impact of such mistakes (and the ever-present potential for many others) has had a devastating effect on my own emotional health, as it does, I believe, for most physicians. For it is not only the obvious mistakes with obvious results that trouble us. Such mistakes as I made with Barb are fortunately rare occurrences for any physician, and an emotionally mature person may learn to cope with them. But there are also those frequent times when an obvious mistake may lead to less obvious consequences, when the physician errs in judgment, never to know how important the error was.

Some years ago, as I was rushing to an imminent delivery, a young woman stopped me in the hospital hall to tell me that her mother had been having chest pains all night. Should she be brought to the emergency room? I knew her mother well, had examined her the previous week, and knew of her recurring angina. "No," I responded, thinking primarily of my busy schedule and the fact that I was already an hour late because of the unexpected delivery. "Take her over to the office, and I'll see her there as soon as I'm done here." It would be a lot more convenient to see her in the office, I thought. About 20 minutes later, as I was finishing the delivery, our clinic nurse rushed into the delivery room, her face pale and frantic. "Come quick! Mrs. Martin just collapsed." I sprinted the 100 yards to the office to find Mrs. Martin in cardiac arrest. Like many physician offices at that time, ours was not equipped with the advanced life-support equipment necessary to handle the situation. Despite everything we could do, Mrs. Martin died.

Would she have survived if I had initially agreed to see her in the emergency room where the requisite staff and equipment were available? No one will ever know for sure, but I have to live with the possibility that she might have lived if I had made a routine decision differently, a decision similar to many others I would make that day, yet one with such an overwhelming outcome.

There is also the common situation of the seriously ill, hospitalized patient who requires almost continuous decision making on the part of the physician. Although no "mistake" may be evident, there are always things that could have been done better: a little more of this medication, starting that treatment a little earlier, recognizing this complication a bit sooner, limiting the number of visitors, and so forth. If the patient dies, the physician is left wondering whether the care provided was adequate. There is no way to be certain, for no one can know what would have happened if things had been done differently. Usually, in fact, it is difficult to get an honest opinion from consultants and other physicians about what one could have done differently. (Judge not, that you not be judged?) In the end, the physician has to swallow the concern, suppress the guilt, and move on to the next patient. He or she may simply be unable to discover whether the mistakes were responsible for the patient's death.

Worst of all, the possibility of a serious mistake is present with each patient the physician sees. The inherent uncertainty of medical practice creates a situation in which errors are always possible. Was that baby I just sent home with a diagnosis of a mild viral fever actually in the early stages of a serious meningitis? Could that nine-year-old with stomach cramps whose mother I just lectured about psychosomatic illness come into the hospital tomorrow with a ruptured appendix? Indeed, the closest I have ever come to involvement in a courtroom malpractice case was the result of my treatment of an apparently minor wrist injury one week after it happened: I misread a straightforward x-ray film and sent the young boy home with a diagnosis of sprain. I next heard about it five years later, when after being summoned to a hearing, I discovered that the fracture I had missed had not healed, and the patient had required extensive treatment and difficult surgery years later.

As practicing primary-care physicians, then, we work in an impossible situation. Each of the myriad decisions to be made every day has the potential for drastic consequences if it is not determined properly. And it is highly likely that sooner or later we will make the mistake that kills or seriously injures another person. How can we live with that knowledge? And after a serious mistake has been made, how can we continue in daily practice and expose ourselves again? How can we who see ourselves as healers deal with such guilt?

Painfully, almost unbelievably, we physicians are even less prepared to deal with our mistakes than the average lay person is. The climate of medical school and residency training, for instance, makes it nearly impossible to confront the emotional consequences of mistakes; it is an environment in which precision seems to predominate. In the large centers where doctors are trained, teams of physicians discuss the smallest details of cases; teaching is usually conducted to make it seem "obvious" what decisions should have been made. And when a physician does make an important mistake, it is first whispered about in the halls, as if it were a sin. Much later, a case conference is called in which experts who have had weeks to think about the situation discuss the way it should have been handled. The environment in which physicians are trained does not encourage them to talk about their mistakes or about their emotional responses to them.

Indeed, errors are rarely admitted or discussed once a physician is in private practice. I have some indication from consultants and colleagues that I am of at least average competence as a physician. The mistakes I have discussed here represent only a fraction of those of which I am aware. I assume that my colleagues at my own clinic and elsewhere are responsible for similar numbers of major and minor errors. Yet we rarely discuss them; I cannot remember a single instance in which another physician initiated a discussion of a mistake for the purpose of clarifying his or her own emotional response or deciding how to follow up. (I do not wish to imply that we don't discuss difficult cases or unfortunate results; yet these discussions are always handled so delicately in the presence of the "offending" physician that there is simply no space for confession or absolution.)

The medical profession simply seems to have no place for its mistakes. There is no permission given to talk about errors, no way of venting emotional responses. Indeed, one would almost think that mistakes are in the same category as sins: it is permissible to talk about them only when they happen to other people.

If the profession has no room for its mistakes, society seems to have even more rigid expectations of its physicians. The malpractice situation in our country is symptomatic of this attitude. In what other profession are practitioners regularly sued for hundreds of thousands of dollars because of misjudgment? A lawyer informed me I could be sued for $50,000 for misreading the x-ray film that led to the young man's unhealed fracture. I am sure the Dailys could have successfully sued me for large amounts of money, had they chosen to do so. Experienced physicians who are honest with themselves can count many potential malpractice suits against them. Even the word "malpractice" carries the implication that one has done something more than made a natural mistake; it connotes guilt and sinfulness.

It is easy, of course, to understand why this situation has arisen. These mistakes are terrible; their consequences are drastic; and the victim or family should be compensated for medical bills, time lost from work, and suffering or death. But in our society, rather than establish a "patient compensation fund" (similar to worker's compensation) from which a deserving patient can be compensated for an injury that results from a legitimate mistake, we insist that the doctor be sued for "malpractice," judged guilty, and forced to compensate the patient personally. An atmosphere of denial is created: the "good physician" doesn't make mistakes.

The drastic consequences of our mistakes, the repeated opportunities to make them, the uncertainty about our own culpability when results are poor, and the medical and societal denial that mistakes must happen all result in an intolerable paradox for the physician. We see the horror of our own mistakes, yet we are given no permission to deal with their enormous emotional impact; instead, we are forced to continue the routine of repeatedly making decisions, any one of which could lead us back into the same pit.

Perhaps the only adequate avenue for dealing with this paradox is spiritual. Although mistakes are not usually sins, they engender similar feelings of guilt. How can I not feel guilty about the death of Barb's baby, the lack of adequate emergency care for Mrs. Martin, the fracture that didn't heal? Whether I "ought" to feel guilty is a moot point; most of us do feel guilty under such circumstances.

The only real answer for guilt is spiritual confession, restitution, and absolution. Yet within the structure of modern medicine there is simply no place for this spiritual healing. Although the emotionally mature physician may find it possible to give the patient or family a clinical description of what happened, the technical details are often so difficult for the lay person to understand that the nature of the mistake is hidden. Or if an error is clearly described, it is presented as "natural," "understandable," or "unavoidable" (which, indeed, it often is). But there is no place for real confessions: "This is the mistake I made; I'm sorry." How can one say that to a grieving mother, to a family that has lost a member? It simply doesn't fit into the physician-patient relationship.

Even if one were bold enough to consider such a confession, strong voices would raise objections. When I finally heard about the unhealed fracture in my young patient, I was anxious that the incident not create antagonism between me and the family, since we live in a small town and see each other frequently. I was tempted to call the family and express my apologies and the hope that a satisfactory settlement could be worked out. I mentioned that possibility to a malpractice lawyer, but he was strongly opposed, urging me not to have any contact with the family until a settlement was reached. Even if a malpractice suit is not likely, the nature of the physician-patient relationship makes such a reversal of roles "unseemly." Can I further burden an already grieving family with the complexities of my feelings, my burden?

And if confession is difficult, what are we to say about restitution? The very nature of our work means that we are dealing with elements that cannot be restored in any meaningful way. What can I offer the Dailys in restitution?

I have not been successful in dealing with the paradox. Any patient encounter can dump me back into the situation of having caused more harm than good, yet my role is to be a healer. Since there has been no permission to address the paradox openly, I lapse into neurotic behavior to deal with my anxiety and guilt. Little wonder that physicians are accused of having a God complex; little wonder that we are defensive about our judgments; little wonder that we blame the patient or the previous physician when things go wrong, that we yell at the nurses for their mistakes, that we have such high rates of alcoholism, drug addiction and suicide.

At some point we must bring our mistakes out of the closet. We need to give ourselves permission to recognize our errors and their consequences. We need to find healthy ways to deal with our emotional responses to those errors. Our profession is difficult enough without our having to wear the yoke of perfection.

Hilfiker D. Facing our mistakes.
N Engl J Med. 1984; 310(2): 118-122.

Reprinted by permission from the author and The New England Journal of Medicine.

Article 4.2

A Primer For Physicians

Douglas Danner. Excerpted from Medical Malpractice: A Primer for Physicians, 1986.

How the Court Action Will Affect You and Your Practice

A malpractice suit does not mean the end of your practice or professional life, but it does mean that a certain amount of your time and energy over the next months or even years will be spent going over records, talking with lawyers and preparing the defense of the claim. This is all time which you would undoubtedly rather devote to other things. While every effort will be made to schedule meetings and hearings at your convenience, you will not be able to ignore the ongoing suit. On the other hand, it should not significantly interfere with your practice or your life.

You can expect to have a very difficult time emotionally until you are able to get the lawsuit into proper perspective. Among the emotions that will stagger you initially are: anger, pain, fear, panic, guilt, embarrassment, helplessness, despair and depression. You will react by taking the insult of the lawsuit personally, you will want to countersue the plaintiff and the plaintiff's lawyer. The key to your survival both personally and professionally is the knowledge that this is an occupational hazard, that you are not the first nor the last to be hit, that there are trusted and respected colleagues of yours who have survived and that your family, your colleagues and your true friends will support you in this crisis. You should recognize that you are not alone and that you will need emotional support from many important resources: your spouse and family, your colleagues and your friends. You should not withdraw physically or emotionally from those closest to you but rather make an extra effort to stay close to them and allow them to support you.

Douglas "Doad" Danner, JD, is an attorney with Powers and Hall in Boston, Massachusetts.

The first involvement of your time will start as soon as you are served with the summons and complaint by the court officer. At that time you should devote the equivalent of several days over several weeks obtaining and studying legible copies of your office and hospital records. You will find the insurance company claim representative to be very experienced in these matters. The claim representative is readily available to guide you completely and will probably obtain from you a detailed recorded statement setting forth everything you know about your care and treatment of the plaintiff.

Depending on your jurisdiction a pretrial Screening Panel hearing may be held but you probably will not be inconvenienced by this. Your attendance is usually not required since only the plaintiff can make an Offer of Proof. Massachusetts has a typical Screening Panel called a Tribunal.

If the plaintiff gets by the Tribunal or files the appropriate bond, your next significant involvement may be in working with defense counsel in answering written interrogatories.

Preparation for and attendance at your pretrial oral deposition will require a significant investment of your time, perhaps the equivalent of several days over several weeks. Your deposition is the most important event prior to trial.

Finally, trial preparation and the trial itself will take your time. If the case has not been resolved by then, this will consume several days in trial preparation, and then your involvement with the trial which may take a few days to a week or more. Since 95% of all cases are resolved prior to the trial, the chances of your involvement at trial are small.

Whether your case may have some unwarranted publicity is not predictable, but recent experience shows that the media is interested in fewer than a dozen cases annually. If the presiding judge feels that there has been any prejudicial pretrial or trial publicity, he will take appropriate action. Accordingly, it is far preferable for you and your trial counsel to avoid all contact with the media.

You personally may be worried and distressed largely because of the attack on your integrity. You may be furious that in spite of your best efforts based on many years of hard work and study, your patient has elected to embarrass you publicly. Our telling you that the patient has nothing personal against you, but just wants money in a situation where you or your insurance company appear to have plenty, is a small consolation to you. Your very first contact with our legal world may be by far the most emotional and once you see that these cases are indeed a risk of medical practice, you will simply adapt your practice to try to avoid them.

Finally, the traumatic impact of your case presents you with a basic challenge to your high intellectual integrity and idealism. Throughout the life of the case and for the rest of your medical practice, in spite of contrary temptations, we earnestly hope that you will:

1. continue to practice the best medicine you can as a compassionate and caring professional.

2. never look at each patient as a potential plaintiff in a malpractice action.

3. never practice defensive medicine by ordering unnecessary diagnostic studies or consultations if they are not in the patient's best interest.

Things NOT to Do Immediately

When you first receive notice that you are being claimed against or sued, your emotions may follow a classical pattern starting with fear, panic, anxiety, nervousness, frustration and self doubt. Your reaction may be one of anger that your integrity is being impugned, your means of making a living threatened and your commitment to patient care questioned.

Here is a specific list of things you should **not** do (unless advised otherwise by your insurance claim representative or your defense attorney):

1. Do not change your records in any way. Of course, in retrospect, we all wish the records had been more detailed or more complete, but changes in the record will be obvious and when pointed out to the jury will seem to be an admission that you had something to hide or cover up. Moreover, experts in document analysis can readily discern the later addition of information to a medical record.

2. Do not transfer your assets. Such transfers will not only appear to be an admission of liability, but they may be void if they are deemed to be transfers made in order to hide assets from creditors or holders of a judgment against you.

3. Do not discuss the case with anyone except your claim representative or your defense attorney. Even off-hand remarks to your partner or office nurse when made under emotional stress may to the ear of a juror sound like an admission of liability. Rehashing the details of the incident with a nurse or another doctor familiar with the events is not a good idea, especially if they are actual or potential co-defendants. Even worse, potentially, would be the appearance of one of these colleagues as a plaintiff's witness, ready to discuss the admissions that you had made.

4. Do not talk to the plaintiff, the plaintiff's friends or family, or the plaintiff's attorney. The time for an amiable reconciliation clearly is past, and further comments by you may be construed as an admission of guilt. Especially do not call to tell them how "sorry" you are about what happened.

5. Do not talk to the media. If a reporter calls you, say that you are under instructions not to discuss the case.

6. Do not overreact to the summons. The process server who is a deputy sheriff is not the one bringing suit. Nothing can be gained by harassing him.

7. Do not be hostile to your insurance claim representative or your defense attorney. You may feel that "the legal system" is attacking you and that as a member of that system, your claim representative and your defense attorney are somehow part of the "enemy." Nothing useful can come of that attitude. The interests of your defense team are in furthering your best interests. To do this efficiently, they need your full cooperation.

8. Do not expect that a counterclaim against the patient for malicious prosecution will be successful. Most defendant doctors are outraged at being sued and want to bring suit against the plaintiff and the plaintiff's attorney for the harm done to their medical practice by the plaintiff's legal action. Such actions are not successful for many reasons. A defendant doctor can only win such an action if the doctor can prove to a jury that the action against the doctor resulted in a verdict for the defendant and that the plaintiff was motivated by actual malice in bringing the original action against the defendant. Actions by a defendant doctor against the plaintiff's attorney will not succeed because of a legal immunity that attorneys have in representing their clients.

If you want to inquire further about such an action against the plaintiff, you should consult with your own personal attorney since the defense trial counsel assigned by the insurance company would not, in any event, be representing you in such an action against the plaintiff.

Things to Do Immediately

When a physician is sued for medical malpractice he must keep his head and not lose his cool. Here is a specific list of things you should do immediately:

1. Notify your insurer at once. Most policies include a provision that all claims and suits must be reported promptly to your insurance company. This is usually done by calling your insurance broker. This applies, of course, when you have formal notice that a court action has been started. Many policies also require you to report incidents which you think may give rise to suit. Even in the absence of anything definite, you should report, for example, letters of unusual recalcitrance in paying bills. To report an incident that turns out not to produce a claim does not in any way impeach your standing as a policyholder; if anything, it enhances it and will not increase your premium. Early notification of the insurance company will allow an early gathering of facts and will strengthen your position.

If the physician has excess liability insurance above the primary limits, notice must also be given to such excess carrier for the coverage to be effective. Once notified, the excess carrier usually will follow the progress of the case by maintaining close contact with your primary carrier.

2. Cooperate with your insurer. Hiding the situation or aspects of it from your insurance company will not protect your insurability, nor is it likely to prevent the facts from being brought into the open during the course of the proceedings.

3. Gather all your records. This should include:

(a) Office notes and records on patient. Dictate or write out all hard-to-read records or abbreviations. Try to recall and document significant telephone conversations with your patient, but keep these separate as they are not part of your original records.
(b) Hospital records in your possession.
(c) Correspondences with the patient or with others concerning the patient.
(d) All financial records including bills submitted for care and treatment of the patient.
(e) X-rays, laboratory or other diagnostic test results.

Maintain these records without changes in their current state. Your attorney will probably also want a typed transcription of the handwritten portions and an explanation of the medical abbreviations used.

4. Dictate or write down immediately all you know about the incidents and the parties involved.
This should include a narrative statement of your entire care in chronological order, from the date you first heard of or saw the patient, describing for each time the patient was seen professionally:

(a) the date, time and place,
(b) the history, physical examination and general information,
(c) the working diagnoses, diagnostic studies recommended and performed, treatment prescribed, and any witnesses to these,
(d) your first intimation of the patient's dissatisfaction such that a suit against you was being contemplated.

Note that by bringing this suit, the patient's "right to privacy" has been waived on these matters (at least between you and your attorney) and thus you should include in your report all the facts known to you about the patient and any other parties involved. Significant scandalous matters, even if hearsay, should be included but identified as such. At the end of this section there is an Example Report Form which may be helpful in identifying the kind of information which the defense team will need to know.

5. Plan to teach your defense team all you can about the medical aspects of the case. As a defense malpractice specialist, your claim representative and your defense attorney will already be well-versed on many areas of medicine. Nevertheless, they will welcome your help on medical matters.

6. If suit has not yet been brought and the patient requests a meeting, consult with your claim representative. Patients sometimes want to talk with their doctors before deciding whether to pursue a formal claim, and occasionally may request to have an attorney present during the conversation. This problem needs delicate handling so you should call your insurance company. As many suits are brought because the patient desires information which he or she feels the doctor did not make available, it can be seen that there might be a potential benefit to both parties from such a meeting. However, there are also risks for the physician, especially if the patient's attorney is to be there.

It is essential to rely on the advice of your insurance company claim representative who may wish to attend the meeting. Otherwise, by talking to either the plaintiff or his or her attorney, without your obtaining prior approval from your insurance company, your insurance coverage might be voided.

7. If your patient's lawyer asks for your records, supply either a copy or an accurate written summary of your care and treatment of your patient which contains all relevant data. If your patient's lawyer sends you a letter including your patient's authorization and a request for a copy of your records, you may wish to consult with your insurance company because of the serious potential this request presents. Obviously you should make no changes in the records. If a written summary is to be supplied, make certain it is completely accurate.

8. Example Report Form.

The following is an outline of the usual information needed by your defense team. It is included here so that you can assemble this information for your conference with your claim representative or your defense counsel.

Date:__________, 19_____

Title of Action:________________________________ vs. ________________________________

Personal and Professional Information:

1. Your full name: ________________________________
2. Your home address: ________________________________
   Home telephone number: ________________________________
3. Your office address: ________________________________
   Office telephone number: ________________________________
4. Age: ________________________________
5. College: Name ______________ Year of graduation __________ Degree ______________
6. Medical School: Name ______________ Year of graduation __________ Degree ______________
7. Place of internship and dates: ________________________________
8. Place of residency and dates: ________________________________
9. Nature of practice: ________________________________
10. Specialty, if any: ________________________________
11. Of what medical societies, associations, and specialty boards are you a member or diplomate? __________
12. Has any state, society, association, or board ever suspended, restricted, or revoked your license or privileges? If so, give details: ________________________________
13. Has any hospital or other institution ever suspended, restricted, or revoked your privileges? __________
    If so, give details: ________________________________
14. Were you practicing under any name other than your own, or practicing in, or associated with, any clinic, group, or partnership at the time any of the services involved in this case were rendered? __________
15. At any time any services in question were rendered, did you have in your employ a licensed physician? __________
    If so, whom: ________________________________

Information about the Patient Who is Suing You:

16. Full name and address: ______
17. Age when treated: ______
18. Occupation: ______ Married or Single: ______
19. Number of minor children and/or other dependents: ______
20. If patient is married or a minor, state name and occupation of spouse or name of parent or guardian: ______
21. Are you related to patient? ______
22. If related, what is the relationship? ______

Your Contacts with this Patient:

23. What was patient's condition and your diagnosis when first seen by you? ______
24. Have you had previous experience in treating this condition? ______
25. If your experience is limited, please explain: ______
26. Was the result obtained in this case unusual or unsatisfactory? ______
    Give details: ______
27. If so, does this result occur in a certain percentage of such cases? ______
    If you are aware of medical literature on this type of result, please identify: ______
28. Did you furnish any treatment to the patient that is not recorded either in your records or other available medical records? If so, please explain: ______
29. If it has been necessary to make any change in the medical records at any time, please explain in detail: ______

______

MAKE NO FURTHER CHANGES IN THE RECORDS UNDER ANY CIRCUMSTANCES!

30. What was the patient's condition when last seen? ______
31. What is the patient's condition now? ______
32. If the patient is dead, state date, place, and cause of death, and name surviving relatives: ______
33. Who signed death certificate? ______
34. Cause of death therein stated: ______
35. When did you first see patient professionally? ______
36. When last? ______
37. By whom were you retained? ______
38. Detail any special arrangement concerning your retention: ______
39. Were you in charge of case? ______
40. If not, in what capacity were you employed? ______
41. Who was in charge? ______
42. Why did you discontinue treatment? ______

Other Doctors

43. Give name and address of each doctor who preceded you on case: ______
44. What was his diagnosis? ______
45. Treatment? ______
46. When did preceding doctor last see patient? ______
47. Attitude toward you? ______
48. What doctor was associated with you in case? ______
49. Attitude toward you? ______
50. Did he approve of your diagnosis and treatment? ______
51. Give name and address of each doctor who succeeded you on case: ______
52. Attitude toward you? ______
53. What doctor is treating case now? ______
54. Attitude toward you? ______

X-rays:

55. Dates when X-ray films were taken: ______
56. By whom interpreted? ______
57. What did each film show (identify by dates)? ______
58. In whose possession are films now? ______

Hospitalization:

59. If patient was hospitalized, state name and location of hospital: ____________
60. State character of hospital (public or private ownership, charitable, or operated for profit): ____________
61. Who owns hospital? ____________
62. Have you any financial or other interest in hospital? ____________
63. Who arranged for hospital service? ____________
64. Give names of nurses on case and state whether hospital or special nurse: ____________
65. Were special nurses paid by patient or hospital? ____________
66. Amount of hospital costs: ____________
67. Balance due: ____________
68. When did patient enter hospital? ____________
69. When discharged? ____________
70. Whose consent was given to discharge? ____________
71. Give details of any of patient's bills under hospitalization, medical, or surgical insurance coverage: ____________

Death Case Information:

72. Was autopsy or post mortem performed? ____________
73. When? ____________
74. Where? ____________
75. Whose consent was obtained? ____________
76. Written or oral consent? ____________
77. Who performed autopsy? ____________
78. What were the findings as to cause of death? ____________
79. Was coroner's inquest held? ____________
80. When? ____________
81. Where? ____________
82. Results? ____________

Workmen's Compensation and Other suits by Patient:

83. Has patient received Workmen's Compensation? ____________
84. Amount? ____________
85. Has patient sued, settled with, or obtained judgment against party causing original injury? ____________
86. Amount? ____________

Claim Background:

87. Related circumstances and substance of all conversations in which patient or family indicated dissatisfaction with your treatment, giving date, place, names of those present and the substance of each conversation: ____________
88. When did such indication of dissatisfaction first occur? ____________
89. When was first definite claim made against you? ____________
90. When did you first learn that there would probably be a claim against you? ____________
91. State name of attorney representing claimant: ____________
92. Has suit been filed against you? ____________
93. In what court? ____________
94. How and from whom did you first learn this? ____________
95. Have you been served with a summons? ____________
96. Date summons served: ____________
97. Have you delivered all such papers you have received to us? ____________
98. State amount paid you for services rendered: ____________
99. Amount due? ____________
100. Have you sued for fees? ____________
101. What was outcome of suit? ____________
102. What attorney or collection agency represented you in fee action? ____________

Prepared by Dr. ____________

Address: ____________

Telephone Number: ____________ Date: ____________

Understanding Your Insurance Coverage

Briefly stated, your insurance policy is a contract which covers you for most kinds of conduct relating to your medical professional services to your patients. There are two separate obligations which your insurance company has: the obligation to defend you and the obligation to pay any judgment rendered against you by the jury up to your policy limits. The significance of this distinction largely relates to the amount of your coverage. No matter what your coverage, you will be defended but a judgment will be paid only to the extent of your coverage. If there is a problem of insurance coverage, you will be notified of this by your insurance company. You may receive a "reservation of rights" letter referring to the coverage question or you may be asked to sign a "non-waiver" agreement whereby your insurance company will agree to defend you but the question of any obligation to pay any judgment will be deferred until the coverage question is resolved.

You have a duty to cooperate in the defense of your case or otherwise the coverage may be voided. You should notify the company of any information which may forecast a suit and obviously you must notify your company of the service of any court process such as the summons and complaint starting the malpractice action.

The company usually has the right to settle your case in its discretion but it exercises that right sparingly and usually asks for your consent to any settlement.

Insurance problems rarely arise and most of these relate to inadequate insurance coverage. If the company feels that your coverage may be inadequate, you will be encouraged to obtain personal counsel at your expense to represent your interests to the extent that they are different from the company's interest. The primary duty of the defense attorney employed by the insurance company is to represent you on all aspects of the case. However, should issues of inadequate coverage arise, you are strongly encouraged to obtain your own personal counsel to assure that there will be no conflict of interest. Your defense attorney will be pleased to work closely with your personal counsel, so you should not hesitate to employ personal counsel.

If any kind of insurance question is bothering you, discuss it first with your insurance agent or broker. If the problem persists, you should contact the insurance company, your assigned defense counsel or your own personal counsel. It is very important to your peace of mind that there be no misunderstandings in this area.

Legal Representation

The typical malpractice insurance policy gives the insurance company the right to select counsel and control the defense. It will select attorneys it knows to have experience and expertise in problems of medical malpractice defense. You should trust your defense counsel's advice. Don't try to substitute your judgment for your lawyer's. In a very real sense, regard yourself as the "patient" and allow your lawyer to assume the role you usually take. Try to conduct yourself as you would have any patient do—give your lawyer your respect and trust, listen well, provide all needed information, follow his protocol, and don't try to do his job or "treat" yourself. At each stage, your lawyer will explain to you the significance of the proceedings and will help prepare you for your role. Do not expect to be told exactly what will happen. A lawyer cannot foretell the future in the trial of cases any more than a doctor can in a medical case.

It is important that you like and have confidence in your defense counsel. If you have a serious problem with your lawyer, or reservations concerning his or her handling of the case, first consult with the lawyer to see if a thorough discussion or explanation will clear up the difficulties. If you are still dissatisfied, you may speak with your insurance company, who may reassure you or discuss the possibility of engaging other counsel. You may consult with your own personal attorney, who may be able to resolve to your satisfaction any problem in this area.

Your employment of your personal counsel is your right but will seldom be necessary.

It will be very rare for personal counsel to sit through the trial at counsel table although local knowledgeable counsel can assist with the jury, especially in rural areas.

You should obtain personal counsel where defense counsel will not be representing your interest, such as where your insurance coverage does not exist or may be inadequate. For example, where punitive damages are alleged, coverage for punitive damages may be denied by the insurance underwriter. As the issues at stake are ones of insurance coverage and insurance law, you should ascertain that your personal counsel is sophisticated in insurance law. The help of your personal counsel is particularly essential where the potential jury verdict may exceed your insurance coverage, such as in lifetime-of-custodial-care cases.

OUTLINE OF THE LEGAL PROCESS

Introduction

A medical malpractice action is commenced like any other tort action, generally by the filing of a complaint in court and then having the court issue a process which is served upon the defendant or various defendants. Often that process says on it that the defendant must appear in court or file an answer. There is never any occasion immediately for the defendant to appear in court, but the papers that are served should be turned over to the insurance company for defense.

Jurisdiction is the word that describes the location where the action is brought because it is essential for the court system to have jurisdiction or control over the parties and the subject matter. For example, the United States District Court cannot take jurisdiction over a medical malpractice case unless the parties, that is the plaintiff and the defendant, are from different states (diversity of citizenship), and the amount at issue is in excess of $10,000. Venue refers to the particular place within a jurisdiction where the case is to be tried. Most plaintiff's attorneys prefer a large metropolitan area on the theory that larger verdicts will be given by juries in those areas. The defendant doctor may prefer to have the case tried in his own local home town because he is well-known and the jury will look upon him as a person rather than a doctor having insurance. Initially the plaintiff's attorney will select the venue, and one of the things that defense counsel will want to consider is whether or not a motion for change of venue should be made. In some instances, the papers can be impounded upon motion to the presiding judge. This means that they are given a designation which will not identify the parties and physically the papers are separated so that they are not available to the general public and the newspapers. Before a judge will impound the papers he must be convinced that serious and apparent irreparable harm will be caused to the defendant physician, so such action is seldom taken.

The Complaint and Answer

The complaint filed by the plaintiff's attorney in court on behalf of the plaintiff or the various plaintiffs is in general terms the statement of the allegations of the plaintiff against the defendant or defendants. The complaint is broken down into counts, each of which sets out a separate cause of action. The causes of action themselves are separated by the type of action such as negligence, assault and battery, breach of contract and lack of informed consent. In addition, the counts are separated by the identity of the plaintiff such as the plaintiff being an adult suing in his own name, a husband suing for consequential damages, a father suing in his capacity as father and next friend for a minor, etc. Counts are also broken down by the various defendants. Thus it is not unusual for there to be many counts where there are multiple causes of action, multiple plaintiffs, and multiple defendants.

The answer filed on behalf of the defendant will generally contain a denial of most of the allegations and certain affirmative defenses such as comparative negligence on the part of the plaintiff, statute of limitations and others. Following the joinder of issue in the case by filing of an answer, there may be various pre-trial or interlocutory motions filed by one side or the other. Quite often the defense attorney will file a motion for Production of Documents.

Interrogatories

Interrogatories are written questions propounded by one party to another before trial. They are an inexpensive method of discovery and are binding on the person giving the answers. Quite often they are helpful to allow either side to learn facts but they have the disadvantage that the person answering will have his answers reviewed by his attorney, and the answers will be the minimum possible to answer the question.

Deposition

Pre-trial oral depositions are by far the most satisfactory pre-trial discovery. The attorney for either party can obtain the pre-trial testimony of any other party or any witness through the use of depositions. The only persons at the depositions are the attorneys, the court reporter, and the witness. The court is not present. Since 19 out of every 20 cases are disposed of prior to trial, the deposition in the medical malpractice case becomes of vital importance and is usually decisive of the case.

Experts

An expert consultant will usually be brought into the case on your behalf after all of the investigation and fact finding has been completed. After the full story is obtained from you and all of those persons that you know and control, and then after the deposition has been taken of the plaintiff and any other crucial witness, your attorney will submit the entire file to an expert in the particular field involved for his consultation and opinion. Sometimes the same doctor is used to make a physical examination of the plaintiff, but often the defendant's expert consultant will testify entirely as to hypothetical questions based upon assumed facts rather than ever having personally examined the plaintiff.

The Trial

A jury trial is conducted quite differently from a deposition. If you have never seen a jury trial, with the approval and guidance of your trial lawyer, you may find it helpful to observe a jury trial before your case is tried. You will learn about the procedures and get acclimated to the proceedings. This knowledge will help eliminate the rehearsal butterflies or pregame jitters.

The trial of a medical malpractice case is not substantially different from other personal injury trials. The trial opens with the impanelling of the jury if either side has claimed a jury. Then the plaintiff's attorney will make an opening statement identifying for the jury what evidence the plaintiff expects to prove. From the plaintiff's point of view the opening is very important indeed, because here is an opportunity for the plaintiff's attorney to set the stage and do his or her best to evoke the sympathy of the jury for the injured plaintiff.

Following the plaintiff's opening statement, your defense counsel probably will make an opening statement on your behalf, explaining how the evidence will show that the jury should not render any verdict against you.

Then the plaintiff, having the burden of proof under the law, proceeds first with presentation of the plaintiff's case. The plaintiff's attorney calls each of the witnesses to stand in turn for questioning (the direct examination). After direct examination, each witness is subjected to interrogation by your attorney (the cross-examination). There may follow redirect and recross examinations in further exploration of matters brought forth as testimony proceeds. Objectionable questions and answers may be challenged by opposing attorneys for ruling by the trial justice. Such rulings are subject to "objection" in which case the disputed ruling may later be appealed to a higher court. The trial, however, proceeds. All testimony is transcribed word for word by a court reporter so that an official transcript may later be made if needed.

Nontestimonial evidence (medical records, x-rays, etc.) may be offered by either side and, if accepted by the court, each is identified and so marked by the court reporter to be retained for study by the jury.

Directed Verdict or Non-suit

A motion for directed verdict or non-suit may be brought by your attorney claiming that the state of the evidence at a particular point in the case is not sufficient to allow the jury to consider the case, and therefore the judge should direct the jury to return a verdict for you. In all cases, the plaintiff has the burden of setting forth a *prima facie* case amounting to sufficient evidence of a legal nature to prove his case. If at the end of the opening statement or at the end of the plaintiff's evidence, or at the end of all of the evidence, your attorney can convince the judge that the plaintiff has not made out a prima facie case, then the judge may direct a verdict against the plaintiff. If the motion for directed verdict on the plaintiff's evidence is denied, then your attorney can appeal later but must continue the trial and put on the defendant's evidence.

If, at the end of all the evidence, the plaintiff has made out a prima facie case, then there will be arguments by counsel to the jury. These are called summations, and each attorney will be given a reasonable time, usually half an hour or so, to argue his client's case to the jury.

Instructions to the Jury

Following arguments, the judge will instruct the jury as to the law of the case, informing the jurors that they are the final arbiters of the facts, liability, and damages. The judge will further instruct the jury as to the various elements of the case that may be considered in arriving at a dollar amount of damages for the plaintiff if the defendant is found liable. As an example, the judge may tell the jury: "Whether a physician is to be compensated for his services has no bearing on the duty that he owes to a person he undertakes to treat and care for as a patient. By taking charge of a case, a physician represents that he possesses, and the law places upon him the duty of possessing, that reasonable degree of learning and skill that is ordinarily possessed by physicians engaged in his specialty. When he consents to treat a patient, he obligates himself to use his best judgment and to use reasonable care in the exercise of his skill and the application of his learning to accomplish the treatment for which he is employed. By undertaking treatment, he does not guarantee a good result, but for an injury to his patient resulting from a physician's lack of requisite knowledge and skill, or his failure to exercise reasonable care or to use his best judgment, he is liable to the patient. The rule in relation to learning and skill does not require the physician to possess that extraordinary learning and skill which belong only to a few men of rare endowments, but such as is possessed by the average physician (in his area of general practice or specialization). He is, however, bound to keep abreast of the times and a departure from approved methods in general use, if it injures the patient, will render him liable, however good his intentions."

After the judge's charge to the jury, the jury will then retire to deliberate.

Appeal

After final judgment, an appeal can be taken on questions of law only and not questions of facts. These questions of law generally relate to the trial judge's rulings on the admissibility of evidence and the trial judge's jury instructions, but they can cover a wide variety of matters. Appeals are rare because of the uncertainty of any change as a result of the appeal, the expense to all parties and the fact that the appeal process takes several years.

Danner D. Medical Malpractice: A Primer for Physicians. Rochester, NY: The Lawyers Co-Operative Publishing Co.; 1986: 3-16.

Reprinted by permission from the author and The Lawyers Co-Operative Publishing Company.

Article 4.3

Physician Management of Patients With Adverse Outcomes

William B. Applegate, MD, MPH. Archives of Internal Medicine, November 1986.

The incidence of iatrogenic complications of medical or surgical care is increasing. Such adverse events may severely strain the patient/physician relationship. The nature of the underlying patient/physician relationship in terms of the style of interaction and the handling of uncertainty and decision making may influence the impact of adverse events on the relationship. Physicians may manage these situations poorly because of perceived threats to their self-image or sense of control, or because of fear of malpractice suits. Patients may consciously or subconsciously blame the physician, fail to express their concerns, or exaggerate their complaints. If possible, continuity of the patient/physician relationship should be maintained through full disclosure of all medical facts, frank and open communication, and a renewed commitment to the therapeutic relationship.

Iatrogenic adverse reactions may develop from a wide array of modern diagnostic or therapeutic practices.[1-3] Despite the enormous power of modern medicine to cure or palliate, untoward side effects still occur. There is a spectrum of such events with varying potential for culpability or feelings of guilt on the part of the physician, and for placing blame on the part of the patient.

Adverse events can occur as haphazard or unpredictable events (eg, a previously ambulatory hospitalized patient falls on the way to the bathroom, breaking a hip). Adverse events can also occur as a result of a diagnostic or therapeutic decision in which the probability of the adverse event was predictable, but justifiably judged to be less than the probability of diagnostic or therapeutic benefit (eg, a stroke resulting from a carotid arteriogram, or side effects of cancer chemotherapy). In addition, adverse events can occur as honest and legitimate errors of judgment in which the physician acted in good faith, made a decision that turned out not to be the best, but involved no negligence or substandard care (eg, stroke after a carotid endarterectomy in a high-risk patient, but a case in which various physicians could reasonably disagree about the initial decision). The final category, decisions in which the physician is, to some degree, obviously culpable of malpractice or negligence will not be discussed here. The focus of this article is on managing adverse events in which the physician would usually not be deemed culpable in a legal sense, but in which there exists definite potential for harm to the patient/physician relationship.

Despite a voluminous literature on iatrogenic complications of various medical procedures and therapies, surprisingly little has been written concerning the impact of an iatrogenic complication or adverse outcome on the patient/physician relationship. It is currently believed that only about 5% of potentially litigious events that occur during the course of medical care ultimately result in lawsuits.[4] Even if the probability of lawsuit is not particularly high once such an event has occurred, what impact can these events have on subsequent patient/physician encounters? Why do some events proceed to the law courts and others do not? Once an adverse event has occurred, how should it be managed?

The perspective of this article is that the underlying patient/physician relationship is the foundation on which the adverse event occurs, that the adverse event is a critical stressor that can either undermine or ultimately strengthen the patient/physician relationship, and that both the previous nature of the relationship and the actual management of the adverse event when it occurs will influence the ultimate course of events.

Nature of the Underlying Patient-Physician Relationship

The malpractice literature contains a number of assertions, but surprisingly little empirical data, on the impact of the underlying patient/physician relationship on malpractice suits.[5] In a national study conducted by the Temple University Institute of Survey Research, nearly 40% of the 1017 respondents reported that they, their spouses, or their dependents had had a negative experience with medical care within the last ten years.[6] Only 8% (37) of those experiencing problems thought about legal advice, while 14 individuals underwent legal counseling, and six made a claim of malpractice. Interestingly, the subgroup who reported negative experiences were more likely to report that today's doctors maintain poor relationships with their patients, with particular concerns about physicians' interpersonal skills and the amount of money charged for services. Blum et al[7] reported on a California study in which patients who sued doctors stated that the doctors had been unresponsive to their concerns and had insisted on large payments despite adverse results.

Medical lawsuits are simply the tip of the iceberg with regard to adverse outcomes and their impact on the patient/physician relationship.Three components of the patient/physician relationship in particular seem likely to determine the type of reaction should an adverse outcome occur. These components are: the style of interaction and communication between the patient and the physician,[8] the handling of uncertainty in decision making and informed consent,[9,10] and the degree to which a trust relationship has been established between the patient and the physician.[11]

As outlined by Szasz and Hollender,[8] the style of the patient/physician interaction can vary as follows: (1) passive-active relationship where the physician determines what is to be done or said and the patient passively accepts it; (2) guidance-cooperation where the physician basically tells the patient what should be done and the patient usually concurs; and (3) mutual participation where patient and physician enter into a mutual partnership to make decisions and work on problems. In recent decades there has been a definite evolution toward mutual participation with sharing of risk and information. The more the physician sets himself or herself up in the dominant role in decision making without adequate collaboration from the patient, the greater is the likelihood that the patient could blame the physician should an adverse outcome occur.[9] If the physician maintains a dominant role in decision making, he or she may assume the mantle of omnipotence, and hence become more culpable in the patient's eyes should an adverse outcome occur.[12] Lazare et al[13] have demonstrated that both the patient and the physician often approach the same clinical problems from different perspectives with regard to the definition or meaning of the problem, the goals and priorities in treatment, and other intangibles, such as values. Since these differences can lead to basic conflict between patients and physicians over a wide range of issues, Lazare et al recommend a negotiated approach to patient care in which the physician elicits the patient's goals, priorities, and values, and negotiates any perceived differences between physician and patient views. If such differences are not negotiated, there is greater potential for anger and hostility on the part of the patient in the future.[13]

Several studies tend to indicate that the degree of communication between patient and physician is important for patient satisfaction and, by extension, could affect the reaction to an adverse event. Korsch et al[14] tape-recorded patient (and mother) encounters with pediatricians in the emergency clinic at the Children's Hospital of Los Angeles. The highest incidence of dissatisfaction among mothers interviewed occurred in visits where the mother's expectations and concerns received little or no attention. In those encounters, the mother often ceased attempts to communicate with the physician, resulting in dissatisfaction.[14] In a study of the relationship of factors that constitute patient attitudes regarding doctors and medical care, Ware and Snyder[15] reported that patient attitudes toward physician conduct are especially influenced by the following physician functions: giving important information, thoroughness in information gathering, and preventive measures and prudence (avoiding risk). In addition, Cousins[16] reported on a survey of patient/physician relationships he distributed in Westwood, Calif. Of the 563 respondents, 85% had changed physicians in the past five years or were thinking of changing. Most changes occurred for a variety of reasons relating to the style and personality of the physician, including the ability to communicate with the patient. In another study, Woolley[17] reported that 65% of patients experiencing a "bad medical outcome" still expressed satisfaction with the care they received. The author of this study concluded that the patients' evaluation of their care was influenced primarily by their assessment of the physician's effort.

Most clinical decisions regarding diagnostic or therapeutic procedures carry some risk and uncertainty with regard to the ultimate outcome. In addition, the course and prognosis of most clinical conditions can usually be estimated at best in terms of a range of probabilities.[10] A basic human psychological tendency is to create a sense of some certainty in the face of an uncertain situation.[12] Patients facing medical uncertainty experience a threat to their sense of well-being, and often react with a sense of fear, helplessness, and doubt.[9] To a varying degree, patients turn to physicians both to treat their illnesses and also to help them change their uncertainty and fears to certainty and hope.[9,10] Those patients who present with the greatest need for certainty may well attribute magical notions of omnipotence to the physician and to medical science. Guthiel et al[9] have pointed out that trust in scientific omnipotence can easily degenerate into paranoid distrust.

Physicians are also vulnerable to the threats inherent in medical uncertainties. For many physicians, a sense of power and control over disease and uncertainty are crucial parts of their self-image as healers.[12,18] Fox[19] suggests that physicians faced with medical uncertainty tend to devise nonempirical or magical techniques to enable them to carry out their tasks with confidence and poise. It may be easier for the physician to cope with multiple uncertainties encountered on a daily basis by developing the mantle of certainty and by assuming a very dominant, almost omnipotent role.

Unfortunately, even though the patient, physician, or both may receive some immediate psychological comfort from a relationship in which the physician appears omnipotent or infallible, this type of relationship does not reflect the true underlying realities of most clinical situations. The patient is likely to be bitterly disappointed if the promised results are not achieved, and the physician's perception of his role may be severely threatened by unexpected outcomes.[9,10] On the other hand, a relationship in which both patient and physician share in the knowledge and discussion of uncertainty allows both patient and physician to approach clinical problems in a realistic fashion, and can actually cement a stronger, mutual therapeutic alliance.[9,10,12] Specifically, the physician should empathize with the patient's need for certainty; at the same time the true nature of the uncertainties involved should be explained, and the patient should participate in determining the course of clinical care. Guthiel et al[9] recommended that a continued commitment to work through the uncertainties (the therapeutic alliance) be substituted for the patient's need for certainty. A sense of mutual commitment to continued work on medical problems will usually lead to mutual trust between patient and physician.[9] Trust and commitment are the glue that cement human relationships, as Mechanic[11] observed.

Informed consent for diagnostic or therapeutic maneuvers should be approached with these concepts in mind.[9] If information is adequately shared with regard to risk and uncertainty, and if mutual collaboration in any decision is attained, then patient and physician become partners in shared uncertainty. The patient can emerge from this process with a more realistic appraisal of the clinical possibilities. The physician can view the informed consent process as an important foundation for mutual disclosure and decisions, rather than as a formality required for medicolegal protection.

Potential Impact of Adverse Outcomes

Once an adverse outcome has occurred, both patient and physician must sort through issues and potential problems that can be a threat to the continued patient/physician relationship.

Problems Related to the Patient

At times the patient may feel that the physician is the cause of, or at least the agent for, his or her suffering.[7] The patient may subconsciously blame the physician, even if the patient consciously admits that the physician's decision that led to the event was warranted at the time of the decision. If the adverse event leads to chronic suffering or incapacity, the possibility exists that such blame could degenerate into a deep sense of anger or hostility.

That possibility increases if the patient has not felt a sense of mutual collaboration in decision making, or has not felt adequately informed with regard to the risks or uncertainties involved in the clinical process.[7,9,11] Anger may be focused on the physician in question, but can also be projected onto other physicians and affect future therapeutic relationships.

In such situations, trust between patient and physician may well be impaired.[11] If the physician tries to give the patient a hopeful prognosis (which may be important both for maintaining patient emotional balance during a period of pain and suffering, and for promotion of a beneficial response to future therapy), the patient may doubt the physician's statements, or feel the physician is covering up, or trying to minimize the extent of the patient's problems.

When trust is impaired, the patient may feel inhibited in openly communicating anxieties, fears, or anger. If the patient's concerns are not addressed, as pointed out by Korsch et al,[14] the patient may cease efforts to communicate. In addition, the patient may not only blame the physician, but also himself (or herself), for agreeing with the decision that led to the adverse event, or may feel that the adverse event was inevitable.[20] Such feelings of fate, or that the patient has "brought this on himself," may lead the patient to obsequiously accept his lot and never express his anguish to the physician. Also, patients who feel powerless because of the nature of their interaction with the physician may not adequately voice their concerns or feelings.[14,20]

If communication between the patient and physician is impaired, because of negative feelings harbored by either party, or because of personality or style of interaction, the patient may begin to feel that the physician is not giving much credence to the patient's concerns. In such situations the patient may either give up and turn away from the physician or, in desperation, inappropriately escalate complaints in an effort to elicit an appropriate level of concern from the physician.[4,9,22] If the physician senses that the patient is inappropriately escalating his complaints, the physician (rather than understanding the need that drives the behavior) may use this evidence as the rationale to discredit or discount the patient's problems or suffering. If the patient feels the physician is not appropriately concerned, and communication is inadequate, or the physician feels the patient is not adequately committed to the relationship, either party may begin to terminate the relationship. As pointed out by Guthiel et al[9] and Press,[4] patients who feel ignored or rejected by their physicians are more likely to consider a lawsuit as a way of forcing the physician to share the responsibility for the outcome and the experience of anger and suffering caused by clinical events.

Problems Related to the Physician

When the physician is faced with a patient who has had an adverse outcome under his or her care, there are several factors that may cause inappropriate management of the situation. A physician whose identity as a healer is heavily invested in feelings of power and control over disease or patients may see an adverse outcome as a threat to that image.[4,18] This is particularly true if the adverse outcome was not just a haphazard event, but rather more directly related to a decision that (in retrospect) could be subject to some question. Feelings of responsibility for the adverse outcome may engender feelings of guilt or professional or personal inadequacy.[4,7]

If the patient expresses dissatisfaction with the outcome, or if conflict with the patient should occur, this may be seen as a further threat to the need to maintain power and control. The underlying style of the physician's interactions with the patient may influence the physician's ability to handle negative feedback. Physicians who have maintained a physician-dominant style of interaction with the patient may attempt to structure their patient interactions to limit effective communication. Although as a rule physicians should try to avoid open conflict with patients, expression of negative feelings must be allowed and, at times, facilitated. If the physician cannot comfortably manage such difficult situations, the physician may then consciously or subconsciously wish to end the therapeutic relationship and may begin, in subtle ways, to drive the patient away.

Physicians may fear that the patient with an adverse outcome may sue them.[5] Such fears may influence the physician to be less than candid about the exact nature or cause of the adverse event, and even cause the physician to deny that the adverse outcome is real. In such circumstances, communication will often be seriously impaired, and, as mentioned earlier, the risk of a malpractice suit may actually increase.[9]

Management After an Adverse Outcome Has Occurred

There are several basic components for the proper management of adverse clinical outcomes. If there is informed consent with sufficient patient participation in decision making, and the patient has knowledge of the risks and uncertainty involved, the reaction to the adverse outcome is likely to be less damaging to the patient/physician relationship.

Regardless of the prior events, once an adverse outcome has occurred, full disclosure of its nature is necessary. Although the patient and the physician are usually aware that an adverse event has occurred, the exact cause may not be obvious to the patient. For example, the patient may be confused whether new symptoms are related to his underlying disease or to complications of therapy. Although it is possible that full disclosure could result in immediate deterioration of the patient/physician relationship, or in legal action, the patient has a right to full disclosure of his medical problems unless the patient is incompetent or unless the disclosure would cause him immediate harm.[23-25] In most cases it is unlikely that disclosure of the full truth would be as disabling as suffering from adverse symptoms in a state of uncertainty.

Lack of full disclosure will usually undermine the patient/physician relationship over time.[26] Patients with adverse outcomes who do not receive adequate explanations will usually sense that the physician is not discussing the problem in an open manner. This is especially true when the physician attempts to deny or minimize the problem. As a result the patient will often feel that his relationship with the physician is impaired or limited. If the physician does not provide full disclosure, he creates an environment for future interactions with the patient that is restrictive, defensive, and, at times, dishonest.[12,26]

The physician must strive to maintain ongoing open communication with the patient and to encourage the patient to express his concerns, fears, or anger. If this aspect of the relationship can be maintained, the physician will be in a position to correct any misconceptions the patient may harbor without losing credibility or trust. The physician should enlist the patient as a mutual participant in sharing information and future decisions. If there is uncertainty about the course of future events, the physician should acknowledge it, empathize with the patient, and be as optimistic as a realistic appraisal of the events allows. Adequate time must be allotted to patient visits to allow a frank interchange to take place. If this is the case, the patient may feel his needs are being met, despite the adverse outcome, and not feel that the physician is trying to drive him away. In some cases, the sharing of frank and open communication between patient and physician over an adverse outcome may actually strengthen the relationship over time, once the initial emotional reaction to the adverse event is worked through.

The physician must periodically assess his own feelings about the adverse outcome and analyze any impact his feelings may have on his behavior toward the patient. The physician should continue to express his commitment to the patient and the management of the patient's problems. Follow-up appointments should be made, and the patient's telephone calls should be answered promptly. If appropriate, consultation with other physicians or other therapeutic modalities should be tried. If a consultation is arranged with another doctor, the physician should clearly describe the rationale for the consultation and state that he wants the patient to return. If the physician demonstrates such clear commitment to the therapeutic relationship, the patient may feel more inclined to continue to work through his clinical problems with the original physician.

Despite these efforts, at times it will not be possible to maintain an adequate patient/physician relationship. An adverse outcome may produce lingering resentments on the part of the patient that are impossible to overcome. If the physician encourages open communication, it may be possible to identify that the patient has irrevocably lost confidence in the physician. Although the realization that the patient has reacted in this manner may be painful to the physician, the matter must still be managed with the patient's best interests at heart. If the patient expresses that he has permanently lost confidence in the physician, and if the probability of further resolution is low, the physician must be prepared to advise the patient that other medical care is available. Whenever possible, the final decision on whether to terminate a therapeutic relationship should be left up to the patient. The physician must carefully examine his own motives prior to making such a recommendation, so that he does not inappropriately drive the patient away. If the patient agrees that it is best for him to seek other medical care, the physician should provide the patient with the names of other physicians, and should give the patient adequate time to make sufficient arrangements. Whenever possible, the physician should state that he would be willing to see the patient at any time in the future.

In conclusion, since the incidence of iatrogenic complications of medical or surgical care is on the rise, many patient/physician relationships may be tested by such an adverse event. Several characteristics of the prior patient/physician relationship may influence the nature of the reaction to the adverse event. These characteristics include the style of interaction between patient and physician, the handling of uncertainty in decision making and informed consent, and the degree to which trust between patient and physician has been established. Relationships in which there is more mutual collaboration in decision making with a realistic understanding of the uncertainties involved may be better prepared to withstand the negative reactions that may occur after an adverse outcome.

If an adverse outcome should occur, continuity of the patient/physician relationship should be maintained through full disclosure of all medical facts, frank and open communication and feedback, and a renewed commitment on the part of both parties to the therapeutic relationship. The physician should encourage the patient to participate fully in future therapeutic decisions, and should be frank with the patient about any future risk or uncertainty associated with medical decisions.

I am indebted to Haavi Morheim, PhD; Linda Nichols, PhD; and Arthur Kellerman, MD, for their review and critique of this manuscript.

References

1. Moser RH: Diseases of Medical Progress: A Study of Iatrogenic Disease. Springfield, Ill, Charles C Thomas Publishers, 1979.

2. D'Arcy PF, Griffin JP: Iatrogenic Disease. New York, Oxford University Press Inc, 1972.

3. Steele K, Gertman PM, Crescenzi C, et al: Iatrogenic illness on a general medical service at a university hospital. N Engl J Med1981;304:638-642.

4. Press I: Predisposition to file claims. Law, Medicine, and Health Care 1984;12:53-62.

5. Richards EP, Rathburn KC: Medical Risk Management. Rockville, Md, Aspen Systems Corp, 1983.

6. Peterson JL: Consumer's knowledge and attitudes toward medical malpractice, in Report to the Secretary's Commission on Medical Malpractice, US Dept Health, Education, and Welfare Publication No. 73-88, 73-89. Government Printing Office, 1973, pp 658-757.

7. Blum RH, Saduch J, Waterson R: Management of the Doctor-Patient Relationship. New York, McGraw-Hill International Book Co, 1960.

8. Szasz TS, Hollender MH: The doctor-patient relationship. Arch Intern Med 1956;97:585-592.

9. Guthiel TG, Bursztajn H, Brodsky A. Malpractice prevention through the sharing of uncertainty. N Engl J Med 1984;31:49-51.

10. Bursztajn H, Feinbloom RI, Hamm RM, et al: Medical Choices, Medical Chances. New York, Delacorte Press, 1981.

11. Mechanic D: Medical Sociology, ed 2. New York, Free Press, 1978, pp 495-570.

12. Katz J: Why doctors don't disclose uncertainty. Hastings Center Rep 1984;14:35-44.

13. Lazare A, Eisenthal S, Frank A, et al: Studies on a negotiated approach to patienthood, in The Doctor-Patient Relationship in the Changing Health Scene, Proceedings of the Fogarty Center International Conference, US Dept Health, Education, and Welfare Publication No. 78-183. Government Printing Office, 1976.

14. Korsch BM, Gozzi EK, Francis V: Gaps in doctor-patient communication: I. Doctor-patient interaction and patient satisfaction. Pediatrics 1978;42:855-871.

15. Ware JE, Snyder MK: Dimensions of patient attitudes regarding doctors and medical care services. Med Care 1975;23:669-682.

16. Cousins N: How patients appraise physicians. N Engl J Med 1985;313:1422-1424.

17. Woolley FR: The effects of doctor-patient communication on satisfaction and outcome of care. Soc Sci Med 1978;12:123-127.

18. Shapiro EC, Lowenstein LM: Becoming a Physician: Development of Values and Attitudes in Medicine. Cambridge, Mass, Ballinger, 1979.

19. Fox R: Experiment Perilous: Physicians and Patients Facing the Unknown. Glencoe, Ill, Free Press, 1959.

20. Kushner HS: When Bad Things Happen to Good People. Boston, GK Hall & Co, 1982.

21. Waitzkin H, Stoeckel J: Information control and the micropolitics of health care. Soc Sci Med 1976;10:263-264.

22. Gabbard GO: The role of compulsiveness in the normal physician. JAMA 1985;254:2926-2929.

23. Pellegrino ED: Toward a reconstruction of medical morality. J Med Philos 1979;4:32-56.

24. Cowles J: Informed consent. New York, Coward, McCann, and Geoghegan, 1976.

25. Childress JF: Who Should Decide? New York, Oxford University Press Inc, 1982, p 127.

26. Radovsky SS: Bearing the news. N Engl J Med 1985;313:586-588.

Applegate WB. Physician management of patients with adverse outcomes. Arch Intern Med. 1986; 146: 2249-2251.

Reprinted by permission from the author and the Archives of Internal Medicine.

Article 4.4

Current Concepts in Risk Management

James F. Holzer, JD. International Anesthesiology Clinics, 1984.

Although eliminating all risk in medical practice is virtually impossible, hospitals and physicians have become increasingly aware of the need to reduce and control those mishaps and iatrogenic events that are preventable. This awareness has grown in part from the dramatic rise in medical malpractice claims and suits in the United States. Data from studies reported in other chapters of this issue clearly demonstrate that anesthetic mishaps, although relatively few in number, present considerable risk of loss in the areas of hospital cost, human suffering, and the integrity of the medical profession.

To counter such losses, many hospitals and medical societies have developed formal programs to systematically identify and control risks that may lead to patient injury or financial loss for providers. Over 1,000 risk management professionals are currently working in a variety of health care settings, including hospitals, health maintenance organizations, large group practices, hospital associations, and medical societies sponsoring professional liability insurance programs.

These experts are now recognizing that losses from preventable anesthetic mishaps pose one of the most significant risks in medicine today. Although estimates of death and injury due to anesthesia vary widely, potentially compensable anesthetic mishaps do occur, many causing patients to suffer lasting sequelae. To the health consumer, injuries from such mishaps appear to be more catastrophic in nature since anesthesia is rarely a therapeutic intervention by itself, but merely a supportive measure of a primary surgical intervention. It has been suggested that anesthesia consequently puts patients at risk while offering no direct curative benefit.[19]

James F. Holzer, JD, is Vice President of Loss Prevention, Risk Management Foundation of the Harvard Medical Insititutions, Cambridge, Massachusetts, and a lecturer on the Faculty of Medicine at Harvard Medical School in Boston.

Scope of Anesthesia Risk

The frequency and severity of anesthetic mishaps in the U.S. is reported in other chapters of this issue. More recent studies conducted separately by independent research firms and the Harvard Risk Management Foundation in Boston, Massachusetts, confirm that anesthesia malpractice claims continue to generate significant financial losses for providers and medical liability insurance programs. In a study of U.S. medical malpractice trials during 1981, Jury Verdict Research, Inc., of Solon, Ohio, reported that jury awards for negligence against physicians and hospitals nearly doubled since 1975.[9] The category of surgical misadventures, which included numerous anesthetic mishaps, accounted for an average verdict of $247,305 against physicians, ranging from a low verdict of $2,500 to a high of $1.5 million. Contributing to this staggering financial loss were numerous suits for improperly administered or monitored anesthesia.[8] Mishaps involving anesthesia also contributed to a number of injuries to mothers during obstetrical or gynecological procedures. The average jury verdict against hospitals and doctors for OB/GYN injuries was $407,814. One such case involved a mother who, after giving birth to a healthy child, received 100% nitrous oxide. Unknown to the hospital and physicians at the time, there was an apparent cross connection in the pipes delivering oxygen and nitrous oxide. The patient's survivors sued the medical corporation, the hospital's architects, the contractors who built the facility, and the hospital. Only the hospital was found to be liable. The jury awarded the family seven million dollars, of which five million was for punitive damages.[9]

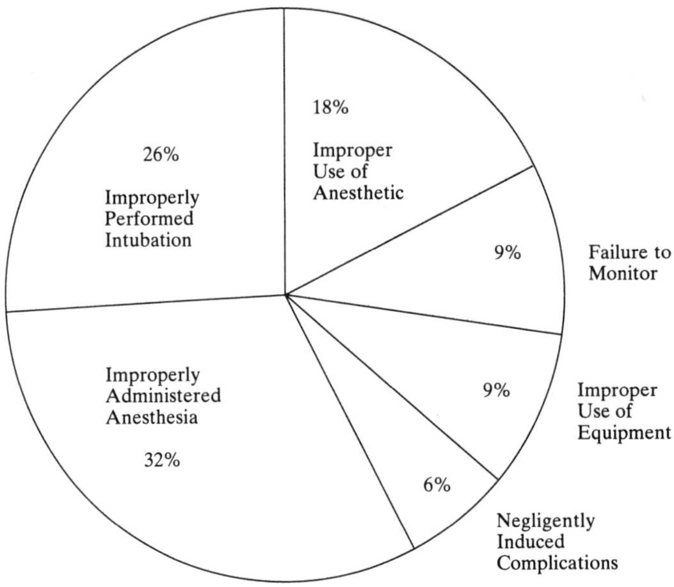

Figure 1. Allegations associated with anesthesia claims, April, 1976, to February, 1983. Compiled by the Harvard Risk Management Foundation.

Also reported was a case involving a 23-year-old woman who suffered a cardiac arrest and died while undergoing surgery for hammertoes. The suit was brought by her husband and child against the defendant anesthesiologist for failure to properly plan the operation, failure to use an endotracheal tube, a cardioscope, or precardial stethoscope, and failure to properly resuscitate the patient. The jury awarded the plaintiff $859,664.[8]

Although anesthetic mishaps are typically classified as low-frequency events, the severity of such mishaps is high in terms of financial loss. A recent study by the Harvard Risk Management Foundation of ten Boston-area teaching hospitals indicates that anesthetic mishaps accounted for less than 2% of the medical malpractice claim files created from April, 1976, through February, 1983. However, the average financial loss for an anesthesia claim file was approximately $110,000. Losses include indemnity-expense reserves for all open and potential claim files, and actual indemnity-expense payments on closed files.

Allegations of Anesthesia Negligence

Approximately one-third of the anesthesia claim files in the Harvard study alleged that anesthesia was improperly administered (Fig. 1). There were a wide variety of injuries associated with this allegation, including cosmetic disfigurement, emotional trauma, numbness or weakness of a limb, and cardiac arrest resulting in death.

The second most frequent anesthesia claim involved damaged teeth from intubation. In spite of the high frequency of this event, the relative financial loss per claim was under $2,000.

The alleged improper use of an anesthetic agent accounted for 18% of the claims surveyed. This category related most frequently to the occurrence of hepatitis following the use of halothane.

Failure of the anesthesiologist to monitor the patient during surgery and improper use of anesthesia equipment were associated with the more catastrophic injuries, including death, cardiac arrest, and brain damage. However, these events occurred less frequently.

Injuries Associated with Anesthesia Claims

Consistent with national insurance data, the most frequent injury associated with anesthesia claims in the Harvard study was damage to patients' teeth (Fig. 2). This mishap was alleged to have occurred most often during intubation procedures and

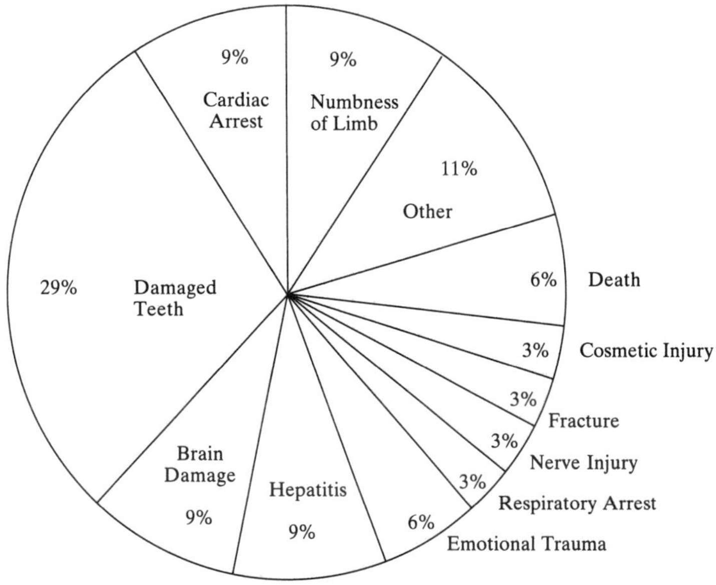

Figure 2. Alleged damage or injury associated with anesthesia claims, April, 1976, to February, 1983. Compiled by the Harvard Risk Management Foundation.

accounted for 29% of the anesthesia claims. There was no clear trend involving the more serious injuries, although allegations of brain damage, cardiac arrest, hepatitis, and numbness of a limb together constituted over one-third of the claims surveyed. Over 20% of the anesthesia claims involved the administration of a spinal agent, of which 50% of the patients suffered some type of weakness or numbness in their leg or arm.

Data such as the type displayed in Figures 1 and 2 are routinely made available to the anesthesia services of the Harvard teaching hospitals as part of their ongoing quality assurance and risk management efforts. The use of these data for risk reduction and educational purposes will be discussed later in this chapter.

Medical Risk Management

It has been argued that the complex social and legal problems stemming from the occurrence of preventable medical mishaps will never be satisfactorily addressed until these mishaps are effectively related to issues of quality of care.[18] As a result, a multidisciplinary effort among hospitals and physicians is being formalized in the U.S. through a relatively new administrative intervention called *risk management. Risk*, in the medical setting, is generally defined as any exposure in the hospital to potential injury or financial loss.[14] It is important to remember that not all risk exposures involve mishaps and not all mishaps constitute legal negligence. Too often, health care providers are quick to equate an adverse medical outcome with a compensable event (e.g., negligence). A study by the California Medical Association in 1977 suggests that the theoretical occurrence of legal negligence is a very small segment of all iatrogenesis.[2] Furthermore, insurance industry data indicate that less than one-third of all medical malpractice claims and suits result in judgments against the defendant doctor or hospital. For an iatrogenic event or anesthetic mishap to constitute legal negligence, the party bringing the lawsuit must prove that:

1. There was a legal duty between the provider and patient.

2. The provider's treatment of the patient fell below an acceptable standard of care.

3. The patient suffered an ascertainable injury which was directly caused by a breach of care.

Consequently, an anesthetic mishap is not necessarily considered negligence solely because it could have been prevented. It is clear, therefore, that reducing the risk of exposure to a malpractice suit is but a small segment of a comprehensive medical risk management and quality assurance effort to control the occurrence of anesthesia mishaps.

Historical Overview of Risk Management

The term *risk management* was coined by the insurance industry in 1963 and related primarily to the funding and control of predictable losses in a business activity.[12] It gradually became a specialty within the field of general management and is now recognized by many corporations and medical facilities as a vital component to the financial stability of an organization and the quality of its product. Risk management has been traditionally defined as the process of planning, organizing, directing, and controlling the resources and activities of an organization and its functions in order to minimize the adverse affects of accidental losses to that organization at the least possible cost.[5] Since the concept grew out of the insurance and corporate sectors of industry, the focus of such efforts was understandably the preservation of financial resources.

In adopting the overall concept of risk management, the health care industry shifted the focus somewhat to patient safety and quality of care. This shift is consistent with the characteristics of a conventional risk management philosophy in that its activities are directed toward the goals of the organization, in this case *to do no harm.*

Application to the Health Care Industry

In the early 1970s, insurance companies providing malpractice coverage for hospitals and physicians suddenly became aware of an impending insurance crisis, the magnitude of which would force many companies to drop out of the medical liability insurance field. The so-called crisis centered on actuarial projections of significant future malpractice losses and the inability of companies to fund adequately for these losses without exorbitant premium increases. Although the number of claims and actual losses was still quite small at that time, it became evident that they were only a small portion of all potentially compensable events in the medical setting. In 1975 and 1976, surging malpractice premiums forced many hospitals, medical societies, and state legislatures to consider alternative ways to fund liability exposure. Some of the alternatives included "joint underwriting pools" which required insurance companies to share risks for malpractice losses; "captive insurance programs," whereby groups of hospitals or a medical society organized programs to share in funding their risks, and "self-insurance programs" which allowed a hospital to fund its anticipated losses usually through a trust fund or other financial mechanism.

At the same time, the health profession encountered a new wave of consumerism placing its services and operations under closer public scrutiny. "Patients' Rights" laws were enacted in many states and the rapidly escalating cost of health care became an issue of national concern. Shortly thereafter, the Joint Commission on Accreditation of Hospitals placed new emphasis on quality assurance in hospitals, requiring that quality assurance activities be more problem focused and results oriented.

By 1980, the interrelationship of these factors heralded the beginning of formal risk management programs in many hospitals and medical institutions whose interests in identifying and resolving preventable mishaps were now inextricably linked to the management of its insurance losses, quality control efforts, and good relationships with patients.

Relationship of Risk Management and Quality Assurance

Although the development of the risk management process in the medical setting is still a relatively new phenomenon, there are nonetheless unique applications that make medical risk management a specialty within its own right. The traditional definition of risk management may have little application in the medical sciences. Thus, a working definition for hospitals and physician groups might be:

> The process of applying sound management technique to identification, assessment and resolution of problems to prevent medical mishaps, and minimize the adverse affects of injury and loss to patients, employees, visitors and the hospital corporation.

Historically, risk management and quality assurance were treated as having separate and distinct operational objectives and functions. It is now clear that they are merely different approaches to the common problem of ensuring optimal quality of care and patient safety.[14] There is a growing rationale to integrate the two functions since both share many common objectives. According to the Joint Commission on Accreditation of Hospitals, the essential components of a sound quality assurance program in the aggregate include[6]:

1. Identification of important or potential problems or related concerns in the care of patients

2. Objective assessment of the cause and scope of problems and concerns, including the determination of priorities for both investigating and resolving problems

3. Implementation of decisions or actions that are designed to eliminate identified problems

4. Monitoring activities designed to assure that the desired result has been achieved and sustained

5. Documentation that reasonably substantiates the effectiveness of the overall program

The risk control function utilizes a strikingly similar methodology. For an anesthesia service, the essential activities in this process include:

1. Problem Identification: A formal mechanism should exist for the timely identification of all actual or potential anesthetic mishaps. These data include not only those events which result in actual injury, but any "incident" or unusual occurrence which could have potential injury or loss.

2. Problem Assessment: Once the problem-oriented data are collected, a system is developed to review and prioritize problems according to degree of potential risk.

3. Problem Resolution: After prioritizing problems, the anesthesia staff works with representatives of the institutional risk management-quality assurance program to seek alternatives and solutions for dealing with identified losses. Risk control alternatives generally break down into three areas: *risk avoidance*, to eliminate the possibility of particular categories of losses; *loss prevention*, to reduce the chance that a mishap or loss will occur; and *loss reduction*, to reduce the severity and impact of losses once they occur.[5]

4. Problem Evaluation: Once action is taken to address a potential problem, the results of the intervention are monitored and evaluated by anesthesia staff and risk management-quality assurance personnel. This effort focuses on setting standards of acceptable clinical performance and outcome, comparing actual results with desired standards, and modifying the risk management approach, if necessary, to comply more fully with the desired objectives.

Applying the Risk Management Process in Anesthesia

As a general rule, a risk management program can be programmatically designed around a variety of existing organizational models. Common to all models is the establishment of an institutional risk management and/or quality assurance office to coordinate related data and activities within the facility and the involvement of the hospital medical staff to facilitate the resolution of problems related to provider performance and acceptable standards of medical practice. In a pilot study conducted by the American College of Surgeons, the patient safety activities of five community hospitals were examined to determine management structure and the process of related programs.[1] In each hospital system, a central office, such as a department of risk management-quality assurance, collected data from all parts of the hospital necessary for risk identification. The data included such things as the results of medical audits, incident reports, patient complaints, and malpractice claims. It also received information from committees or offices responsible for such medical review activities as infection control, peer review, and patient care evaluation. Data were then communicated to an appropriate risk management-quality assurance committee to ensure the necessary action and follow-up. In some cases, committees were multidisciplinary in nature, bringing together key members of hospital administration and the medical staff.

The activities of a multidisciplinary risk management-quality assurance committee can vary depending on the sophistication of the institutional program. In some instances, committees will review actual raw data for the purpose of prioritizing problems and developing ideas to reduce, prevent, or avoid actual or potential losses. In most cases, however, committees act solely as a coordinating body to oversee the risk management or quality assurance process and to ensure that any planned activity is monitored and documented. Thus, the risk management process itself is centered in departments and clinical service areas charged with the responsibility for ensuring the safe and optimal delivery of patient care. It is clear then that medical risk management is not a function delegated solely to some centralized hospital department or committee but rather is an essential activity of each clinical area and medical specialty. For an anesthesia service, this means the creation of a formalized program within the department to identify, assess, and resolve the wide range of factors contributing to preventable mishaps under the control of the anesthesia staff.

Problem Identification

There is a natural tendency for individuals planning the start of a new risk management program to reinvent the wheel. This can be avoided since most of the activities necessary to undertake a departmental program are already in place. However, these activities have often been conducted in an independent and uncoordinated manner. Therefore, it is necessary to first inventory all existing departmental activities relating to the identification and review of anesthesia incidents. The objective of this inventory is eventually to centralize and integrate these independent functions into a consolidated program of formal review and action.

The process of risk identification is hardly a new phenomenon to many anesthesia services. Regularly scheduled case conferences, morbidity and mortality rounds, and departmental grand rounds are examples of ongoing activities generating beneficial risk management data. Although the scheduling of such conferences may be coordinated through one office, the data and results of such conference reviews are generally not consolidated with other problem-oriented information. Although more sensitive in nature, problems uncovered through the peer review or credentialing process are often isolated and not integrated into an aggregate risk data base. However, perhaps the single most isolated and protected piece of information relates to the existence of actual or potential medical malpractice claims. The desire to keep such information locked away is understandable. The emotional impact on an anesthesiologist who is formally accused of contributing to a catastrophic injury cannot be underestimated. Many anesthesiologists and other physicians perceive irreparable damage to their professional reputation and integrity, even though the vast majority of claims and suits will be terminated in favor of a medical provider. Nonetheless, information relating to a particular mishap and subsequent claims investigation is vital to the overall risk management effort of an anesthesia service. Professional liability insurance companies can often provide such data in the aggregate so as to minimize the identification of individuals named in a lawsuit.

Another means of problem identification is the hospital incident report. Unfortunately, it is frequently regarded as the key to an effective risk management program when, in fact, it has proved to be of limited use in clinical services such as anesthesia and surgery. The incident report was another tool borrowed from the insurance industry and made a routine part of hospital management operations. It has been most effective in identifying trends relating to a segment of occurrences and outcomes, such as patient falls, medication problems, and equipment failures. It has also been a useful tool in the reporting and follow-up of employee injuries for workmen's compensation purposes. Incident reporting has been least effective in the identification of incidents during surgery, diagnostic treatment, and physician care. The reluctance of physicians to actively use an incident reporting system stems, in part, from the difficulty in defining a "physician-related incident" and the incorrect assumption that such reports are indicative of negligence rather than a mechanism for loss prevention. Given the general reluctance of physicians to use incident reports, any effort by an anesthesia service might be better spent in designing a critical incident reporting system expressly for anesthesia events or in examining other problem identification systems which may be more effective in the long run.

One such system was developed as an outgrowth of the California Medical Feasibility Study which examined the practicability of a no-fault insurance system to compensate patients who incur hospital-related injuries. The system used a set of general outcome criteria designed to identify adverse medical events that might otherwise go undetected.

The screening criteria have been adapted subsequently for use as an early warning system to uncover potentially compensable adverse events occurring in a hospital. The criteria can be modified somewhat to meet the special needs of institutional programs of specific clinical services such as anesthesiology. Data retrieval is usually coordinated by quality assurance or utilization review staff who review medical records concurrent with a patient's hospitalization. Once an outcome on the criteria set is identified, the reviewer will examine the medical record for further information. In many instances, a physician or other provider involved in the case is consulted and may assist in the follow-up investigation. Although all outcomes on the criteria set are not, by themselves, indicative of potentially compensable events, the criteria tested during the California Medical Insurance Feasibility Study were found to be effective in identifying a significant number of important adverse occurrences.[2,3]

The set of criteria in Table 1 was revised and adapted by Joyce Craddick, M.D., from a basic set for the Good Samaritan Hospital in Phoenix, Arizona, and exemplify the type of problem identification system that an anesthesia department can design to meet its specialized risk management objectives.[16]

Table 1

Criteria	Instructions for Data Retrieval
1. Blood pressure variability during anesthesia, i.e., greater than 30 mm Hg increase or decrease	Look in anesthesia note for rationale of variability such as removal of aortic clamp
2. Any hypotensive episodes below 25% range	Compare pre- and postoperative blood pressure range with anesthesia blood pressure
3. Length of stay in recovery room greater than standard **Exceptions**: a. Holding for bed in intensive care unit b. During night c. Complicating medical problems, i.e., history of heart or lung disease.	General anesthetic (2 1/2 hr) Spinal anesthetic (3 1/2 hr)
4. Postoperative respiratory problems within 48 hours, e.g., aspiration, atelectasis, arrest	See progress notes, chest x-ray studies
5. Intraoperative death, or death within 48 hours of surgery	
6. Incidents during surgery, e.g., cardiac arrest, broken teeth, scleral edema	See operative report and anesthesia notes
7. Anesthesia equipment problems, e.g., missing, broken, or malfunctioning equipment	See anesthesia record and clinical engineering records

Quality assurance reviews are also an effective means of identifying potentially compensable events since they can focus on factors other than adverse outcomes. In several instances, the data sources may be located outside the anesthesia department, requiring a coordinated multidisciplinary effort with the hospital risk management quality assurance staff. The Joint Commission on Accreditation of Hospitals publishes a suggested list of indicators to assist anesthesia services in reviewing the quality and appropriateness of care. This is shown in Table 2.

Table 2

List of Indicators

Anesthesia Indicators	Currently Reviewed Yes	No
1. Postanesthesia infections determined to be related to anesthesia	_____	_____
2. Complications (e.g., spinal headache, paresis, nerve injury, postoperative pneumonitis)	_____	_____
3. Adequacy of preanesthesia information (e.g., drug history, including allergic reactions, etc.); previous anesthesia experience	_____	_____
4. Mortality	_____	_____
5. Morbidity	_____	_____
6. Quality of recovery care, especially outside the unit (e.g., ambulatory care, dental clinic)	_____	_____
7. Emergency cases	_____	_____
8. Recovery time for elective surgery	_____	_____
9. Prolonged stay in recovery room	_____	_____
10. Overmedication or undermedication preoperatively, overmedication or undermedication postoperatively	_____	_____
11. Previous recommendations from JCAH surveys or others	_____	_____
12. Indications for choice of anesthesia	_____	_____
13. Cases needing reintubation	_____	_____
14. Rise in blood pressure over 40 mm Hg of the resting reading (what was done and why)	_____	_____
15. Drop in blood pressure over 40 mm Hg of the resting reading (what was done and why)	_____	_____
16. Blood use in surgery	_____	_____
17. Adequacy and consistency of preoperative and postoperative evaluations	_____	_____
18. Pediatric versus adult cases	_____	_____

Data Sources

1. Infection control reports
2. Utilization review minutes
3. Medical records review functions
4. Medical records
5. Previous recommendations from JCAH survey or others
6. Insurance carrier reports
7. Patient and family complaints
8. Staff interviews and questionnaires

Source: From Reference 7. JCAH=Joint Commission on Accreditation of Hospitals.

Problem Assessment

One of the most important problem identification and assessment mechanisms is perhaps the least structured. It simply involves training anesthesia staff to report immediately any anesthesia mishap that could lead to a potential claim or legal action. This is often accomplished through a less formal channel of communications, usually between a provider who witnessed the mishap and the department head or chief of service. Early identification of such events places the risk management staff and claims investigators in a better position to assess the potential liability of an adverse occurrence and to take appropriate action. The cost involved in investigating and settling an anesthesia claim is more equitable for all parties concerned when the investigation is done as soon after the mishap as possible. This point will be examined further in a case study presented later in this article.

The assessment of aggregate problem data is likewise a critical function of an anesthesia risk management program. Although most hospitals will undertake multidisciplinary reviews of general risk, this effort is only as good as the clinical reviews by the departments involved. Given the present preoccupation with medical malpractice among health providers in the U.S., there occasionally is a tendency to look only at those mishaps that involve potential negligence and to classify other adverse outcomes as less important in nature. Since the concept of medical risk management involves more than malpractice prevention, the focus of a departmental risk management-quality assurance program should not be claims centered, but should be directed toward those events which the airline industry characterizes as "near misses." Thus, the process of problem assessment in an anesthesia service should be directed more toward meeting the goals of loss prevention and avoidance rather than loss reduction or transfer. In addition, national and regional data on anesthesia mishaps should be analyzed, as well as information specific to a particular institution. This affords the reviewer an opportunity to prioritize departmental problems based on national trends and outcome.

Problem Resolution

The most difficult part of a risk management program to implement is the creation of a formal mechanism to resolve identified risks and problems. Most corrective interventions require significant changes in physicians' practice, procedure, and behavior. Effecting change can occasionally present major political and behavioral obstacles, particularly in a health care facility. Nonetheless, it is far more effective to address these obstacles than to prolong corrective action in the hope that a mishap or injury will not occur.

The process of taking appropriate action should involve a small number of senior anesthesia staff who coordinate the problem identification and assessment phases of the risk management-quality assurance program for the department. The chief of service or a senior anesthesiologist is customarily involved in this effort. Senior staff representing operating room nurses and certified registered nurse anesthetists, as well as personnel involved in clinical engineering and hospital assurance, should also assist in the process as needed. When the issue of provider performance is in question, it may be appropriate for the chief to dispense with a multidisciplinary review and to act instead through established channels created by medical staff bylaws, such as credentialing and peer review. A summary of risk management activities of the anesthesia task force should be presented periodically to a larger institutional group such as a medical executive board, the hospital risk management-quality assurance committee, or a risk management subcommittee of the board of trustees.

The process of problem resolution can include the following interventions:

1. Changing formal hospital or departmental policies and procedures

2. Changing staffing patterns and work schedules

3. The purchase, modification, or elimination of equipment and devices

4. More comprehensive review of provider performance for recredentialing anesthesiologists and related support staff

5. Imposing sanctions or practice limitations on providers where appropriate

6. The creation of underwriting incentives in situations in which a hospital or physician group operates a liability insurance program. Examples of this include insurance premium discounts for

equipping devices with alarms or fail-safe mechanisms; insurance premium adjustments for anesthesiologists with advanced training or certification in selected areas; retrospective rating increases for providers involved in an abnormal number of claims, suits, or patient complaints; and nonrenewal or cancellation of insurance coverage in extreme cases.

Education

In many instances, general trends uncovered by problem assessment can best be addressed through extensive professional education within the anesthesia department. The mere awareness that a problem exists can oftentimes result in positive changes in practice and behavior. The importance of vigilance can be more effectively demonstrated by the review of serious mishaps which, for no other reason, occurred from the lack of alertness and attentiveness by anesthesia staff. The educational process can also give staff the opportunity to participate in the review and resolution of problems in their department. At the same time, national and regional data on the frequency, severity, and causes of anesthesia malpractice claims can be examined.

At a minimum, anesthesia services of community hospitals should conduct one educational program per year on risk management and malpractice issues. Anesthesia services at teaching hospitals should strive to use regularly scheduled sessions such as case conferences and grand rounds to provide ongoing risk management education throughout the academic year. At a minimum, these facilities should schedule a general session devoted to risk management, quality assurance, and medical malpractice, concurrent with the orientation of new anesthesiology residents and fellows. At one of the Harvard teaching hospitals, the chief of anesthesia also extends this education to other services interested in anesthetic mishaps, such as a department of surgery.

Case Study

The following case study is based on an actual malpractice claim against a large teaching hospital. Staff from the Harvard Risk Management Foundation handled all aspects of the claim, including investigation, disposition, and assistance in loss control follow-up.[15]

A 47-year-old woman suffered from severe juvenile rheumatoid arthritis. She was admitted to the hospital to undergo a bilateral total hip replacement. The operation proceeded without incident, and several days later, the patient was discharged and told to return to the hospital for therapy every day for approximately three weeks. Two weeks later, the patient developed gastric bleeding. Arteriography was subsequently performed under general anesthesia in the arteriography suite of the hospital. During the nine-hour surgery that followed, the origin of the bleeding was determined and corrected. A senior anesthesiologist, present for most of the procedure, was relieved toward the end of the procedure by an anesthesiology resident. After all clinical problems were rectified, the resident was told to terminate the anesthesia and give the patient 100% oxygen. Without looking at the machine, the resident turned off the oxygen instead of the nitrous oxide. The machine was an older British-made model that differed significantly from other anesthesia machines in use at the hospital. Among the differences were the location and configuration of the dials, and the lack of any built-in fail-safe or alarm systems. Moments later, the patient's vital signs dropped. Efforts at resuscitation were begun but the patient went into cardiac arrest, suffered irreversible brain damage, and died several days later.

The chief of anesthesiology, hospital administrator, and hospital risk manager were notified immediately of the mishap. Within hours, representatives of the Risk Management Foundation began a thorough claims review and investigation. Relatives of the patient were naturally given a full explanation of the event. Subsequently, doctors and claim representatives met with members of the patient's family including the father who was an attorney, in an attempt to settle the matter through the hospital's malpractice insurance program. The case was equitably settled out of court within weeks of the mishap.

This case clearly demonstrates the benefits of a well-structured risk management program and the value of good communications between the anesthesia department and the risk managers. The timely and equitable settlement was a direct result of the immediate reporting and follow-up of the incident. All parties involved dealt honestly with the patient's family, and the excellent physician-patient relationship contributed to early disposition of the matter. Without these factors present, it is unlikely that the matter would have been settled as quickly and as satisfactorily as it was.

Shortly after the mishap, the case was reviewed carefully by members of the anesthesia service, clinical engineers, radiology staff, and risk management-quality assurance personnel. The British-made machine was immediately taken out of service. Hospital policy on the use of oxygen analyzers was reviewed, and an immediate effort was undertaken to assure that each anesthesia machine was equipped with a functioning alarm device. Since the analyzers monitor the mixture of oxygen and nitrous oxide leaving the machine, such a device would most likely have prevented the anesthesiology resident from delivering an hypoxic and lethal mixture to the patient. Since the alarm devices have been proved effective in preventing such mishaps and are readily available from manufacturers, the failure to use such a device would undoubtedly have been of probative value in a legal malpractice suit. Of course, there is no substitute for an anesthetist's careful attention to detail and vigilance in monitoring. Some anesthesiologists, however, believe that the use of alarms makes staff rely too heavily on medical instrumentation to monitor patients. Most insurance companies and defense lawyers nonetheless believe that hospitals and anesthesia services are exposing themselves to potential liability by failing to equip anesthesia machines with oxygen analyzers. Using analyzers selectively on some machines, and not others, presents an even greater degree of risk of liability. Obviously, the periodic testing and maintenance of such devices is critical to both the prevention of related mishaps and the legal defense for adverse events stemming from the operation of anesthesia equipment.

The hospital involved in this case study also replaced a certain number of anesthesia machines with newer models. These devices now incorporate such fail-safe systems as oxygen ratio monitors which ensure a constant safe ratio between nitrous oxide and oxygen, and other design modifications which prevent oxygen from being turned off completely. The use of such devices is discussed in other chapters of this issue.

A representative from the anesthesia department also reported on the mishap to the hospital's multidisciplinary risk management-quality assurance committee. The committee assisted in monitoring and documenting the loss prevention follow-up. In addition, the case study has been routinely included for presentation at all orientation sessions for new anesthesiology residents at the hospital. The Risk Management Foundation also published and circulated an analysis of the case to other Harvard teaching hospitals.

CURRENT ISSUES IN ANESTHESIA RISK MANAGEMENT

Informed Consent

The doctrine of informed consent has been firmly established in almost every legal jurisdiction in the U.S. Although every hospital and health provider has recognized the moral and legal obligation involved in obtaining a patient's permission to undergo medical treatment, the approaches to obtaining such consent vary considerably. The issue is of relevance to the risk management process since legal consent is predicated in part on the disclosure of significant material risks involved in a particular treatment.

As a general rule, physicians are under a legal duty to divulge sufficient information to enable the patient to make an informed judgment whether to give or withhold consent for the carrying out of a medical or surgical procedure, including anesthesia. Failure to so inform a patient would constitute professional misconduct in many states. The type of information which must be shared with the patient depends on how material it is to the patient's decision. In most jurisdictions, the obligation to give adequate information does not require the disclosure of *all* risks of proposed therapy, recognizing that there are limits to what society or an individual can reasonably expect of a physician or anesthetist in this regard.[4] The type of information to be disclosed customarily includes the nature of the patient's condition, the nature and probability of risks involved, the benefits to be reasonably expected from the procedure, the likely outcome of no treatment, and the alternatives to the medical treatment, including its risks and benefits.

In the ideal situation, patient consent is first given orally and then immediately documented on a form signed by the patient and physician. When possible, obtaining consent for anesthesia should be the sole responsibility of the anesthesiologist. It is strongly advised that this duty not be delegated to another physician or health care professional since, as a practical matter, only an anesthesiologist would be able to adequately explain related risks and answer any questions a patient might have prior to giving consent. Although the anesthesia consent can be documented on the same form as the permission for surgery, the process of obtaining this consent should be clearly distinguished from the process of obtaining the surgical permission.

The specific medical risks to be disclosed are not matters within the expertise of a court. Therefore, the law will look to the medical profession and patient to determine what information is to be considered legally material. In 1982, the Texas Medical Disclosure Panel developed minimum standards for obtaining consent in certain surgical procedures.[10] Although the use of the proposed form and suggested risks to be disclosed is voluntary, physicians who elect to use the form and standards are afforded the opportunity to present a stronger defense if sued by a patient alleging lack of informed consent. The risks of general, spinal, and epidural anesthetics were included in the language of the proposed disclosure and consent form, and include the following[17]:

1. Respiratory problems
2. Drug reaction
3. Paralysis
4. Brain damage
5. Death
6. Other risks ranging from minor discomfort to injury to vocal cords, teeth, or eyes
7. Headache and chronic pain resulting from spinal or epidural anesthetics

The anesthesia department, as part of its risk management effort, is advised to work with hospital attorneys and risk management staff to develop an appropriate policy and procedure governing the acquisition and documentation of patient consent. It is hoped that this process will reduce the number of informed consent claims as well as improve the rapport and flow of information between the patient and provider.

Product Liability

As discussed in other chapters (see especially the chapter, "Equipment-Related Anesthetic Incidents"), a significant number of anesthetic mishaps are directly related to medical equipment problems. Insurance and trial statistics indicate that there continues to be a significant increase in medical product liability claims. Although manufacturing and design defects are commonly alleged, many medical mishaps involving instrumentation are related to the improper use or maintenance of equipment.

In a report issued by the National Association of Insurance Commissioners, 2,569 closed medical malpractice claims were reviewed involving the improper maintenance and operation of hospital equipment. These claims involved equipment-related injuries in anesthesia and at least six other high-risk areas. The average indemnity paid for all equipment-related claims was $47,111.[11]

In seeking risk management alternatives to these problems, many anesthesia departments have developed formal programs to address the following needs: selection and inspection of new equipment; orientation and continuing education on use of equipment; recognition of anesthesia equipment defects and hazards; insurance that anesthesia equipment is used in an appropriate manner (as intended by the manufacturer); and preventive maintenance of devices.

Anesthesia equipment involved in mishaps should never leave the custody of the hospital or department without approval from the risk management staff or insurance company representatives. Such equipment should be taken out of service immediately and sequestered until such time as the device has been evaluated fully by the necessary parties involved in the investigation of the mishap. As a general rule, it is advisable not to have a representative of the manufacturer examine or work on the involved equipment without the presence of a third party who is a qualified expert in the engineering and operation of the device. Such outside experts might be mutually arranged by representatives of the insurance carrier and manufacturer.

Factors Influencing the Filing of a Lawsuit

Efforts are under way by the insurance industry and medical profession to identify the reasons for the dramatic rise in the frequency of medical malpractice claims since 1975. As of this writing, there is an unfortunate lack of meaningful data to demonstrate the real causes behind what appears to be a complex social phenomenon. It has been theorized that the reasons for the rapid rise in claims is related more to nonclinical factors than to any increase in substandard medical performance by providers. Insurance industry experts suggest that the factors common to many malpractice claims stem mainly from the rapport, or lack thereof, between the patient and provider. Over 92% of physicians surveyed in 1982 by the American Medical Association believed that better rapport between doctors and patients is a very effective method for reducing the risk of malpractice suits and claims. In an informal telephone survey by the Chicago Hospital Risk Pooling Program, patients who successfully sued or filed a claim against their physician were asked why they initiated the action. The majority of respondents stated that anger and frustration were chief reasons for filing a malpractice claim. Many of the claimants perceived a "we-they" relationship with their physician, indicating that the inducement to sue might have been related more to the lack of rapport than to the mishap or negative outcome.

The tendency of some anesthesiologists to remain behind the scenes does little to establish any form of relationship with the patient, no matter how brief. Patients can recall both pleasant and negative experiences during their hospitalization. Oftentimes, some of the briefest encounters are the most positive. Although it is not possible for anesthesiologists to develop as close a rapport with patients as a surgeon or an internist, the combination of brief positive encounters in the operating room can leave equally favorable impressions.

Another factor common to many claims involving significant financial loss is the failure to appropriately document care and treatment. Faulty documentation, inappropriate wording, incomplete information, and missing or falsified records have all contributed to staggering indemnities in recent years. These problems can be addressed best by designing an anesthesia record that logically consolidates all necessary clinical and problem-oriented information to assure consistency and quality of documentation. Projects are under way in several U.S. hospitals to study such a system.

Conclusions

Although anesthetic mishaps are relatively few in number, the increasing severity of such events demonstrates the need for an aggressive approach to prevent those risks which are potentially avoidable and to reduce the impact of losses from mishaps that do occur. The risk management process, although simple in approach, requires a firm commitment of time, staff resources, and total medical staff support to be a truly effective and results-oriented program. The risk management process can be logically integrated with departmental quality assurance functions to achieve maximum benefits and cost effectiveness. The existence of a hospital-wide risk management-quality assurance program should greatly expedite departmental activities. The thrust of a risk management effort in anesthesia begins, however, in the department itself, and ends with the total involvement and commitment of all members of the anesthesiology staff. Anything less will undoubtedly result in an even more dramatic rise in preventable mishaps, patient injuries, and costly litigation.

References

1. American College of Surgeons: Patient Safety Manual. Chicago, IL: American College of Surgeons, 1979, pp 19-26

2. California Medical Association and California Hospital Association: Report on Medical Insurance Feasibility Study. San Francisco: Sutler Publications, 1977.

3. Craddick, JW: The medical management analysis system. Qual Rev Bull 5:4, 1979.

4. Harnish v. Children's Hospital Medical Center, 387 MA 152, 1982.

5. Head GL: The Risk Management Process. New York: Risk and Insurance Management Society, 1978, pp 8-16.

6. Joint Commission on Accreditation of Hospitals: Accreditation Manual on Hospitals, 1981. Chicago: Joint Commission on Accreditation of Hospitals, 1981, pp 151-154.

7. Joint Commission on Accreditation of Hospitals: Making Quality Assurance Work for You. Chicago: Joint Commission on Accreditation of Hospitals, 1982, sect. 2, p 53.

8. Jury Verdict Research, Inc: Injury Valuation Reports: Tables of Verdict Expectancy Values for Doctor's Malpractice, No. 251, Solon, OH: Jury Verdict Research, Inc., 1981, pp 1203-1236.

9. Jury Verdict Research, Inc: Injury Valuation Reports: Tables of Verdict Expectancy Values for Doctor and Hospital Malpractice, No. 253. Solon,

OH: Jury Verdict Research, Inc., 1981, pp 1283-1320.

10. Medical Disclosure Panel: Informing Patients About Medical Risk. Tex Med 78:3, 1982

11. National Association of Insurance Commissioners: Malpractice Closed Claim Study 1975-1978. Milwaukee: National Association of Insurance Commissioners, 1980.

12. Orlikoff JE, Fifer WR, Greeley HP: Malpractice Prevention and Liability Control for Hospitals. Chicago: American Hospital Association, 1981, pp 28-29.

13. Professional Negligence Awards Increase 450%: Hosp Risk Mgt 7:95, 1982.

14. Richards EP, Rathbun KC: Medical Risk Management. Rockville, MD: Aspen Systems Corporation, 1983, pp 11-48.

15. Risk Management Foundation of the Harvard Medical Institutions: Closed Claim Abstract: Anesthesia Mishap. Risk Management Foundation Forum Vol. 3, No. 2, 1982.

16. Risk Management Foundation of the Harvard Medical Institutions and Medical Malpractice Joint Underwriting Association of Massachusetts: Workbook: New Dimensions in Quality Assurance and Risk Management—Occurrence Monitoring/Generic Screening. Boston: New England Hospital Assembly, 1981.

17. Rosenberg CL: Will this law resolve the informed consent dilemma? Medical Economics Jan 24, 1983.

18. Somers HM: The malpractice controversy and the quality of patient care, New York: Milbank Memorial Fund Quarterly/ Health and Society, Spring, 1977, Vol 55, pp 193-233.

19. Tabatzbi C: On the quality of anesthesia care. Qual Rev Bull 7:8,1981.

Holzer JF. Current concepts in risk management. Int Anesthesiol Clin. 1984; 22: 91-116.

Article 4.5

The Malpractice Stress Syndrome

Rev. Edward G. Reading. Maryland Medical Journal, March 1987.

The impact of malpractice suits on the physician and family is called the "malpractice stress syndrome."

There has been an increasing awareness within the medical profession and among the public-at-large that malpractice litigation is part of the new American way of life. The amount of awards and the rates for coverage have been well publicized. The impact of these expenses on the cost of health care is being felt by all. The relationship of these expenses to the national economy and national debt has been part of numerous commentaries. This understanding of the malpractice issue is one centered on economics, law, and the health-care system. Attention has not been given to the issue of the person who is at the center of this complex multifaceted issue—the individual physician who is experiencing an assault on his personal and professional identity, competence, and integrity.

Doctor Sara Charles conducted two studies: physicians who were sued for malpractice in Cook County, Illinois; and sued and unsued physician-members of the Chicago Medical Society. She is coauthor, with her husband, Eugene Kennedy, of the book, Defendant: A Psychiatrist on Trial for Medical Malpractice, published in 1985. In Doctor Charles studies on physicians involved in malpractice litigation, a number of significant issues have surfaced which bring to light the personal impact of malpractice stress.

Reverend Edward Reading MDiv, CAC, is the founder of the Litigation Stress Support group in New Jersey and has lectured nationally on this topic. Rev. Reading has also helped other states begin similar programs.

Isolation. Of the physicians involved in the study, 31.4 percent felt "alone in my effort to vindicate myself"; but only 10 percent sought moral support from peers. In ways similar to how people tend to avoid persons with terminal illness, other physicians frequently avoid the physician being sued. Physicians express sorrow, sympathy, and pity for another physician being sued, but there generally is a failure to express "empathy," in part due to an aversion of facing personal vulnerability.

Negative Self-Image. Defendant physicians feel misunderstood (41.2 percent), defeated (34 percent), decreased self-confidence (31.4 percent), lower self-esteem (27.3 percent), and shame (14.4 percent).

Emotional Impact. More than 50 percent of the responding physicians in these studies experienced anger, inner tension, depressed mood, frustration, irritability, and insomnia. In one study of Cook County physicians who were sued, it was found that 39.1 percent had experienced "major depressive disorders," and 26.6 percent of the physicians had these symptoms for more than two weeks. More than 20 percent experienced pervasive anger accompanied by at least four of the following symptoms: depressed mood, inner tension, frustration, irritability, insomnia, fatigue, gastrointestinal symptoms, and headache.

Other Effects. About 36 percent of sued physicians reported difficulty in concentrating, 29 percent experienced decreased sex drive, and 27 percent noted decreased appetite. Between 5 and 8 percent developed physical illness, between 7.4 and 9 percent experienced exacerbation of previously diagnosed illness, e.g. angina, duodenal ulcer, spastic colon, and hypertension. In two studies it was found that some physicians escaped experiencing no symptoms (4.2 and 17.9 percent, respectively).

If we note all of these issues, we can see a very complex combination of physiological, emotional, and spiritual issues impacting on the physician. The ripple effect also brings a high risk to domestic stability. Additionally, the isolation experienced by the physician is experienced by the other members of the physician-family. Stress on the physician and family members is prolonged by the litigation process itself. While one study found that 50 percent of the claims filed were dropped - many remained active for 24 to 38 months.

Professional therapists have not understood fully the impact of stress caused by litigation. Further, learning how to treat the problem still is one of trial and error. For the physician who is used to treating a person with problems, it frequently is difficult for that physician to follow the adage, "Physician, heal thyself."

A new need has been recognized in the medical community. The impact of malpractice suits on the physician and the medical family can be described as "Malpractice Stress Syndrome." As has been identified with many other "stressing" diseases or situations, the Malpractice Stress Syndrome has an impact far beyond the physician. The members of the medical family most definitely are involved—and, in some cases, even more than the physician. If we take the experiences of successfully proved self-help groups, and take a look at their principles, characteristics, benefits, and practical considerations and procedures, we find guidance in establishing self-help groups for the physician and members of the medical family who are involved in "Malpractice Stress Syndrome."

In the case of malpractice stress, self-help groups help physicians realize they can live with a sense of some emotional security and stability, even when the medical practice is falling apart, and with potentially devastating press coverage. The fear associated with financial insecurity is another aspect with which a self-help group can assist. These groups provide successful "role models" within the group, making advice available from more experienced members to those of lesser experience. They provide a network of new friends and acquaintances to replace the old "non-understanding" friends and to remind the members that they are not alone. The groups provide psychological, emotional, social, and spiritual support for each other to remain healthy through an emphasis on personal satisfaction, self-esteem, productivity, and community involvement (which prevents unhealthy isolation).

The Impaired Physicians Program of the Medical Society of New Jersey works closely with a number of self-help groups, including A.A. and N.A. for alcoholics and other chemically dependent persons, Al-anon, Narc-anon, Ala-teen, and Tough Love for family members, Emotions Anonymous, Gamblers Anonymous, and suicide survivors groups. Many of our program participants are involved in I.D.A.A. (International Doctors in A.A.). Self-help groups can, and do, work. Self-help groups can be successful with helping people cope with Malpractice Stress Syndrome.

It is important to note that while the Impaired Physicians Program refers some of our physicians to these groups, we do not run them or determine their policies or procedures. Successful self-help groups need to remain independent of "outside controls."

While the Malpractice Stress Syndrome can cause physician impairment, it is prudent not to try to deal with it solely through the Impaired Physicians Program at this time in history. The primary reason for this is the common misunderstanding of the concepts of "impaired physician" as alcoholism/drug abuse and addictions.

I would like to stress another primary reason to keep these "malpractice support groups" out of the domain of the Impaired Physicians Program/ Committees. Because of the "still existent stigma" associated with these programs—that they are primarily for drunks and druggies—it might be used in a negative way, in the malpractice case by the attorney prosecuting the case.

One group which is helpful in assisting medical professionals and their families in dealing with and surviving, malpractice stress in the Litigation Stress Support Group. This group was organized in 1985 by the Auxiliary of the Medical Society of New Jersey, staff of the Medical Society of New Jersey, and the Medical Inter-Insurance Exchange of New Jersey. The Impaired Physicians Program provides assistance in the beginning stages of group development as a "prevention effort" for dealing with physician impairment. The group is based on self-help, or mutual-help principles which provide peer-group support. The group helps the participants deal with the personal, family, and professional stresses which surface when malpractice litigation becomes an "active participant" in the life of the medical family.

The group is not a lobby group, it is not a peer group for individual cases, and it is not a professional therapy group (although it can be therapeutic). The group is one which says that "You are not alone"; "Others have gone through the same thing you're going through, and they've survived"; and "So can you!"

Each meeting is divided into two parts. The first is educational in nature about some aspects of litigation, family living, and dealing with stress. The second part is a group discussion based on the principles of mutual self-help. Each meeting lasts approximately 90 minutes.

Participation in the group is open to medical professionals who are in the process of malpractice litigation, spouses/family members/significant others of medical professionals who are involved in litigation, and medical professionals/family members who presently are not involved in any litigation but have been through it and survived, and who are willing to share their experiences and offer strength and hope to those presently involved.

Participation in the group is strictly confidential: there is no official membership list. Many members are available through a telephone network to "talk" one-to-one, till the next group meeting.

Reading EG. The malpractice stress syndrome. Md Med J. 1987; 36(3).

Annotated Bibliography

Iatrogenic Disease

Couch NP, Tilney NL, Rayner AA, Moore FD. *The high cost of low-frequency events: the anatomy and economics of surgical mishaps.* N Engl J Med. 1981; 304: 634-637.
Physicians at a large Boston teaching hospital identified 36 adverse outcomes due to error in 5,612 consecutive surgical admissions. Patterns of error and total cost of care are analyzed.

D'Arcy PF, Griffin JP. *Iatrogenic Disease.* 2nd ed. New York, NY: Oxford University Press Inc.; 1979.
The editors, professors of pharmacology in Great Britain, give detailed descriptions of drug-induced illness by organ system. The appendix includes an extensive table of drug interactions.

Goldman L, Sayson R, Robbins S, Cohn LH, Bettman M, Weisberg M. *The value of the autopsy in three medical eras.* N Engl J Med. 1983; 308: 1000-1005.
Study of autopsies from 1960, 1970, and 1980 at a large university hospital showed that 22 percent of autopsies revealed a clinically missed major diagnosis. The authors caution physicians not to rely too heavily on high-technology diagnostic procedures.

Lambert EC. *Modern Medical Mistakes.* Bloomington, IN: Indiana University Press; 1978.
The physician-author gives an historical accounting of major errors in medical treatment during this century.

Steel K, Gertman PM, Crescinze C, et al. *Iatrogenic illness on a general medical service at a university hospital.* N Engl J Med. 1981; 304: 638-642.
The authors found that 36 percent of 815 consecutive patients on a general medical service in a large Boston teaching hospital had an iatrogenic illness. They discuss the reasons and ramifications.

The Physician and Adverse Outcomes

Applegate WB. *Physician management of patients with adverse outcomes.* Arch Intern Med. 1986; 146: 2249-2251.
Article 4.3

California Medical Association and California Hospital Association, Mills DH, ed. *Report on the Medical Insurance Feasibility Study.* San Francisco: Sutter Publications; 1977.
This study of 20,864 hospital records was undertaken to determine the incidence of adverse events in patients caused by medical care. It estimated that 0.8 percent of all hospitalized patients suffer injury caused by negligence.

Hiatt HH, Barnes BA, Brennan TA, et al. *A study of medical injury and medical malpractice: an overview.* N Engl J Med. 1989; 321: 480-484.
This article describes the goals, methods and initial data findings of the landmark study of that analyzed 30,195 hospital discharge records from New York in 1984.

Hilfiker D. *Facing our mistakes.* N Engl J Med. 1984;310:118-122.
Article 4.1

Kapp MB. *Decision-making in critical care: is the law an impediment or a scapegoat?* Crit Care Med. 1986; 14: 247-250.
An attorney describes the law as a system of checks and balances that helps to ensure rigorous analysis of life and death decisions for vulnerable patients. He admonishes physicians to be aware of the prevailing legal parameters that affect their decisions in the critical care setting.

Katz J. *Why doctors don't disclose uncertainty*. The Hastings Center Report. 1984; 14: 35-44.
Katz, a physician and professor of law and psychoanalysis at Yale, notes that many common drugs and diseases have not undergone the scrutiny of systematic research. Our system of medical education leads us to discount and ignore our lack of information. This is an attempt to diminish the stressful effect of uncertainty and to support our desire to deliver good news to patients. He includes methods for coping with uncertainty.

Kushner HS. *When Bad Things Happen to Good People*. New York, NY: Schoken Books; 1981.
Rabbi Kushner reflects on the loss of his own 13-year-old son, who died of an obscure illness. He helps to sort out anger, guilt, and frustration, with emphasis on the role of God and religion. This book may be useful for patients and physicians facing adverse medical outcomes.

Medical Practice Study: Executive Summary. New York, NY. New York State Health Department; February 1990.
This landmark study of 30,195 hospital records analyzes the incidence of adverse events and negligent care. Malpractice claims data were correlated. Estimates are made of the cost of a no-fault system for the compensation of patient injuries.

Rodovsky SS. *Bearing the news*. N Engl J Med. 1985; 313: 586-588.
Dr. Rodovsky briefly describes the common practice of withholding medical information from patients, such as a diagnosis of cancer. During the past 20 years, this practice has diminished, and most physicians now rarely withhold such a diagnosis. He encourages physicians to accept their own mortality and to admit to themselves their own failures. This, he contends, will make it easier to communicate bad news.

Sager MS, Voeks S, Drinka P, Langer E, Grimstad P. *Do the elderly sue physicians?* Arch Intern Med. 1990; 150: 1091-1093.
Court records were reviewed from malpractice claims in the state of Wisconsin for 1983 and 1984. Only 10 percent of suits were initiated by elderly persons. Discussion of this relatively low rate is included.

Winterscheid LC. *Adverse medical outcomes and tort reform*. J Fam Pract. 1986; 23: 15-16.
In this editorial, the author differentiates undesirable medical outcomes from poor outcomes caused by negligence. He assails the current tort system and makes specific recommendations to improve it.

Risk Management

Brennan TA, Localio AR, Leape LL, et al. *Identification of adverse events occurring during hospitalization*. Ann Intern Med. 1990; 112: 221-226.
This group of attorneys and physicians describe a system of record review that has a high degree of sensitivity for identifying adverse patient outcomes and negligent medical care. The use of such a system might improve hospital-based quality assurance programs.

Danner D. *Medical Malpractice: A Primer for Physicians.* Rochester, NY: The Lawyers Cooperative Publishing Co.; 1986.
In this practical primer written by a nationally recognized member of the medical malpractice defense bar, there is a brief section on how to "keep a bad situation from getting worse," which lists things not to do once a patient complaint or accusation is made. Other sections, such as the one on "admission of fault made by the physician," further address what to do when malpractice is charged. (See also Article 4.2)

Guthrie MD. *The medical staff and risk management.* In: Troyer GT, Salmon SL, eds. Handbook of Health Care Risk Management. Rockville, MD: Aspen Systems Corp.; 1986: 347-359.
Written from the perspective of the hospital risk manager, this chapter presents an overview of the physician's involvement in a hospital risk management program. Prevention of adverse events is stressed with some attention on how to respond to poor outcomes.

Holzer JF. *Current concepts in risk management.* Intern Anesthesiol Clin. 1984; 22: 91-116.
Article 4.4

Joint Commission on Accreditation of Healthcare Organizations. *1989 Accreditation Manual for Hospitals*; Chicago, IL. Joint Commission on the Accreditation of Healthcare Organizations; 1988.
These guidelines include expanded requirements for hospital risk management programs and require active physician participation in the identification of high-risk areas for patient injury and remediation of such risks.

Morlock L, Lindgren OH. *Malpractice, clinical risk management, and quality assessment.* In: Goldfield N, Nash DB, eds. Providing Quality Care. Philadelphia, PA: American College of Physicians; 1989.
This book chapter reviews some of the history of rising malpractice claim frequency and insurance costs of the 1970s and 1980s. The authors describe the convergence of quality assurance, utilization review, and risk management activities. State-of-the-art techniques are briefly reviewed.

Richards EP, Rathburn KC. *Medical Risk Management.* Rockville, MD: Aspen Systems Corp.; 1983.
This book is pertinent for physicians in private practice in an office setting as well as for hospital programs in risk management. It includes chapters on quality assurance, physicians' services, medical records, and teaching hospitals.

Wright RH. *What to do until the malpractice lawyer comes: a survivor's manual.* Am Psychol. 1981; 36: 1535-1541.
This article presents step-by-step advice of what to do when a malpractice claim is received or anticipated. While the advice is specific to the practicing psychologist, many of the main points are generalizable to the medical profession. A checklist of appropriate and inappropriate responses is included.

Malpractice Stress Syndrome

Charles SC, Kennedy EC. *Defendant: A Psychiatrist on Trial for Medical Malpractice*. New York, NY: Free Press of MacMillan; 1985.
The authors chronicle the emotional and professional turmoil of a malpractice suit in New York.

Charles SC, Wilbert JR, Kennedy EC. *Physicians' self-reports of reactions to malpractice litigation*. Am J Psychiatry. 1984;141:563-565.
This study of physicians sued in Cook County, Illinois, between 1977 and 1981 reveals the psychological impact and changes in medical practice induced by medical malpractice lawsuits.

Reading EG. *The malpractice stress syndrome*. New Jersey Med. 1986; 83: 289-290.
Article 4.5

"With a certain degree of sadness," "but I took care of this patient," "the cost of doing business." Illinois Med J. 1985; 167: 378-383.
Authors from the state medical journal interview three physicians whose lives have changed due to their involvement as defendants in malpractice trials.

Chapter 5

The Impaired Physician

Case: Operating Under the Influence

A medical student observes an anesthesiologist administer an inappropriate mixture of gases during a procedure and alter the medical record to cover up her mistake. The student suspects that the anesthesiologist was abusing drugs at the time.

John, a third-year medical student, is now on his initial anesthesiology rotation. He is assisting Dr. North, a popular young attending physician. They are administering general anesthesia to a 45-year-old man for an elective cholecystectomy.

John notices that Dr. North has pinpoint-size pupils, appears quite lethargic, and has slow, labored movements. He asks if she is feeling well. Dr. North comments that she is just feeling tired and that her contact lenses are bothering her. After taking a routine blood pressure, John proclaims his findings, "50 over palp.!" He quickly takes it again at Dr. North's request and declares, "45 over palp.!" John observes the anesthesia controls and queries, "Dr. North, why are we using such a high concentration of enflurane and halothane in this patient?" Dr. North adjusts the controls to decrease the flow of anesthetic agents and increase the flow of oxygen. While reading the anesthesia record, John continues to narrate that the patient may have had that incredibly low blood pressure for as long as six to eight minutes. He dutifully takes another pressure reading and begins to enter it into the record. "No, don't write that!" Dr. North commands. Instead, she falsely records higher blood pressures and lower gas mixtures. She tells the student that this whole episode will have no ill effect on the patient, that the pressure was not dangerously low, and that only two to three minutes had actually elapsed.

Postoperatively, the patient is in the intensive care unit. He is in a semi-comatose state, is unable to speak, and is having difficulty breathing. John learns from another medical student that Dr. North has a history of drug abuse. He also is told that Dr. North was recently involved as a defendant in a malpractice case. John believes that Dr. North was under the influence of narcotics during the operation and that the patient was harmed due to her resulting incompetence. He struggles with his own plan of action: Should he remain silent or report Dr. North's possible impairment?

Discussion Questions

1. Do you believe Dr. North is an "impaired physician?"

2. In your opinion, what did Dr. North do that would support this suspicion? Did these actions harm the patient?

3. What responsibility does the medical student working with Dr. North have concerning the medical record?

4. What is the student's responsibility concerning Dr. North's conduct? To whom should he talk?

5. What are the factors that cause or contribute to the professional impairment of physicians and medical students?

6. Are impaired physicians and medical students commonly encountered by patients or fellow health care workers?

7. At what point do fellow physicians or society at large have a responsibility to change a physician's behavior? Should members of the medical profession be held to a different standard of behavior than the rest of society?

Overview

Recognition that physician colleagues may be functioning with a handicap of body or mind is probably as old as the profession of medicine itself. However, what has been termed a "conspiracy of silence" has long plagued those who minister to the health of others. That is, physicians have been slow to assist or intervene on behalf of fellow physicians who may be mentally, physically, or emotionally impaired. In recent years, however, both medicine and society have achieved a better understanding of the problem. By the early 1970s, a few states had "sick doctor statutes" that led to the development of a general definition of an impaired physician.

The impaired physician "is one who is unable to practice medicine with reasonable skill and safety to patients because of physical or mental illness, deterioration through the aging process or loss of motor skill, or excessive use or abuse of drugs including alcohol."[1]

Since this description was formulated, some experts have sought to add to it problems that can affect education or family life as potential sources of impairment. In 1972, the Council on Mental Health of the AMA identified the scope of the problem of impaired physicians in its report "The Sick Physician."[1] This report set goals for education, legislation, and rehabilitation programs. It made dealing with the problem of impaired physicians a priority for the profession. There are now good resources in the literature and well-developed programs in each state for individuals seeking to help themselves or a colleague. Some useful articles are reprinted here; other resources are listed in the annotated bibliography at the end of this chapter.

The Problem of Impaired Physicians

Many surveys have attempted to quantify the problem of impaired physicians. These studies typically sample only a small population of impaired physicians or medical students, making the generalization of their data difficult. Overwhelming denial, which is a hallmark of the problem, may also be an impediment to accurate self-reporting, on which most of the studies rely. Several studies estimate the prevalence of narcotic addiction to be 10 to 100 times greater in the medical profession than in the general population.[2,3] The common practice of self-medicating and ready access to drugs that cause psychiatric or physical dependence are occupational hazards that will always be present in the delivery of health care. In the mid-1970s, studies indicated that alcoholism contributed to the impairment of approximately 25,000 physicians.[4,5] A more recent study showed that 920 of 1,000 impaired physicians studied had a primary diagnosis of chemical dependence. Anesthesiologists, and family and general practitioners, were found to be overrepresented in the study population compared with their numbers as a proportion of all U.S. physicians.[6] In total, it is estimated that 12 to 14 percent of physicians will experience problems with alcohol or other drugs at some time during their lives.[7]

Analyzing the impact of mental illness on physicians is even more difficult. It is widely perceived that physicians are slow to seek professional help for mental health problems. It is estimated that the equivalent of one to two medical school classes of physicians meet premature death by suicide each year. The incidence of physician suicide is estimated to be between 28 and 40 per 100,000, about three times greater than that of the general population.[8] Within the profession, women physicians have a higher incidence of suicide than their male counterparts.[9-11] The educational process of becoming a physician selects those who tend to be hard-working perfectionists and idealists. Physicians undergo rigorous training, which tests their intellectual, physical, and emotional limits while delaying gratification. These physician characteristics may be an important component of their subsequent morbidity and mortality.[12] A valuable discussion of the role stress plays in the daily life of a physician is found in Dr. Jack McCue's article "The Effects of Stress on Physicians and Their Medical Practice" (see Article 5.1).

Residency Training

Although most professional attention has been directed toward substance abuse and psychiatric disability, there is a growing sensitivity to the needs of physicians impaired with physical disability, senility, environmental stress, and educational deficiency.[13-15] In January 1987, a Manhattan grand jury found that house staff at a New York hospital had improperly cared for a young woman who died shortly after admission through the emergency room.[16] In the now-famous Libby Zion case, no criminal indictments were brought against the hospital or its physicians. However, the court did, in effect, indict the system of residency training throughout the United States. It concluded that the long working hours of interns and residents lead to impairment of judgment and performance that jeopardizes the health of patients.

The Libby Zion incident has sparked debate about physician work load and training programs across the country.[17-20] The American Association of Medical Colleges proposed reforms, among them a recommendation that residents work no more than an average of 80 hours per week, including moonlighting. In the 1988 edition of the *Guide to the Essentials of a Modern Medical Practice Act*, the Federation of State Medical Boards recommended restricting moonlighting to physicians with at least two years of residency training.

There is some debate as to who should be responsible for regulating work hours. The New York State Health Commissioner has promulgated regulations to modify working hours and increase supervision of resident physicians. As of July 1, 1989, in New York state, residents are instructed to work no more than 24 consecutive hours and a maximum of 80 hours per week.[18] A number of state legislatures have entertained legislation; elsewhere, state public health and other agencies have proposed regulations. Individual hospitals and medical schools have made changes in an attempt to stave off further state regulation. On a national level, residency programs are regulated by the Accreditation Council for Graduate Medical Education (ACGME), which determines the "General Requirements" for all programs. "Special Requirements" for each medical and surgical specialty are devised by one of 24 Residency Review Committees (RRCs). The RRC for internal medicine has now revised its requirements, including stipulations for work hours, call schedules, and amount of time required in outpatient services, effective October 1989. All RRCs have been asked to revise their accreditation requirements, with particular attention paid to resident work hours and supervision.

Most observers agree that implementing restrictions on resident work hours will require the costly hiring of ancillary personnel and additional staff physicians. Disagreement concerning the benefits of the continuity of care and intensive experience gained from longer hours may never be resolved.

In Article 5.2, "House Officer Responses to Impaired Physicians," David Reuben and Sarah Noble describe the barriers to reporting colleagues with disabilities. As might be expected, house officers were much more reluctant to confront attending physicians than were other residents. The importance of developing a system of confidential reporting is illustrated. The article contains case scenarios of incompetent, alcoholic, and depressed physician, and challenges the reader to decide how he or she would respond if confronted by an impaired colleague.

New stresses, most acutely felt by medical students and physicians in training, include the decreased status of physicians as perceived by the public; large educational debt; and a predicted oversupply and maldistribution of physicians.[22-24] The perceived threat of malpractice, rising malpractice insurance premiums, competition in the health care delivery system, and governmental financial constraints are also growing forces that affect even the most experienced clinicians.

Caring for the Impaired Physician

The identification and treatment of substance abusing physicians has been particularly hampered by denial on the part of the individual physician, his or her family, colleagues, support staff, and, in the past, society at large. Some of these elements are illustrated in the case that introduces this chapter. Dr. North denied the readily identifiable physical effects that drugs were having on her body even when confronted by the medical student. She even altered the facts of a dangerously low blood pressure and inappropriate anesthesia gas mixtures in the medical record, a practice that is never acceptable. Unfortunately, her apparent drug problem had affected her ability to safely care for patients. Warning signs were likely present before this patient was harmed but were denied or ignored by the impaired physician, her family, and colleagues. It is important to stress that performance in the care of patients is usually the last area of a physician's life to be affected. Sensitivity to the warning signs of impairment due to substance abuse or other causes is the first step in salvaging the life and career of an afflicted physician and protecting the safety of his or her patients. G. Douglas Talbott, MD, and Earl B. Benson, MD, describe the early warning signs of impairment due to substance abuse in Article 5.3, "Impaired Physicians: The Dilemma of Identification." See also Table 5.1, "Warning Signs of Physician Impairment Due to Alcoholism or Drug Addiction," from their article.

During the past 15 years, state medical societies in all 50 states, with support from the AMA, have set up programs to help impaired physicians. By and large, these programs have been most successful in dealing with physicians afflicted by substance abuse. For example, Dr. Talbott describes the goals and structure of the service sponsored by the Medical Association of Georgia in Article 5.4, "Elements of the Impaired Physicians Program." In the first five years of the Georgia program, 156 physicians were successfully rehabilitated and returned to practice. Data from the Committee on Impaired Physicians of the Massachusetts Medical Society show that 125 physicians received help for substance abuse between 1978 and 1987. Although substance abuse has been the main focus of most of these programs, assistance to physicians with other forms of impairment and the issue of physician suicide have evolved as additional concerns.

In the case that introduces this chapter, the medical student working with Dr. North has a responsibility to report his experience to his course director, who is presumably another staff anesthesiologist. If the student's claim is ignored by the course director, he should notify the chairman of the department of anesthesiology. Further follow-up through the department of surgery or the medical school dean's office may be required if fellow anesthesiologists continue to ignore or deny the problem. Some institutions have established special committees to deal specifically with the problem of impaired physicians and nurses. Reporting an impaired colleague is no small step for a medical student or any member of the health care team. In an atmosphere of trust where physicians have been educated about the problems of impairment and malpractice, an acceptable system should be developed to help impaired physicians and maintain high standards of medical practice. Education and carefully designed institutional programs can assist in overcoming the denial that is the hallmark of the problem of impairment.

Education for medical students, physicians' families, and other health care workers is a focus of professional society programs in many states. Some medical schools have developed programs to assist students with substance abuse and stress experienced in the medical school environment. The structure and experience of a model program in Louisiana is detailed in two articles by Simkin and Binder referenced in the annotated bibliography at the end of this chapter. A list of helpful suggestions for coping with stress can be found in Table 5.2. These coping methods are useful for both students and practicing physicians.

Summary

Considerable interest has arisen regarding the problem of impaired physicians within the profession of medicine. The public demands accountability from the profession. In response, the profession has developed resources and rehabilitation programs to assist impaired physicians. Improved education, particularly reaching medical students and physicians' families, is still needed. Physicians and patients both will benefit from a united effort to diminish the impairment of the medical professional.

References

1. The sick physician: report of the Council on Mental Health of the American Medical Association. *JAMA*. 1973; 223: 684-687.

2. Schreiber SC. Emotional problems of physicians: nature and extent of problems. *Arizona Med*. 1977; 34: 323-325.

3. Winich C. Physician narcotic addicts. *Social Problems*. 1961; 9: 174-186.

4. Steindler EM. *The Impaired Physician*. Chicago, IL: American Medical Association; 1975.

5. Green RC Jr, Carroll GJ, Buxton WD. *The Care and Management of the Sick and Incompetent Physician*. Springfield, IL: Charles C Thomas Publisher; 1978.

6. Talbott GD, Gallegos KV, Wilson PO, Porter TL. The Medical Association of Georgia's impaired physicians program: review of the first 1,000 physicians: analysis of specialty. *JAMA*. 1987; 257: 2927-2934.

7. Talbott GD, Benson D, Benson E. Impaired physicians: the dilemma of identification. *Postgrad Med*. 1980; 68: 56-64.

8. Results and implications of the AMA-APA physician mortality project. AMA Council on Scientific Affairs. *JAMA*. 1987; 257: 2949-2953.

9. Ross M. Suicide among physicians. *Psychiatry in Medicine*. 1971; 2: 189-198.

10. Ross M. Physician suicide risk: practical recognition and management. *South Med J*. 1975; 68: 699-702.

11. Steppacher R, Mauser J. Suicide in male and female physicians. *JAMA*. 1974; 228: 323-328.

12. Gabbard GO. The role of compulsiveness in the normal physician. *JAMA*. 1985; 254: 2926-2929.

13. Tye L. Some older doctors run afoul of law. *Boston Globe*. July 7, 1979: 1,10.

14. Wainapel SF. The physically disabled physician. *JAMA*. 1987; 257: 2935-2938.

15. Reuben DB, Noble S. House officer responses to impaired physicians. *JAMA*. 1990; 263: 958-960.

16. Asch DA, Parker RM. Sounding board: the Libby Zion case. *N Engl J Med*. 1988; 318: 771-775.

17. Tye L. Hospitals ask: is the doctor all in? *Boston Globe*. June 11, 1987: 1.

18. Segal MM. Shorter shifts won't cure hospital-care problems. *The Wall Street Journal*. June 18, 1987.

19. McCall TB, Levinsky NG, Glickman RM. Sounding board: (1) the impact of long working hours on resident physicians, (2) compounding the error, (3) house-staff training: the need for careful reform. *N Engl J Med*. 1988; 318: 775-782.

20. Stress and impairment during residency training: strategies for reduction, identification, and management: report from the Resident Services Committee, Association of Program Directors in Internal Medicine. *Ann Intern Med*. 1988;109:154-162.

21. NY Comp. Codes § Regs. tit. 10, chV(a), part 405(1989).

22. Health care in transition: consequences for young physicians: report of the Council on Long-Range Planning and Development. *JAMA*. 1986;256:3384-3390.

23. Uncertainty and the future of young physicians. *JAMA*. 1986;256:3391. Editorial.

24. Tye L. Boston hospitals lure fewer trainees: high cost of living deters interns, residents. *Boston Sunday Globe*. July 5, 1987:1,10.

Table 5.1

Warning Signs of Physician Impairment Due to Alcoholism or Drug Addiction

Clues to Alcoholism or Drug Addiction in Six Areas of a Physician's Life[1]

Community
- Isolation and withdrawal from community activities, leisure activities and hobbies, church, friends, peers
- Embarrassing behavior at clubs/parties
- Arrests for driving while intoxicated, legal problems
- Unreliability and unpredictability in community and social activities
- Unpredictable behavior, e.g., inappropriate spending, excessive involvement in political activities

Family
- Withdrawal from family activities, unexplained absences from home
- Fights, child abuse
- Development in spouse of disease of "spousaholism"
- Abnormal, antisocial, illegal behavior by children
- Sexual problems: impotence, extramarital affairs, contracultural sexual behavior
- Assumption of surrogate role by spouse and children
- Institution of geographic separation or divorce proceedings by spouse

Employment
- Numerous job changes in past five years
- Frequent geographic relocations for unexplained reasons
- Frequent hospitalizations[2]
- Complicated/elaborate medical history[2]
- Unexplained intervals between jobs
- Indefinite or inappropriate references
- Working in job inappropriate for qualifications
- Reluctance of job applicant to let spouse and children be interviewed
- Reluctance to undergo immediate preemployment physical examination

Physical Status
- Deterioration in personal hygiene
- Deterioration in clothing and dressing habits
- Multiple physical signs and complaints
- Numerous prescriptions and drugs
- Frequent hospitalizations
- Frequent visits to physicians and dentists
- Accidents
- Emotional crisis

Office
- Disruption of appointment schedule
- Hostile, withdrawn, unreasonable behavior to staff and patients
- "Locked-door syndrome"
- Excessive ordering of supplies of drugs from local druggist or by mail
- Complaints by patients to staff about doctor's behavior
- Absence from office unexplained or due to frequent illness

Hospital
- Making rounds late or inappropriate, abnormal behavior during rounds
- Decreasing quality of performance, e.g., in staff presentations, writing in chart
- Inappropriate orders or over-prescription of medications
- Reports of behavioral changes from hospital personnel ("hospital gossip")
- Involvement in malpractice suits and legal sanctions against hospital
- Reports from emergency department staff of unavailability or inappropriate responses to phone calls

1 Areas are usually involved sequentially, although two or three may seem to be involved simultaneously.

2 Information obtained from employment applications.

Derived from G. Douglas Talbott's
Impaired Physicians: The Dilemma of Identification.

Table 5.2

Suggestions for Coping With Stress

- Schedule personal time for *your* interests
- Maintain contact with family and friends at home
- Develop new support systems, including non-medical people
- Work on nurturing personal relationships
- Urge your partner to develop other support systems
- Select a physician or professor you can talk to as a confidant or mentor

Learn to use these physical or mental coping aids

Physical Coping:

- Exercise
- Deep muscle relaxation
- Sleep and diet
- Biofeedback

Mental Coping:

- Meditation
- Imagery
- Self-hypnosis

A Primer on Medical Student Impairment. Chicago, IL: AMA Department of Medical Student Services, 1986.

Article 5.1

The Effects of Stress on Physicians and Their Medical Practice

Jack D. McCue, MD. The New England Journal of Medicine, February 1982.

Each day physicians encounter stresses that are an intrinsic part of medical practice. Those who are vulnerable may become unable to practice medicine without the intrusion of seriously neurotic or inappropriate behavior: that is, they become impaired physicians. In nonimpaired physicians, adaptations to the unalterable stresses of medicine may be productive and may actually improve the quality of medical care. Unfortunately, adaptations are often unproductive, resulting in poorer quality or uneconomical care, or they may adversely affect the personal lives of the physician and his or her family. A description of physicians' stresses and adaptations would facilitate educational, personal, and societal changes that could improve the quality of medical care.

INTRINSIC STRESSES

I believe that the stresses of medical practice result from one or more of the following situations peculiar to medicine: working with intensely emotional aspects of life governed by strong cultural codes for behavior, e.g., suffering, fear, sexuality, and death; inadequate training for fundamental professional tasks, e.g., handling "problem" patients; and demands from society or patients that cannot be reasonably met, e.g., the need for certainty when current medical knowledge allows only approximation.

Suffering

The social graces that ordinarily make human interactions enjoyable are stripped away by sickness and pain. Medicine is selected as a profession by students who expect to be rewarded by satisfying encounters with their patients, yet their chosen career consists of routinely interacting with persons who are anxious, uncomfortable, and often unable to express gratitude or affection. The admonition to medical students not to judge patients who are in a state called illness by their behavior rings true—the acutely ill problem patient may be a social paragon after discharge from the hospital.

Patients expect greater sympathy for their suffering and more skill in relieving their symptoms than most modern physicians can provide; today's physicians are poorly educated in palliative treatment and have experienced only trivial illness themselves. Physicians are further hampered by poor communication; since objective measurement of discomfort is rarely possible, and since language serves most patients and physicians poorly in attempts to explain degrees of discomfort, the physician usually relies on fallible intuition. Repeated contacts with a patient could enhance the accuracy of intuitive judgments, but sub-specialization, the rarity of visits to a physician when patients are under 40, and our nomadic society have made long-term patient-physician relationships less common.

Descriptions of pain may elicit suspicion rather than the compassion expected by patients. Fear of manipulation by patients with drug-acquisitive behavior is especially common among residents and nurses, who tolerate the complaints of patients more willingly than the disapproval of their peers. The paradox of the patient's trying to prove the presence of pain to a skeptical physician whose avowed professional mission is to relieve suffering is frustratingly common, and it is stressful to both patient and physician.

The physician is entrusted not only with the relief of pain but also with decisions to inflict pain (with diagnostic procedures or toxic chemotherapy), to proscribe pleasures, or to deny the palliative treatment of discomfort. The occasions to inflict pain or deny palliation have multiplied with the increase in opportunities to make precise diagnoses and sophisticated in vivo measurements and to sustain vegetative functions in terminally ill patients.

Fear

The primary and ultimate reason for consulting a physician is fear: Even the simplest blood-pressure check is a cautious inquiry into the patient's mortality.[1] The calm and relaxed patient is uncommon enough to make the physician suspect abnormal behavior. Fearful persons are fatiguing and unpleasant to work with, and their fear is often contagious, especially when a physician becomes personally involved or identified with their problems.

Skillful treatment of illness and fear requires reassurance, the most important medicine dispensed by a physician.[2] Reassuring patients effectively, especially when they are excessively anxious, requires special techniques[3] and skills; since these are rarely taught well in medical training, physicians are forced to spend their time doing what they have been poorly trained to do.

Sexuality

The physician is entitled and required to probe into areas of the body that are hidden from all others, and into private aspects of a patient's life that are disguised with psychological defenses and denial. The patient has intensely ambivalent feelings about the physician's privileged role; the desire to trust and respect this person who is allowed to violate cultural and social taboos is countered by anger at being forced into a child-parent relationship. There is also fear that those privileges and powers could be abused. The physician, too, is ambivalent; the civilized desire to respect the patient's modesty and avoid the anxiety of emotional and physical nakedness is countered by the obligations that accompany special privileges and responsibilities.

Perhaps those most vulnerable to the stresses of embarrassment are students and interns,[4] who must probe clinically when neither they nor their patients consider them fully vested with the privileges of a physician. Practicing physicians experience comparable embarrassment when caring for friends, family members, and other physicians; emotional distancing is lost, and the desire to preserve modesty conflicts with the need to acquire clinical information.

Embarrassment never completely disappears from the act of obtaining a clinical history and physical. Attempts by physicians to avoid the stress of embarrassment for either party may result in an incomplete evaluation of the patient and guilt feelings on the part of the physician, because internal demands for careful data collection have been ignored.

Death

It is sardonically observed that physicians who strive to keep patients alive are ultimately doomed to fail. That death is usually seen as a failure of medical care both by the patient's family and the physician is only part of its impact on a doctor; death's cultural meaning is so great that the vocabulary connected with it is a smokescreen of euphemisms (e.g., "cemetery," "undertaker," or "passing away"). Most physicians work continuously in the fear of death or in its presence, but familiarity does not remove its sting. Observe, for example, the heavy sadness and sense of failure of physicians who quickly leave the room after an unsuccessful attempt at cardiac resuscitation.

Communication among the patient, family, and physician frequently breaks down when the patient is dying. Telling the truth about dying is a major social issue, in part because nobody is comfortable talking about the realities of death, although seminars on dying and ethical discourses on patients' rights to a dignified death have facilitated communication. Still, even families who are meticulously informed about the prognosis and are consulted for all major decisions may turn against the physician in anger when the patient dies.

Technologic innovations permit prolongation of dying, making the cessation of a machine's function, rather than of a physiologic function, the proximate cause of death. The physician is placed in the absurdly stressful situation of "killing" a patient by discontinuing the use of life-supporting gadgets or drugs. The ethically insecure physician confronted with these numbing moral ambiguities resorts to the deceit of continuing therapy but with deliberate carelessness—e.g., not checking respirator settings or not looking for complications known to be likely—to ensure the ultimately compassionate outcome of hastening the patient's death.

Problem Patients

The stereotypes of "clingers," "demanders," "help rejecters," and "deniers" [5-9] are familiar to all physicians. They elicit anger, avoidance, fear, and despair. The biomedical model fits these patients poorly, since they cannot or will not get better. Most problem patients have important psychiatric disorders, which are at the basis of their frustrating interactions with physicians, but the time and energy required to care for them well deter physicians from making psychiatric diagnoses.[10,11] Furthermore, physicians are rarely taught the techniques needed to take care of this type of patient[12,13] or to understand their own complicated feelings toward them.

Problem patients seek medical care much more often than the ordinary patient does and may even constitute a large percentage of the clinic patients seen by residents. Only recently has society given many of these problem patients the right to medical care on demand; previously, only problem patients who could pay for it had easy access to care for non-biomedical illness. It is likely that the amount of time spent by primary-care physicians in caring for problem patients has increased dramatically over the past three decades.

Uncertainty

Much of medical training consists of learning to cope with pervasive uncertainty[14] and with the limits of medical knowledge. Making serious clinical decisions on the basis of conflicting, incomplete, and untimely data is routine. Balancing the demands of patients (the physicians' ultimate bosses) for definitive diagnoses with those of society's heath-care planners for cost-effective use of resources can make the diagnosis and treatment of even a sore throat a bewildering series of uncertain decisions.[15,16] The physician is palpably relieved to encounter a typical presentation of a definable illness—for once, the stress of gambling without knowing the odds (or often even the game) is avoided.

The stress of uncertainty tempts both physician and patient to collude in oversimplifications and lies. Although the illusion of certainty may allay fears, falsehoods break down communication and bring new moral and emotional consequences for the physician.[17] A common adaptation, developing standard clinical routines or habits, may reduce the stresses of making decisions, but it can increase the costs of medical care with little clinical benefit (e.g, obtaining cultures in all adults with sore throats) or result in irrational and possibly hazardous medical care (e.g., treating all productive coughs with antibiotics). Furthermore, both patient and physician are often uncomfortable today in what once seemed to be a stable, predictable relationship. The dizzying changes brought on by social and governmental activism, the courts, economic competition, and nostalgia for the wise, paternalistic general practitioner have made many encounters unsettling explorations of the roles and obligation of the doctor and patient (What kind of doctor/patient are you going to be?). Patients reward physicians who conform to their preconceptions about how doctors should behave and look. Doctors who happen to be of the wrong sex or race, or who dress unconventionally, will have fewer job offers and slowly growing practices. Demands for conformity to social conventions for behavior and appearance also have a profound effect on the physician's personal and family life.[18]

EFFECTS OF STRESS ON PHYSICIANS

Students and Residents

Despite rigorous screening by medical schools' admissions committees, the dropout rate for medical students hovers around 10 percent; it is higher among less talented students[19] and those with psychiatric problems.[20] It has been estimated that up to half the students who eventually graduate need psychotherapy[19]; a smaller but substantial percentage actually receive it.[19,21,22] Suicides are second in number only to accidents as a cause of death among medical students,[23] and drug abuse is common.[24,25]

The dramatic stresses of postgraduate training are better described than those of medical school[26-28]: role ambiguity, periods of transition, responsibility beyond one's abilities, social isolation, and sleep deprivation. Two studies have shown that about one third of interns have frequent or severe episodes of emotional distress or depression[29,30] and that 25 percent of these interns have suicidal ideation.[29]

Seriously Impaired Physicians

Physicians who commit suicide, violate laws, transgress basic medical ethical precepts, or have socially deviant behavior fall into two groups: those with diagnosable psychiatric conditions and those whose peculiar vulnerability to the demands of medical practice is expressed in neurotic or irrational acts ("medical misfits"). It is certain that physicians who harm themselves also directly or indirectly harm their patients.

Ample evidence indicates that physician impairment is common. The suicide rate of physicians is two to three times that of the general population,[23,31] equal in number to the loss of about two medical-school classes yearly. Alcoholism is at least as prevalent among physicians as in the general population,[32,33] and underreporting of physician-alcoholics is likely. Drug addiction may be 30 to 100 times more common among physicians than in general population[25]; a controlled study showed that heavy drug use, including use of alcohol, was 1.6 times more frequent among doctors than in a comparable group of non-physicians.[32] Physicians are also more likely to have had 10 or more visits to a psychiatrist than are controls.[32]

Unhappy and Maladapted Physicians

Many physicians who are not seriously impaired are still troubled and dissatisfied with their work.[34] Questionnaires returned by 416 internists showed a fall in "adequate compensation financially and in psychic satisfaction" from 83 percent in 1973 to 67 percent in 1979; only 59 percent wanted their child to be an internist.[35] Marriages and sexual relationships are often unsatisfactory for physicians,[32,33,36] although divorce may be no more common than in the general population.[37-39]

Physicians who are not consciously unhappy may still have maladaptive or self-destructive responses to the stresses of medical practice. Home life can evolve into a professional "support system," practice procedures can be designed to minimize business stresses rather than to deliver optimal care, and altruistic goals can be replaced by greed and self-interest.

It is unlikely that optimal medical care can be delivered by unhappy or maladapted physicians. Empathic concern for a patient's distress, placing the patient's interests before those of the physician, and considering all the ramifications of a therapeutic or diagnostic intervention ("cost-benefit analysis") require concentration by a physician who enjoys the work and brings to it an emotional stability derived from his or her personal life.

ADAPTATIONS TO PHYSICIAN STRESS

Emotional Withdrawal

Retreat from family life is probably the most common adaptation to the demand of medical practice.[37] A progressive emotional separation from family life in the early years of practice becomes a de facto divorce; the willingness and finally the ability to share feelings and experiences are lost. Spontaneous home activities are interrupted by the telephone or pocket pager; late office hours, hospital rounds on days off, and subtle or unconscious encouragements for patients to call after hours erode the time and energy needed for personal development. The consequences of emotional withdrawal can be grave. Failure in professional life results in disappointment, but failure in personal and family life results in heartache and anguish.[40] Why do intelligent and successful physicians tolerate the failure of an unrewarding family life and surrender nonmedical interests, becoming narrow and boring? The first reason is peer pressure. The diligent, self-sacrificing physician who surrenders a personal life to patients wins respect from colleagues, first in residency and later in private practice. Even physicians with reasonable working habits often praise colleagues who abandon their personal lives to their profession. The second reason is fear of failure and of success. Physicians who put all their energy into medicine ensure that their efforts are above criticism—their failures must be attributed to misfortune. Being always on call avoids the risk that patients will criticize them for being unavailable when needed, as well as the discordant cycles of alertness and relaxation. Long hours and publicly visible fatigue justify economic prosperity to the physician who is uncomfortable with success in fee-for-service practice. A final factor is self-importance. Insecure physicians can maximize ego gratification at the hospital, where they issue orders, make critical decisions, and receive praise from their patients; at home, the physician is just another suburban husband or wife.

Social Isolation

Retreat from the nonmedical world usually begins in medical school and progresses to a nearly total avoidance of nonmedical socializing by private practitioners. Physicians are often defensively locked into self-important, authoritarian professional roles, which nonphysicians rarely let them drop. Isolation may be a response to the resulting "role fatigue."[41] For example, at social events a physician is expected to answer medical questions graciously and to respond as a physician when someone describes a symptom. Society enjoys seeing a physician fail to meet its high standards and thinks it amusing when a physician exposes a vulnerable human side. Not being allowed to relax, to fail, or to escape the public eye causes an avoidance of nonphysicians, a refusal to wear "Dr." name tags, or to identify oneself as a physician in introductions, and a retreat to homogeneous upper-middle-class suburbs where many other physicians live.

Physicians may socially withdraw to avoid having their financial success observed by their patients. The physician is expected to place patients' interests before his or her own.[42] Although most physicians do this, Americans are clearly a self-oriented people,[43] and it is difficult for American physicians to behave totally differently. Patients seek out busy and successful physicians, yet they are jealous of their prosperity and accuse the successful physician of practicing medicine for its financial rewards. Furthermore, nobody is entirely comfortable with a piecework fee-for-service system that compensates a physician approximately in proportion to patients' suffering and misfortune.

Denial of Professional Problems

Physicians and patients often conspire to deny the complexities, uncertainties, limitations, and tragedies intrinsic to medical practice. The pervasiveness of the routine laboratory test suggest that more than a lack of cost awareness or an intellectual laziness is responsible. Unlike other aspects of medical education, teaching laboratory-cost containment is rarely successful without long-term efforts toward modification of physicians' behavior and coercive administrative changes.[44] Ordering tests that are known to be unnecessary[45] and subsequently ignoring even abnormal results cannot be ascribed to physicians' ignorance; other factors must be involved. For example, many laboratory tests are used as hedges against fears and uncertainty. Unnecessary electrocardiograms for benign chest pain are placebos that give false reassurance and thereby decrease disability.[46]

The denial of business responsibilities to avoid executive stresses—those involving the role of employer, the efficient use of time, and the proper management of finances[18]—can also increase the costs of medical care. Lack of training in ways to manage a small business and the misconception (held by patients and physicians) that good business procedures indicate too much interest in financial rewards can result in fee schedules that are unfair to patients and physicians, deprive the physician of needed personal time, and make the doctor less accessible to patients.

Walking away from crises, refusing to acknowledge critical illness, and being unable to recognize one's insensitive or inadequate care are examples of denial found in impaired physicians. Unless this type of denial leads to flagrantly bad outcomes, however, impaired private practitioners are hard to identify or help.

Irony

Residents' most publicly maligned adaptation to stresses such as hopelessness, problem patients, or tiring work for no apparent benefit is probably their least harmful. The teacher who thinks that a resident who refers to a patient as an "alkie" or a "troll" is practicing bad medicine is guilty of dreadful naivete. Lay people and faculty see this attempt by residents to establish group support with code words as callous and cynical. Instead, they should look at the residents' actual behavior and the hopelessness behind ironic terms such as "tubing out" or "gork." Interestingly, although dry humor persists in private practice, ironic naming is virtually nonexistent outside educational programs.

COPING WITH STRESS

The reluctance of physicians and patients to discuss the effects of stress on physicians honestly—a conspiracy of silence[1] —is a major obstacle to investigating the effects of stress on physicians. Having spent up to a third of their adult lives preparing to practice medicine, physicians are understandably reluctant to acknowledge psychological discomfort with fundamental professional activities or the conflict between long-held expectations and the realities of daily medical practice. Patients, on the other hand, like to believe that caring for their illnesses is inherently satisfying, and they rightfully point to the physician's generous financial and social rewards.

The lack of adequate descriptions of the effects of medical practice on the physician and of how these effects alter the delivery and content of medical care also impedes investigation. Medical sociology has had relatively little input from physicians[47,48] and has contributed only fragmentary and often superficial commentary on what happens in the physician's half of a medical encounter. For example, a look at possible unsalutary stressful effects on the physician in fee-for-service medicine, as compared with other methods of heath-care delivery, is needed.

Much must be done to coordinate medical-school admissions policies with society's needs and the available jobs, and to assist students and residents in their career decisions. The categories of students selected for medical school at matriculation have been delineated by Funkenstein[49]: students-scientists or bioscientists, student-practitioners with biosocial orientation and interpersonal skills, and student-psychiatrists with biosocial orientation and behavioral skills. The proportions of students in each category have been determined not by society's needs for academicians, practitioners, or psychiatrists, but by larger societal trends and medical-school admissions policies. The jobs available to students when they graduate, therefore, may have little relation to their talents, emotional strengths, or even their education. The near absence of influential practitioner role models in university programs[50] means that the great majority of residents enter primary-care practice[51,52] with only a vague concept of what they will encounter. Furthermore, it is likely that some of their career decisions are attempts to avoid stressful or unpleasant experiences in medical school and residency, rather than rational or positive decisions recently studied.[53]

The resident is under close scrutiny by many educators. Friction with colleagues or a seeming inability to provide the quality of care that medical-school performance or native intelligence would predict should alert faculty to a possibly impaired or vulnerable resident. Easy access to private, nonjudgmental counseling must be available. Unless impairment is severe, once a resident enters private practice, the opportunity to identify the problem and to provide career or psychological counseling rarely occurs.

During medical training, feelings and emotions are suppressed to prevent the loss of control (or "equanimitas") and to conserve the energy required for survival.[26] Honest discussion of the psychological difficulties of medical practice or of how physicians feel during difficult encounters with patients are important in helping physicians identify maladaptive behavior. Open, direct exploration of productive adaptations to stresses would help to avoid suppression of feelings or excessive emotional distancing from patients; such approaches would ultimately result in better, more economical medical care.

References

1. Fox RC. Address delivered to faculty and residents at Cleveland Metropolitan General Hospital, May 5, 1981.

2. Balint M. The doctor, his patient and the illness. New York: Pitman, 1964.

3. Sapira JD. Reassurance therapy: what to say to symptomatic patients with benign diseases. Ann Intern Med. 1972; 77:603-4.

4. Lief HI, Fox RC. Training for "detached concern" in medical students. In: Lief HL, Lief VF, Lief NR, eds. The psychological basis of medical practice. New York: Harper & Row, 1963:449-60.

5. Groves JE. Taking care of the hateful patient. N Engl J Med. 1978; 298:883-7.

6. Goodwin JM, Goodwin JS, Kellner R. Psychiatric symptoms in disliked medical patients. JAMA. 1979; 241:1117-20.

7. Lorber J. Good patients and problem patients: conformity and deviance in a general hospital. J Health Soc Behav. 1975; 16:213-25.

8. Papper S. The undesirable patient. J Chronic Dis. 1970; 22:777-9.

9. Lipsitt DR. Medical and psychological characteristics of "crocks." Int J Psychiatr Med. 1970; 1:15-25.

10. Shemo JPD, Withersty DJ, Spradlin WW, Waldman RH. Psychiatry as an internal medicine subspecialty: an educational model. J Med Educ. 1980; 55:354-61.

11. Duffy DL, Hammerman D, Cohen MA. Communication skills of house officers: a study in a medical clinic. Ann Intern Med. 1980; 93:354-7.

12. Drossman DA. The problem patient: evaluation and care of medical patients with psychosocial disturbances. Ann Intern Med. 1978; 88:366-72.

13. Schildkrout E. Medical residents' difficulty in learning and utilizing a psychosocial perspective. J Med Educ. 1980; 55:962-4.

14. Fox RC. Training for uncertainty. In: Merton RK, Reader GC, Kendal PL, eds. The student physician. Cambridge, Mass.: Harvard University Press, 1957: 207-47.

15. Tompkins RK, Burnes DC, Cable WE. An analysis of the cost-effectiveness of pharyngitis management and acute rheumatic fever prevention. Ann Intern Med. 1977; 86:481-92.

16. Komaraff AL. A management strategy for sore throat. JAMA. 1978; 239:1429-32.

17. Bok S. Lying: Moral choice in public and private life. New York: Pantheon, 1978.

18. McCue JD. Private practice: surviving the first year. Lexington, Mass.: Collamore Press, 1982.

19. Duffy JC. Emotional issues in the lives of physicians. Springfield, Ill.: Charles C. Thomas, 1970.

20. Thomas CB. What becomes of medical students: the dark side. Johns Hopkins Med J. 1976;138:185-95.

21. Hunter RCA, Lohrenz JC, Schwartzman AE. Nosophobia and hypochondriasis in medical students. J Nerv Ment Dis. 1964; 139:142-52.

22. Bojar S. Psychiatric problems of medical students. In: Blaine GB, McArthur CC, eds. Emotional problems of the student. New York: Appleton-Century-Crofts, 1971:350-63.

23. Ross M. Suicide among physicians. Psychiatry Med. 1971; 2:189-98.

24. Thomas RB, Luber SA, Smith JA. A survey of alcohol and drug abuse in medical students. Dis Nerv Syst. 1977;38:41-3.

25. Modlin HC, Montes A. Narcotic addiction in physicians. Am J Psychiatry. 1964; 121:358-65.

26. Tokarz JP, Bremer W, Peters K. Beyond survival. Chicago: American Medical Association, 1979.

27. Mumford E. Interns: from students to physicians. Cambridge, Mass.: Harvard University Press 1970.

28. Friedman RC, Bigger JT, Kornfield DS. The intern and sleep loss. N Engl J Med. 1971; 285:201-3.

29. Valko RJ, Clayton PJ. Depression in the internship. Dis Nerv Syst. 1975;36:26-9.

30. Ford CV. The emotional distress of interns and residents. Presented at the 134th American Psychiatric Association annual meeting, New Orleans, La., May, 1981.

31. Rose KD, Rosow I. Physicians who kill themselves. Arch Gen Psychiatry. 1973; 29:800-5.

32. Vaillant GE, Sobowale NC, McArthur C. Some psychologic vulnerabilities of physicians. N Engl J Med. 1972; 287:372-5

33. Scheiber SC. Emotional problems of physicians: 1. Nature and extent of problems. Ariz Med. 1977; 34:323-5.

34. Mawardi BH. Satisfactions, dissatisfactions, and causes of stress in medical practice. JAMA. 1979; 241:1483-6.

35. Rubin W. The internist: a self-profile. Challenges, opportunity to help patients attractive. Int Med News. 1980; 13(2):1, 36-7.

36. Rose KD, Rosow I. Marital stability among physicians. Calif Med. 1972; 116(3):95-9.

37. Fine C. Married to medicine: an intimate portrait of doctors' wives. New York: Atheneum, 1981.

38. Garvey M, Tuason VB. Physician marriages. J Clin Psychiatry. 1979;40:129-31.

39. Werber R. A doctor's wife interviews 100 doctors' wives. Physician manager. 1980; 20(11):63-8.

40. Brent RL, Brent LH. Medicine: an excuse from living, Res Staff Physician. 1978; 24(12):61-5.

41. Halenar JF. Doctors don't have to burn out. Med Econ. 1981; 58(21):148-61.

42. Parsons T, ed. The social system. Glencoe, Ill.: Free Press, 1951: 428-49.

43. Lasch C. The culture of narcissism. New York: WW Norton, 1979.

44. Eisenberg JM, Williams SV. Cost containment and changing physicians' practice behavior: can the fox learn to guard the chicken coop? JAMA. 1981; 246:2195-201.

45. Sox HC, Margulies I, Sox CH. Psychologically mediated effects of diagnostic tests. Ann Intern Med. 1982; 95:680-5.

46. Greenland P, Mushlin AI, Griner PF. Discrepancies between knowledge and use of diagnostic studies in asymptomatic patients. J Med Educ. 1979; 54:863-9.

47. Petersdorf RG, Feinstein AR. An informal appraisal of the current status of 'medical sociology.' JAMA. 1981; 245:943-50.

48. Ruderman FA. What is medical sociology? JAMA. 1981;245:927-9.

49. Funkenstein DH. Medical students, medical school and society during five eras: factors affecting the career choices of physicians 1958-1976. Cambridge, Mass.: Ballinger, 1978.

50. McCue JD. Training internists: insights from private practice. Am J Med. 1981:71:475-9.

51. Gaffney JC, Glandon GL. Profile of medical practice 1979. Chicago: American Medical Association. 1979.

52. Mendenhall RC, Tarlov AR, Girard RA, Michel JK, Radecki SE. A national study of internal medicine and its specialties. II. Primary care in internal medicine. Ann Intern Med. 1979; 91:275-87.

53. Weil PA, Schleiter MK, Tarlov AR. National study of internal medicine manpower. V. Comparison of residents in internal medicine—future generalists and subspecialists. Ann Intern Med. 198; 94:678-90.

McCue JD. The effects of stress on physicians and their medical practice. N Engl J Med. 1982; 306(8): 458-463.

Article 5.2

House Officer Responses to Impaired Physicians

David B. Reuben, MD, and Sarah Noble. Journal of the American Medical Association, February 1990.

Although physician impairment may have substantial personal and clinical consequences, it is commonly held that physicians fail to act in the case of impaired colleagues. To learn about initial responses when confronted with impaired house officers and attending physicians, we administered five case scenarios to all 76 internal medicine house officers at a large, urban, teaching hospital. House officer responses to an alcohol impaired physician differed depending on whether that physician was an attending physician or a house officer. Seventy-two percent of house officers would tell the chief resident about the alcohol-impaired attending physician, whereas 96% would confront the alcohol-impaired house officer personally. The most common response to the incompetent attending physician (67%) and the incompetent house officer (49%) was to tell the chief resident; only 25% would confront an incompetent house officer. In contrast, 71% would confront a depressed house officer.

Although the American Medical Association Council on Mental Health has referred to physician impairment as "the inability to practice medicine adequately by reason of physical or mental illness, including alcoholism or drug dependence,"[1] the problem can be approached more broadly to include the effects of stress on practice[2] and *physician incompetence*, defined as the inability to provide sound medical care because of deficient knowledge, poor judgment, or substandard clinical skills. In each of these situations, a potentially remediable physician problem may lead to less than optimal care of patients.

Ideally, once one of these problems is suspected, a well-defined series of steps can be initiated to ensure that the impaired physician is encouraged to enter a treatment program, counseling, or further training. For example, in the case of substance abuse, every state medical society has developed a program to monitor and rehabilitate impaired physicians.[3] This rehabilitation begins with referral by the affected physician or by family members, friends, colleagues, and patients. Although confidentiality protects the persons who report the physicians, a "conspiracy of silence" has been described in which only the most overt cases of physician impairment are reported.[4,5]

Given this discrepancy between recognition of impairment and initiation of appropriate referral, the process of obtaining help for the impaired physician must be examined more closely. To begin this examination, we surveyed house officers to learn how they would respond when confronted with an impaired colleague or attending physician. Specifically, we wanted to learn the following: (1) What initial steps would house officers take when faced with an impaired physician? (2) Would house officers take different steps based on whether the impaired physician was an attending physician vs. a house officer? (3) Would house officers take different steps depending on whether the physician was impaired (within the guidelines of the American Medical Association's statement) vs. incompetent?

Methods

The study used a convenience sample: the entire population of internal medicine house officers (N=76) at Rhode Island Hospital, Providence, a 729-bed voluntary hospital and a major affiliate of the Brown University Program in Medicine, Providence. We developed an instrument that included five case scenarios (Table I) that depicted an alcohol-impaired attending physician (case 1) and house officer (case 4), an incompetent attending physician (case 2) and house officer (case 5), and a depressed house officer (case 3). Following each case was a list of possible initial courses of action, including (1) confronting the physician personally, (2) telling the chief resident, supervising resident, chief of medicine, or some other faculty member, (3) reporting the incident to the Rhode Island Medical Society Impaired Physician Committee, (4) deciding to take no action, or (5) another course of action that the respondent specified. House officers were directed to select one or more choices for each case scenario.

The instrument was pretested by residents and reviewed by faculty with expertise in physician impairment. The case scenarios were then administered to medical house officers using a double-envelope method to track responses but preserve confidentiality. This method uses an outer envelope with the respondent's name that is discarded after the response is recorded and an inner envelope that contains the instrument but no identifying information.

Data were entered into a personal computer, with 100% second-entry verification, and analyzed using SPSS software. Testing for statistical significance was performed using McNemar's Test[6] to compare house officer responses to different cases and the χ^2 test to compare responses between male and female house officers and between training levels (postgraduate years). In all statistical testing, two-tailed testing was performed, with $P<.05$ being considered significant. We did not adjust our level of significance for multiple testing because we were testing independent hypotheses that were generated prior to data analysis, and we report all of our principal comparisons.[7] Using a power calculation formula for McNemar's Test,[8] we estimate that with a sample size of 76 and an α value of .10, if one third of our sample differed in their responses to two cases presented, our power would be 0.62.

Results

All 76 medical house officers participated in the study. The respondents included 42 male house officers (55%) and 34 female house officers (45%). Thirty-two house officers (42%) were in their first postgraduate year and 22 (29%) were in each of the subsequent years of training.

Responses to Alcohol-Impaired Physicians

When faced with the case scenario of an alcohol-impaired physician (Table 2), almost all of the house officers (96%) would confront the physician personally if he or she was a house officer, but only 9% would confront an attending physician. In the latter situation, house officers would most commonly tell the chief resident (72%); one fourth would tell the chief of medicine and 17% would report the physician to the state's impaired physician committee. In contrast, no house officer would report another house officer to this committee and only one would tell the chief of medicine.

Responses to Incompetent Physicians

When faced with the case scenario of an incompetent physician (Table 3), the most common response was to tell the chief resident regardless of whether the incompetent physician was a house officer or an attending physician. As in the cases of alcohol impairment, house officers were more likely to confront other house officers personally than attendings, but only one fourth stated that they would take this action. House officers were also more likely to tell the chief of medicine about an incompetent attending than an incompetent house officer.

Responses to Various House Officer Problems

House officers were significantly less likely to confront a depressed compared with an alcohol-impaired house officer (Table 4). Nevertheless, the most common response in either of these cases was confronting the impaired house officer personally. In contrast, when faced with an incompetent house officer the most common response was to tell the chief resident or supervising resident.

Analysis of Responses by House Officer Gender and Level of Training

Responses did not differ by gender or levels of training, with the following exceptions. Male house officers were more likely than female house officers to tell the chief resident about an incompetent attending (81% vs. 48%, $P<.05$), and with progressive advancement of level of training there was an increasing likelihood of a house officer reporting an incompetent resident to the chief resident (32% for first-year, 45% for second-year, and 77% for third-year house officers; $P<.05$).

Comment:

Physician impairment, defined broadly to include any condition that may adversely affect the physician's personal health or the care provided to patients, remains an important problem because of

Table 1

Case Scenarios

1. It is 11:30 pm. A patient is admitted to the ER with upper GI bleeding. You are the resident in charge. You call the GI attending and he is abusive on the telephone. The abuse continues when he arrives at the ER to endoscope the patient. You smell alcohol on his breath. The doctor treats your patient but you begin to wonder about his behavior. The next day you talk to a colleague who tells you that he has had similar problems with this same physician. What would you do initially?

2. During the first week of your residency you had an argument with an attending physician regarding case management and you asked your resident whether you were wrong. Your resident told you that you were correct and the attending physician is widely regarded as incompetent. Over the next 6 months, you have cared for several of the physician's patients. In each case, you and your resident have believed that the attending physician mismanaged the case. You are worried that this is the usual situation and the physician may be dangerous. What would you do initially?

3. It is 9:30 pm. You are on call and have just responded to a page. After the page, you go to the cafeteria and see a colleague sitting alone with an empty, vacant look. You go over to sit with your fellow resident and ask, "What's wrong?" The resident quietly tells you that he has had it and cannot take the stress anymore. Nothing provides enjoyment. He has had frequent crying spells and difficulty sleeping, even after call. What would you do initially?

4. During internship, you and another resident had become close friends. At first, you and your colleague shared just a few drinks after call. Now he seems to be hung over when he comes to the hospital in the morning; he admits to drinking heavily every night when not on call. You are worried about the quality of your friend's work. What would you do initially?

5. You are working with a co-intern and it soon becomes obvious that the intern is disorganized and is not learning how to manage patients effectively. You feel that your colleague just can't grasp basic concepts despite good teaching from the residents. Each resident has worked with this cointern for only 1 month at a time and has been reluctant to confront or report the intern. You believe that the program director and the faculty are not aware that your co-intern is unable to perform adequately. What would you do initially?

Table 2

House Officer Responses to Alcohol-Impaired Physicians[a]

	Impaired Attending		Impaired House Officer	
Response	No.	%	No.	%
Confront physician	7	9	73	96[a]
Tell chief resident	55	72	16	21[b]
Tell chief of medicine	19	25	1	1[b]
Tell another faculty member	4	5	0	0
Report to impaired physician committee	13	17	0	0
Wait for more evidence	4	5	1	1
Take no action	0	0	1	1
Other	4	5	2	3

a Totals are greater than 100% because respondents could select more than one option.
b $P<.05$ between responses to impaired attending and house officer.

Table 3

House Officer Responses to Incompetent Physicians[a]

	Incompetent Attending		Incompetent House Officer	
Response	No.	%	No.	%
Confront physician	8	11	19	25
Tell chief resident	50	67	37	49
Tell chief of medicine	30	41	7	9[b]
Tell another faculty member	5	9	0	0
Take no action	6	8	8	11
Other	6	8	7	9

a Totals are greater than 100% because respondents could select more than one option.
b P<.05 between responses to incompetent attending and house officer.

Table 4

House Officer Responses to House Officer Problems[a]

	Alcohol Impairment		Incompetence		Depression	
Response	No.	%	No.	%	No.	%
Confront physician	73	96	19	25	53	71[b]
Tell chief resident	16	21	37	49[c]	26	34
Tell supervising resident	11	14	33	43[d]	13	17
Tell chief of medicine	1	1	7	9	4	5
Tell another faculty member	0	0	0	2	2	3
Take no action	1	1	8	11	1	1
Other	2	3	7	9	8	11

a Totals are greater than 100% because respondents could select more than one option.
b P<.05 for all comparisons for this response.
c P<.05 between responses to incompetent and alcohol-impaired house officers.
d P<.05 between responses to incompetent and alcohol-impaired house officers and between responses to incompetent and depressed house officers.

the trust that society has placed in physicians to provide medical care for its ill. Despite its importance, the prevalence of physician impairment is unknown. As Brewster[9] notes, each data source (e.g., surveys, hospital admissions, and mortality rates) that has been used to establish prevalence rates for alcohol and other drug problems has its own set of limitations. She concluded that the overall prevalence of physician problems with alcohol and other drugs may not be different from that of the general population. The prevalence of other mental impairments such as depression among practicing physicians is not known.

In contrast, depression is a well-recognized cause of impairment during residency training, especially during the first year of training, with reported rates as high as 30%.[10-12] The prevalence of alcohol and drug impairment among house officers is not known, but recent data from a cohort of medical students suggest that approximately 10% of students met criteria for excessive drinking for at least one 6-month period,[13] and a survey of medical students' drug use identified 5% as having drug dependence at any time.[14]

To learn about how impaired physicians might be referred for treatment, we studied house officers, a population that has frequent interactions with attending physicians and other house officers. Therefore, our subjects were likely to have been placed in real situations similar to the case scenarios. In contrast to the commonly held notion that there is underreporting of physician impairment, our data suggest that the vast majority of house officers would have taken some initial action, either confronting or reporting the impaired physicians in each of the case scenarios.

We found that the initial response to physician impairment differed significantly depending on whether the impaired physician was an attending physician or a house officer. House officers would most likely tell a figure of authority about an alcohol-impaired attending but would almost universally personally confront an alcohol-impaired peer. This difference in initial action is understandable given the disparity of roles and stature between house officers and attending physicians.

Incompetence, per se, has received little attention in studies of physician impairment but places house officers in a similar situation, i.e., whether to report this problem and to whom. Responses of house officers to the scenario of the incompetent attending physician were similar to those of the alcohol-impaired physician. On the other hand, house officers were much less likely to confront incompetent house officers compared with alcohol-impaired or depressed peers. Thus, house officers seem to differentiate incompetence from other impairments among their peers but not among attending physicians. Perhaps they feel uncomfortable relating personal judgments of their peers' competence through direct confrontation but are more likely to act when a comrade's health is endangered by alcohol or depression.

Given these findings, what are the implications in terms of helping the impaired physician? The pivotal role of the chief resident as the most likely person to hear about physician impairment in all our scenarios demands that chief residents be knowledgeable about the resources available to help the impaired physician. The study also provides valuable information that may facilitate the management of physician impairment. Given that personal confrontation is the most common approach to these problems when occurring in peers, house officers must become more facile and confident in discussing these problems among themselves. For example, an initial confrontation might just be a friendly expression of concern. If the problem is not corrected, the house officer might become more directive in subsequent confrontation with the peer.

The limitations of our study must be considered. We have addressed the issue of responder bias by obtaining a 100% response rate. In our study design, however, we relied on standardized case scenarios to answer our research questions. The use of case scenarios does not permit us to comment on what house officers would do if situations similar to the case scenarios actually occurred. In fact, well-intentioned house officers may not take the steps they indicated because of psychological or institutional barriers. Finally, the issue of our study's generalizability must also be raised. The importance of the chief resident at our institution may have reflected the value that our house officers placed on the current chief resident. This possibility further supports the influence that a strong chief resident could have at other programs. In addition, our study only examined house officer responses to physician impairment. The actions of attending physicians, physicians' families, and patients when faced with physician impairment must be determined in future studies.

In conclusion, there seems be a network of personal confrontation that is most important in attempting to help the impaired house officer, but house officers rely on more senior physicians when faced with an impaired attending physician. Whether any of these efforts are effective in linking impaired physicians to assistive programs remains to be determined.

We thank the internal medicine house staff of Rhode Island Hospital, Providence, for participating in the study; Patricia S. O'Sullivan, PhD, for statistical advice; Dennis H. Novack, MD, and Richard J. Goldberg, MD, for reviewing the instrument; Dr O'Sullivan, David C. Lewis, MD, Alan Wartenberg, MD, Robert M. Arnold, MD, and Gail A. Greendale, MD, for reviewing an early draft of the manuscript; and Brenda Manchester for manuscript preparation.

References

1. American Medical Association Council on Mental Health. The sick physician: impairment by psychiatric disorders, including alcoholism and drug dependence. JAMA. 1973;223:684-687.

2. McCue JD. The effects of stress on physicians and their medical practice. N Engl J Med. 1982;306:458-463.

3. Lewis DC. Doctors and drugs. N Engl J Med. 1986;315:826-828.

4. Spickarad A, Billings FT. Alcoholism in a medical-school faculty. N Engl J Med. 1981;305:1646-1648

5. Samkoff JS, McDermott RW. Recognizing physician impairment. Pa Med. 1988;91:36-38.

6. Marascuilo LA, McSweeney M. Nonparametric and Distribution-Free Methods for the Social Sciences, Monterey, Calif: Brooks/Cole Publishing Co; 1977:167-169.

7. Rothman KJ. Modern Epidemiology. Boston, Mass: Little Brown & Co Inc; 1986:149.

8. Schlesselman JJ. Case-Control Studies: Design, Conduct, Analysis. New York, NY: Oxford University Press Inc; 1982:162.

9. Brewster JM. Prevalence of alcohol and other drug problems among physicians. JAMA. 1986;255:1913-1920.

10. Valko RJ, Clayton PJ. Depression in internship. Dis Nerv Syst. 1975;36-29.

11. Reuben DB. Depressive symptoms in medical house officers. Arch Intern Med. 1985;145:286-288.

12. Girard DE, Elliot DL, Hickman DH, et al. The internship: a prospective investigation of emotions and attitudes. West J Med. 1986;144:93-98.

13. Clark DC, Eckenfels EJ, Daugherty SR, Fawcett J. Alcohol-use patterns through medical school. JAMA. 1989;257:2921-2926.

14. McAuliffe WE, Rohman M. Santagelo S, et al. Psychoactive drug use among practicing physicians and medical students. N Engl J Med. 1986;315:805-810.

Reuben DB. House officer responses to impaired physicians. JAMA. 1990; 263(7): 958-960.

Reprinted with permission from the authors and the American Medical Association.

Article 5.3

Impaired Physicians: The Dilemma of Identification

G. Douglas Talbott, MD and Earl B. Benson, MD. Post Graduate Medicine, 1980.

CONSIDER

- **According to estimates, what percentage of physicians have been, are, or will be addicted to alcohol and/or other drugs?**
- **In what ways may physicians try to hide their addiction? How may family and associates unwittingly aid and abet them?**
- **What clues in the physician's behavior may help in early identification of the problem?**

Doctors disabled by alcohol and/or other drugs are often difficult to detect, owing to both the conspiracy of silence surrounding them and their own self-deception. Now, investigators in Georgia have compiled lists of characteristic behaviors in six major areas of life that make identification easier. These lists are presented here, along with preliminary results of an aggressive intervention and treatment program.

Impaired physicians—those doctors afflicted with alcohol and/or other drug addiction—have but recently been recognized as a significant problem within the medical community.

Specific statistics regarding number of identifiable impaired physicians in a total physician population are lacking, as the data available in any given state are grossly descriptive if not anecdotal in nature.

G. Douglas Talbott, MD, is founder and director of Talbott-Marsh Recovery Campus; chairman of the Georgia Impaired Health Professional Program and clinical professor of psychiatry at Emory University Medical School in Atlanta, Georgia.

However, because of the longevity and depth of the "Georgia experience," data from this state may shed light on the situation.

In 1975, the Medical Association of Georgia implemented the Disabled Doctors Program for physicians impaired by alcohol and drug abuse. As of July 1, 1980, 297 of the state's 6,500 physicians (including residents, interns, house staff, and fellows in academia) had been contacted as prospective candidates for the program; 240 entered the program, and 57 were judged inappropriate or rejected. Based on these figures and our experience and perception, we conclude that one of eight physicians in Georgia has been, is, or will be afflicted with the disease of chemical dependency. However, we strongly believe that more critical and precise statistics are needed.

Results of the program to date are impressive. As of July 1, 1980, 156 physicians have been successfully rehabilitated and returned to practice, having been followed for two years or longer. However, since the inception of the program, identification of impaired physicians has presented a major problem. This is due, principally, to two factors: (1) the conspiracy of silence among professionals and lay people alike and (2) self-deception on the part of the impaired physician. Neither the medical profession nor the lay population in the United States is yet comfortable with the presence of disabled doctors, so many of them are ignored or not recognized until late in the disease course when punitive action is taken. Compounding the problem is the fact that disabled doctors often deny that they have a problem, which prevents them from reaching out for help.

The staff of the Disabled Doctors Program and particularly the authors have repeatedly encountered peers and colleagues who are unaware of the fact that 12% to 14% of the physicians in their community, their medical society, their hospital staff have had, do have, or will have problems with alcohol and drugs. Repeatedly we have heard arguments by unknowledgeable and naive colleagues that problems of this kind do not exist in their community. Obviously, this is not true.

To aid in identification of impaired physicians, we have compiled six lists of characteristic behaviors. We have found that impaired physicians demonstrate alcohol and drug addiction by behavioral abnormalities in six areas of life, which are affected in sequence. The last area affected is the medical setting, ie, in the hospital, during staff rounds, in the emergency room, at medical society meetings. Long before this, changes appear in community involvement, family life, employment patterns, physical status, and office conduct.

We have found these lists to be very valuable in identifying impaired physicians. Behavioral abnormalities in each of the six areas are...described in more detail in the following sections.

Community Involvement

Isolation and withdrawal from the community and its activities often signal the onset of significant development of alcoholism or drug addiction in the physician. This is part of the "target syndrome," in which the impaired physician ends up like the bull's-eye of a target after having eliminated the successive rings of community activities, leisure activities, church, friends, peers, distant family, and finally, nuclear family. Embarrassing behaviors —getting traffic tickets, being arrested for driving while intoxicated, getting drunk at parties and at the country club, fighting publicly with spouse and peers—are part of this syndrome.

The physician who was once a pillar of the church and community may now behave unpredictably and unreliably. He or she may become an instant participant in a new field, e.g., real estate, politics, art, often spending money in amounts out of proportion to the usual pursuit of a hobby or leisure activity. The community and friends gradually lose respect for the physician and lose confidence in his or her emotional and behavioral stability.

Family Life

Alcoholism and drug addiction have been accurately characterized as family diseases. This is especially true when the alcoholic or addict is a physician. As part of the target syndrome, the impaired physician withdraws from family activities, relationships, and communication. Family fights erupt, and child abuse—if not physical, certainly emotional—may even occur. The spouse becomes sick with the disease of "spousaholism."

The best way to identify impaired physicians is not to ask which physicians in the community drink addictively or are habituated to other drugs but instead to look at those physicians who are separated from their families or whose children have serious emotional, legal, or scholastic problems. Often we find that such physicians also have drug problems. The same holds true for physicians engaged in extra-marital affairs or contracultural sexual behavior.

Employment Patterns

At this point in the evolution of the disease, the impaired physician typically seeks employment elsewhere. In reviewing applications for jobs in clinics, partnerships, and public and private facilities as well as applications for staff appointments in community and teaching hospitals, we identified nine criteria indicative of alcohol and drug addiction. The presence of any three of these should alert the employer to the possibility that the applicant has such a problem.

Numerous job changes and frequent relocations speak to the "geographic cure" so often attempted by alcoholics and drug addicts. A complicated medical history with frequent hospitalizations is often a sign of chemical dependency. Unexplained intervals between jobs and inappropriate references can be significant clues also. It is interesting how frequently such references are not checked or documented. A disabled doctor in our program a few years ago gave his dog's veterinarian as his primary professional reference, and nobody at the facility where he was applying checked the reference.

Inappropriate jobs may be another clue. A doctor in our program had been a professor of cardiovascular surgery but was doing routine physical examinations in insurance assessment on a full-time basis. This was obviously inappropriate for his qualifications and in this case reflected meperidine addiction.

Reluctance of the physician to involve his or her family in the interview or to undergo immediate physical examination is also suspicious. In the latter situation, the physician hopes to avoid the examination or at least to postpone it until needle marks or recent bruises fade away.

Physical Status

Next, physical signs and symptoms of the disease of chemical dependency become evident. Poor personal hygiene and unkempt appearance (e.g., long, dirty fingernails; unshaven face; untrimmed hair; dirty, unpressed clothes) are strong clues to the presence of alcoholism or drug addiction in a previously well-dressed or fastidious physician. Numerous and constant physical complaints, frequent visits to fellow physicians, multiple prescriptions and medications (often self-prescribed), and frequent hospitalizations may provide additional clues. Repeated car accidents or accidents while on vacation or involved in hobbies or leisure activities also may be evidence of alcoholism or drug addiction. Likewise, wide mood swings and emotional crises too often are manifestations of such a problem.

Office Conduct

As our experience with the Georgia program grew and our understanding of the problem increased, we began to dialogue with physicians' office personnel and to hold educational seminars and forums for them throughout the state. We found a number of criteria relating to office practice that may help in identifying impaired physicians.

The doctor may arrive late or have unexplained and often lengthy absences from the office, making a jumble of the appointment schedule. His or her behavior may become angry, hostile, or otherwise inconsistent with previous behavior, which prompts complaints by patients and, later, staff. The doctor may give inappropriate orders. We have repeatedly found nurses, usually long-time employees, who act as enablers, monitoring verbal and written orders and correcting them if necessary. Frequently, doctors lock themselves in the office or bathroom to inject or ingest the drug of choice. We have found this so often that we have named it the locked-door syndrome. Repeatedly we have noted a conspiracy of silence among the office staff and even an attitude of complacency or detachment by patients despite their knowledge that something is wrong with the doctor.

Hospital Duties

The last place where the impaired physician's problem becomes apparent is the hospital. Making rounds at midnight or 2 a.m., writing inappropriate orders, going into the wrong rooms, reading the wrong chart, writing illegibly can all be signs of alcoholism or drug addiction. A change in behavior is the important clue. For example, since physicians notoriously write poorly, it is not the writing itself but a significant change in writing that is important.

Hospital gossip about the aberrant behavior of an impaired physician often reaches the ear of the administrator via a telephone operator, parking lot attendant, janitor, elevator operator, or other hospital employee. It is important for the administrator to question emergency department personnel, as they are aware of unanswered emergencies; slowed, slurred verbal responses on the phone at night; inappropriate orders; and other signs that the physician is chemically dependent. Involvement in malpractice suits and legal sanctions against the hospital is another important clue. In assessing physicians involved in legal actions against or with the hospital, we have found a high incidence of alcoholism and drug addiction.

Since the hospital is the last area of the impaired physician's life to be affected, the disease is usually advanced by the time we receive complaints from hospital personnel.

Results of Georgia Program

Where lists of the characteristic behaviors of impaired physicians have been made available, the level of awareness of the problem has increased considerably. Since early intervention is highly desirable in view of the fact that disabled doctors have difficulty in reaching out for help, such lists should be distributed, with appropriate educative efforts, to medical societies and auxiliaries, hospital administrators, hospital and office staffs, and physicians' families.

In Georgia's Disabled Doctors Program, once a physician has been identified as impaired and this information has been verified, he or she is confronted with the problem. (Confrontation dynamics and techniques have been described thoroughly elsewhere and will not be discussed here.) The success rate of active intervention is impressive. Comparing the results of confrontation in the first 90 and the last 90 physicians involved in our program, we found success rates of 73% and 97%, respectively. (Our rates cannot be compared with those of other state programs because of differences in extent of experience and in techniques used.) Confrontation success is defined as the patient coming into treatment; confrontation failure, as complete rejection of involvement in the program. Identification and subsequent intervention, motivation, and therapy would be far less attractive if the recovery rate were not so high.

Since we are dealing with a chronic, progressive disease, the rate of recovery in impaired physicians must be viewed with reservations unless the data refer to at least a five-year period and to a statistically significant number of physicians. In the Georgia program, we have yet to meet these criteria. Preliminary data have been compiled for 100 physicians followed for four years and for an additional 100 physicians followed for two years. The recovery rates for the two groups are 86% and 93%, respectively. Recovery is defined as serene sobriety with effective and productive return to family, job and community. If relapse extends beyond 36 hours or occurs more than twice, the patient is eliminated from the recovery group.

Further details of the Disabled Doctors Program are available elsewhere. It is important to emphasize here the unique nature of this program and the fact that it is being refined and improved yearly.

Summary

Physicians addicted to alcohol and/or other drugs demonstrate characteristic behaviors in six areas of life. First they withdraw from community and family. Next they change jobs, often repeatedly. Then their physical status begins to deteriorate. Finally they can no longer function effectively at office or hospital. By learning the warning signs, those who come in contact with physicians can detect such problems earlier, while there is still a good chance of recovery.

Talbott GD. Impaired physicians: the dilemma of identification. Post Graduate Medicine. 1980; 68.

Article 5.4

Elements of the Impaired Physicians Program

G. Douglas Talbott, MD. Journal of the Medical Association of Georgia, November 1984.

MAG's Impaired Physicians Program (IPP) consists of four elements which have evolved from experience over the past 10 years: identification, intervention, treatment, and re-entry. All four elements are essential to the successful rehabilitation of Georgia's impaired physician.

Identification

The identification of impaired physicians is profoundly affected by their characteristic massive denial. Their almost phobic inability to reach out for help, combined with the conspiracy of silence evidenced by family, peers, friends, and even patients, makes identification very difficult. After analysis of the progression of the disease in the first 100 patients in IPP, it became apparent that the signs and symptoms used as identification criteria occurred first in the home and family setting, then sequentially in the community and the church and in financial, legal, and health problems. Symptoms were apparent last at the office or the hospital. When impaired physicians arrive in an altered state of consciousness at their job, it is usually very late in the disease and the rest of their lives is already in turmoil.

Symptom inventories in the form of checklists have been prepared[1] and are utilized for early identification of the impaired physician. Inherent in identification is verification which is accomplished by confirming the diagnosis with the IPP network of recovering physicians, spouses, administrators of hospitals, medical society staff, nurses, and friends in self-help groups. Such verification is possible because of extensive education efforts throughout the states to establish this Program as a non-punitive, advocacy, disease model.

Intervention

The second element of the program, intervention, is dictated by the denial characteristics of impaired physicians and their inability to reach out for help. In the vast majority of physicians, motivation for treatment is dependent upon intervention. Following hundreds of interventions with impaired physicians, guidelines have been established,[2] the use of which has recently been demonstrated in a videotape. Basic to this approach is the requirement that this intervention be implemented by at least two physician intervenors; ideally, one of these is recovering from the disease of chemical dependence. The intervenors, who are carefully trained in the facts of this psychosocial biogenetic disease, must also be carefully instructed and practiced in dealing with denial, anger, and hostility.

Representing the Medical Association of Georgia, these intervenors, who are selected because of absence of personal or professional relations with the impaired physician, must have also carefully done their homework. This homework consists mainly of careful documentation of evidence of the disease and is accomplished by interviewing and mobilizing for the intervention the support systems of that particular impaired physician. In addition, intervenors prepare specific goals and objectives of the intervention with particular attention to the assessment and treatment plans to be presented.

When such homework is accomplished, then the support systems are brought together for instruction on the disease, for definition of their roles at interven-

G. Douglas Talbott, MD, is founder and director of Talbott-Marsh Recovery Campus; chairman of the Georgia Impaired Health Professional Program; and clinical professor of psychiatry at Emory University Medical School in Atlanta, Georgia.

tion, and for role playing and rehearsal of the actual events. Attention to a realistic assessment of the situation and to likely responses by the physician to the intervention helps participants make a tough-minded commitment to follow through with whatever agreements have been made for negative sanctions if the person refuses help. It also helps them unequivocally accept the physician's decision to go into treatment. Careful attention is given to the selection of participants and of the time and place for the structured intervention. Adequate time is allowed in the intervention for meeting the physician's objections and for dealing with extenuating circumstances so that the goal of getting the physician into immediate assessment or treatment is accomplished. In the Georgia program, repeated interventions are utilized if the primary confrontation fails. Intervention without the implied authority and consequences of the MAG and/or the licensing board is usually doomed to failure.

Treatment

The treatment element of the Georgia Impaired Physicians Program is divided into an initial 72-hour assessment followed by four phases of treatment. The initial assessment has been found to be a very effective goal of intervention. This allows the intervention team, rather than play the role of judge and jury for the impaired physician, to emphasize that they want the impaired physician to see the "experts" who will define the problem and recommend the specific treatment course.

Five-member teams of medical specialists, psychologists and neuropsychologists, psychiatrists, family therapists, and addictionologists consult to establish the diagnosis. They differentiate chemical dependence from primary psychiatric disease and assess other medical problems; then they present specific treatment plans to the impaired physician and the family. Various treatment options are utilized for patients in the Georgia Program. These include referral to their community Alcoholics Anonymous/Narcotics Anonymous program and the prescribed plan for attending "90 meetings in 90 days," referral to outpatient alcohol and/or drug treatment only, referral to a psychiatric rather than a chemical dependence program, referral to counseling, and return to their practice or, as is true of the majority of assessment cases in the Georgia Program, referral to full treatment in the MAG Impaired Physicians Program.

With the signing of a treatment contract impaired physicians are regarded as entering a 2-year treatment program, including after-care monitoring, and surveillance upon returning. IPP's treatment regimen consists of four phases. Phase 1 is a 4-6 week intensive inpatient treatment program which may or may not be completed at Ridgeview Institute, where the majority of the treatment team is located. The Ridgeview model (as do the other approved programs) stresses the disease precept of chemical dependence and emphasizes family therapy, AA/NA, a strong personal spiritual program, group therapy, non-chemical coping skills training, and detailed education on the psychosocial biogenetic characteristics of the disease of alcoholism and drug addiction. In Phase 1, true peer group therapy is initiated to deal with special problems and influences that uniquely affect those in the medical profession. In the peer groups, physicians meet with physicians, dentists with dentists, pharmacists with pharmacists, and nurses with nurses. They consist of people in various phases of treatment. These special peer groups continue throughout the 4 months and beyond for those people in the area.

Following Phase 1, the impaired physician enters into Phase 2, which consists of outpatient therapy and supervised living in a recovery residence. The outpatient program at a SAFE (Substance Abuse Free Existence) Center is an extension of the medical model established at Ridgeview. Determined by the severity of an individual's disease, this phase lasts 1-2 months and provides further practice in non-chemical coping, development of a stronger spiritual program, and deeper involvement in AA/NA with intense family therapy. Caduceus Outpatient Recovery Residences (CORR) utilize rented apartments and houses in the metropolitan Atlanta area, and these recovery residences serve as a site for surrogate family living. For 90 days, impaired physicians live there, going to 90 meetings of AA/NA, participating in supervised group therapy four times a week, and learning in that ambience to care again, to trust, to socialize, to communicate and to assume personal accountability for their own behavior.

Phase 3 is completed when impaired physicians, while continuing to live in the recovery residence, are judged able to move from strict patient status to that of counselor-trainees under strict supervision. As they become frustrated and try forcefully to get the addict or alcoholic they are supervising to break through denial, to deal with depression, anger, or hostility, or to mend family wounds, they can see themselves. This "mirror image" therapy is a very constructive experience lasting for a minimum of 2 months. Concomitant with this work, impaired physicians also teach, dialogue, and interact with medical students at Emory University School of Medicine. Dealing with these students in a variety of seminars, lectures, and workshops restores professional dignity while cleansing the impaired physician of the embarrassment, shame, and guilt that society assigns to this disease. In turn, the medical students acquire a new dimension regarding this disease—that indeed it could happen to them.[3]

Re-Entry

The last phase of the treatment process, re-entry, is considered a separate element. Having already signed a treatment contract and having completed the 4 months of treatment, impaired physicians enter into a 20-month aftercare contract which provides for a primary monitoring physician and for random drug screens. It also states the agreed on schedule of AA/NA meetings and choice of "sponsor" in the AA/NA program. In addition, the elements of a personal spiritual program and further recommendations for a family therapy program are carefully detailed.

Another document, called "Relapse Guidelines," is also signed. Rather than a firm contract, the Guidelines give certain suggestions to guard against relapse and to interrupt it if it does occur. Georgia's Program recognizes that chemical dependence is a relapsing disease and, while the Program does not give permission for relapse to occur, it recognizes that possibility. Procedures such as obtaining drug screens, calling the primary monitoring physician, calling the treatment center, and mobilizing the impaired physician's support systems are outlined for physicians to utilize before, and certainly after, using a mood-altering chemical. The guidelines also suggest procedures for families or supervisors to use when they are concerned about the physician's relapse.

Just as the effectiveness of the initial phase of treatment is dependent on its intensity to break through denial, the value of the aftercare phase lies in its extension to provide support during transition to community-based support. Twenty months allows for structured contacts to be maintained through the first 2 years after which, according to our data, the risk of relapse drops significantly.[4]

In addition to the aftercare contract and the relapse guidelines, the re-entry phase is ideally characterized by continuous contact with the Caduceus Club network, the primary care physician, and the treatment center. In actuality, many physicians are miles from other recovering physicians. Other than frequent calls to contacts at IPP, they rely on AA/NA networks and sponsors for the support they need to stay sober. International Doctors in Alcoholics Anonymous (IDAA) offers further personal and professional support. Composed of physicians and Ph.D. psychologists, IDAA has an annual meeting and other informal meetings in conjunction with various conferences.

The long-term goal of Georgia's Impaired Physicians Program is that each physician who completes the treatment regimen will have acquired an emotional and spiritual commitment to "go to any lengths" to stay sober and live a productive and rewarding life, 24 hours at a time. The tools for preventing relapse or for turning it into a higher quality recovery program are provided in the four elements of the Program discussed in this paper.

References

1. Talbott GD, Benson LB. Impaired physicians: The dilemma of identification. Postgrad Med 1980; 68: 56-64.

2. Talbott GD. The impaired physician and intervention: A key to recovery. J Fla Med Assoc. 1982; 69: 793-797.

3. Talbott GD. The role of the medical student in the treatment of impaired physicians. J Med Assn Ga. 1982;11:275-277.

4. Unpublished study.

Talbott GD. Elements of the impaired physicians program. J Med Assoc Ga. 1984; 73: 747-751.

Reprinted with permission from the author and the Journal of the Medical Association of Georgia.

Annotated Bibliography

Physician Suicide

Results and implications of the AMA-APA physician mortality project: stage II. AMA Council on Scientific Affairs report. JAMA. 1987; 257: 2949-2953.
This detailed study carried out jointly by the AMA and the American Psychiatric Association compares interviews with family members of physicians who died by suicide and those who died of natural causes. The profile of a suicide-prone physician is described and recommendations are made.

Ross M. *Physician suicide risk: practical recognition and management.* South Med J. 1975; 68: 699-702.
Data from the American Psychiatric Association Task Force on Suicide Prevention is presented with emphasis on recognition and management of physicians at risk for suicide.

Ross M. *Suicide among physicians.* Psychiatry in Medicine. 1971; 1: 189-198.
A review of the international literature since 1900 yields comparison of physician suicide rates throughout the world and ranks Holland first, Britain second and the United States third for the frequency of physician suicide.

Steppacher RC, Mausner JS. *Suicide in male and female physicians.* JAMA. 1984; 228: 323-328.
This study of 530 suicide deaths among physicians between 1965 and 1970 showed that female physicians had a much higher incidence than their male colleagues.

The Physician-in-Training and Impairment

Blackwell B. *Prevention of impairment among residents in training.* JAMA. 1986; 255: 1177-1178.
This editorial, using the survey reported by Smith, Denny and Witze (see below) as a springboard, describes additional stress factors of internship and expands the discussion of possible impairment prevention resources. See also the accompanying editorial.

Clark DC. *Alcohol and drug use and mood disorders among medical students: implications for physician impairment.* Quality Rev Bull. 1988; 14: 50-54.
This prospective analysis of a medical school class from first-year students through first-year residents describes the natural history of alcohol and other drug use and depression. Early substance abuse did not correlate with impaired work activities. Students did appear to have an elevated risk for depression compared with the general population.

McAuliffe WE, Rohman M, Santangelo S, et al. *Psychoactive drug use among practicing physicians and medical students.* N Engl J Med. 1986; 315: 805-810.
This article presents comprehensive self-reported data on psychoactive drug use in samples of physicians and medical students in one New England state during 1984-1985. Prevalence, type and extent of drug use and subjects "at risk" are considered within the context of policy implications for physician education about drug use and the risks of impairment. Includes extensive bibliography. Alcohol use is not included in this evaluation.

On the Horizon: Regulation of Physician Training Programs. Chicago,IL: American Medical Association Medical Education Group; 1989.
This book is the recording of the proceedings of a joint conference sponsored by the AMA, the American Hospital Association, and the Association of American Medical Colleges. Twenty-five speakers and panelists represent views of academicians, residents, hospital managers, and state regulators.

Reuben DB, Noble S. *House officer responses to impaired physicians.* JAMA. 1990; 263: 958-960.
Article 5.2

Simkin DR, Binder J. *Student section of impaired professional program established.* J LA State Med Soc. 1985-1986; 136(12): 24-25 and 137(1): 23-24.
This two-part article presents a synopsis of William Marchand's literature review on the impaired student problem, examines how some states include students in their impaired physician program, and describes the development of the student section of the Impaired Physician Program in Louisiana.

Smith JW, Denny WF, Witzke DB. *Emotional impairment in internal medicine house staff: results of a national survey.* JAMA. 1986; 255: 1155-1158.
Results of a survey sent to 436 directors of internal medicine residency programs in the United States to identify the scope of debilitating emotional impairment are reported. The definition of impaired resident was limited to presence of emotional problems necessitating a leave of absence from the training program. Recovery was noted by return to the program, with program drop-outs and successful suicides reported. Potential stress factors and other predispositions as well as potential prevention programs are briefly described. Several references specific to the impaired intern, resident or house officer are listed.

Stress and impairment during residency training: strategies for reduction, identification, and management: Report of the Resident Services Committee of the Association of Program Directors in Internal Medicine. Ann Intern Med. 1988; 109: 154-160.
This report describes three categories of stress: stress in training, situational stress, and personal stress. It makes specific recommendations for limiting resident work loads and improving the educational features of training programs.

Organized Medicine and the Impaired Physician

American Society of Anesthesiologists. *Questions and Answers About Clinical Dependence and Physician Impairment.* Park Ridge, IL: The American Society of Anesthesiologists; 1986.
This booklet presents, in question-and-answer format, concise information about the manifestations of alcohol and other drug abuse, practical advice about confronting and assisting an impaired physician, and programs for rehabilitation and long-term recovery. The appendices include helpful step-by-step guides on such topics as re-entry and physician monitoring at the level of the hospital medical staff following treatment for chemical dependence. This pamphlet is of special interest to anesthesiologists; however, many of the practical suggestions have broader applicability.

Dodd JL. *Impaired physicians: an Iowa perspective.* Iowa Med. 1984; 74: 517-522.
This article reviews briefly the origins of "sick doctor laws," studies of categories of impairment, and reported recovery rates. The author also describes an incidence study of physicians who were under probation by the Iowa Board of Medical Examiners on January 1, 1983. A brief description of the Iowa Board of Medical Examiners program for dealing with impaired and unethical physicians is included.

Green RC, Carroll GJ, Buxton WD. *The Care and Management of the Sick and Incompetent Physician.* Springfield, IL: Charles C Thomas Publisher; 1978.
Three physician members of the Virginia State Board of Medicine analyze drug addiction, alcoholism, psychiatric illness, and behavioral problems among physicians. They include a history of the development of peer review and physician disciplinary bodies in the United States as well as a chapter on the legal rights of impaired physicians.

Rakatansky H. *Special report: the Committee on Impaired Physicians of the Rhode Island Medical Society.* R I Med J. 1985; 68: 119-121.
This article presents a status report on the functions and results of the Impaired Physician Committee of the Rhode Island Medical Society. Illness considered by the committee, statistics on cases referred, and family issues are described. Legal liability and record keeping are briefly discussed.

Talbott GD. *Elements of the impaired physician program.* J Med Assoc Ga. 1984; 73: 747-751.
Article 5.4

Impairment Related to Physical Problems

Feinstein RJ. *When should the sick doctor stop caring for patients, and who will make that decision?* J Fla Med Assoc. 1986; 113: 95-99.
The author believes that the sick physician cannot be relied on to make a decision about when to stop caring for patients and offers many vivid examples to support his contention. A brief discussion of practical approaches to this issue, including intervention by the treating physician or groups of trained colleagues, is included.

Wainapel SF. *The physically disabled physician.* JAMA. 1987; 257: 2935-2938.
Information on 215 physicians and 92 medical students with a wide range of physical disabilities is analyzed and the literature is reviewed.

Wainapel SF, Bernbaum M. *The physician with visual impairment or blindness.* Arch Ophthalmol. 1986; 104: 498-502.
Following a review of the literature, the authors present a survey of 31 current practitioners who identified themselves as blind or with severe vision impairment. Characteristics of these 31 physicians are detailed and an extensive list of resources and technology for the visually disabled physician is included. Barriers to professional practice are discussed.

Impairment Related to Emotional Problems

McCue JD. *The effects of stress on physicians and their medical practice.* N Engl J Med. 1987; 306: 458-463.
Article 5.1

Scheiber SC, Doyle BB, eds. *The Impaired Physician.* New York, NY: Plenum Medical Book Company; 1983.
This comprehensive text presents a detailed analysis of the problems, prevention, and treatment of impaired physicians. Special issues, such as the physician as patient, stress and women physicians, suicide, and the rights of the individual physician versus the concerns and responsibilities of organized medicine, are included. The psychiatric approach to problem analysis and treatment is highlighted.

Substance Abuse

American Society of Anesthesiologists. *Questions and Answers About Chemical Dependence and Physician Impairment.* Park Ridge, IL: American Society of Anesthesiologists; 1986.
See annotation under "Organized Medicine and the Impaired Physician."

Brewster JM. *Prevalence of alcohol and other drug problems among physicians.* JAMA. 1986; 255: 1913-1920.
After a comprehensive review of the literature, the author concludes that the data are insufficient to support a conclusion that the overall prevalence of problems associated with alcohol and other drugs among physicians is greater than that found among the general population. The author concludes with recommendations for further study. There is a very extensive reference list, including a literature review back to 1869.

Clark DC. *Alcohol and drug use and mood disorders among medical students: implications for physical impairment.* Quality Rev Bull. 1988; 14:50-54.
See annotation under "The Physician-in-Training and Impairment."

LeClair B, Skorina JK. *One hundred alcoholic women in medicine.* JAMA. 1987; 257: 2939-2944.
This interview study of 95 physicians and five medical students shows concomitant addiction to drugs to be very high. The prevalence of suicide attempts, alcoholic family members, and marital instability are discussed.

McAuliffe WE, Rohman M, Santangelo S, et al. *Psychoactive drug use among practicing physicians and medical students.* N Engl J Med. 1986; 315: 805-810.
See annotation under "The Physician-in-Training and Impairment."

Talbott GD. *Elements of the impaired physicians program.*
J Med Assoc Ga. 1984; 73: 747-751
Article 5.4

Talbott GD, Benson EB. *Impaired physicians: the dilemma of identification.* Post Graduate Medicine. 1980; 68.
Article 5.3

Talbott GD, Gallegos KV, Wilson PO, Porter TL. *The Medical Association of Georgia's impaired physician program: review of the first 1000 physicians: analysis of specialty.* JAMA. 1987; 257: 2927-2930.
Among the first 1,000 physicians referred to this model program to assist impaired physicians, 92 percent had a primary diagnosis of chemical dependence and 59 percent had a major psychiatric illness.

Stress Management

Callan JP. *The Physician: A Professional Under Stress.* Norwalk, CT: Appelton & Lange; Century-Crofts; 1983.
This is an excellent book for an overview of the strategies for coping with the physician's lifestyle. It covers medical school through retirement and deals with family life, impairment, and minority issues.

Coombs RH, St. John J. *Making It in Medical School.* New York, NY: SP Medical and Scientific Books; 1979.
This book also deals with the stress of medical education and how to cope with it. It utilizes a pleasant mixture of humor and anecdotes to make its points.

Howell JB II, Schroeder DP. *Physician Stress: A Handbook for Coping.* Baltimore, MD: University Park Press; 1984.
This book discusses personal issues from burn-out to family problems and how to deal with various work-related issues, such as difficult patients. What makes the book different is its format. After the discussion/text, it presents a self-assessment test and then provides various "corrective protocols" for dealing with the problem. In appropriate areas, these protocols are divided into student, resident, and physician sections. There is also an excellent discussion of personal coping mechanisms.

Tubesing DA. *Kicking Your Stress Habits.* Duluth, MN: Whole Person Associates, Inc.; 1981.
This creative workbook teaches about stress and how to cope with it by having the reader do instead of just read. It also teaches time management and relationship skills.

Virsheep B. *Coping in Medial School.* Chapel Hill, NC: Health Sciences Consortium, Inc.; 1981.
This book is completely dedicated to helping the medical student understand what will take place in medical school and how to deal with it constructively. It also presents a series of exercises to deal with problems or to explain a principle.

Chapter 6

Professional Liability Insurance

Case: Choosing the Right Coverage

A senior resident in obstetrics/gynecology plans to enter clinical practice in the near future. She now faces a new dilemma—the purchase of a professional liability insurance policy.

Dr. West is an obstetrician/gynecologist planning the transition from residency training to clinical practice. She plans to take a position at a community hospital, with a residency training program in a nearby state. She needs to choose a professional liability insurance policy. She already knows that obstetrician/gynecologists pay some of the highest malpractice insurance premiums and has read recent statistics reporting that 14 percent are sued each year and almost 60 percent have been sued at least once. The $52,000 annual premium that was quoted to her will be a great financial burden. She considered not purchasing any insurance at all until each of the community hospitals with which she interviewed informed her that she must have malpractice insurance to perform deliveries and perform surgery at their facilities. She would like to minimize her outlays in the first years of practice, as she has office start-up expenses and a large educational debt.

Dr. West has reviewed malpractice insurance policies from two providers—the joint underwriting association sponsored by the state government and the captive insurance company operated by the state medical society. Dr. West learned that both companies offer a choice between occurrence coverage and claims-made coverage. A claims-made policy is initially more attractive to her due to its lower cost compared with an occurrence policy. The option of reducing her policy limits to $500,000 per occurrence/$1 million per year versus $1 millon/$3 million also made a significant difference in the premium charged. The continuation of a research project and the initiation of teaching duties will limit Dr. West's clinical practice to 60 percent of her professional time. She hopes to get a "limited-practice" policy with a lower premium, as her patient care hours are less than full time. Dr. West has learned that recent changes have been made in the state medical malpractice law, including a limitation on pain-and-suffering awards and regulation of attorneys' contingency fees. She wonders whether these legislative reforms will result in lower liability insurance premiums for her in future years.

Discussion Questions

1. What are the differences between claims-made and occurrence professional liability insurance policies?

2. Who or what determines whether a physician is required to purchase malpractice insurance in your state—the individual hospital, medical staff bylaws, or state law?

3. What responsibilities does the physician have with respect to risk management education?

4. What are the relative benefits of purchasing professional liability insurance from a joint underwriting association, a hospital or medical society-sponsored captive insurance company, or a commercial insurance carrier?

5. How does one determine the most appropriate policy limits for his or her practice?

6. Have the widespread changes in malpractice claims processing and insurance reform made by state legislatures in the mid 1980s had an impact on malpractice premiums?

Overview

It is now acknowledged in the medical community that it is not only the incompetent, careless or negligent physician who is charged with fault. Highly skilled and talented physicians also frequently become the target of a malpractice suit. According to studies by the AMA, the number of claims filed against physicians increased from an average annual rate of 3.0 per 100 physicians before 1980 to 10.2 in 1985, although the rate has dropped to 6.4 in recent years.[1,2] The General Accounting Office of the United States Government estimated that approximately 73,500 medical malpractice claims involving approximately 103,300 health care providers were closed in 1984.[3] The cost of this activity has accelerated far in excess of the inflation rate. Total malpractice insurance costs for physicians increased from $1.7 billion in 1983 to $3.4 billion in 1984, according to the United States Government.[4] In a AMA survey of non-federal patient care physicians, 37 percent reported having been sued for malpractice at least once as of 1988.[1] These data speak loudly; developing a basic understanding of professional liability insurance should now be on the agenda of every clinician.

The tremendous increases in the frequency and expense of lawsuits and the costs of liability insurance since the 1960s has been termed by many as a "liability crisis." In fact, the problem appears to be cyclical, characterized by periods in which the frequency of claims, the magnitude of jury awards, and the attendant cost of insurance escalate dramatically, followed by years in which these indicators appear to plateau. During the crisis of the mid-1970s, virtually every commercial insurance company, with the exception of the St. Paul Fire and Marine Insurance Company, withdrew from the medical liability market, forcing physicians to establish their own "captive" companies. The crisis of the mid-1980s was much more one of affordability than availability. During this time, even the physician-owned companies, most of which are operated on a not-for-profit basis, and joint underwriting associations were forced to assess huge premium increases to stay solvent. Both crisis periods were met by vigorous legislative tort reform efforts as well as increased risk management activity by physicians and insurers.

For a discussion of the legal definition of medical malpractice, refer to Chapter 2; Chapter 4 offers some insight into the management of clinical cases that may develop into a malpractice suit and the appropriate physician response once legal action is formally launched against a physician. Discussion of professional liability insurance follows in this chapter.

Professional Liability Insurance

A professional liability or "malpractice" insurance policy provides coverage for legal liability incurred while rendering professional services. Professional liability policies can differ a great deal from company to company, and every physician should be aware of the details of his or her policy, including the type of coverage provided, the policy limits, and any obligations required under the policy agreement. The insurance company typically has the obligation, within the terms of the particular policy, to defend the physician and to pay or "indemnify" him or her for any settlement or judgment rendered in favor of a plaintiff for an amount up to the policy limits. The insurer may be authorized under the policy terms to settle claims without the consent of the insured policyholder, but the physician is customarily consulted concerning this important decision.

Physicians often voice concern over the loyalty of the defense attorney provided them by their insurance company. Attorney Donald P. Wilcox describes the relationship of the physician and the defense lawyer provided by the malpractice insurance company in Article 6.1, "Possible Claim? Role of Insurer and Legal Counsel." The attorney provided by the insurer has a fiduciary obligation to exercise his or her skills solely in the interest of the physician. The American Bar Association has delineated this position quite clearly in its *Model Rules of Professional Conduct.*[5] It is paramount that the physician who is the target of legal action work constructively with his attorney and the insurance company. Ideally, the defendant physician should become a key resource regarding medical information by, for example, providing pertinent literature reviews. There may be occasions, however, when the insurer or the appointed attorney have a potential conflict of interest. In such a case, the physician defendant should consider retaining a personal attorney in addition to the defense attorney provided by the insurer. Attorney Wilcox also provides guidance on this subject in his article.

Policy Types

There are essentially two types of professional liability insurance policies: an occurrence policy and a claims-made policy.

Occurrence Policy

An occurrence policy is the simpler type of insurance to understand. It provides coverage for claims arising from any incident that occurred during the policy period. It does not matter when the patient notifies the physician of a claim, as long as the injury or the physician's act or omission giving rise to the injury occurred while the insurance policy was in effect. There typically is no need for the physician to purchase additional coverage when he or she retires or changes insurance providers, and moving from practice location to practice location is easier with this type of policy. Until the late 1970s, occurrence coverage was standard in the medical liability market. Today, it is unavailable in most states.

Claims-made Policy

A claims-made policy, by definition, provides coverage for *claims made* against the physician during the policy period, usually one year, theoretically, when the alleged act of malpractice occurred or when the patient's injury was suffered is not the significant event where claims-made coverage is concerned. However, most claims-made policies exclude coverage of incidents that occurred before the physician purchased his or her first policy with the current insurer. In other words, claims-made coverage typically requires that (1) the alleged malpractice took place during some policy period, and (2) the physician is still insured with the same insurer at the time the claim is made.

A claims-made policy is typically priced so that each year the policyholder pays for protection against claims that may be reported during that year. The first year's premium is lower than subsequent premiums because it is less likely that all claims resulting from treatment rendered during the first year will be reported by patients that same year. When the claims-made policy is renewed for a second year, the "exposure period" covered under the policy expands and the premium increases accordingly. The second-year premium is priced to cover the projected costs of (1) claims reported and occurring during the second year of coverage and (2) claims that are reported in the second coverage year but arise from treatment that occurred during the first coverage year.

Claims-made premiums thus typically continue to increase annually until a "mature" level is reached, reflecting a leveling off in the cost and number of claims reported. For most claims-made policies, this takes place in the fourth or fifth policy year. The exposure period covered under the policy continues to expand year by year as the policy is renewed.

Once a claims-made policy is terminated, the policyholder is not covered for any claim that might be reported after the termination date—even if a claims-made policy was in effect when the incident occurred. This can result in problematic gaps in coverage when a physician moves from one state to another, changes employers, or makes some other career decision that involves changing liability insurers. For protection against claims made after termination of claims-made insurance with a given company, the physician typically must purchase an "extended reporting endorsement," also known as "tail" coverage. In essence, tail coverage is a separate policy that provides coverage for incidents that have occurred, but have not yet been brought to the physician's attention as a claim. If the physician is changing companies, the new carrier may offer what is called "prior acts" or "nose" coverage as an alternative to purchasing tail coverage from the old company. It is important to note that while tail coverage is offered by all insurers when claims-made insurance is terminated for any reason (including cancellation by the insurer), prior acts coverage (i.e., tail coverage from a new insurer) may not always be available. It should also be remembered that the offer of tail coverage usually must be accepted within a certain time, usually 60 or 90 days after termination, after which it may be impossible to obtain the needed coverage at any price.

Although claims-made policies have lower annual premiums than do occurrence policies, tail coverage can be expensive, often two to three times the yearly mature premium rate for claims-made coverage. A balloon payment of this magnitude may present a significant obstacle to a physician wishing to make a career move. As a practical matter, physicians making practice changes may have little choice but to obtain tail coverage, because their new insurer or employer may require it. Proof of tail coverage may also be required by hospital or medical staff credentialing procedures and, in at least one state (Massachusetts), it is a condition of obtaining a license to practice.

The market for medical malpractice insurance has become increasingly competitive in recent years, which has prompted a number of companies to provide "free" tail coverage (building its cost into the claims-made premium) under certain circumstances, almost always including death, retirement, or disability. The physician should become familiar with his or her own insurer's tail coverage arrangements before any practice changes are implemented.

Insurance Providers

The number and type of malpractice insurance providers is constantly changing. Prior to the malpractice insurance "availability crisis" of the 1970s, commercial (profit-making) insurance carriers wrote the vast majority of professional liability insurance policies for physicians. With the exception of the St. Paul Fire and Marine Insurance Company, which continues to offer medical liability coverage in 42 states, this segment of the industry abruptly withdrew from the market in 1975-1976. New entities, such as state-sponsored joint underwriting associations and provider-owned companies, were created to fill the void left by the departure of commercial insurers. Most of the 43 member companies of the Physician Insurers Association of America (PIAA) are not-for-profit companies started by medical societies and physician groups during this time. As of 1989, they provided policies to more than half of practicing physicians (approximately 177,000). Their gross premiums now exceed $2 billion annually.[6] Some individual hospitals and consortia of hospitals have formed their own "captive" insurance companies, with the advantage of tailoring policies and risk management programs to their own institutions.[7] One example is the Controlled Risk Insurance Company, Ltd. (CRICO), which insures 5,000 physicians affiliated with the teaching hospitals of Harvard Medical School.

Even newer arrangements have been developed with the purpose of lowering the overhead cost of liability protection, presumably resulting in lower premiums. A "self-insured trust" may cover a group of physicians and/or hospitals who share the risk of being sued. Annual contributions to the trust may be adjusted by rebates or additional assessments based on the group's losses in a given year. Similarly, "risk retention groups" and "risk purchasing groups" are federally sanctioned mechanisms whereby providers that are similarly situated (usually practicing in the same specialty field) may pool their risk on a nationwide basis and either self-insure or purchase traditional insurance at group rates. These groups, as well as trusts, are exempt from some aspects of state regulation, and the resulting savings in overhead can mean lower costs for physicians. It should be noted, however, that risk-retention and risk-purchasing groups are generally not protected by state-operated "guaranty funds," which back state-regulated insurance companies. If insolvency occurs and the group folds, physicians could be left with no insurance coverage whatsoever.

Physicians who do not meet the enrollment requirements of standard-line companies may be referred to "surplus-line" companies, which are free to charge whatever premium they consider appropriate for a given applicant.[8] Physicians purchasing such insurance have typically lost their standard coverage due to an excessive claims history, loss of hospital privileges, or governmental disciplinary sanctions for serious infractions. In some states, joint underwriting associations chartered by the state serve as the insurer of last resort.

See the Appendix for a partial listing of insurance providers. The listing includes 10 of the larger private insurance companies, state-run joint underwriting associations, and the 43 PIAA companies. The names of additional insurance resources should be available through your state medical society or the state insurance commissioner's office.

Every entity that provides insurance coverage must undertake the difficult task of estimating how much money it will have to pay out over the next several years due to claims during that period of time, a process known as "underwriting." Factors such as past claims experience, inflation, and risk management interventions must all be weighed to determine what the actual cost of insurance will be for the physician. The underwriting and rate-making process relies on a specialized area of applied mathematics called "actuarial analysis."[9] Medical liability insurance is a particularly difficult line of insurance to underwrite due to the rapid escalation in jury awards and the excessively lengthy period of time the tort system takes to resolve suits.

The recommended limits for professional liability coverage will vary depending on practice setting and specialty. Often, hospitals require each member of their medical staff to have a specific minimum amount of coverage. A typical policy limit is designated as "$1 million/$3 million," meaning an individual is covered to a maximum of $1 million per claim and $3 million total claims in a given policy year. In some states, the physician may have very narrow options as to available policy limits.

Regardless of the type of coverage chosen, it is important for physicians to understand the scope of professional activities covered by their policy, the limits of coverage, and their responsibilities under the policy. For example, most states require insurance carriers to report all claims closed with a payment to the plaintiff to the state medical licensing board, and a few require reporting of all claims, even if they are ultimately resolved in the physician's favor. Reporting to the National Practitioner Data Bank of information regarding malpractice claims is now also required (see Chapter 7 for a discussion of the Data Bank). Most applications for liability insurance require physicians to report previous malpractice claims. Some insurance companies offer less expensive policies for academic physicians, semi-retired physicians, or others who practice medicine only part time. Some companies have a system of penalties for those physicians with a higher-than-average number of malpractice suits (a practice known as "experience rating") or offer discounts for those who incorporate specialty-specific liability control standards into their practice or participate in continuing education specific to malpractice risk management. Consultation with an insurance professional or hospital risk manager is advised for a detailed interpretation of the terms of any specific malpractice insurance policy.

A final option, usually exercised when the availability or affordability of insurance appears to be too great a burden, is to "go bare" or practice medicine without liability insurance. This rather dramatic option is exercised by very few physicians and is prohibited in some states. In Article 6.2, "Malpractice Insurance: What Can Happen if You Don't Have It," Attorney William Hunt examines the hazards of "going bare." Although Hunt's discussion refers to the specific laws in Hawaii, the points he raises are, in general, applicable in all jurisdictions.

Making the Decision

In the case that introduced this chapter, Dr. West is in the process of purchasing a professional liability insurance policy. She has done a comparison of policies from two sources. She is embarking on a career in obstetrics and gynecology, considered by liability insurers to be one of the highest-risk specialties. She should choose a policy with sufficient coverage limits given the common occurrence of high payouts in obstetrics/gynecology cases. In most situations, a $1 million/$3 million policy will likely suffice. However, in some locations with a history of higher jury awards, additional coverage might be advisable. Local medical societies should be consulted about the liability laws and litigation climate of a given state and their recommended limits.

Choosing between an occurrence and a claims-made policy can be more difficult, if occurrence coverage is even available. In the majority of states, it has been completely supplanted by the claims-made form of policy. If an occurrence policy is available, it will cost Dr. West more, but it may be well worth the expense. She will not have to purchase a separate policy for tail coverage, which would be necessary if she bought a claims-made policy. This will also increase her flexibility if she decides to leave her current position for one in another location. The cost of purchasing tail coverage some time in the future can be unpredictable and should be expected to require a substantial outlay of funds.

Because she will not be seeing patients full time, Dr. West has inquired about purchasing a limited-practice policy. Among the companies that do sell limited-practice policies, most restrict this option to physicians working less than half-time. In this case, she has examined the coverages offered by a joint underwriting association and one from a captive insurance company. She should consider each company's track record for policyholder service as well as its financial stability and premiums. Dr. West could also explore other options, such as a hospital or HMO offering an insurance program that includes full or partial premium payment for staff or employee physicians. If she does this, she should find out if the coverage is occurrence or claims-made, and if it is the latter, she should make sure that her contract specifically states who is to bear the responsibility for the cost of tail coverage.

The Malpractice Crisis and Malpractice Reform

After the crisis periods of the mid-1970s and mid-1980s, it became obvious to all parties involved that medical liability litigation and insurance issues were leading indicators of a general liability insurance problem affecting our entire society. Professional liability is costly for all purchasers of health care as well as for physicians and hospitals directly. In Article 6.3, "Medical Malpractice: 'Crisis' and Reform" Francis X. Campion, MD, details some of the similarities between crises past and present.

Organized medicine's proposed solution—legislative reform of the tort system—was just about the same in both the 1970s and 1980s. Repeated analysis and experience with tort reform, however, has yielded some new thinking. There has emerged an expanding recognition of basic problems in the adversarial legal system that impede compensation of persons injured in the course of medical care. Five major criticisms of the current system cited by the United States General Accounting Office include: (1) the difficulty in differentiating adverse events or outcomes from malpractice, (2) the considerable time and effort required to establish provider fault, (3) the legal fees that consume a high percentage (approximately 40 percent) of the total cost of the tort system, (4) the unpredictability of jury decisions as to liability and size of awards, and (5) excessive awards and settlements, particularly for noneconomic losses such as pain and suffering.[10] These factors have stimulated some groups to investigate ways to redesign the entire system for resolving medical liability claims.

"No-fault" compensation funds, which do away with the requirement that negligence be proved, have recently been instituted to address specific adverse occurrences; these include a federally mandated initiative to compensate children who incur injuries related to vaccinations.[11] Special insurance pools for obstetricians and family practitioners have been devised in Virginia and Florida to assist children with catastrophic birth-related injuries.[12,13] The premise underlying the no-fault concept is that limited funds are better spent in compensating patients with adverse outcomes regardless of fault than in fighting for years in the tort system about whether or not the poor outcome was caused by negligence. In January 1990, Dr. David Axelrod, New York State Health Commissioner, proposed consideration of an across-the-board no-fault medical malpractice system for his state. Across-the-board no-fault legislation has already been introduced in Massachusetts, where it is supported by the state medical society.[14, 15]

Skeptics of a no-fault system contend that it would be too costly to compensate every adverse outcome, that it is unfair to impose the cost of financing it solely on health care providers, and that the fault-based tort system's role in deterring bad medical practice would be lost. Proponents argue that the tort system serves its twin goals of compensation and deterrence haphazardly at best and wastes money. Only recently have reliable statistics become available regarding the effectiveness of the tort system and the feasibility of a no-fault system. The Harvard Medical Practice Study, discussed in Chapter 4, found that only 2 percent of persons who had an injury due to medical negligence had filed malpractice claims within five years after the injury.[16,17] With respect to the deterrence issue, Harvard's analysis revealed "no evidence that the threat of a lawsuit decreased the rate of injury."[17] Given limitations of the study, this point could not be proved conclusively. However, an accompanying survey of physicians did show that physicians who believed they were at greater risk of a malpractice suit were more likely to have changed their practice pattern during the previous 10 years. In particular, these physicians reported that they were now more likely to order additional diagnostic tests and to have reduced the scope of their clinical practice. The Harvard study also sets forth an economic analysis concluding that a no-fault system of reimbursing patients for injuries related to medical care could be financially competitive with the present tort system. Ironically, data generated by the Harvard Study have added fuel to both sides of the ongoing debate over a no-fault "solution."

Other proposals suggest retaining a fault-based standard of care but removing the decision-making process from the jury and placing it with expert judges who hear only medical liability claims. In January 1988, the AMA/Specialty Society Medical Liability Project (a coalition comprising the AMA and more than 30 national medical specialty societies) proposed that such a model be tested in one or more states in a demonstration project. The Medical Liability Project recommends that the claim-resolution process be removed from the jury and court system to a state administrative agency and coordinated with the state's licensing and disciplinary efforts. This bold proposal has prompted both praise and criticism from commentators. The Executive Summary of the Medical Liability Project is reprinted as Article 6.4. In 1989, the Physician Insurers Association of America published another model for a fault-based administrative system, also urging that it be tested in a demonstration project.

Other proposals include the encouragement of arbitration, mediation, and other private dispute resolution mechanisms. All of these alternatives have the common goal of reducing the "transaction cost" of resolving claims so that more compensation dollars can be delivered more cost-effectively to injured patients.

Current Trends in Claims and Insurance

Recent statistics give some cause for optimism. Since approximately 1986, there has been a significant slowing of the rate of growth of malpractice claims and premiums for most specialties. As mentioned previously, the frequency of claims, as measured by the AMA, peaked at 10.2 per 100 physicians per annum in 1985. That frequency actually declined to 9.2 in 1986, 6.7 in 1987, and 6.4 in 1988.[1,2] While certainly an improvement, this figure is still more than double the rate of 3.0 per 100 physicians in 1980, as measured by the AMA. Despite the improvement in claim frequency, the cost of malpractice insurance continued to rise through the end of the 1980s. Nationwide, physicians paid an average premium of $10,500 in 1985, $12,800 in 1986, $15,000 in 1987, and $15,900 in 1988. Insurance premiums continue to rise despite reductions in claim frequency, because the magnitude of medical malpractice judgments and settlements continues to rise.

There is considerable speculation as to the cause of the apparent slowdown in claims frequency. In California and Indiana, where strong tort reform has been enacted, it appears to be playing a measurable role. California physicians' premiums currently average about one third less than those of their colleagues in New York and Florida, where tort reform movements have met with only limited success. Prior to 1975 reform legislation, premiums in California were comparable to those in New York and Florida. Another notable factor is the tremendous increase in patient safety/risk management initiatives in the 1980s, led by liability insurers, hospitals, and medical societies. Then again, the decrease in claims may be only a temporary phenomenon, part of a social or economic cycle that is not yet clearly understood. A similar drop in claim frequency was noted between 1976 and 1978, between the crisis periods of the mid-1970s and the mid-1980s.

Attorney James Holzer, vice president for loss prevention at the Risk Management Foundation of the Harvard Medical Institutions, gives a measured analysis of these recent trends. In Article 6.5, "Liability Insurance Issues in Anesthesiology," he cautions that despite the reduction in claim frequency, there still is no clear improvement in the magnitude or cost of settling claims. The magnitude and cost of claims are equally important factors as claim frequency in the calculation of physician premiums. Holzer uses the example of anesthesiology claims and premiums to illustrate this lesson. He describes the topic of insurance rates and premium "relativities" by which insurance companies categorize physician specialties or classes according to their financial risk of being sued and accruing insurance loss. A convincing argument is made for continued, aggressive risk management techniques that could potentially be linked to an actual reduction in insurance premiums.

References

1. *Socioeconomic Characteristics of Medical Malpractice 1989*. Chicago, IL: American Medical Association Center for Health Policy Research, 1989: 18-20.

2. Reynolds RA, Rizzo JA, Gonzalez ML. The cost of medical professional liability. *JAMA*. 1987; 257: 2776-2781.

3. *Medical Malpractice: Characteristics of Claims Closed in 1984*. Washington, DC: 1987; U.S. General Accounting Office document (GAO) HRD-87-55.

4. *Medical Malpractice: Insurance Costs Increased but Varied Among Physicians and Hospitals*. Washington, DC: 1986; U.S. General Accounting Office document (GAO) HRD-86-112.

5. *Model Rules of Professional Conduct*. Chicago, IL: American Bar Association House of Delegates; 1983.

6. *PIAA 1990 Membership Directory and Professional Services Section*. Lawrenceville, NJ: Physician Insurers Association of American; 1990.

7. Burda D. Liability reshapes hospital/physician relationships. *Hospitals*. 1987; 61(7): 56-60.

8. Schwartz WB, Mendelson DN. Physicians who have lost their malpractice insurance. *JAMA*. 1989; 262: 1335-1341.

9. O'Leary JF, Kahan R. Medical liability insurance crisis revisited. *Int Anesthesiol Clin*. 1984; 22: 117-131.

10. *Medical Malpractice: No Agreement on the Problems or Solutions*. Washington, DC: 1986; U.S. General Accounting Office document (GAO) HRD-86-50.

11. Inglehart JK. Compensating children with vaccine-related injuries. *N Engl J Med*. 1987; 316: 1283-1288.

12. Virginia Birth-Related Injury Compensation Act. 1987, C.540, ss 38.5001.

13. Florida Birth-Related Injury Compensation Plan. Florida S6-XXXXX Fifth Special Session, 1988 New Laws, p 101.

14. Manuel B. Professional liability: a no-fault solution. *N Engl J Med*. 1990; 302: 627-631.

15. Relman AS. Changing the malpractice liability system *N Engl J Med*. 1990; 302: 626-627.

16. Hiatt HH, Barnes BA, Brennan TA, et al. A study of medical injury and medical malpractice: an overview. *N Engl J Med*. 1989; 321: 480-484. Special Report.

17. *Medical Practice Study: Executive Summary*. New York, NY: New York State Health Department; 1990.

Table 6.1

Questions to Ask When Purchasing Professional Liability Insurance

1. Does the insurer's obligation include both the payment of damages as well as defense costs?

2. What are the per claim and annual caps on coverage? Are they adequate for your practice?

3. What restrictions to practice exist under this policy? Is "moonlighting" in another facility covered? Are specific procedures prohibited? Does the policy cover both office and hospital practice?

4. Is the insurance company committed to receiving consent from the insured party before settling a claim?

5. Are all persons for whom the insured party is legally responsible covered by the insurance policy (such as office employees or students)?

6. Is coverage for punitive damages included?

7. Is the insured physician required to participate in educational programs regarding risk management?

8. Are penalties or discounts reflected in the insurance premium of individual physicians based on their claims history?

9. Is the insurance carrier financially stable? (Check AM Best's Review)

10. Are less expensive insurance policies available for physicians just entering practice, physicians who share research and clinical duties, or for semi-retired physicians?

11. Are prior acts covered by the policy?

12. Does the insurance carrier have a good track record in handling claims and the defense of lawsuits?

13. What will the cost of purchasing "tail coverage" for a claims-made policy be at a given time in the future? Under what circumstances is tail coverage provided at no additional charge?

14. Are there any time limitations or restrictions on the purchase or duration of tail coverage?

15. Is the insurance carrier covered by a state guaranty fund?

Article 6.1

Possible Claim? Role of Insurer and Legal Counsel

Donald P. "Rocky" Wilcox, JD. Texas Medicine, July 1986.

This column addresses the actions physicians should take in the event of a suit or claim potentially covered by insurance. It also discusses the carrier's obligation to defend and pay up to the limits of the policy, and the duty of the insurer's attorney to represent and defend the insured. Finally, it addresses the role of the physician's personal attorney in assisting in the insured physician's defense.

Insured Physician's Duties

When an insured physician becomes aware of any alleged occurrence, injury, or damages to which his or her insurance may apply, the physician should notify the insurance carrier as soon as practical. The notice should include identification of the insured, and any available information about the time, place, and circumstances of the occurrence. It also should list the names and addresses of the injured and other potential claimants and available witnesses. If the insured fails to notify the carrier, the carrier may escape coverage responsibility.

The insurance policy (the contract between the physician and the insurer) routinely requires full cooperation and assistance from the insured. Cooperation with insurer includes making available all records relating to the incident. The insured also will need to cooperate in defense preparation, including attending hearings, depositions, trials and appeals, securing and giving evidence, and assisting in obtaining the cooperation of witnesses. The insured also may be required to cooperate in any settlement made in accordance with the provisions of the policy, and to cooperate in obtaining contribution, indemnity, or other recovery from or against any person who shares liability in a covered incident.

The typical insurance contract provides that the insured physician may not make any payment, assume any obligation or liability by contract or otherwise, incur any expense with respect to any such occurrence, injury, damages, or claim or suit without the carrier's prior written approval. The insurer controls defense strategy. While the plaintiff's attorney may encourage a physician to discuss the case, a physician should never do so until he has discussed the matter with his attorney. Some physicians mistakenly believe that they will be able to call a plaintiff's attorney and "talk him out of bringing a lawsuit." Such attempts further educate the plaintiff's attorney about the case and, simultaneously, may allow the physician to be led into damaging admissions without having the benefit of legal counsel.[1]

Carrier's Duty to Pay and Defend

The insurance carrier will reserve the right to defend at its expense any claim or suit seeking covered damages. The defense may include appeals, writs of error, and other legal proceedings that the carrier determines to be reasonable and appropriate. The typical policy provides that upon receipt of notice from the insured, the carrier immediately assumes responsibility for the defense of covered claims and shall retain legal counsel.

Sometimes the policy provides that the carrier may not compromise or settle any claim or suit without the consent of the insured. However, many policies also provide that if the carrier wishes to settle and the insured elects to contest or continue the defense, the carrier's liability shall not exceed the amount for which the claim could have been settled.

Donald P. "Rocky" Wilcox, JD, is general counsel for the Texas Medical Association.

In Texas and in other jurisdictions, an insurer normally exercises its right to defend if there is a "potentially" covered claim. One authority observes:

> Assuming the defense of an insured, therefore, may create a conflict of interest on the part of the insurer. To illustrate, an injured third party, under certain circumstances, will allege alternative causes of action. One may be covered under the terms of the policy, such as a negligence cause of action, and the other may not....
>
> Whenever a conflict becomes evident to an insurer, it faces an election. It may withdraw from the defense of the insured or under certain circumstances, it may continue to represent him. In either event, a failure to act in utmost good faith will render the insurer liable to the insured...[2]

The court in *Employers Casualty Co v Tilley* stated that when the insurer assumes exclusive control of the insured's defense, the counsel hired to defend the case becomes the attorney of record and the legal representative of the insured.[3]

As such, the attorney owes the insured the same unqualified loyalty he would have owed if he had been employed by the insured originally. The attorney of record is bound by a "rigid rule" of conduct designed to avoid any potential conflict of interest.[4]

Rules of Conduct

The "Comment" section under Rule 1.7 of the Model Rules of Professional Conduct (American Bar Association, House of Delegates, August 1983) provides under the caption "Interest of Person Paying for a Lawyer's Service" the following:

> A lawyer may be paid from a source other than the client, if the client is informed of that fact and consents and the arrangement does not compromise the lawyer's duty of loyalty to the client. See Rule 1.8(f). For example, when an insurer and its insured have conflicting interests in a matter arising from a liability insurance agreement, and the insurer is required to provide special counsel for the insured, the arrangement should assure the special counsel's professional independence. So also, when a corporation and its directors or employees are involved in a controversy in which they have conflicting interests, the corporation may provide funds for legal representation of the directors or employees, if the clients consent after consultation and the arrangement ensures the lawyer's professional independence.

Rule 1.08 of the ABA Model Rules of Professional Conduct provides in part: A lawyer shall not accept compensation for representing a client from one other than the client unless: (1) the client consents after consultation; (2) there is no interference with the lawyer's independence of professional judgement or with the client-lawyer relationship; and (3) information relating to representation of a client is protected as required under Rule 1.6 (Confidentiality of Information).

Preserving Client Secrets

The ABA Committee On Ethics and Professional Responsibility, Informal Opinion 1476, Duty of Lawyer to Preserve Confidences and Secrets of Client in Multiple Representation from Co-clients, Aug. 11, 1981, provides that:

> A lawyer retained by insurer to represent employer and employee who learns from employee-client that employee may not be entitled to coverage may not disclose the pertinent facts to the employer or the insurer without the employee-client's consent after full disclosure of the consequences of such revelation.

In the question presented, an insurance company retained the lawyer to defend both an insured employer and an employee of the insured. The lawyer sought the advice of the ABA Committee on Ethics as to his professional responsibility with respect to disclosure to the insurance company of information gained in the course of preparing the defense. The committee concluded:

> We are mindful that a typical liability insurance policy does not give the insured the right to choose the lawyer retained and compensated by the insurance company. Moreover, the insured is required as a condition of the insurance protection to cooperate and assist in the defense and implicitly to reveal to the lawyer all pertinent information known to the insured....
>
> The employer is also the lawyer's client, and the employer's liability to the plaintiff may be affected by the scope-of-employment circumstances. The lawyer would be unable to represent the employer-client in denying the employer's legal responsibility for the employee's conduct without concurrently acting adversely to the interest of the employee-client in preserving the employer's insurance protection. Possibly, the employee-client and the insurance company would be willing to forego a scope-of-employment defense and stand with the employee, in which case the interests of the lawyer's clients would not differ. The lawyer's dilemma, however, is that in seeking this consent the lawyer might disclose the information that he should preserve in confidence. He should not do so without the employee's consent after full advice as to the possible consequences. If the matter cannot be resolved by agreement of insurance company, employer, and employee, then the lawyer may have a duty to withdraw from the litigation....If the lawyer so

withdraws, he should recommend to the insurance company that separate counsel be retained to represent only the employee's interests.

Of course, the lawyer also should not represent the insurance company in asserting that the employee-client is outside policy coverage.[5]

But, in the Tilley case[3] (p 559), decided in 1973, the Texas court "approved" different advice. The court cited two principles from a 1970 ABA National Conference of Lawyers and Liability Insurers list of "Guiding Principles" for liability insurers furnishing legal counsel for their insureds.

IV. CONFLICTS OF INTEREST GENERALLY—DUTIES OF ATTORNEY. In any claim or in any suit where the attorney selected by the company to defend the claim or action becomes aware of facts or information which indicate to him a question of coverage in the matter being defended or any other conflict of interests between the company and the insured with respect to the defense of the matter, the attorney should promptly inform both the company and the insured, preferably in writing, of the nature and extent of the conflicting interests.

V. CONTINUATION BY ATTORNEY EVEN THOUGH THERE IS A CONFLICT OF INTEREST. Where there is a question of coverage or other conflict of interest, the company and the attorney selected by the company to defend the claim or suit should not thereafter continue to defend the insured in the matter in question unless, after a full explanation of the coverage question, the insured acquiesces in the continuation of such defense...[3], (p 559).

The mandate in Guiding Principle IV approved by the court in Tilley[3] is for the attorney to inform both the carrier and the insured of the nature and extent of the conflicting interest. However, the ABA Committee on Ethics and Professional Responsibility, Informed Opinion 1476, issued 11 years later, states that the lawyer is free to disclose confidences and secrets of his client only with the client's consent after full disclosure of the consequences of such revelation. In other words, the information the lawyer gains in his representation of the client may not be disclosed to the carrier "when the revelation might result in denial of insurance protection to the employee" except with the client's informed consent.

The Physician's Personal Attorney

Sometimes the defending physician retains his own personal attorney to assure that his interests are fully protected. This might happen even if a coverage question is not involved. The physician's personally selected attorney may perform the following functions:

1. Review policy terms and explain policy coverage to the physician;

2. Insure that the physician's personal assets—in the event of inadequate coverage—are protected over the interests of the insurance carrier; and

3. Work out policy coverage questions or other potential conflicts-of-interest between the physician and the carrier. (These necessarily are raised when the carrier provides a non-waiver agreement or notice. Such an agreement or notice provides that no subsequent action shall be construed as a waiver of the carrier's right, if any, to deny liability under the policy.)

The physician's personal attorney also may assure that the best possible defense is provided by having a calming effect on the physician defendant (if necessary), maintaining a constructive interest on the part of the physician, and serving as a buffer or sounding board for the carrier, the carrier's selected attorney, and the physician. The physician's selected attorney also may make a formal recommendation or written demand, if the case warrants such action, against the insurer. This may become critical if the probable verdict or judgment exceeds the limits of the professional liability insurance coverage.

The physician's selected attorney also may work with the carrier's selected defense counsel to evaluate and prepare the defense. But, the physician's selected attorney must not go behind the back of the carrier's selected attorney in working with the plaintiff's attorney. The physician's selected attorney should counsel the physician regarding allegations that are not covered by insurance, such as antitrust and punitive or exemplary damages. If it seems unlikely that the case can be defended within policy limits, the physician's personal attorney should counsel the physician with respect to a demand against the carrier.[6] Finally, if there is a settlement, the physician's selected attorney should participate in settlement negotiations, making sure that no settlement stone is left unturned.

Conclusion

The insured physician must cooperate with the insurer and its selected counsel in claim defense. To the extent the defense lawyer retained by the insurance company is perceived by the physician as not having his or her interests of primary concern, the physician may continue to seek out his or her own counsel. Professional ethics at the national and state levels suggest that the carrier-selected lawyer's primary concern and loyalty is to the physician he is defending and not to the insurance carrier. Under the more stringent ABA ethical statement, the lawyer is not free to provide information to the carrier which might cause denial of insurance protection without the informed consent of the client. Because this ethical requirement is the natural evolution in defining the proper role of the carrier-retained defense lawyer, we can anticipate that Texas courts will follow this ABA statement in the future.

References

1. Tottenham T: Ten steps to the courthouse. Tex Med 1985 (December); 81:56.

2. Dohoney B: The liability insurer's duty to defend. Baylor L. Rev 1985;33:451-484.

3. Employers Casualty Co v Tilley, 496 SW2d 552 (Tex 1973).

4. Barreda Corp v Ballinger, 116 SW2d 422(Tex Civ App—Beaumont 1938, writ dism'd).

5. Committee on Professional Responsibility: Recent ethics opinions. ABA-ABF.

6. Stowers Furniture Co v American Indemnity, 15 SW2d 544 (Tex Comm of Appeals 1929) and Texas Pacific Indemnity Company v City of Beaumont, 488 SW2d 539 (Tex Civ App—Beaumont 1972, no writ).

Wilcox DP. Possible claim? Role of insurer and legal counsel. Tex Med. 1986; 82: 70-72.

Article 6.2

Malpractice Insurance —What Can Happen if You Don't Have It

William S. Hunt, Esq. Hawaii Medical Journal, June 1985.

Perhaps the primary concern of practicing physicians today is the cost of premiums for medical malpractice insurance. As all physicians know, due to a number of factors, premiums are increasing each year, and the likelihood that they will level off in the near future appears slim. In response to this situation, a number of doctors are presently contemplating, or have already decided, to practice without medical malpractice insurance protection. This article discusses the risks involved in taking such action.

Since nearly all medical malpractice claims are based on a negligent act, some physicians may be under the impression that if they are careful, they will not be sued.

Unfortunately, this is not necessarily so. Any attorney with experience in medical malpractice litigation is aware that a great number of claims result as much from a lack of communication with the patient as from actionable negligence.

Although the physician may eventually convince the patient and his attorney that a bad result was not his or her fault, it may require a trial and jury verdict to do so. Thus, simply relying upon caution and perhaps luck is no guarantee you won't become a defendant in a malpractice action, regardless of your specialty.

William S. Hunt, Esq, an officer and a director of the Honolulu law firm of Paul, Johnson & Alston, has practiced law in Honolulu since 1972. He has served as chairman on numerous medical claim conciliation panels.

A physician who has no insurance, and is sued, faces two avenues of financial exposure: first, certain and often substantial attorneys' fees and costs; and second, a less-certain but frequently substantial payment of a settlement or judgment. Depending on the particular case, either or both of these can be overwhelming.

Hawaii Revised Statutes, Chap. 671, et. seq., deals with medical torts and provides that any person who alleges he is a victim of "professional negligence" must file a claim with the Medical Claim Conciliation Panel. A decision must be rendered by the panel before he may file a lawsuit.

Thus, a defendant physician may require the services of an attorney for two proceedings, the panel hearing and the ultimate trial, if there is one. The panel hearings are more informal and don't require as much preparation as a trial, but attorneys' fees and costs for defending a case before the panel nevertheless can reach several thousand dollars.

Although the panel has returned decisions in favor of the physician a majority of the time, this does not prevent the plaintiff from then filing a lawsuit.

Once a lawsuit is filed, defense attorneys' fees and costs and expert witness fees can quickly exceed the amount spent for a defense at the panel hearing. Thus, even if a plaintiff withdraws his claim, or agrees to settle for a nominal amount, the physician usually will have expended thousands of dollars in attorneys' fees that are not generally recoverable from the plaintiff.

Some physicians are attempting to deal with the problem of attorneys' fees by organizing physician-run associations that provide funds for the defense of a member who is sued, often up to a certain maximum amount. Such entities do not offer coverage for payment of settlements or judgments, as would the usual insurance policy.

Since some amount of payment is made by the defendant physician for settlement or judgment in a number of the cases filed, joining such a protective association reduces the risk of substantial out-of-pocket payments by the individual physician.

In addition to the likelihood of having to pay attorneys' fees and the possibility of a judgment against him for his negligence, the physician without insurance also faces the possibility of being held responsible for payment of compensation for injuries jointly caused by the negligence of another doctor, or by a member of the hospital's staff, such as nurses, technicians, and others. Under the Hawaii Uniform Contribution Among Tortfeasors Act, HRS & 663-11, et seq., each defendant found, after a trial, to be jointly liable with another defendant can be required to pay the entire judgment to the plaintiff by himself.

In other words, if a plaintiff wins a verdict for $100,000 and you are found to be only 1% at fault, and your co-defendants are found 99% at fault, the plaintiff can nevertheless *collect the entire judgment amount from you.* It would then be up to you to collect contributions or reimbursement from the other defendants, if they have the money.

The theory behind this law is that the plaintiff who has been insured and is found to be entitled to compensation should not be denied that compensation as long as at least one of the responsible defendants has the ability to pay it.

Many hospitals now require physicians to carry some medical malpractice insurance before being given privileges to practice at that hospital, to ensure that the doctor will be able to contribute his or her share of any judgment based upon the joint liability of the doctors and hospital.

Similarly, individual physicians who have substantial assets but no insurance coverage may be required to pay a large judgment, even though that physician was not primarily—or even significantly—responsible for the patient's injury, because the other co-defendants cannot pay their share.

Once a judgment is obtained against an uninsured physician, there are several means available to the plaintiff in collecting it. Most often, the plaintiff's attorney will conduct an "Examination of Judgment Debtor." This procedure requires a defendant who has had a judgment entered against him to answer questions under oath concerning his income and assets.

Generally, any assets held by the defendant individually, or even jointly with another, may be attached, pursuant to procedures supervised by the court, and used to pay the judgment.

The major exception to this is property held in "tenancy by the entirety." Tenancy by the entirety refers to assets owned jointly by a husband and wife. Although it is a term generally used with regard to land, it is also applicable to other assets, such as bank accounts and automobiles.

Thus, while a judgment creditor may be able to attach the usual bank account opened jointly by a husband and wife, this would not necessarily be the case with an account held by them as tenants by the entirety.

Of course, there are exceptions to every rule. The protection of tenancy by the entirety does not apply to existing debts on property owned by one spouse and then transferred into ownership in tenancy by the entirety.

Also, it may not apply in situations where the spouse transfers the property in anticipation of a specific adverse judgment. Depending upon the circumstances, a court could find such a transfer as a fraud upon creditors and allow the property to be attached anyway.

Even if a physician has no attachable assets, a plaintiff may be able to collect a judgment by garnishment of the physician's future income.

This is easier to do if the physician is employed by a group or other entity that has a separate payroll department. Even with self-employed physicians, a diligent plaintiff's attorney would not have great difficulty in obtaining a court order requiring the physician to pay the plaintiff a significant percentage of his monthly income until the judgment is satisfied.

Furthermore, an individual physician is not protected from such garnishment merely because he is an employee of his own corporation. While incorporating may have other benefits, it will not shield a physician from a claim based upon professional negligence.

The final defense of an uninsured physician against a large personal injury judgment is to declare personal bankruptcy. Although bankruptcy law is a highly specialized area fraught with exceptions and exclusions, it generally can be said that a personal injury judgment may be avoided by filing for personal bankruptcy. This alternative has many drawbacks, since it generally requires selling off most of the physician's assets and does significant damage to the physician's reputation and credit. Also, by law, it can be done only once every 6 years.

In summary, there are serious risks involved in practicing without malpractice insurance, and although some of them can be reduced with careful planning, they are still substantial and cannot be eliminated.

Hunt WS. Malpractice insurance—what can happen if you don't have it. Hawaii Med J. 1985; 44(6): 209-210.

Reprinted with permission from the author and the Hawaii Medical Journal.

Article 6.3

Medical Malpractice: "Crisis" and Reform

Francis X. Campion, MD.

Is the medical malpractice crisis of the 1980s different from the malpractice crisis of the 1970s? Why weren't the troubles of medical malpractice put to rest with the reforms of the 1970s? Have the extensive malpractice reforms of the 1980s slowed the rise in suits or insurance premiums? These questions are important to ponder if our society is to develop a long term solution for the multiple woes collectively termed "malpractice crisis."

Labelling any set of circumstances a "crisis" is done from a particular viewpoint. From the perspective of many physicians, particularly those in higher-risk, procedure-oriented specialties such as obstetrics, anesthesiology, orthopedic surgery, and neurosurgery, a crisis of serious import is ongoing. The chief complaints are costly malpractice insurance premiums and a high incidence of malpractice suits.

In Massachusetts, the cost of insurance purchased from the state-run Joint Underwriters Association rose 375 percent between 1981 and 1987. In Southern California, malpractice rates for physicians rose 122 percent between 1980 and 1986.[1] In the

Table 1

Malpractice Insurance Rates[a] as of January 1, 1986 for Selected Specialties

	AR	CA[b]	FL[c]	IN[d]	NY[e]	NC
General practice (minor surgery)	$1,907	$10,024	$10,448	$2,328	$9,220	$2,760
Internal medicine	1,907	5,924	10,448	2,328	7,233	2,760
General surgery	6,063	28,576	35,794	7,760	20,642	8,896
Anesthesiology	5,407	20,492	31,837	7,760	13,598	7,924
Obstetrics/gynecology	9,940	42,928	59,537	11,380	35,133	16,904
Orthopedic surgery	7,985	33,632	47,667	10,605	36,472	11,812
Neurosurgery	12,612	37,984	75,367	11,380	43,019	18,595

a Rates are those applicable to the state's leading insurer of physicians for the predominately purchased coverage limits and policy form for the rating category in which there was the greatest total number of physicians insured.

b Rates applicable to Southern California.

c Rates applicable to entire state except for Dade and Broward Counties.

d Includes surcharge rate to participate in the Patient's Compensation Fund.

e Rates applicable to entire state except for Nassau, Suffolk, Bronx, Kings, Queens, Richmond, Rockland, Sullivan, New York, Orange, Ulster and Westchester Counties.

Source: United States General Accounting Office.

state of New York, not including the New York City metropolitan area, rates rose 271 percent during the same period.[2] Of course, liability insurance rates vary dramatically among different medical specialties according to their risk and past malpractice experience. The actual cost of insurance to a physician depends on the amount of coverage that individual desires as well as the terms of the policy. Such variation has made comparison between different physician groups and different geographic regions difficult. A well-regarded series of studies by the United States General Accounting Office (GAO) shows that insurance rates differ considerably from state to state (Table 1). Costs can vary significantly even between neighboring counties within a single state. One recent estimate shows a sampling of the annual costs of a $1 million/$3 million occurrence policy as of February 1987: $2,300 for a Massachusetts psychiatrist, $5,316 for a New Jersey internist, $84,645 for an obstetrician on Long Island and $152,881 for a Dade County (Florida) neurosurgeon.[3]

The likelihood of being sued is high. The annual claims per 100 physicians rose dramatically from 3.2 per 100 physicians prior to 1981, to 10.2 in 1985. It declined somewhat to 6.7 per 100 physicians in 1987 (Table 2). Thirty-seven percent of physicians reported having been sued at least once. These data were calculated from the annual survey of non-federal patient care physicians conducted by the American Medical Association.[4]

The rapid rise in malpractice claim frequency between 1980 and 1986 was a prime cause of the spiraling cost of insurance. Perhaps equally important was the increasing severity or cost of settling the average claim. The GAO study revealed that in 1984, 102 insurers closed an estimated 73,500 claims against 103,300 health care providers.[5] In 1984, there were 35.7 malpractice claims per 100 physicians in New York, representing a 32 percent increase from four years previous. The St. Paul Fire and Marine Insurance Company, the

Table 2

Annual Claims per 100 Physicians by Specialty and Census Division, 1985-1987

	1985	1986	1987	Average Annual Rate of Change 1985-1987
All Physicians	10.2	9.2	6.7[b]	-19.0%[c]
Specialty				
General/Family Practice	5.7	7.6	5.7	0.0
Internal Medicine	6.2	5.5	4.5	-14.8
Surgery	16.8	15.8	12.7	-13.1
Pediatrics	7.2	6.8	4.5	-20.9
Obstetrics/Gynecology	25.8	13.0[a]	8.0	-44.3[c]
Radiology	12.8	11.5	8.0	-20.9
Psychiatry	2.9	4.5	1.6	-25.7
Anesthesiology	7.5	8.7	4.6	-21.7
Pathology	3.3	1.1	4.9	21.9
Other	10.4	9.1	5.9	-24.7

a 1985-1986 change statistically significant at the p = .05 level.
b 1986-1987 change statistically significant at the p = .05 level.
c Total 1985-1987 change statistically significant at the p= .05 level

Source: Socioeconomic Characteristics of Medical Practice, 1988. Chicago, IL: American Medical Association

nation's largest private malpractice insurance underwriter, reported a 56 percent increase in claims frequency between 1980 and 1984 (Table 3). According to the GAO, only 43 percent of the estimated 73,500 claims closed in 1984 led to an indemnity payment to the alleged injured party. These payments went as high as $2.5 million for a single claim and totaled $2.6 billion. The median and average payments were $18,000 and $80,741, respectively. St. Paul paid out 102 percent more per claim in 1984 than they did in 1980. Table 4 shows that paid claims rose between 63 percent and 124 percent in five selected states during that period. In the GAO study, claims closed with indemnities of $250,000 or more represented only 9 percent of paid claims but accounted for 61 percent of the total indemnity.

The cost escalation of recent years differs from the crisis of the 1970s which was characterized by a dearth of insurance carriers willing to continue to sell liability insurance to doctors. Arguments over who is to blame for the "affordability" crisis sound similar to those arguments heard during the "availability" crisis of the 1970s. Opinion is aptly described in the first of the GAO studies designed to assist Congress in developing policy concerning professional liability. It was published in February 1986 and is entitled, "Medical Malpractice: No Agreement on the Problems or Solutions."[6] The three major players, attorneys, insurance companies, and doctors, follow slightly different reasoning. It is generally unfair to characterize all attorneys or the entire insurance industry just as one recognizes the incredible heterogeneity of medical opinion on so many topics. It is useful to do so, however, in an attempt to understand this complex issue.

A common opinion of many medical malpractice plaintiff attorneys is that no medical liability crisis exists. They contend that the rising number of malpractice suits reflects an increasing awareness by consumers of their legal rights. Furthermore, they believe that there are still many instances of misdiagnosis and negligence which are never contested by injured patients. With this reasoning, trial attorneys predict an overall improvement in medical care will result when the cost of defending malpractice cases finally forces doctors to weed out the prime offenders and improve their level of care.

Some physician and insurance groups have called for the restructuring of the tort system itself by introducing pre-trial tribunals which would screen all cases and theoretically limit the number which actually get to court. In the 1970s this was a

Table 3

Frequency of Claims Reported per 100 Physicians in Selected States, 1980-84

State	1980	1981	1982	1983	1984	1980-84 percent increase
AR	6.6	8.4	8.8	7.7	8.6	30
CA	20.4	22.3	22.5	24.6	26.0	27
FL	20.8	31.6	32.3	29.1	26.1	25
IN	5.3	6.0	7.9	9.8	10.2	92
NY	27.1	28.9	31.4	38.1	35.7	32
NC	a	7.5	8.7	8.9	8.9	19[b]
(St. Paul) Country-wide	10.6	11.4	13.3	15.1	16.5	56

a Data not available.
b Percent computed from 1981 to 1984.

Source: United States General Accounting Office.

common type of malpractice reform. Trial lawyers consistently resist efforts to restructure the legal system or to change the way it is funded. They believe the current contingency fee system ensures access to the courts for all citizens, regardless of their ability to pay. Any other arrangement, they argue, would compromise this fundamental right to seek justice in a court of law.

The insurance industry tends to blame lawyers for bringing increasing numbers of frivolous suits, those cases which contain questionable or no real medical negligence. These suits are often cheaper to settle out of court but, in aggregate, are quite costly to the insurance industry. The cost of settling out of court naturally rises as the awards delivered by jury verdicts increases. Insurance leaders would also like to change the way settlements are paid out. If payments were made in a structured fashion over time, instead of single lump sum payments, then patients would benefit by guaranteed security and insurance companies would possibly pay less in the long run. Insurance spokesmen also complain of the exorbitant fees which lawyers receive. In most states, lawyers receive a 30 to 40 percent share of the final settlement awarded to their client. If they lose the case they receive nothing and by the same reasoning have a great incentive to strive for even higher awards. In this era, when million dollar cases are not uncommon, lawyers stand to take home a considerable amount of money which the jury has intended for the pain and suffering of the plaintiff. Estimates vary as to how much of a typical jury award actually is paid to the injured party. According to one estimate about 56 percent of the award is received by the plaintiff and the remaining 44 percent goes to paying the lawyer and other expenses of the legal proceeding.[7] Many insurance companies are seeking ways to limit the monies which go directly to lawyers.

Table 4

Average Paid Claim for Physicians in Selected States 1980-84[a]

State[b]	1980	1981	1982	1983	1984	1980-84 percent increase
AR	$31,619	$35,974	$50,783	$20,182	$51,685	63
CA	32,963	43,570	60,123	55,419	61,774	87
FL	80,556	74,572	123,384	112,862	140,594	75
NY	46,789	76,203	80,865	105,552	104,810	124
NC	c	36,064	36,967	48,938	62,043	72[d]
Country-wide (St. Paul)[e]	28,059	36,824	45,421	53,380	56,739	102

a These amounts may be understated in some states if insurance companies only initially began writing malpractice policies in the state for recent years. Generally, those claims closed earlier are smaller than those closed later.

b Information on Indiana is presented separately on pp. 19-20 because we could not compute an overall average paid claim that combined the experiences of primary insurers with that of the state's Patient Compensation Fund.

c Data not available.

d Percent computed from 1981 to 1984.

e For purposes of computing this average, the St. Paul Company limits each paid claim to a maximum of $1 million.

Source: United States General Accounting Office.

Doctors too, are being reprimanded by the insurance companies. Chart reviews, stricter credentialing, and mandatory physician education concerning risk management are being imposed by the insurance industry. Some insurance carriers are charging higher premiums for those doctors who have a higher than average number of claims against them.

Doctors have been willing to point the finger as well. They complain that lawyers advertise for patients with poor medical outcomes who can easily garner the sentiments of any jury composed of non-health professionals. They reason that this leads to large numbers of frivolous suits which are ultimately paid for by doctors through their malpractice insurance premiums. Physicians also complain of a group of doctors known, derogatorily, as "hired guns" who are paid by lawyers to give "expert testimony" to support their client's charge of malpractice. These doctors will purportedly travel to any part of the country and offer any medical testimony for the right price.

There is also great debate over the measurement of those "non-economic damages" known as pain and suffering. Doctors say that lawyers run up the cost of pain and suffering simply out of greed. As the size of the final settlement grows, so grows the check which the lawyer takes home. Of course doctors also complain of the cost of their malpractice insurance premiums directly to their insurance carriers. Insurance companies are forced to use a great deal of speculation in estimating the amount of money they will require to pay out future settlements. It is on a set of best guesses and mathematical formulas that malpractice premiums are based. Doctors easily find points of disagreement and claim that the insurance companies are collecting far too much money. Also, doctors often feel they have been unfairly dealt with when their insurance company decides to settle before trial. The feeling is that the insurance company has taken the economically expedient path but has not allowed justice to prevail.

Crisis Spawns Change

In the mid-1970s, the malpractice insurance availability crisis led to innovation in providing insurance. Twenty years ago there were more than 40 commercial companies which offered professional liability insurance to physicians. Today there are only six. During the 1970s some state governments initiated insurance pools of their own so that any licensed physician in their state would be guaranteed access to liability insurance. Many state medical societies have chartered their own mutual insurance companies. There are now at least 41 physician owned or sponsored companies providing liability insurance to half the nation's physicians.[8] Even smaller entities, such as groups of university-affiliated hospitals, pooled their resources to self-insure their physicians and impose their own risk management activities in a controlled environment. The resulting corporation is often referred to as a captive insurance company. Other methods of insurance regulation and tort reform were also instituted at the state level during the 1970s. Many of these principles are again under discussion. They form the nucleus of changes which have been instituted since 1984 in states across the country.

Change has developed rapidly. The national media has sensitized the public to the existence of a general cost crisis in all forms of liability insurance.[9] The cost of liability insurance for municipal governments, product manufacturers, and even little league baseball teams rose several hundred percent during the early 1980s. A special White House commission called for sweeping changes in the nation's tort system, the judicial system designed to compensate individuals for civil wrongdoing and personal injury. The White House working group on tort reform noted that the number of product liability suits filed against manufacturers rose 758 percent between 1974 and 1985. Claims against state and local governments increased 141 percent between 1979 and 1983.[10] Some experts cite changes in tort law itself which have made it easier for persons to successfully bring claims against other individuals and institutions.[11] In particular, there has been a lessening in the burden of proof required to show fault or causation.

In many states, coalitions of interest groups, including physician organizations, have provided the impetus for change. It is focused at the state level where laws concerning liability, insurance regulation, and physician licensing take place. Between 1971 and 1985 all 50 states passed some legislation regarding medical malpractice.[12] In 1986 alone, 37 states passed tort reform legislation. In 20 of these states, there were specific changes concerning medical malpractice.

Here is a sampling of some of the more popular areas of malpractice reform:

Modifications to Tort Laws

Caps on non-economic damages have been instituted in at least 18 states, limiting reimbursement for such damages as pain and suffering to between $250,000 and $1,000,000 depending on the state. Caps on all damages (economic and non-economic) now exist in Indiana and Texas.

Attorney's contingency fees will be calculated on a sliding scale such as in Massachusetts; 40 percent of the first $150,000, 33.3 percent of the next $150,000, 30 percent of the next $200,000, and 25 percent of any amount by which the recovery exceeds $500,000.

Pretrial hearings may require the plaintiff to present his/her case before a screening tribunal. A tribunal typically consists of a physician, judge, and attorney whose purpose is to differentiate those claims which are completely frivolous from those which have at least some evidence. In the case of a frivolous claim, the plaintiff may be required to post a bond to cover some defense costs if he/she desires to press the claim into court.

Statute of limitations specifies the number of years after a wrongdoing that an individual has to pursue legal action in the courts. Many states have set different limits for claims concerning birth injuries, minors, and adults. In some cases the time runs from the moment of injury, in others the time runs from the moment of discovery of the injury.

Abolition of the collateral source rule allows the jury to consider other sources of remuneration which the plaintiff receives for medical bills, disability, etc. Under many existing collateral source rules the plaintiff receives reimbursement from the malpractice insurance company for expenses already paid for by health insurers, worker's compensation, union benefits, and other agencies.

Restriction of joint and several liability would limit the number of parties from which a plaintiff could seek full remuneration for damages. In the past, plaintiffs could press charges and pursue remuneration from physicians and hospital corporations only peripherally related to an actual act of malpractice. This has often been described as suing the person or corporate entity with the "deep pockets."

Insurance Reform

Structured payments to the plaintiff are made over several years instead of one lump sum payment. This assures a steady flow of money to the injured party for a period of time specified by the court. Such a plan can buffer insurance companies from disproportionate losses in any one year and helps in planning their future cash flow.

Experience rating allows malpractice insurers to charge higher premiums for physicians who have had an above average number of malpractice claims against them. Physicians with commendable records may benefit from reduced rates.

Insurance requirements may force physicians to purchase some form of liability protection in order to practice medicine within a state. In the past, hospitals had such discretion when considering requirements for staff privileges.

Insurance ceilings have been raised in many states, allowing physicians to purchase in excess of $1 million dollars worth of liability insurance. Policy limits usually specify the amount of coverage for a single malpractice claim and the amount for all claims against a single physician in one year such as the $1 million/$3 million policy.

Physician Reform

Risk management programs are now mandatory in many hospitals, HMOs, and nursing homes in some states. This may entail the hiring of a staff person known as the risk manager to oversee chart reviews, the development of patient care protocols, and educational programs related to malpractice loss reduction.

Physician licensing boards have been given greater authority and stricter requirements concerning the licensing of medical doctors. More thorough credentialing, review of physicians with repeated malpractice claims, and increased authority for investigation will make the licensing board the final common pathway for disciplining physicians.

Mandatory reporting of physician disciplinary actions by hospitals, HMOs, nursing homes, and insurance carriers to the licensing board is now required in some states. Controversy still continues over what type of information must be reported with particular concern for the confidentiality of such sensitive information.

As of September 1, 1990, national reporting is required as part of the mandate of the Health Care Quality Improvement Act of 1986. This federal initiative forms a centralized, nationwide database containing information on physician malpractice history and disciplinary action. Every health care facility is responsible for knowing the file contents on each of their staff physicians and for submitting information on a regular basis.

Peer review was, in the past, the responsibility of those conscientious physicians willing to shoulder the burden of potential libel suits from disgruntled physicians. Under the Health Care Quality Improvement Act of 1986 physicians who participate in the review of their colleagues, in good faith, will be protected from lawsuits alleging defamation of character, unfair trade practices or similar charges.

The Impact of Reform

What effect will any of these reforms have on malpractice insurance rates? Most observers acknowledge that insurance rates will likely never decline to their pre-1980 level. At best, recent reforms will slow the growth in insurance costs. In fact, as of 1990, there are data to support a stabilization of malpractice premiums and claims. There was a similar, but short-lived trend in the late 1970s after reform efforts. Reforms in the 1970s primarily made changes in the tort system. The specific impact of those measures has been very difficult to discern due to a lack of comparable statistics from states and insurance companies. However the federal government did finance a study by the Rand Corporation in 1983 to measure the effects of the widespread changes which were instituted in and around 1975.[13] They compared closed insurance claims from 1970 with those between 1975 and 1978. The good news was that nationwide claim frequency declined 27 percent between 1975 and 1976 and dropped a further 9 percent in 1977. A rise of 2 percent was measured in 1978. The mean number of malpractice claims per 100,000 population grew from 2.76 in 1970 to a peak of 10.04 in 1975 and settled at 6.23 in 1978. The mean number of paid claims per 100,000 population declined from 3.64 in 1975 to 2.68 in 1978. The bad news was that the severity of paid claims continued to increase at a rate of 30 percent between 1975 and 1978. The average cost of settling a claim in 1978 was $36,766. The gamut of reforms were analyzed to determine which may have been responsible for this measured decrease in frequency and increase in severity. The study did show a link between the introduction of a cap on noneconomic damages and a decrease in severity but not frequency of claims. A repeal or modification of collateral source rules correlated with a similar pattern of change. None of the other popular reform measures showed a statistically significant change in claims. One recent study of 12 different reform measures enacted in the 1970s showed only one, the institution of pre-trial screening, had a statistically significant association with lower malpractice premiums.[14] In California, a 1975 law instituting a $250,000 ceiling on awards for pain and suffering and limits on attorneys' fees is praised as having saved that state's physicians millions of dollars in insurance premiums.[15]

By 1978 the major problem of malpractice insurance availability had largely been put to rest. Many state sponsored joint underwriting associations and physician-owned insurance companies had been formed. The mild improvement in malpractice claims frequency was of brief duration and never translated into significant insurance premium reductions on a large scale. As described, the cost of liability insurance, frequency of malpractice suits, and severity of those suits all began an upward spiral after 1980. In fact, $1.57 billion dollars were spent on medical liability insurance in 1983 but the insurance companies were still short after paying out $2.0 billion in losses.[16] The rush of legislation in statehouses between 1982 and 1987 had much the same agenda as seen just 10 years prior.

In the late 1980s, professional liability insurers reported the first drop in claims frequency in more than 10 years. The St. Paul reported a drop in claim frequency from 17.3 to 13.0 per 100 physicians between 1985 and 1988. This has led the company to decrease malpractice insurance premiums 5 to 30 percent in 34 of the 42 states in which it sells policies.[17] The AMA annual survey also showed a drop in claim frequency from 10.2 to 6.7 per 100 physicians between 1985 and 1987 (Table 3).

Though claim frequency has dropped recently, there is no clear trend on the severity of claims.[18] The severity includes claims paid, claims closed without payment, open claims and defense costs. The St. Paul reports the average cost of reported claims rose 15 percent between 1986 and 1988. In 1988 the average claim cost $39,298.[17]

Despite the moderate decrease in insurance premiums announced by the St. Paul, the cost of insurance for most physicians continues to rise. The rate of increase has modified somewhat compared to the dramatic rises seen in the early 1980s. The AMA reports the average physician premium in 1985 was $10,500 and $15,000 in 1987.[4]

This time around, some people are rethinking the entire process of reimbursing injured persons. Many believe that the current tort system does not meet the needs of our society. The increasing use of technology and our ability to treat those who had no chance of survival just 20 years ago, carries with it an inherently higher risk of undesirable outcomes even when that care is delivered by the most competent individuals. Society has come to expect medical cures but has not developed an adequate system for compensating individuals who are unfortunately impaired by their medical care. The current system forces the injured party to prove fault on the part of another individual in order to be compensated for their loss. Critics of the fault-based system have charged that (a) it does not adequately differentiate maloccurrence from malpractice, (b) considerable time and effort are required to establish provider fault, (c) legal fees consume too high a percentage of awards and settlements, (d) the outcome of claims and the size of awards are unpredictable, and (e) awards and settlements are frequently excessive, particularly for noneconomic losses such as pain and suffering.[6]

Various configurations of alternative fault and "no fault" insurance systems are receiving serious discussion.[6,7,19,20] Other systems include administrative systems, specialized physician-patient contracts, and methods of binding arbitration. Insurance systems which make compensation based on occurrence and require no proof of fault include worker's compensation and many automobile insurance policies in this country. No-fault systems designed to compensate injuries incurred during medical care are functioning in other countries, most notably Sweden and New Zealand.[21,22,23] Proponents claim that such a system in the United States would allow injured persons to receive compensation quicker, be more efficient in terms of cost, and be more fair for patients, doctors, and hospitals. Congress has already instituted such a system to compensate children with injuries related to vaccine inoculations.[24] In 1987 the state of Virginia formed a program to compensate severely brain-damaged babies on a no-fault basis. Funding is provided primarily from physicians.[25]

In 1988, Florida passed similar legislation to pay for custodial and rehabilitative care for children with birth-related neurological injuries. The legislature acknowledged, "any birth other than the normal birth frequently leads to a claim against the attending physician. Because obstetric services are essential, it is incumbent upon the legislature to provide a plan designed to result in the stabilization and reduction of malpractice insurance premiums for providers of such services in Florida."[26]

The long waited Harvard Medical Practice Study, which reviewed the hospitalization records of 30,195 patients in New York state, estimated the incidence and severity of patient injury caused by medical care.[27] The investigators concluded that a no-fault system for compensating patients who had expenses related to hospital injuries would be cost-competitive with the present tort-based system of malpractice litigation. Such a system would pay for health care, lost wages and other injury-related expenses incurred six months after injury. Six months is the time at which most disability programs begin payment. They estimated expenses at $900 million per year for the state of New York, exclusive of administrative costs. This compares with the $1 billion in liability insurance premiums paid by hospitals and physicians in the state. No-fault systems are now gaining supporters and are being seriously considered in New York and Massachusetts.[28]

In 1988, the American Medical Association unveiled plans for a model system which would replace the existing court system for malpractice.[29] Their proposal is to develop a comprehensive administrative system centered around a powerful medical licensing board on the state level. Medical liability claims would be settled by a panel of experts, eliminating the long time delays and expense of the existing jury system. Pilot projects are under consideration in Vermont and Utah. Any new system in this country will likely need to preserve at least some access to the courts and be closely linked to the medical licensing process. Both considerations are accomplished by the AMA proposal.

In the spring of 1990, legislators began consideration of an alternative system of malpractice claim resolution for Medicare beneficiaries.[30] Connecticut congresswoman, Nancy Johnson, drafted plans allowing patients and physicians to settle disputes through arbitration. Under such a system, a panel of legal and medical experts would be empowered to determine fault and apportion liability. Her plan also incorporates a cap on non-economic damages and a statute of limitations for the filing of claims. It is expected to meet with opposition from trial attorneys, but receive support from consumer groups.

The impact which the increasing number of lawsuits and cost of insurance has on society becomes more evident daily. Many physicians acknowledge that their style of practice has been affected by the omnipresent potential for a lawsuit regardless of the accuracy of their diagnoses or quality of their care. This threat has probably led to the increased utilization of diagnostic tests and the practice of "defensive medicine." The financial costs of such changes in practice style and the rising premiums themselves are important components of the growing price tag of health care in the United States.[31] Many physicians have decided not to perform certain high-risk surgical procedures or to deliver babies. Some have retired early to pursue other, less stressful and less costly endeavors. The loss of these human resources to the community has become an issue in many parts of the country. All physicians must weigh these stresses in their own personal lives and styles of practice. Many have described the doctor-patient relationship as the final common target of these forces. The potential exists for lasting damage to be done to that fragile relationship. However, a combination of institutional reform and personal physician commitment will be required if we are to preserve the high standard of medical care to which we are accustomed.

References

1. Medical Malpractice: Case Study on California. United States General Accounting Office. Document No. GAO/HRD-87-21S-2, Dec. 1986, p. 12.

2. Medical Malpractice: Case Study on New York. United States General Accounting Office. Document No. GAO/HRD-87-21S-5, Dec. 1986, p. 12.

3. Secretary Gold Cites Impact of Malpractice Reform Law on New Rates. Press release from the Commonwealth of Massachusetts Executive Office of Consumer Affairs and Business Regulation, March 4, 1987.

4. Socioeconomic Characteristics of Medical Practice 1988. Chicago: American Medical Association Center for Health Policy Research, 1988; pp.18-22.

5. Medical Malpractice: Characteristics of Claims Closed in 1984. United States General Accounting Office. Document No. GAO/HRD-87-55, p. 2.

6. Medical Malpractice: No Agreement on the Problems or Solutions. United States General Accounting Office. Document No. GAO/HRD-86-50, Feb. 1986.

7. Tancredi LR. Compensating for medical injuries: is there an effective alternative to the tort system of medical malpractice? NY State Med J. July 1986:370-376.

8. Physician Insurers Association of America 1989 Membership Directory and Professional Services Section. PIAA, Lawrenceville, NJ, 1989.

9. Church J, et al. Sorry your policy has been canceled. Time. March 24, 1986:16-26.

10. Rust M. Report backs tort law changes. Am Med News. April 4, 1986:2.

11. Bok DC. A flawed system. Harvard Magazine. May-June 1983:38-45.

12. Siegel DR. An overview of medical malpractice legislation. NY State Med. July 1986:377-391.

13. Danzon PM. The Frequency and Severity of Medical Malpractice Claims. Santa Monica, CA: Rand Corporation; 1982.

14. Sloan FA. State responses to the malpractice insurance 'crisis' of the 1970s: an empirical assessment. J Health Politics, Policy Law. 1985;9:629-646.

15. McGinn PR. MDs look forward to lower liability rate hikes. Am Med News. January 1, 1988:9.

16. Professional Liability in the '80s. Report No. 1 of the AMA Special Task Force on Professional Liability and Insurance, Chicago, October 1984.

17. The St. Paul's 1989 Annual Report to Policyholders. Saint Paul, MN: The St. Paul Companies; 1989.

18. Holzer JF. Liability insurance issues in anesthesiology. Intl Anes Clinics. 1989;27(3):205-212.

19. O'Connell J. Medical malpractice: is no-fault a remedy? Massachusetts Medicine. Jan./Feb. 1986:39-43.

20. O'Connell J. A new approach to medical malpractice insurance. RI Med J. 1986;69:81-83.

21. Cooper JK. Sweden's no-fault patient-injury insurance. N Engl J Med. 1976;294:1268-1270.

22. Oldertz C. The Swedish patient insurance system—8 years of experience. Medico-Legal J. 1984;52:43-59.

23. Smith R. Compensation for medical misadventure and drug injury in the New Zealand no-fault system: feeling the way. Brit Med J. 1982;284:1457-1459.

24. Inglehart JK. Compensating children with vaccine-related injuries. N Engl J Med. 1987;316:1283-1288.

25. Virginia Birth-related Neurological Injury Compensation Act. 1987, c.540, ss 38.5001.

26. Florida Birth-related Neurological Injury Compensation Plan, Florida S6-xxxx Fifth Special Session, 1988 New Laws, p. 104.

27. Medical Practice Study: Executive Summary. New York State Health Department, New York, February 28, 1990.

28. Manuel BM. Professional liability: A no-fault solution. N Engl J Med. March 1, 1990;322(9):627-631.

29. O'Brien C. AMA, specialties tort model as alternative to tort system. Am Med News. January 15, 1988:1.

30. Gianelli DM. Draft bill seeks arbitration of Medicare malpractice claims. Am News; April 20, 1990; pp.1,32.

31. Reynolds RA, Rizzo JA, Gonzalez ML. The cost of medical professional liability. JAMA. 1987;257:2776-2781.

Article 6.4

A Proposed Alternative to the Civil Justice System for Resolving Medical Liability Disputes: A Fault-Based Administrative System

Executive Summary

AMA/Specialty Society Medical Liability Project. January 1988.

The American Medical Association ("AMA"), 31 national medical specialty societies and the Council of Medical Specialty Societies have joined together to create the Medical Liability Project to propose a fair and efficient system of resolving medical liability disputes. Specifically, we propose a system in which such disputes would be adjudicated by an expert administrative agency. This agency can be either a modification of the current state licensing board or a new agency. This Medical Board would also have the power to take appropriate action to identify and rehabilitate or discipline physicians whose practice patterns pose a threat to patients. Because of the radical nature of our proposal, we recommend that it be tried as an experiment in one or more states.

We have endeavored to create a system that is fair and equitable to patients and physicians alike. Medical liability is only a part of the much larger and more important issues concerning the quality of medical care being provided by physicians. Accordingly, in addition to changes in the legal standards for determining medical liability, the proposal includes specific provisions designed to enhance the state medical board's credentialing and disciplinary functions. The administrative scheme proposed in this Report recognizes that physicians, patients and the public have distinct interests which must be respected and evenly balanced in any reasonable attempt to solve the medical liability crisis.

Part I: The Administrative Alternative to the Current Medical Liability System And Improved Credentialing and Disciplinary Processes

A. Rationale for the Alternative

Our proposal arises out of two basic facts. First, the current judicial system for determining professional liability does not compensate a significant number of patients who have been injured by medical negligence. Individuals who have claims which do not involve a substantial potential recovery have difficulty enlisting the services of private attorneys. Thus, the existing system imposes barriers to the courts which preclude plaintiffs from receiving any compensation for injuries caused by medical negligence.

Second, the current tort system, which relies heavily upon juries, is not optimally suited for resolving medical negligence issues. Under the current system, there have been consistent increases in the size of damage awards, especially for non-economic damages. By their magnitude, these awards are threatening the availability and affordability of insurance coverage and health care in many geographic areas in the United States and in many medical specialties. Moreover, juries have tended to award plaintiffs significantly greater amounts in malpractice cases than in cases which concern identical injuries not involving physicians. In addition, the use of juries can be a time-consuming and inefficient way to resolve medical liability disputes. Currently, less than half of the total dollars spent on malpractice insurance ever reach the injured patient.

Because the existing judicial system is not entirely fair either to patients or physicians and is not an effective or efficient method of medical liability dispute resolution, it is reasonable to consider whether an alternative could be developed which would be fairer and more efficient. However, the system of trial by jury has strong historical roots in this country and there are significant constitutional and political limitations on the range of alternatives to the civil justice system that can be implemented even on a limited basis. In particular, there must be a meaningful *quid pro quo* provided to patients in order to justify withdrawing their claims from the jury system—as there is in no-fault automobile and workers compensation systems.

The Medical Liability Project does not suggest a general rejection of the tort system, nor does it advocate the abandonment of traditional tort reform. However, the Project has concluded that a persuasive case can be made for employing on an experimental basis an administrative alternative to the tort system for resolving medical liability disputes. The Medical Liability Project therefore proposes that in one or more states broad authority to handle medical liability disputes be granted to an existing medical disciplinary board or to a new agency so that an administrative system of medical liability compensation can be established. This Medical Board would provide several advantages to patients. The most important of these is that the system should permit more injured parties to be compensated than does the current system. At the same time, windfall damage awards would be eliminated, medical liability disputes would be resolved more quickly and efficiently, and certainty and predictability of compensation for medical liability would be increased.

B. The Claims Resolution Function

The administrative system for adjudicating medical liability can divided into three parts: (1) the pre-hearing and initial hearing stage; (2) the final decision of the Board; and (3) judicial review. The proposed system would provide a significant benefit to patients by making available to any patient who has a claim of reasonable merit an experienced attorney from the Medical Board's general counsel's office who will litigate the claim on behalf of the patient free of charge.

Under proposed pre-hearing procedures, claims reviewers from the Medical Board will quickly evaluate claims and dismiss those without merit. For claims with merit, the claims reviewers will submit the matter to an expert in the same field as the health care provider. The expert will review the claim and make a judgment as to whether it has merit. The claims reviewer also will assist the patient in evaluating the claim and any settlement offers.

If the claim is not settled, it will be assigned to one of the Medical Board's hearing examiners. In order to encourage reasonable and timely settlements, blind settlement offers by the parties will be required prior to hearing. A party would be subject to sanctions if the outcome of the case is not an improvement over a settlement offer that the party has rejected. The hearing examiner also will oversee expedited discovery and ensure that the parties have valid expert evidence available to support their case. At the hearing itself, the examiner will have broad authority to conduct the proceedings, including authority to call an independent expert to provide assistance in deciding the case. The hearing examiner will be required to render a written decision within 90 days of the hearing. In that decision, the hearing examiner will determine whether the health care provider is liable for the claimant's injury and, if so, will determine the size of the damage award.

The hearing examiner's decision will be subject to review by the Medical Board. The Board will have discretion to award fees and costs incurred in an appeal if the appeal presented no substantial question. The Medical Board will hear these cases as an appellate body in panels of three members. The Medical Board will make a full independent determination whether the health care provider's conduct was inadequate and caused the claimant's injury. Appeal from the Medical Board's decision will be to the intermediate appellate court of the state, where the review will be limited to whether the Board acted contrary to statute or the Board's own rules.

This proposed scheme will provide experienced and expert personnel at every level in the decision-making process. Over time, they should be better able than a jury to evaluate medical negligence claims. In addition, the involvement of the Board will increase the ability of the decision-making process to be consistent in both liability determinations and the size of damage awards. The proposed administrative system also should be able to resolve disputes more quickly than the current system and thereby save both plaintiffs and defendants the substantial expense incurred in litigating cases for years in court.

In addition to acting as an adjudicator of medical liability claims, the Medical Board also will develop rules and substantive guidelines to complement the statutory standards. The Board will have administrative authority to initiate rulemaking and to solicit public comments. A rule promulgated by the Board will have the force of law and will be subject to judicial review by an appellate court to determine if it is arbitrary, capricious or in excess of the Medical Board's authority.

C. The Performance Monitoring Function

1. In conjunction with its expanded authority to handle medical liability claims, the Board's performance monitoring function will be strengthened. Specifically, all settlements and awards based on medical liability will be reported to the Board's investigative branch. This does not mean that every or even many liability determinations will lead to disciplinary actions. What it means is that every liability determination will give rise to an initial screening of the physician's practices as reported to the Medical Board. The primary purpose of this endeavor, as with all performance monitoring, will be education and rehabilitation. Thus, our proposal is intended to enhance the Board's ability to discover physicians who are impaired, lacking appropriate medical skills or otherwise unable to provide acceptable medical care.

2. In conjunction with the proposals for monitoring physician performance by the Medical Board, our proposal calls for enactment of three categories of changes designed to further strengthen physician credentialing. First, reporting requirements will be increased by requiring hospitals and other health care institutions to conduct periodic physician performance reviews (a modified version of those required by the Joint Commission on the Accreditation of Healthcare Organizations) and to report to the Medical Board any conclusion that a physician's performance has been substandard. Insurers will be required to report cancellations and failures to renew for reasons that are not class based. All physicians will be required to report instances of suspected incompetence, impairment, or drug or alcohol dependence to the hospital credentials committee or other credentialing entity. In order to facilitate physician reporting, the state will provide immunity to physicians who report suspected problems in good faith. All of these reporting requirements are designed to increase substantially the amount of information available on physician performance. Second, this information must be maintained in a form that is accessible to those who conduct professional review activities under the proposed system. To facilitate this process, the Medical Board will create and maintain a clearinghouse (or utilize the one established pursuant to the Health Care Quality Improvement Act of 1986) for reports from insurers, reports from hospitals and other entities and disciplinary actions taken by other states. Much of the information that will be collected under this proposal overlaps with the required reporting under current federal law. The licensing board will review this information, on a routine basis, every two years. Immediate review is required in the event of certain negative reports. The Board will also have authority to conduct an on-site review of the medical practices of all physicians against whom a medical liability determination (or settlement) has been made where there is reason to believe that the physician's practices pose a threat to patient health. In addition, certain credentialing entities, such as hospitals, will be required to check with the clearinghouse in connection with credentialing and privilege reviews.

Finally, the Project calls for the furtherance of quality assurance/risk prevention goals by requiring all physicians to complete a number of continuing medical education "credit hours" per year. A certain percentage of these hours must be directly relevant to clinical practice. In addition, all physicians will be required to participate in a risk management program. This change is designed to ensure that physicians maintain and enhance their professional skills.

In addition to the settlements and awards that are automatically reported, performance complaints—from hospitals, physicians, the public or employees of the Medical Board—will be sent to a claims reviewer at the Board for investigation. As with claims of medical liability, the claims reviewer will evaluate these complaints and, if appropriate, make a recommendation to the Board's general counsel's office to pursue complaints that appear meritorious. A member of the general counsel's office will then make a decision whether to initiate a disciplinary charge. Once a disciplinary charge is initiated, a member of the general counsel's office will prosecute the charge before a hearing examiner who, after an appropriate due process proceeding, will make a decision as to what, if any, action is appropriate. The examiner's action is subject to review by the Board, which is required to provide notice of any disciplinary action to credentialing entities, insurers and other state Medical Boards.

D. The Structure of the Board

In order to perform the complex and sensitive functions outlined above, the existing Medical Boards will be restructured or a new agency will be created. Membership on the Board will have to become full time, probably for a five year term. Members will be selected by the governor—from a list of nominees selected by a nominating committee —and approved by the legislature. The Project recommends a seven person Board, of which at least two but no more than three members are physicians. It is also crucial that the Medical Board members be widely recognized as experienced and neutral, and that they be committed to attempting a bold new approach to the problems of medical negligence. To ensure the Board's quality, all of its employees, from claims reviewers to hearing examiners, must be selected and retained on the basis of their ability and commitment to resolving claims efficiently and fairly.

Proper implementation of the administrative model also will require that substantial issues of funding be addressed. With respect to the increased funding requirements of the Board itself, because of the substantial benefits to the public and expected lower overall costs, use of general revenues will be necessary and appropriate. In addition, the state could make an initial assessment against insurance companies, which provide medical liability insurance within the state, or physicians and other health care providers.

Part II: The Legal Elements of Medical Liability

In order to ensure that the administrative model of medical liability passes constitutional muster, it will be necessary to codify the liability rules to be applied by the Medical Board under the administrative system. It will not be enough simply to incorporate by reference existing common law standards. The statute establishing the Medical Board will have to define specifically the standards under which a claim for medical liability is established, although as noted previously, the Board will be expected to exercise its rulemaking authority to fill in the interstices of the statute. The need for codification of the rules governing medical liability provides an opportunity to revise existing rules in a way that furthers the patient's interests in fair compensation, the physician's interest in predictable awards and the public's interest in standards of liability and damages that can be consistently and efficiently applied. Set forth below is a summary of the most important proposed rules of medical liability.

The rules governing standard of care based on custom and locality would be abolished in favor of a standard that focuses on whether the challenged actions fall within a range of reasonableness, to be determined by reference to the standards of a prudent and competent practitioner in the same or similar circumstances. The hearing examiner would be required to consider a variety of factors in determining the range of reasonableness, including the expertise of and means available to the health care provider, the state of medical knowledge, the availability of facilities and access to transportation and communications facilities. With respect to proof of liability, the statute also would set standards for evidentiary matters such as the qualifications of experts, the use of manufacturer's instructions on drugs and medical devices and the use of medical literature.

A significant modification in the causation standard is also proposed. Traditionally, recovery has been denied unless the physician was at least 50% responsible for the patient's loss. The causation standard would be modified to allow recovery if the physician's negligence was a "contributing factor" in causing the injury. Damages under this standard would be apportioned according to the physician's degree of fault.

The informed consent doctrine would be codified under the current "minority" rule which requires that the adequacy of the disclosure should be measured from the perspective of the reasonable patient. The privilege to withhold information (for therapeutic reasons) and standards for determining individual responsibility for disclosure also would be included in the statutory "informed consent" doctrine.

In the area of damages, non-economic damages (and punitive damages) would be capped at an amount that is tied to a percentage of the average annual wage in the state. Special damages would be awarded under a series of guidelines designed to ensure that those damages represent a realistic "replacement cost." For example, in determining the "lost income" of an unemployed minor, the hearing examiner would be required to award damages based on the average annual income in the state multiplied by the average work life expectancy, absent clear and convincing proof that the loss would be greater or smaller.

The rule of joint and several liability would be abolished so that defendants would be liable for damages only in proportion to their actual liability. In addition, any award of future damages, where the present value of such damages exceeds $250,000, would be made in accordance with a periodic payment schedule. Finally, damages generally would be reduced by collateral source payments.

Article 6.5

Liability Insurance Issues in Anesthesiology

James F. Holzer, JD. International Anesthesiology Clinics, 1989.

Will Rogers said, "There is nothing as easy as denouncing. It don't take much to see that something is wrong, but it takes some eyesight to see what will put it right again."

Denouncing lawyers and the insurance industry has become a conditioned reflex on the part of many health care providers adversely affected by the malpractice insurance crisis. During the 1980s, the casualty insurance market has had little encouraging news for physicians facing yearly increases in their liability insurance premiums at rates well above that of inflation.[1] The grim news was foretold in this publication five years ago when it was suggested that physicians could anticipate premium increases on the order of 35 to 40% annually.[2]

Although annual malpractice premiums have indeed increased at a significant rate, there is evidence to suggest modest improvement ahead for the medical profession overall and, perhaps, dramatic improvement for anesthesiologists. In the opinion of many insurance and risk management experts, anesthesia loss experience has improved markedly in recent years, thanks in large part to the foresight of U.S. anesthesiologists who squarely addressed the liability problem early in the decade. Although data are insufficient to statistically correlate risk management activities and improved loss experience, it is my perception as a risk manager and insurance underwriter that recent trends discussed in this chapter make the correlation a reasonable assumption.

James F. Holzer, JD, is Vice President of Loss Prevention, Risk Management Foundation of the Harvard Medical Insititutions, Cambridge, Massachusetts, and a lecturer on the Faculty of Medicine at Harvard Medical School in Boston.

Declining Malpractice Claim Frequency

From all indications, the annual rate of professional liability claims against physicians in most specialties is declining. Data from the American Medical Association (AMA) and several notable commercial and provider-sponsored insurance companies indicate that the drop in claims frequency began in 1985 and continued through 1988.

In its annual random sample of physicians practicing patient care in the United States, the AMA Center for Health Policy Research reports the average annual rate of professional liability claims declined from 10.2 per 100 physicians in 1985 to 6.7 per 100 in 1987 (Table 1). This means that since 1985, claims have been decreasing at an average annual rate of 19%.[1] A similar decline in claims frequency was reported by the St. Paul Fire & Marine Insurance Company (St. Paul), one of the country's largest commercial underwriters of professional liability insurance for physicians. According to its most recent annual report, claims against its policyholders dropped from 18.1 per 100 physicians in 1985 to 15.4 claims per 100 in 1987, the lowest such rate recorded by the company since 1982.[3] This trend has also been favorably recognized by casualty actuaries advising commercial and captive insurance companies on levels of required premium.[4]

Sharing in this favorable trend are anesthesiologists. According to the AMA report, claims frequency against anesthesiologists declined at an average annual rate of 21.7%, dropping from 7.5 claims per 100 physicians in 1985 to 4.6 claims per 100 in 1987. The percent of anesthesiologists sued annually also dropped from 7.5% in 1985 to 4.2% in 1987. The low-to-moderate claims frequency rate against anesthesiologists is also confirmed in a study by the U.S. General Accounting Office (GAO). It showed that, while anesthesiologists represented 3.5% of all practicing physicians in the country, they accounted for 4.3% of doctors named in claims closed during 1984.[5] Unfortunately, the AMA study also indicates that 32% of anesthesiologists nationwide have been sued at least once during their careers as of 1987. This compares with a career suit rate of 37% for physicians in all specialties and 57% for obstetricians and gynecologists[1] (Table 2).

Although the national decline in claims frequency is welcome news, physicians and insurers understand that these data alone are insufficient to predict long-term permanent relief. As will be shown, the severity of claims, their average cost, and the numerical difference in premiums among specialties are equally meaningful in determining a physician's future insurance profile—particularly for anesthesiologists.

Many insurance company representatives and actuaries agree that, although moderation in overall premium levels could be realized in future years, it may be premature to attribute the decline in frequency to any one factor. Indeed, a similar drop in claims frequency occurred during the period from 1976 to 1978, but it proved to be the calm before the storm. Some actuaries theorize that today's decline in frequency may be attributable in part to nationwide tort reform efforts that are causing a leveling off of so-called frivolous suits. Tillinghast actuary James Wood, experienced in the professional liability insurance market, indicates that more than half of all medical malpractice claim files are closed with no payment (58.4% for anesthesiology, according to the GAO). Consequently, he believes a reduction in the frequency of frivolous claims may have little or no impact on the size of paid claims, and thus no affect on the total aggregate cost of professional liability claims.[3-5] Wood also reports that there were nearly 100 tort reform initiatives during 1987 but only a handful in 1988. This could be significant, as there was a surge in tort reform proposals the last time claims frequency declined (1976-1978), and a sharp increase in claims and suits when reform initiatives tapered off after 1978. Professional liability insurance companies remembering the mid-1970's will no doubt resist the temptation to underreserve claims or underprice their product until the overall severity and claims cost show a similar decline. The "good news" is that such decline in cost and severity may already be occurring for anesthesiology in selected insurance markets.

Severity and Cost of Claims

Despite the drop in the number of professional liability claims against U.S. physicians, there is still no clear trend concerning changes in the overall severity and cost of claims. However, there are encouraging signs that malpractice jury verdicts against physicians may be decreasing. Nationally, the average malpractice verdict against physicians dropped 6% in 1987 compared with the year before and was accompanied by a significant decline in the number of jury awards of $1 million or more.[6] In California, where significant tort reform was promulgated in 1985, one doctor-sponsored insurance company reported the average indemnity for large claims (those closed with payment of $50,000 or more) decreased in 1987 by 31% from the previous year. Claims in excess of $1 million also dropped from 30 in 1985 to 12 in 1987, the lowest number of such cases since 1978.[7]

These reports are tempered somewhat by the fact that medical liability suits are among the highest verdicts compared with other types of personal liability legal actions. The 1987 decline notwithstanding, the average malpractice jury verdict against U.S. hospital and physicians in all specialties was nearly $925,000 (Table 3). And despite the drop in claims frequency, St. Paul representatives reported that their average cost per claims increased by more than $20,000 for the 1986-1987 period compared with a year earlier. The number of large losses for St. Paul policyholders also continued to increase, with 21% of its paid claims in 1987 alone exceeding $100,000.[3]

One reason severity figures from insurance companies continue to be high is that insurance losses typically combine the amount of reserves on open cases, indemnity payments on closed claims, and the (rising) cost of litigation including defense attorney fees. Nationally, defense costs are actually increasing faster than indemnity costs, according to one actuary.[4] Consequently, loss figures from insurance companies, although more conservative, may also be more indicative of market trends, since they incorporate projections of future claims costs.

Unfortunately, this confusing array of national data on combined physicians losses does little to clarify the liability insurance picture for individual specialties. Only when insurance companies look closely at

Table 1

Annual Claims per 100 Physicians by Specialty[a]

	Years			Average Annual Rate of Change 1985-1987
	1985	1986	1987	
All physicians	10.2	9.2	6.7[c]	-19.0%[d]
Specialty				
General/family practice	5.7	7.6	5.7	0.0
Internal medicine	6.2	5.5	4.5	-14.8
Surgery	16.8	15.8	12.7	-13.1
Pediatrics	7.2	6.8	4.5	-20.9
Obstetrics/gynecology	25.8	13.0[b]	8.0	-44.3[d]
Radiology	12.8	11.5	8.0	-20.9
Psychiatry	2.9	4.5	1.6	-25.7
Anesthesiology	7.5	8.7	4.6	-21.7
Pathology	3.3	1.9	4.9	21.9
Other	10.4	9.1	5.9	-24.7

a Used with permission from the American Medical Association.
b 1985-1986 change statistically significant at the p = .05 level.
c 1986-1987 change statistically significant at the p = .05 level.
d Total 1985-1987 change statistically significant at the p = .05 level.

Table 2

Percent of Physicians Sued Annually (1985-1987) and in Career by Specialty[a]

	Percent Sued Annually			Average Annual Rate of Change 1985-1987	Percent Sued in Career as of 1987
	1985	1986	1987		
All physicians	8.5%	7.6%	6.0%[c]	-16.0%[d]	37.0%
Specialty					
General/family practice	5.5	6.3	5.1	-3.7	34.9
Internal medicine	5.4	4.8	4.3	-10.8	28.5
Surgery	13.6	12.3	11.0	-10.1	50.3
Pediatrics	6.6	5.7	3.9	-23.1	31.7
Obstetrics/gynecology	20.0	10.9[b]	6.7	-42.1[d]	57.3
Radiology	11.2	10.5	6.5	-23.8	40.8
Psychiatry	2.9	4.1	1.6	-25.7	20.2
Anesthesiology	7.5	8.2	4.2	-25.2	31.5
Pathology	3.3	1.9	4.9	21.9	21.3
Other	7.5	7.4	5.7	-12.8	37.4

a Used with permission from the American Medical Association.
b 1985-1986 change statistically significant at the p = .05 level.
c 1986-1987 change statistically significant at the p = .05 level.
d Total 1985-1987 change statistically significant at the p = .05 level.

the severity and claims cost profiles of specific specialties can changes in the malpractice climate, which might be brought about by improved risk modification activities, be discerned.

Early analyses of malpractice claims closed between 1975 and 1978 showed that anesthesia injuries accounted for 3% of all paid claims but a disproportionately large 11% of all dollars paid out.[8] Nearly ten years later, although the frequency of anesthesia events as a percentage of total claims grew at a moderate rate, the percent of the total paid indemnity attributable to anesthesia declined markedly. In the GAO's 1984 closed claim study, allegations of anesthesia error accounted for 5.3% of paid claims and only 5.6% of indemnity payments.[5] National figures from St. Paul released in 1988 showed a similar pattern, with anesthesia allegations accounting for 3.5% of total claims during its 1986-1987 period and only 3.6% of the total incurred loss.[3]

Despite the apparent moderation in anesthesia claims severity, the average cost of an anesthesia liability claim remains high. According to the GAO report, claims alleging an anesthesia error had an average indemnity of $84,451 and had the largest recorded payment of almost $2.5 million (Table 4). Anesthesia-related claims were also associated with the greatest range of payments and had the highest percentage of paid claims by type of error (62.5%).[5] Anesthesia claims resulting from cardiac arrest reported by St. Paul during its 1986-1987 period had an average cost of over $116,000.

Although some of the favorable claims data in anesthesia seem to be offset by troubling negative information, there is a growing sentiment among risk managers in 1989 that the specialty may be turning the corner on its liability insurance problems. As will be discussed, liability premiums for anesthesiologists appear to reflect improved loss experience compared with many other specialties. Further, some provider-sponsored insurance programs, such as the one at the Harvard medical institutions, report a marked reduction in anesthesia premiums as well as in certain types of anesthesia loss, following the implementation of aggressive risk management programs.

The Risk Management Foundation of the Harvard Medical Institutions coordinates Harvard's professional liability insurance program for its twelve-member teaching facilities and more than 5,000 affiliated physicians. Prior to the spring of 1985, when the Harvard anesthesia department heads adopted the first set of clinical standards developed by its Risk Management Committee (RMC), the foundation had reported total anesthesia losses of approximately $5.5 million from April 1976 to April 1985.[9,10] As shown in Table 5, this amounted to a Loss Per Anesthetic (LPA) for the nine-year period of $5.24. Following implementation of minimal monitoring standards, anesthesia losses based on claims filed through December 31, 1988, and arising out of care rendered during policy years 1986, 1987, and the first nine months of the policy year 1988 showed significantly lower LPAs of $2.00, $1.84, and $.78 respectively. The average cost per claim also declined during the twelve-year period. For the policy periods 1976 to 1985, the average anesthesia-related loss was approximately $153,000. In the thirty-three-month period following adoption of the standards, the average cost per claim was approximately $34,000. (Subsequent to final preparation of the data for Table 5, a claim was filed involving serious injury in the recovery room following a 1987 surgical procedure. Since the suit was filed after December 31, 1988, the claim is not included as part of the Table 5 analysis.)

It is important to note that insurance figures on Average Cost Per Claim and LPA include incurred losses on open claims and are subject to periodic evaluation and modification until the claim file is closed. As such, so-called claims development factors, future changes in reserves, and late reporting must be considered when reviewing insurance loss data for specialties with small claims frequency like anesthesiology.

Insurance Rates and Premium Relativities

Average professional liability insurance premiums were considerably higher nationwide despite the decline in claims frequency. According to the AMA study, premiums for all physicians have increased at an average annual rate of 19.5% since 1985. The average physician's premium in 1987 was $15,000 compared with $12,800 in 1986 and $10,500 in 1985. For anesthesiology, the average annual rate of premium increase was approximately 13%,

Table 3

Medical Malpractice Awards

Year	Frequency of Plaintiff Verdicts Reported	Average Verdict Award	Rewards of One Million Dollars or More
1987	279	$ 924,416	62
1986	272	1,478,028	92
1985	233	1,179,095	79
1984	356	640,619	71
1983	322	887,938	69
1982	234	962,258	45
1981	186	850,396	45
1980	146	404,726	20

Reproduced with permission from Jury Verdict Research.

Table 4

United Stated General Accounting Office - Characteristics of Claims Closed in 1984

	Paid Claims		Indemnity Payments			
					Range	
Type of Error	Number	Percent of Total[a]	Median	Average	Lowest	Highest
All claims[b]	31,786	43.3	$18,000	$ 80,741	$ 1	$2,472,020
Surgery	7,235	38.7	25,000	76,255	108	1,616,185
Diagnosis	7,647	44.0	30,000	95,747	28	1,315,996
Treatment	5,291	36.2	12,500	42,316	1	1,000,000
Obstetrics	3,186	57.8	65,000	216,464	187	2,000,000
Medication	1,448	47.9	13,500	51,263	100	709,000
Medication administration	1,231	45.0	6,000	33,379	18	1,000,000
Anesthesia	1,699	62.5	1,500	84,451	20	2,472,020
Physiology/behavior monitoring, biomedical equipment, intravenous, blood products, and other	4,046	46.1	8,000	27,122	9	800,000

a Shows paid claims as a percentage of total claims within each of the types of error. For example, an estimated 2,720 claims involved anesthesia errors. Of these, 1,699 (about 62.5 percent) were closed with payment.

b Detail does not add to total because some paid claims were not classified by their allegation of negligence.

Table 5

Risk Management Foundation of the Harvard Medical Institutions: Liability Insurance Loss for Anesthesia[a]

Policy Period (based on occurrence)	No. of Claims	Approximate Insurance Loss	Average Cost per Claim	Loss per Anesthetic
1976-85	36[b]	$5,500,000	$152,777	$5.24
1986	5	210,357	40,071	2.00
1987	8	206,250	25,781	1.84
1989 (9 mo)	2[c]	87,500	43,750	.78

a Used with permission
b Includes "11 major intraoperative accidents"
c Includes claims reported during the first nine months of the 1988 policy year

somewhat less than the national average for all physicians combined. The average annual premium for anesthesiologists was approximately $23,000 in 1987 compared with $18,000 in 1985.[1]

The St. Paul Fire & Marine Insurance Company reported more modest rate increases for the same period. The average rate increase for physicians' policies, effective July 1, 1988, was 5.5% compared with an average 30% increase a year earlier. Factored into the 1988 rate hike were changes in premium relativity for different specialties, an average 2.9% premium decrease for basic limit policies ($100,000 per claim/$300,000 per policy), and a 9.4% average increase in rates for policies in excess of the basic limits. In their 1988 report, St. Paul representatives point to decreasing claims frequency as a reason for the rate moderation, but cautioned policyholders that premiums have to keep pace with losses. In other words, average cost per claim and aggregate losses for specific risk groups and specialties, rather than claims frequency alone, may be the key factors in determining premium levels in the next decade. The moderating trend in physician premiums appears to be continuing in 1989 as evidenced in a recent Wall Street Journal article reporting that St. Paul policyholders will actually experience an average rate decrease in 1989.[11]

If aggregate losses and cost per claim become driving forces behind insurance company rate-setting, then perhaps some of the best barometers of rates for specialties like anesthesia will be actuarial reports showing "indicated relativities" by class. Premium relativities are used by professional liability insurance companies to determine the statistical differences between the various physician classes and specialties based on their susceptibility to claims and the degree of risk of financial loss. In determining indicated relativities, an actuary evaluates such things as claim losses by physician group for a specified period of time, the number of "physician covered years," and the dollar loss per covered year. Each group is compared against the loss information for all specialties combined, and against each other. Assuming there is sufficient reliable data over a credible period of time, the actuary determines the indicated relativity, which is then weighted and used by the insurance company to ultimately determine the premium rate. It is worth noting that claims frequency is not directly factored into this report. Thus, the present preoccupation with declining frequency could be a fatal attraction to both insurance companies and physicians.

The final relativities selected each year by the insurer are eventually used to determine premium by class or risk group. Typically, physicians who perform no surgical, obstetrical, or invasive procedures are assigned a relativity of 1.0. Physicians insured by the same company and in higher or lower risk categories are assigned an appropriate relativity based on their loss experience. The premiums for these groups can then be determined and looked at relative to the premium established for the so-called Class 1 physician (having a relativity of 1.0). An obstetrician, for example, with a relativity of 7.5 pays approximately seven and a half times the premium of a Class 1 internist who performs no surgery.

Anesthesia Relativities
Examining the indicated and assigned premium relativities of anesthesiologists in different risk pools may provide additional insight into the changing and (one hopes) improved liability insurance picture of the specialty. For purposes of illustration, premium relativity changes for anesthesiologists and other selected specialties will be reviewed in three different insurance risk pools: the St. Paul Fire & Marine Insurance Company, the Medical Malpractice Joint Underwriting Association of Massachusetts (JUA), and the Harvard medical malpractice insurance program. Each insurance company or program's experience includes degrees of risk management and loss prevention activities in anesthesia.

St. Paul Relativities and Premiums
During its 1988 policy year, St. Paul made what it termed "the first major adjustment in rating classes for physicians and surgeons since 1985."[3] Consistent with other professional liability carriers, the company indicated that claims against some of its "lower-rated" doctors were increasing at a rate greater than those against traditionally higher-rated surgical specialists. This change may have been due, in part, to the shift in provider services from inpatient to ambulatory settings, as well as to improved loss experience. Anesthesiology appeared to benefit from this adjustment as well. The St. Paul relativity for the specialty dropped from 4.5 to 4.0, resulting in a premium level of approximately four times the rate charged an internist in Class 1. This represented a drop in relativity (not premium) of 11%. The St. Paul's 1988 published relativities also declined for other physician groups with the exception of Class 1 and Class 2 doctors performing no surgery and only minor surgery, respectively. The approximate premium levels after July 1, 1988, for St. Paul-insured anesthesiologists ranged from a low of $10,756 in Arkansas to $55,104 in Nevada for a mature claims-made policy with $1 million/$3 million limits. Ultimately, however, premium levels depend not only on the assigned relativities but also on the state or locale in which a physician practices, the limits of liability selected, and the number of years insured under claims-made coverage.

Massachusetts JUA Relativity and Premium Levels
In 1975, surging malpractice premiums forced many hospitals, medical societies, and state legislatures to find alternative ways to fund professional liability exposure. In several states, including Massachusetts, legislatures established joint underwriting pools that afforded providers a guaranteed market from which to purchase malpractice coverage.[12] Although the solvency of some of these pools remains in question, the majority of physicians (including anesthesiologists) in Massachusetts continue to buy their liability insurance from this program. In recent years the Massachusetts JUA has adopted more aggressive risk management and risk modification activities at the urging of its board of directors and the legislature.

After a thorough analysis of the Massachusetts JUA's losses, a new rating structure was developed and approved for phase-in over a three-year period. Due in part to the work of anesthesia societies on the state and national levels, anesthesiologists will benefit from an appreciable phased-in decrease in premium relativity, coupled with an incentive discount for participating in predetermined loss prevention activities. Anesthesia relativities (but not necessarily premiums) will reportedly drop 40% over the three-year period from 5.0 in 1987, to 4.0 in 1988, to 3.0 in July of 1989 (Table 6). JUA-insured anesthesiologists may also receive an additional 15 to 20% risk management discount discussed later in this chapter. Although the premium level for each specialty is still uncertain, the state insurance commissioner recently approved an 8.6% average increase for rates effective July 1, 1989. Under the decision, the average rate for doctors in internal medicine will be approximately $5,700 for occurrence policies with limits of $1 million per claims, $3 million per policy.[13] Assuming a relativity of 3.0, anesthesiologists would pay an approximate annual premium of $17,100. Risk management discounts could further reduce the premium by $2,600 to $3,400.

The Harvard Rating Structure
Anesthesia loss experience in the Harvard medical system has improved to the extent that anesthesiologists insured under the program will see their 1989 premiums cut by almost one-third over the previous year's rate. The assigned premium relativities based on historical losses for the specialty had a decline similar to that of the JUA experience. And although the Harvard program does

Table 6

Selected Premium Relatives for Massachusetts Physicians[a]

Specialty	1987 Relativity Harvard	1987 Relativity JUA	1988 Relativity Harvard	1988 Relativity JUA	1989 Relativity Harvard	1989 Relativity JUA
Internal medicine	1.0	1.0	1.0	1.0	1.0	1.0
Anesthesiology	4.0	5.0	3.4	4.0	2.5	3.0
General surgery	5.2	5.0	4.8	4.75	4.8	4.5
Obstetrics/gynecology	7.2	7.0	7.5	7.5	7.5	8.0
Neurosurgery	8.3	8.0	7.5	8.0	7.5	8.0

a Used with permission.
JUA = Massachusetts Medical Malpractice Joint Underwriting Association.

not incorporate any risk management discounts, the base premium for Harvard's Class 1 physician (relativity 1.0) will be approximately $1,000 less than the expected Class 1 rate for JUA-insured doctors. This should result in a comparably lower Harvard anesthesia premium which, for 1989, will be only two and a half times (relativity 2.5) the Class 1 rate. Further, the limit of coverage for Harvard-insured physicians in 1989 is $5 million per individual per claim and $10 million per individual annual aggregate.

As shown in Table 6, the numerical relativities used in the Harvard insurance program to determine the premium differences among various physician risk categories have been reduced in anesthesiology for 3 consecutive years. Relativities dropped from 5.2 in 1985, to 4.0 in 1986 and 1987, to 3.4 in 1988, to 2.5 in 1989. This means that, as of the new policy year beginning April 1, 1989, anesthesiologists (Premium Class 3) will pay an annual premium of $11,750—approximately half of what they would have been assessed in their 1985 rating group (Premium Class 5). The rating adjustments were in part due to the development and use of clinical standards by the Department of Anesthesia at Harvard Medical School, referenced earlier in the chapter, and to improved loss experience since the standards were adopted by the Harvard anesthesia chiefs in 1985. In comparison, most of the relativities for other specialty groups insured under the Harvard program remained constant or moderated only slightly during the three-year period. However, the aggregate premium level for all physicians did decrease twice as a result of the Harvard insurance company's favorable performance overall.

Moderating Influences

Although it may be too early to predict any dramatic turnabout in the U.S. medical liability insurance market, it is clear that certain moderating influences will affect the next decade of malpractice litigation. Although average premium levels continue to escalate for many physicians nationwide, rating and relativity adjustments based on historical loss experience appear to show improvement in several risk groups. A recent report by A.M. Best, a respected independent insurance analyst in the United States, described medical liability insurance as the "industry's most improved line of business," based on 1987 operating results of liability insurance carriers. The industry has traditionally used a so-called combined ratio to compare a company's premium receipts against its total losses and expenses for a specific line of insurance. A combined ratio over 100 indicates an underwriting loss, although investment income and other more profitable insurance lines may offset such losses on a company's balance sheet. According to estimates by Best, the combined ratio for medical liability insurance lines, including insurance written for both physicians and hospitals, dropped from 166 in 1985 to 121 projected for 1987. The St. Paul's combined ratio showed similar improvement, dropping from 121.8 in 1986 to 109.0 in 1987.[3]

The big question, of course, is what factors are influencing this trend. Unfortunately, there is considerable speculation but little credible data or research. However, it is my belief that the favorable trends reviewed here may be attributable to various programs and activities whose value at the time was also statistically unvalidated. It may again be useful to heed nonscientific supposition in identifying which activities providers and insurers should support during the next ten years.

Tort Reform

Articles on this topic in the year 2000 will no doubt continue to speculate on whether tort reform, risk management, or simply practicing better medicine has most improved the medical malpractice situation. There is, nonetheless, compelling evidence that jurisdictions with caps on noneconomic damages (e.g., pain and suffering, loss of consortium) are seeing reductions in average indemnity payments. Other reform measures such as malpractice screening panels and limitations on attorneys' fees may be discouraging so-called nonmeritorious or frivolous claims. As stated earlier, Tillinghast actuary James Wood and St. Paul representatives believe today's moderation in claims frequency mirrors a similar trend in the mid-1970's, which ultimately proved short-lived. Wood believes that extensive tort reform activity during the 1976-1978 period may have exerted a moderating influence on claims frequency back then and could well be a factor today. He cautions that the resumption of increased claims frequency after 1978 coincided with fewer tort reform initiatives.

Improved Risk Identification

Despite the insurance and medical professions' historically disjointed approach to coordinating malpractice loss data, attempts by both groups to become involved in joint risk identification and loss prevention activities have improved. Anesthesiology has clearly been at the forefront in identifying, analyzing, and addressing preventable loss through organizations such as the American Society of Anesthesiologists (ASA) and the Anesthesia Patient Safety Foundation. For example, a database of over 1,000 closed claim files for anesthesia-related patient injuries has been established through the work of the ASA's Committee on Professional Liability.[14] These efforts have encouraged other medical specialty organizations to conduct similar studies in conjunction with insurance carriers committed to risk management and patient safety. Fortunately, most nonprofit provider-sponsored insurance companies and commercial underwriters like St. Paul are now making it more feasible for specialty groups to enter into data-sharing arrangements with carriers. When analysis of this information produces risk management activities that demonstrably change practice and behavior, such as standard-setting, it follows that malpractice insurance loss will decrease, as appears to be happening in anesthesiology.

Clinical Standards

The development of clinical standards based on review of malpractice claims loss may be the single most helpful risk management tool available to the majority of clinical specialties. Anesthesiology has once again shown leadership in developing tools and strategies that take aim at recurring mishaps and thus enhance patient safety. For example, standards developed in part from claims information provided to Harvard anesthesia chiefs by the Risk Management Foundation helped precipitate the development of clinical standards for other specialty groups—both at Harvard and at a number of national medical specialty societies. As discussed earlier, Harvard anesthesia losses declined markedly following implementation of the first set of standards on Minimal Monitoring in 1985. Since then, the anesthesia Risk Management Committee has created standards for Anesthetizing Locations Outside the Operating Room, Apparatus Checkout, and Postanesthesia Care, as well as a protocol for handling anesthesia mishaps.[10] Other provider-sponsored insurance carriers have supported similar activities with anesthesiologists, including the development of clinical guidelines, the establishment of peer review committees, patient safety newsletters, and professional liability workshops.[15] Practitioners reluctant to participate in such efforts should bear in mind that even a *possible* connection between these activities and improved anesthesia loss experience is not lost on insurance company underwriters.[16]

Risk Management Discounts

Using the carrot-and-stick approach, some insurance programs, including the Massachusetts JUA, offer anesthesiologists premium discounts for agreeing to use such equipment as pulse oximeter and end-tidal CO_2 analyzers. Insured anesthesiologists must also agree to allow the carrier to conduct on-site audits without prior notice or approval. In return, policyholders receive a 15% reduction on their claims-made policies and a 20% discount on occurrence policies. Anesthesiologists would lose the discount and pay a deductible of $5,000 if a claim against them resulted in an indemnity payment *and* if it was determined they had failed to use both monitoring devices as they had agreed. These arrangements with carriers may become more common in the 1990s, but it remains to be seen whether such intervention is perceived by providers as a permanent and necessary policy or merely a temporary requirement to satisfy a third-party carrier.

Improved Claims Management

A somewhat disturbing finding in a recent study by Cheney[14] is that perhaps more than 40% of malpractice claims in which the anesthesia care was judged to be appropriate resulted in a payment to the plaintiff.[14] Although the author points out that factors other than the standard of care are involved in closing a claim with payment, it is clear that standards developed by anesthesia (and other specialty groups) need to be communicated with greater vigor to defense attorneys and claims adjustors than they currently are. In addition, there continues to be a need for better documentation of the preanesthetic assessment, perianesthetic course and postoperative recovery. Often the "facts" of the case as represented in the medical record do not adequately reflect the true facts as they occurred. Clearly, lack of adequate documentation contributes to the payment of medical liability claims on behalf of physicians who did not provide substandard or negligent care.

Patient/Consumer Orientation

Most health care risk managers agree that a sizeable portion of malpractice claims are precipitated by patients' surprise over unexpected adverse outcomes and by poor patient-physician rapport. Although it is often difficult for anesthesiologists to develop a close rapport with patients, it is believed that honest and courteous communication with the patient plays an important role in avoiding certain types of nonmeritorious claims. The process of obtaining informed consent gives anesthesiologists and other providers one opportunity to reinforce the patient's role in making decision about his or her health care and to help patients themselves weigh both the risks and benefits of treatment.

Shortly after the Massachusetts Supreme Judicial Court delivered a landmark decision on informed consent, anesthesia departments at most Harvard hospitals reviewed and updated their consent protocols and documentation procedures. A model form was created that spelled out the risks, benefits, and alternatives to anesthesia. Among the risks specifically enumerated on the form were injury to

---

Consent for Anesthesia

To the parent/guardian and/or patient: This consent form is designed to confirm the discussion of the proposed anesthesia you will receive during your proposed surgical, medical or diagnostic procedure(s).

Dr. ________________________ has explained to me and/or my child that a member of the Department of Anesthesia will administer anesthesia appropriate to my condition and will monitor vital bodily functions during the procedure(s). I understand that anesthesia involves risks in addition to the risks of the procedure itself. These risks may include adverse drug reactions, brain damage, nerve injury or death. Additional risks may include such things as injury to teeth or dental work, damage to vocal cords, respiratory problems, minor pain and discomfort, damage to arteries or veins, or headaches.

I also realize that the following additional anesthesia-related risks may occur in conjunction with the particular procedure(s) proposed for me:

____

____

____

Additional comments or observations:

____

____

____

I am aware that in the administration of anesthesia other unexpected risks or complications may occur.

This information has been explained to me and I understand it. I voluntarily give my authorization and consent to the administration of anesthesia by a member of the Department of Anesthesia.

Date: __________	Signed: ______________ (Parent or Guardian Necessary if Patient is Under 18 Years of Age and Not an Emancipated Minor)
Witnessed: _____ (Telephone Consents)	Signed: ______________ Patient (if 12 Years or Older and Appropriate

---

Model anesthesia consent form. From the Risk Management Foundation of the Harvard Medical Institutions. Used with permission.

teeth, damage to vocal cords, respiratory problems, damage to veins, and headaches, as well as other major risks connected with surgery (Figure). Although consent forms offer no guarantee of avoiding suits, they give anesthesiologists an opportunity to improve dialogue with patients and may well address some of the claims loss historically encountered in the specialty.

Conclusion

The medical profession is beginning to see subtle changes in its professional liability exposure, as evidenced by: (1) a moderation in claims frequency; (2) a decrease in the average medical liability jury award; (3) downward adjustments in premium relativities for certain "higher-rated" physician groups; (4) rating discounts for participation in selected risk management activities; and (5) improved performance of medical liability insurance companies with lower combined ratios. In certain regions and risk pools, anesthesiologists may be experiencing these moderating factors more than other clinical specialties. Improved anesthesia loss experience in some insurance programs appears to correlate with involvement by insured anesthesiologists in risk management and loss prevention activities. The reduction of anesthesia losses also coincides with the implementation of risk management intervention such as standards development, although studies have not yet been published that establish a statistical correlation.

As with much of the activity in risk management to date, loss prevention techniques will continue to be developed and implemented on an empirical basis until the database and time period are large enough to validate more scientific conclusions. It appears, however, that the physician specialties most actively involved in addressing the medical liability insurance problem from a number of innovative perspectives are indeed gaining the collective "eyesight to see what will put it right again."

References

1. Slora EJ, Gonzales ML. Medical professional liability claims and premiums, 1985-1987. In: Gonzalez ML, Emmons DW, eds. Socioeconomic characteristics of medical practice 1988. Chicago: American Medical Association, 1988:18-22.

2. O'Leary JF, Kahan R. Medical liability insurance: crisis revisited. Int Anesthesiol Clin 1984:22:117-131.

3. St. Paul Fire & Marine Insurance Company. Physicians' and surgeons' update. St. Paul, MN, St. Paul: 1988:1-12.

4. Rosenbaum DH, ed. Captive insurance company reports. Stamford, CT: Tillinghast, January 1989;1.

5. US General Accounting Office. Medical malpractice: characteristics of claims closed in 1984. Washington, D.C., General Accounting Office, 1987.

6. Jury Verdict Research, Inc. Current award trends, 1989 edition. Solon, Ohio: Jury Verdict Research, 1989.

7. Neupauer R. 1987 California large loss trend study/ malpractice. Oakland: Medical Underwriters of California, 1988.

8. National Association of Insurance Commissioners. Malpractice closed claims study 1975-1978. Milwaukee: National Association of Insurance Commissioners, 1980.

9. Eicchorn JH, Cooper JB, Cullen DJ, et al. Standards for patient monitoring during anesthesia at Harvard Medical School. JAMA 1986;256:1017-1020.

10. Eicchorn JH, Cooper JB, Cullen DJ, et al. Anesthesia practice standards at Harvard: a review. J Clin Anesth 1988;1:55-65.

11. Shiffman J. Medical-malpractice insurance rates fall. Wall Street Journal 1989 April 28:B1.

12. Holzer JH. Current concepts in risk management. Int Anesthesiol Clin 1984;22:91-116.

13. The Boston Globe. Malpractice rates in Massachusetts and other states. Boston, March 18, 1989, p. 27.

14. Cheney FW, Posner MA, Caplan RA, et al. Standard of care and anesthesia liability. JAMA 1989;261:1599-1603.

15. Pierce EC. Improving anesthesia safety today and in the future: steps taken by the profession to reduce risk. In: Gravenstein JS, Holzer JF, eds. Safety and cost containment in anesthesia. Boston: Butterworth, 1988:105-118.

16. Wood MD. Monitoring equipment and loss reduction: an insurer's view. In: Gravenstein JS, Holzer JF, eds. Safety and cost containment in anesthesia. Boston: Butterworth, 1988:47-54.

Holzer JF. Liability insurance issues in anesthesiology. Int Anesthesiol Clin. 1989; 27: 205-212.

Reprinted with permission from the author and Little, Brown and Company.

Annotated Bibliography

Malpractice Insurance

Crane M. *How much of a gamble is this malpractice coverage?* Medical Economics. December 4, 1989: 56-61.
Self-insurance trusts are distinguished from traditional malpractice insurance companies. Governmental regulations allow for lower capitalization for trusts, resulting in lower insurance premiums for physicians willing to assume additional personal risk.

Hunt WS. *Malpractice insurance: what can happen if you don't have it.* Hawaii Med J. 1985; 44: 209-210.
Article 6.2

Inglehart JK. *Compensating children with vaccine-related injuries.* N Engl J Med. 1987; 316: 1283-1288.
The federal immunization program providing vaccination for millions of children each year is a tremendous public health success. Unfortunately, a small number of children are injured by these vaccines and resulting lawsuits have threatened the supply of vaccines. A new federal law establishes a no-fault system of insurance for compensating these children.

Oldertz C. *The Swedish patient insurance system: eight years of experience.* Med Leg J. 1984; 52: 43-59.
An insurance official describes the cost and claims experience of Sweden's no-fault/patient-injury insurance system after eight years of operation.

Schwartz WB, Mendelson DN. *Physicians who have lost their malpractice insurance.* JAMA. 1989; 262: 1335-1341.
This article outlines the characteristics of 921 physicians who lost their standard malpractice insurance coverage due to poor claims history, loss of hospital privileges, or government sanction. They seek coverage through the "surplus-line" insurance carriers, which are described as well.

Schwartz WB, Mendelson DN. *The rate of physician-owned insurance companies in the detection and deterrence of negligence.* JAMA. 1989; 262: 1342-1346.
This study describes the disciplinary process carried out by physician-owned insurance companies and concludes that these companies play an important role in deterring substandard practice.

Smith R. *Compensation for medical misadventure and drug injury in the New Zealand no-fault system: feeling the way.* BMJ. 1982; 284: 1457-1459.
New Zealand's Accident Compensation Corporation compensates individuals injured due to accidents of many different types, including medical misadventure and the administration of drugs. Many questions remain unanswered relative to this no-fault system.

Socioeconomic Characteristics of Medical Practice 1989. Chicago, IL: American Medical Association Center for Health Policy Research; 1989.
This annual survey of non-federal practicing clinicians offers the latest figures on physician employment. One section is devoted to costs of malpractice insurance and incidence of malpractice suits.

Wilcox DP. *Possible claim? role of insurer and legal counsel.* Tex Med. 1986; 82: 70-72.
Article 6.1

Malpractice Reform

AMA/Specialty Society Medical Liability Project. *A Proposed Alternative to the Civil Justice System for Resolving Medical Liability Disputes: A Fault-Based Administrative System.* Executive summary
Article 6.4

Campion FX. *Medical malpractice: 'crisis' and reform.*
Article 6.3

Cooper JK. *Sweden's no-fault patient-injury insurance.* N Engl J Med. 1976; 294: 1268-1270.
Experience from the first year of operation of the Swedish no-fault system are extrapolated to the American population. Such a system would yield a greater number of claims but at an average cost per claim that is lower than current values.

Curran WJ. *Medical malpractice claims since the crisis of 1975: some good news and some bad.* N Engl J Med. 1983; 309: 1107-1108.
Attorney Curran summarizes the results of the first RAND Corporation report described below. He cites increases in both claims and malpractice insurance premiums of the early 1980s as evidence for a continuing crisis in professional liability.

Danzon PM. *Medical Malpractice: Theory, Evidence, and Public Policy.* Cambridge, MA: Harvard University Press; 1985.
Danzon compares and contrasts the medical malpractice problems of the 1980s with those of the 1970s with the use of data from her RAND Corporation studies (cited below). A critical discussion of reform measures and alternatives to the current system is included.

Danzon PM. *The Frequency and Severity of Medical Malpractice Claims.* Santa Monica, CA: RAND Corporation Institute for Civil Justice; 1982 Document #R-2870-ICJ.

Danzon PM, Lillard LA. *The Resolution of Medical Malpractice Claims.* Santa Monica, CA: RAND Corporation Institute for Civil Justice; 1982 Document #R-2793-ICJ.
These two publications represent the most rigorous attempt at analyzing the medical malpractice crisis of the mid-1970s. Their data bases include the results of closed medical liability insurance claims from 1970 and 1975-1978 in the first report and 1974-1976 in the second report. They describe the effects of the malpractice reform that swept through the country at that time. These reports can be ordered from the RAND Publication Department, 1700 Main St., Santa Monica, CA 90406.

Edwards FJ. *Medical Malpractice: Solving the Crisis.* New York, NY: Henry Holt; 1989.
Dr. Edwards gives an illustration of the current tort system by detailing eight specific medical malpractice cases. Inequities and the high cost of the system lead the author to endorse an arbitration system as an alternative approach to settling malpractice cases.

Halley MM, et al. *Medical Malpractice Solutions: Systems and Proposals for Injury Compensation.* Springfield, IL: Charles C Thomas Publisher; 1989.
The attorney and physician authors' main conviction is that the malpractice crisis is principally one of cost to society. They review systems in other countries and describe details of the Model Medical Malpractice Compensation Act which has been submitted to the Kansas legislature.

Hiatt HH, Barnes BA, Brennan TA, et al. *A study of medical injury and medical malpractice.* N Engl J Med. 1989; 321: 480-484.

Medical Practice Study: Executive Summary. New York, NY: New York State Department of Health; 1990.
This journal article and later summary of results present the finest information to date on the incidence of medical maloccurrence and negligence. The study was funded by the State of New York and executed by the Harvard School of Public Health. It analyzed 31,000 patient hospitalization records in New York state from the year 1984.

Holzer JF. Liability insurance issues in anesthesiology. Int Anesthesiol Clin. 1989; 27: 205-212.
Article 6.5

Manuel BM. *Professional liability: a no-fault solution.* N Engl J Med. 1990; 322: 627-631.
Dr. Manuel is a strong advocate of a no-fault professional liability insurance system. He describes the benefits of such a system, comparing it with familiar models of worker's compensation and no-fault automobile insurance systems. See also the accompanying editorial.

O'Connell J. *A new approach to medical malpractice insurance.* RI Med J. 1986; 69: 81-83.
O'Connell highlights four alternatives to the tort-based medical liability insurance system: two systems that could bypass the courtroom, a no-fault insurance system and a contractual-based insurance system.

Professional Liability in the '80s. Reports 1, 2, and 3 of the American Medical Association Special Task Force on Professional Liability and Insurance. Am Med News. October 26, 1984; November 23, 1984; March 22, 1985.
Together these reports summarize data concerning malpractice claims from the 1970s and the 1980s as well as the cost of insurance. They include discussions about the origins of the insurance affordability crisis of the 1980s and conclude with an action plan with 18 specific recommendations concerning education, legislation, tort reform, and risk management.

Reynolds RA, Rizzo JA, Gonzalez ML. *The cost of medical professional liability.* JAMA. 1987; 257: 2776-2781.
The authors have estimated the additional health care costs for which medical liability is responsible for the year 1984. The costs include professional liability insurance, costs of practice changes made in response to increasing risk of liability, and costs of incurring claims that are not covered by malpractice insurance.

Siegel Dr. *An overview of medical malpractice legislation.* NY State J Med. 1986; 7: 377-391.
This article includes descriptions of medical malpractice legislation enacted on the state level for purposes of malpractice reform. A table cross-references 42 different types of legislation passed between 1971 and 1985 in each of the 50 states.

Tancredi LR. *Compensating for medical injuries: is there an effective alternative to the tort system of medical malpractice?* NY State J Med. 1986; 7: 370-376.
Tancredi gives an elegant discussion of the goals of any system designed to compensate persons injured in the course of receiving medical care. He describes the inadequacies of the current tort system and describes a more fair and efficient system based on "designated compensable events."

Chapter 7

Peer Review

Case: Surgical Complications

An HMO's review committee discovers a high complication rate following colonic resections by a 45-year-old general surgeon. After an explanation of the review, the physician is questioned about his experience and asked to participate in a re-education plan.

Dr. Thomas is a 45-year-old general surgeon who joined the staff of an HMO two years ago. Prior to joining the HMO, he was a member of a private group practice. He recently received a letter from the HMO's tissue committee notifying him that a review of surgical cases had identified a higher than average number of surgical complications. The letter asked that he arrange a meeting with Dr. Marshall, chairman of the department of surgery of the HMO. Dr. Marshall explained to Dr. Thomas that the hospital utilization review department keeps a standardized profile of every abdominal surgery in the hospital. The profile includes indications for surgery, recording of informed consent, pre-operative and post-operative diagnosis, unexpected findings, instrument counts, intraoperative complications, post-operative wound infections, hospital lengths of stay, and other parameters. A review of Dr. Thomas' case profiles showed that he had an unexpected rate of complications with bowel surgeries. During a total of eight partial colonic resections over the prior two years, four patients had incidental splenectomies and three required re-operation for dehiscence of the bowel anastomoses. This was the highest complication rate for any surgeon on staff for intestinal surgery.

Initially, Dr. Thomas was angry with the report and denied its validity. He was defensive about his surgical technique and stated that he had no complaints from his patients or their families. He responded that the committee should leave him alone and review the record of a plastic surgeon who was recently charged with malpractice in a case involving complications after breast reconstruction.

His anger mellowed after Dr. Marshall explained that there was no blame being placed on him. The surgeon went on to discuss Dr. Thomas' prior experience with colonic surgery. Dr. Thomas stated that he rarely did major abdominal procedures, such as colonic resection, while he was in his former group practice. He mainly performed breast surgeries and minor abdominal operations, such as hernia repairs and appendectomies; a particularly well-known cancer surgeon in their group performed most of the colon surgery. Dr. Thomas stated that one of the appealing aspects of taking on his new position at the HMO was that he would have the opportunity to take on more abdominal procedures. His goal was eventually to perform at least 10 to 15 colon surgeries annually instead of the four per year that he had done in the first two years at the HMO.

Dr. Marshall acknowledged this goal and stated that the expanded case load would likely be possible as the HMO took on more subscribers. However, the chairman explained that Dr. Thomas' complication rate prohibited the expansion of his colonic surgery case load at the present time. He offered Dr. Thomas the option of assisting another staff surgeon on the next 10 colonic resections. Subsequently, his performance would be reviewed and a determination would be made regarding his readiness to perform the surgeries on his own. The chairman communicated his belief that this re-education plan was in their patients' best interests. He also reminded Dr. Thomas that the hospital had an ethical and legal obligation to review physician performance and take corrective action when indicated. The chairman told him that it was fortunate that no malpractice cases had arisen from the complications and that he hoped that the experience of assisting another, more seasoned colon surgeon would lower Dr. Thomas' complication rate and reduce his exposure to potential malpractice claims.

Dr. Marshall informed Dr. Thomas that the only other alternative was to prohibit Dr. Thomas from performing colon surgery altogether. This would entail sharing the surgical review data with the members of the medical staff credentials committee, participating in a hearing before that committee, and facing the possibility of having formal action taken to limit Dr. Thomas' surgical privileges. Given the options, Dr. Thomas chose to assist in the next 10 colon surgeries and submit to the chairman's periodic personal review of his intestinal surgery cases.

Discussion Questions

1. Is the type of surgical review that identified the high rate of complications in Dr. Thomas' experience common in hospitals? What other forms of peer review exist?

2. Does the hospital have the legal authority to restrict Dr. Thomas' surgical privileges? What individuals or committees within the hospital organization have the authority to review and restrict physician privileges? What are Dr. Thomas' rights or remedies in opposing such an action?

3. Could the HMO or the hospital be held liable for damages in a future malpractice case against Dr. Thomas if it did not take corrective action against him at present? If so, why? What duty to the patient would the HMO or the hospital have breached?

4. Does Dr. Thomas have to report the re-education plan agreed to when he seeks privileges at another hospital or applies for a medical license in another state? Is this plan considered a formal restriction of privileges or a "disciplinary action"?

5. Does the current re-education plan need to be reported to the state medical licensing board? Will it be reported to the National Practitioner Data Bank?

6. Could Dr. Marshall or the hospital tissue committee incur potential liability under the federal antitrust law for taking some action against Dr. Thomas? Does Dr. Thomas have reason to believe that the actions taken against him were done so in bad faith or constitute anti-competitive action?

7. What members of the tissue committee should review the data on surgical complications? Should it include surgeons? Should it be limited to non-surgeons who are not in direct competition with the surgeons being reviewed?

8. What laws protect the hospital tissue committee from a charge of violating the antitrust laws? What guidelines exist to help peer review committees avoid such an allegation?

Overview

"Peer review" has long been a familiar term within the medical community. By definition, it is the self-policing of the profession and, historically, it has been the heart of physicians' quality assurance activity. The process consists in an ongoing monitoring and evaluation of one another's professional performance, with the understanding that physicians who engage in peer review have a duty to restrict the activity of colleagues who endanger patient safety or quality of care. Particularly in recent years, peer review activity has come to evoke a spectrum of emotions, from a sense of duty to fear of liability and frustration with the medicolegal framework within which peer review operates. It remains, however, a responsibility that society has entrusted to members of the medical profession to discharge in good faith for the health of the profession and the protection of patients.

Historically, peer review was largely shielded from supervision or intervention from those outside the profession. Dramatic changes in the past two decades, however, have focused increased scrutiny on physician peer review. The public has developed an active consumerism regarding medical care, with many patients clamoring for access to physician credentials and detailed information concerning clinical expertise. A few widely publicized malpractice cases have suggested a glaring lack of rigorous peer review and an apparent willingness of some physicians to look the other way even when substandard clinical practice is evident.[1,2] Competition among physicians and a relaxation of rules limiting advertising have created turf disputes in local communities and between the different specialties. Expanded application to the medical profession of federal antitrust law by the U.S. Supreme Court has encouraged litigation in connection with peer review actions alleged to have been conducted in bad faith. Court decisions that allow plaintiffs to recover damages from hospitals as well as physicians have put pressure on hospitals for effective credentialing. Reform measures enacted in the mid-1980s include new state and federal laws requiring reporting of peer review decisions to strengthened state licensing boards and a national data bank.

The Peer Review Process

Identification of physicians practicing substandard care takes place in a variety of practice settings and typically induces a variety of formal and informal responses. The most informal may be the subtle reforming of referral patterns, for example, to exclude patients from an aging surgeon with diminished manual dexterity or from an internist suffering from an early dementia. Additionally, verbal reports to hospital chiefs of staff may provide an informal source of information.

Of course, more formalized procedures of reporting and review are in place in every accredited hospital as well. Credentials committees, peer review committees, and tissue committees exist for the formal review of physicians by physicians. Also, systematic "utilization review" of admissions and treatment procedures characterized as "outliers" due to excessive length of hospital stay or complications is carried out in virtually every hospital by the quality assurance department. Other types of case review, such as morbidity and mortality rounds, clinicopathologic conferences, and residents' reports, exist primarily for educational purposes, but also promote quality of care.

By way of hospital regulations and medical staff bylaws, every hospital has a procedure to grant medical staff membership and delineate practice privileges for physicians. Hospitals can also limit or restrict an individual physician's privileges. The most drastic available measure is to exclude a physician from the hospital staff completely.

To correct the problem of physicians being excluded from one hospital for reasons relating to quality of care or competence only to apply for privileges in a neighboring hospital, at least 37 states now require the reporting of hospital disciplinary actions to the state licensing board. A disciplinary or licensing board can then act to limit or suspend a physician's license to practice medicine within the state. To impede the interstate travel of incompetent physicians, licensing boards exchange information about disciplinary actions through the Federation of State Medical Boards office in Texas. A recently enacted federal law strengthens and expands such information exchange. The Health Care Quality Improvement Act of 1986[3] mandated the creation of the National Practitioner Data Bank, which became operational September 1, 1990. The Data Bank collects information on malpractice awards, adverse credentialing decisions, and disciplinary actions taken by state medical societies and licensing boards.

Every peer review committee should take certain precautions, which include providing a fair hearing procedure and the opportunity to respond to charges, to ensure that the process is carried out in "good faith" and not for an economic motive or a personal prejudice unrelated to patient care. In addition to establishing the National Practitioner Data Bank, the Health Care Quality Improvement Act extends limited immunity from the antitrust laws to peer review participants acting in good faith. Marva West Tan expands on these principals in Article 7.1, "Practical Safeguards for Peer Reviewers."

Hospital Liability

Tort law has historically imposed a duty on health care institutions to maintain safely functioning equipment and facilities and to oversee the competence of their employees. Nursing and other personnel on the hospital payroll are typically covered for claims against them by the hospital's liability insurance. Moreover, during the past 25 years, the courts have significantly expanded the legal responsibilities of hospitals to patients, particularly with respect to physician credentialing. Attorney William Smith outlines the court decisions that have shaped the expansion of the hospital standard of care in Article 7.2, "Hospital Liability for Physician Negligence." In particular, he discusses *Darling v. Charleston Community Hospital*, the 1965 Illinois case that established for the first time that a hospital may be directly responsible for the quality of care provided by members of its medical staff if it had reason to know, through peer review and other supervision, that a physician was practicing substandard medicine. Prior to this time, physicians or the medical staff were considered independent contractors, and hospitals were considered liable only for the negligence of their own non-physician employees. Cases in other states adopted the reasoning of the *Darling* case and extended it. For example, under the doctrine of "ostensible agency," a hospital now "may be liable for injury to a patient if the patient could reasonably conclude that the physician providing hands-on care was controlled by the hospital, and if that impression was created by or furthered by the hospital and if the patient, in some way, relied upon the impression."[4-6]

Today, it is also common for hospitals to directly employ and salary physicians. As is true for other hospital personnel, under these circumstances, the tort law doctrine of "respondeat superior" places the responsibility for physician negligence directly with the hospital. In this setting of increased potential liability, hospitals need to pay particular attention to the credentialing of new physicians to the medical staff and to the periodic review of physician performance through peer review.

Medical Staff Privileges

Although the ultimate authority for licensing and disciplining physicians rests with state regulatory boards, hospitals have substantial power to restrict the activities of incompetent, unethical, or impaired physicians through the granting of medical privileges. The AMA emphasizes the importance of staff privileges in its Current Opinions of the Council on Ethical and Judicial Affairs (opinion 4.07.1989).[7]

> The mutual objective of both the governing board and the medical staff is to improve the quality and efficiency of patient care in the hospital. Decisions regarding hospital privileges should be based upon the training, experience and demonstrated competence of candidates, taking into consideration the availability of facilities and the overall medical needs of the community, the hospital and especially patients. Personal friendships, antagonisms, jurisdictional disputes or fear of competition should be disregarded in fulfilling this responsibility. Physicians who are involved in the granting, denying or termination of the hospital privileges have an ethical responsibility to be guided primarily by concern for the welfare and best interests of patients in discharging this responsibility.

A thorough investigation of credentials is critical to this process. Most hospitals require letters of recommendation, proof of education, and valid medical licenses as minimum criteria for the granting of staff privileges. It is important that the documents be reviewed carefully and verified with their original sources.

Unfortunately, such thorough scrutiny does not always take place. Failure to comply with accepted standards of credentialing may expose the hospital to avoidable liability. This might occur if a physician on the staff is determined liable in a malpractice action and it is demonstrated by the plaintiff attorney that the physician was inappropriately granted hospital privileges outside his or her area of proved expertise. The American Hospital Association has developed the following checklist of the materials a physician should reasonably be expected to present when applying for medical staff privileges.[8]

- Certified transcripts of premedical college education

- A valid medical school diploma with certified transcripts; if the documents are not in English, notarized translations should accompany the copies

- Written verification, from the appropriate institutional authorities, of any clinical training obtained in U.S. hospitals; verification should include the name of the medical school granting the educational credits, the disciplines in which training was obtained, and an evaluation of the student's performance

- Valid certificate(s) from appropriate medical specialty certifying board(s), if applicable

- A valid and current unrestricted license to practice in the state, verified by the appropriate state agency

- A limited permit to practice medicine should be verified by the appropriate state agency; in most instances, these permits specify the institution and time period in which the physician may practice

- Verification of other state medical license(s), if applicable

- Written and telephone verification of prior employment/staff privileges at other institutions; telephone follow-up also may be appropriate; general letters of recommendation should not be considered an acceptable substitute

The *1989 Accreditation Manual for Hospitals* by the Joint Commission on Accreditation of Healthcare Organizations (JCAHO) requires hospitals to monitor, at a minimum, final malpractice judgments and settlements against members of the medical staff; JCAHO encourages hospitals to pursue more detailed information if desired.[9] Some states have expanded the JCAHO requirements, mandating that hospitals keep reports of open and closed claims.[10] Many hospitals already require a physician to report and explain any prior or ongoing medical malpractice claim against them; such reporting can be painful for the applicant. Questions frequently arise as to exactly what information needs to be reported to hospitals when applying for staff privileges. The recommendations of the Risk Management Foundation of the Harvard Medical Institutions are contained in Article 7.3 "Answers to Physicians' Questions About Reporting Claims Experience." Physicians should contact the credentials committee at the hospital to which they are applying for specific requirements.

The Health Care Quality Improvement Act of 1986, discussed at greater length later in this chapter, imposes additional information-gathering requirements on the credentialing process through the establishment of the National Practitioner Data Bank. This law requires that all health care facilities access information from the Data Bank on each staff member at the time medical staff privileges are first requested and every two years thereafter.

As part of an "Agenda for Change" recently announced by JCAHO, it will be re-evaluating and strengthening its quality assurance requirements in the coming years. The clear purpose of its publication of *Hospital Accreditation Program Scoring Guidelines 1989* is to ensure that hospital medical staff members are appropriately trained and practicing within the limits of their expertise. Table 7.1 is a list of primary sources from which verification of medical credentials can be requested.

Licensure and Discipline

Although requirements for obtaining a license to practice medicine vary somewhat among the 54 licensing jurisdictions in the United States (including the District of Columbia, Puerto Rico, Guam, and the Virgin Islands), the following general requirements are shared: (1) completing a premedical and medical education curriculum that is satisfactory to the board; (2) possessing good moral character; (3) completing a period of accredited residency training in the United States or, in some jurisdictions, in Canada; and (4) passing a written examination acceptable to the board.[11] Generally, physicians must pay annual fees to state licensing and/or disciplinary boards to maintain their licenses. These fees may be allocated directly to the operating expenses of the state board or may become part of the general state fund for allocation by the legislature.

Sometimes the licensing and performance monitoring functions of the state are housed in separate agencies; more often, these duties are discharged by a single board. There also may be separate boards for each health care profession (medicine, dentistry, nursing, etc.) or these functions may be consolidated. In recent years, licensing boards have been criticized for their failure to aggressively monitor physician performance and, where necessary, take action to revoke the licenses of incompetent or unethical practitioners. In many states, boards have been hindered by the lack of adequate funding and by inefficient organizational structures or operating procedures.[12] There is now a clear trend to bolster the funding of state boards and broaden their responsibilities. Some agencies have been expanded to include more members of the legal profession and the public to ensure that the interests of health care consumers are primary. Other boards have expanded their access to incident reports and other medical records from health care facilities for the purpose of investigation. In addition to processing applications for medical licenses, boards also follow up on consumer complaints and reports from health care facilities of adverse credentialing actions against physicians.

The tension between public demands for access and the need for confidentiality of information presents a thorny issue for policy-makers. Only in an environment where the participants are protected from legal action will individual clinicians and hospital peer review committees be comfortable with the disclosure necessary for effective policing of the profession. For example, if the board allows public access to hospital incident reports or fails to protect the identity of witnesses who prefer to remain anonymous, the cooperative efforts of the public and health care providers (who risk being sued for defamation or anticompetitive behavior) may be chilled. States must come to terms with this issue if the "bad doctor" problem is to be successfully addressed.

Some state medical boards have initiated programs for peer review, quality assurance, risk management, and impaired physician rehabilitation.[13] In Massachusetts, regulations require health care facilities to report certain medical outcomes to the board, regardless of whether legal action or the possibility of physician negligence is involved. Reportable outcomes include fetal deaths, maternal deaths during birth, and deaths resulting from ambulatory surgery. The Oregon Board of Medical Examiners sponsors physician education programs to heighten awareness of inappropriate prescribing practices and proper treatment of patients with substance abuse problems.

In Article 7.4, "An Overview of State Medical Discipline," Richard Kusserow et al summarize a 1986 study of medical board effectiveness conducted by the Office of the Inspector General of the United States Department of Health and Human Services. Between 1982 and 1984, there was a 62 percent increase in the number (953 to 1,540) of disciplinary actions against physicians by state medical boards. While the Office of the Inspector General found these results to be encouraging, Kusserow et al note that the rise was primarily due to increases in lesser penalties such as reprimands and censures as opposed to license revocations, suspensions, and probations. Also notable is that the majority of disciplinary actions arose from consumer complaints and reports from law enforcement agencies; only a small number arose from the professional review activities of medical societies, Peer Review Organizations (PROs), health care institutional peer review committees, and individual practitioners.

Antitrust Law: The Patrick Case

Peer review decisions can have serious consequences for everyone involved. The actions of a chief of staff, members of a hospital medical staff or peer review committee, or a person providing information to such a committee can as a practical matter terminate a colleague's career. On the other hand, physicians willing to engage in such a review may risk liability under state tort law for libel or slander, or under federal antitrust law, for damaging another physician's reputation or career. Antitrust exposure is particularly threatening because it carries the threat of punitive damages that may not be covered by liability insurers. Historically, members of the "learned professions," including medicine, law, architecture, and dentistry, were exempted from antitrust laws,[14] but a series of legal decisions have wholly removed this special status. To ameliorate the inherent conflicts that hospital peer review committees face and to increase potentially beneficial reporting, state confidentiality and immunity laws have been promulgated to protect physicians who participate, in good faith, in peer review processes. These state laws are not an effective defense to federal antitrust action because, under our constitutional system, federal law is supreme and, as such, it overrules state law.

In the highly publicized case of *Patrick v. Burget*, an Oregon surgeon sued several of his colleagues under the federal antitrust laws, alleging that a peer review decision that revoked Dr. Patrick's hospital admitting privileges was unfairly motivated by economic considerations. Dr. Patrick's colleagues and peer reviewers were also his competitors in the rural area where they all practiced. While there was significant evidence of instances of substandard care attributable to Dr. Patrick, there was also evidence of a long-standing difficult relationship between him and some of the peer review committee members. Initially, the federal court in Oregon delivered a verdict finding that the members of the medical staff did violate antitrust laws when it revoked Dr. Patrick's privileges. Punitive damages totaling more than $2 million were awarded against individual physician defendants, who appeared to have no applicable insurance coverage. Citing a legal doctrine known as the "state action" exemption, a federal appellate court reversed this decision on the basis that Oregon's state law regulation of the peer review process would be completely undermined if federal antitrust law was applied and permitted to overrule state law protecting peer review.[15]

On appeal to the U.S. Supreme Court, the appellate court was reversed on the issue of peer review exemption from antitrust law because, the court concluded, the state of Oregon had not displayed active participation in supervising the peer review process. This action by the Supreme Court does not mean that physicians participating in peer review are wholly unprotected by the law. It does mean, however, that peer review decisions cannot be made until extensive due process is accorded to the physician being reviewed, that such decisions must be based only on professional competence concerns and never on anti-competitive criteria, and that the federal courts intend to carefully review claims of improper or wrongly motivated peer review.

In Article 7.5, "Peer Review After *Patrick*," attorney Jack Bierig discusses the implications of *Patrick v. Burget*. He argues that as long as physicians act in good faith during peer review and take particular care to avoid any actions regarded as purely anti-competitive, they can then proceed without fear of antitrust liability. He comments that the doctrine of "state action" is too fiscally and legally cumbersome and not a reliable means of protection from antitrust liability.

Despite this opinion, at least two states now provide mechanisms for "active supervision" of peer review cases through their medical licensing boards.[13] Oregon hospitals may now request the state licensing board to appoint a special committee to hear sensitive peer review cases. In the first two years following the Patrick decision, the board reviewed four cases at the request of hospitals. In Colorado, the licensing board established a committee on anti-competitive conduct. Physicians who feel they have been denied staff privileges unjustly, because of unfair economic motives, must present their case to the committee prior to suing the peer review committee or hospital. These measures provide excellent support to physicians who serve on hospital peer review committees by lessening the threat of antitrust litigation.

Health Care Quality Improvement Act

When the Patrick trial court awarded an uninsured multi-million dollar judgment against the physician defendants, it sent a chill down the spines of physicians across the nation who were engaged in peer review activities. In response to this reaction, Congress passed legislation to help clarify and support the peer review process. The Health Care Quality Improvement Act of 1986 extends immunity from antitrust liability to physicians who participate in peer review in good faith to further enhance the quality of health care.[16] To offer guidance to peer review committees, the bill sets forth elements of due process, including specific notice and hearing provisions, that would constitute "good faith" peer review, although it makes clear that alternative due process procedures may also be satisfactory. In particular, it restricts from the peer review any physician who is in direct economic competition with the physician in question. In Article 7.6, "Health Care Quality Improvement Act of 1986," the AMA Office of the General Counsel has summarized the main provisions of the legislation. The law applies only to doctors of medicine, osteopathy, and dentistry. Physicians who contest a peer review decision with a frivolous or unreasonable suit charging antitrust may be penalized by the assessment of the opposing party's legal fees.

As previously mentioned, this bill also provides for the establishment of the National Practitioner Data Bank. The director of the

National Practitioner Data Bank recently outlined the function of the bank,[18] which, as of September 1, 1990, began collecting information on malpractice claims, adverse licensure actions, professional society membership revocations, and hospital privilege sanctions reported on every "physician" (including medical doctors, osteopathic doctors, and dentists). Any monetary settlement made to a patient must be reported, regardless of the size of the award. The method of settlement—arbitration, court decision, or out-of-court agreement—does not alter the reporting requirement.

State licensing boards must report revocations, suspensions, and surrender of medical licenses for reasons relating to professional competence or conduct. Health care entities that perform a formal peer review process (hospital, HMOs, etc.) must report adverse clinical privileges actions taken against physicians that are, again, based on professional conduct or competence concerns and longer than 30 days in duration. Professional societies that perform peer review must also report certain actions.

Hospitals must request data on a physician's profile at the time of initial privilege delineation and every two years thereafter. State medical boards and professional societies may, but are not required to, access data. Individual physicians will be notified each time a report is made to their file and will receive a copy of the report filed. They are not notified of queries to their file. A 60-day period will be allowed after each new entry to a file for a physician to formally dispute the facts contained in that entry. Communications concerning the reporting and requesting of data will be kept confidential by the Data Bank through the use of special forms and identification code numbers. The enabling legislation already has been amended to clarify that attorneys representing plaintiffs in medical malpractice suits will not routinely have access to the Data Bank. However, there continues to be serious concern regarding the confidentiality of the system, the data requirements, and reporting procedures. These concerns are being actively pursued by the physician community through organized medicine. The Data Bank is operated by the UNISYS Corporation under contract with the federal government.[19]

PROs

The term "peer review" has come to have at least one additional meaning. The federal government has developed a network of 54 "Peer Review Organizations" commonly identified as "PROs" to monitor the federally funded Medicare program. PROs were designed to fulfill section 1156 of the Social Security Act, which calls for a peer review organization to ensure high-quality and economically delivered health care for persons participating in Title XVIII (Medicare and Medicaid) programs. The express purpose of PROs is utilization review with the goals of reducing unnecessary hospital admissions, reviewing the appropriateness of certain high-volume procedures, and validating Diagnosis Related Group

(DRG) assignments.[20] The existing law permits the Department of Health and Human Services to impose a civil monetary penalty and exclude a physician from further participation in the Medicare program based on a PRO review of that physician's performance. Since the inception of PROs, considerable debate has developed over their principal objective—quality improvement or cost containment. In any interpretation it should be understood that the use of the term "peer review" by this federal program can more appropriately be described as "utilization review." It should not be confused with the more problematic "peer review," which is carried out by medical staff committees and licensing boards.

The Institute of Medicine of the National Academy of Sciences released its evaluation of the quality assurance function of the PROs in its 1990 report "Medicare: A Strategy for Quality Assurance."[21] It calls for sweeping changes of the current system over a 10-year period. The recommendations call for a transformation of the current PROs to the Medicare Program to Assure Quality or "MPAQ," centered around Medicare Quality Review Organizations. The stated goals of the MPAQ are continuous improvement of the quality of care, strengthening the ability of health care organizations and practitioners to assess and improve their own performance, and overcoming systemic and policy barriers to high-quality care.[21,22]

The job of peer review is a difficult but necessary one. It is important for physicians to know the scope of their peer review activity responsibilities as outlined by the hospitals, clinics, HMOs, or group practices with which they are affiliated. Effective maintenance of high standards within the profession requires that all physicians be cognizant not only of their contractual duties but also of the ethical responsibility owed to their patients, their colleagues, and ultimately themselves to be vigilant against practices that endanger patient safety or fall below accepted standards of conduct.

References

1. Lehman BA. Medical discipline: policing doctors: where does the buck stop? *Boston Globe*. September 9, 1985: 41,42.

2. Feinstein RJ. The ethics of professional regulation. *N Engl J Med*. 1985; 312: 801-804.

3 Health Care Quality Improvement Act. 42 U.S.C. §11101 et seq. (1986)

4. Reed ME. A hospital's liability for negligence. *American College of Surgeons Bulletin*. May 1983: 18-20.

5. Jeddeloh NP. The ostensible agency doctrine and theories of corporate liability. *Occurrence*. 1988; 10: 1-3.

6. Jeddeloh NP. The ostensible agency doctrine: more to the point than Darling. *Hospital Law*. 1987; XX: 40.

7. Current opinions of the Council on Ethical and Judicial Affairs. Chicago, IL: American Medical Association; 1989.

8. *Verification of physician credentials. Technical Advisory Bulletin.* Chicago, IL: American Hospital Association. September 1985.

9. *1989 Accreditation Manual for Hospitals.* Chicago, IL: The Joint Commission on the Accreditation of Healthcare Organizations; 1988: MS.1.2.3.1.3.3.1.

10. Massachusetts Board of Registration in Medicine Patient Care Assessment Regulations, 243 CMR 3.05(3).

11. Report on medical licensure: report of the AMA Council on Medical Education. *JAMA*. 1988; 259: 1994-2001.

12. Siegel DR. An overview of state medical malpractice legislation. *NY State J Med.* July 1986: 377-391.

13. Weinstein M. Pro-active medicine boards not just for licensing any more. *Observer.* January 1990: 1012.

14. Curran WJ. Legal immunity for medical peer-review programs. *N Engl J Med.* 1989; 320: 233-235.

15. Bierig J. Peer review after Patrick. *J Health Hosp Law.* 1988; 21(6): 135-139.

16. Health Care Quality Improvement Act of 1986, Public Law No. 99-660, 100 Stat. 3743, secs 401-431 (1986).

17. Hanson J. Conference Proceedings, American Medical Association National Leadership Conference. Phoenix, AZ: February 24-26, 1990.

18. Holzer JF, ed. *Forum* (bi-monthly publication of the Risk Management Foundation of the Harvard Medical Institutions). 1990; 11(3): 1-11.

19. Dons PE, et al. Peer review organizations: promises and pitfalls. *N Engl J Med.* 1985; 313: 1131-1137.

21. Institute of Medicine, Lohr KN, ed. *Medicare: A Strategy for Quality Assurance.* Washington, DC: National Academy Press; 1990: 1,2.

22. Lohr KN, Schroeder SA. A strategy for quality assurance in Medicare. *N Engl J Med.* 1990; 322: 707-712.

Table 7.1

Verification of Certain Credentials Can Be Obtained From the Following Sources

Exchange-Visitor Foreign Medical Graduate Program
Foreign Medical Graduate Examination in the Medical Sciences
ECFMG Certification
Educational Commission for Foreign Medical Graduates
3624 Market Street
Philadelphia, PA 19104
215/386-5900

Federation of State Medical Boards
2626-B West Fenway, Suite 200
Forth Worth, TX 76102
817/335-1141

Federal Work Permit and Visa Status
Local office of the Immigration and Naturalization Service

Licensure and Credentialing Irregularities
AMA Physician Masterfile
American Medical Association
515 North State Street
Chicago, IL 60610
312/464-5000

Medical College Admission Test
American College Testing Service
2255 North Dubuque Road
P.O. Box 168
Iowa City, IA 52243
319/337-1000

Medical Sciences Knowledge Profile
Division of Student Services
Association of American Medical Colleges
One Dupont Circle N.W.
Washington, DC 20036
202/828-0400

National Practitioner Data Bank
c/o Unisys Corporation System Development Group
8301 Greensboro Drive, Suite 1100
McLean, VA 22102
Data Bank Help Line
1-800-767-6732

Article 7.1

Practical Safeguards for Peer Reviewers

Marva West Tan, RN. Forum, September-October 1987.

Competitive pressures to demonstrate quality control coupled with legislative mandates to reduce malpractice are pushing medical staffs nationwide to conduct more meaningful peer review. Even with safeguards for peer reviewers such as the recently enacted Health Care Quality Improvement Act of 1986 and state statutes which offer varying degrees of protection from liability, peer reviewers are understandably nervous about possible legal retaliation from a disciplined physician. There are several steps that peer reviewers can take to reduce their potential exposure to claims arising out of peer review activities. These protections are basic but are often overlooked or incompletely followed by peer reviewers enmeshed in attempts to resolve a complex, sensitive physician practice question.

Quality as the Goal

In the majority of legal challenges to peer review actions, the aggrieved practitioner will allege that peer review activities were motivated by economic competition or personality conflicts, or based on discriminatory actions rather than a desire to improve quality of care. Don't provide a disciplined physician with any factual basis for such a claim. Flippant, off-the-cuff remarks about a physician's race, ethnic background or financial status have no place in peer review and may come back to haunt peer reviewers. Keep the focus of all peer review on valid goals: improving the quality of patient care, resolving questions about professional practice and correcting identified clinical problems.

Keep Bylaws Current

Too frequently the medical staff is not familiar with bylaw sections detailing its own peer review and disciplinary processes. Unfamiliarity with bylaws and discrepancies between written bylaws and current practice can create enormous procedural headaches when an unofficial department chairman or committee, i.e. one without bylaw authority, undertakes a peer review evaluation or initiates disciplinary action. Avoid these problems by keeping bylaws updated to reflect actual medical staff organization and functioning and any changes in local or federal law. Also, carefully read institutional and medical staff bylaws before initiating in-depth evaluations of a practitioner and certainly before taking any disciplinary action.

Follow Your Bylaws

Don't jump the gun and invent your own bylaws as you go. Frustrated medical staff members, particularly those who have been grappling with a knotty practitioner problem for months or years, have been known to take matters into their own hands and act without bylaws authority. Or, physicians may take actions according to the process detailed in their bylaws but without giving "adequate attention to developing a sufficiently objective basis for action."[1]

To avoid allegations that a practitioner's due process rights were violated, follow your bylaws, including all due process provisions, to the letter in any peer review evaluation and subsequent disciplinary action. Set up a procedural checklist and a paper tracking system to accompany the peer review process. The checklist should address the process, notices and steps required and time frames defined in the bylaws including a fair hearing plan.

Keep communications with the physician to be evaluated factual and objective. Neither berate the physician for poor performance nor assure him or her that a review is being undertaken merely to satisfy quality review requirements, i.e. give no assurances that there will be no resultant action. The latter may prove, upon evaluation, to be embarrassingly untrue and the former fuels antagonism and adversarial feelings.

If bylaws simply do not provide a good basis for peer review activities, then a major overhaul of bylaws is indicated. This may not be realized until a complex physician practice problem is encountered. Seek out legal counsel for clarification and interpretation of bylaws and advice on how to proceed while planning a bylaws update.

Avoid Locker Room Conferences

Restrict discussions of cases, events and concerns related to peer review to settings which take advantage of any statutory projections for peer review activities, such as peer review committee meetings. Resist the urge to discuss problem cases with colleagues in casual locations such as institutional hallways or dining rooms. Such informal meetings can bring the objectivity of the evaluation into question and may provide a basis for a legal challenge. Also, discussing sensitive matters in an uncontrolled setting increases the likelihood that confidentiality will be violated.

Select Unbiased Peer Reviewers

Choose physicians who are committed to an objective, independent evaluation to serve as the peer reviewers. Well qualified senior medical staff are typically selected to fulfill this role. Most medical staffs prefer to utilize physician peer reviewers of the same specialty as the physician in question for any initial clinical analysis.

To avoid allegations of bias, partners of the physician under review or physicians in direct economic competition should not be appointed as evaluators. Avoid selection of any physician who might have a conflict of interest, e.g. a close friend or relative of the studied physician. If possible, it is desirable that the peer reviewers not know who they are evaluating. This can be accomplished by obliterating physician and patient identifiers on photocopied medical records or other documents. To the degree possible, the physician evaluators should not be the same physicians as those who have raised practice questions, nor should physician evaluators also serve as hearing and appeal officers.

As an additional precaution against charges of bias or conflicts of interest, some medical staffs have recruited the services of an outside expert to assist them in peer review. Outside experts may prove particularly helpful to either the small medical staff or in instances where there is no local physician reviewer available, such as review of the sole urologist on staff. If the disciplinary action results in a hearing and appeal, and if local bylaws permit, consider the use of an objective, outside hearing officer such as an attorney. An objective hearing officer may be better able to keep the hearing procedurally on course. Also, an outside hearing officer may not be subjected to the same sorts of economic and political pressures as is a medical staff member. Also, in order to qualify for immunity under the Health Care Quality Improvement Act of 1986, specific requirements regarding the composition of the hearing body must be met, including the provision that the hearing officer and panel may not be in direct economic competition with the physician involved.[2] And finally, although there is always tremendous pressure to resolve practice questions, medical staff, governing bodies and administrative leadership should stress to peer reviewers that there is no pressure for them to arrive at any preconceived conclusion.

Base Decisions on Objective Information

To the extent possible, rely on objective documented information as a basis for the evaluation of practice questions. While informal polling of medical staff members may be an effective way to better delineate the nature of a practice problem, it may not be the optimal way to carry out an actual evaluation. Medical staff members may actively seek a way to blow off steam about a problematic colleague in such interview sessions. However, their short-term relief may be countered by an accusation from the evaluated physician of a biased, subjective review.

While the majority of peer review involves qualitative rather than quantitative evaluation, efforts can be made to strengthen objectivity, validity and reliability of the assessment. Use of criteria, standards, or guidelines developed by professional associations to measure clinical practice enhances study objectivity and validity. In evaluations based on medical records, data abstraction reliability can be assessed through reabstraction of all or a sample of the records. Likewise, peer reviewer findings and conclusions can be assessed for interrater reliability through "blind" double review of a sample of cases or other study data.

Recommendations for disciplinary actions should reflect the evaluation findings and be tailored to the severity of the problem. A wide range of possible disciplinary actions is available, e.g. counseling, monitoring, partial limitation of privileges. The options should not be limited to either a total revocation of privileges or no action at all.

Preserve the Practitioner's Dignity

Confronting a practitioner firmly but fairly with confirmed problems and a corrective strategy or disciplinary action requires skill and tact. On many medical staffs, one physician is acknowledged as the expert in resolving medical staff difficulties and is frequently sought out for advice when such situations arise. Because the manner in which peer review recommendations are presented to the practitioner may be a crucial determinant in the practitioner's response, strive always to employ an approach sensitive to the physician's dignity and self-esteem.

Move Beyond the Barriers

While hard data on the frequency and severity of claims arising out of peer review activities are not readily available, peer reviewers have a realistic concern that they may be sued by a disgruntled colleague whom they have disciplined. This fear has frequently been cited as a reason for not conducting effective peer review. Consumers, state medical boards, legislators and purchases of health care are no longer willing to accept this excuse. By taking advantage of all statutory protections and employing practical safeguards in all local peer review activities, physicians must demonstrate quality of care and take responsibility for improved self-regulation and self-discipline.

References

1. Thompson RE. Ten common errors in dealing with marginal practice. The Hospital Medical Staff. Feb, 1983, Vol. 12, No. 2, p. 5.

2. Health Care Quality Improvement Act of 1986, Pub. L. No. 99-660, 100 Stat. 3743, Sec. 412 (6) (3).

Tan MW. Practical safeguards for peer reviewers. Forum. 1987; 8(5): 2, 6.

Reprinted with permission from the Risk Management Foundation of the Harvard Medical Institutions, Inc.

Article 7.2

Hospital Liability for Physician Negligence

William B. Smith, JD. Journal of the American Medical Association, January 1984.

Once upon a time, the law recognized that hospitals were places in which physicians practiced medicine. The hospital merely furnished the facilities for the treatment that independent practitioners provided to their patients. If the physician's treatment was not up to the standard of care of the medical profession, he alone might be liable to the patient.

This article will attempt to show how our society — and American law — has departed from that former state of affairs. Hospitals have always been liable for their own negligence and the negligence of their employees. The hospital has always had the legal obligation to maintain its equipment and facilities in good condition and efficient working order. Thus, when defective equipment or supplies used in the hospital injured the patient, the hospital could be held liable. Over the years hospital equipment has become more complex, more powerful, and more sophisticated, thus requiring more careful use and maintenance. The hospital's exposure to the risk of liability has increased accordingly.

The hospital employs nurses and technicians and other personnel to work in the laboratories and treatment areas. If, as a result of their negligence, a patient is injured, the hospital can be held liable under the legal doctrine of *respondeat superior*.
This doctrine applies to all employers and holds the employer responsible for the negligent conduct of the employee acting within the scope of his employment. As hospitals increasingly have employed physicians to practice medicine in the hospital, their exposure to liability under the legal doctrine of *respondeat superior* has increased correspondingly.

Corporate Liability

Darling v Charleston Community Hospital, 211 NE2d 253 (Ill 1965) was probably the first case to impose liability on the hospital for deficiencies in the quality of medical care provided to patients by the independent physicians practicing in the hospital. Referring to the hospital licensing act, the standards of the Joint Commission on Accreditation of Hospitals and the hospital's own bylaws, the court held the hospital liable to a patient for substandard care provided by an independent physician who treated the patient in the hospital emergency room and admitted the patient to the hospital for further treatment under his care. The court held that the hospital had a duty to patients in the hospital to oversee the competency of treatment provided by independent physicians practicing in the hospital. Subsequently, a number of cases have recognized hospital liability to patients for failing to exercise reasonable care in granting hospital staff privileges to independent physicians and in reviewing the competency of the independent physicians practicing in that hospital. See eg, *Mitchell County Hospital v Joiner*, 189 SE2d 412 (Ga 1972) [failure to investigate physician's professional qualifications]; *Purcell v Zimbelman*, 500 P2d 335 (Ariz 1972) [failure to act on knowledge of prior lawsuits based on same type of surgery negligently performed on plaintiff]; *Ferguson v Gonyaw*, 236 NW2d 543, 550 (Mich App 1976) [court held that "[o]ne of the hospital's primary functions is to screen its staff of physicians to 'insure' that only competent physicians are allowed to practice in the hospital"].

In *Johnson v Misericordia Community Hospital*, 301 NW2d 156 (Wis 1981), a patient sued his physician and the hospital after the physician unsuccessfully attempted to remove a pin fragment from the patient's right hip. During the surgery the patient's common femoral nerve and artery were damaged. His right thigh muscles were permanently paralyzed, with resultant atrophy and weakness and loss of function. At the trial, the undisputed expert testimony established that the surgical procedure was not conducted in accord with sound orthopedic practice. The jury rendered a substantial verdict for the patient against both the physician and the hospital.

The basis of the patient's lawsuit against the hospital was that the hospital was negligent in granting orthopedic privileges to the surgeon in question because it should have known that he was not competent to perform surgery. The evidence disclosed that there had been no review or investigation of the physician in question when he applied for medical staff privileges at the hospital. The evidence further disclosed that the physician's application was inaccurate and incomplete. If the application had been checked, the hospital would have discovered that the physician's medical staff privileges at several other hospitals had been denied, restricted, and terminated on several occasions, including a limitation on surgical privileges at another hospital just two months before his application to the hospital in question; that the physician had ten pending malpractice cases filed against him in the local county court; and that the physician's peers in the community did not consider him to be a competent orthopedic surgeon.

In affirming the judgment, the Wisconsin Supreme Court made several observations that include some important advice for both hospitals and the physicians on the medical staffs of the hospitals.

> In summary, we hold that a hospital owes a duty to its patients to exercise reasonable care in the selection of its medical staff and in granting specialized privileges. The final appointing authority resides in the hospital's governing body, although it must rely on the medical staff and in particular the credentials committee (or committee of the whole) to investigate and evaluate an applicant's qualifications for the requested privileges.
>
> However, this delegation of the responsibility to investigate and evaluate the professional competence of applicants for clinical privileges does not relieve the governing body of its duty to appoint only qualified physicians and surgeons to its medical staff and periodically monitor and review their competency. The credentials committee (or committee of the whole) must investigate the qualifications of applicants. The facts of this case demonstrate that a hospital should, at a minimum, require completion of the application and verify the accuracy of the applicant's statements, especially in regard to his medical education, training and experience. Additionally, it should: (1) solicit information from the applicant's peers, including those not referenced in his application, who are knowledgeable about his education, training, experience, health, competence and ethical character; (2) determine if the applicant is currently licensed to practice in this state and if his licensure or registration has been or is currently being challenged; and (3) inquire whether the applicant has been involved in any adverse malpractice action and whether he has experienced a loss of medical organization membership or medical privileges or membership at any other hospital. The investigating committee must also evaluate the information gained through its inquiries and make a reasonable judgment as to the approval or denial of each application for staff privileges. The hospital will be charged with gaining and evaluating the knowledge that would have been acquired had it exercised ordinary care in investigating its medical staff applicants and the hospital's failure to exercise that degree of care, skill, and judgment that is exercised by the average hospital in approving an applicant's request for privileges is negligence. This is not to say that hospitals are insurers of the competence of their medical staff, for a hospital will not be negligent if it exercises the noted standard of care in selecting its staff. 301 NW2d at 174-75.

The Hospital's Expanding Duty of Care

In *Elam v. College Park Hospital*, 183 Cal Rptr 156 (Cal App 1982), a podiatrist was granted hospital staff privileges after an appropriate review of his credentials. Furthermore, the hospital's medical care evaluation committee regularly reviewed the charts of the podiatrist at its monthly meetings and never had reason to consider the podiatrist incompetent or not qualified to practice podiatric surgery. The podiatrist was selected by a patient to perform surgery, after which the patient sued both the podiatrist and the hospital, charging that the surgery was negligently conducted. The action against the hospital asserted that the hospital had a duty to the patient not only to select staff physicians carefully but also to review and supervise their work to ensure their competence.

The court agreed, finding that this duty arose from two sources. First, a number of California statutes and standards of the Joint Commission on Accreditation of Hospitals recognize the accountability of hospitals through their governing boards for the quality of medical care provided to patients. With regard to staff supervision, the court concluded that the hospital's duty to regulate physician conduct was implied by required renewal of staff privileges at least every two years on the basis of competency review and by required periodic review of the medical records of hospital patients. Although these reviews were conducted by "peer" committees of the medical staff, the court noted that the hospital was responsible for establishing the review procedures. The court found the second source of the hospital's duty in its changing social and economic role:

> The community hospital has evolved into a corporate institution, assuming "the role of a comprehensive health center ultimately responsible for arranging and coordinating total health care" [reference omitted]. The patient treated in such a facility receives care from a number of individuals of varying capacities and not merely treated by a physician acting in isolation. The patient relies upon the effectiveness of this "highly integrated system of activities. . . ." 183 Cal Rptr, at 163 [citations omitted].

The only negative aspect of the hospital's conduct was evidence that approximately 4 1/2 months before the surgery in question the hospital learned that the podiatrist was being sued for malpractice by a former patient for surgery performed in the hospital. The court held that the hospital has a duty of reasonable care to protect patients from foreseeable harm and refused to dismiss the patient's claim. In returning the case for trial, the court suggested several issues that should be considered with reference to the hospital's peer-review monitoring system. In particular, the court asked if the hospital should have conducted an investigation of the podiatrist through its peer-review committee when it learned of the earlier malpractice case. The court also questioned whether the peer-review committee had been negligent in its periodic review of the podiatrist's work in the hospital and whether, if the review had been more careful, it would have recommended revocation or suspension of the podiatrist's hospital staff privileges.

Conclusion

The extension of hospital liability to the patient for the physician's negligence does not reduce or diminish the physician's liability to the patient. The hospital's liability is additional to that of the physician.

The extension of the hospital's liability to patients for the careful selection, review, and supervision of the physicians who are permitted to practice in the hospital presents those physicians who are granted the right to practice in the hospital substantial personal and professional challenges. Not only must those physicians maintain their own skills and ability at the highest level of competence, but they must serve objectively as reviewers of their peers. In both instances the physician must bear in mind that the objective is to benefit the patient—all those who may seek care and treatment from the physician or one of his or her peers in the hospital. The cooperation of all physicians practicing in the hospital is needed to meet the challenge adequately. In doing so, physicians might be mindful of the advice of the Judicial Council of the American Medical Association. In *Current Opinions of the Judicial Council—1982*, opinion 4.07 states:

> **STAFF PRIVILEGES**. The mutual objective of both the governing board and the organized medical staff is to improve the quality and efficiency of patient care in the hospital. Decisions regarding hospital privileges are based upon the individual physician's training, experience and demonstrated competence. Physicians who are involved in the granting, denying or termination of the hospital privileges of other physicians have an ethical responsibility to be guided primarily by concern for the welfare and best interests of patients in discharging this responsibility. Personal friendships or antagonisms should be disregarded in fulfilling this responsibility.

Smith WB. Hospital liability for physician negligence. JAMA. 1984; 251(4): 447-448.

Reprinted with permission from the author and the American Medical Association.

Article 7.3

Answers to Physicians' Questions About Reporting Claims Experience

Peggy B. Martin, Marva West Tan, RN, and Sally T. Trombly, RN, MPH.
Forum, May-August 1988.

Now that more and more health care institutions are considering professional liability experience as part of the credentialing process, physicians are becoming concerned about their responsibility to report accurate information. In an effort to ease the reporting process, the Risk Management Foundation has provided answers to some questions frequently received from physicians about their roles and responsibilities.

What constitutes a claim?
The insurance industry defines a claim as *any* demand for compensation. A suit is further defined as any claim that has been formalized by the legal process. Distilling these into a working definition to guide physicians can be difficult. For one, the types of claims to be reported vary from one health care institution to another. One institution's bylaws may specify that only closed claims need to be reported; another set of bylaws may cast a broader net and require the reporting of all professional liability-related activities.

The Risk Management Foundation defines a claim as any instance in which:

- The insurer has been notified by the health care provider that an incident has occurred that may lead to a claim being filed.

- A suit for damages has been filed by the injured person (plaintiff).

- The injured person or family member has made either an oral or a written claim for damages, or a statement charging an insured with malpractice and demanding an investigation or explanation.

- An attorney has sent a letter of representation (other than a request only for medical records) to an insured or to the insurer's claims department.

- As a result of a loss arising out of clear negligence, the insurer has decided to approach a patient or family for purposes of exploring the possibility of a settlement and avoiding a likely formal claim or suit.

As definitions vary, physicians who are required to report their malpractice claims experience, should check with their own malpractice insurer/insurers and medical institution to determine their individual malpractice history.

What information must I report to the hospital?
State law may dictate what information a physician must provide concerning his or her involvement in a malpractice case. The Patient Care Assessment Regulations of the Massachusetts Board of Registration in Medicine, for example, specify that each physician must authorize his malpractice carrier to release information to each health care facility where he or she is seeking appointment or reappointment. Also as of January 1, 1989, the Joint Commission on Accreditation of Health Care Organizations (JCAHO) in the revised Medical Staff section of its *Accreditation Manual for Hospitals* will require "medical staff bylaws and rules and regulations to specify circumstances in which an individual is to report involvement in a professional liability action." The JCAHO standard goes on to say that, "at a minimum, *final* judgments or settlements involving the individual are reported."[1] Thus according to this, each institution's bylaws will have to include requirements for reporting physician malpractice history even if the state does not already set forth such requirements.

Because inconsistencies exist between these and other regulations, physicians may, understandably, be uncertain about which categories of claims are reportable and which are not. This is further complicated by a physician's fear that he or she may be unknowingly reporting more data than is required. Physicians should not assume, however, that they should report only negative information about their liability experience such as cases they have "lost," or cases that have been closed.

If your institution requires reporting on additional categories, a question of falsification or deliberate omission of vital information may be raised. Such situations are uncomfortable and could result in adverse-credentialing recommendations. Therefore, it is *very* important that physicians seek clarification from the responsible person at the health care facility where they are currently or where they wish to be affiliated.

Is it my responsibility to see that malpractice history information is sent from my insurance carrier?
In some states, as in Massachusetts, physicians are asked to sign a release to enable the hospital to obtain various information to be used for the initial credentialing or reappointment process. Such information includes data from your malpractice carrier, from other hospitals at which you already have privileges, and from people whom you have specified as references. While the hospital must make "reasonable attempts" to get all the information necessary, many hospital bylaws and applications for appointment and reappointment state that the burden of responsibility is on the applicant to see that all necessary information is sent to the hospital. It is important to recognize that physician appointment will likely be delayed or jeopardized if the required information is not all assembled. Therefore, a physician can speed the credentialing process by completing required forms, applications, and authorizations and returning them in a timely manner to the health care facility. In addition, physicians should check with the person at their own institution who handles institutional credentialing.

Mandatory Use of Malpractice Experience for Credentialing

Institutions which credential physicians who hold licensure in more than one state should be aware that the regulatory requirements concerning the use of professional liability experience in this process vary. In New England, for example, Massachusetts has detailed requirements for credentialing physicians (243 CMR 3.05) which include the gathering of professional liability experience.

The Rhode Island Board of Medical Licensure and Discipline maintains a confidential file available to licensed health care facilities in connection with the granting of staff privileges (as well as to the individual physician). This file contains physician information relative to malpractice suits, disciplinary actions, sanctions by third party health insurers, and felony convictions.[2] Use of this file, while available, is not mandated by statute.

New Hampshire's Board of Registration in Medicine collects information from the court system regarding both filing and final disposition of actions for "medical injury" and from insurers regarding reservable claims and suits in connection with the action.[3] Although the New Hampshire Board is required by statute to conduct an investigation of any licensee with three reservable claims or actions for medical injury brought within a five year period, there is no legislated requirement that the physician's liability experience be part of the credentialing process.

Maine, Vermont and Connecticut currently have no specific statutes as part of physician licensing which require the consideration of professional liability experience by the credentialing health care institution.

Variations by state become more relevant as the duty to obtain necessary information for appropriate credentialing is increasingly mandated by outside accreditation agencies and regulators, and supported by consumer demand and current case law. Many physicians, besides those practicing in areas bordering state lines, maintain dual (or more) licensure. This expands the potential sources of credentialing information available and can not be overlooked by responsible health care facilities.

Sally T. Trombly, RN, MPH.

This person, often known as the Medical Staff Registrar, is responsible for collecting all credentialing information and making sure each physician has met all the reporting requirements.

How will I know what is being sent from my malpractice carrier to health care facilities?
In states which require carriers to send malpractice information to health care facilities, insurance carriers may provide physicians with a copy either before or after it is sent. The Risk Management Foundation, for example, keeps its insured physicians informed by sending 1) notification to the physician that an inquiry has been made from a specific health care facility, 2) a release for doctors to sign and return to RMF before the Foundation will release malpractice history, and 3) a copy of the physician's malpractice history information that will be released to the health care facility making the inquiry. At the very least, the health care facility receiving the information should be able to answer any questions about a physician's malpractice history once it has received all the information.

What if I get confused and fail to report a claim?
Failure to provide a piece of required information may be the basis for nonapproval of privileges according to many institutional bylaws. However, because these reporting requirements are new, it is likely that errors will be made. Errors may occur if malpractice history information is collected from several sources (i.e., if you have changed malpractice insurance carriers, or if you have or are seeking appointment in more than one health care facility and in more than one state). To avoid errors of this type, be certain what information you need to report. If you discover you have omitted a piece of required information, call the person in the health care facility responsible for collecting the information. They should be able to tell you how to proceed.

How can I be sure that my malpractice history will be kept confidential after the health care facility receives it?
Peer review information that you send to a health care facility for the purpose of initial appointment or reappointment should be placed in your credentials file. This should be kept separate from a personnel file that typically contains payroll and other employee benefits information. Because this file, in most states including Massachusetts, is designated solely for peer review information and is used by a medical peer review body, such as a Credentialings Committee, it is presumed to be protected from discovery. (It should be noted that information about court decisions is already public record.)

It is important to note that these credentialing guidelines may not be applicable to all states. Because space does not permit a complete recitation of all circumstances or issues, it is suggested that you direct questions to the key people involved in the credentialing process at your own health care facilities, and to those individuals working for your malpractice carrier.

Physicians who hold privileges in facilities in more than one state and/or are insured by more than one insurance carrier should make a special effort to assure that they understand the reporting process and their responsibilities.

References

1. Joint Commission on Accreditation of Health Care Organizations. Joint Commission Perspectives. Vol. 8, No. 1/2 (Jan.-Feb. 1988) p. 9 (M.S. 5.3.2, and M.S. 5.3.2.1).

2. R.I. Gen. Laws Title 5-Chapter 37 (1987).

3. N.H. Rep. Stat. Ann. Chapter 329:17. (1986 Amendment).

Martin PB et al. Answers to physicians' questions about reporting claims experience. Forum. 1988; 9(3-4): 2-3.

Reprinted with permission from the Risk Management Foundation of the Harvard Medical Institutions, Inc.

Article 7.4

An Overview of State Medical Discipline

Richard P. Kusserow, Elisabeth A. Handley, MPA, and Mark Yessian, PhD.
Journal of the American Medical Association, February 1987.

The Office of Inspector General's responsibility for financially penalizing and excluding health care professionals from Medicare and Medicaid participation led to an interest in examining the state medical boards' licensure and discipline processes. This article discusses the results of the subsequent study and focuses only on medical discipline issues. We found that the rate of disciplinary actions taken by boards has been increasing. However, revocations and suspensions, the most serious category of actions, have remained relatively constant. Additionally, consumers and law enforcement agencies are the most active sources of possible violations. Individual health care professionals, hospitals, peer review organizations, and medical societies provide strikingly few reports. To rectify these problems, we encourage states to increase physician license renewal fees to fund expansion and improvement of boards' enforcement activities and to consider ways to limit the legal liability of those making good faith referrals.

In the two decades following the advent of the Medicare program, we have observed state medical boards undergoing great change. Their responsibilities have expanded tremendously from the licensure and discipline of physicians to include a growing number of other health care professionals such as nurses, podiatrists, physician assistants, physical therapists, and emergency medical technicians. Additionally, consumer awareness has grown with a concomitant rise in consumer reporting to state boards. These factors have resulted in an increasing work load.

Boards are increasingly strained to handle the growing disciplinary work load before them. It is not uncommon for them to have backlogs of hundreds of cases pending assignment while investigators are weighed down with active caseloads of 60 to 70 or more cases. Board officials offered a number of factors that have contributed to this. Not only must they regulate more professions, they must also deal with a rising number of cases due to an increase in consumer complaints, more active law enforcement involving physicians, and mandated reporting of malpractice cases in some states.

Little Rise in Board Resources

In response to their expanded responsibilities and work loads, nearly all states have been raising their fees in recent years. In most states, medical board revenues derive entirely from fees imposed on physicians. Two thirds of this fee income comes from renewal fees paid by licensed physicians. The remainder is from fees charged to those seeking licensure on the basis of a license held in another state or endorsement of a certificate received from the National Board of Medical Examiners. Boards are typically part of the state budget process and subject to the same budgetary and personnel controls as other state agencies.

Renewal fees, usually good for two to three years, have increased from an average annual level of about $31 in 1979 to $51 in 1985. (These data were obtained from annual reviews done by the American Medical Association and from a state-by-state survey conducted by the Office of Inspector General.) However, they have barely kept pace with inflation. Moreover, many state boards are not necessarily allowed to spend all the money they collect from fees. Instead, this money goes into the state's general revenue funds.

Severe budgetary constraints are precluding boards from enhancing the number or quality of investigators and from taking better advantage of computer technology that could improve their productivity. Laborious and costly procedures geared to quieter times, long since past, contribute to the time and complexity of internal review and due process hearings.

Combined, these factors leave boards in an extremely vulnerable position, with investigatory and administrative resources well below the level necessary to handle the job before them effectively. Thus, although medical licensure and discipline is about a $50 million a year enterprise, many board officials feel as though they can make only limited progress in improving their licensing and disciplining performance. (This estimate is based on a 50-state survey done by the Office of the Inspector General.)

Inspector General's Role

In the last few years, the involvement of the Office of Inspector General of the US Department of Health and Human Services (DHHS) in a number of activities made it increasingly aware of the limitations within which state medical boards were operating. The Inspector General is charged by law with the responsibility of policing the Medicare and Medicaid programs for fraud and abuse.

From the scandals involving fraudulent medical credentials from two Caribbean medical schools, it became apparent that the credentials verification capabilities of most states might be seriously flawed. Because of the Office of Inspector General's role in prosecuting criminal cases and imposing exclusions on hundreds of health care providers, it was also clear that communication between those in a position to witness unprofessional practice and those with the authority to do something about it was inadequate. In many cases, information about practitioners with recurrent cases of misbehavior or malpractice never reached medical boards.

The Office of Inspector General became aware of loopholes through which poor health care providers could slip. Many physicians under investigation would voluntarily surrender their licenses in one state and then would continue practicing medicine by moving to another state where they also had a license. Under current law, the Office of Inspector General found that it had no authority to exclude these physicians from Medicare and Medicaid participation except in the state in which the license had been initially revoked or suspended.

Given these developments, our responsibility for financially penalizing and excluding from Medicare and Medicaid participation health care professionals who have committed fraud or abused our programs and beneficiaries, the Inspector General's Office conducted a program inspection. Its purpose was to help DHHS and other interested parties gain a broadly based and up-to-date overview of state medical licensure and discipline and to recommend possible solutions to alleviate problems we discovered. The study specifically examined pressures being exerted on licensure and discipline processes, the changes taking place, and the effects being achieved.

The study took place between July 1985 and March 1986 and involved visits to 14 states, where we met with medical board officials and many others, including representatives of medical societies, hospitals, and peer review organizations (PROs). We also had telephone discussions with medical board directors in another ten states, and met with representatives of the American Medical Association, the Federation of State Medical Boards (FSMB), the American Association of Medical Colleges, the Educational Commission for Foreign Medical Graduates, and other major national organizations concerned with medical licensure and discipline. Altogether, the states we visited or had telephone discussions with account for 72% of the physicians licensed in the United States.[1]

While our study addressed medical licensure and discipline, this brief article focuses only on the latter. It provides an overview of the study's major findings concerning medical discipline and then offers a few concluding observations and recommendations.

Other Forces Influencing Boards

Boards have had to contend with increased work loads and responsibilities without a concomitant real increase in resources. There are several other significant factors that have played a role in states' abilities to license and discipline physicians.

Foreign Medical Graduates

First among these is the factor of foreign medical graduates (FMGs), about half of whom are Americans. There have always been foreign medical schools for American students to attend and foreign medical students who were interested in doing their residency training in the United States. Largely because of the discovery of "phony doctor" networks and the establishment of proprietary foreign medical schools geared to US citizens in the Caribbean basin, state boards became increasingly interested in the adequacy of education received by FMGs. As one state board executive director said, "The quality of the education being received by FMGs is a much bigger issue than the phony credential one. It is an issue that is less within our control. And one that is not confined to the Caribbean schools."

While they noted that there are a number of excellent foreign schools, board officials stressed that many of the schools, especially the newer ones, are far inferior to US and Canadian medical schools, which undergo accreditation. They expressed particular concern about inadequate clinical training and minimal admission requirements.[2,3]

Meanwhile, the number of FMGs receiving initial state licenses was rising, from 3131 in 1981 to 4753 in 1983. This represented an increase from 16.6% to 23.1% of all those receiving initial licenses. Although this level was well below the peak year of 1973, when 7419 FMGs (44.5%) were granted initial licenses, the resumption of growth contributed to the uneasiness being felt by many state board officials. (Licensing data were obtained from the American Medical Association.)

While many have been questioning the adequacy of education received by FMGs, the federal government has continued to subsidize some FMGs, education by granting US Department of Education and Veterans Administration loans to students attending questionable foreign schools. In addition, Medicare funding for residency training of FMGs (as well as graduates of US medical schools) continues.

Because of these concerns, boards began devoting significant resources to addressing the adequacy of education received by FMGs. In fact, a few states (such as California, New York, and New Jersey) have visited foreign schools to assess their quality. By 1983 and 1984, in the states accounting for the great majority of practicing physicians in the United States, the licensing of FMGs had become the premier policy issue facing the state medical boards. Discipline, which typically accounts for two to three times greater expenditures than licensing, remained an area of concern, but was overshadowed by the FMG problem.

Changed Public Perception and Malpractice

In recent years, public perception about the adequacy of board disciplinary actions has shifted. Newspaper exposes have berated boards for not better protecting the public. Headlines scream, "Doctor Sued 14 Times, But No State Hearing," (*Chicago Tribune*, May 10, 1982, p1) and "Doctors Practice While Wheels Turn" (*Detroit Free Press*, April 1, 1984, p 11a). (The Detroit Free Press' examination was a particularly extensive one. It led to a seven-part report published between April 1 and 8, 1984.) This has placed a lot of pressure on boards to examine their practices.

The editor of the *New England Journal of Medicine*, Arnold S. Relman, MD, expressed this view in a March 1985 editorial: "All the evidence suggests that most if not all the States have been too lax—not too strict—in their enforcement of medical professional standards."[4]

The public is also frustrated with the length of time that due process takes, and blames boards for "dragging their feet" on cases. As one high-level official noted, "The public perceives that bad doctors shouldn't be practicing medicine, but we must give these doctors due process. Not everyone understands this."

Physicians' status in society has also been eroding, partially as a result of the liability crisis as it relates to malpractice claims. Many Americans' view of physicians has shifted from reverence to questioning. Indeed, a large number of patients who feel they have been wronged by physicians have been willing to litigate in increasing numbers, with higher dollar awards made by courts and the skyrocketing cost of liability insurance. All of this has put renewed pressure on state medical boards to "weed out" bad doctors.

Organizational Changes

Boards have experienced other significant changes in recent years in addition to rising work loads greater than the resources to deal with them. Both the organizational structure and size of boards have changed.

While in 1969, only 16 boards were housed under the aegis of a central agency, currently 31 of them are. This has both advantages and disadvantages. While under the aegis of a central agency, a board has greater protection against lawsuits that have a chilling effect, but may have a harder time competing for scarce resources than if it stands alone. Boards have broadened their base, with nearly all boards now having at least one or two nonphysician members, whereas one half had none in 1965. The size of the boards has also increased, with board members finding it necessary to devote considerably more time to the role than did their predecessors, at greater personal sacrifice to their own practices. Paid an average per diem of only about $50, these members are typically appointed by the governor for terms of three to six years. In the more populated states, board members often spend at least 30 days per year on board business.

State Boards' Response

State boards have reacted to burgeoning work loads and pressures. Recently, states have strengthened the investigatory powers of boards (for instance, the granting of subpoena powers); expanded their disciplinary authorities (most notably, the authorization to immediately suspend physicians posing a "clear and present danger" to the public); widening their access to disciplinary actions taken in other places (through mandatory reporting laws); and broadened the grounds on which they can take disciplinary action. The latter development, following an earlier wave of such activity in the 1970s, has led to more detailed specifications of unprofessional conduct, covering such matters as sexual abuse, incompetence, and violations of controlled substance laws. Since 1982, at least 20 states have amended their laws to clarify the grounds on which physicians can be disciplined.

States' responses to overworked investigators and board members have focused mainly on ways of easing the burden on board members. Among the changes instituted are allowing boards to draw on the work of hearing officers, to delegate the conduct of hearings to individual members, and to hire medical or legal consultants to help guide the use of investigatory resources. In Colorado, a change that splits board members' time between inquiry and hearing panels appears to be especially promising.

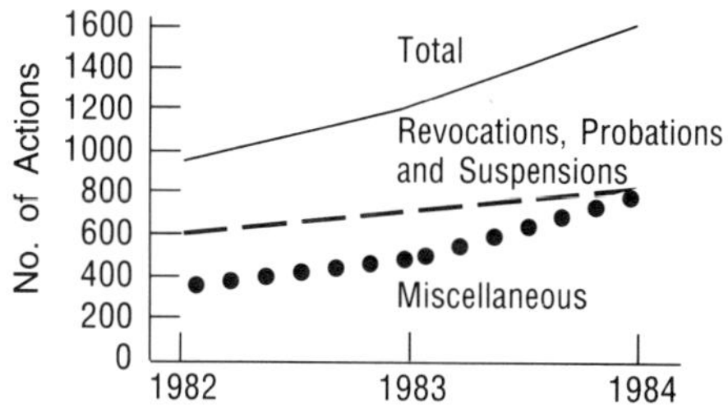

Trends in selected categories of state disciplinary actions from 1982 through 1984. Source: Federation of State Medical Boards

Incidence of Disciplinary Actions

Over the past few years, the number of disciplinary actions taken against physicians has been increasing. National tabulations made by the FSMB reveal an increase of 62% in actions (excluding simple administrative actions), from 953 in 1982 to 1540 in 1984 (Figure). (The numbers used for 1982 and 1983 are unofficial FSMB figures.)

However, a closer look at the Figure indicates that the most serious actions, such as revocations, suspensions, and probations, have not grown nearly as much as the other actions, increasing only slightly from 600 in 1982 to 788 in 1984. This has occurred despite the fact that approximately 15,000 to 20,000 new physicians enter practice each year. The miscellaneous or tier-2 category accounts for the bulk of the increase and includes reprimands, censures, and stipulated agreements. Indeed, it is likely that the increase in this category is even greater than the FSMB's summary suggests, because many stipulated (or plea bargain) agreements are made on a confidential basis, with the information not reported to the FSMB.

Some observers have dismissed these second-tier actions, which are often handled in informal proceedings, as being relatively inconsequential. In actuality, however, they are often quite significant and may involve a voluntary surrender of license for a period of time or a restriction of prescription privileges. Moreover, these actions represent a practical response by boards faced with insufficient investigatory resources and the memory of the many costly cases that have lingered during the hearing and judicial process for years while the physician involved has continued to practice. Unfortunately, it has also masked many serious cases and has permitted many physicians to continue practicing who would otherwise have lost their licenses.

Types of Violations

The inappropriate writing of prescriptions is by far the most common violation on which disciplinary actions are based, accounting for about one half of all actions taken by state boards. These are serious matters involving not only excessive or unnecessary prescribing of drugs to patients, but also unlawful distribution to drug addicts. They are also the easiest kinds of cases for investigators to develop, especially in states with triplicate prescription laws.

The second major type of violation is the self-abuse of drugs and/or alcohol. In most states, this category is expanding, both in absolute and proportionate terms. Together with overprescribing, it accounts for three fourths or more of all disciplinary actions.

Throughout the nation, programs designed to help impaired physicians have been expanding and receiving increased attention. Typically these programs are run by medical societies or other private organizations. While the exact approaches vary, they generally involve group sessions, signed agreements stipulating the terms of participation, and periodic monitoring to ensure that participating physicians are adhering to the agreements. Some programs, such as the one in Oregon, stress inpatient care, while others focus on outpatient treatment.

While these programs have been generally well received, they have met with some criticism and skepticism. Some interested parties are concerned about physicians being treated too sympathetically for behavior that can be harmful to their patients. The result in some states has been a tightening of monitoring practices and a closer examination of the responsibilities these programs have to report violations to the boards. Since a substantial number of physicians have enrolled in these programs voluntarily (without any board involvement), the issue of reporting violations to the boards has become an especially sensitive one because physicians signed up with the understanding that their participation would be confidential.

The remaining types of violations underlying disciplinary actions cover a wide range. Among the most prominent are cases involving conviction for a felony or fraud. Much less prominent are cases involving incompetency or sexual abuse, which are among the most difficult kinds of cases to develop.

The minimal response in the area of physician incompetency is placing boards in an increasingly untenable position as the incidence of malpractice cases and public concern about the implications of these cases increase. As noted before, it is increasingly believed that boards can and should do something about this situation.

Why, then, the minimal response to date? At least three factors seem to be involved: (1) the complexity, length, and cost of cases concerning alleged incompetence, even where a malpractice judgment has been rendered; (2) the substantial burden of proof that tends to call for the "clear and convincing" evidence rather than the "preponderance of evidence"; and (3) the considerable variations among physicians themselves about what constitutes acceptable practice in many facets of medicine. One board's executive director summed up his frustrations in this area by noting:

> We just can't seem to do anything with malpractice. In fact, we've never had a disciplinary action based on malpractice. It's such tender legal ground, even though we have a statute. So when there is a malpractice case, we tend to look for another basis for disciplinary action.

Yet, in the course of addressing rising malpractice costs, some states are taking initiatives that could prove to be consequential. Particularly noteworthy are two amendments Wisconsin made in 1985 to its medical practice act. One allows for a court finding of physician negligence in patient care to serve as conclusive evidence that a physician is guilty of negligence of treatment. This frees the board from the need to hold a probable cause hearing in such cases. Another more significant amendment provides the board with a lesser burden of proof in disciplinary proceedings, one that calls for a "preponderance of evidence" rather than "clear and convincing evidence."

Also of note are laws in California and Oregon that authorize boards to compel a physician to take a clinical competency examination if there is reasonable cause to believe that his or her skill level is inadequate. The California effort allows a physician two chances to pass an oral examination conducted by a panel of two physicians. The Oregon effort, under way for a number of years, may involve oral or writ-ten examinations, but generally employs the latter because they offer a firmer legal basis for subsequently denying a license or imposing discipline.

Source of Disciplinary Actions

Earlier we mentioned that during the past few years, the number of consumer complaints received by boards has been rising, often quite substantially. The greater visibility of boards and the establishment of toll-free complaint lines in some states have contributed to this development.

These consumer complaints, together with information provided by government agencies (mainly law enforcement agencies), account for most of the disciplinary actions eventually taken by boards. Strikingly few such actions first come to a board's attention as a result of referrals from those who would most naturally make referrals and who are the most qualified to make referrals—medical societies, PROs, health care institutions, and individual health care professionals. The reason for this seems mostly to stem from a lack of affirmative legal duty to report individuals and from the fear of being sued for reporting someone.

The Secretary of Health and Human Services, Otis R. Bowen, MD, released our report when he addressed New York University's graduating medical class on June 5, 1986. He noted the lack of referrals made by health care professionals and urged students, "Speak up when you see poor medicine being practiced. Not to do so is to render a grave disservice to patients and the profession alike."

Board officials, when commenting on this situation, often pointed to the PROs as an especially unproductive source of information. The following comment from the executive director of the board in a heavily populated state would probably be endorsed by many of his colleagues across the country: We get very little from the PROs. They take care of their own problems in-house until they get out of hand. We should be getting a lot more information from them."

Aware that much important information is not being passed on to boards, many states have initiated, expanded, or tightened reporting laws. The majority of states currently have reporting laws. Since 1982, at least 17 states have taken action to require reporting. (Annual reviews by the FSMB serve as a basis for this and other information concerning changes in state licensure and discipline laws). Most of these laws focus on hospitals. They usually require hospitals to inform boards of any changes in a physician's staff privileges or (in some states) of any resignations from the staff. A growing number require the reporting of malpractice judgments or settlements, often if they exceed a certain amount (eg, $10,000 in Georgia, $25,000 in New Jersey, $30,000 in California). A few states have laws that direct individual practitioners to report poor performance.

Nevertheless, reporting laws have not had the expected impact. When asking why, one often hears reference to the "brotherhood of silence," an inherent resistance to reporting one's peers. Another reason often cited is a fear of legal liability, even in states that have granted criminal and civil immunity to those who report information in good faith.

Information Sharing

States now provide the FSMB (and thereby other states) with regular reports on disciplinary actions they have taken. This represents considerable progress compared with the situation two to three years ago.

However, the extent of the actions reported varies from state to state. Many boards do not report licensure denials. More notably, many do not report tier-2 disciplinary actions if they did not involve a formal hearing or were imposed with the understanding that they would be confidential. The rationale for holding back on these cases is that confidentiality or lack of publicity were key to the agreements that enabled discipline to be imposed without a formal hearing. Yet, the failure to report such cases means that other states are prevented from obtaining information that could prove to be important to them if a disciplined physician relocates to their jurisdiction and practices on an unsuspecting public.

Furthermore, from state to state and even within states, there are considerable inconsistencies in the type of disciplinary actions taken in relation to the charges and even in the meaning of the different types of actions. The FSMB has promoted some consistency by establishing a standardized coding system for the different types of violations that boards use in reporting their actions to the FSMB. Unfortunately, many states fail to use it or use it irregularly, leaving it to the FSMB to choose what appears to be the most appropriate code. To foster greater consistency within the state, California developed a manual of disciplinary guidelines and model disciplinary orders a number of years ago, and regularly revises it to keep pace with developments. The FSMB has also devised and distributed *A Model for the Preparation of a Guidebook on Medical Discipline.*

While the FSMB's data base serves as the primary vehicle for the states to keep abreast of disciplinary actions taken in other states, follow-up communication among the states themselves is the means for obtaining more detailed information concerning the specifics of a case. In this context, substantial and effective information sharing is being achieved through the mailing of final board orders on a case through informal networking among board investigators and administrators. Where problems in gaining access to information have occurred, they have concerned cases still pending formal board action or tier-2 cases in which the action was agreed to be confidential.

Finally, within the states, boards typically inform medical societies and Medicaid state agencies of all formal disciplinary actions. They are less likely to do so with respect to other entities such as PROs, insurance companies, and hospitals. Most do not actively inform the general public or the medical community of their actions. However, a few boards, such as Florida's, regularly identify disciplined physicians in newsletters published by the board, medical society, or other parties, believing that publicizing the information has preventive value.

Conclusions and Recommendations

We have shown how boards have been confronted with increased work loads, inadequate financial support, and many conflicting pressures. Yet, their ability to act as necessary is predicated on their resource level. Accordingly, we believe physician license renewal fees should be set at a level sufficient to support expansion and improvement of the enforcement activities of the boards. (A recent report by the Public Citizen Health Research Group called for an increase in annual physician renewal fees to at least $500, "with all of the money going to identification and discipline of doctors who are incompetent or otherwise practicing bad medicine."[5]) These fees should be dedicated to board activities and not be diverted to general revenue funds. At the end of 1985, the average annual renewal fee rose to $51, a level that barely kept pace with inflation in the 1980s.

Of the issues previously addressed, the board's inability to help abate the flood of malpractice cases is the most troublesome. In recent years, the small increases in funding made available to boards have often been made with the expectation that boards would help stem the tidal wave of cases. Some of the recent initiatives have been noted; however, without doubt, the public's expectations have been rising much faster than boards have been able to respond.

Medical malpractice that is not rectified is a twofold problem for American society. Clearly, the safety and well being of patients seeking medical care is threatened when incompetent physicians remain in practice—however large or small their numbers. (We believe that the current level of litigation over-represents the number of physicians who perform negligently. Not all physicians who are sued for malpractice are guilty of negligence or misconduct, in our opinion. However, it is important to eliminate poor practitioners through disciplinary action, whenever possible.) Additionally, all patients pay higher prices due to the escalating costs of premiums and awards and the defensive medicine practiced to minimize the likelihood of successful malpractice suits. Many observers also believe that incompetent physicians also unnecessarily add billions of dollars annually to the nation's health expenditures.

In a speech read before the American Medical Association on Feb 21, 1986, Otis R. Bowen, MD, the first physician to be Secretary of Health and Human Services, made it clear that the development of an effective system of medical discipline is crucial to a resolution of the nation's malpractice problem:

> We cannot expect Americans to endorse any solution to the malpractice issue unless we address the central question of the physician's responsibility. If we ignore the "bad apple" in our profession, then we contribute to the malpractice problem. We then do not deserve any legislative relief.

For boards to play an important part in addressing this problem, it is clear that there must be substantial changes in the legal ground rules governing their handling of malpractice cases. The fear of being sued has had a chilling effect on reporting of incompetence. Perhaps states should consider ways to limit the liability of those making good-faith referrals at the same time that they create affirmative legal duties to report professional misconduct or incompetency. No less clear than the chilling effect of potential litigation is the fact that the resources available to boards must be increased. At present, most boards lack sufficient resources to devote serious attention to such cases without jeopardizing their other disciplinary and licensing responsibilities. We are hopeful that an increase in renewal fees, which boards are allowed to keep, could help eliminate this problem.

We in the federal government can provide some help in improving medical discipline efforts without undermining the central state role in this arena. One form of assistance we can provide is to assure more affirmative action within our own domain. That is, we can help ensure that PROs and Medicare carriers provide more extensive and timely reporting to state medical boards of cases involving physician misconduct or incompetence. In fact, based on our report, Secretary Bowen has directed that regulations and instructions intended to foster this objective be developed.

Another potentially significant form of federal assistance is represented by the Medicare and Medicaid Patient and Program Protection Act (HR 1868), passed by the US House of Representatives in 1985 in response to concerns about physicians being sanctioned in one state and then moving their practice to another state. Parallel legislation (S 1323) is now being considered in the US Senate and is widely supported. (The Medicare and Medicaid Patient and Program Protection Act failed to be enacted by the 99th US Congress, but we expect it to be reintroduced in this upcoming session.)

Passage of this legislation would close many existing loopholes, facilitate more efficient sanctioning by DHHS, and promote more extensive and effective sharing of disciplinary action among the states and DHHS. It would provide a much-needed vehicle for fostering (1) further and more timely reporting of disciplinary actions to a central clearinghouse, (2) more extensive nationwide distribution of information on such actions, and (3) more consistent definitions of the type of violations committed by physicians. This last issue is important when one considers that currently there is total reciprocity among states for licensing, but not for disciplinary decisions.

The federal government's reliance on state medical boards to provide the front line of protection for millions of Medicare and Medicaid patients creates an important stake in the improvement by the individual state regarding state medical discipline. A spirit of partnership involving federal and state government and the medical profession is vital if we are to accelerate and sustain progress in this direction.

References

1. Medical Licensure and Discipline: An Overview. US Dept of Health and Human Services, 1986.

2. Policies on U.S. Citizens Studying Medicine Abroad Need Review and Reappraisal. U.S. General Accounting Office, 1980.

3. Federal, State, and Private Activities Pertaining to U.S. Graduates of Foreign Medical Schools. U.S. General Accounting Office, 1985.

4. Relman AS: Professional regulation and the state medical boards. N Engl J Med 1985;312:784-785.

5. Wolfe SM, Bergman H, Silver G: Medical Malpractice: The Need for Disciplinary Reform, Not Tort Reform. Washington, DC, Public Citizen Health Research Group, 1985.

Kusserow RP et al. An overview of state medical discipline. JAMA. 1987; 257(6): 820-824.

Reprinted with permission from the authors and the American Medical Association.

Article 7.5

Peer Review After *Patrick*

Jack Bierig. Journal of Health and Hospital Law, June 1988.

In 1981 physicians at Columbia Memorial Hospital in Astoria, Oregon, commenced what became the most notorious peer review proceeding in medical history.[1] This proceeding led to a recommendation that the staff privileges of Timothy Patrick, M.D., a general surgeon, be terminated. As a result Dr. Patrick resigned from the staff to avoid having his privileges revoked. He brought an antitrust action against the physicians involved in the peer review process.

Based on a jury verdict, the district court entered a judgment of approximately $2,000,000 in antitrust damages plus $228,600 in attorney's fees. On appeal the principal issue was whether the "state action" doctrine of *Parker v Brown*[2] immunized the challenged peer review activities from the antitrust laws. The Ninth Circuit Court of Appeals held that it did.[3] However, on May 16, 1988, in *Patrick v. Burget* the Supreme Court in an 8-0 decision held that it did not.[4]

Today, there are few physicians in Astoria, Oregon. Those who conducted the peer review process have been devastated emotionally and ruined financially.[5] The case and its consequences have received enormous publicity in the medical press.[6] And physicians across the country question whether they should serve on credentials committees or otherwise participate in peer review—lest they suffer a fate similar to the *Patrick* defendants.[7]

Part 1 of this article explores the antitrust exposure of physicians who engage in credentialing activities after *Patrick*. It discusses the risks of an antitrust judgment against such physicians, the costs of having to defend an antitrust action, and the prospects for reducing those costs without resort to the state action defense. Part II considers steps that can be taken to make the state action doctrine applicable to peer review proceedings and whether such steps are worthwhile.

The article concludes that the risks of antitrust liability based on good faith peer review activities are not substantial. While such activities can result in significant litigation costs, there are a number of avenues for reducing these costs. Creating a system that would clearly provide state action immunity for credentialing decisions would involve review by a state agency of all decisions that are adverse to the physician. On balance, the costs of securing such immunity appear to outweigh the benefits.

1. The Antitrust Consequences of Peer Review After Patrick

A. Risk of Liability

Despite the decision in *Patrick*, physicians face little risk of antitrust liability for participating in good faith credentialing of their peers. Indeed, perhaps the most notable fact about *Patrick* is that it is the only case which has imposed antitrust liability based on the credentialing of a physician. Although scores of antitrust actions have been brought by physicians who have been denied privileges, there are no other reported cases in which the plaintiff has prevailed.[8]

The reasons that participation in good faith peer review should not result in liability were summarized in a 1986 letter to the General Counsel of the American Medical Association from Charles F. Rule, Assistant Attorney General for the Antitrust Division of the U.S. Department of Justice:

> [A] hospital may legitimately decide to deny privileges to an incompetent practitioner, based on good faith peer review conducted by the medical staff. Although the denial of privileges might make it difficult or even impossible for the practitioner to engage in his profession, such a denial does not impair competition. Rather, because the denial will enhance the quality and efficiency of health care and thereby strengthen the hospital's competitive position, peer review serves the underlying goals of the antitrust laws.[9]

This letter concludes, "[T]he antitrust laws do not stand in the way of physician's participation in hospital peer review conducted to identify and restrain incompetence in the provision of health care."[10]

Patrick should not alter this conclusion. In two separate respects *Patrick* involved a most atypical peer review proceeding. First, the case arose in a geographic market in which denial of privileges to a physician could adversely affect competition. Specifically, Columbia Memorial Hospital (CMH) was the only hospital in the Astoria area. Most of the physicians at CMH, moreover, were affiliated with one medical group, Astoria Clinic. Because the only effective competition could come from physicians who were on the CMH staff but independent of the Clinic, denial of staff privileges at CMH to an independent physician could adversely affect competition among local physicians and could thereby implicate the antitrust laws.

Second, the case is filled with facts which permit a jury to infer that the challenged privilege determination did not involve a good faith effort to evaluate the medical credentials of a staff physician. Quite to the contrary, these facts suggest that the proceeding was little more than an effort to eliminate a physician who posed a competitive threat to the Astoria Clinic. The facts are described in some detail in the opinions of both the Ninth Circuit and Supreme Court. Suffice to say that they provoked both tribunals to characterize the conduct of defendant physicians as "shabby, unprincipled, and unprofessional."[11]

Thus, the result in *Patrick* can be explained by the rare confluence of (1) a market in which peer review could adversely affect competition and not just a competitor and (2) bad faith conduct by the defendants.[12] That result should not be predictive of liability in the vast majority of peer review cases. In contrast to the situation in *Patrick*, many geographic markets include more than one hospital. Most have several competing groups of physicians. In these circumstances denial of privileges to a single physician may harm that physician, but it cannot suppress competition. In most peer review situations, moreover, the physicians attempt in good faith to make reasonable judgments about whether privileges for a particular physician would further quality health care at the hospital.

B. Risk of Involvement in Protracted Antitrust Proceedings

Even with the assurance that they will ultimately prevail in antitrust cases based on credentialing decisions, many physicians are reluctant to participate in such decisions. They do not want to risk the substantial attorney's fees, disruptions, and other costs of having to defend a protracted antitrust case. And they have no particular incentive to accept any antitrust exposure. For unlike most antitrust defendants, they generally derive no direct economic benefit from the challenged conduct.

The decision of the court of appeals in *Patrick* made available a defense that might have permitted the dismissal of peer review antitrust cases at a preliminary stage of litigation.[13] It thereby helped to allay the legitimate concerns of physicians about the costs of having to defend plenary antitrust proceedings. The decision of the Supreme Court has, at least for now, curtailed the state action defense as a vehicle for early dismissal of peer review antitrust cases. However, recent developments provide alternative avenues for early dismissal of these cases and thereby for reducing litigation costs.

The first relevant development is the increasing judicial recognition that summary judgment can be particularly useful for resolving antitrust cases.[14] Prior to *Matsushita Electric Industrial Co. v. Zenith Radio Corp.*, courts were reluctant to enter summary judgment in antitrust cases. *Matsushita*, however, makes it clear that when plaintiff's claims are economically implausible, there is no need for a trial. As explained above, physician credentialing cases are often defective from an economic standpoint. Accordingly, courts should grant summary judgement for defendants in peer review antitrust litigation whenever discovery fails to demonstrate a triable factual issue relating to an adverse effect on competition.[15]

Matsushita notwithstanding, there will continue to be cases in which summary judgment is denied to peer review defendants.[16] These cases may misapply the Supreme Court's admonition in *Matsushita* that weak factual claims should be weeded out through summary judgment. They may also confuse the distinction between (a) credentialing decisions that adversely affect a competitor and (b) credentialing decisions that affect competition itself. Or they may be correctly decided where there is a legitimate question of fact regarding the competitive significance of a particular credentialing decision. In any event cases such as *Miller v. Indiana Hospital* demonstrate that liberalized use of summary judgment is not, of itself, sufficient to reduce the litigation costs of peer review antitrust litigation.[17]

Therefore, the second development which may permit early termination of peer review antitrust litigation is enactment by Congress of the Health Care Quality Improvement Act of 1986.[18] Subchapter 1 of this Act reflects two congressional findings. First, the "threat of private money damage liability under federal laws, including treble damage liability under federal antitrust law, unreasonably discourages physicians from participating in effective professional peer review."[19] Second, there is "an overriding national need to provide incentive and protection for physicians engaging in effective professional peer review."[20]

In light of these findings, Congress sought to protect those who engage in good faith peer review "after adequate notice and hearing procedures are afforded to the physician involved or after such other procedures as are fair to the physician under the circumstances."[21] Defendants are presumed to have met this standard unless the presumption is rebutted by a preponderance of the evidence.[22] Defendants who meet this standard "shall not be liable" in private treble damage actions.[23] Moreover, upon prevailing, such defendants are entitled to recover their costs,

> including a reasonable attorney's fee, if the claim or claimant's conduct during the litigation of the claim was frivolous, unreasonable, without foundation, or in bad faith.[24]

To be sure, the "adequate notice and hearing procedures" set forth in the Act are quite extensive.[25] Particularly for initial applicants for staff privileges, some of these procedures are impractical, e.g., representation by an attorney and the right to call, examine, and cross-examine witnesses.[26] However, the Act does not require that all these procedures be given as a prerequisite for immunity. It also permits "such other procedures as are fair."[27] Thus, participants in peer review proceedings that take place after the effective date of the Act, October 14, 1987, and who accord with fair procedure may be able to obtain dismissal of private treble damage actions at an early stage. Whether they succeed in doing so will depend on how courts interpret the statutory phrase "such other procedures as are fair." However, given the Congressional findings underlying the Act[28] and given the statutory presumption that peer review proceedings meet the applicable standards, courts should dismiss peer review antitrust cases before trial unless the plaintiff can present substantial evidence of bad faith or unfair procedure.

Of course, even increased use of summary judgment and even a liberal construction of the Health Care Quality Improvement Act will not prevent physicians from being named as defendants in antitrust litigation arising out of the credentialing process. However, the risk of being named as a defendant would exist even if *Patrick* had come differently. Moreover, this risk has always existed under most state antitrust laws.[29] It also exists under the due process jurisprudence of many states for credentialing incumbent staff members.[30] Finally, in some states, it exists even for credentialing of initial applicants.[31]

Ultimately, it may make sense for hospitals to indemnify physicians or to provide insurance for their good faith participation on credentialing and other peer review committees. Many hospital insurance policies already cover physicians for their service on hospital committees. To the extent that they do, these policies provide physicians with some assurance that they will not incur substantial out-of-pocket costs. To the extent that these policies do not provide coverage, it may be advisable for hospitals to pick up the litigation costs of physicians who engage in peer review on their behalf.

II. The State Action Doctrine in the Peer Review Context

The question decided in *Patrick* was whether the state action doctrine protects "physicians in the State of Oregon from federal antitrust liability for their activities on hospital peer-review committees."[32] Under this doctrine private conduct is immune from the federal antitrust laws if it satisfies two criteria first articulated in *Parker v. Brown*,[33] and restated in *California Retail Liquor Dealer's Ass'n v. Midcal Aluminum, Inc.*:[34]

1. It must be undertaken pursuant to a "clearly articulated affirmatively expressed state policy,"[35] and

2. it must be "actively supervised" by the state.[36]

In *Patrick* the Supreme Court did not "consider the 'clear articulation' prong of the Midcal test" because it held that "the 'active supervision' requirement [was] not satisfied."[37]

The Court ruled that the "active supervision prong of the *Midcal* test requires that state officials have and exercise power to review particular anticompetitive acts of private parties and disapprove those that fail to accord with state policy."[38] It found that this standard was not satisfied by a statutory scheme that (a) required hospitals to establish peer review procedures and (b) gave a state agency authority to revoke a hospital's license for non-compliance. This general authority did not extend to review of specific privilege determinations at Oregon hospitals.

Similarly, the Court ruled that the active supervision requirement was not met by a statute that required reporting to the State Board of Medical Examiners decisions to terminate or restrict privileges. In the Courts' view such reporting merely enabled the board to determine whether to take additional action against the physician. The board did not review privilege decisions and never asserted the authority to reverse them.

Finally, the Court held that the active supervision requirement was not satisfied by judicial review of privilege determinations by Oregon state courts. The Court explicitly declined to decide "the broad question whether judicial review of private conduct ever can constitute active supervision."[39] It had no need to resolve that question because, in its view, the judicial review of privilege termination decisions in Oregon fell "far short of satisfying the active supervision requirement."[40] This view was predicated on the proposition that the Oregon courts will not decide the merits of a challenge to a credentialing decision, but rather will determine only whether "reasonable procedure was afforded."[41] This limited review does not involve a determination whether a particular credentialing decision "accorded with state regulatory policy" and therefore, does not constitute active state supervision.

The *Patrick* decision raises two questions relating to the state action doctrine as applied to credentialing decisions:

1. What steps must a state take in order to immunize private credentialing decisions from the federal antitrust laws?

2. Do the benefits of these steps outweigh the costs?

These questions are addressed below.

A. Bringing Private Credentialing Decisions Within the State Action Doctrine

The decision in *Patrick* suggests two potential approaches to satisfying the active supervision prong of the state action doctrine. The first, substantive review of credentialing decisions by state courts, may not be sufficient. The second, evaluation of such decisions by a state agency, will inject a new layer of bureaucracy into the peer review process.

1. Judicial Review

In *Patrick* the Supreme Court expressly reserved the issue of whether judicial review can ever constitute active supervision—noting that the limited procedural review afforded by the Oregon courts clearly did not satisfy this requirement. In some states courts will undertake a more substantive review.[42]

It is unclear whether even this level of judicial review will satisfy the state action doctrine. Initially, as the Court noted in *Patrick*, "[a]ll of our prior cases concerning state supervision over private parties have involved administrative agencies."[43] A properly empowered agency can review all peer review decisions made in the state or at least all such decisions that are adverse to the practitioner under review. A court, by contrast, can review only those cases that are put before it by a plaintiff. Thus, insofar as the power to institute review is concerned, administrative supervision is more "active" than judicial supervision.

Substantively, the key issue is whether there is review of "the merits of a privilege termination decision to determine whether it accorded with state regulatory policy."[44] The effect of the type of review envisioned by *Greisman v. Newcomb Hospital*[45] and the cases that follow it may be to ensure that a credentialing decision comports with state policy to promote quality medical care at hospitals. However, the review does not focus on the consistency of a particular decision with specified state policies governing credentialing. Thus, in terms of a purpose analysis, judicial review may or may not satisfy the active supervision requirement.

In *Patrick* the court had an opportunity to decide that judicial review can in appropriate circumstances satisfy the active supervision requirement. It did not do so. In these circumstances, whether substantive judicial review of credentialing decisions will suffice to implicate the state action doctrine is a question for litigation. And as long as the issue remains open, a state action defense based on judicial review will give those involved in peer review little comfort.

2. Administrative Review

The safest approach for a state that wants to satisfy the active supervision criterion is to enact a statute requiring (a) reporting of adverse credentialing decisions to an administrative agency and (b) review of such decisions by the agency for compliance with standards specified in the statute. Statutory standards could include (a) evaluation of the practitioner's professional record and willingness to comply with reasonable hospital and medical staff policies, (b) consideration of the need for additional practitioners in the specialty of the practitioner under review, (c) provision of fair procedure, and (d) any other factors deemed necessary to effectuate state policy. The statute might even provide that credentialing decisions are deemed approved unless questioned by the state agency within a specified period of time, e.g., sixty days after reporting. In this connection it should be noted that the active supervision requirement contemplates more than that state officials have power to review privilege determinations. Rather, such officials must actually "exercise this power."[46] There can be no assurance that the active supervision requirement will be met unless the administrative agency to which credentialing decisions are reported actually overturns such decisions from time to time.

B. Does It Make Sense to Bring Private Credentialing Decisions Within the State Action Doctrine?

Assuming that the state clearly authorized private credentialing decisions even when they have anti-competitve effects, the foregoing system of administrative review would appear to permit successful invocation of the state action defense. But this system in essence would involve a new overlay of agency review of privilege determinations. Any decision to revoke, restrict or deny privileges would be subject to administrative review. Decisions that currently go unquestioned might become the subject of administrative proceedings. And a new question would arise relating to the effect of an agency determination on any subsequent judicial proceedings.

Is it sound policy to create such a system in order to qualify for state action immunity from the antitrust laws? Each state will have to answer this question for itself. However, in the opinion of this author, the answer is no.

As noted in Part I, the likelihood of an antitrust judgment based on a good faith credentialing decision is exceedingly remote. In addition, the costs of antitrust litigation arising in this context should be reduced by increased use of summary judgment and by thoughtful application of the Health Care Quality Improvement Act. Finally, the possibility of an award of attorneys' fees against a plaintiff whose claim is found to be "unreasonable" may deter the bringing of federal antitrust actions based on peer review decisions that appear to comply with the Health Care Quality Improvement Act. In these circumstances, the potential benefits of state action immunity do not appear to justify the costs that are likely to be associated with a system of administrative review of credentialing decisions.

References

1. 56 U.S.I.W. 4430 (U.S. May 16, 1988); rev'g.800F.2d 1498 (9th Cir. 1986).

2. 317 U.S. 341 (1943)

3. 800 F.2d 1498 (9th Cir. 1986)

4. 56 U.S.L.W. 4430 (U.S. May 16, 1988)

5. See O'Brien, Town Left With Little Care, American Medical News, Feb. 26, 1988, at 1 col. 1.

6. Id.

7. Id. at 19, col. 2.

8. Liability was imposed in one case based on the credentialing of an osteopath by physicians. Weiss v. York Hospital, 745 F.2d 786 (3d Cir. 1984), and in another case based on the credentialing of a nurse anesthetist. Oltz v. St. Peter's Community Hospital, 656 F. Supp. 760 (D. Mont. 1987). Neither of these cases involves the ordinary peer review of a physician's application for staff privileges.

9. Letter to Kirk B. Johnson, General Counsel, American Medical Association, from Charles F. Rule, Assistant Attorney General, Antitrust Division, U.S. Department of Justice (Dec. 2, 1986).

10. Id.

11. 56 U.S.L.W. at 4431, n.3, quoting 800 F.2d at 1509.

12. 56 U.S.L.W. at

13. See, e.g., Marrese v. Interqual, Inc., 748 F.2d 373 (7th Cir. 1984); Doe v. St. Joseph's Hospital, 788 F.2d 411 (7th Cir. 1986); Ezpeleta v. Sisters of Mercy Health Corp., 800 F.2d 119 (7th Cir. 1986).

14. Matsushita Electric Industrial Co. v. Zenith Radio Corp., 475 U.S. 574, 586-587 (1986) Collins v. Associated Pathologists, Ltd., F.2d. 1988-1 Trade Cases ¶67,971 at 57, 951-952 (7th Cir. 1988).

15. See Collins v. Associated Pathologists, 1988-1 Trade Cases at 57,951.

16. See, e.g., Miller v. Indiana Hospital, 843 F.2d 139 (3rd Cir. 1988).

17. Id.

18. 42 U.S.C.A. §§ 11101, et seq. (West. Supp. 1988).

19. 42 U.S.C.A. § 11101(4)

20. 42 U.S.C.A. § 11101(5).

21. 42 U.S.C.A. § 11112(a).

22. 42 U.S.C.A.§ 11113.

23. Id.

24. Id. The meaning of the phrase "frivolous, unreasonable, without foundation, or in bad faith" has not yet been litigated. However, the congressional findings to the effect that peer review should be encouraged suggests that the word "unreasonably" should be liberally construed to allow imposition of attorneys' fees in most cases involving good faith credentialing.

25. See 42 U.S.C. § 11112(b).

26. See 42 U.S.C. § 11112(b)(3)(C).

27. 42 U.S.C. § 11112(a)(3). In fact, the Act explicitly provides that failure to provide all the "adequate notice and hearing procedures" set forth in § 11112(b) "shall not, in itself, constitute failure to meet the standards" necessary to qualify for immunity.

28. 1986 U.S. Code Cong. & Admin. News, p. 6287, 6391.

29. See, e.g., Nashville Memorial Hosp. Inc. v. Brinkley, 534 S.W.2d 318 (Tenn. 1976).

30. See, e.g., Jain v. Northwest Community Hospital, 385 N.E.2d 108, 112(Ill. 1978)

31. See, e.g., Greisman v. Newcomb Hospital, 192 A.2d 817 (N.J. 1963); cases discussed in Barrows v. Northwestern Memorial Hospital, 505 N.E.2d 1182 (Ill. App. 1987) and cases cited therein.

32. 56 U.S.L.W. 4430

33. 317 U.S. 341 (1943).

34. 445 U.S. 97, 105 (1980).

35. See, e.g., Southern Motor Carriers Rate Conference v. United States, 471 U.S. 48 (1985).

36. See e.g., 324 Liquor Corp. v. Duffy, 479 U.S. 335, ___,1075 S. Ct. 723, 725 (1987).

37. 56 U.S.L.W. at 4432.

38. Id.

39. Id. at 4432-33.

40. Id. at 4433.

41. Id. at 4433 (citing Straube v. Emanuel Lutheran Charity Board, 600 P.2d 381, 386 (Ore. 1979)).

42. Greisman v. Newcomb Hospital, 192 A.2d 817 (N.J. 1963); See also Barrows v. Northwestern Memorial Hospital, 505 N.E.2d 1182, 1187 (Ill App. Ct. 1987) rev'd, No. 65066 (Ill. Sup. Ct. May 26, 1988); Woodard v. Porter Hospital, Inc., 217 A.2d 37, 40 (Vt. 1966)); Silver v. Castle Memorial Hospital, 497 P.2d 574 (Hawaii 1972).

43. 56 U.S.L.W. at 4432.

44. Id. at 4433.

45. Greisman v. Newcomb Hospital, 192 A.2d 817 (N.J. 1963).

46. 56 U.S.L.W. at 4432-33.

Bierig J. Peer review after *Patrick*.
J Health Hosp Law. 1988; 21(6): 135-139.

Reprinted with permission from the author and the Journal of Health and Hospital Law.

Article 7.6

Health Care Quality Improvement Act of 1986

American Medical Association Office of General Counsel. Excerpted from The Citation, January 1987.

In enacting the Health Care Quality Improvement Act of 1986, Congress found (1) that there is an increasing occurrence of medical malpractice and the need to improve the quality of medical care; (2) that the threat of liability for money damages, particularly treble damages under federal antitrust law, unreasonably discourages physicians from participating in peer review; and (3) that there is need to provide incentive and protection for physicians engaging in effective peer review.

The Act is intended to protect the public from incompetent physicians by (1) providing immunity from liability for damages resulting from good faith peer review activities; and (2) establishing a central data bank that serves as a nationwide repository for information related to professional conduct and competence, licensure status, and the malpractice claims experience of physicians.

Damages

If specified standards of due process and fairness are met, the Act gives hospitals, HMOs, group medical practices, professional societies, peer review committees and their respective participants immunity from damages for good faith peer review actions that adversely affect a physician's clinical privileges or membership in a group practice or professional society. However, the Act does not apply to damages under any federal or state law relating to the violation of any person's civil rights.

A witness, complainant or other person who provides information to a peer review body regarding the professional conduct or competence of a physician is not liable in damages under any federal or state law unless such information is false and the person providing it knew that it was false.

Standards For Peer Review

To assure immunity under the Act from liability for damages, a peer review action must be taken in the reasonable belief that the action is in furtherance of quality health care, and after adequate notice and hearing procedures are afforded to the physician involved, or after such other procedures as are fair to the physician under the circumstances.

The adequate notice and hearing requirement shall be deemed to be met if the following conditions are observed or waived voluntarily by the physician:

1. The physician involved is given notice that a peer review action has been proposed against him, the reasons for the proposed action, and that he has the right to request a hearing.

2. If a hearing is requested notice of the date of the hearing must be given, which shall not be less than 30 days following the date of the notice, and also a list of the witnesses expected to testify at the hearing on behalf of the peer review body.

3. The hearing should be conducted before a hearing officer or a panel of individuals who are not in "direct economic competition" with the physician involved.

4. In the hearing the physician has the right (a) to representation by an attorney or other person of his choice; (b) to have a copy of the record of the proceedings upon payment of reasonable charges; (c) to call, examine, and cross-examine witnesses; (d) to present relevant evidence regardless of its admissibility in a court of law; (e) to submit a written statement at the close of the hearing; (f) to receive the written recommendation of the hearing officer or peer review panel, including a statement of the basis

for the recommendation; and (g) to receive a written decision of the governing board or whoever is responsible for taking action on the recommendation, including a statement of the basis for the decision.

Attorneys' Fees

If a physician challenges an adverse peer review action by bringing a suit that the court finds to be frivolous, unreasonable, or in bad faith, a defendant who has met the standards specified in the Act and substantially prevails in the suit shall be entitled to an award of the cost of the suit, including reasonable attorneys' fees. The Act does not provide for payment of attorneys' fees and costs to a physician who is successful in litigation brought to restore privileges that were unreasonably terminated.

Effective Dates

With respect to federal law, such as the Sherman Antitrust Act, the provisions of the Act relating to immunity from liability for damages were effective on October 14, 1986, the date of enactment of the Act. This immunity shall extend to the states for peer review actions commenced on or after October 14, 1989, unless a state by legislation elects such treatment earlier, or by legislation elects that this immunity shall not commence on or after October 14, 1989.

Reporting of Information

The Act requires state medical boards to report disciplinary actions, the surrender or revocation of a license, or any other action restricting a physician's right to practice in the state, to a central data bank. Insurance carriers and self-insurers are required to report payments in settlement or satisfaction of medical malpractice judgments or claims to the central data bank and the appropriate state board or risk fines up to $10,000 for each failure to report. No report is required until a partial or full payment of the claim is made.

Hospitals are required to report to the state board the denial, revocation or other action that adversely affects the clinical privileges of a physician for more than 30 days, and to request the central data bank for information whenever a physician or other licensed health care practitioner applies for privileges. At least once every two years a hospital must request information with respect to all physicians and health care practitioners who have been granted privileges.

A group medical practice, HMO, or professional society that meets the standards of due process and fairness specified in the Act and reports to the state board peer review actions that adversely affect the membership of a physician is immune from damages under the Act.

The information required to be reported under the Act must be reported at least annually and shall be first reported not later than October 14, 1987. The central data bank which will serve as a repository for this information will be a private or governmental agency as determined by the Secretary of Health and Human Services.

Confidentiality of Information

Within the parameters of broad exceptions, information reported under the Act may not be disclosed under penalty of $10,000 for each violation. Reported information is considered confidential with the following exceptions:

1. A physician or other practitioner is entitled to access to information concerning him which has been reported to the central data bank or a state medical board.

2. Reported information that is pertinent may be disclosed to persons involved in peer review activity or medical malpractice actions.

3. Such information also may be disclosed in accordance with regulations promulgated by the Secretary of Health and Human Services.

4. The Act does not prevent the disclosure of reported information by a person authorized under state law to make such disclosure.

Subject to the foregoing conditions of confidentially and exceptions, the Act intends that reported information shall be used solely with respect to activities in furtherance of the quality of health care.

Comment

The enactment of the Health Care Quality Improvement Act of 1986 is a major legislative achievement in providing a mechanism for improving the quality of medical care in hospitals and promoting more effective peer review. Although physicians challenging termination of their clinical privileges commonly allege lack of good faith, nevertheless, it is likely that physicians participating in peer review actions will have less cause to fear threat of liability for damages, particularly uninsurable treble damages in antitrust litigation.

At the same time, the Act is not unfair to physicians whose privileges are wrongfully terminated. Even though they cannot get damages without establishing bad faith, they are not foreclosed from seeking restoration of clinical privileges or other non-monetary relief. They may still litigate under federal antitrust laws if they can prove the usual requisites of interstate commerce and monopoly or restraint of trade, and obtain injunctive relief, attorneys' fees and costs. Of most benefit to physicians contemplating suit for loss or denial of privileges is the fact that the standards in the Act are far more specific than those reflected in the variable case law, and provide better guidance as to whether a physician has a meritorious case.

In situations where a physician is justifiably found to be incompetent but has threatened to sue and is tempted to do so, there is a strong deterrent in the Act which provides for the payment of attorneys' fees if the physician brings a frivolous or unreasonable suit. This is not a harsh provision. Courts are reluctant to find that a losing plaintiff has instituted a frivolous suit except where this is clearly the case.

In the vast majority of instances where denial or termination of clinical privileges occur, the action is probably entirely justified. However, there are also numerous instances where the action is motivated by institutional politics, personality conflicts, influential competitors and hospital economics. The articulation of sound peer review standards of due process and fairness in a federal law should be helpful to physicians who have been dealt with unfairly, even in suits brought in state courts.

The Act is intended to eliminate incompetent physicians from practicing in hospitals. A physician is defined to mean a doctor of medicine, osteopathy or dentistry authorized to practice in the state. The term does not include podiatrists or other limited health care practitioners who face no impediment in suing for damages. The term physician does include hospital residents even though they may be unlicensed. The Act may, therefore, encourage more prudence on the part of hospitals in the selection of residents.

Hospitals will have to review their medical staff bylaws to see if they conform to the standards for peer review actions specified in the Act. Although the Act permits some leeway for other procedures that may be "fair to the physician," a prudent approach is to follow the Act precisely.

Hearings conducted by peer review panels will now take on more of the character of hearings conducted by governmental administrative agencies. Lawyers will debate and argue the relevance of evidence and examine and cross-examine witnesses. Expert witnesses will be called with greater frequency to evaluate the physician's competence and performance as in a malpractice trial. The employment of a reporter to prepare a verbatim transcript of the proceedings will be standard practice. Minutes of the hearing will not suffice.

Conclusion

This legislation will take on greater importance as competition for hospital privileges escalates because of an increasing physician population accompanied by the closing of numerous hospitals and major hospital departments. Furthermore, the true impact will be felt in years to come after the central data bank has accumulated massive information.

Annotated Bibliography

The Peer Review Process

Crane M. *How much do you risk when you review a colleague's work?* Medical Economics. September 4, 1989: 23-38.
Physicians undertaking peer review responsibilities should discuss with their hospital attorney the legal protections they may or may not have under their personal malpractice policy and the hospital's general liability insurance policy.

Jessee WF, Brenner LH. *Approaches to improving health care: dealing with the problem physicians.* Quality Rev Bull. 1984; 10: 393-396.
The authors, a physician and an attorney, describe the elements of due process that should be present in all peer review proceedings.

Plumeri PA. *Colleagues: to protect or not?* J Clin Gastroenterol. 1984; 6: 549-552.
A gastroenterologist makes the diagnosis which was missed by a family physician. The patient asks the specialist whether the family physician was negligent and informs him that she is contemplating legal action. The article includes an excellent discussion of how to respond with a medical opinion only, while avoiding legal determinations and advice.

Tan MW. *Practical safeguards for peer reviewers.* Forum (bi-monthly publication of the Risk Management Foundation of the Harvard Medical Institutions). 1987; 8(5): 2,6.
Article 7.1

Hospital Liability

Jeddeloh NP. *The ostensible agency doctrine and theories of corporate liability.* Occurrence (quarterly publication of the Chicago Hospital Risk Pooling Program). 1988; 10(2): 1-3.
Attorney Jeddeloh compares the various legal theories established in case law regarding hospital liability for physician negligence. He argues that the "ostensible agency doctrine" is a more realistic approach than is the "corporate negligence theory" for hospitals.

Reed ME. *A hospital's liability for negligence.* American College of Surgeons Bulletin. May 1983: 18-20.
Attorney Reed reviews the *Darling v. Charleston Community Hospital* case and subsequent cases that establish hospital liability for physician negligence.

Smith WB. *Hospital liability for physician negligence.* JAMA. 1984; 251: 447-448.
Article 7.2

Medical Staff Privileges

Martin PB, Tan MW, Trombly ST. *Answers to physicians' questions about reporting claims experience.* Forum (bi-monthly publication of the Risk Management Foundation of the Harvard Medical Institutions). 1988; 9(3,4): 2-3.
Article 7.3

Roberts JS, Radany MH, Nash DB. *Privilege delineation in a demanding new environment.* Ann Intern Med. 1988; 108: 880-886.
This review of the legal and ethical need for proper physician credentialing addresses the type of organizational framework needed to carry out privilege delineation in a typical hospital.

Role and function of the hospital medical staff: American Hospital Association guidelines. Chicago, IL: American Hospital Association; 1986.
These guidelines briefly summarize the organization, strategies planning, education, research, and other functions of the hospital medical staff.

Verification of physician credentials: American Hospital Association technical advisory bulletin. Chicago, IL: American Hospital Association; September 1985.
This official position statement describes the data that need to be reviewed by hospitals regarding medical students, resident physicians, foreign medical graduates, and physician applicants for staff positions. Addresses for sources of credentialing information are given.

Licensure and Discipline

Kusserow RP, Handley EA, Yessian MR. *An overview of state medical discipline.* JAMA. 1987; 257: 820-824.
Article 7.4

Report of medical licensure: report of the Council on Medical Education of the AMA. JAMA. 1988; 259: 1994-2001.
This report updates AMA policy on a range of issues regarding medical licensure. It addresses the use of NBME and FLEX examinations, the licensing of foreign medical graduates, continuing education, and re-examinations regarding license renewal.

Roberts JS, Radany MH, Nash DB. *Privilege delineation in a demanding new environment.* Ann Intern Med. 1988; 108: 880-886.
The authors provide an excellent review of the legal and ethical needs for proper physician credentialing. Discussion includes the organizational framework needed to carry out medical staff appointments in a typical hospital and the resources available for investigating a physician's credentials.

Weinstein M. *Pro-active medical boards not just for licensing any more.* Observers (publication of the American College of Physicians). December 1989:1; January 1990: 10-12.
New trends in licensing boards' activities include physician education, peer review, risk management, quality assurance, and the rehabilitation of impaired physicians. New programs in Oregon, Missouri, and Massachusetts are described.

Antitrust Law

A Compendium of State Peer Review Immunity Laws. Chicago, IL: American Medical Association; 1988.
A guidebook of laws in all 50 states and the District of Columbia for use by health care lawyers and physicians involved in peer review programs.

AMA Office of General Council. *Health Care Quality Improvement Act of 1986.* The Citation. January 15, 1987.
Article 7.6

Bierig J. *Peer review after Patrick.* J Health Hosp Law.1988; 21: 135-139.
Article 7.5

Curran WJ. *Legal immunity for medical peer-review programs.* N Engl J Med. 1989; 320: 233-235.
Attorney Curran reviews the Health Care Quality Improvement Act, the *Patrick* decision, and subsequent court rulings. He states that trepidation on the part of physicians participating in peer review still exists.

Dolin LC. *Antitrust law versus peer review.* N Engl J Med. 1985; 313: 1156-1157.
A physician describes the peer review process of a negligent colleague gone awry. He advocates federal law declaring immunity for physicians involved in the peer review process.

Francisco CJ. *The federal antitrust laws: a primer for physicians.* Tex Med. 1989; 85: 56-58.
This article defines terms and gives brief synopses of the Sherman Act, the Federal Trade Commission Act, the Clayton Act, the *Patrick v. Burget* case, the Health Care Quality Improvement Act of 1986, and other elements of antitrust law.

Health Care Quality Improvement Act of 1986, Public Law No. 99-660, 100 Stat. 3743, secs 401-431 (1986).
This legislative package bolstered the principles set forth in the United States Supreme Court decision in *Patrick v. Burget.* It delineates specific requirements of peer review, offers antitrust liability protection to physicians participating in good faith peer review, and establishes the National Practitioner Data Bank.

Holzer JF, ed. *Forum* (bi-monthly publication of the Risk Management Foundation of the Harvard Medical Institutions) 1990; 11(3): 1-12
This entire issue investigates the requirements and ramifications of the National Practitioner Data Bank.

Inglehart JK. Congress moves to bolster peer review: the Health Care Quality Improvement Act of 1986. N Engl J Med. 1987; 316: 960-964.
A synopsis of the political background of this landmark legislation is given. This law grants immunity from liability to protect physicians participating in good faith peer review. An analysis of the legislation's shortcomings is included.

Peer Review Organizations (PROs)

Dans PE, et al. *Peer review organizations: promises and pitfalls.* N Engl J Med. 1985; 313: 1131-1137.
This article includes a history of federally mandated peer review, including PSROs of the past and PROs of the present. Although originally intended to monitor hospital use and quality of care for Medicare patients, these organizations are now primarily viewed as agents of cost containment. The authors suggest some steps that could make PROs acceptable measures of quality of care.

Institute of Medicine. In: Lohr KN, ed. *Medicare: A Strategy for Quality Assurance.* Washington, DC: National Academy Press; 1990:1,2.
This evaluation of the PROs' quality assurance performance highlights the program's main function of utilization review. It calls for a major transformation of the PROs into "Medicare Quality Review Organizations" over the next 10 years. The emphasis would shift to a primary goal of quality assurance.

Lohr KN, Schroeder SA. *A strategy for quality assurance in Medicare.* N Engl J Med. 1990; 322: 707-712.
A summary of the recommendations of the Institute of Medicine report cited above.

Appendix

Physician-owned Insurance Companies

Alabama
Mutual Assurance, Inc.
115 Office Park Drive
P.O. Box 590009 (ZIP 35259)
Birmingham, AL 35233
(205) 871-7280
Sponsors: Alabama Medical and Dental Associations

Arizona
Mutual Insurance Company of Arizona
2602 E. Thomas Road
Phoenix, AZ 85016
(602) 956-5276
Sponsors: Arizona Medical Association, Arizona Osteopathic Medical Association

California
Medical Insurance Exchange of California
6250 Claremont Avenue
Oakland, CA 94618
(415) 428-9411
Also Licensed: Alaska, Hawaii, Idaho, Nevada
Sponsor: Medical society in each state

NORCAL Mutual Insurance Company
50 Fremont Street
San Francisco, CA 94105
(415) 777-4200
Sponsor: Northern California Physicians Council

Southern California Physicians Insurance Exchange
9441 West Olympic Blvd.
Beverly Hills, CA 90210
(213) 551-5900
Sponsors: County medical societies of Kern, Los Angeles, Orange, Riverside, San Bernadino, San Luis Obispo, Santa Barbara and Ventura, and California Association of Maxillofacial Surgeons

The Doctors' Company
An Interinsurance Exchange
401 Wilshire Boulevard
Santa Monica, CA 90401
(213) 451-3011
Sponsors: Montana Medical Association, Wyoming Medical Society, Denver Medical Society

Colorado
COPIC Insurance Company
5575 DTC Parkway #200
Englewood, CO 80111
P.O. Box 17540 TA
Denver, CO 80217-0540
(303) 779-0044

Connecticut
Connecticut Medical Insurance Company
10 Alexander Drive
P.O. Box 757
Wallingford, CT 06492
(203) 284-0212
Sponsor: Connecticut State Medical Society

District of Columbia
National Capital Reciprocal Insurance Company
2170 Wisconsin Avenue, N.W.
Washington, D.C. 20007
(202) 342-6690
Sponsor: District of Columbia Medical Society

Florida
Florida Physicians Insurance Company
1000 Riverside Avenue
Jacksonville, FL 32204
(904) 354-5910
Sponsor: Florida Medical Association

Florida Physicians Insurance Trust
1545 Raymond Diehl Road
Tallahassee, FL 32312
(904) 422-2255

Physicians Protective Trust Fund
2121 Ponce de Leon Boulevard, Suite 350
Coral Gables, FL 33134
(305) 442-8119

Georgia
MAG Mutual Insurance Company
Eight Piedmont Center, Suite 600
3525 Piedmont Road
Atlanta, GA 30305-1533
(404) 842-5600
Sponsor: Medical Association of Georgia

Illinois
Associatied Physicians Insurance Company
2300 North Barrington Road
Hoffman Estates, IL 60195
(708) 310-9900

Illinois State Medical Inter-Insurance Exchange
Illinois State Medical Insurance Services, Inc.
Twenty North Michigan Avenue, Suite 700
Chicago, IL 60602-4890
(312) 782-1654
Sponsor: Illinois State Medical Society

Iowa
Iowa Physicians Mutual Insurance Trust (IPMIT)
1239 Eighth Street West
Des Moines, IA 50265
(515) 223-2816
Sponsor: Iowa Medical Society

Kansas
Kansas Medical Mutual Insurance Company
1631 South Topeka Blvd.
Topeka, KS 66612
(913) 232-2224
Sponsor: Kansas Medical Society

Kentucky
Kentucky Medical Insurance Company
3532 Ephraim McDowell Drive
Louisville, KY 40205
(502) 459-3400
Sponsor: Kentucky Medical Association

Louisiana
Louisiana Medical Mutual Insurance Company
111 Veterans Memorial Boulevard Suite 1700
Metairie, LA 70005
(504) 831-3756
Sponsor: Louisiana State Medical Society

Maine
Medical Mutual Insurance Company of Maine
43 Baxter Boulevard
Portland, ME 04101
(207) 775-2791

Maryland
Medical Mutual Liability Insurance Society of Maryland
225 International Circle
Hunt Valley, MD 21030
(301) 785-0050

Michigan
Michigan Physicians Mutual Liability Company
1305 Abbott Road
East Lansing, MI 48826
(517) 351-1150
Sponsor: Michigan State Medical Society

Michigan
Physicians Insurance Company of Michigan
4295 Okemos Road, Box 2510
Okemos, MI 48864-2510
(517) 349-6500

Minnesota
Midwest Medical Insurance Co.
2221 University Avenue SE
Suite 220
Minneapolis, MN 55414
(612) 623-1132
Sponsor: Minnesota Medical Association

Mississippi
Medical Assurance Company of Mississippi, Inc.
735 Riverside Drive, Suite 301
Jackson, MS 39296-4915
(601) 353-2000
Sponsor: Mississippi State Medical Association

Missouri
Medical Defense Associates
3444-P South Campbell
Springfield, MO 65807
(417) 887-3120

Missouri Medical
Insurance Company
(MOMEDICO)
10795 Watson Road
St. Louis, MO 63127
(314) 965-1003
Sponsor: Missouri State Medical Association

Risk Control Associates, Inc.
1111 South Glenstone, Suite 3-102
Springfield, MO 65804
(417) 862-0650

New Jersey
The Medical Inter-Insurance Exchange of New Jersey
Two Princess Road
Lawrenceville, NJ 08648
(609) 896-2404
Sponsors: Medical Society of New Jersey and New Jersey Association of Osteopathic Physicians and Surgeons

New Mexico
New Mexico Physicians Mutual Liability Company
7770 Jefferson, N.E., Suite 400
Albuquerque, NM 87109
(505) 828-0237

New York
Medical Liability Mutual Insurance Company
2 Park Avenue, Suite 2500
New York, NY 10016
(212) 576-9800
Sponsor: Medical Society of the State of New York

North Carolina
Medical Mutual Insurance Company of North Carolina
222 North Person Street
Raleigh, NC 27611-6088
(919) 828-9334
Sponsors: North Carolina Medical Society, North Carolina Dental Society

Ohio
Physicians Insurance Company of Ohio
13515 Yarmouth Drive, N.W.
Pickerington, OH 43147
(614) 864-7100
Sponsor: Ohio State Medical Association

Oklahoma
Physicians Liability Insurance Company
5005 N. Lincoln
Oklahoma City, OK 73105
(405) 524-0801
Sponsor: Oklahoma State Medical Association

Oregon
Northwest Physicians Mutual Insurance Co.
1155 Mission Street, S.E.
Suite 205
Salem, OR 97302-6208
(503) 371-8228

Pennsylvania
Pennsylvania Medical Society Liability Insurance Company
777 East Park Drive
Harrisburg, PA 17111
(717) 558-7500
Sponsor: Pennsylvania Medical Society

Tennessee
State Volunteer Mutual Insurance Company
101 Westpark Drive, Suite 300
Brentwood, TN 37027
(615) 377-1999

Texas
American Physicians Insurance Exchange
1301 Capital of Texas Highway, South B320
Austin, TX 78746
(512) 328-1520
Sponsor: Arkansas Medical Society

Texas Medical Liability Trust
Farm Credit Bank Building
6210 Highway 290 East
Suite 400
Austin, TX 78723
(512) 454-6781

Utah
Utah Medical Insurance Association
540 East 500 South
Salt Lake City, UT 84102
(801) 531-0375
Sponsor: Utah Medical Association

Washington
Washington State Physicians Insurance Exchange & Association
1730 Minor Avenue, Suite 1800
Seattle, WA 98101-1499
(206) 343-7300
Sponsor: Washington State Medical Association

Wisconsin
Physicians Insurance Company of Wisconsin
328 East Lakeside Street
Madison, WI 53715
(608) 256-6677
Sponsor: The State Medical Society of Wisconsin

From
Physician Insurers Association of America 1990 Membership Directory.

Physician Insurers Association of America
Pennington Professional Park
65 South Main Street, Bldg. D
Pennington, NJ 08534
(609) 737-7193

Medical Malpractice Joint Underwriting Associations

Florida Medical Malpractice JUA
325 John Knox Road, G-104
Tallahassee, FL 32303-4176
904/385-8114

Kansas Insurance Services
System, Inc.
Citizens National Bank Building
200 South Main, Suite 205
Fort Scott, KS 66701
316/223-5252

Maine Medical Malpractice JUA
P.O. Box 9147, JFK Station
50 Stanford Street
Boston, MA 02114
617/742-5070 (inactive JUA)

Medical Malpractice JUA
of Massachusetts
P.O. Box 9178, 101 Arch Street
Boston, MA 02205
617/330-1755

Minnesota Medical
Malpractice JUA
c/o Volunteer Attorney Program
802 Torrey Building
Duluth, MN 55802
218/723-4005

New Hampshire Medical
Malpractice JUA
c/o Johnson and Higgins
Three Center Plaza, Third Floor
Boston, MA 02108
617/742-5300

New Jersey Medical Malpractice
Reinsurance Association
P.O. Box 868, 560 Main Street
Chatham, NJ 07982
201/966-0966 (inactive JUA) or
201/635-1700

New York Medical Malpractice
Insurance Association
110 Williams Street
New York, NY 10038
212/962-0286

Ohio Medical Professional
Liability Underwriting Association
6230 Busch Boulevard, Suite 303
Columbus, OH 43229
614/436-4530 (inactive JUA)

Pennsylvania Professional
Liability JUA
P.O. Box 329
580 W.Germantown Pike
Suite 207
Plymouth Meeting, PA 19426
215/828-8990

Medical Malpractice JUA
of Rhode Island
100 Bignall Street
Warwick, RI 02888
401/461-8840

South Carolina Medical
Malpractice Liability Insurance
JUA
P.O. Box 4366
1612 Marion Street
Columbia, SC 29240
803/256-6311

Texas Medical Malpractice
Liability Insurance
Underwriting Association
250 One La Posada Drive
Suite 250
Austin, TX 78752
512/452-4370

Virginia Medical Malpractice JUA
P.O. Box 31656
Richmond, VA 23294
804/672-2101

Wisconsin Health Care Liability
Insurance Plan
c/o
Employers Insurance of Wausau
2000 Westwood Drive
P.O. Box 8017
Wausau, WI 54402-8017
715/842-6685

From Alliance of American Insurers, National Association of Independent Insurers, and personal contacts.

State Patient Compensation Funds

Florida Patient Compensation Fund
P.O. Box 13359
Tallahassee, FL 32317-3359
904/386-3105

Indiana Patient
Compensation Division
Inpatient Compensation Division
311 W. Washington Street,
Suite 300
Indianapolis, IN 46204
317/232-5066

Kansas Health Care
Stabilization Fund
Kansan Insurance Department
420 SW 9th Street
Topeka, KS 66612-1678
913/296-3071

Louisiana Patient
Compensation Fund
P.O. Box 94214
Baton Rouge, LA 70804
504/34205323

Nebraska Excess Liability Fund
941 O Street, Suite 400
Lincoln, NE 65808
402/471-2201

New Mexico Patient
Compensation Fund
c/o NM Department of Insurance
P.O. Drawer 1269
Santa Fe, NM 87504-1269
505/827-4563

Pennsylvania Professional
Liability Catastrophe Loss Fund
P.O. Box 12030
Harrisburg, PA 17108
717/783-3770

South Carolina Medical
Malpractice Patients'
Compensation Fund
P.O. Box 11534
Columbia, SC 29211-1534
803/737-6262

Wisconsin Patient
Compensation Fund
P.O. Box 7873
123 W. Washington Avenue
Madison, WI 53707-7873
608/266-9895

From telephone calls to PIAA members, state medical societies, state insurance offices, etc.

Ten Largest Commercial Medical Malpractice Insurance Carriers

A.M. Best Ranking[a]	Company[b]	Coverage Provided
1	St. Paul Group 385 Washington Street St. Paul, MN 55102 (612) 221-7911	Physicians and other health care providers, hospital and other medical facilities
3	CNA Insurance Companies CNA Plaza Chicago, IL 60685 (312) 822-500	Physicians
4	The Medical Protective Company 5814 Reed Road Fort Wayne, IN 46835 (219) 485-9622	Physicians, dentists
5	Farmers Insurance Group 4680 Wilshire Blvd. Los Angeles, CA 90010 (213) 932-3200	Hospitals
6	American International Group (AIG) 70 Pine Street New York, NY 10270 (212) 770-7000	Hospitals
10	Health Care Group 746-760 Alexander Road Princeton, NJ 08540 (609) 452-9404	Physicians, hospitals
11	PIE Mutual Insurance Company North Point Tower 1001 Lakeside Avenue Cleveland, OH 44114-1149 (216) 736-8400	Physicians
13	Pennsylvania Hospital Insurance Company (PHICO) One Phico Drive P.O. Box 85 Mechanicsburg, PA 17055-0085 (717) 766-1122	Hospitals, hospital-employed physicians, and groups
15	Physicians Reciprocal Insurance Company 11 East Shore Road Manhasset, NY 11030 (516) 365-6690	Physicians
19	Health Care Indemnity 500 West Main Box 1438 Louisville, KY 40201 (502) 580-3797	Humana hospitals

a From 1989 Best's Insurance Management Reports Property/Casualty. A.M. Best Company ranks insurance companies by size of gross written premium. This listing excludes physician-owned insurance companies.

b Companies listed may not offer coverage in all states.

Glossary of Medical-Legal and Insurance Terms

Abandonment — A legal term referring to the termination of a physician-patient relationship by the physician without reasonable notice and without an opportunity for the patient to acquire adequate medical care elsewhere. If the abandonment results in some type of damage to the patient it may constitute medical malpractice.

Actuary — A mathematician who uses statistical analysis to compute insurance risks and premiums.

Ad damnum clause — The part of a plaintiff's complaint that states the damages that are claimed.

Admissibility (in evidence) — Refers to evidence that may be properly received and considered in a legal proceeding. The determination as to admissibility is based on legal rules of evidence and is made by the trial judge.

Admission Against Interest — Statements by a party to a lawsuit that are indicative of his or her own guilt. An admission against interest is admissible in evidence as an exception to the hearsay rule. (*See* Hearsay Rule.)

Affidavit — Voluntary, written statement of facts made under oath before an officer of the court or before a notary public.

Affirmative Defense — A response to allegations in a complaint which constitutes a defense, even assuming the alleged facts to be true. Common examples of affirmative defenses include the statute of limitations and the contributory negligence of the opposing party.

Allegation — Statement of a party to an action, made in a pleading, setting out what the party expects to prove.

Answer — A document filed with the court that contains a defendant's response to allegations set forth in the plaintiffs complaint. (*See* Complaint).

Appeal — The process by which a decision of a trial court is brought for review to a court of higher jurisdiction, typically known as an appellate court.

Appellate Court — The court that reviews trial court decisions to determine whether errors of law were committed by the trial judge.

Arbitration — An alternative to a court trial for resolution of a dispute (e.g. a liability claim) between two or more parties, whereby the case is heard and resolved by an individual known as an arbitrator or a panel of arbitrators. Arbitration may be entered into by agreement or may be mandated by statute, and the arbitration decision may be binding or non-binding. A binding decision cannot be retried in the courts.

Battery — The unauthorized and intentional touching of a person by another. In medical malpractice cases, battery typically refers to contact of some type with a patient who has not granted an informed consent to the contact. Battery can be either a civil or a criminal offense.

Breach of Contract Failure without legal excuse to complete or perform any promise which forms the whole or part of a legally binding contract.

Burden of Proof The responsibility in a legal proceeding of presenting sufficient evidence to prove a fact or facts in dispute. The plaintiff typically has the burden of proof.

Captain of the Ship A legal doctrine which holds one responsible for the acts of those under his or her supervision and control, most commonly used when the physician in charge of a medical team is liable for all the negligent acts of the members of the team.

Captive Insurance Company A provider-owned insurance company, where the provider may be a hospital or a group of physicians.

Carrier An insurance company.

Case A legal action or cause of action; a matter in dispute; a suit or lawsuit.

Case Law Legal principles derived from judicial decisions, also known as common law. Case law differs from statutory law, which is enacted by legislatures.

Causation A legal term referring to the causal connection between the defendant's alleged breach of duty and the injury suffered by the plaintiff. It is necessary to show causation in order to prove negligence. (*See* Negligence, Proximate Cause.)

Cause of Action A set of alleged facts that forms the basis for a plaintiff to file a complaint.

Certificate of Merit A tort reform mandated by law in several states that requires the plaintiff or his attorney in a medical malpractice case to file an affidavit or other sworn statement with (or shortly after) the Complaint stating that the case has been reviewed by a qualified expert who determined that on its face it is not frivolous.

Claim In common parlance, any demand for compensation. What constitutes a claim that must be reported to an insurance company varies, but is always defined in the policy.

Claims-Made Insurance Policy Provides coverage for claims arising from incidents that both occur and are reported to the insurance company while the policy is continually in force. A claims-made policy is in force beginning with the starting date of the initial policy period and continues in force from that date through each subsequent renewal. When a claims-made policy is terminated, future claims arising from incidents that occurred during the policy period are not covered. (*See* Extended Reporting Endorsement, Nose Coverage.)

Collateral Source Rule A rule of law that prevents the admissibility of any evidence about or the subtraction from the damage award of any payments that the plaintiff has received from such collateral sources as workers' compensation, health insurance, government benefits, or sick pay benefits.

Common Law That body of law that has been developed, interpreted, and refined by court decisions, as opposed to statutory law.

Community Standard Rule *See* Locality Rule.

Comparative Negligence A legal doctrine that attempts to apportion liability for an injury or loss according to the amount of fault attributable to each responsible person, including each defendant, any potential defendants not named in the lawsuit, and the plaintiff. In some jurisdictions the comparative negligence of the plaintiff may be used as an affirmative defense to reduce the amount of damages, generally by an amount equal to the plaintiff's percentage of fault. Most states have adopted some form of comparative fault.

Complaint A legal document that is the initial pleading filed by the plaintiff in a civil lawsuit. A complaint, sometimes known as a declaration, gives a defendant notice of the alleged facts constituting the cause of action. The complaint, accompanied by the summons, is served on the defendant by a process server or, in some states, by certified mail.

Contingency Fee A fee agreement between the plaintiff and an attorney, whereby the plaintiff agrees to pay the attorney a percentage of the damages recovered. If no damages are recovered, no fee is owed to the attorney.

Contract An agreement between competent, consenting parties that creates, modifies or terminates rights and responsibilities. To be legally enforceable, a contract must be supported by "consideration," which may be thought of as a promise for or transfer of something of value, usually money or services.

Contributory Negligence A legal doctrine that has been supplanted in most states by the doctrine of comparative negligence. The old rule held that the contributory negligence of a plaintiff in any amount could be asserted as an affirmative defense by the defendant, completely barring recovery of damages by the plaintiff. In contrast, comparative negligence only reduces the amount of damages owed to the plaintiff. Some states have adopted a hybrid know as modified comparative fault, which bars recovery when the plaintiffs share of negligence exceeds a certain proportion of total fault, typically 50 percent.

Counterclaim A defendant's claim against a plaintiff or another defendant, usually asserted with the answer to the complaint.

Court Costs Litigation costs of an opposing party that may be awarded to the winning party in a lawsuit. Attorney's fees are not included. Court costs are usually not awarded in medical malpractice cases.

Damages The sum of money a court or jury awards as compensation for a tort or breach of contract. The law recognizes certain categories of damages, including general, special, and punitive/exemplary damages.

General damages: typically intangible damages, such as pain and suffering, disfigurement, interference with ordinary enjoyment of life, and loss of consortium (marital services).

Special damages: out-of-pocket damages that may be quantified, such as medical expenses, lost wages, and rehabilitation costs.

Punitive/exemplary damages: damages awarded to the plaintiff in cases of intentional tort or gross negligence to punish the defendant or act as a deterrent to others.

Decedent A deceased person named or otherwise involved in a legal action, who normally would have been the plaintiff if still living.

Declaration *See* Complaint.

Defamation The willful injuring of another person's reputation or character by false and malicious statements, either written (libel) or spoken (slander). Like negligence and battery, defamation is a tort.

Defendant In a lawsuit, a party against whom suit is brought.

Defense Attorney The attorney who defends the person who is sued (defendant).

Deposition A "discovery" procedure whereby each party may question another party or anyone who may possibly be a witness. Depositions are conducted before the trial under oath and are admissable at trial under certain circumstances. (*See* Discovery.)

Designated Compensable Events Defined medical injuries that would be compensated according to a schedule of benefits. Several tort reform proposals advocate an insurance mechanism that would remove medical malpractice cases from the court system into an administrative system that would compensate designated compensable events. (*See* No-fault Compensation.)

Discovery Pretrial procedures to learn of evidence in the possession of an opposing party in order to minimize the element of surprise at the time of trial.

Dismissal An act of termination by a court.

Doctor-Patient Privilege The right of the patient to prevent disclosure of communications made between the patient and physician. May not be recognized in all jurisdictions and may be limited in others. (*See* Privileged Communications.)

Due Process Legal procedures that have been established in systems of jurisprudence for the enforcement and protection of private rights. The right to due process incorporates adequate notice of claims against one, a fair trial and the opportunity to cross-examine hostile witnesses.

Duty An obligation recognized by the law. A physician's duty to a patient is to provide the degree of care ordinarily exercised by physicians. (*See* Standard of Care.)

Evidence Facts presented at trial through witnesses, records, documents, treatises, etc., for the purpose of proving or defending a case. Evidence is admitted at trial through a complex system of legal rules.

Experience Rating The practice of basing insurance premiums on past loss history.

Expert Opinion A type of evidence, the testimony of a person who has special training, knowledge, skill, or experience in an area relevant to resolution of the legal dispute.

Expert Witness One who has special training, knowledge, skill, or experience and who can provide information beyond the knowledge of the average person.

Extended Reporting Endorsement Commonly known as tail coverage, the extended reporting endorsement is a supplemental policy obtained from a claims-made carrier to provide coverage for any incident that occurred while the claims-made insurance was in effect but had not been brought as a claim by the time the insurer/policyholder relationship terminated. Tail coverage is generally needed at the time of death or retirement or upon the decision to change claims-made carriers. (*See* Nose Coverage.)

Fact Finder The person or group of persons in a judicial or administrative proceeding that has the responsibility for determining the relevant facts in a controversy. In the civil justice system the fact finder typically is the jury, but in a "bench" trial where the jury is waived, the judge serves as the fact finder.

Federal Court A system of trial and appellate courts established by the U.S. Constitution, which only accepts certain types of cases. Malpractice cases generally are filed in state courts and may not be brought in the federal courts unless the plaintiff is from one state and the defendant(s) from another.

Fraud Intentionally misleading another individual in a manner that causes damage or injury to that person. Fraud is a tort.

Frequency of Claims Refers to the number of claims that are filed. Frequency and average severity of claims are the fundamental variables used in determining insurance premiums. (*See* Severity of a Claim.)

General Liability Insurance A type of liability insurance, other than automobile, workers' compensation and employer's liability, that covers damage or bodily injury. In a health care setting, general liability insurance would cover such incidents as a visitor slipping on a wet floor of a hospital or the theft of a patient's belongings.

Good Samaritan Statute Statute enacted to encourage individuals to stop and assist victims of accidents by granting immunity from liability for any negligence resulting from attempts to give such emergency aid without the expectation of payment.

Guaranty Fund Established by law in every state, this fund is typically maintained by the state commissioner of insurance to protect policyholders in the event that their insurer becomes insolvent or otherwise unable to meet its financial obligations. The fund is usually financed by an assessment against all property and casualty insurers regulated by the state.

Guardian Individual recognized by law or appointed by the court to manage the affairs or protect the legal interests of one who is incompetent by reason of age, physical or mental status, and is therefore considered incapable of managing his/her own affairs.

Hearsay Rule An out-of-court statement offered as evidence to prove the truth of the facts contained in the statement. Hearsay is generally not admissible. There are, however, many exceptions to the hearsay rule. (*See* Admission Against Interest.)

Hold Harmless Agreement A clause in some contracts and leases that attempts to shift liability from one party to another (for example, from a medical equipment manufacturer to a health care provider who purchases the equipment). Courts may modify or refuse to uphold such agreements if they are deemed harmful to the public or if the parties are perceived to have unequal bargaining power.

Hypothetical Question A question that solicits the opinion of an expert witness at a trial or deposition based on a combination of assumptions and facts already introduced in evidence.

Immunity (from Liability) Legally granted freedom from responsibility for damages due to an act or omission that ordinarily would impose such liability. Generally, immunity is awarded only in a narrow range of circumstances necessary to achieve some important public good. Good Samaritan statutes are an example.

Indemnity Refers to a total shifting of the economic loss to the party directly responsible for that loss. To indemnify is to compensate for damage, loss, or injury.

Indemnity Agreement An agreement whereby one party attempts to shift responsibility for economic loss or potential liability to another party. (*See* Hold Harmless Agreement.)

Informed Consent A legal doctrine that requires a physician to obtain consent for treatment rendered or an operation performed after explaining the risks involved and the treatment options; without an informed consent the physician may be held liable for violation of the patient's rights, regardless of whether the treatment was appropriate and rendered with due care. (*See* Battery.)

Insurance A contractual relationship (policy) which exists when one party (insurance company or carrier) in consideration of a fixed sum (premium), agrees to reimburse another (insured or policyholder) for loss caused by designated contingencies. (*See* Policy.)

Insurance Company A company, also known as a provider or a carrier, that is licensed by a state to sell some or all types of insurance. There are four types of insurance companies, including (1) "stock" companies, (2) "mutual" companies, (3) "reciprocal" companies and (4) "syndicates."

Interinsurance Exchange An association of insurance policyholders, also known as a reciprocal exchange, in which the policyholders join together and "exchange" their rights and obligations, thereby insuring one another.

Interrogatories A "discovery" procedure in which one party submits a series of written questions to the opposing party, who must answer in writing under oath within a certain period of time. The answers are admissible at trial under certain circumstances. (*See* Discovery.)

Joint Underwriting Association A government-administered risk pooling arrangement, commonly referred to as a JUA, established by law in a number of states to provide professional liability insurance to health care providers. A JUA is structured to be financed by assessments against its participants, but typically also has the authority to assess property and casualty insurers licensed to do business in the state in the event of a deficit.

Joint and Several Liability A legal doctrine designed to protect the plaintiff from insolvent defendants, whereby each individual defendant in a lawsuit is responsible for the entire amount of damages awarded against all defendants. Generally, a defendant who is forced to pay more than his share has the right to file a cross-claim against other defendants for contribution.

Judgment The final entry in the record of a case, which is binding upon the parties unless it is overturned or modified on appeal. A judgment typically consists of a finding in favor of one or more of the parties and an assessment of damages and costs. In a jury trial, the judgment may follow or, under certain circumstances, modify the jury's verdict.

Jury Trial A trial in which six to 12 registered voters are impaneled to hear the evidence, determine the facts, and render a verdict. In most states the verdict must be unanimous.

Liability Obligation that a person has incurred or might incur through any breach of a legally enforced duty; responsibility for conduct falling below a certain standard which is the causal connection of the plaintiff's injury.

Libel Intentional defamation of a person's reputation or character by either printed, written or published work created in a way as to hold the individual up to ridicule, contempt, shame, disgrace or to otherwise degrade him/her in the estimation of the general population. (*See* Defamation.)

Limits of Coverage The maximum amount an insured can collect under the terms of a policy. Professional liability policies typically specify limits per claim and a cumulative limit for all claims incurred during the term of a contract, e.g. $1 million (per claim)/$3 million (per term).

Litigation The process of resolving a dispute in a court of law to determine factual and legal issues, rights and duties between the parties to the controversy, and to award damages or other relief.

Locality Rule The test historically used by courts to determine the standard of care owed by health care providers to patients. The rule holds that health care providers have the duty to render care consistent with the care of other competent or prudent practitioners under the same or similar circumstances in the same or similar community. Most states have displaced the locality rule with the requirement that care must be consistent with national standards. (*See* Standard of Care.)

Loss of Consortium A claim for damages by the spouse of an injured party for the loss of services, comfort, society, and interference with sexual relations.

Malpractice Professional negligence. (*See* Negligence.)

Minor A person below the age of adulthood, as established by state law. Minors usually are considered by law to be incompetent to enter legal contracts. (*See* Guardian.)

Motion Written or oral court plea requesting that a judge make an order or ruling affecting the lawsuit.

Mutual Insurance Company A company organized as a "cooperative" activity by a group of persons, whereby all participants share the losses and profits of the business. A mutual company has no formal stockholders or capital stock.

National Standard of Care A duty to exercise that degree of care and skill expected of a reasonably competent practitioner in the same specialty acting under similar circumstances. In most places, the national standard has replaced the locality rule as the standard of care applied in medical malpractice suits.

Negligence A tort which is proved by showing (1) the existence of a duty owed to the plaintiff(s), (2) breach of the duty by the defendant(s), and (3) an injury that (4) was caused by the breach. In medical malpractice cases, the breach of duty element is proved by showing that a health care provider failed to exercise the standard of care practiced by reasonably prudent health care providers with similar training under similar circumstances. (*See* Standard of Care.)

No-fault Compensation A method for compensating persons injured during the course of medical treatment regardless of whether the injury was caused by the negligence or fault of a health care provider.

Nose Coverage A supplement to a "claims-made" insurance policy that may be purchased by a professional from a new carrier when the professional changes carriers and had claims-made coverage with the previous carrier. A nose policy, also known as "prior acts" coverage, covers incidents that occurred prior to the beginning of the new insurance relationship, but have not yet been brought to the professional's attention as a claim. Nose coverage is an alternative to an "extended reporting endorsement," also known as "tail coverage," which is purchased from the original carrier when a change in carriers is made. (*See* Claims-Made Policy and Extended Reporting Endorsement.)

Occurrence Policy A type of policy in which the policyholder is covered for any incident that occurs during the term of the policy, regardless of when a claim arising from the incident is filed. Occurrence policies have been largely supplanted by "claims-made" coverage in the medical liability insurance market.

Outrageous Conduct Refers to conduct so gross that the law may award damages for emotional or psychic suffering even though no physical harm is caused.

Pain and Suffering Element of non-economic damages (i.e. not related to out-of-pocket expenses) that allows compensation for mental anguish and/or physical pain endured by the plaintiff in connection with the injury for which the plaintiff is seeking redress.

Patient Compensation Fund A fund established by law in a few states that pays benefits to patients injured in the course of medical treatment. Benefits may be awarded on either a fault basis or a no-fault basis, depending on the state program. The fund's benefits may either supplement the payment made by a defendant in a medical malpractice claim or be the primary compensation, again depending on the state program.

Periodic Payments Damages paid over a period of time instead of in a lump sum. Periodic payments may be mandated when the damages exceed a certain amount. Some periodic payment awards cease upon the death of the plaintiff.

Perjury The deliberate giving of false testimony under oath.

Plaintiff The party who initiates a lawsuit by filing the Complaint; the claimant.

Pleadings First phase of a lawsuit, consisting in the complaint, the answer, and any affirmative defenses or counterclaims, during which the issues in dispute are identified and clarified.

Policy The contractual agreement between an insurance company and its insured. The policy sets forth the rights and obligations of both parties to the agreement.

Premium The amount of money an insured pays for an insurance policy. The premium is calculated by the insurance company's underwriters to bring in enough money to establish reserves for future losses, pay current losses, cover the company's operating expenses including the cost of defending claims, and generate a profit if the company is organized as a profit-making business. (*See* Underwriting.)

Premium Credits A reduction in premium that acknowledges an expected reduction in risk due to claims history, completion of a risk management course or a variety of other factors. (*See* Experience Rating.)

Preponderance of Evidence The greater share (more than 50 percent) of the weight of the total evidence in support of or in defense of a legal claim. In medical malpractice cases, a plaintiff must prove negligence by a preponderance of the evidence in order to prevail.

Pretrial Screening A tort reform established in a number of states to require or encourage plaintiffs to participate in a procedure for determining if the claim is unfounded or has merit prior to pursuing litigation in the courts. States differ in the structure of the pretrial screening process, the type of evidence that will be reviewed and in the rules regarding whether the pretrial screening conclusion is admissible as evidence in subsequent litigation.

Prima Facie Case A case that is sufficient to meet the plaintiff's initial burden of proof and requires the defense to offer evidence on its own behalf.

Prior Acts An insurance term referring to incidents that may have occurred, but not yet been filed as claims, prior to the onset of the company/insured relationship. Companies typically require the new insured to purchase either supplemental "tail" or "nose" coverage to protect against claims arising from prior acts. (*See* Extended Reporting Endorsement, Nose Coverage.)

Privileged Communications A legal doctrine designed to protect special confidential communications, such as those existing between lawyer and client and between physician and patient. Although legal protections vary, the general rule is that the communicator controls the privilege. The recipient of the communication cannot be legally compelled to disclose it, nor can he voluntarily do so without the communicator's permission.

Proximate Cause An act or omission that, unbroken by any intervening cause, produces an injury. Proximate causation is one of the four elements that a plaintiff must prove in a negligence claim. In a medical malpractice case, failure to adhere to the standard of care must be the proximate cause of the injury to the patient.

Rate An insurance term reflecting the basis or classification upon which the premium is based; often used as a synonym for premium. (*See* Premium.)

Reciprocal Insurance Company A company organized as a "cooperative" activity in which an "attorney in fact" operates on behalf of the policyholders, who agree to share each others' losses. Like a mutual company, a reciprocal company has no stockholders or capital stock.

Reinsurance A contract whereby an insurance company will itself buy insurance from a second company (the reinsurer) to cover part of the risk the first company has insured. The amount of risk a company will reinsure varies from carrier to carrier.

Release The statement signed by one party relinquishing a legal claim against another party, usually in exchange for a money payment. (*See* Settlement.)

Reporting Requirement The contractual obligation of the insured to promptly report to the carrier any claim for damages asserted against the insured. What constitutes a claim that must be reported varies from company to company, but is always defined in the policy.

Reservation of Rights An insurance term that refers to the situation arising when there is a question as to whether there is a coverage for an incident. Typically, an insurer is obligated to defend a claim during the time the coverage issue between insurer and policyholder is being resolved.

Reserve Money set aside and invested by insurance companies to pay estimated future losses. A company's claims department typically specifies a reserve amount for every claim that is filed, which may be modified as the claim proceeds in the courts.

Res Ipsa Loquitur "The thing speaks for itself." A case in which the personal injuries and/or property damage would not have occurred without negligence. In medical malpractice cases, it allows a patient to prove his or her case without the necessity of an expert witness to testify that the defendant physician violated the standard of care. It is applicable only in those instances in which negligence is clear and obvious, even to a layman, such as a case in which a surgeon leaves a sponge or other foreign object in the patient following surgery.

Respondeat Superior "Let the master answer." The legal principle that makes an employer liable for civil wrong, including negligence, committed by employees within the course and scope of their employment.

Retrospective Rating *See* Experience Rating, Premium Credits..

Risk Classification An insurance term referring to a classification based on the actual and predicted number and size of losses that can be expected from a physician's specialty and procedures, which is used in determining the premium to be charged.

Risk Purchasing Group A group of similarly situated persons or entities that are permitted under federal law to organize across state lines to buy insurance. The insurer selling to the group must be licensed in at least one state, but need not be licensed in every state where a member of the group resides.

Risk Retention Group A group of similarly situated persons or entities that are permitted under federal law to organize across state lines for the purpose of pooling their liability risk and self-insuring. If the group is licensed in one state, it is permitted to solicit business and sell insurance nationwide without fulfilling each state's licensure requirements.

Settlement An agreement between opposing parties whereby the claimant accepts "consideration," usually a money payment, in exchange for a release of any legal right against the party upon whose behalf the payment is made.

Severity of a Claim Also known as claim magnitude, this is the dollar value of a claim as determined by jury verdict or settlement agreement. Claim frequency and average severity are the principal variables used in determining insurance premiums. (*See* Frequency of Claims.)

Standard of Care A term used in the legal definition of medical malpractice. A physician is required to adhere to the standards of practice of reasonably competent physicians, in the same or similar circumstances, with comparable training and experience. (*See* Locality Rule, National Standard of Care.)

Statute of Limitations The time period established by law in which a plaintiff may file a lawsuit. Once this period expires, the plaintiff's lawsuit is barred if the defendant asserts the affirmative defense of the statute of limitations.

Statutory Law Laws enacted by the legislature, in contrast to case law.

Stipulation An agreement made by both parties to the litigation regulating any matter related to the case, proceeding, or trial. For instance, litigants can stipulate to extend the time period for pleadings or to admit certain facts into evidence at trial.

Structured Settlement Settlement agreement between the parties to a lawsuit or a claim, in which the damages are paid to the plaintiff over a period of time instead of in a lump sum. These settlements are usually financed through the purchase of an annuity. (*See* Periodic Payments.)

Subpoena Court order requiring a witness to appear at a certain proceeding to give testimony or produce documents.

Subrogation A legal term referring to the substitution of one person for another in reference to pursuing a legal claim. For example, where one insurer pays damages that may also be covered by another insurer's policy, the paying insurer will obtain a subrogation right from the insured to pursue the insured's claim against the insurer who has not yet paid.

Suit *See* Case.

Summary Judgment Granting of a judgment in favor of either party prior to trial. Summary judgment is only granted when there is no material fact in dispute and one of the parties is entitled to judgment as a matter of law.

Summons A legal document which is attached to the complaint in a lawsuit and must be served on the defendant. It orders the defendant or the defendant's attorney to file an Answer within a specified period of time.

Syndicate Insurance Company A company organized by group of entities who each agree to share in selling insurance to the syndicate's policyholders and pledge their personal assets to cover the losses of the policyholders.

Tail Coverage *See* Extended Reporting Endorsement.

Testimony Oral evidence taken under oath and presented during a judicial proceeding to prove a fact.

Tort A civil wrong for which an action can be filed in court to recover damages for personal injury or property damage resulting from negligent acts or intentional misconduct.

Tort Reform A term used to collectively describe a number of legislative and judicial modifications to traditional tort law.

Tortfeasor One who commits a tort.

Trial Court The court of first jurisdiction where the pleadings are filed, the witnesses appear, testimony is taken and a judgment is entered; also referred to as the lower court.

Trier of Fact *See* Fact Finder.

Underwriting The process by which a company evaluates and classifies risks and measures and calculates the cost of protection, within the framework of the rules, rates and coverage forms that are permitted by law in a particular state.

Verdict The formal decision or finding made by a jury or judge. The verdict is in favor of the plaintiff or defendant. Damages are awarded when a judgment is entered on a verdict in favor of the plaintiff.

Vicarious Liability Civil liability for the torts of others. Physicians may be vicariously liable for the negligent acts of their employees committed within the scope of their employment. (*See* Respondeat Superior.) In the hospital setting, a surgeon may be vicariously liable for the negligent acts of all members of the surgical team. (*See* Captain of the Ship.)

Work Product Materials used by an attorney in preparation for litigation. These materials are not subject to discovery.

Wrongful Birth An action recognized in some states that allows parents to seek damages after the birth of an impaired child on the theory that if they had received proper genetic counseling or testing, the child's birth could have been avoided.

Wrongful Death An action for money damages that exists in favor of a surviving spouse, children, parents or estate when a person dies due to the wrongful acts of another.

Wrongful Life An action brought by an impaired child who contends that if his or her parents had been correctly counseled about likely birth defects, he or she would have never been conceived or would have been aborted.

Index

ABA. *See* American Bar Association

abandonment of patient by physician, *15, 34-41, 349*

abortion: minors' rights concerning, *136-37*

abortion rate: in minors, *137*

abuse. *See* alcohol abuse; child abuse; drug abuse; spouse abuse; substance abuse

access to care, restrictions on, *94*

access to the courts, *71, 272, 279*

Accreditation Council of Graduate Medical Education, *217-18*

Accreditation Manual for Hospitals (1989), *304, 319*

ACGME. *See* Accreditation Council for Graduate Medical Education

active listening, *20*

active supervision requirement, *333*

actuarial analysis, *255*

Adams, E.K., *70*

adequate notice requirement under Health Care Quality Improvement Act of 1986, *336*

admissibility, *349*; of medical records as evidence, *25*

admission policies (medical schools), *228-29*

adolescents. *See* minors

adverse outcomes, *9, 17, 49,* **159-213**, *293*; as grounds for malpractice action, *82*; bibliography, *210-13*; causes of, *162*; clinical response to, *163*; components of, *161*; disclosure of, *190*; emotional effects of, 167; free treatments in response to, *164*; frequency of, *162*; iatrogenic, *186*; impact on physicians, *189*; importance of medical records in, *165*; importance of physician-patient relationship in, *163-64*; inevitability of, *168*; liability for in tort system, *63*; management of, *186-92*; probability of according to specialty, *65*; screening for and reporting of, *90*

Alberts v. Devine (privileged communications), *14*

alcohol abuse: by physicians, *326*; consent by minors to treatment, *135*; indications of in physicians, *237-40*; prevalence of among physicians, *226*; reporting of in physicians, *281*

Alcoholics Anonymous, *242*

alcohol-impaired physicians: responses to, *232, 233;* prevalence of, *226, 234-35*. *See also* alcohol abuse

alcoholism. *See* alcohol abuse

A.M. Best, *291, 348*

AMA/Specialty Society Medical Liability Project, *53, 258, 277, 279-83*

American Academy of Ophthalmology, *55*

American Academy of Orthopaedic Surgeons, guidelines for expert witnesses, *57-58*

American Academy of Pediatricians, *57-58, 77*

American Association of Medical Colleges, *217, 323*

American Association of Neurological Surgeons, guidelines for expert witnesses, *57-58*

American Bar Association Committee on Ethics and Professional Responsibility, *263, 264*

American Bar Association Council on Ethical and Judicial Affairs, *303*

American Bar Association Model Rules of Professional Conduct, *252, 263*

American Bar Association National Conference of Lawyers and Liability Insurers, *264*

American Board of Medical Specialties, *101*

American Cancer Society, *91*

American College of Cardiology, *55*

American College of Obstetricians and Gynecologists: survey on expert witnesses, *57*; survey on litigation outcomes, *66*

American College of Surgeons, *91, 197*

American Diabetes Association, *55*

American Heart Association, *55*

American Hospital Association, *304*

American Medical Association: *323, 328*; annual survey data: data on claims frequency, *270, 284, 286*; practice parameters, *54, 55, 83*

American Medical Association Center for Health Policy Research, *284*

American Medical Association Code of Ethics, *28*

American Medical Association Council on Ethical and Judicial Affairs, *19, 58, 303*

American Medical Association Council on Mental Health, *216, 231*

American Medical Association Judicial Council, *25-26, 318*

American Medical Association Office of the General Counsel, *308, 330, 336-38*

American Medical Association Physician Recognition Award, *5*

American Society of Anesthesiologists, *53, 292*; guidelines of, *77*; standards issued by, *89*

American Society of Anesthesiologists Committee on Professional Liability, *292*

anesthesia: allegations of negligence in, *194*; alleged injuries due to, *194-95*; cost of implementing standards in, *80*; Harvard standards of, *53, 55, 76-81, 82, 84-85, 292*; indicators of quality in, *200*; insurance claim losses, *85, 193, 194, 289*; insurance issues, *284-94*; morbidity and mortality rates, *76*; requirements, in Arizona, *89*, and Massachusetts, *89*; risk management in, *197-205*

Anesthesia Patient Safety Foundation, *292*

anesthesiology. *See* anesthesia

angioplasty, *54*

anticompetitive behavior, *306, 308*

Antitrust Division of the US Department of Justice, *330*

antitrust litigation: consequences of *Patrick*, *307-9, 330-35*; early termination of, *331-32*; exposure of peer reviewing physicians, *330-35*; and the medical profession, *301, 307*; physician immunity from, *281, 302, 307-8*

Appelbaum, Paul A., MD, *143-44; 146-52*

Applegate, William B., MD, MPH, *186-92*

appropriate address of patients, *17*

appropriate language in medical records, *23*

appropriateness of use of procedures, *96-98*

arbitration, *70, 259, 276, 277, 309, 349*

ASA. *See* American Society of Anesthesiologists

aseptic necrosis, *153-54*

assets, transfer of, *177*

attorneys' fees, *49*; recovery of in antitrust actions, *332-37*

authority of physician, *126-30, 148*

automobile insurance *276, 280*

autonomy of patient, *128*

autopsy, benefits of, *18*

awards in malpractice suits, *64-67, 288*

Axelrod, David, Dr. (New York State Health Commissioner), *258*

battery, of patient by physician, *112-13, 349*

Bierig, Jack, *330-35*

bioethics, *146*

birth-related injuries: as most costly group of claims, *66*; compensation for, *72, 276*; insurance pools for, *257*

Blue Cross/Blue Shield, adoption of clinical guidelines, *55*

Blum, R.H., *187*

Bowen, Otis R., *327, 328, 329*

breach of contract, *35, 350*

breach of duty or standard of care, *51, 56, 82*

Brewster, J.M., *234*

Broder, I., *67*

Brodsky, Archie, BA, *131-33*

burden of proof, *71, 184, 273, 326, 350*

Burszatjn, Harold, MD, *131-33*

business skills: need for in medical practice, *228*

Caduceus Outpatient Residences, *242*

California Hospital Association, *162*

California Medical Association, *162, 195*

California Medical Feasibility Study, *198-99*

California: physician competency laws, *326-27*

California Retail Liquor Dealers Assn v. Midcal Aluminum Inc. (state action doctrine of peer review), *332-33*

Campion, Francis X., MD, *269-78*

Canterbury v. Spence (informed consent) *128*

captive insurance companies, *196, 251, 254, 273, 284, 350*

Caribbean medical schools, *323*

case law, *50, 350*

causation, *350*; probabilistic, *72*; proof of, *51*; revision of standard, *282*; scientific notions of, *69*

cause of action: definition of, *183, 350*

cerebral palsy: as causation issue, *69*

charitable immunity, abolition of, *70*

Charles, Sara, Dr., *207*

chemical dependency. *See* drug abuse, alcohol abuse.

Chicago Medical Society, *207*

Chicago Risk Pooling Program, *205*

child abuse: and parental consent laws, *137*; reporting of, *31*

Childrens Hospital of Los Angeles, *187*

civil justice system: alternatives to, *279-80*

claims-made insurance policy, *252-54, 350*

claims, malpractice: allegation frequencies, *59, 62, 102-4*; closure with no payment: rates of, *285*; cost of, *102-4, 270, 272, 285*; data concerning,*58-59*; definition of, *319, 350*; for minor or emotional injuries, *161*; frequency of, *64-67, 204-5, 259, 270-71, 275-76, 284-87*; most expensive, *102-4*; reasons for, *205*; results of, *195*; review projects underway at Harvard, *86*

clear and convincing evidence, *326*

clear and present danger, power to suspend physicians posing, *325*

clinical judgment, *129*

clinical practice standards. *See* standards of care

CME. *See* continuing medical education

COBRA. *See* Consolidated Omnibus Budget Reconciliation Act of 1986

co-defendants, discussions with, *177*

Code of Ethics. *See* American Medical Association Code of Ethics

cognitive services, reimbursement for, *151*

collateral source: payments, *70, 274, 283*; rule, *350*

collection recommendations, *53*

Columbia Memorial Hospital, *330-31*

comatose patients: and informed consent, *141*

Committee on Impaired Physicians of the Massachusetts Medical Society, *219*

communication: as cause of malpractice suits, *9, 266*; between physician and family, *225*; between physician and patient, *1, 187-91, 225*; effects of poor (on physicians), *224*. *See also* physician-patient relationship

communication skills, improving, *10*

companionship, loss of. *See* loss of consortium

compensation funds, state, list of, *347*

compensation to patients as percentage of malpractice costs, *279* competitive threat, *331*

complaint (legal), *183, 351*

computerization of medical records: implications of, *13*; problems with, *31*

confidentiality: ethical and legal aspects, *27*; of information under Health Care Quality Improvement Act of 1986, *337*; legal definition of clinical, *27*; limits of, *29*; of malpractice history, *321*; of National Practitioner Data Bank, *309*; of participation in impaired physician programs, *326*; in peer review, *307*; of physician-lawyer relationship, *263*; of physician-patient relationship, *14-15;* waiver of by patient, *29, 30*

conflict of interest: between insurer and insured physician, *263, 264*

confrontation of impaired or incompetent physician, *315*

consent. *See* informed consent

consent forms: inadequacies of, *116*; samples, *119-24*; sample for anesthesia, *293-94*

Consent to Treatment: A Practical Guide, *113*

Consolidated Omnibus Budget Reconciliation Act of 1986, *89*

conspiracy of silence, *216, 228, 237, 241*

consultation: limitation of practice to, *39-40*

consulting physician: responsibilities of, *36, 37*

consumer participation, *21*

consumer (patient) complaints: as source of disciplinary actions, *327*

consumer rights, *271*

contingency fees, *49, 272, 351*; reform of, *274*

continuing medical education, *281*; credits for in professional liability and risk management, *4, 5*

contraception, minors' rights regarding, *136*

contract, *351*; between physician and patient, *15, 276*

Controlled Risk Insurance Co., Ltd., *254*

conversations, documenting important, *12*

conviction of physicians for felony or fraud, *326*

Cooper, Jeffrey B., PhD, *76-81*

COPIC, *87*

corrections to medical record, *13*

cost-benefit analysis, *95, 227*

cost containment: role in practice parameters, *53*

cost of care: discussions concerning, *18*; physician responsibilities regarding, *11*

Council of Medical Specialty Societies, *101, 279*; guidelines for expert witnesses, *58*

counts (legal): definition of, *183*

Cousins, N., *187-88*

Craddick, Joyce, MD, *199*

credentialing: accepted standards, *304*; administrative review of decisions, *334*; judicial review of decisions, *333-34*; processes, *279-80*; role of proposed Medical Board in, *281*; use of malpractice experience in, *320*

credentials (physician): checklist for medical staff privileges, *304*; availability of information on, *301*; sources for verification of, *312*; proper investigation of, *303-4*

CRICO. *See* Controlled Risk Insurance Co., Ltd.

Crile, George Jr., *129*

criticism of other physicians, *12, 17, 24*

cross-examination, *184*

Cullen, David J., MD, *76-81*

culpable dereliction of duty, *37*

Curran, William J., JD., *153-55*

customary care, definition of, *68*

damages, *351*; legally compensable, *82*; payment schedule, *283*; punitive, *50, 307*. *See also*: economic damages; non-economic damages; treble damage liability

Danner, Douglas, *116, 163, 176-85*

Danzon, P.M., *70*

Darling v. Charleston Community Hospital (hospital liability), *303, 316*

death, coping with, *225*

debt (educational), effects of, *218*

decision analysis, *95*

decision-making: autonomy of adolescents, *134*; preservation of patients', *111*; assessing patients' capacity for, *143*

deep pocket defendants, *69, 274*

defamation of character, *275, 306*

Defendant: A Psychiatrist on Trial for Medical Malpractice, *207*

defendant, *351*; physician, rights of, *336-37*

defense attorney, *351*; dealing with, *177-78*; loyalty obligations of, *252, 263*

defensive medicine, *1, 69, 133, 177, 277, 328*

delay in diagnosis: as allegation of malpractice, *56*

delivery of baby: duty to attend, *36*

Department of Anaesthesia of Harvard Medical School, *76-81, 291*

deposition, *176, 183-84* , *352*

depressed physicians, responses to, *232*

depression during residency, prevalence of, *234*

depressive disorders: as part of malpractice stress syndrome, *207*

deviation from customary standard of care, *56, 90*

DHHS. *See* Health and Human Services, US Department of

diabetes, guidelines for treatment of, *55*

diagnosis related groups, *309-10*

directed verdict, motion for, *184*

direct examination, *184*

Disabled Doctors Program of the Medical Association of Georgia, *237-40*

discharge: against medical advice, *143*; instructions, *18*; sharing of information during, *31*

disciplinary action: grounds for, *325*; incidence of, *306, 325-26*; inconsistencies in, *327-28*; lack of referrals for by physicians, *327*; processes for, *279-80*; publicizing of, *328*; public perceptions of, *324*; reporting of, *302, 309, 327*

discipline (medical): overview of, *322-29*

disclosure standards (in informed consent), *112, 128*

discovery, *352* methods of, *183-84*

discretion of physician, in informed consent, *127*

discrimination against physicians by patients, *226*

dissatisfaction with work, among physicians, *227*

Doctors' Co., The, *86-87*

doctrine of informed consent. *See* informed consent

documentation. *See* records

Doran v. Priddy (duty of consulting physician), *35-36*

Dostoyevsky, F., *126*

DRGs. *See* diagnosis related groups

drug abuse: consent by minors to treatment of, *135*; prescription, *32*; incidence in physicians, *226-27, 326*; indications of in physicians, *237*; reporting of in physicians, *281*

drug-acquisitive behavior, *224*

drug addiction. *See* drug abuse

due process: rights of disciplined physicians, *313*; under peer review procedures, *308*

duty of care, *352*; hospitals, *316-18*; physicians, *55-56*

duty to person harmed, *50*

Easter v. Lexington Memorial Hospital, Inc. (patient abandonment), *35*

economic damages, *51, 67*

Educational Commission for Foreign Medical Graduates, *323*

Education, US Department of, *324*

Eichhorn, John H., MD, *76-81*

Elam v. College Park Hospital (hospital liability), *317*

elective interventions, *129*

emancipated minor, *134*. *See also* minors

emergency department physicians, liability risks of, *59-60*

emotional distress, *52*

Employers Casualty Co. v. Tilley (loyalty owed insurer by insurer-provided attorney), *263, 264*

epidural analgesia, *78*

epilepsy, breach of confidentiality concerning, *29*

errors of judgment, *51, 186*

ethical standards concerning confidentiality, *27-28*

ethics manual of American College of Physicians, *15*

event model. *See* informed consent

evidence, *352*; admissibility, *50*; nontestimonial, *184*; testimony of expert witnesses as, *57*. *See also* rules of evidence

examination of judgment of debtor, *267*

expectations: of patients, *10, 17, 48, 59, 68, 148, 150*; of physicians, *10, 11, 48, 148*; of society, *276*

experience rating for insurance purposes, *256, 274, 352*

expert consultants, *184*

expert medical testimony, *35, 51, 68-69*; of "hired guns," *57, 273*; uses in establishing standards of care, *82-83*. *See also* expert witnesses

expert witnesses, *352*; economists as, *71*; qualifications and guidelines for, *57-58, 101*. *See also* expert medical testimony

exposure period, *253*

failure, admissions of, *164*

failure to act, *48, 51*

family life among physicians, *227*

family members, as surrogate decision makers, *144*; involvement in medical decisions, *25, 115*

family planning facilities, federal regulation of, *136*

fantasies of certainty, *131-33*

fault-based administrative system for medical liability, *279-83*

fear (patients'): physician's role in alleviating, *224-25*

Federation of State Medical Boards, *217, 302, 323, 325, 327, 328*

fee-for-service system, discomfort with, *227*

fees, attorneys', *272, 292*. *See also* contingency fees

Feinstein, Alvan, *129*

Ferguson v. Gonyaw (hospital liability), *316*

fetal assessment in labor, standards for, *88*

financial needs of patient, discussion of, *21*

follow-up contact, *21*

foreign medical graduates, *323-34*

fourth amendment, *27, 28*

Fox, R., *188*

Frederick, Dr., *153-54*

frequency of malpractice claims. *See* claims

frivolous (non-meritorious) claims or suits, *9, 272, 292, 293, 308, 338*. *See also* malicious prosecution

FSMB. *See* Federation of State Medical Boards

GAO. *See* General Accounting Office

garnishment of income, *267-68*

gatekeepers, *94*

General Accounting Office, US: *270, 284-85*; criticisms of malpractice system, *257*; data on malpractice claims, *288*; studies regarding insurance availability, *271*; study on data for anesthesia allegations, *287*

genetic screening: liability implications of, *71*

geographic limitations on scope of practice, *39*

glaucoma: guidelines for treatment of, *55*; sample surgery consent form, *120*

good faith peer review, *308, 330*

Good Samaritan Hospital, *199*

Greisman v. Newcomb Hospital (peer review and credentialing), *333-34*

guaranteed outcomes, *17*

guaranty funds, *255, 353*

Guide to the Essentials of a Modern Medical Practice Act, *217*

guilt, admissions of, *164*

gunshot wounds: breach of confidentiality concerning, *29*

Gutheil, Thomas G., MD, *131-33, 188, 189*

Hamlet, *130*

Handley, Elisabeth A., MPA, *322-29*

Hankoff, L.D., MD, *27-33*

harm to a third party: confidentiality concerns, *29, 32*

Harnish v. Childrens Hospital Medical Center (informed consent), *154*

Harvard Anesthesia Standards. *See* anesthesia

Harvard Medical Practice Study, *2, 162, 258, 276*

Harvard Medical School, *53*

Harvard Obstetrical Standards, *85*

Harvard Radiology Standards, *85*

Harvard rating structure for specialty risks, *290*

Harvard Risk Management Foundation. *See* Risk Management Foundation

Harvard School of Public Health, *2, 162*

Health and Human Services, US Department of, *136, 310, 329*

health care expenditures, *1*

Health Care Quality Improvement Act of 1986, *72, 275, 281, 302, 305, 308-9, 313, 332, 334*; review of, *336-38*

health maintenance organizations, *94*

hearings: in peer review panels, *338*; requirement for under Health Care Quality Improvement Act of 1986, *336-37*

HHS. *See* Health and Human Services, US Department of

high-risk specialties, *48*; claims losses of, *83*; premiums for, *59*

Hilfiker, David, MD, *161, 171-75*

Hippocratic oath, *28*

"hired gun" physicians, *57, 273*

Hirsh, Harold, MD, JD, FCLM, *34-41*

HIV antibody testing: discrimination due to, *114*; sample consent form for, *124*

HMOs. *See* health maintenance organizations

"holding self out": theory of, *36*

Hollender, M.H., *187*

Holzer, James F., JD, *82-93, 193-206, 284-94*

homicidal patients: confidentiality concerning, *30*

Hospital Accreditation Program Scoring Guidelines 1989, *305*

hospital-owned insurance, *201-2*

hospitals: liability regarding physician negligence, *316-18*; responsibilities regarding physician credentialing, *302-3*

house calls: legal implications of refusal to make, *37-38*

Howard, J., *148*

human immunodeficiency virus. *See* HIV

Hunt, William S., Esq., *266-68*

Hyg, S.M., *153-55*

iatrogenic illness, injury, disease, morbidity, or complications: and physician-patient relationship, *186*; incidence of, *64, 72*; patient dissatisfaction resulting from, *9*; probability of, *161*; publicity concerning, *168*

IDAA. *See* International Doctors in Alcoholics Anonymous

identification of impaired/incompetent physicians, *301*

illness models, *148*

immunity from antitrust laws. *See* antitrust

immunity: from damages under Health Care Quality Improvement Act of 1986, *336*; from liability, *353*

impaired physicians, **214-48**; behavioral abnormalities of, *237-40*; bibliography, *244-48*; chemical dependency, *216*; definition of, *216, 231*; dilemma in identifying, *237-40*; education about, *219*; employment patterns, *237-38*; identification of, *241*; malpractice stress syndrome, *208*; physically disabled, *217*; physical signs of impairment, *238*; prevalence of, *234*; programs to help, *219, 326*; responses to among house officers, *231-37*; self-deception of, *237*; statistics, *237*; treatment of, *242-43*; voluntary enrollment in treatment programs, *326*; warning signs, *218-19, 222*

Impaired Physicians Program of the Medical Association of Georgia, *241-42*

Impaired Physicians Program of the Medical Society of New Jersey, *208*

impairment, reporting of, *281*

inadequacy, physician feelings of, *189*

incapacitated patients: clinical presentations, *141*

incapacity: clinical, *114-15, 140-41*; mental, *139*; transient *141-42*

incest: and parental consent laws, *137*

incident reports, limitations of, *198*

incompetency, definition of, *114-15*. *See also* legal incompetency

incompetent physicians: cost of, *328*; definition of, *231*; prevalence of, *234-45*; reporting of, *235, 281*; responses to, *232, 234, 326*

incorporation, benefits of, *268*

indemnification of physicians for peer review activities, *332*

independent contractors, physicians' status as, *303*

information sciences, *95*

informed consent, **109-58**, *353*; and HIV antibody testing, *113*; and incompetent patients, *114*; and medical uncertainty, *113*; and mentally incompetent patients, *139-45*; and physician-patient relationship, *111-12, 126-30, 147, 188*; and psychiatric patients, *139*; and risk management, *203-4*; bibliography, *156-58*; clinical impact, *131*; courtroom implications, *111*; doctrine of, *112, 126-27, 140, 203, 282*; documentation of, *115, 116*; event model of *146-47*; expansion of, *70*; implementation of, *146-52*; inception of, *146*; in Massachusetts, *153*; list of "do's and don'ts," *118*; minimum standards for obtaining, *204*; not required, *114, 140*; patient-oriented standard, *115*; process model of, *147-51*; therapeutic use of, *131-33*; unrealistic burdens on physicians, *153*; voluntary waiver of, *114*; when required, *125* . *See also* consent forms

informed judgment, *203*

Ingelfinger, Franz, *153*

injury rates, *2*

Inspector General of the US Department of Health and Human Services, *306*

Institute of Medicine of the National Academy of Sciences, *310*

insurance: **249-97**, *353*; availability of, *271, 273, 275*; bibliography, *295-97*; ceilings, *274*; choosing correct policy, *249*; claims-made policies, *252-54*; considerations in evaluating data, *287*; cost of, *269-70*; cost statistics, *251*; going without, 256, *266-68*; issues in anesthesiology, *284-94*; limited practice coverage, *256*; nose coverage, *253*; occurrence policies, *252*; physicians duty to insurer, *262*; prior acts coverage, *253*; questions to ask when purchasing, *261*; rates by specialty, *269*; reasons for surcharges and cancellations, *87*; recommended limits, *255*; relative cost of policies, *253-54*; reforms, *274*; requirement to have, *254*; scope of coverage, *255-56*; tail coverage, 253; variations in policies, *251-54*; what it covers, *182*.

insurance claim representatives, dealing with, *177-78*

insurance companies, *354*; captive, *196, 251, 254, 273, 284*; duty to pay and defend, *262-63*; largest commercial (list) *348*; losses, *1, 92, 275*; physician/hospital owned, *83, 86, 201-2, 273, 275, 342-45*; types of, *254*

insurance premiums. *See* premiums

insurance providers. *See* insurance companies

International Doctors in Alcoholics Anonymous, *243*

interrogatories, definition of, *183, 354*

involuntary/underwriter-generated standards of care, *87*

irrational alliance, *132*

irrational refusal of treatment, *143*

isolation: as part of malpractice stress syndrome, *207*

Jacobson, Peter D., JD, MPH, *63-75*

jargon, use of, *26*

JCAHO. *See* Joint Commission on Accreditation of Healthcare Organizations

Johnson, Nancy (congresswoman from Conn.), *277*

Johnson v. Misericordia Community Hospital (negligent credentialing), *316-17*

joint and several liability: legal doctrine of, *56, 283, 354*; restriction of, *274*. *See also* joint liability

Joint Commission on Accreditation of Hospitals, *196, 200, 316, 317*; standards of care issued by, *77*

Joint Commission on Accreditation of Healthcare Organizations, *166, 304, 305, 319*

joint liability, *267*

joint underwriting associations, list of, *346*

joint underwriting pools, *196*

juries: average verdicts, *83*; behavior, *69*; decrease in verdicts, *285*; instructions to, *185*; size of awards made by, *279*

jurisdiction: definition of, *183*; variation in, *50*

Jury Verdict Research, Inc., *67, 193*

Justice, US Department of, *330*

Katz, Jay, MD, *126-30*

Kennedy, Eugene, *207*

Korsch, B.M., *187*

Kusserow, Richard P., *322-29*

lawyers' tactics, changes in, *71*

Lazare, A., *187*

legal incompetency, definition of, *140-41*. *See* also incompetency

legal system: evolution of in regard to medical malpractice, *63-75*; substantive changes in, *70-71*

Levy, S., *148*

liability, *354*; control standards, *53, 89-91*; crisis, *251, 271*; due to poor medical records, *23*; expansion of, *70-71*; legal elements of, *282*; legal standards for, *279*; proposed revisions to rules of, *282*; standards for assessment of, *68*; statistics, *2*

Liacos, Justice, of Massachusetts Supreme Judicial Court, *154*

Libby Zion case, *217*

licenses: renewal fees, *322, 328*

licensing: authority of boards, *274-75*; reciprocity, *329*; requirements, *305*

licensure actions, adverse, *309*. *See* also disciplinary actions

licensure denials: reporting of, *327*

Lidz, Charles W., PhD, *139-45, 146-52*

limitations on scope of practice, *37-40*

limitation to practice of specialty, *39*

limited scope of care, *16*

Litigation Stress Support Group, *208*

locality rule, *68-69, 70, 83, 354*

loss of chance of survival, *70*

loss of consortium, *49, 52, 154, 292, 355*

loss prevention: as component in development of standards of care, *83*. *See also* risk management

lost income, *283*

lump-sum settlement payments, *272, 274*

magical thinking, *131-33*

Maier, Ward R., MD, *76-81*

Maine standards, *87*

maladapted physicians, *227*

malicious prosecution, counterclaims for, *178*

malpractice claims. *See* claims

malpractice: criminal repercussions (lack of), *50*; crises in, *269-78*; data trends in, *64-67*; definition of, *48, 49*; legal process, *163*; legal requirements of a defense, *23*; reform, *257-59, 269-78*; risk, *20-22*

malpractice history: national reporting of, *275*. *See also* National Practitioner Data Bank

malpractice insurance. *See* insurance

malpractice stress syndrome, *162, 167-68, 207-9*

malpractice suits. *See* suits

Martin, Peggy B., *319-21*

Massachusetts Board of Registration in Medicine, *319*

Massachusetts Eye and Ear Infirmary, *153, 154*

Massachusetts Medical Society, *154, 219*

Massachusetts: regulations concerning risk management, *89*

Massachusetts Society of Eye Physicians, *154*

Massachusetts Supreme Judicial Court, *293*

Matsushita Electric Industrial Co. v. Zenith Radio Corp. (summary judgment in antitrust cases), *331*

mature minor rule, definition of, *135*

mature minors, *114*. *See also* minors

McAfee, R.E., *91*

McCue, Jack D., *224-30*

McIntosh v. Milano (protection of third party), *29*

Mechanic, D., *188*

media: talking to, *177*

Medicaid, *309*. *See also* Medicare

Medical Association of Georgia, *219, 237-43*

Medical Claim Conciliation Panel (Hawaii), *266*

medical history, *27*

Medical Insurance Feasibility Study, *162*

Medical Inter-Insurance Exchange of New Jersey, *208*

Medical Liability Project. *See* AMA/Specialty Society Medical Liability Project

Medical Malpractice: A Primer for Physicians, *163, 176-85*

medical malpractice insurance. *See* insurance

Medical Malpractice Joint Underwriting Association of Massachusetts, *89, 290-91*

medical malpractice. *See* malpractice

medical malpractice stress syndrome. *See* malpractice stress syndrome

Medical Mutual Insurance Co. of Maine, *87*

medical practice guidelines/parameters/protocols/standards: *53-55*; admissibility as evidence, *89-90*; anesthesia, *77-80*; clinical, *52, 53-55, 287, 291, 292*; compatibility with practicing medicine, *94-100*; consensus-based, *91*; cost of implementing, *80;* federally imposed, *89*; fetal assessment in labor, *88*; for liability, *82-93*; Maine, *87*; national, *83*; need for, *64*; need for expanded use of, *72*; potential detrimental effects and risks, *98-99*; prevalence of, *77*; recommendations concerning, *98-99;* resistance to, *76, 81, 89*

Medical Practice Study. *See* Harvard Medical Practice Study

medical records. *See* records

medical schools: foreign, *323-24*

Medical Society of New Jersey, *208*

medical uncertainty, *128-30, 131-33, 168, 226*; and physician decision making, *168*; threat to patients posed by, *188*

Medicare, *309*

Medicare and Medicaid Patient and Program Protection Act, *329*

Medicare/Medicaid: policing, *323*

Medicare Program to Assure Quality, *310*

Medicare Quality Review Organizations, *310*

Meisel, Alan, JD, *139-45, 146-52*

mental anguish, *52*. *See also* non-economic damages

mental illness: and decision-making capacity, *142*; in physicians, *216-17*

mental retardation: and decision-making capacity, *142*

Michigan State Medical Society: guidelines for record-keeping, *13, 23*

Miller v. Indiana Hospital (summary judgment in antitrust cases), *332*

Mills, D.H., *65*

minors, *355*; consent issues concerning, *113-14, 134-38*; pregnancy rates in, *137*; treatment statutes, *134-35*

mirror image therapy for impaired physicians, *243*

Mitchell County Hospital v. Joiner (negligent credentialing), *316*

Model Guide for the Preparation of a Guidebook on Medical Discipline, *328*

monitoring, minimal standards in anesthesiology, *292*

MPAQ. *See* Medicare Program to Assure Quality

multiple clinicians, *17, 22, 53*

Munetz, Mark R., MD, *139-45*

Murray v. United States (patient abandonment), *40*

Mutual Insurance Co. of Arizona, *89*

mutual monitoring and informed consent, *148-49*

narcissistic alliance, *132*

Narcotics Anonymous, *242*

Natanson v. Kline (informed consent), *128*

National Academy of Sciences, *310*

National Association of Insurance Commissioners, *204*

National Cancer Institute, *91*

National Practitioner Data Bank, *49, 256, 302, 305, 308-9*

Nattland, Candice, PsyD, *27-33*

negative self-image: as part of malpractice stress syndrome, *207*

negligence, **46-108**, *355*; and hospital liability, *316-18*; assessment of in tort system, *63*; bibliography, *105-8*; components of, *20, 50, 82*; malpractice awards for, *193*; necessary conditions to prove, *195-96*; perceived, *11*; prevalence of, *162*; proportion of incidents resulting in claim, *163*; rates of, *2*

neurosurgery, liability risks of, *59*

New England Journal of Medicine, *324*

New York State Department of Health, *162*

New York State Health Commissioner, *217, 258*

New Zealand: medical compensation in, *276*

Noble, Sarah, *231-37*

no-fault: automobile insurance *276, 280*; compensation, *355*; compensation funds, *257-58*; insurance for medical injury, *198-99, 276*; medical liability, *153*

noncompliance: with anesthesia standards, *80*; with medical instructions, *10*

non-economic damages, *51-52, 273*; cap on, *70, 274, 275, 277, 282-83, 292*; increases in, *279*; proportion of jury verdicts, *67*

non-meritorious claims. *See* frivolous claims

non-suit, motion for, *184*

nonverbal communication, *17*

nose coverage (insurance), *253, 355*

notification to insurer, *178*

Nye, D.J., *66*

obligation to treat: legal vs. moral, *15*

obstetrical standards of care, *85, 86*

obstetricians, effect on malpractice statistics, *66*; liability risks of, *59*; rates of malpractice claims among, *59*

obstruction of justice, duty to avoid, *29*

occurrence policy, *252, 355*

O'Connor, Justice, of Massachusetts Supreme Judicial Court, *154*

offer of proof, in malpractice suits, *176*

Office of the Inspector General of the US Department of Health and Human Services, *323*

omnipotence, disavowal of, *132*

ongoing claims: required reporting of, *304-5*

opening statements, by attorneys, *184*

Oregon Board of Medical Examiners, *306*

Oregon: physician competency laws, *326-27*

organ donation, *18*

ostensible agency, *303*

overuse of procedures, 96-98

pain and suffering, *355*. *See also* non-economic damages

parental consent: to minor's abortion, *136*; treatment without obtaining, *134*

Parker v. Brown (state action immunity for peer review), *330, 332-33*

patient autonomy, re-establishing, *151*

Patient Care Assessment Regulations of the Massachusetts Board of Registration in Medicine, *319*

patient expertise, *148*

patient-oriented care, *21*

patient participation, *21*

patient questions, list of, *21-22*

patient rights, *11, 19, 30, 196*

patient values, *148*

Patrick, Timothy, MD, *330-35*

Patrick v. Burget (peer review and antitrust), *307, 330-35*

peer review, **298-340**; bibliography, *339-41*; confidentiality of, *307*; consequences of, *307*; definition of, *301*; due process in, *307*; guidelines for conducting, *313-15*; immunity for, *306* (*see also* antitrust); qualifications for, *314*; need for, *64*; need for insulation of, *72*; responsibility of, *275*; risks to reviewers, *307*; standards for under Health Care Quality Improvement Act of 1986, *336*; unreasonable discouragement of, *336*

Peer Review Organizations, *306, 309-10*

peer support during adverse outcome, *167-68*

performance complaints, *281*

performance monitoring, *281, 305-6*

perinatal injury: review panel, *87*

personal attorney, physician's, role of, *264*; when to hire, *182-83, 252*

Peterson, M.A., *66, 67*

Philip, James H., MD, *76-81*

phony doctor networks, *324*

physical handicaps and decision-making capacity, *143*

physician error, emotional repercussions of, *171*

physician impairment. *See* impaired physician

Physician Insurers Association of America, *254, 258-59*

physician-owned insurance companies, *201-2, 273, 275, 342-45*

physician-patient interaction, styles of, *187*

physician-patient relationship, **6-45**, *293*; bibliography, *42-45*; duration of, *34*; in adverse outcomes, *187-91*; legal protection of, *14*; maturation of, *11*; proof of establishment, *50*; role of trust, *20*; statistics on, *9*. *See also* confidentiality, communication

PIAA. *See* Physician Insurers Association of America

Planned Parenthood, *136*

poor communication. *See* communication; physician-patient relationship

poor outcomes. *See* adverse outcomes

posttrial reductions, use in malpractice statistics, *67*

practice guidelines. *See* medical practice guidelines

practice parameters. *See* medical practice guidelines

precedent, *50*

Precourt v. Frederick (informed consent), *115-16; 153-54*

pregnancy: rate in minors, *137*

premium relativities (Mass.), *291*

premiums, *1, 356*; credits, *356*; discounts, *5, 201-2; 256, 292-93*; increases in, *48, 284, 287, 289*; moderation of, *291*; reductions in, *66, 276*

preponderance of evidence, *326, 332, 356*

prescribing practices: recommendations, *53*

prescription violations, *326*

President's Commission for the Study of Ethical Problems in Medical Biomedical and Behavioral Research, *139*

Press, I., *189*

prior acts, *356*; coverage (insurance), *253*

privacy, definition, *27*

private dispute resolution, *259*

privileged communications, *356*; between physicians and patients, *14*; legal and ethical standards, *27-28*. *See* also confidentiality

privileges (staff): granting by hospitals, *316-18*; hospitals' powers and responsibilities regarding, *303*; judicial review of decisions regarding, *333*; limitation or restriction of, *302*. *See also* antitrust litigation

problem patients, *225-26*

process model. *See* informed consent

prodefendant changes in law, *70*

product liability, *48, 204, 273*

product-related injuries, *48-49*

professional liability insurance. *See* insurance

professional sanctions, need for, *66*

Professional Standard Review Organization program, *98*

proplaintiff reforms of the law, *70*

PROs. *See* Peer Review Organizations

proximate cause, *51, 56, 69, 82, 356*

psychiatric treatment, confidentiality in, *29, 32*

psychiatrist-patient privilege, *28*

psychiatry: standards of treatment, *55*

psychotherapy, confidentiality in, *29*

Public Citizen Health Research Group, *328*

Public Health Service Act of 1970, *136*

public interest, breach of confidence to preserve, *29*

publicity, in malpractice suits, *177*

punitive damages, *50, 307, 351*

Purcell v. Zimbelman (negligent credentialing), *316*

purchase of medical records, *25-26*

quality assurance, *166, 196-97, 199*

radiology: malpractice claims rate, *85*

radiology standards of care, *85, 91*

Rand Corp., *55, 275*

Reading, Edward G., Rev., *207-9*

reasonable care: by hospital in selecting medical staff, *317*. *See also* privileges

reasonable care standard, *77*

records (medical): *11-14*; admissibility as evidence, *25*; appropriate language in, *23*; as malpractice defense, *23-26*; changes in, *177*; inadequate documentation of care, *53, 205, 293*; mechanical requirements, *23*; purchase or sale of, *25-26*; release or transfer, *13-14*; standard formats and guidelines, *12-13*; release to other physicians, *25*; supplying to plaintiff, *179*; what not to write, *12*; which relevant to a malpractice suit, *178*

reform, legal. *See* tort reform

refusal of treatment: irrational but competent decisions, *143*; rights of minors, *135-36*

refusal to attend, *36*

refusal to treat, *35*

rehabilitation of physicians, *279*

relativities, use of in evaluating premiums, *289-91*

Relman, Arnold S., MD, *324*

reporting: of information under Health Care Quality Improvement Act of 1986, *337*; of malpractice history, *319-21*; of privileged communications, *15*; of physician malpractice, *327*; procedures (peer review), *301-2*

report to defense: sample form, *179-81*

Residency Review Committees, *218*

respondeat superior, *70, 303, 316, 357*

Reuben, David B., *231-37*

rights of patients. *See* patient rights

right to privacy, waiver of patients, *178-79*. *See also* confidentiality

risk management; *166-167*; concepts in, *193-206*; development of, *195, 196*; education, *202*; multidisciplinary nature of, *197-98*; problem assessment, *201*; problem identification, *198-200, 292*; programs, *274*; recommendations, *2*; requirements for accreditation, *166*; scientific validation of guidelines, *91*

Risk Management Foundation of the Harvard Medical Institutions, *84, 86, 193, 194, 202, 287*

Risk Management Principles & Commentaries for the Medical Office, *53*

risk manager, role of, *166-67, 193*

risk purchasing groups, *254-55, 357*

risk retention groups, *254-55, 357*

Rogers, Will, *284*

Roth, L.H., *143-44*

Rozovsky, Fay A., JD, MPH, *113*

RRCs. *See* Residency Review Committees

Rule, Charles F., *330*

rules (federal) of discovery and evidence, adoption of by states, *71*

rules of evidence, changes in, *71*; complexity and variability of, *89*. *See also* evidence

SAFE (Substance Abuse Free Existence) Center, *242*

sale of medical records, *25-26*

sample consent forms. *See* consent forms

scheduling: physician role in facilitating, *20*

scope-of-employment, lawyers, *263*

screening: for potentially compensable adverse outcomes, *199*

screening panels or tribunals, pretrial, *176, 271-72, 274, 275, 292*

second opinions, use of, *26*

Secretary of Health and Human Services, *327, 328*

Seeman, Robert G., *76-81*

self-determination of patients, *127*

self-help groups for malpractice stress syndrome, *208*

self-insurance programs, *196*

self-insured trust, *254*

settlement *49, 63, 357*; rights of insurance companies, *182, 252, 262*

severity of claims, *276, 285, 357*

sexual abuse: and parental consent laws, *137*

Shakespeare, *130*

Shanley, M.G., *67*

sharing of medical information, *30*. *See also* records

Sheridan v. Quarrier (patient abandonment), *39*

Sherman Antitrust Act, *337*

sick doctor statutes, *216*

Silent World of Doctor and Patient, The, 127

single visit, limitation of practice to, *39-40*

Smith, William B., JD, *316-18*

Snyder, M.K., *187*

S.O.A.P. (Subjective information, Objective data, Assessment, and Plan), *12*

Social Security Act, *309*

Sommers, Paul A., PhD, *20-22*

specialty, risk according to, *64-65*. *See also* claims: frequency

Specialty Society Medical Liability Project. *See* AMA/Specialty Society Medical Liability Project

spouse abuse, *31*

staff privileges. *See* privileges

standard of care, *358*; community, *83*; compliance with, *52*; establishing applicable, *50-51*; prevailing, *51*; revisions to rules regarding, *282*

standards of disclosure, *112, 128*

standards of practice. *See* medical practice guidelines

state action defense, *331, 334*

state action exemption, *307*

state medical boards: changes in responsibilities and resources, *322-23*; membership of, *325*; organizational changes in, *324-25*

status of physicians/medical profession, *218, 307, 324*

statute of limitations, *49, 70, 274, 277, 358*

statutorily-imposed standards of care, *89*

Stevens, John Paul, Justice, *136*

Stewart, Potter, Justice, *143*

St. Paul Fire and Marine Insurance Co., *58-59, 66, 83-84, 251, 254, 270-71, 276, 284, 287, 289, 290, 291*

stress: adaptations to: *224, 227-28*; intrinsic to medical practice, *224*; methods for coping with, *223*; on physicians, *217, 218, 224-30*

strict liability, *48-49, 68, 153*

students (medical): career choices open to, *229*; drop-out rate, *226*

subpoena, *358*; powers of state medical boards, *325*

substance abuse: by physicians, *214-15, 218-19;* prescription practices regarding treatment of, *306*; programs for physicians, *219*. *See also* alcohol and drug abuse

suffering of patients: physicians' role in alleviating, *224*

suicidal patients: confidentiality concerning, *30*

suicide: among physicians, *217, 226*

suits, malpractice: definition of, *319*; immediate effects on physicians, *176*; number of claims, *251*; publicity in, *177*; targets, *251*; trial preparation for, *176*; value in deterring poor medicine, *258*. *See also* claims

summations, *184*

summons, *358*; dealing with, *177*

support groups, for malpractice, *208*

Supreme Court, US, *301*

surgical consent, *109-10*

surplus-line insurance companies, *255*

surrogate decision maker, *139, 141, 142*; absence of family members or close friends to serve as, *145*; finding and assessing appropriateness of, *144*

Sweden: medical compensation in, *276*

Szasz, T.S., *187*

tail coverage (insurance), *253, 358*

Talbott, G. Douglas, MD, *241-43*

Tan, Marva West, RN, *313-15, 319-21*

Tarasoff v. Catlin (breaching confidences), *14, 28*

technology: impact on liability, *53, 68, 94-95, 276*

Temple University Institute of Survey Research, *187*

tenancy by the entirety, *267*

termination of: life support, *18*; physician relationship by patient, *35*; privileges (motivations for), *338*; therapeutic relationship, *191*

testimonial compulsion, *27*

Texas Medical Disclosure Panel, *204*
therapeutic alliance, *131, 133, 188*
therapeutic options, discussion of, *150*
third party harm. *See* harm to a third party
Thomas, Lewis, *129*
thoracentesis: sample consent form for, *121-22*
threats to self or others, *29*
tier-2 disciplinary actions: reporting of, *327*
Tillinghast, *285, 292*
time costs, *130*
time pressure: effects on physicians, *96*
Title X (of Public Health Service Act of 1970), *136*
Title XVIII (of Social Security Act), *309*
tort reform, *70, 84, 257, 273, 274, 285, 292, 358*
tort, *358*; system, *49-50, 63-75*. *See also* negligence
transaction cost of malpractice claims, reduction of, *259*
transient incapacity, *141-42*
treatment goals, *149, 187*
treble damage liability, *332*. *See also* damages; antitrust litigation
trial by jury, tradition of, *279*
Trombly, Sally T., RN, MPH, *319-21*
tuberculosis: breach of confidentiality concerning, *29*
uncertainty. *See* medical uncertainty
uncompensated care, *15-16*
unfair trade practices, *275*. *See also* antitrust litigation
unilateral severance of physician-patient relationship, *34*
Unisys Corp., *309*
unrealistic wishes, *132*
unreasonable claims: award of attorneys fees in, *334*
Utah: malpractice insurance, *87*
Utah Medical Insurance Association, *87*
utilization review, *310*
vaccination injuries: compensation for, *72, 257, 276*
vaccination standards, *55*
Vann v. Harden (patient abandonment), *36*
variability of observations, *95-96*
venereal disease: confidentiality concerning, *29, 32*; consent by minors to treatment, *135*; reporting requirement, *32*
verdict, *359*; outcomes, data on, *66*
verdicts, averages, *193*
Veterans Administration, US, *324*
voluntary practice standards, *86*
Ware, J.E., *187*
warning signs of physician impairment, *222*
Washington State Physicians Insurance Exchange, *87*
White House working group on tort reform, *273*
Wilcox, Donald P. "Rocky," JD, *262-65*
Wisconsin: amendments to medical practice act, *326*
withholding information from patient, *129, 282*
Wood, James, *285, 292*
Woolley, F.R., *188*
workers' compensation, *29, 30, 276, 280*
wrongful action, *48*
wrongful life/birth, *70-71, 359*
wrongful termination of privileges, *338*
Yessian, Mark, PhD, *322-29*
Zuckerman, S., *70*